GENTILE CHRISTIAN IDENTITY
FROM CORNELIUS TO CONSTANTINE

GENTILE CHRISTIAN IDENTITY
from CORNELIUS *to* CONSTANTINE

*The Nations, the Parting of the Ways,
and Roman Imperial Ideology*

Terence L. Donaldson

WILLIAM B. EERDMANS PUBLISHING COMPANY
GRAND RAPIDS, MICHIGAN

Wm. B. Eerdmans Publishing Co.
4035 Park East Court SE, Grand Rapids, Michigan 49546
www.eerdmans.com

© 2020 Terence L. Donaldson
All rights reserved

Hardcover edition 2020
Paperback edition 2024

ISBN 978-0-8028-8532-6

Library of Congress Cataloging-in-Publication Data

Names: Donaldson, Terence L., author.
Title: Gentile Christian identity from Cornelius to Constantine : the nations, the
    parting of the ways, and Roman imperial ideology / Terence L. Donaldson.
Description: Grand Rapids, Michigan : William. B. Eerdmans Publishing Com-
    pany, 2020. | Includes bibliographical references and index. | Summary:
    "A comprehensive historical account of the origins and effects of gentile Chris-
    tian identity construction"—Provided by publisher.
Identifiers: LCCN 2020013782 | ISBN 9780802885326 (pbk.)
Subjects: LCSH: Church history—Primitive and early church, ca. 30–600. | Iden-
    tification (Religion) | Identity (Psychology)—Religious aspects—Christianity. |
    Gentiles. | Christians.
Classification: LCC BR165 .D66 2020 | DDC 270.1—dc23
LC record available at https://lccn.loc.gov/2020013782

To my early mentors,

Larry Hurtado (in memoriam)

and Richard Longenecker

Contents

	Abbreviations	ix
	Preface	xiii
1.	**Three Orations and a Question**	1
	Eusebius's *On the Holy Sepulchre*	1
	Aelius Aristides's *Regarding Rome*	7
	Paul's Speech in Acts 25:23–26:32	11
	The Construction of Gentile Christian Identity	13
2.	**Positioning the Question**	37
	The Parting of the Ways	37
	Ethnicity and Social Identity	54
	Identity, Ethnicity, and Power in the Roman Empire	69
3.	***Ethnē* as an Identity Ascribed to Non-Jews: By Jews**	103
	Jewish Identity Construction in the Greco-Roman World	103
	Ethnē and Ascribed Identity	129

4. *Ethnē* as an Identity Ascribed to Non-Jews:
   By Jewish Christ-Believers 151

   Earliest Jewish Christ-Communities and the Gentiles 152

   Ascribed Identities 194

5. The Nations in Roman Imperial Discourse 244

   Vocabulary and Usage: General Considerations 245

   Roman Imperial Ideology and the Nations 277

6. *Ethnē* and Gentile Christian Identity
   (Before 135 CE) 310

   Setting Up the Questions 311

   Ethnē and Identity: Up to 70 CE 322

   Ethnē and Identity: Between the Destruction
   of Jerusalem and the Bar Kokhba Revolt 329

7. *Ethnē* and Gentile Christian Identity
   (After 135 CE) 387

   Ethnē as an Identity Term in the Writings of Justin Martyr .. 389

   Constraints: Celsus and Marcion 422

   Ethnē and Christian Identity Construction after Justin 434

   Afterword 475

   Bibliography 483

   Author Index 511

   Subject Index 517

   Index of Ancient Sources 529

Abbreviations

AB	Anchor Bible
ACW	Ancient Christian Writers
ANF	*Ante-Nicene Fathers*
CBQ	*Catholic Biblical Quarterly*
CBQMS	Catholic Biblical Quarterly Monograph Series
CIL	*Corpus Inscriptionum Latinarum*
CP	*Classical Philology*
CRINT	Compendia Rerum Iudaicarum ad Novum Testamentum
ECF	Early Church Fathers
ECL	Early Christianity and Its Literature
ESCJ	Studies in Christianity and Judaism/Études sur le christianisme et le judaïsme
FC	Fathers of the Church
FRLANT	Forschungen zur Religion und Literatur des Alten und Neuen Testaments
HNT	Handbuch zum Neuen Testament
HTR	*Harvard Theological Review*
ICC	International Critical Commentary
IG	*Inscriptiones Graecae. Editio Minor*
IK Knidos I	Packard Humanities Institute, Searchable Greek Inscriptions, Regions: Asia Minor: Caria: IK Knidos I https://inscriptions.packhum.org/book/480?location=1040

ABBREVIATIONS

ILS	*Islamic Law and Society*
Int	*Interpretation*
ISL	*Inscriptiones Latinae Selectae*
JBL	*Journal of Biblical Literature*
JJMJS	*Journal of the Jesus Movement in Its Jewish Setting*
JQR	*Jewish Quarterly Review*
JSJ	*Journal for the Study of Judaism in the Persian, Hellenistic, and Roman Periods*
JSJSup	Journal for the Study of Judaism Supplements
JSNTSup	Journal for the Study of the New Testament Supplement Series
JSPSup	Journal for the Study of the Pseudepigrapha Supplement Series
JTS	*Journal of Theological Studies*
Knidos	Packard Humanities Institute, Searchable Greek Inscriptions, Regions: Asia Minor: Caria: McCabe, Knidos https://inscriptions.packhum.org/text/259743?&bookid=502&location=1040
LCL	Loeb Classical Library
LNTS	The Library of New Testament Studies
LSJ	Liddell, Henry George, Robert Scott, Henry Stuart Jones, *A Greek-English Lexicon*. 9th ed. with revised supplement
NHC	Nag Hammadi Codices
NovTSup	Supplements to Novum Testamentum
NPNF	*Nicene and Post-Nicene Fathers*
NTL	New Testament Library
OAF	Oxford Apostolic Fathers
OECT	Oxford Early Christian Texts
OGIS	*Orientis Graeci Inscriptiones Selectae*
PLO	Porta Linguarum Orientalium
SBLDS	Society of Biblical Literature Dissertation Series
SBT	Studies in Biblical Theology
SC	Sources chrétiennes
SEG	Supplementum epigraphicum graecum
SNTMS	Society for New Testament Studies Monograph Series
SPCK	Society for Promoting Christian Knowledge
StPB	Studia Post-biblica
NovTSup	Supplements to Novum Testamentum
TDNT	*Theological Dictionary of the New Testament*

TLG	*Thesaurus Linguae Graecae: Canon of Greek Authors and Works*
TSAJ	Texte und Studien zum antiken Judentum
VC	*Vigiliae Christianae*
VCSup	Supplements to Vigiliae Christianae
WBC	Word Biblical Commentary
WGRW	Writings from the Greco-Roman World
WUNT	Wissenschaftliche Untersuchungen zum Neuen Testament
ZNW	*Zeitschrift für die neutestamentliche Wissenschaft und die Kunde der älteren Kirche*

Preface

One of the things that precipitated this book project was a seemingly idle question that came to me once while I was reading Romans 11 and arrived at verse 13: "I am speaking to you gentiles." What, I wondered, would Paul's non-Jewish readers have made of this term? People are not naturally inclined to think of themselves as the "other" to someone else's "us." It is unlikely that "barbarians" would have found anything appealing in a term being foisted on them by self-congratulatory Greeks; one would expect that non-Jews who were attracted to Christ would have found this Jewish term for the non-Jewish other to be similarly unappealing. Its probable lack of appeal notwithstanding, many gentiles were indeed attracted to the movement; once they had come to identify with Christ, they found themselves in an environment where this identity term was one that they could hardly avoid or ignore. What then did they make of it?

My initial probing of the material suggested that, while the term was not very significant for the most part in the earliest gentile Christian literature, a different picture emerged from the writings of Justin Martyr and other early apologists. Since student days I had been interested in (and frequently appalled by) the *adversus Judaeos* tradition of the early gentile church, and so I had some awareness of the place of the term *ethnē*—gentiles, (members of) the non-Jewish nations—in these arguments against the Jews. Coming at the material again from this particular angle, however, I was struck by both the sheer frequency of the term and its evident importance for the apologetic enterprise—not only for the troublesome question of how the gentile church might position itself with respect to Israel, the Jews, and Judaism, but also for their attempts to address

Greco-Roman opinion makers more generally. These initial impressions led me to believe that a more thoroughgoing investigation was in order.

While this project built on my earlier work in a number of ways, it also led me into a number of areas where I could claim no special expertise (including ethnicity, social identity theory, postcolonialism, Greco-Roman ethnography, Roman imperial ideology, and ante-Nicene Christian literature to a certain extent). In an early conversation about the project with a respected senior scholar, I expressed some apprehension about the challenges it presented. His response stuck with me: "Don't be afraid of heading into less familiar territory," he told me; "that's how you learn things."

In the time since then, I have certainly learned a great deal. To be sure, specialists in these various areas will readily recognize the limits to my knowledge. In addition, since the parameters of the study encompass a broad array of ancient literature (Jewish, Greco-Roman, Christian), I have not been able to engage with the correspondingly broad array of pertinent secondary literature to the extent that would have been possible in a more circumscribed study. Nevertheless, despite these limits and constraints, I feel that because of the specific focus of the project—*ethnē* as an identity term—and because of the work I have already done in related areas, this book has some contribution to make to our understanding. Of course, it will fall to others to assess its value.

During the years in which I was engaged in this project, I had various opportunities to present aspects of my work in academic settings: in papers presented at the annual meetings of scholarly societies (Canadian Society of Biblical Studies, Society of Biblical Literature, Studiorum Novi Testamenti Societas); in invited lectures or papers at several institutions (Barnard College, University of Toronto, McMaster University, Baylor University); and, during a sabbatical at the University of Cambridge, in papers presented in established seminars (New Testament Seminar; Hebrew, Jewish, Early Christian Studies Seminar). I am grateful to the organizers and conveners of these various sessions for the opportunity to share aspects of my research in progress. I also want to express my appreciation for the critical interaction that took place in these sessions and for those whose questions, comments, and learned critique helped to sharpen my own thinking in significant ways. Closer to home, students in my graduate seminar "Early Christian Self-Definition" have had the opportunity to read several chapters of the book, along with related papers, and have made their own contributions to the book in its final form.

My early thinking about this project was facilitated by a sabbatical *cum* administrative leave in 2011–12, eight months of which were spent at the University of Cambridge. The completion of this project provides me with another opportunity to express my thanks to Wycliffe College and the Toronto School of The-

Preface

ology for granting me this period of sustained research and reflection. I am also grateful to the Faculty of Divinity at the University of Cambridge for granting me a visiting fellowship, and especially to James Carleton Paget, Judith Lieu, and William Horbury for their assistance, hospitality, and various kindnesses. Thanks are also due to Clare Hall—a wonderful institution for visiting scholars—for accommodation and the chance to interact with a diverse and stimulating group of scholars and graduate students from around the world.

During this period, my work on this project was also supported and enhanced by two research grants from the Social Sciences and Humanities Research Council of Canada (2009–13 and 2015–19), for which I am also grateful. Among other things, this funding allowed me to hire several research assistants—Adam Panacci, David Ney, Mari Leesment, and Bruce Worthington—who provided invaluable help, especially by carrying out preliminary surveys of primary literature. Bruce also checked all the primary and secondary references in chapters 1 through 6, thus relieving me of a lot of tedious work and saving me from a number of errors in the process. Any that remain, of course, need to be added to my account.

In addition, I want to express my appreciation to the staff at Eerdmans for their fine work at every stage of the process: to Michael Thomson, who sought me out when the project was in its early stages and provided continuing support in his regular visits to Toronto; to Trevor Thompson, who succeeded Michael as senior acquisitions editor and who accepted a manuscript that was considerably longer and somewhat later than was first envisioned; to Linda Bieze, who as project editor has guided the manuscript through the editorial and production stages with a sure hand; to Justin Howell, who as copy editor has helped me identify some imperfections and thus produce a more polished final version; and to Laura Hubers, who has overseen the design of the cover (with its effective use of the Peutinger Map) and the marketing material.

For support of a quite different kind, I am deeply grateful to my immediate family: to Lois first of all, my wife and life partner, for her unfailing wisdom, resourcefulness, support, and love; to our adult children Meredith (with her husband David) and Graeme (with his wife Amanda), for the many ways in which they enrich our lives; and to our grandchildren, Iver, Florence, and Elsie, for reawakening us to the joys of discovery and the wonder of the world.

Finally, I am dedicating this book to two of my early mentors, Larry Hurtado (in memoriam) and Richard Longenecker. Larry supervised my first piece of sustained research—a master's thesis on Matthew's Gospel and anti-Judaism—and taught me a great deal about Christian origins and the nature of research in the process. Dick, my doctoral supervisor, stimulated my interest in Second Temple Judaism and introduced me to ways of looking at early Christianity with

Jewish questions in view. In different ways I learned a great deal from both of them and both continued to represent important models for me as I followed my own scholarly career.

Small portions drawn from the following articles and chapters have been adapted for reuse in the present work:

"'We Gentiles': Ethnicity and Identity in Justin's *Dialogue*," *Early Christianity* 4 (2013): 216–41. Incorporated material appears in chapters 1 and 7.

"'Gentile Christianity' as a Category in the Study of Christian Origins," in *Harvard Theological Review* 106 (2013), 433–58. Incorporated material appears in chapter 3.

"Paul, Abraham's Gentile 'Offspring' and the Torah," in *Torah Ethics and Early Christian Identity*, ed. David M. Miller and Susan Wendel (Grand Rapids: Eerdmans, 2016), 135–50. Incorporated material appears in chapter 3.

"'Nations,' 'Non-Jewish Nations' or 'Non-Jewish Individuals': Matt 28:19 Revisited," in *Matthew within Judaism: Israel and the Nations in the First Gospel*, ed. Anders Runesson and Daniel M. Gurtner, Early Christianity and Its Literature (Atlanta: SBL Press, 2020), 169–94. Incorporated material appears in chapters 3 and 4.

This material has been reused with the permission of the respective publishers, for which I am grateful.

CHAPTER 1

Three Orations and a Question

Eusebius, Aelius Aristides, and Paul were disparate personages—a fourth-century bishop of Caesarea Maritima, a well-to-do second-century sophist and orator from Mysia in the Roman province of Asia, an itinerant first-century Jewish "apostle of Christ to the gentiles." One thing they had in common, however, was an oration addressed in one way or another to the Roman Empire (self-composed in the case of Eusebius and Aristides, composed by a later chronicler in the case of Paul). Taken together, these three orations focus our attention on a significant question about the construction of early gentile Christian identity.

EUSEBIUS'S *ON THE HOLY SEPULCHRE*

In 335 CE, in the context of an ecclesiastical gathering in Jerusalem to mark the dedication of the recently completed Church of the Holy Sepulchre—a project initiated by Constantine shortly after his defeat of Licinius eleven years earlier and his consequent emergence as sole ruler of the Roman Empire—a remarkable oration was delivered by Eusebius, the bishop of nearby Caesarea, in praise of the emperor and his accomplishments. After a brief description of the "lofty and noble structures" that Constantine had built to commemorate and honor the site of the Savior's death and resurrection, Eusebius observed that some had questioned why so much effort and energy was devoted to the project. Apologist that he was, he saw these objections as providing him with an opportunity to proclaim in words what (he believed, and not without reason) Constantine was intending to proclaim in the imperial language of edifice and architecture (*In Praise of Constantine* 18.3). And so, addressing himself to the emperor, he set himself the task of proclaiming to everyone "the reasons and motives of your God-loving works" (11.7).

The address that follows—commonly referred to as *On the Holy Sepulchre*—is a kind of theological ethnography carried out within the framework of an encomium on the emperor and his accomplishments.[1] Eusebius lays out an apologia for the religion of the emperor in which the history of redemption is intertwined with the history of the nations. His argument contains a number of connected themes: the multiplicity of nations itself as the locus of the malady for which the Savior offers "his heavenly cure";[2] the mission of the disciples to all the nations as the means by which this cure is made available; the Roman Empire, which established peace among the nations of the world, as an important element in the success of this mission; and the emergence of a unified empire under Constantine as the visible manifestation of the divine plan to overcome the division of the nations and to gather them into a harmonious unity, thus fulfilling the prophetic promise that Christ "shall have dominion from sea to sea, and from the river to the ends of the earth" (*In Praise of Constantine* 16.7).

While Eusebius does not portray the existence of multiple nations as inherently negative, he nevertheless establishes a close association between ethnic diversity and the various "evils which of old afflicted the whole human race [*to pan tōn anthrōpōn genos*]" (*In Praise of Constantine* 13.8). The root of the problem, as he portrays it, is "the polytheistic error of the nations [*tōn ethnōn*]" (15.8), an error that had two stages of development. The initial part of the problem had to do with the inability of human beings to recognize the Creator of the world, which led "each race [*genos*]" (13.5) to devise a multiplicity of other deities, variously identified with heavenly bodies, human passions, deified mortals, and even animals (13.1–6). Here Eusebius goes into considerable detail, listing a broad array of nations by name and describing their various religious practices.

The problem, however, went beyond mere human follies and fancies. Evil demons took advantage of the situation, using polytheistic worship as a means

---

1. In the manuscripts, this oration is combined with a panegyric to Constantine on the occasion of the thirtieth anniversary of his reign, under the joint title *In Praise of Constantine*; the Holy Sepulchre oration constitutes chs. 11–18. While there is a more recent English translation (H. A. Drake, *In Praise of Constantine: A Historical Study and New Translation of Eusebius' Tricennial Orations* [Berkeley: University of California Press, 1976]), the version by Arthur Cushman McGiffert (vol. 1 of *Nicene and Post-Nicene Fathers*, Series 2 [Grand Rapids: Eerdmans, 1989]) is preferable for present purposes.

2. The phrase is found in 11.5.

of insinuating themselves into human affairs (*In Praise of Constantine* 13.4–6) and thus infecting "the whole human race" (13.14) with a malady that first came to expression in human sacrifice (13.7–8) and then manifested itself in a variety of other noxious symptoms (13.9–14). Political disputes, open conflict and warfare, plunder and highway robbery, incest and other forms of sexual deviance, treachery and murder, brutality and dissolution—such was the hopeless situation of division, conflict, and vile immorality that "the nations of the whole world [*ta kath' holēs tēs oikoumenēs ethnē*], both Greek and barbarian, driven mad by demonic forces" (13.9), had created for themselves.

While this list of vices and evils is commonplace for the most part, one item stands out—political disputes or, more precisely, "fierce contention over laws and forms of government [*nomois te kai politeiais*]" (*In Praise of Constantine* 13.9). One might wonder what place there could be in a list such as this for disputes over *politeia*, especially a place at the head of the list. But it is a measure of its significance that Eusebius returns to it a little later, when he is speaking of the positive benefits that have resulted from the death and resurrection of the Word of God. Here it appears not simply at the head of the list, but as the (penultimate) cause of the others. What has produced wars, atrocities, and suffering of every kind is the fact that "all the nations of old upon the earth [*panta ta palai epi gēs ethnē*], the entire human race [*genos*], were cut up into provincial, national, and local governments, tyrannies and many kinds of rule" (16.2). However, the multiplicity of nations, with their various forms of government, was not the ultimate cause of human evil, strife, and misery. For Eusebius, a nation's *politeia*—its form of government or corporate way of life—was an essential element of its character as a nation, and the *politeia* of every nation of the world was founded on "the delusion of polytheistic error" (16.3). Thus the ultimate cause of the various evils plaguing humankind was the polytheistic (and thus demonic) foundation on which ethnic diversity was constructed.

This, then, was "the inveterate malady which had asserted its dominion over the whole human race" (*In Praise of Constantine* 13.14) and which, Eusebius goes on to proclaim, Christ had come to remediate. To be sure, the remedy had already been available to some extent through the words of the prophets, together with the example of those few men of old who had been able to discern the truth about God. But the tyranny of the "ruthless and soul-destroying demons and spirits" had progressed to such an extent that a superior form of help was needed (13.15).

Christ's work, in part, was to reveal himself as the Word of God and thus to reveal the nature of the true God and creator of all things. Revelation, however, was not sufficient in itself; the power of the demons needed to be broken. This is precisely what was accomplished through the death and resurrection of the Savior:

> For as soon as the one holy and mighty sacrifice, the sacred body of our Savior, had been slain on behalf of the human race, to be as a ransom for all nations [*pantōn ethnōn*] heretofore involved in the guilt of impious superstition, thenceforward the power of impure and unholy daemons was utterly abolished, and every earth-born and delusive error was at once weakened and destroyed. (*In Praise of Constantine* 15.11)

If Eusebius here locates the site of the victory in Christ's death, he can also link it with the resurrection. When he picks up the theme in the next chapter, he declares that when Christ "was raised, as a trophy of victory over the ancient demons and as a means of averting evil, the works of these demons were at once destroyed" (16.3). Either way, however, the defeat of the demons was the goal and outcome of the divine operation.

Given that the demons' sphere of operation was the nations themselves, it is not surprising that the next step in Eusebius's history of redemption is the worldwide mission to the nations. Indeed, it is the defeat of the demons that opens the way for the "one God [to be] proclaimed to all" (*In Praise of Constantine* 16.3). This mission is carried out by the disciples, "who were destined . . . to communicate to all humankind that knowledge of God which he before ordained for all the nations [*pasi tois ethnesi*]" (15.7). It was a sign of Christ's own power that he was able to take "obscure and unlettered men" and turn them into "the legislators and instructors of the human race," composing "writings of such authority that they were translated into every language of Greeks and barbarians, and were read and pondered by all the nations [*pasi tois ethnesi*]" (17.9). Thus not only did Christ promise that "his gospel must be preached in all the world as a testimony to all the nations [*pasi tois ethnesin*]"; through the mission of his disciples he fulfilled it as well, "for within a little time the whole world [*hē sympasa oikoumenē*] was filled with his doctrine" (16.8).

The disciples, however, were not the sole agents of the worldwide success of the gospel. God was also at work through a second channel—the Roman Empire itself, which had its own role to play in overcoming the ethnic fractiousness of the human race. Eusebius attaches considerable significance to the fact that the emergence of "the doctrine of Christ" coincided with the emergence of the empire under Augustus: "so at the self-same period, the entire dominion of the Roman empire being nested in a single sovereign, profound peace reigned throughout the world" (*In Praise of Constantine* 16.4). Coincided, yes; but coincidence, no. For Eusebius, it was precisely "by the express appointment of the same God" that these "two roots of blessing, the Roman empire, and the doctrine of Christian piety, sprang up together for the benefit of humankind" (16.4). Working together, they were able to address the twin causes of the human malady—the

Three Orations and a Question

division of the human race into hostile, warring nations; and the demonic forces at work in the polytheistic structures of the nations themselves:

> But two mighty powers, starting from the same point, the Roman empire, which henceforth was swayed by a single sovereign, and the teaching of Christ, subdued and reconciled these contending elements. Our Savior's mighty power destroyed at once the many governments and the many gods of the demons, and proclaimed to all humankind [*pasin anthrōpois*], both Greek and barbarian, to the extremities of the earth, the sole sovereignty of God himself. Meantime the Roman empire, the causes of multiplied governments being thus removed, effected an easy conquest of those which yet remained; its object being to unite all nations [*pantoiōn ethnōn*] in one harmonious whole; an object in great measure already secured, and destined to be still more perfectly attained, even to the final conquest of the ends of the habitable world [*tēs oikoumenēs*], by means of the salutary doctrine, and through the aid of that Divine power which facilitates and smooths its way. (16.5–6)

Even so, the "two roots of blessing" are not placed on a completely equal footing. Rome's ability to unite the nations under one sovereign was dependent on the prior victory of the "Savior," whose defeat of the demons effectively removed the underlying "causes of multiplied governments."

While Eusebius may acknowledge that the divine purposes have not yet been "perfectly attained," he nevertheless places the emphasis on the "great measure" to which these purposes have been "already secured." The worship of the one God has spread throughout the inhabited world: "the ears and tongue of all humankind on earth [have been filled] with the praises of his name" (*In Praise of Constantine* 16.8); "spiritual and rational sacrifices are offered as a sacred service by all the nations [*hapantōn tōn ethnōn*] to the One Supreme God" (16.10); "in every region of the world of humankind," Christ is "acknowledged by all the nations [*tōn ethnōn hapantōn*] as the only Son of God" (17.13). Accompanying the spread of true worship, people from every walk of life and every nation have been converted to piety, virtue, and peaceable relations with others: "multitudes from multitudes of nations" (*myria myriōn ethnōn*) have been instructed to live "a just and virtuous life" (17.6); "the whole human race, subdued by the controlling power of peace and concord, received one another as brethren, and responded to the feelings of their common nature" (16.7). Such transformation took place not only among individuals but among the nations as well: "the inveterate strife and mutual hatred of the nations [*tōn ethnōn*]" was a thing of the past (16.7); people could travel freely "from West to East, and from East to West," as if the whole world was "their own native country [*patridas*]" (16.7); indeed, with the one

GENTILE CHRISTIAN IDENTITY

God as their Father, and "true religion as their common mother, . . . the whole world [*tēn sympasan oikoumenēn*] appeared like one well-ordered and united family" (16.7).³ And all of this, Eusebius declares, is a fulfillment of the prophetic promises, especially those "which speak as follows concerning the saving Word. 'He shall have dominion from sea to sea, and from the river to the ends of the earth.' And again, 'In his days shall righteousness spring up; and abundance of peace.' 'And they shall beat their swords into ploughshares, and their spears into sickles: and nation shall not take up sword against nation [*ethnos ep' ethnos*], neither shall they learn to war any more'"⁴ (16.7).

It was, then, a remarkable oration, striking alike for its context as well as its content. Speaking in Jerusalem, "that city from which as from a fountain-head the Savior Word has issued forth to all humankind" (*In Praise of Constantine* 11.2), Eusebius addresses himself to the sole emperor of the Roman world, as he stands within a magnificent new edifice constructed by the emperor himself in honor of that Savior Word, whose devotee and subject he has now become. In vivid terms, Eusebius presents us with a vision in which the mission of the disciples and the empire of Rome function as divinely intended partners in a grand project, one in which all the nations of the inhabited world are gathered into a single unified dominion. What may have appeared at the outset to have been two distinct or even oppositional projects—the mission of the disciples to preach the gospel "to all nations [*panta ta ethnē*]" (16.8) and the campaign of the Roman Empire "to unite all nations [*pantoiōn ethnōn*]" (16.5)—turn out in the end to have been a single enterprise directed by the one God of all the nations, each of them dependent in its own way on the prior victory of Christ over the baleful influence of the demons. "Two mighty powers"—"the teaching of Christ" and "the Roman empire" (16.5)—one spreading outward from Jerusalem and the other from Rome, have joined forces, with the result that the "kingdom [*basileia*] of God" (16.6) and the "kingdom [*basileia*] of the Romans" (16.4) have merged into a single kingdom, at once earthly and divine, thus bringing to (almost complete) fulfillment the prophetic promises of an age of peace and righteousness among the nations of the world.

Although this remarkable vision was presented in the context of an oration for a very specific occasion, it drew on themes that were deeply embedded in Eusebius's work as a whole.⁵ To be sure, in this oration, they are presented in accents that were missing in works written while the Eastern Empire was still ruled

---

3. Literally, "one well-ordered household and kin group" (*mias eunomoumenēs oiketeias te kai syngeneias*).
4. Respectively, Ps 72:8; Ps 72:7; Isa 2:4.
5. Especially his *Preparation for the Gospel* and *Demonstration of the Gospel*, though

by Licinius, a time when Christians were at best tolerated and at worst (toward the end of his rule) persecuted once again. Nevertheless, Eusebius's vision of the church as a universal people drawn from all the nations of the inhabited world, together with his belief in the providential role played by the Roman Empire, were by no means simple rhetorical flourishes worked up for the needs of the moment. To be sure, the historical moment was a fleeting one; had Eusebius lived to see the internecine conflicts among Constantine's successors during the next quarter century, he might have been more inclined to put clearer theological daylight between the dominion of the Christ and the dominion of the Caesar.[6] Still, despite the ironies that are all too painfully apparent from the standpoint of our own historical moment, it remains a remarkable oration.

AELIUS ARISTIDES'S *REGARDING ROME*

We will return to Eusebius a little later. For now, however, let us shift the scene and consider an earlier oration, also in praise of the Roman Empire and the accomplishments of its emperor, this one delivered in the imperial court in Rome. The speaker on this occasion was Aelius Aristides, the highly learned orator and writer from Mysia, a member of a wealthy family with citizenship in Smyrna as well, and a leading figure in the Second Sophistic. He delivered the oration, *Regarding Rome*, on one of his two visits to Rome (144 or 155 CE), during the reign of Antoninus Pius.[7]

Following the conventions of the genre, Aristides begins his encomium by

---

the themes of these works were anticipated by the shorter *General Elementary Introduction* and rendered in a more popular form in his *Divine Manifestation*.

6. One should not exaggerate the degree to which Eusebius conflates the two, seeing him as so dazzled by the recent turn of events and Constantine's benefactions to the church that he simply becomes a cheerleader for the empire. Even in *In Praise of Constantine*, there is an element of reserve and undercurrent of qualification; see further below.

7. Since the first visit was cut short by one of Aristides's recurring illnesses, Behr argues that the speech took place during the second visit; Charles A. Behr, *P. Aelius Aristides: The Complete Works* (Leiden: Brill, 1981–86), 1:1–3 and 2:373, n. 1; also Daniel S. Richter, *Cosmopolis: Imagining Community in Late Classical Athens and the Early Roman Empire* (Oxford: Oxford University Press, 2011), 131. For the alternative opinion, see Laurent Pernot, "Aelius Aristides and Rome," in *Aelius Aristides Between Greece, Rome, and the Gods*, ed. William V. Harris and Brooke Holmes, Columbia Studies in the Classical Tradition 33 (Leiden: Brill, 2008), 175–201, here 176. For present purposes, it is not necessary to resolve the question of dating. Quotations, together with the enumerated paragraph sections, are from Behr's translation.

describing the difficulties facing any orator who would aspire to find words of praise commensurate with the glories of the city being praised (*Regarding Rome* 2–5). After touching on the geographical extent of the empire (6–13)—the course of the sun from its rising to its setting "is always in your land" (10)—he proceeds by way of comparison, setting the Roman Empire alongside "the empires which have gone before" (13), first the Persian (15–23) and then the Greek (24–57).[8] The remainder of the oration consists of a more topical treatment of Roman superiority, dealing severally with civic and imperial administration, justice, military organization, benefaction, political constitution, and the like (57–106). He ends with a brief but elegant acclamation of the emperor and a prayer to the gods "that this empire and this city bloom forever" (107–9).

The dominant image that emerges from *Regarding Rome* is of the empire as an ideal, universal realm of peace, harmony, and good government, a common fatherland encompassing all races and nations, and thus a realization of the Greek philosophical and political vision of a single, civilized world (*oikoumenē*). Of particular interest here is the way in which this image is conveyed by means of the language of nation (*ethnos*), race (*genos*), and related terminology.[9]

In his comparison of Rome with the empires that went before, Aristides begins with the most readily apparent difference, its extent. If one starts at the westernmost boundary of the Persian Empire, he says, and measures from that point, what remains of the Roman Empire to the west is larger in itself than the whole of the Persian Empire. Nothing lies outside the Roman grasp, "neither city, nor nation [*ethnos*], nor harbor, nor land," unless, he adds, it was useless to begin with. What for previous rulers were the ends of the earth are for Rome just the fence around the courtyard. Rome has not only discovered and explored "the ocean," but (and here modern readers are permitted a smile) has even conquered "the island" that it contains (i.e., Britain).[10]

More impressive than the circumference of its boundaries, however, is the surpassing quality of its governance (*Regarding Rome* 29). Alexander may have conquered a lot of territory (24), but it was the Romans who discovered how to govern (51, 58). Earlier empires simply "did not know how to rule" (23). Despotic rule might work in a household, but when Rome's predecessors attempted to extend it "to cities and nations [*eis poleis te kai ethnē*]" (23), the result was simply "hatred and plotting on the part of those who were treated in this way," together

---

8. Any others, he says, are too inconsequential to mention, in comparison with these.

9. Cities are important for Aristides as well, but they are not conceived as a separate category. Rather, the one (the city) is embedded in the other (the race or nation); cities are "the cities of each of the races" (*tas poleis hekastō tōn genōn*) (67).

10. All of this from section 28.

with "revolts, civil war, continual strife and unceasing contention" (20). Rome, however, has discovered an ideal "form of government [*politeian*]," one that did not exist before (91).[11] Under the efficient administration of "the rulers who are sent to the cities and the nations [*eis tas poleis te kai ta ethnē*]," "everything is accomplished by edict and by a sign of assent more easily than one would strike the chord of a lyre" (31). The governors consider their subjects not as "foreigners" (*allotriōn*), but as members of their own "household" (*oikeiōn*) (65). Likewise with the army, although it contains soldiers drawn from many races (*genōn*), everything is arrayed in an orderly fashion under "one man, whose authority is all pervasive and who oversees everything—nations [*ethnē*], cities, legions, the generals themselves," and so on down the line to the individual soldier (88).

A particular aspect of Rome's good government is its generosity in benefaction. While other rulers and empires "ruled over, as it were, only the naked bodies of their nations [*tōn ethnōn*], . . . you have filled your whole empire with cities and adornments" (*Regarding Rome* 92). With former sources of strife and conflict now a thing of the past, the only contention among "races" (*genōn*; 95) and cities (97) involves civic pride: every city "is full of gymnasiums, fountains, gateways, temples, handicrafts, and schools" (97).

Consequently, the empire is a worldwide domain of peace and security. Just a few "cohorts and cavalry troops are sufficient to guard whole nations [*ethnōn holōn*], and not even many of these are quartered throughout the cities of the races [*tōn genōn*]"; as a result, "many of the nations [*polla tōn ethnōn*]" do not even know where the nearest military garrison is located (*Regarding Rome* 67). In place of the disorder, strife, and bloodshed of the past, "total security, universal and clear to all, has been given to the earth itself and those who inhabit it" (104). "Now it is possible for both Greek and barbarian" to travel freely from one end of the empire to the other, just as if "he were going from one country of his to another" (100). It is no wonder, then, that "the whole inhabited world [*hapasa hē oikoumenē*] speaks in greater harmony than a chorus, praying that this empire last for all time" (29).

Although individual races and nations continue to exist, Aristides declares that they have been gathered up into a new form of shared identity. Rome governs as if the whole inhabited world were a single city, with each nation being a free citizen of this universal *polis* (*Regarding Rome* 36). Again, "what a city is to its boundaries and its territories, so this city is to the whole inhabited

11. If it did, the Greeks would have discovered it, since they surpassed all others in knowledge (51). Its newness, however, consists in the fact that it combines the best of the already-existing forms of government—tyranny (in conjunction with oligarchy), kingship (with aristocracy), and democracy—while avoiding the weaknesses of each (90).

world" (61). Rome has turned into reality "that well-known saying, that the earth is the mother and the common fatherland [*patris*] of all" (100). It is now possible for people everywhere to become citizens of Rome; "no one is a foreigner [*xenos*] who deserves to hold office or to be trusted" (60). By giving others a share in the empire, Rome has even brought a new kind of race into being:

> You used the word "Roman" to belong not to a city, but to be the name of a sort of common race [*genous onoma koinou tinos*], this not being one among the others but a balance to all the remaining ones. You do not now divide the races [*ta genē*] into Greeks and barbarians, ... but you have divided people into Romans and non-Romans. So far have you extended the use of the city's name. (63)

This new race can even be described as the "golden race [*genous*]" envisaged by Hesiod, for if Hesiod could have foreseen the empire of Rome, he would have placed the golden race not at the beginning of human generations but at the end (106).

In comparing the Roman Empire with what went before, Aristides uses the metaphor of illness and healing: "it can be said in medical terms that the inhabited world was, as it were, ill at the start and has now recovered" (*Regarding Rome* 97). A more striking comparison, however, is with the role of Zeus among the pantheon. Before the rule of Zeus was established, "everything was filled with faction, uproar and disorder," but when Zeus came to rule, "the Titans were banished to the deepest corners of the earth," and "everything was put in order." Likewise with the Roman Empire, before, there was confusion and factionalism; after, "there entered in universal order and a glorious light" (103).

This comparison, though, leads Aristides to an additional point: "it seems that the gods, watching from above, in their benevolence join with you in making your empire successful and that they confirm your possession of it" (*Regarding Rome* 104). The gods themselves take great pleasure in the establishment of universal order—indeed, they actively support the enterprise—not least because Rome has put an end to a state of cultic disorder that involved even child sacrifice and has reestablished "the altars of the gods" (103–4). Beginning with Zeus, who approves of their "care for the inhabited world [*tēs oikoumenēs*] that he had made," Aristides provides a roll call of the pantheon—Hera; Athena and Hephaestus; Dionysus and Demeter; Poseidon; Apollo, Artemis, and the Muses; Hermes; Aphrodite; Asclepius and the Egyptian gods; Ares—each with his or her own reasons for approval and support. Even "the Sun, who watches over all things, has seen under you no act of violence or of injustice nor things of the sort which were frequent in former times" (105).

Just before bringing his encomium to an end with a prayer to the gods, Aristides turns to the emperor and makes one final comparison. "The present ruler" stands head and shoulders above his predecessors, precisely because of the degree to which he has given outsiders a place within the household of the empire: "he has treated as equals his partners in the administration of the empire, whom he regards as kinsfolk [*oikeious*], and . . . he has more of them than any of his predecessors" (*Regarding Rome* 107).

As should be readily apparent, there are striking points of connection between this oration and the one delivered by Eusebius almost two centuries later. Before turning our attention to these, however, let us shift the scene one more time and consider a third oration, this one even earlier.

PAUL'S SPEECH IN ACTS 25:23–26:32

Toward the end of the Acts of the Apostles (25:23–26:32), we are presented with an account of a speech delivered by the apostle Paul in the city of Caesarea, to an audience consisting of Porcius Festus (the Roman governor of Judea, 60–62 CE), Agrippa II (client-king of territories east of the Jordan, with additional authority over the temple in Jerusalem), his sister (and, it was rumored, consort) Bernice, together "with the military tribunes and the prominent men of the city" (25:23). When Festus took up his office, Paul had already spent two years in Roman custody because of charges brought against him by "the chief priests and the elders of the Jews" (25:15). The charges arose from controversies having to do with Paul's preaching among the gentiles (literally, "the nations [*ethnē*]"),[12] which were precipitated in part by a visit of Paul to the temple in Jerusalem. Wanting to move the case forward, Festus arranged a hearing, at the end of which Paul, objecting to a suggestion that his case be decided by a tribunal in Jerusalem, appealed instead to Caesar, a request readily granted by Festus (25:6–12). Not long afterward, when Agrippa and Bernice came to Caesarea to pay their respects, Festus described both the case and his own bewilderment: instead of the sorts of charges he was expecting, what were brought forward were "points of disagreement about their own religion [*deisidaimonias*, "modes of fearing the gods"] and about a certain Jesus, who had died but whom Paul asserted to be alive" (25:19). In response to Agrippa's expression of interest in meeting Paul, Festus invited him to a hearing that he had arranged for the purpose of getting a better sense of what report he might forward to the emperor's tribunal—"for it seems to me unreasonable to

---

12. The term *gentiles* will require more careful consideration as we proceed.

send a prisoner without indicating the charges against him" (25:27). This is the gathering in which Paul's speech is delivered.

We encounter this speech in the context of a third-party narrative, and thus it differs in character from those of Eusebius and Aristides, which come to us as the compositions of the orators themselves. We will not concern ourselves here with questions of history, asking about Luke's possible sources, trying to reconstruct events that might lie behind the account or asking how closely the content of the speech might reflect Paul's own lines of thought. For present purposes, it is sufficient to take the speech as it stands, as Luke's own narrative reconstruction of what, in his perception of things, Paul might have said in such a situation.[13] Further, instead of an encomium on the Roman Empire and its ruler, Paul's speech is a defense (cf. *apologeisthai* [Acts 26:2]) against the charges facing him. In addition, the defense is addressed not to the emperor but to Agrippa and Festus.[14] Nevertheless, given that both Agrippa and Festus were agents of Rome and that Paul has appealed to Caesar, the oration is addressed indirectly to the emperor as well.

Paul's defense unfolds as a narrative of his own conversion, call, and subsequent activity as a preacher to the gentiles. His accusers (he says) are well aware of his story. He was raised "among my own nation [*tō ethnei mou*] and in Jerusalem" (Acts 26:4). He lived as a Pharisee, the strictest of the Jewish groups (v. 5). As a member of this group, he was convinced that he needed to oppose those associated with "the name of Jesus of Nazareth" (v. 9) and so persecuted them ferociously, not only in Jerusalem but in foreign cities as well. In the course of this activity, while he was on his way to Damascus, he was accosted by "a light from heaven, brighter than the sun" (v. 13), and heard a voice, which turned out to be that of the risen Jesus himself. After briefly acknowledging the matter of the persecution, Jesus announced to Paul that he was appointing him as a servant and witness, and sending him to the gentiles [*tōn ethnōn*], "to open their eyes so that they may turn from darkness to light and from the power of Satan to God" and thus be forgiven of their sins and granted a place among the holy ones (v. 18). From that day to this, says Paul, he has carried out this commission, preaching a message that is nothing other than what Moses and the prophets had foretold: "that the Messiah must suffer, and that, by being the first to rise from the dead, he would proclaim light both to the people [of Israel] and to the Gentiles [*tō te laō kai tois ethnesin*]" (v. 23). Thus, as he says at the outset of the speech, what he was really on trial for was his commitment to "the promise made by God to our ancestors" (v. 6).

---

13. Nor will we concern ourselves with the identity of the author; *Luke* is used here as a matter of convenience.

14. Actually, he addresses himself to Agrippa directly (v. 2), engaging Festus only in response to Festus's own interjection (v. 24).

As Paul's speech comes to an end, what had been an account of his preaching activity quickly switches into another instance of it. In response to Festus's bemused interjection—"You are out of your mind, Paul! Too much learning is driving you insane!" (Acts 26:24)—he changes from defendant to witness (in the evangelistic rather than the juridical sense of the term), attempting to convince Festus and all his hearers to become Christians. While his attempt met with no apparent success, it did at least lead Festus and Agrippa to conclude that he was "doing nothing to deserve death or imprisonment," and that, if he had not appealed to Caesar, he could have been set free (vv. 31–32). Whether Paul ever had the opportunity to present his defense in the context of an imperial tribunal in Rome is something about which Luke is silent.

The Construction of Gentile Christian Identity

These three orations span more than two centuries, take place in quite different urban locales (Caesarea, Rome, Jerusalem), and are written by authors with significantly diverse background, training, and conviction. The diversity would be even greater if we were to include Paul directly, and not just through later Lukan reflection—for example, if we were also to consider his letter to the church in Rome and the defense of his preaching to the gentiles that we find there. Brought into juxtaposition with each other, these orations crackle with sparks of interaction—points of connection, striking similarities and contrasts, unexpected ironies, provocative implied questions, and the like.

The most striking contrast, of course, has to do with the composition and context of the Christian movement as reflected in the Acts narrative, at one end of the period, and in Eusebius's oration at the Church of the Holy Sepulchre, at the other. At the outset—at the time of Paul's Damascus experience, say—what eventually came to be called Christianity consisted of a cluster of renewal movements located within the boundaries of the Jewish world. This world itself was a variegated phenomenon, and the groups of Jewish Christ-believers both reflected and added to the variety. The membership of the movement was almost entirely Jewish, and although non-Jews began to be included, the terms of their inclusion was a matter of considerable controversy. Indeed, variegation within the movement was largely generated by disagreements about the inclusion of gentiles, together with differing stances toward the wider non-Jewish world more generally. Judea was subject to Rome, of course, and so the movement from the very beginning stood in an implicit relationship to the Roman Empire. Still, the most obvious aspect of this relationship was the fact that its founder had suffered an ignominious Roman execution.

By the time of Eusebius, Christianity (now a standard term) had spread throughout the Mediterranean world and had become sufficiently well established among the general population that,[15] not only was it adopted by the emperor himself, but Constantine felt sufficiently confident of popular support that he could embark on an active policy of advancing the status and interests of the church in the empire as a whole.[16] One who had been executed by Rome as a troublemaker in a dusty outpost of the empire had now become a deity worshiped by the emperor himself and a substantial proportion of his subjects. While Eusebius was prone to exaggeration, still it is not without significance that he could, without hesitation or fear of ridicule, challenge anyone to refute his claim "that whole myriads in crowds together of women, and children, slaves and free, obscure and illustrious, barbarians and Greeks alike, in every place and city and district in all the nations [*pasi tois . . . ethnesi*] under the sun," had wholeheartedly embraced the Christian teaching (*Preparation for the Gospel* 1.4.11). Needless to say, the population of the movement with which Eusebius identified was now almost entirely gentile. Of course, few Christians from "all the nations under the sun" would have thought of themselves as *ethnē* in the specifically Jewish sense of the term—that is, as members of non-Jewish nations or gentiles. A more accurate way of putting it would be to say that the population of the movement included very few Jews. While forms of (what is usually described as) Jewish Christianity continued to exist,[17] for a member of the orthodox mainstream such as Eusebius, they were now a marginal oddity.[18] To be sure, the continuing existence of a recognizable Jewish

---

15. Eusebius uses *Christianity* some twenty-two times.

16. Barnes's comment is apropos: "The early history of the Christian church in the West is so badly documented that no narrative of its expansion can be written. The surviving evidence, however, clearly indicates that Christianity had thoroughly permeated provincial society long before Constantine became emperor"; Timothy D. Barnes, *Constantine and Eusebius* (Cambridge, MA: Harvard University Press, 1981), 53.

17. Both the term *Jewish Christianity* and the way in which it might be defined are subject to considerable debate and discussion. For recent studies, see especially Oskar Skarsaune and Reidar Hvalvik, eds., *Jewish Believers in Jesus: The Early Centuries* (Peabody, MA: Hendrickson, 2007); Matt Jackson-McCabe, ed., *Jewish Christianity Reconsidered: Rethinking Ancient Groups and Texts* (Minneapolis: Fortress, 2007); and James Carleton Paget, *Jews, Christians and Jewish Christians in Antiquity*, WUNT 1.251 (Tübingen: Mohr Siebeck, 2010).

18. See Annette Yoshiko Reed, "'Jewish Christianity' as Counter-History? The Apostolic Past in Eusebius' *Ecclesiastical History* and the Pseudo-Clementine *Homilies*," in *Antiquity in Antiquity: Jewish and Christian Pasts in the Greco-Roman World*, ed. Gregg Gardner and Kevin L. Osterloh, TSAJ 123 (Tübingen: Mohr Siebeck, 2008), 171-216, esp. 204-7. This is not to overlook the fact that, at the popular level, interactions between Jews and Christians continued to take place, in ways that often distressed leaders of the orthodox mainstream; see especially Adam H. Becker and Annette Yoshiko Reed, eds.,

Christianity serves as a reminder that diversity was a feature of the movement in Eusebius's day no less than in Paul's. At this later stage of development, however, diversity was driven by substantially different issues, and the days were long past when division would have taken place over the question whether gentile believers would need to become full torah-observers in order to be admitted. At this stage, for an orthodox Christian like Eusebius, the issue would have been turned on its head: it would have been controversial—even heretical—to suggest that Jews could be admitted to the church while continuing to be full torah-observers.

It is a dizzying experience to move from the world of Acts 26 to that of Eusebius's *On the Holy Sepulchre*, and from the Caesarea of Paul's day to the Caesarea of its bishop, Eusebius, during the reign of Constantine.[19] Or at least it should be. Given the Christian foundations of Western culture, however, the natural tendency of those whose perceptions have been shaped by this culture is to take this transition for granted, to see the Christianization of the Roman world as the natural outcome of an inevitable process. For many in the Western world, it takes a prodigious act of imagination to extricate ourselves from this inherited context and to put ourselves into a position where we can perceive the sheer improbability of it all.

Once the inevitable has become the improbable, of course, questions of causality and explanation immediately present themselves. As Rodney Stark has put it:

> Finally, all questions concerning the rise of Christianity are one: How was it done? How did a tiny and obscure messianic movement from the edge of the Roman Empire dislodge classical paganism and become the dominant faith of Western civilization?[20]

Stark is just one of the latest in a long line of scholars who have attempted to answer the question, a line that begins with Eusebius himself and continues

---

The Ways That Never Parted: Jews and Christians in Late Antiquity and the Early Middle Ages (Minneapolis: Fortress, 2007).

19. In a piece of delightful irony from later in the Byzantine period, the text of Rom 13:3—"Do you wish to have no fear of the authority? Then do what is good, and you will receive its approval"—appears in a mosaic on the floor of an administrative building in Caesarea; in this reuse of the text, advice sent to the Christians in Rome by someone who not long afterward was a Roman prisoner in Caesarea was transformed by the powers that be into a piece of imperial propaganda encouraging citizens of Byzantine Caesarea to be duly subservient to the state. See Terence L. Donaldson, ed., *Religious Rivalries and the Struggle for Success in Caesarea Maritima*, ESCJ 8 (Waterloo, ON: Wilfrid Laurier University Press, 2000), 1.

20. Rodney Stark, *The Rise of Christianity: A Sociologist Reconsiders History* (Princeton: Princeton University Press, 1996), 3.

on through Gibbon, Voltaire, Harnack, Nock, Lietzmann, Frend, MacMullen, and many others.[21] It is certainly not my intention here to make any attempt to append myself to this list; I will leave this to those with the expertise and qualifications necessary for the task. Rather, I want to make a small contribution by picking up and examining one thread that is present throughout the whole process.

We begin, again, with Eusebius. As we have seen, he places great emphasis on what might be called the transethnic character of the Christian movement. As Johnson has observed, the idea of "the church from the nations" plays a significant role in Eusebius's agenda.[22] For him it is an essential characteristic of the Christian movement that its members have been drawn from all the nations, that it has established itself among all the nations, and so on. In fact, Eusebius goes beyond such partitive expressions ("from," "among") to speak of nations apparently in their entirety: the Son of God has been recognized "by all the nations" (*In Praise of Constantine* 17.12); Christian worship is offered "by all the nations" (16.10); the writings of the apostles are accepted as the oracles of God "by all the nations" (17.8; *panta ta ethnē* in each case). The language is hyperbolic but nevertheless revealing. There is an irreducible ethnic—and transethnic—element in Eusebius's ecclesiastical demographic; the nations represent a fundamental building block in the construction of *Christianismos* as he understands it.[23]

---

21. For an insightful recent treatment of the discussion, see Jan N. Bremmer, *The Rise of Christianity through the Eyes of Gibbon, Harnack and Rodney Stark* (Groningen: Barkhuis, 2010). Selected works: Edward Gibbon, *The History of the Decline and Fall of the Roman Empire*, ed. J. B. Bury (London: Methuen, 1909–26); Voltaire, *Histoire de l'établissement du Christianisme*, in *Oeuvres complètes*, vol. 31 (Paris: Garnier frères, 1877–85), 43–116; Adolf von Harnack, *The Mission and Expansion of Christianity in the First Three Centuries*, trans. James Moffatt (London: Williams & Norgate, 1908); Arthur Darby Nock, *Conversion: The Old and the New in Religion from Alexander the Great to Augustine of Hippo* (London: Oxford University Press, 1933); Hans Lietzmann, *A History of the Early Church*, trans. Bertram Lee Woolf (London: Lutterworth, 1961); W. H. C. Frend, *The Rise of Christianity* (London: Darton, Longman and Todd, 1984); Ramsay MacMullen, *Christianizing the Roman Empire (A.D. 100–400)* (New Haven: Yale University Press, 1984); Stark, *Rise of Christianity*; also Jonathan Hill, *Christianity: How a Despised Sect from a Minority Religion Came to Dominate the Roman Empire* (Minneapolis: Fortress, 2011).

22. Aaron P. Johnson, *Ethnicity and Argument in Eusebius' Praeparatio Evangelica* (Oxford: Oxford University Press, 2006), 203.

23. To be sure, as we will see in more detail a little later, Eusebius also understands Christians to constitute a "new nation" (*Ecclesiastical History* 1.4.2), which is at the same time the ancient "nation" of the Hebrews (1.4.5), and he also expects converts to abandon all those aspects of their own ethnic identities that involved the gods of their fathers

Further, this aspect of Christian reality is embedded in a larger construction—a theological ethnography, as I have called it—that undergirds much of Eusebius's work and is visible in condensed form in *On the Holy Sepulchre*, even if some aspects of it are left largely in the shadows and need to be filled in from his other writings. Tracing the history of the nations in their political, moral, and religious characteristics, he lays a foundation both for his account of the history of redemption and for his work in redrawing the internal boundaries within "the whole human race," a boundary-making project that enables him to position Christianity favorably with respect to other pertinent demographic categories (Romans, Greeks, barbarians, and Jews).

Placing Eusebius alongside Paul, however, brings another ethnic boundary into view. The message of Christ, Paul says, is one to be proclaimed both to "the people"—that is, the people of Israel, the Jews—and to "the Gentiles" (Acts 26:23). Further, he himself was imprisoned because of Jewish perceptions that he had violated the boundary between Jews and gentiles. *Gentiles*, of course, renders *ethnē*, the same term that runs through Eusebius's theological ethnography, normally rendered as *nations*. The transition reflected by the contrast between Acts 26 and Eusebius's *On the Holy Sepulchre*, then, is one in which a mission to the gentiles (*ethnē*) carried out by Paul and other Jewish Christ-believers (which the Roman governor dismisses as irrelevant madness) develops into a transethnic "church from all the nations [*ethnē*]" (which the Roman emperor adopts as his own and promotes with enthusiasm). Before reflecting further on this transition, however, a brief digression is necessary to consider this Jewish use of *ethnē* as a way of marking the boundary between us and them, and on the limitations of the English term.[24]

This boundary language first appears in the Hebrew Scriptures, where it functioned solely in corporate terms—to speak of "the people [*hāʿām*] of Israel" in contrast to "the (other) nations" (*haggôyîm*). When the Scriptures were translated into Greek, these terms were rendered as *ho laos* and *ta ethnē*, respectively. In the later Hellenistic period, however, *ethnē* came to be used not only with reference to nations but also to (non-Jewish) individuals. In such instances, of course, *nations* is a quite inappropriate rendering of *ethnē*. To take a pertinent example from Paul's letters (Gal 2:12), when Paul says that Peter used to eat "with the *ethnē*," he was describing a situation in which Peter's table companions were individual non-Jews, not nations. The usefulness of the term *gentiles*, which

---

(*Demonstration of the Gospel* 8.3.13). But this does not override the importance of the nations themselves.

24. We will consider it in more detail in ch. 3.

derives from the Latin adjective *gentilis* and came into English (and other languages) via the Vulgate, is that it denotes non-Jewish individuals.

Its usefulness comes with an attendant cost, however. The cost is highest in passages such as Acts 26:23, where *ta ethnē* clearly refers to nations (since it is paired with *ho laos*) rather than individuals: the message preached by Paul pertains both to the people Israel and to the non-Jewish nations. But even in a passage such as Gal 2:12, to say that Peter used to eat with the gentiles serves to obscure or even eliminate the corporate-ethnic overtones that usually hover about the term *ethnē*. The issue at play in Galatians is that Peter had at one point been willing to cross the boundary that separated the Jewish people from their ethnic other, the non-Jewish nations. In passages such as these, it would be more accurate to speak of non-Jewish nations (where ethnic entities are in view) or members of non-Jewish nations (when the reference is to individuals). Such phrases, however, are probably too cumbersome to serve as fully acceptable substitutes, and so I will not attempt to avoid *gentile* and *gentiles* in what follows. Nevertheless, where clarity is necessary, I will use more accurate formulations; where the common terms appear, they should be seen as convenient shorthand for more complex realities.[25]

To return to Paul and Eusebius, Eusebius is well aware of the special use of *ethnē* as a way of referring to non-Jewish nations and individuals. The usage does not appear in his *On the Holy Sepulchre*; although he mentions the Jewish race (*genos*) or nation (*ethnos*) on two occasions (16.5; 17.8), he does not set it in explicit contrast with the *ethnē*.[26] Elsewhere, however, he frequently uses *ethnē* in contexts where the term is explicitly set over against the Jews or the Jewish nation. In most of these instances, the term appears with reference to Christian preaching to non-Jews and the emergence of gentile Christianity.[27]

---

25. For a full discussion of the path that leads from the Hebrew *gôyîm* through the Greek *ethnē* and the Latin *gentilis* to the English *gentiles*, together with a discussion of the problems pertaining to the English term, see my "'Gentile Christianity' as a Category in the Study of Christian Origins," *HTR* 106 (2013): 433–58.

26. Yet he comes close in *In Praise of Constantine* 17.8. After describing the destruction of Jerusalem "as the immediate consequence of their impiety," he immediately goes on to speak of "the establishment of his church throughout the world," in the context of which he refers to the writings of the apostles, which were "read and pondered by all the nations [*para pasi tois ethnesi*]" (17.9).

27. He can use the term in a more negative sense as well. For example, describing the purposes of his two works *Preparation for the Gospel* and *Demonstration of the Gospel*, he says that the first was a response to "the attacks of the polytheistic Gentiles [*tōn . . . ethnōn*]," while the second addressed "the accusation of the Jews" (*Demonstration of the Gospel* 1.1.15–16).

The prophets foretold "that the advent of Christ and the falling away of the Jews would be followed by the call of the Gentiles [*tōn ethnōn*]" (*Preparation for the Gospel* 1.3.14). Until that falling away had fully manifested itself, the earliest apostles were not yet in a position "to transmit the word of faith to Gentiles [*ethnesin*]," and so they "announced it only to Jews" (*Ecclesiastical History* 2.1.8). Subsequently, however, while Peter continued to preach "to those of the circumcision," Paul, "in his preaching to those from the Gentiles [*tois ex ethnōn*], laid the foundations of the churches from Jerusalem round about unto Illyricum" (*Ecclesiastical History* 3.4.1). The usage is frequently encountered, and the point is not controversial.[28]

It is clear, then, that Eusebius would see the church from the nations of his own day as the culmination of the mission to the gentiles that was foretold by the prophets, commanded by Christ and initiated by Paul and other Jewish preachers. Indeed, in one passage, he explicitly connects the two in a very personal way. Responding to questions about why (non-Jewish) Christians should use and venerate Jewish Scriptures, he says that "we have accepted and loved as belonging to ourselves the sacred books of the Hebrews" precisely because of these prophecies "relating to us Gentiles [*hēmōn tōn ethnōn*]" (*Demonstration of the Gospel* 1.4.1). He continues by quoting not only a number of these "prophecies" (Pss 9:20; 96:3–8, 10; 98:1–3; Isa 2:3) but also Jesus's command to the disciples that they go and "make disciples of all the *ethnē*" (Matt 28:19–20). In this context, then, his use of the first-person plural ("us Gentiles") thus serves both to characterize the church in his own day as a gentile entity and to identify this church with the early Christian mission to the gentiles.

Thus, although Eusebius does not make an explicit contrast between Jews and gentiles in *On the Holy Sepulchre*, we are certainly justified to see a connection between the story that unfolds in his oration and Paul's narrative in Acts 26 concerning his call to proclaim Christ among the non-Jewish *ethnē*, the gentiles. In this regard, other points of connection immediately present themselves. Like Eusebius, Paul understands the mission to the gentiles to be a fulfillment of prophetic promises—precisely "what the prophets and Moses said would take place" (v. 22). Further, Eusebius's emphasis on the power of the demons has a certain counterpart in Paul's address—the gentiles are under "the power [*exousias*] of Satan" and need to have their eyes opened so that "they may turn from darkness to light" (v. 18). Also, as we have noted, Paul's address is placed within a Roman imperial framework, with the emperor himself being called on to render a decision about the degree of tolerance to be given to Paul's mission.

---

28. For other instances, see, e.g., *Demonstration of the Gospel* 1.7.6; 2.1.1; *Ecclesiastical History* 1.3.6; 1.6.1, 4; 2.1.13; 3.7.5; 4.6.3.

Of course, there are differences as well, both the obvious differences in the composition and status of the Christian movement between the first and fourth centuries (not to mention the ethnic identities of Paul and Eusebius), and more specific differences in detail. In Paul's address, for example, more latitude is given to a mission to the Jews: the message of light pertains "both to the people [of Israel] and to the Gentiles" (v. 23); Paul proclaimed his message throughout Judea "and also to the Gentiles" (v. 20).[29]

While it is not my purpose at this juncture to carry out a detailed comparison, it will aid our initial reflections if we fill in some gaps by looking at the place of the Jews in Eusebius's theological ethnography as it appears in other works. Central to this is a distinction he makes between the Hebrews and the Jews, though to describe this we need to look again at the larger picture.

In much of his work, Eusebius is concerned to construct an identity for the Christian movement by locating it with respect to the various nations and ethnic groupings that constitute what he frequently refers to as the human race. Nations are characterized by their way of life (*politeia*), which, in turn, is founded on their mode of religion (*tropos theosebeias* or *tropos eusebeias*).[30] While each nation has its own specific character, he argues that there are three broad types (*Demonstration of the Gospel* 1.2.8–16). The most widespread type, fully in view in *On the Holy Sepulchre*, is found among all those nations that are fully enslaved to the demons. As we have seen, this mode of religion developed in two stages. At the outset, it involved simply the worship of created entities as gods. In *On the Holy Sepulchre*, Eusebius attributes the development of this mode of worship simply to the nations' inability to perceive and recognize the creator of all (*In Praise of Constantine* 13.5). Elsewhere, however, the picture is a little more detailed. The worship of "things seen in the heavens, the sun and moon and stars," he says, was something allowed to the nations as a kind of accommodation to human weakness, either by God directly (citing Deut 4:19) or by the angelic guardians assigned to the nations (citing Deut 32:8).[31] Even so, this divine ac-

---

29. Of course, in the context of Luke-Acts as a whole, this "both . . . and" is much more complex, especially in view of Paul's repeated pattern of turning away from the Jews and concentrating on gentiles (Acts 13:44–48; 18:5–7; 28:23–28), the final instance of which brings the narrative to an emphatic conclusion.

30. The former phrase appears, e.g., in *Demonstration of the Gospel* 1.2.8; 1.6.30; 1.6.54, 60; the latter, e.g., in *Demonstration of the Gospel* 1.1.4, 8; 1.9.2; 1.10.6; 5.1.28; 6.13.26.

31. According to Deut 4:19 (cited in *Preparation for the Gospel* 1.9.15), God has allotted the worship of the heavenly bodies "to all the nations everywhere under heaven." In Deut 32:8 (cited in *Demonstration of the Gospel* 4.7.1), the boundaries of the nations have been fixed "according to the number of the angels of God" (Eusebius follows the LXX reading;

commodation did not extend to the worship of other created beings, including divinized humans, animals, and other named gods. In the second stage, the demons took advantage of this situation of divine accommodation corrupted by human weakness. Infiltrating polytheistic worship, they soon had brought all nations under their sway. Outside *On the Holy Sepulchre*, this story is repeated and elaborated, as Eusebius describes the rebellion of Lucifer/Satan and the fall of his band of renegade angels (*Preparation for the Gospel* 7.16.8; *Demonstration of the Gospel* 4.9.1–12).

From earliest times, however, there was one nation that followed "the opposite course" (*Preparation for the Gospel* 7.3.1), that of the Hebrews. Observing the visible world, they were able to perceive "the Maker and Creator of the universe" who stood behind it and whom they worshiped as the only God. Beginning with the appearance of the Word "to one or two of the God-fearing [*theophilōn*] men of old," the Hebrews eventually became "a whole nation [*ethnos*]" (*Ecclesiastical History* 1.2.21, 22). Living fully in accordance with nature and in freedom from the tyranny of the passions, they "enjoyed a free and unfettered mode of religion [*eusebeias*]," so that they "had no need of laws to rule them" (*Preparation for the Gospel* 7.6.4). With the implication in this statement that a life ruled by laws is an inferior mode of religion, one begins to see the sort of distinction Eusebius will make between the Hebrews and the Jews. Indeed, the Hebrew nation consists essentially of the Genesis patriarchs, though the line continues with Moses, the prophets, and some others, as we will see.

Although the nation of the Jews takes its name from Judah (*Preparation for the Gospel* 7.6.2), it comes into being only with the giving of the law by Moses. It is only when "the system of Moses' Law had . . . been brought into being" that one can begin to speak of Jews and Judaism; the Hebrews who lived before this, therefore, "were not Jews" (*Demonstration of the Gospel* 1.2.4, 5). The law of Moses, which brought the Jewish nation into being, was necessitated by the debilitating effects of the sojourn in Egypt. After the death of Joseph, the noble example of their Hebrew forebears gradually faded under the corrosive influence of the Egyptian way of life, so that they "came round in their modes of living to customs similar to those of the Egyptians" and eventually were virtually indistinguishable in character from them (*Preparation for the Gospel* 7.8.37). So it was that when Moses arrived on the scene, he found them "unable through moral weakness to emulate the virtue of their fathers, inasmuch as they were enslaved by passions and sick in soul" (*Preparation for the Gospel* 7.8.38). The law, then,

---

in place of "angels," "sons of the gods" is found in Qumran material, while the MT reading is "sons of Israel"). In both passages, however, this concession to the nations (*ethnē* in both cases) is not to be followed by Israel.

is to be seen as a remedial—rather than ideal—mode of religion and way of life. It is medicine to heal a race "worn away by the terrible disease of Egypt" (*Demonstration of the Gospel* 1.6.31), a "polity [*politeia*] that corresponded to their condition" (*Preparation for the Gospel* 7.8.39), and thus "a lower and less perfect way of life" (*Demonstration of the Gospel* 1.6.31) than that which characterized the Hebrews who preceded them. Even so, aspects of the ideal mode of religion that most of them, in their weakened state, were not able to understand were nevertheless present in the law in the form of "symbols and shadows" (*Preparation for the Gospel* 7.8.39).

It is only in the form of these symbols and shadows that the law has any relevance to the wider world of the nations as a whole. Eusebius is fond of pointing out that much of the law cannot be fulfilled outside Judea. Pilgrimage festivals, purification after childbirth, removing corpse defilement, and many other requirements of the law all require residence in the land and proximity to the temple, which means that it was never intended as a mode of religion and way of life for "god-fearing people from all the nations [*tous ex hapantōn tōn ethnōn theosebēsontas*]" (*Demonstration of the Gospel* 1.2.16).

Still, at the level of symbol and shadow, the law has had some influence. Pointing to what in his view are the admirable qualities of the Greek philosophical tradition—its monotheistic high points ("knowledge of the worship of the One Supreme God"; *Preparation for the Gospel* 10.1.1), condemnation of the mythological accounts of the gods, concern for virtue and the soul, and so on—he argues that the Greeks got all these things from the Hebrews, who had possessed them long before the Greek nation appeared. "The wise men of the Greeks have been zealous imitators of the Hebrew doctrines," he declares (*Preparation for the Gospel* 10.14.19).

To the extent that Eusebius praises the Greeks, however, he does so just to shift them to a less favorable location in his map of the nations than the one to which they themselves would lay claim. The Greeks are inveterate borrowers. What is good in their tradition they took from the Hebrews; the rest—especially their polytheistic mode of religion (with its demonic underpinnings)—they adopted from the barbarians (*Preparation for the Gospel* 10.1.1–3). Even more, Eusebius on occasion classes the Hebrews among the barbarians,[32] which has the effect of turning the traditional Greek-barbarian binary on its head.

Eusebius thus takes the two traditional ethnic maps of the world—one divided into Jews and gentiles, the other into Greeks and barbarians—and redraws them to produce three groups of nations. While he does not erase the Greek/

---

32. *Preparation for the Gospel* 7.1.3; 10.1.1–3; 10.3.26.

barbarian distinction entirely,[33] there is no difference between them as far as their mode of religion and way of life are concerned. Together they constitute the first group, consisting of "all the nations" under the power of demonic polytheism. Thus the Jew/gentile distinction remains, but the Jews, defined by the law of Moses, represent only a partial advance on the gentiles. With the law of Moses functioning as a kind of first aid for polytheists, they "have reached the first step of holiness" (*Demonstration of the Gospel* 1.6.62) and thus constitute the second group.

The third group are the Christians, those from all the nations who have ascended to the heights "by the stair of Gospel teaching" (*Demonstration of the Gospel* 1.6.62). In his life and person, Christ, the quintessential Hebrew of the Hebrews,[34] has fully revealed the mode of religion and way of life first grasped by the Hebrews; in his death and resurrection, he has demolished the power of the demons and has made this mode of religion and way of life accessible to the nations. Christianity, as a consequence, is "exactly that third form of religion," which, says Eusebius, "I have already deduced as the most ancient and most venerable of all religions, and which has been preached of late to all nations [*pasi tois ethnesi*] through our Savior" (*Demonstration of the Gospel* 1.2.9). As such it is "the most ancient organization [*politeuma*] for piety" and "the most venerable philosophy" (*Demonstration of the Gospel* 1.2.10). Thus even as this "third form of religion" has drawn its members from all the nations of the world, it is at the same time also a renewal of the ancient nation of the Hebrews.[35] In this sense, Eusebius can also describe it as a "new nation [*neon ethnos*]" (*Ecclesiastical History* 1.4.2). All of this was fully anticipated by the Hebrews themselves; Eusebius carries out an extensive exegetical argument, especially in the *Demonstration of the Gospel*, in which a whole array of scriptural references to the *ethnē* are read as anticipations of the conversion of the gentiles and the creation of the church from the nations.[36]

---

33. E.g., he frequently describes the church as including both Greeks and barbarians; *Ecclesiastical History* 10.4.20; *Preparation for the Gospel* 1.1.6; 1.4.9, 11, 13; 1.5.1; 2.5.2; 12.32.7; *Demonstration of the Gospel* 1.6.63, 75; 3.2.40; *In Praise of Constantine* 11.5; 16.6.

34. Eusebius uses the phrase to describe Joseph (*Preparation for the Gospel* 7.8.36) and Moses (*Preparation for the Gospel* 7.7.1). Although he does not use the term for Jesus, it is at least implied by his description of "the law and life of our Saviour Jesus Christ" as "a renewal of the ancient pre-Mosaic religion, in which Abraham, the friend of God, and his forefathers are shown to have lived" (*Demonstration of the Gospel* 1.5.2).

35. See also *Preparation for the Gospel* 1.5.2; 1.6.30, 54, 62.

36. A significant portion of *Demonstration of the Gospel* (2.1.1–2.2.19) is given over to a series of prophetic texts, with the aim of showing "how full they are of predictions of good and salvation for all nations [*pasi tois ethnesin*], and how strongly they asserted that

For all intents and purposes, then, Christianity for Eusebius is a gentile entity.[37] To be sure, he can make statements reminiscent of Paul's both/and ("both to our people and to the Gentiles"; Acts 26:23). For example, with reference to God's promises to Abraham, he says that "in days to come not only Abraham's descendants, his Jewish seed, but all the tribes of the earth and all the nations [*panta ta ethnē*] will be counted worthy of God's blessing" (*Demonstration of the Gospel* 1.2.12). Later, at the end of his collection of proof texts in the *Demonstration*, he claims to have demonstrated "that the presence of Christ was intended to be the salvation not only of the Jews, but of all nations [*tois pasin ethnesin*] as well" (*Demonstration of the Gospel* 2.2.20).[38] These promises of salvation, however, have been fulfilled without remainder in the experience of the Jewish believers in the early days of the church—"a small and scanty number," consisting only of "the disciples, apostles and evangelists of our Savior, and all the others of the circumcision who believed on Him at the time of the falling away of their whole nation."[39] Except for this small remnant, now a thing of the past, the Jewish nation as a whole has been "lost" (*Demonstration of the Gospel* 1.1.8).

The second of Eusebius's three modes of religion, then, was a temporary thing, an "intermediate period" (*Demonstration of the Gospel* 1.6.31) lasting only until the coming of Christ.[40] He puts considerable emphasis on Gen 49:10, Jacob's deathbed blessing of Judah: "A ruler shall not be wanting from Judah, and a leader from his thighs, until the things stored up for him come, and he is the expectation of nations [*ethnōn*]." In Eusebius's reading, the period in which the Jews were able "to live under the native rulers of the nation," a period that began with Moses, came to an end with the accession of the foreigner Herod, which coincided both with the emergence of Augustus as the first Roman emperor and, of course, with the birth of Christ, the "expectation of the nations" himself (*Ecclesiastical History* 1.6.1–4).

Except for the tiny remnant, "the Jewish nation as a whole" (*to pan Ioudaiōn*

---

their promises to the Gentile world [*tois ethnesin*] could only be fulfilled by the coming of Christ" (*Demonstration of the Gospel* 2.1.1).

37. Occasionally he can use *ethnē* in an unqualified sense to refer to non-Christian outsiders (e.g., "the terrible rage of the heathen [*tōn ethnōn*] against the saints" (*Ecclesiastical History* 5.1.4), in which case it might have the sense of an identity that Christians have left behind.

38. He also speaks of promises that the gentiles will have an "equal share" of things promised to Israel (*Demonstration of the Gospel* 2.3.30, 32), though he elsewhere says that the Christians are "better" rather than "equal" (*Demonstration of the Gospel* 2.2.21).

39. Respectively, *Demonstration of the Gospel* 2.3.48 and 2.3.78.

40. See also *Preparation for the Gospel* 7.8.40.

ethnos) rejected Christ, preferring to cling to an obsolete mode of religion and way of life.[41] The consequences were swift. Quoting Josephus, Eusebius recounts some of the woes experienced by the Jews in their war with Rome, so that his readers may be able to see "how the punishment of God followed close after them for their crime against the Christ of God" (*Ecclesiastical History* 3.5.7).[42] The punishment represented by the destruction of Jerusalem itself was compounded in that, now deprived of the temple and thus also of the possibility of fulfilling the law, they were subject to the curse prescribed by the law itself for those who did not fulfill it.[43] The destruction of the temple by the Romans thus functions for Eusebius as a historical demonstration of the temporary nature of the mode of religion based on the law of Moses.

While the punishment of the Jews and the gathering of the church from the gentiles are thus linked in Eusebius's construction, at one level it is not a simple cause-and-effect process, with the rejection of the Jewish nation serving as the precondition of the mission to the gentiles, who are brought in to take their place. Part of Moses's intent in concentrating the functioning of the law around the temple was that when the temple was no more, the Jews "of necessity ... would have to receive the new covenant announced by Christ" (*Demonstration of the Gospel* 1.6.38). In other words, the new covenant theoretically could have been a both/and mode of religion; the Jews could have—should have—recognized the temporary character of the Mosaic *politeia* and joined with the other nations of the world in turning to Christ. At the same time, however, Eusebius believes that the fate of the Jews was also anticipated by the prophets: "Yes, the Hebrew oracles foretell distinctly the fall and ruin of the Jewish nation [*tou Ioudaiōn ethnous*] through their disbelief in Christ, so that we should no longer appear equal to them, but better than they" (*Demonstration of the Gospel* 2.2.21). This statement is followed by an equally lengthy list of prophetic proof texts (*Demonstration of the Gospel* 2.3.1–29). In the end, then, a both/and outcome was only a theoretical possibility. From the outset, the prophets knew that the salvation of the gentiles would be accompanied by the failure of the Jews; they foresaw that "though one nation were lost, every nation and race of men [*pan ethnos kai genos anthrōpōn*] would know God, escape from the demons, cease from ignorance and deceit and enjoy the light of holiness" (*Demonstration of the Gospel* 1.1.8). In fact, Eu-

---

41. The phrase is from *Ecclesiastical History* 1.1.2, where Eusebius indicates that in the history to follow he will recount "the fate which has beset the whole nation of the Jews [*to pan Ioudaiōn ethnos*] from the moment of their plot against our Saviour."

42. One wonders why the Romans should not be liable to similar punishment for their part in this "crime."

43. I.e., in Deut 27:26; see *Demonstration of the Gospel* 1.6.38–39.

sebius sees the fulfillment of these prophecies in his own day—the emergence of a worldwide church drawn from all the nations, and the ongoing woes of the Jewish nation as it mourns the loss of its land and temple—as "the works of our Savior in our own age" (*In Praise of Constantine* 17.1) and thus as an incontrovertible "demonstration" of the truth of the gospel itself.[44]

The destruction of the temple brings us back to the Roman Empire, which occupies an important place in Eusebius's religious history of the human race. After the conversion of Constantine, the redrawn map of the human race that Eusebius had developed in earlier works is placed even more firmly within a framework provided by the Roman Empire. Rome is now no longer simply the providential means by which God had brought to an end the "intermediate period" of the Mosaic law and facilitated the spread of the gospel to all the nations. Now that the transethnic mission of the gospel had coalesced with Rome's project of extending its sovereignty to the ends of the inhabited world, the empire has become a partner with the church in an overarching mission of drawing all the nations, Greek and barbarian alike, into the new nation founded on the mode of religion and way of life first exemplified by the ancient Hebrews.

To gain perspective on this merger of evangelic mission and imperial ideology, let us return to Aelius Aristides. As has been noted, one cannot read Aristides's *Regarding Rome* alongside Eusebius's *On the Holy Sepulchre* without being struck by the similarities, both in the overall shape of these two orations in praise of Rome and in specific details. To be sure, there are significant differences that will occupy our attention in a moment. But Aristides, no less than Eusebius, commends Rome for the extent to which it has achieved its goal "to unite all nations in one harmonious whole."[45]

As we have seen, both of them emphasize the unprecedented extent of the Roman Empire, even using the same image of the daily course of the sun to make the point.[46] Both draw attention to the peace and harmony that characterize the empire, attributing this to the rule of the emperor as a single sovereign and the

---

44. The title of his work is deliberately chosen. He rests his apologetic argument ultimately on historical demonstrations of the truth of the gospel—the end of the line of Jewish rulers, the destruction of the temple, the emergence of the Roman Empire, and, at the heart of it all, the spread of the religion of the Hebrews to all the nations of the world.

45. Using Eusebius's language in *In Praise of Constantine* 16.6.

46. Aristides: "the course of the sun and your possessions are equal and . . . the sun's course is always in your land" (*Regarding Rome* 10); Eusebius: who else "has ever held his course from the rising to the setting sun?" (*In Praise of Constantine* 17.13).

establishment of a common *politeia*.⁴⁷ Both praise the emperor for his generous benefactions in the form of magnificent building projects.⁴⁸ In both works, the population of the empire is described as a single family or race inhabiting a common native land,⁴⁹ and both illustrate this by pointing to the fact that people are able to travel freely from one end of the empire to the other.⁵⁰ Common to both works is a contrast between the present state of affairs and the violence and disarray that were endemic in the world in previous times;⁵¹ common, too, are the images of healing and enlightenment that are used to describe this contrast.⁵² Also, despite their differences on this point, both Aristides and Eusebius describe the contrast in religious terms: with divine help and approval, the Roman Empire has restored proper worship, putting an end to a state of religious disorder that even involved widespread child sacrifice.⁵³

---

47. For the single sovereign, see *Regarding Rome* 88 and *In Praise of Constantine* 16.4; for the common *politeia*, see *Regarding Rome* 90 and *In Praise of Constantine* 13.9.

48. See *Regarding Rome* 92–94; *In Praise of Constantine* 11.2.

49. Aristides: "and you used the word 'Roman' to belong not to a city but to be the name of a sort of common race [*genos*]" (*Regarding Rome* 63); Eusebius: "Thus the whole world appeared like one well-ordered and united family" (*In Praise of Constantine* 16.7).

50. Aristides: "Indeed, you have best proved that well-known saying, that the earth is the mother of all and the universal country [*patris*] of all. Now it is possible for both Greek and barbarian, with his possessions or without them, to travel easily wherever he wishes, quite as if he were going from one country of his to another" (*Regarding Rome* 100); Eusebius: "each one might journey unhindered as far as and whithersoever he pleased: men might securely travel from West to East, and from East to West, as to their own native country [*patridas*]" (*In Praise of Constantine* 16.7).

51. Aristides: The inept and abusive form of rule in the past resulted in "hatred and plotting on the part of those who were treated in this way, revolts, civil war, continual strife and unceasing contention" (*Regarding Rome* 20); Eusebius: "All nations, whether Greek or barbarian, throughout the world . . . were infected with sedition as with some fierce and terrible disease: insomuch that the human family was irreconcilably divided against itself. . . . Nay, more than this: with passions aroused to fury, they engaged in mutual conflicts, so frequent that their lives were passed as it were in uninterrupted warfare" (*In Praise of Constantine* 13.9–10).

52. Aristides: "and it can be said in medical terms that the inhabited world was, as it were, ill at the start and has now recovered"; "the confusion and faction ceased and there entered in universal order and a glorious light in life and government and the laws came to the fore" (*Regarding Rome* 97, 103); Eusebius: "the inveterate malady which had asserted its dominion over the whole human race"; "and irradiated mankind with the bright and glorious beams of his doctrine" (*In Praise of Constantine* 13.14; 17.12).

53. On child sacrifice, see *Regarding Rome* 104; *In Praise of Constantine* 13.4–5.

GENTILE CHRISTIAN IDENTITY

Of course, this description elides significant points of contrast. For Eusebius, the one whose rule is coextensive with the course of the sun is "our Savior";[54] he also is the one who enlightens the nations, and so on down the line. While the emperor has come in to join forces with Christ in this grand program of uniting the nations, Christ as the divine Word is the primary agent in it all. The major portion of the story of redemption history that Eusebius narrates in *On the Holy Sepulchre* could be told without reference to a Christian emperor. As indeed it had been, in the more detailed accounts that we have drawn on above (especially *Preparation for the Gospel* and *Demonstration of the Gospel*), works—it should be noted—that were completed prior to Constantine's victory in 324 CE, when Eusebius and the eastern part of the empire were still under the rule of Licinius.

In comparing Eusebius's *On the Holy Sepulchre* with Aristides's *Regarding Rome*, then, we should recognize the existence of two layers in Eusebius's work. At the top layer, representing the period after the emergence of Constantine as the sole emperor, it can be said that Eusebius and Aristides are carrying out analogous enterprises; both are engaged in the praise of Rome and its role in uniting and enlightening the nations. This layer, however, is simply superimposed on an earlier construction, without occasioning much rebuilding of what was already there. To be sure, Rome had a place in the earlier construction as well. There Eusebius had assigned it a providential role—emerging at the same time as Christ; punishing the Jews and destroying the temple; providing the worldwide infrastructure that facilitated the spread of the gospel. Nevertheless, Rome was able to play this role effectively only because Christ had already done the redemptive heavy lifting; it was only because the demonic forces had been defeated by Christ in his death and resurrection that Rome was able to extend its domain and rule so effectively. In his later work, including *On the Holy Sepulchre*,[55] the role of the Roman Empire, with a Christian emperor at its helm, was upgraded from that of a useful beneficiary of Christ's redeeming work to that of a partner with the church in the task of establishing the benefits of Christ's work among the nations. Nevertheless, even in *On the Holy Sepulchre*, the success of the empire was dependent on what Christ had already accomplished. It was only because Christ had first "destroyed at once the many governments and the many gods of the powers of darkness" that "the Roman empire, the causes of multiplied governments being thus removed," was able to effect "an easy conquest of those [nations] which yet remained" and

---

54. Eusebius avoids *Christ* and other specific designations in the Holy Sepulchre oration.

55. Also the oration delivered in Constantinople in 336 CE as part of the celebrations commemorating the thirtieth anniversary of Constantine's accession to power (constituting the first part of *In Praise of Constantine*) and the *Life of Constantine*.

move decisively toward its goal "to unite all nations [*pantoiōn ethnōn*] in one harmonious whole" (*In Praise of Constantine* 16.6).

While Eusebius differs greatly from Aristides at the level of his basic construction, the points of similarity remain pertinent, though in a somewhat different way. Although Aristides is from one of the provinces, it is fair to see his *Regarding Rome* as a representation of imperial ideology—an oration that praises the empire by reflecting back to a Roman audience Rome's own image of itself, at least the self-portrait that it presents for public display. The points of similarity with Eusebius suggest that we might see the latter's narrative of the redemptive unification of the nations as an attempt to mimic imperial ideology—a kind of counternarrative that draws on elements of the story that Rome tells about itself in order to present the Christian movement in terms that would both resonate with and compete with the dominant imperial narrative. In material written after Constantine's victory over Licinius, the two narratives are merged, the Roman Empire being assigned a new role in the Christian narrative alongside that of the church, with the intention that the counternarrative might itself become the official story of a Christian empire.

As was observed at the outset, *On the Holy Sepulchre* is essentially an apologetic work; Eusebius was using the occasion and the broad audience it afforded him to make a persuasive case for the religion of the emperor. In the opening section of his earlier work *Preparation for the Gospel*, Eusebius describes the apologetic challenges he sets out to meet in this work and its sequel, *Demonstration of the Gospel*. The challenges come on one side from the Greeks and on the other from the Jews. Both sets of challenges have to do with Christian identity; both sets operate within the framework of ethnicity.

The Greeks, says Eusebius, accuse Christians of deserting their ancestral family and kinfolk and revolting against (*apostantes*) "those ancestral gods by whom every nation and every city [*pan ethnos kai pasa polis*] is sustained." What is worse, they have exchanged these forms of worship, established from "the earliest time, among all Greeks and barbarians," for "the foreign mythologies of the Jews," those "impious enemies of all nations [*pasin ethnesi*]." What is doubly worse is that they have not really become Jews; while they have based their claim on Jewish mythologies, they refused to follow those customs that characterize the Jews as a distinctive people. Thus the Christians are neither Greek, nor barbarian, nor Jewish. They have cut themselves off from the ethnic map of the human race and are wandering in "a pathless desert."[56]

From their side, says Eusebius, the Jews complain that the Christians, who are "strangers and aliens" (*allophyloi ontes kai allogeneis*), nevertheless lay claim

---

56. For this whole paragraph, see *Preparation for the Gospel* 1.2.1–4.

to the Scriptures of the Jews, but then simply misunderstand and misuse them. The most egregious misuse is that Christians claim the Scriptures for their own but refuse to follow the law that lies at the heart of the Scriptures. How can they think that they can ignore and even break the law and still expect to receive "the better rewards which have been promised to those who keep the Law"? Further, the Christians claim that Jesus is the messiah promised by the prophets. But the prophets were Jewish; they promised a messiah who "would come as Redeemer and King of the Jews, and not of alien nations [*tōn allophylōn ethnōn*]"; the Jewish people would be in a much better position to recognize the messiah when he came than would gentile outsiders. In reading the Scriptures, the Christians unfairly—even fraudulently—claim all the blessings for themselves and leave the Jews only with the sins and the prophetic warnings of judgment "against their nation [*tou ethnous*]." In short, say the Jews, the Christians thrust themselves in and "try violently to thrust out the true family and kindred from their own ancestral rights."[57]

Eusebius is a shrewd debater, showing himself to be both fully conversant with the criticisms of his opponents and not afraid to set them out in accurate and compelling terms. From his summary of Greek and Jewish objections, one can readily get a sense of the role of ethnicity in the three-sided debate. For his opponents on both sides, religion was thoroughly embedded in ethnicity—part of the ancestral customs of a nation. Even the recognition of larger ethnic groupings—Greeks and barbarians—did not override the ethnic character of religious practice and belief. If the Jews stood somewhat outside the categories of Greek and barbarian, they nevertheless were a recognizable nation, with their own ancestral customs. Straddling the boundaries and blurring the categories, the Christians were seen as occupying an undefined space somewhere off the map of the ethnically constructed *oikoumenē*, attempting "to cut out for themselves a new kind of track in a pathless desert" (*Preparation for the Gospel* 1.2.4).

Looking at Eusebius's theological ethnography from this perspective, one gets a clearer sense of what he was trying to accomplish with his own redrawing of the ethnic map. With his invention of the "Hebrews" as a primordial race of pure ethical monotheists, he is able both to place the traditional ethnic groupings (Greeks, barbarians, Jews) into new subordinate positions by redefining their identities in terms of their relationships with the Hebrews and to create a primary place at the center of the map for Christians, a new nation that is at the same time the full manifestation of the ancient Hebrew nation.

Further, looking at Eusebius from the perspective of Aristides's *Regarding Rome*, one can also discern how Eusebius has made use of Roman imperial

---

57. For this paragraph, see *Preparation for the Gospel* 1.2.5–8.

ideology in his apologetic remaking of the map. Playing off Rome's image of itself as the means by which "all the nations" not only are conquered but also are civilized and drawn into a new peaceable and harmonious form of kinship, Eusebius constructs a counterimage of the church as a superior means by which this transethnic ideal might be realized. While his apologetic construction of the "church from all the nations" did not require a Christian emperor for its cogency, once Constantine had emerged as the sole ruler of the empire it did not take much to turn the counterimage into a single combined image: "two mighty powers"—"the teaching of Christ" and "the Roman empire"—working in concert to gather all the nations into "one well-ordered and united family" (*In Praise of Constantine* 16.5–7).

Before moving on, one final glance at Aristides will be useful. To this point, his oration in Rome has been used simply as a convenient example of imperial ideology. It is possible, however, that there is more going on in the work. Several aspects of *Regarding Rome* suggest that we might see it as something of an analogous attempt to use the dominant imperial narrative as a means of creating space within the empire for a subjugated group. Despite his Roman citizenship, Aristides was intensely proud of his Greek intellectual heritage. Further, as a representative of the movement that came to be known as the Second Sophistic, he was engaged in a lifelong project to recover the glory of the Greek past and to enhance its esteem among the educated elite in the Roman world. His *Regarding Rome* should not be seen in isolation from this cultural and biographical context.

On reading the oration, one is certainly struck, of course, by Aristides's effusive praise for the accomplishments of the empire. Reading it more carefully, however, one might form the impression that he praises Rome only within certain limits and with a discernible reserve.[58] While he recognizes the failings of the Greeks in the administration of their empire, especially in comparison with the Romans, this is the only area mentioned in the oration in which the Romans excel. While the Romans were superior in "the knowledge of how to govern," the Greeks "far excelled all others in knowledge" more generally (*Regarding Rome* 51). Apart from matters of governance, Aristides brings nothing else forward for praise, even though it would have been quite appropriate in the context. He has nothing to say about the city of Rome itself—its architecture, monuments, schools, literature, or cultural achievements. He says nothing about Roman history and does not acknowledge Roman claims to a common ancestry with the Greeks. He mentions no Roman by name; even the gods who take delight in the good order of the Roman Empire are Greek. In his encomium, his

58. Here I am depending on Pernot's perceptive article, "Aelius Aristides and Rome."

interest in Rome is restricted to its role as governor of the "cities and nations." Apart from this he has little to say.

This is not to suggest that Aristides set out to be deliberately subversive. As Pernot has suggested, it should be seen as a case not of outright opposition but of ambivalent feelings:

> It is neither a matter of frontal attacks, nor of being "pro-Roman" or "anti-Roman." We are not speaking of opposition or dissidence, phenomena that did exist in other contexts in the Roman Empire. It is more a question of psychological complexity and subtle undertones.[59]

What is on view in the oration is the perspective of a Roman subject who appreciates the empire for providing the secure framework within which a Greek scholar and orator can proceed with his work, but who reserves the right to his own opinion on the cultural superiority of his own "native affinities" (*Regarding Rome* 59).

To the extent that this reading is justified, Aristides's oration in the court of Antoninus Pius helps to cast that of Eusebius into even sharper relief. Of course, we should not minimize the differences. Eusebius lived near the eastern boundary of the empire and was a member of a controversial group that until recently had been subject to severe imperial repression; Aristides belonged to the elite stratum of a long-established Roman province and was well connected with influential circles in Rome. Christianity had been widely despised, Greek culture widely admired. Nevertheless, despite these considerable differences, both orations represent attempts by well-educated provincials, standing at some distance from the center of the Roman world, to negotiate and preserve a space within the empire for the subjugated groups to which they belong. And in pursuing this goal, both Aristides and Eusebius draw on Roman imperial ideology about the nations and use it for their own rhetorical ends.

Thus, in reading Eusebius alongside Aristides and (Luke's) Paul, our attention is necessarily drawn to issues of identity, ethnicity, and the emergence of gentile Christianity. Paul's speech in Acts 26 gives us a glimpse of the Christian movement in its early days,[60] when gentiles (*ethnē*) were first being admitted into a movement that was still largely Jewish and centered on Jerusalem. Eusebius's speech at the dedication of the Church of the Holy Sepulchre almost three centuries later, in a Jerusalem from which Jews were now banished, brings into view a church that has become well established in all corners of the Roman Empire and

---

59. Pernot, "Aelius Aristides and Rome," 177.
60. Albeit a retrospective glimpse, through the eyes of Luke.

that has come to think of itself as a new kind of race or nation drawn from all the non-Jewish nations (*ethnē*) of the inhabited world. Read alongside Eusebius's work, Aristides's speech in praise of Rome helps open a window onto the process by which the gentile church formed a distinctive identity and negotiated a place for itself within the Roman Empire as a whole. And taken together, the three works raise a whole variety of questions about stages in the intervening process that do not come directly into view in these works.

Again, it is not my purpose here to attempt any sort of grand narrative dealing with the Christianization of the empire. But Christian success in the empire would not have been possible without the emergence and development of a distinctively gentile Christianity. If the earliest Jewish groups of Christ-believers had not taken the step of including non-Jews within their membership; if the movement had not taken root in significant ways in areas beyond Judea and outside the Jewish diaspora; if gentile congregations in various parts of the Mediterranean basin had not developed a certain translocal solidarity and socioreligious cohesiveness; and if this had not produced a sense among Christians that they belonged to a distinctive new people drawn from all the nations—then the world that becomes visible through the lens of Eusebius's Holy Sepulchre oration would have been difficult to imagine.

Of course, this way of framing the matter requires immediate qualification and refinement. For one thing, it gives the false impression of a smooth, linear, and homogeneous process, leaving little space for diversity and conflict at each stage, including that represented by Eusebius himself. For another, it might convey a certain impression of inevitability, as if the emergence of a Christian empire could have been predicted from the emergence of a distinctively gentile Christianity.[61] In addition, it might encourage an inappropriate teleological reading of the evidence, as if gentile Christians developed a particular form of self-definition with the conscious purpose of "dislodg[ing] classical paganism and becom[ing] the dominant faith of Western civilization."[62] Further, it casts into shadow the spread of the Christian movement outside the boundaries of the Roman world, particularly to the east. Eusebius provides us with a convenient retrospective vantage point from which to begin, but this brings with it some blind spots that will need to be avoided.

---

61. Daniel Richter speaks of his "dissatisfaction with how reception studies often treat end points as the inevitable result of beginnings. Such an approach blinds the student of the past both to the nature of the substratum as well as to the many possible directions in which things could have gone" (*Cosmopolis*, 6).

62. To use a phrase from the passage by Rodney Stark, cited above, though with no intention of implying that he read the evidence in this way.

More generally, this way of framing the matter might suggest that I am setting myself up for a grand narrative after all, a full account of "the mission and expansion of Christianity" from its Jewish beginnings to its gentile triumph,[63] or from Cornelius of Caesarea to Eusebius of Caesarea. My goals here, however, are narrower and more specific. Most specifically, I am interested in the term *ethnē* as it was used and understood by gentile Christians, from the time of the earliest non-Jewish Christ-believers to the emergence of a sense among gentile Christians that they were a community drawn from, or somehow representative of, "all the nations." This means that I am also interested in issues of identity and self-definition—the part played by the term as gentile Christians worked out their identity in relation to the Jewish people on one side and the wider Greco-Roman world on the other. This in turn brings with it an interest in issues of ethnicity and identity more generally—how "nations" were perceived in antiquity and the role played by ethnicity as various groups worked to construct the boundaries that differentiated themselves from others and to negotiate a space for themselves in the complex world of the Roman Empire.

Despite my fourth-century starting point, in what follows I will concentrate primarily on an earlier period, as gentile Christian identity developed from its beginnings through its more formative stages. By the time of the Severan dynasty (193–235 CE), one discerns an increasing self-confidence within the Christian movement—based partly on numerical growth, partly on the intellectual firepower of its thinkers, partly on the development of organizational structures—such that the successes witnessed by Eusebius a century or so later begin to seem at least within the realm of possibility. My interest is in the kind of identity and self-definition that made this increasing self-confidence possible, which means that I will focus on developments up to the early third century.

Nevertheless, Eusebius will continue to provide us with a vantage point from which we can look back at earlier developments. Again, this is not to suggest that he represents the inevitable culmination of those developments, nor is it to overlook other choices and lines of development. Rather, his role will be heuristic. His fully articulated theological ethnology will help us discern potentially significant details in earlier works that might otherwise have been overlooked or undervalued; it will also be helpful, by way of contrast, to identify other self-definitional options that had been available and to trace other lines of development among diverse manifestations of the Christian movement.

As will be clear from the discussion to this point, my questions about early gentile Christian identity touch on several contiguous fields of discourse. In the next chapter, I will look at the three most pertinent areas and attempt to locate

63. To allude to Harnack's grand narrative.

my project within them. The first of them concerns Judaism and the process often referred to (though not without some uneasiness about the term) as *the parting of the ways*. In the first century and a half of its existence, what eventually became known as Christianity developed from a cluster of renewal movements located within the boundaries of the Jewish world (itself a variegated phenomenon) into a phenomenon that was increasingly gentile and independent of Judaism (albeit with its own variegation). We will need to give due consideration both to the complexities of the process and to the debates about how best to characterize it. Nevertheless, the construction of identity among the first gentile Christ-believers and early gentile Christian communities was a fundamental component of this process, and the process of identity construction inevitably involved considerations of how gentile Christianity related to three distinct but overlapping entities: scriptural Israel, Jewish Christ-believers, and the Jewish nation itself.

A second contiguous field of discourse is the study of ethnicity and identity. Traditionally, the success of Christianity has often been linked with its supposed "universalism"—that is, its ability to transcend, and thereby render irrelevant, the normal categories of race and ethnicity by which identity in the ancient world was generally defined and within which religion was normally embedded. The genius of the movement (it was supposed) lay in the fact that it abolished ethnic distinctions ("there is no longer Jew or Greek") and invited people of all races into a new inclusive community ("you are all one in Christ Jesus").[64] As the example of Eusebius demonstrates, however, such a concept of universalism significantly misinterprets a central aspect of early Christian self-definition. Although it is clear that Eusebius understood the church to be a new, unified community incorporating people across ethnic boundaries, it is equally clear that ethnic categories and conceptions continue to be fundamental for his understanding. In his *Preparation for the Gospel* and *Demonstration of the Gospel*, for example, *ethnos* appears well over a thousand times.[65] In recent years, the place of ethnicity in early Christian self-definition has increasingly been recognized. This recent work makes fruitful use of theoretical constructs drawn from contemporary social-scientific studies of ethnicity and identity, and it draws on a wide range of studies dealing with issues of ethnicity and identity in Greco-Roman antiquity. Any study of a movement that sees itself as a community drawn from and embedded in the nations will necessarily give attention to this work.

The third field of study within which my project needs to be located concerns the Roman Empire. Imperial reality inevitably impinges on issues of identity,

---

64. To use the oft-cited language of Paul in Gal 3:28.
65. By my count, about 175 for *Preparation* and 965 for *Demonstration*.

as subject nations and other groups find themselves forced to revisit their own identity-forming boundaries, now located within larger boundaries inscribed by the empire itself. Put differently, nations and other groups subject to imperial rule find it necessary to rewrite the narratives by which their identities have been shaped, in order to bring them into considered relationship with the dominant imperial narrative put forward by the ruling power. Of course, subject nations, groups, and individuals can choose to relate to the dominant ruling power in a whole variety of ways, ranging from attraction and assimilation, at one end, to subversion and explicit resistance, at the other, with many points in between (acquiescence, compromise, mimicry, withdrawal, passive resistance, and so on). With respect to the Christian movement itself, a lively area of current discussion concerns the significance of the Roman imperial context for a proper understanding of early Christian development, and any attempt to investigate the origins and development of gentile Christian identity needs to draw on and engage this work in appropriate ways.

CHAPTER 2

Positioning the Question

As has been indicated, I propose to carry out my investigation into the construction of early gentile Christian identity in conversation with three contiguous fields of discourse: the historical process commonly described as the "parting of the ways"; the social-scientific study of ethnicity and identity; and the dynamics of identity construction in the Roman Empire.

THE PARTING OF THE WAYS

Questions about the development of a distinct identity among gentile Christ-believers in the first two or three centuries after Christ inevitably spill over into questions about what has often been described as the parting of the ways—the process by which "Christianity" emerged from its Jewish matrix and became recognizably distinct from "Judaism." By the time Judaism and Christianity had become distinct socioreligious entities—that is, by the time it becomes appropriate to remove the quotation marks from the terms—the group that identified itself as Christianity was ethnically non-Jewish. Further, as we have seen, this group was prepared to identify itself also as gentile; we Christians were also we gentiles. Thus one cannot ask about the development of gentile Christian identity without also asking about the parting of the ways; the one is a significant aspect of the other.

To be sure, the two sets of questions cannot simply be collapsed into one without remainder. For one thing, presumably it is possible to speak of a distinct sense of identity among groups of gentile believers in the early stages of the movement, when the phenomenon of Christ-belief was still perceived on all sides as existing within a Jewish context. For another, even when gentile Christianity had emerged as a distinct entity, sociologically distinct from the Jewish world and characterized by its own developing institutional structures, the ways had certainly not yet fully parted for those various groups of Jewish Christ-believers who continued to identify themselves in some manner with the world of Judaism. In addition, as we have already seen, gentile Christian identity formation also involved a negotiation with patterns of identity found within the larger Greco-Roman world. While this negotiation inevitably had to address questions about the relationship between the Christian movement and the Jewish world in which it originated, its scope was certainly larger than this. Nevertheless, the two processes—the development of gentile Christian identity and the parting of the ways—overlap and intertwine significantly. To pursue our question, then, it will be important to situate it with respect to this related process.

The parting of the ways is generally understood as referring to a construction of Christian origins that was widely adopted in the years after the Second World War and has remained dominant until relatively recently. Perhaps the earliest occurrence of the term was in James Parkes's 1934 book *The Conflict of the Church and the Synagogue*.[1] The occurrence was not incidental; Parkes's work was in many ways a precursor of the later approach. As an Anglican priest involved in Continental relief work after World War I, Parkes became puzzled and disturbed by the pervasive and deeply rooted strains of anti-Semitism that he encountered in Christian Europe. His attempts to discern "the causes of anti-Semitism" led him eventually to the *adversus Judaeos* tradition of the early church fathers, an anti-Judaic construction that (as he perceived the process) emerged in the work of the second-century apologists just as the separation between Judaism and Christianity had become complete.[2] "The Parting of the Ways" appears as the title of the chapter in which he traces this process of separation—from the death of Paul, at which point "Christianity was still a Jewish sect," to "the middle of

---

1. James Parkes, *The Conflict of the Church and the Synagogue: A Study in the Origins of Antisemitism* (London: Soncino, 1934). A related term was used earlier as the title of a collected volume of essays, written by scholars associated with Jesus College (Cambridge) and edited by F. J. Foakes-Jackson, *The Parting of the Roads: Studies in the Development of Judaism and Early Christianity* (London: Edward Arnold, 1912). Except for one chapter by a Jewish scholar (Ephraim Levine, "The Breach between Judaism and Christianity"), however, the work displays few of the concerns or characteristics of the later phenomenon.

2. Part of the subtitle of an earlier book: *The Jew and His Neighbour: A Study of the Causes of Anti-Semitism* (London: Student Christian Movement Press, 1930).

the second century," when it had become "a separate religion busily engaged in apologetics to the Greek and Roman world, and anxious to establish its antiquity, respectability and loyalty."[3]

Parkes's work is marked by many of the features that came to characterize the later approach: a concern to provide a sympathetic portrayal of first-century Judaism;[4] an emphasis on the Jewishness of Jesus and the early church;[5] a recognition of both the vitality and the diversity of first-century Judaism, together with a belief that the early Christians need to be seen as constituting a group or movement within a variegated Judaism;[6] the significant role in the parting of the ways played by the wars with Rome in 66–70 and 132–35 CE,[7] which resulted in the end of the temple-centered Jewish state, the emergence of Pharisaism/rabbinism as the dominant form of Judaism, and the resultant concern to define the boundaries of the Jewish community more narrowly and sharply; the success of the gentile mission as the other most significant factor in the separation of Christianity from its Jewish matrix; the creation of various measures of exclusion (the Birkat Haminim, official letters), by which Jewish Christians were pushed

---

3. Ch. 3 (pp. 71–120); the quoted material appears on p. 77.

4. See his defense of torah religion against Christian caricature (pp. 35–37) and his criticism of those whose portrait of Judaism is drawn from Christian sources ("it is no juster to go to Christian sources to understand Judaism than to go to the Jews to understand Christianity" [p. 37]). Against the tendency to see Christianity and Judaism as representing "two fundamentally different conceptions of religion"—an approach found even among Christian interpreters sympathetic to Judaism (such as Travers Herford, to whom this characterization is attributed)—Parkes argues: "But this opposition is only true upon the assumption of certain Protestant interpretations of Christianity. It would be truer to say that the Christian through Jesus, the Jew through Torah, sought the same thing—'the immediate intuition of God in the individual soul and conscience'—and that to preserve for succeeding generations the possibilities of that intuition each religion has 'hedged it round' with the discipline of a system and the humility of an authority" (p. 37).

5. Jesus "wished to change things in current teaching, but not to abandon Judaism itself" (p. 34). As for the Jewish believers, even with the first admission of gentiles there was "as yet no question of the Law not being valid for Jewish Christians" (p. 49) and the creation of the Birkat Haminim demonstrates that "the Judeo-Christians still frequented the synagogue" until late in the first century (p. 78).

6. In the early decades of the Christian movement, they were seen by the rest of the Jewish world as "a 'party', not a separate religion" (p. 49). "At the death of Paul, Christianity was still a Jewish sect" (p. 77).

7. The revolt during Trajan's rule (115–17 CE), for which detailed evidence is scarce and incomplete, features much less prominently in the discussion.

to the margins and beyond the boundaries;[8] the end of the Bar Kokhba revolt as the date by which the separation can be said to be complete;[9] on the Christian side, the development of an anti-Jewish interpretation of Scripture and recent history by which it defended its claim to be the true Israel and the inheritor of all that was of value in Israel's tradition;[10] and the significance of this *adversus Judaeos* tradition for the subsequent development of anti-Semitism within the Christian world, whose main roots thus need to be found in Christian apologetic and theology, rather than (say) in negative Greco-Roman attitudes toward Jews and Judaism.[11]

8. On the previous three points: "The loss of the Temple meant that Judaism had now only the Law as a basis for its continued independence. Had the Judeo-Christians been the only members of the new faith, the breach between them and the Jews might have been healed, for they also desired to observe the Law. But the rabbis at Jabne were not unaware of their contact with Gentile Christians who did not observe the Law at all. They knew the teaching of Paul, and condemned it utterly. It was only a step from this condemnation to the refusal to accept as orthodox the conformity of the Judeo-Christians. This step was taken by the insertion into the daily Blessings recited in the synagogue of a declaration about heretics so worded that the Judeo-Christians could not pronounce it" (p. 77).

9. While the separation was complete from the Jewish side by the end of the first century (see the previous note), many Jewish Christians still desired to remain within the world of the synagogue: "The fact that the test [i.e., the Birkat Haminim] was a statement made in the synagogue service shows that at the time of making it the Judeo-Christians still frequented the synagogue. There would be no point otherwise in trying to prevent them from leading the prayers. In other words, at the time when official Judaism, represented by the rabbis at Jabne, had decided that the presence of these people could not be tolerated, the Judeo-Christians, however much they disagreed from other Jews on the question as to whether the Messiah had or had not come, still considered themselves to be Jews; and it is not too much to suppose from this that there were also Jews who considered that a disagreement on this point did not make fellowship with them impossible. They must have been generally accepted, or it is incredible that they should have continued to frequent the synagogue. They were evidently there as ordinary members, since it needed the introduction of this formula to detect them" (p. 78). It was the Second Jewish Revolt, and especially the acclamation of Bar Kokhba as messiah, that led to the recognition of a definitive separation on the part of the Jewish Christians: "A breach would, however, from their point of view, occur if the rest of the Jews decided definitely on another Messiah, and this is what happened in the time of Barcochba" (p. 78).

10. See his description of "the creation of an official attitude to Judaism" (pp. 95–106).

11. In his concluding chapter, "The Foundations of Antisemitism," after examining various putative explanations for the phenomenon, he concludes: "There is no other adequate foundation than the theological conceptions built up in the first three centuries. But upon these foundations an awful superstructure has been reared, and the first stones

Positioning the Question

The significance of Parkes's work can readily be seen in its contrast with earlier constructions of the process, which all too often have been fraught with theological assumptions, ideological agendas, triumphalistic historiography (especially on the Christian side of things), and apologetics in the guise of scholarship (on both sides).[12] Here we must content ourselves with some broad characterizations rather than anything like a thorough account. In the spirit of Parkes's parting of the ways, it will be convenient to use other spatial imagery as a way of constructing a rudimentary typology.

The first two categories to be identified represent approaches that received their classical formulation in the early centuries of the Christian movement and, in their unreconstructed forms, continued to represent dominant Christian belief up to the beginning of the modern period, when the emergence of more critical biblical and historical scholarship led to new approaches.[13] The more widespread of the two is centered on the idea of *replacement*, a model in which something seen to be defective or outmoded is replaced by something better. As we have had occasion to see already, this model was essential for Eusebius, who understands Christ to have revealed and brought into being the true form of religion, a form of religion that replaced the law of Moses, which had had a certain preparatory role to play both in warning Israel away from polytheistic error and in pointing ahead by means of "symbols and shadows" to the realities of Christ. This model was by no means unique to Eusebius, of course; as Parkes has

---

of that superstructure were laid, the very moment the Church had power to do so, in the legislation of Constantine and his successors. . . . And the old falsification of Jewish history . . . has persisted up to the present time in popular teaching. Scholars may know to-day of the beauty and profundity of the Jewish conception of life. They may know that '*some* Jews' were responsible for the death of Jesus. But the Christian public as a whole, the great and overwhelming majority of the hundreds of millions of nominal Christians in the world, still believe that 'the Jews' killed Jesus, that they are a people rejected by their God, that all the beauty of their Bible belongs to the Christian Church and not to those by whom it was written; and if on this ground, so carefully prepared, modern antisemites have reared a structure of racial and economic propaganda, the final responsibility still rests with those who prepared the soil, created the deformation of the people, and so made these ineptitudes credible" (pp. 375–76).

12. See the section "From Supersessionism to Common Origins and 'Parted Ways,'" in *The Ways That Never Parted: Jews and Christians in Late Antiquity and the Early Middle Ages*, ed. Adam H. Becker and Annette Yoshiko Reed (Minneapolis: Fortress, 2007), 4–16.

13. For an attempt to set these two approaches within a more thoroughgoing characterization of the various ways in which early Christian groups conceived of their relationship with Israel (including scriptural Israel, contemporary Judaism, Jewish Christ-believers), see my "Supersessionism and Early Christian Self-Definition," *JJMJS* 3 (2016): 1–32.

shown, it represented the "official attitude to Judaism" that was hammered out in the *adversus Judaeos* tradition of the early centuries of the movement. This model is often described today as supersessionism, a term that originally was used in a positive sense by Christian apologists but increasingly functions as a negative characterization of the model.[14] In this approach, the destruction of the temple and the resultant dispersion of the Jews is taken as a divine demonstration of the supersession—either as bringing the temple-centered old covenant to an end, or as punishment for the sin of rejecting the Messiah, or both.[15] With respect to the emergence of gentile Christianity—which, along with the destruction of the temple, figures prominently in parting-of-the-ways approaches—the non-Jewish character of the church is virtually axiomatic in this approach. The emphasis falls on the rejection of the Jews and their replacement by the Christians, seen as the new Israel but assumed without question to be non-Jewish.

The concept of supersession or replacement, however, concedes a certain positive value to the entity that is being superseded or replaced, something that Christian proponents have often been reluctant to do. Again, as we have seen, Eusebius, for example, made a distinction between Jews, on the one hand, and the Hebrews, on the other. Jews and Judaism were characterized by the law of Moses, which, except for its value as symbolic prophecy, had the purely negative role of curbing the polytheistic excesses that the descendants of Jacob/Israel picked up in Egypt. The Hebrews, by contrast, a group that comprised the patriarchs of Genesis and the spiritual heroes of the Old Testament, were in effect Christians before Christ, in that they recognized the truth of monotheistic worship from the outset and, later, perceived the true symbolic meaning of the Scriptures. Rather than constituting new Israel, the church in this construction represented true Israel, a form of religion or belief that existed from the beginning and that could readily be differentiated from the Jews or "Israel according to the flesh." The official attitude to Judaism contained a strain, then, that construed the relationship between Christianity and Judaism in more antithetical terms; one might describe it as an *antipodal* model.[16] Within proto-orthodox forms of

---

14. On the term itself, see my "Supersessionism and Early Christian Self-Definition," 2–8.

15. In his very helpful discussion of supersessionism, Soulen designates these as "economic" and "punitive" forms of supersessionism respectively; to these he adds a third category—"structural" supersessionism—a form of Christian theology that moves structurally from the fall to the redemption in Christ, without finding any meaningful place for Israel at all. See R. Kendall Soulen, *The God of Israel and Christian Theology* (Minneapolis: Fortress, 1996).

16. Later we will have occasion to look at Marcion's more extreme antipodal construction, in which the distinction between the Jews and his own group of Christ-believers

Christianity and consequently up to the modern period, the antipodal model coexisted (somewhat awkwardly) with replacement approaches.

Under the impact of the Enlightenment and the emergence of historical-critical forms of scholarship, other models appeared. The architects of these historical-critical reconstructions of early Christianity usually saw their work as representing a sharp departure from the dogmatic approaches of an earlier period—and so it was, in many ways. At the same time, however, looking back on the period with our postmodern sensibilities, we can also perceive the extent to which these new models also represent versions of the replacement and antipodal models, albeit transposed into a historical key and covered with a thin veneer of supposed objectivity.

In one common model, Christianity and Judaism are understood in essentialist terms, the essences in question being non-ethnic universalism and ethnic particularism. Although Christianity emerged from within Judaism, its genius (so this model assumes) was the recognition that religion was not to be confined within ethnic boundaries and tied to specific cultic sites and practices, but instead, to use the language of F. C. Baur, was to be "placed in a freer, more universal, and purely spiritual sphere, where the absolute importance which Judaism had claimed till then was at once obliterated."[17] Baur himself provides the image of a *breakthrough*—Christianity by virtue of its essential character being able to break through the limiting walls of Judaism in order to become a wider, universal religion:

> How these bounds were broken through, how Christianity, instead of remaining a mere form of Judaism, although a progressive one, asserted itself as a separate, independent principle, broke loose from it and took its stand as a new enfranchised form of religious thought and life, essentially different from all the national peculiarities of Judaism is the ultimate, most important point of the primitive history of Christianity.[18]

While Baur's reconstruction was built on the foundations of German Idealism, the idea of a breakthrough from ethnic particularism to unrestricted universalism is a model that is much more widely distributed within modern scholarship.

Overlapping to a certain extent but placing more emphasis on aspects of Israel's past is an approach that sees Christianity as the continuation of one side

---

was grounded in a duality of Gods—the Father God of Christ, who came for the sake of the gentiles, and the subordinate creator God of the Jews.

17. F. C. Baur, *Paul: The Apostle of Jesus Christ* (London: Williams & Norgate, 1876), 2:125.
18. Baur, *Paul*, 1:3.

of a *bifurcation* already present within Judaism. One might think of this as a historicized adaptation of the antipodal model. The classical liberalism of the nineteenth and early twentieth century, for example, often sought biblical underpinnings for itself by positing the presence within the religion of Israel of two antithetical movements—one priestly and cultic, the other prophetic and ethical. For Walter Rauschenbusch, although the two movements "[grew] side by side, on the same national soil and from the same historic convictions, . . . they are two distinct and antagonistic religions." Needless to say, in his view, the religion of Jesus, properly understood, is a continuation of the prophetic form.[19] Harnack's reconstruction of first-century Judaism, in which it appears as an entity divided between the fierce nationalism of the Maccabees and their spiritual successors (apocalypticists, Zealots, Shammai), on the one hand, and the universalistic spirit of second Isaiah and his successors, on the other (Hellenistic Judaism, diaspora missionary activity, Philo, Hillel, etc.), is another example.[20] Once again, Jesus, together with most of his disciples and followers, represent the continuation of the more progressive stream (though proponents of this approach often portray their own contemporary opponents as latter-day manifestations of the other side of the bifurcation).

Bifurcation models could be constructed by drawing different lines of demarcation, however. Albert Schweitzer, for example, who strongly criticized many of the Idealist reconstructions of his teachers, nevertheless carried out his own reconstruction on the basis of an equally bifurcated view of Judaism. In his case,

---

19. Walter Rauschenbusch, *A Theology for the Social Gospel* (New York: Macmillan, 1917), 276. To be sure, both classical liberalism and German Idealism were characterized by a sharp thesis of decline, the emergence of catholic orthodoxy seen as representing a kind of reassertion of priestly and particularistic forms of religion within the Christian movement.

20. In Harnack's view, first-century Judaism was influenced by two tendencies, one "progressive," the other "nationalist." The progressive strand, the older of the two, which goes back as far as second Isaiah, "gave vivid expression, even within Palestine itself, to the universalism of the Jewish religion as well as to a religious ethic which rose almost to the pitch of humanitarianism." Under the influence of this tendency, Judaism "was already blossoming out by some inward transformation and becoming a cross between a national religion and a world-religion (confession of faith and a church)." With the Maccabees and their reaction to the policies of Antiochus IV, however, "an opposite tendency set in. Apocalyptic was keener upon the downfall of the heathen than upon their conversion, and the exclusive tendencies of Judaism again assert themselves, in the struggle to preserve the distinctive characteristics of the nation." Adolf von Harnack, *The Mission and Expansion of Christianity in the First Three Centuries*, trans. James Moffatt (London: Williams & Norgate, 1908), 9–16; cited material from pp. 16, 9, 17.

the line was to be drawn between the legalism of the rabbis and the eschatology of the apocalyptic movement. In his vivid and inimitable style, he contrasts the "green and fresh" grass of the apocalyptic writers with the "yellow wilted grass" on a "sun-scorched plain" that we find in the rabbinic writings.[21] In works of enduring significance despite their idiosyncratic elements, he locates both Jesus and Paul within the supposedly lush fields of apocalyptic and thus portrays early Christianity, in its best and early manifestations, as the continuation of one of these two streams that flowed through the Jewish world of the first century.[22]

In his work on Paul, Schweitzer sets himself in opposition to approaches that would understand Paul, and the gentile churches that he founded, as representing a translation of early Christian preaching into the thought forms and religious patterns of the Hellenistic world. He concedes that this was something that occurred eventually, though he laments the development.[23] In the work of those he opposes, however—history-of-religions scholars and others—we find an additional model, one that sees emergent Christianity as the *confluence* of two streams, one flowing from the terrain of Judaism, the other from the Hellenistic world. In some history-of-religions approaches, most notably Bultmann's synthesis of a number of earlier developments, a significant role is assigned to an already-existing hellenized form of Judaism, through which Hellenistic ideas flowed into early Christianity. Here we can see an interweaving of two models—that of a bifurcation within Judaism and that of a confluence of Jewish and Hellenistic streams. Purer forms of the confluence model exist, however. In Otto Pfleiderer's reconstruction of Paul's religion, for example, he identifies two distinct patterns of thought and influence—one drawn from his Pharisaic background; the other, emerging after his conversion and, more influential, drawn from the Hellenistic world.[24] The model appears in a particularly striking form in an essay by W. R. Inge.[25] Modifying Clement of Alexandria's description of Christianity as "a river which receives tributaries from all sides," he argues instead that there are only two, and these utterly dissimilar:

---

21. Albert Schweitzer, *Paul and His Interpreters* (London: A. & C. Black, 1950), 49.
22. Similar models of bifurcation can be found in others who worked with apocalyptic literature in this period—for example, Johannes Weiss in Germany and R. H. Charles in Britain.
23. While "Paul did not Hellenize Christianity," he put it into "a form in which it was capable of being Hellenized" and indeed was (beginning with John's Gospel and Ignatius). Albert Schweitzer, *The Mysticism of Paul the Apostle* (London: A. & C. Black, 1931), 334.
24. Otto Pfleiderer, *Primitive Christianity* (London: Williams & Norgate, 1906), 1:87–91.
25. Actually, the introductory essay (pp. 1–14) in the collection *The Parting of the Roads*, cited above.

> Catholic Christianity was the result of the confluence of two great streams, which differed in their origin and in the color of their water more widely than the Rhone and the Saône, or than the White and the Blue Niles. These two streams, the Semitic and the European, the Jewish and the Greek, still mingle their water in the turbid flood which constitutes the institutional religion of civilized humanity; but to this day the waters flow side by side in the same bed, perfectly recognizable—so alien are the two types to each other.[26]

Though he sees the Greek tributary as the larger (and clearly the more desirable) of the two, they have continued to coexist, primarily because Christ himself "was above the antithesis."[27]

In contrast to the situation in more recent decades, Jewish scholarship in the period prior to Parkes played a much smaller part in any general scholarly discussion of Christian origins. Painting with a broad brush, however, one might say that Jewish scholars who were engaged in wider discussion (e.g., Claude Montefiore and Joseph Klausner) tended to see the emergence of Christianity as a small sideroad branching off from a main thoroughfare, which then became a separate thoroughfare of its own once it entered gentile territory. In other words, the tendency was to see a contrast between a dominant form of Judaism, which eventually became "normative" in the rabbinic period,[28] and a marginal Jewish movement that became successful once it moved into the wider non-Jewish world. The primary early traveler on the sideroad, of course, was Paul, the apostle to the gentiles. While scholars such as Montefiore and Klausner may have been prepared to see Jesus more favorably—as one who never left the main thoroughfare at all—in their view of Paul, they differ very little from many of their predecessors.[29] Because Paul grew up in the diaspora rather than in Judea, he was shaped by an inferior form of Judaism and thus failed in essential ways

---

26. William Ralph Inge, "Essay I: Introductory," in *The Parting of the Roads: Studies in the Development of Judaism and Early Christianity*, ed. F. J. Foakes-Jackson (London: Edward Arnold, 1912), 4.

27. He continues: "His character and view of life were unlike those of the typical Jew; but we can hardly call them Hellenic"; Inge, "Essay I: Introductory," 10.

28. The term has become common through its use by George Foot Moore, whose three-volume work *Judaism in the First Centuries of the Christian Era* (Cambridge, MA: Harvard University Press, 1927-30) represents a classic and still-useful treatment by a sympathetic Christian scholar.

29. Claude G. Montefiore, *The Synoptic Gospels* (London: Macmillan, 1927); Joseph Klausner, *Jesus of Nazareth: His Life, Times and Teaching* (London: George Allen & Unwin, 1929). See also Donald A. Hagner, *The Jewish Reclamation of Jesus: An Analysis and Critique of Modern Jewish Study of Jesus* (Grand Rapids: Academie, 1984); Zev Garber,

to understand Jewish life and religion in its purer and more vibrant form. For the same reason, however, he was culturally well positioned to transmute early beliefs about Jesus into a form that would appeal to gentiles.[30]

When seen against this background, then, the newness of Parkes's more soberly historical and less patently self-serving parting of the ways can be clearly seen. To be sure, he was in a sense ahead of his time. His work was overshadowed by subsequent factors—the Second World War of course, the storm-clouds of which were already appearing on the horizon as his book was published; then after the war, the shattering impact of the Holocaust, as Christian scholars in particular came to recognize the anti-Judaism and anti-Semitism that characterized much Christian tradition and scholarship; and the discovery of the Dead Sea Scrolls, which precipitated a reassessment of Judaism in the Second Temple period and beyond, with normative Judaism giving way to reconstructions that emphasized diversity and variegation. Such factors had the effect of spurring scholars to wrestle with a set of questions very similar to those that had driven Parkes's earlier work, though in a significantly different context. While their own work produced results very similar to those of Parkes, these were determined more by the subsequent factors than by the direct influence of Parkes's own work, even though his descriptive phrase has come into common use.[31] Other

---

ed., *The Jewish Jesus: Revelation, Reflection, Reclamation* (West Lafayette, IN: Purdue University Press, 2011).

30. Claude G. Montefiore, *Judaism and St. Paul: Two Essays* (London: Max Goschen, 1914); Joseph Klausner, *From Jesus to Paul* (New York: Macmillan, 1943). See also the thorough survey of Jewish scholarship on Paul by Stefan Meissner, *Die Heimholung des Ketzers: Studien zur jüdischen Auseinandersetzung mit Paulus*, WUNT 2.87 (Tübingen: Mohr Siebeck, 1996).

31. E.g., Morton Scott Enslin, "Parting of the Ways," *JQR* 51 (1961): 177–97; James D. G. Dunn, *The Partings of the Ways between Christianity and Judaism and Their Significance for the Character of Christianity* (Philadelphia: Trinity Press International, 1991); Richard Bauckham, "The Parting of the Ways: What Happened and Why," *Studia Theologica* 47 (1993): 135–51; Martha Himmelfarb, "The Parting of the Ways Reconsidered: Diversity in Judaism and Jewish-Christian Relations in the Roman Empire; A Jewish Perspective," in *Interwoven Destinies: Jews and Christians through the Ages*, ed. Eugene J. Fisher (Mahwah, NJ: Paulist, 1993), 47–61; Judith M. Lieu, "'The Parting of the Ways': Theological Construct or Historical Reality?" *JSNT* 56 (1994): 101–19; James D. G. Dunn, ed., *Jews and Christians: The Parting of the Ways, A.D. 70 to 135* (Grand Rapids: Eerdmans, 1992); Becker and Reed, *Ways That Never Parted*; Thomas A. Robinson, *Ignatius of Antioch and the Parting of the Ways: Early Jewish-Christian Relations* (Peabody, MA: Hendrickson, 2009). While Becker and Reed give due credit to Parkes for his work (see *Ways That Never Parted*, 8–12), Parkes's pioneering role with respect to the term itself is often overlooked. In her 1994 article,

phrases and images have been used with the same intent, especially those involving strained familial relationships.[32]

Speaking in broad terms, it is no exaggeration to say that the parting-of-the-ways model has in large measure provided the conceptual framework for the study of Christian origins since the middle of the last century (even if the framework has left considerable room for variation and for debate over specific points).[33] In recent years, however, there has been increasing reexamination and questioning of the model itself.

For one thing, while the model is appealing for its apparent impartiality and historical evenhandedness, these appearances may well mask significant theological and ideological assumptions. The issue is not simply that none of the ancient participants would have understood themselves to be parting ways with former cotravelers on a single road. There is a place, after all, for etic analysis—scholarly constructions that are brought in from outside to help gain insight into a particular cultural situation but that do not correspond to the terms and categories of insiders (emic analysis).[34] The issue, rather, is that, by assuming two more or less homogeneous entities—rabbinic Judaism and orthodox Christianity—the model serves the interests of normative forms of two contemporary religions, especially those aspects of each that are interested in interreligious dialogue. In the words of Reed and Becker, the model functions as "a reassuringly ecumenical etiology of the religious differences between present-day Christians and Jews."[35]

---

for example, Lieu says that the origin of the term is "unclear" (though she does refer to Foakes-Jackson's *The Parting of the Roads*); see "Parting of the Ways," 101.

32. Alan F. Segal, *Rebecca's Children: Judaism and Christianity in the Roman World* (Cambridge, MA: Harvard University Press, 1986); Stephen G. Wilson, *Related Strangers: Jews and Christians, 70–170 C.E.* (Minneapolis: Fortress, 1995). Cf. Daniel Boyarin, *Border Lines: The Partition of Judaeo-Christianity* (Philadelphia: University of Pennsylvania Press, 2004).

33. The essays in Dunn, *Jews and Christians*, for example, may be taken as representative. They reflect debates on a variety of issues: whether one can identify a date by which parting was (more or less) complete; Yavneh and the degree of rabbinic dominance; the Birkat Haminim; reactions to the destruction of the temple; Greek translations of Scripture; the significance of Christology; the role of Paul; geographical variation; ongoing forms of Jewish Christianity; etc. For an earlier discussion of various issues (official letters, a ban on Christians, the prohibition of heretical books, the Birkat Haminim), see Steven T. Katz, "Issues in the Separation of Judaism and Christianity after 70 CE: A Reconsideration," *JBL* 103 (1984): 43–76.

34. See Lieu, "'Parting of the Ways,'" 101–5.

35. Becker and Reed, *Ways That Never Parted*, 1. Lieu goes further in arguing that, with its interest in establishing continuity, the model serves Christian interests more sub-

Not that historically informed interreligious dialogue is something to be resisted, of course. But the model almost necessarily downplays diversity, not only before the ways have parted (where the idea of diversity has a certain role to play) but especially after. The continuing existence of various forms of Jewish Christianity; the vitality of various heterodox Christian groups; the continuation of vigorous but nonrabbinic Jewish communities in the diaspora; the increasing evidence for ongoing interaction and overlap between members of churches and synagogues into the fourth century (at least), well after the parting had supposedly been complete—all such phenomena are necessarily marginalized in a two-ways construal of history. By the same token, taking such phenomena more fully into account serves to destabilize the structures of the model itself.[36]

Related to this are various questions that have been raised about the need to differentiate between reality and rhetoric in the interpretation of textual evidence. In appealing to second- or third-century texts that seem to suggest a definitive parting (e.g., Ignatius, Justin, Irenaeus on the Christian side; the Mishnah on the Jewish), many interpreters (it has been argued) have failed to recognize the extent to which the proponents of what came to be the normative definitions were not simply reflecting social realities but instead were engaged in rhetorical attempts to define and impose them. Justin's *Dialogue with Trypho*, for example, should not be seen as a straightforward interchange across a well-established boundary between Christianity and Judaism but as an attempt to impose clear boundaries on disputed territory where social definitions and distinctions were in reality much more fluid. The differentiation between rhetoric and reality has been part of the discussion of early Christian history from the time of Walter Bauer and his seminal work on orthodoxy and heresy,[37] but more recently it has become an issue with respect to the parting of the ways. Boyarin, for example, has argued that instead of "a natural-sounding 'parting of the ways,' such as we usually hear about with respect to these two 'religions,'" we should think instead of "an imposed *partitioning* of what was once a territory without border lines," the partition being imposed by Christian and rabbinic "heresiologists" alike.[38]

---

stantively than it does Jewish: "the 'parting of the ways' is essentially a Christian model. Its concern is to maintain the Christian apologetic of continuity in the face of questions about that continuity from a historical or theological angle"; "'Parting of the Ways,'" 108.

36. As is done in the various essays in Becker and Reed, *Ways That Never Parted*.

37. Walter Bauer, *Orthodoxy and Heresy in Earliest Christianity* (Philadelphia: Fortress, 1971); German original 1934.

38. Boyarin, *Border Lines*, 1–2. Boyarin refers explicitly to Bauer. See also Andrew S. Jacobs, "The Lion and the Lamb: Reconsidering Jewish-Christian Relations in Antiquity," in Becker and Reed, *Ways That Never Parted*, 95–118. The issue of rhetoric versus reality

Boyarin takes his critique one step further, however. He argues that the image of two diverging but analogous ways not only privileges the forms of Judaism and Christianity that ultimately became normative but also does so by forcing Judaism to conform to an inappropriate category—religion—which itself is a Christian construct: "[T]he difference between Christianity and Judaism is not so much a difference between two religions as a difference between a religion and an entity that refuses to be one."[39] For Boyarin, the idea of a religion—a group characterized not by traditional categories such as class or ethnicity but by structures of belief—was something that emerged in the second century in the context of a Christian struggle for identity and self-definition. By treating Christianity and Judaism as two forms of the same species, then, the parting-of-the-ways model both imposes a Christian category on Judaism and obscures the extent to which this category was an entirely "new thing, a community defined by adherence to a certain canon of doctrine and practice."[40] For Boyarin, this new identity was a distinctly gentile Christian construction. We will return to this aspect of his work in a few moments, but for the present it provides us with an opportunity to look more generally at the place of gentile Christianity in parting-of-the-ways discourse.

In some of the older essentialist models discussed above, in which Christianity was understood to be categorically distinct from Judaism in its very essence, its existence as a gentile phenomenon was almost a categorical necessity. If Christianity represented a replacement of Judaism, or its antipodal opposite, or a breaking through the boundaries of an ethnic religion, then it was non-Jewish in its essence and thus could continue only as a gentile phenomenon. A defining element of the parting-of-the-ways model, however, is that the ways diverge only over time and through a process of historical development. In this model, the emergence of gentile Christianity is to be seen as a contingent aspect of a process, not a necessary manifestation of a fundamental essence. Furthermore, even if

---

has also emerged more generally with respect to the depiction of Judaism in the *adversus Judaeos* tradition: Does this tradition reflect a real situation where Christians were engaged in active debate with Jews and Judaism represented a significant competitor to Christianity for approval from the wider Greco-Roman world (so Marcel Simon)? Or is it an artificial construct designed primarily for rhetorical purposes of self-definition (so Adolf von Harnack, Miriam Taylor)? For discussion, see, e.g., Judith M. Lieu, *Image and Reality: The Jews in the World of the Christians in the Second Century* (Edinburgh: T&T Clark, 1996); Geoffrey D. Dunn, *Tertullian's* Aduersus Iudaeos: *A Rhetorical Analysis*, Patristic Monograph Series 19 (Washington, DC: Catholic University of America Press, 2008), 16–36.

39. Boyarin, *Border Lines*, 8.
40. Boyarin, *Border Lines*, 16.

some aspects of the model have been subjected to critique, the more fundamental assumption of a developing process has remained intact.

There is variation, however, concerning the significance of gentile Christianity in the process. To be sure, there is general agreement about the end result: once the ways had fully parted, the Christian way was almost entirely a gentile phenomenon. But differences are apparent with respect to the role played by gentile Christianity in the parting itself. One option has been to see the inclusion of gentiles as a categorical cause for the eventual separation. That is, the decision to admit gentiles as gentiles into membership in the community of Christ-believers constituted a decisive step across the boundary that defined the Jewish community, even if it would take a while for the implications of the step to become fully manifest. Bauckham, for example, argues that, since gentiles were categorically excluded from the full participation in temple worship, a group that included gentiles as gentiles in its membership could not remain indefinitely within the boundaries of Judaism. "The temple was the greatest, the most meaningful boundary marker between Jew and Gentile"; thus to grant full membership to gentiles without requiring them to become Jews was to take a step that would be "in the end decisive for the parting of the ways."[41]

Another view, perhaps the dominant one, is to see gentile Christianity not as a categorical cause but rather as an effective cause for the eventual parting of the ways. That is, as long as Jewish Christ-believers themselves continued to observe the torah faithfully and as long as the population of gentile believers remained small, the inclusion of gentiles did not in itself effect any fundamental parting. Many synagogues, after all, had their own circle of gentile adherents and sympathizers. But the success of Paul's mission among the gentiles, his reputation as one who encouraged Jewish believers to abandon torah observance (cf. Acts 21:20–21) and, more generally, the eventual demographic shift from Jewish to gentile membership had the combined effect of making the separation inevitable. As Himmelfarb puts it in her description of the parting of the ways:

> Had Paul never appeared on the scene, the Jerusalem church, so Jewish in its piety, might have remained a variety of Judaism. But Paul's mission to the Gentiles radically altered the demographic balance of early Christianity against the Jerusalem community. . . . What is more, Paul's mission to the Gentiles involved a rejection of the Torah.[42]

---

41. Bauckham, "Parting of the Ways," here 143, 148. Jossa also tends to move in this direction; see Giorgio Jossa, *Jews or Christians? The Followers of Jesus in Search of Their Own Identity*, WUNT 1.202 (Tübingen: Mohr Siebeck, 2006).

42. Himmelfarb, "Parting of the Ways Reconsidered," 48. Parkes takes a similar view of

A third assessment of the place of gentile Christianity is to see it not as a cause but as a result of the parting of the ways. In Segal's view, for example, "[o]nce the communities of Judaism and Christianity had separated, . . . Christianity slowly became a church of Gentiles."[43] Although Segal sees Paul's gentile mission as a factor in the separation, in his view the demographic shift from Jew to gentile was more a result than a cause.

My particular interest here, however, has to do with gentile identity and self-definition. Throughout this whole process (however it may be characterized), how did gentile believers come to conceive of their own identity, especially with respect to the identity imposed on them from the Jewish side—namely, that of *ethnē* (= non-Jews)? Given the historical context within which gentile Christianity emerged, any investigation of this question must necessarily be carried out in tandem with a consideration of the parting of the ways. On the one hand (we need to ask), what effect did the process of separation have on the developing sense of identity among gentile Christ-believers? On the other, what role was played in the process by their own developing sense of who they were? For the most part, these questions have not received sustained attention, either by those who work within the partings paradigm or by those who raise questions about its adequacy.

With respect to the former, the conception of a parting of the ways, by virtue of its choice of category, tends to downplay the importance of ethnicity and to conceive of the process in essentialist rather than ethnic terms. Because it operates on the basis of a differentiation between two ways—almost inevitably understood to be Christianity and Judaism—it tends to marginalize the more originary ethnic differentiation, the one between Jews and gentiles. Likewise, once the ways have parted, gentile Christianity inevitably appears as a redundancy, and little attention is paid to the ongoing role of ethnicity in Christian self-definition (a new *ethnos* or *genos* drawn from "all the nations").

Among those who have questioned the parting-of-the-ways model, Boyarin can be singled out as one who has made significant use of gentile Christian identity in the construction of an alternative model:

> In my historical reconstruction, a serious problem of identity arose for Christians who were not prepared (for whatever reason) to think of themselves as

---

the significance of Paul; *Conflict of the Church and the Synagogue*, 77 (pertinent material quoted in n. 8 above). See also Philip S. Alexander, "'The Parting of the Ways' from the Perspective of Rabbinic Judaism," in Dunn, ed., *Jews and Christians*, 23–24; and Lawrence H. Schiffman, *Who Was a Jew?* (Hoboken, NJ: Ktav, 1985).

43. Segal, *Rebecca's Children*, 161–62.

Positioning the Question

Jews, as early as the second century, if not the end of the first. These Christians, whom I will call by virtue of their own *self*-presentation, Gentile Christians ("The Church from the Gentiles," *ek tōn ethnōn*), were confronted with a dilemma: Since we are no longer "Greeks" and not "Jews," to what kind of group do we belong? . . . These Christians had to ask themselves: What is this *Christianismos* in which we find ourselves? Is it a new *gens*, a new *ethnos*, a third one, neither Jew nor Greek, or is it an entirely new something in the world, some new kind of identity completely? For one important strand of early Christianity, beginning with Justin Martyr, the option of seeing *Christianismos* as an entirely novel form of identity was chosen. Christianity was a new thing, a community defined by adherence to a certain canon of doctrine and practice.[44]

For Boyarin, identity formation among gentile Christians is to be seen as a fundamental factor in the partition, the second-century imposition (from both sides) of a boundary between Jews and Christians. But as has been observed already, he conceives of this "entirely novel form of identity" as something set over against ethnicity. What Justin was instrumental in inventing was a new entity called religion, something categorically distinct from the form of ethnic identity preserved among the Jews. While Boyarin recognizes the fact that Christians such as Justin saw themselves as gentile Christians ("'The Church from the Gentiles,' *ek tōn ethnōn*"), he seems to see this as a non-identity, a gap to be filled and a problem to be solved. Instead, I suggest, the evident interest on the part of gentile Christians to present themselves as a new *ethnos* drawn from all the *ethnē* suggests that Christians also, in their own way, refused to abandon an *ethnos*-based identity for a religious one.[45]

Further, the concern on the part of gentile Christians to identify themselves as a people drawn from all the nations directs attention to the fact that the process of parting involves not just two entities (Jews and Christians) but the wider world of the nations within which both exist. However we map the ways and their partings, we need to remember that the terrain they traverse is not empty countryside but the larger world of the nations. And terrain tends to have an important effect on the way paths and roads develop. As we have observed already,

44. Boyarin, *Border Lines*, 16–17.
45. To allude to this statement of Boyarin, cited in part above: "While Christianity finally configures Judaism as a different religion, Judaism itself, I suggest, at the end of the day refuses that call, so that seen from that perspective the difference between Christianity and Judaism is not so much a difference between two religions as a difference between a religion and an entity that refuses to be one"; *Border Lines*, 7–8.

gentile Christian self-definition was carried out in dialogue with conceptions of the nations and of transethnic ideals in this wider world. Such conceptions were significant in their own ways for Jews as well; Jewish self-definition vis-à-vis the nations was an essential element of the Jewish world. The parting-of-the-ways model assumes just two elements (at least once the parting is complete): Jews and Christians. But all along the stages of the process, there was a third crucial entity—the wider world of the nations—that was an important additional factor in the process.

Thus, while our focus in this study will be gentile Christian identity rather than the parting of the ways per se, we will necessarily engage with this related discussion as we proceed. We will do so in the expectation that, by paying attention to the specific issue of gentile Christian self-definition, we may arrive at a better understanding of the process of Christian/Jewish differentiation itself.

Ethnicity and Social Identity

Central to our investigation of gentile Christian identity construction is the term *ethnē* itself (together with related Hebrew, Aramaic, and Latin terms). A number of aspects and uses of the term have already come into view, and others will emerge as we proceed. While we will leave any more detailed consideration for later, here a brief preliminary survey will be useful.

At the most basic level, we need to take account (1) of *ethnos* as a generic term used to denote identifiable nations or ethnic groups. The framework for much of the phenomena we will investigate, however, was set (2) by the specific Jewish use of the plural *ethnē* (and the Hebrew *gôyîm* before it) as a collective term for the other nations, all nations other than that of the Jews. Arising from this us-them binary is (3) the curious use of the term to refer not only to a collectivity of non-Jewish ethnic groups, but also to a plurality of non-Jewish individuals. Within the earliest stages of the Christian movement, Jewish Christ-believers used the term not only of non-Jewish outsiders (both ethnic groups and individuals), but also (4) of quasi-insiders—those non-Jews who had also become Christ-believers. With respect to the obverse of this terminological coin, we will want to ask (5) how the first non-Jewish Christ-believers themselves perceived and responded to this usage. What sense did they make of this ascribed identity? To the extent that they accepted it, how did they understand and define it? Although we have little direct evidence for this in the early stages—that is, when non-Jews were a minority in a still distinctively Jewish movement—there is considerable evidence (as we have begun to see) for (6) the use of *ethnē* as an identity term on the part of non-Jewish Christians when gentile Christianity existed as a distinct non-Jewish entity. In addition, as we have noted in passing with Eusebius and will see in more detail later, (7) some non-Jewish Christians reserved the term for non-Jewish unbelievers, so that *ethnē* came to designate an identity that they had left behind when they came to believe in Christ. Finally, we have also seen that gentile Christians such as Eusebius can not only describe themselves as *ethnē*, or as drawn from all the *ethnē*, but (8) can also consider themselves as constituting a new *ethnos*.

Thus in our considerations of *ethnē* as an identity term, we will need to reckon with various denotations and usages. Even though the idea of ethnicity is always present in some sense, the term was used to refer not only to ethnic groups per se but also to other types of groups or collectivities. Further, even though we are interested primarily in the appropriation of the term by non-Jews themselves, it emerged in the first instance as a term ascribed to them by others, as a Jewish way of identifying them as outsiders. Leading on from this, the term is used both to mark various types of us-them boundaries (between Jews and non-Jews, between Jewish and non-Jewish Christ-believers, between non-Jewish Christ-believers and polytheists) and to forge connections between Christian self-understanding and the transethnic aspirations of the wider world of the *ethnē*.

The issues we want to explore, then, lead us naturally into social-scientific studies of ethnicity and social identity, where analogous issues are explored in more general and theoretical terms. To be sure, this is not the place for anything like a full discussion of the field; nor is it my intention to carry out this investigation within any full-blown theoretical framework. Nevertheless, social identity theory offers a useful heuristic, helping us sharpen our questions and place our data into new interpretive light, and so some discussion is in order.

Because ethnic groups have often been perceived in the past as constituting a distinct social category, characterized by inherited traits in a way that sets them apart from other types of groups, it might be thought that we are dealing here with two separate domains of discourse. As we will see, however, in recent years theoretical considerations of ethnicity have led naturally into the study of social identity more generally.

Since the time of Herodotus, ethnic identity has been associated with a number of shared characteristics that persist over time—kinship and genealogical descent, a common language, a homeland or shared territory, common religious practices, a shared history and way of life, mutual interests, and the like.[46]

---

46. See, e.g., Jonathan M. Hall, *Ethnic Identity in Greek Antiquity* (Cambridge: Cambridge University Press, 1997), 45; Irad Malkin, ed., *Ancient Perceptions of Greek Ethnicity*, Center for Hellenic Studies Colloquia 5 (Cambridge, MA: Harvard University Press, 2001), 6; Denise Kimber Buell, *Why This New Race? Ethnic Reasoning in Early Christi-*

Because at least some of these characteristics seem to be immutable—simply a given aspect of a person's existence—ethnic identity has often been seen in essentialist terms, that is, as an objective reality inherent in and determined by these shared characteristics. Since the seminal work of Fredrik Barth,[47] however, a broad consensus has developed that ethnic identity needs to be seen more as the negotiated result of a process of social construction than as an objective reality produced naturally by a set of contributing factors such as those listed above. To be sure, group members often perceive or portray their ethnic identity as fixed and immutable, but studies of the ways in which these factors shift and undergo redefinition over time betray the extent to which such perceptions or portrayals themselves are part of the process by which such identity is constructed and maintained.

Barth's work focused on the relationship between ethnic groups and the boundaries that differentiated them from others. From the perspective of the essentialist approach described above, such a boundary was simply an objective reality, the outer edge of an equally objective ethnic entity whose emergence and continued existence was a purely self-contained matter, even as it bumped into the hard outer edges of neighboring ethnic groups. Reacting against this "simplistic view that geographical and social isolation have been the critical factors in sustaining cultural diversity,"[48] Barth in effect turned the relationship between boundary and ethnic identity on its head.

In his view, ethnic identity is something that is constructed at the boundary of a group, the result of a process of social interaction between members of the group and outsiders. In this process of identity negotiation, various cultural factors—including those usually categorized as ethnic—come into play as indicators

---

anity (New York: Columbia University Press, 2005), 37. Herodotus's statement is more made in passing than as an attempt at definition: "For there are many great reasons why we [the Athenians] should not do this [consider an accommodation with the Persians], even if we so desired; first and chiefest, the burning and destruction of the adornments and temples of our gods, whom we are constrained to avenge to the uttermost rather than make covenants with the doer of these things, and next the kinship of all Greeks [*to Hellēnikon*] in blood and speech, and the shrines of gods and the sacrifices that we have in common, and the likeness of our way of life" (*Histories* 8.144).

47. The key conceptions were set out in the introductory chapter of Fredrik Barth, ed., *Ethnic Groups and Boundaries: The Social Organization of Culture Difference* (Boston: Little, Brown, 1969), and developed in subsequent work. Jenkins has pointed out, however, that there were important precursors; see Richard Jenkins, *Social Identity*, 4th ed. (New York: Routledge, 2014), 46.

48. Barth, *Ethnic Groups and Boundaries*, 9.

Positioning the Question

of group identity. They play this role, however, not intrinsically and necessarily but because the members of the group come to see them as significant:

> The features that are taken into account are not the sum of "objective" differences, but only those which the actors themselves regard as significant. Not only do ecologic variations mark and exaggerate differences; some cultural features are used by the actors as signals and emblems of differences, others are ignored, and in some relationships radical differences are played down and denied.[49]

For Barth, then, the core of ethnic identity is the shared sense on the part of group members that they belong to an ethnic group. Cultural and ethnic characteristics are to be seen, in effect, as a stockpile of identity-related raw material from which members draw the necessary resources as they engage in the process of differentiating themselves from outsiders. The characteristics used in the process serve as functional indicators of ethnic identity rather than as essentialized producers of it.[50] Since the process of differentiation is dynamic and ongoing, the selection and function of the indicators can change over time. As Barth sums it up: "The critical focus of investigation from this point of view becomes the ethnic *boundary* that defines the group, not the cultural stuff that it encloses."[51]

It is important to observe that, for Barth, the process of identity construction taking place at the boundary is an interactive one, with parts to be played by those on both sides. How a group comes to view itself is shaped in part by how it is viewed by those outside. Ethnic identity emerges from the interaction between a characterization ascribed by outsiders and a sense of group identity perceived by insiders—or, more simply, between "self-ascription and ascription by others."[52] As Jenkins has described it, "One of his [Barth's] key propositions is that it isn't enough to send a message about identity: that message must be accepted by significant others before an identity can be said to be 'taken on.'"[53]

Before moving on, we might also observe two further aspects of Barth's work

---

49. Barth, *Ethnic Groups and Boundaries*, 14.
50. Jonathan Hall describes this as a distinction between *criteria*—"the definitional set of attributes by which membership in an ethnic group is ultimately determined"—and *indicia*—"the operational set of distinguishing attributes which people tend to associate with particular ethnic groups once the criteria have been established"; *Ethnic Identity in Greek Antiquity*, 20–21.
51. Barth, *Ethnic Groups and Boundaries*, 15.
52. Barth, *Ethnic Groups and Boundaries*, 13.
53. Jenkins, *Social Identity*, 46.

that he touched on in passing but that have been picked up and amplified in subsequent scholarly discussion.[54] The first is that ethnic identity can be seen as a special instance of social or group identity more generally. For Barth, a process of interaction between self-ascribed and externally ascribed identities is something that characterizes all groups; an ethnic group is a particular kind of group, one in which the ascription of ethnic categories is to the fore: "A categorical ascription is an ethnic prescription when it classifies a person in terms of his basic, most general identity, presumptively determined by his origin and background."[55]

The idea of a person's "basic, most general identity" leads to a second significant aspect, the relationship between social and individual identity. This statement might be taken to imply that for Barth some aspects of individual identity are foundational for social or ethnic identity. Elsewhere, by contrast, he talks about the permeability of ethnic boundaries and the changes of identity that individuals experience as they migrate across a border.[56] Either way, however, his work opened up preliminary lines of connection between social and ethnic identity, on one side, and individual identity, on the other.[57]

Barth's critique of a thoroughgoing essentialist (or primordial) approach has been widely accepted. There is a broad consensus that ethnic identity needs to be seen as a product of social construction, something that characterizes groups more generally. Nevertheless, there is also a range of opinion on how one is to view those aspects that tend to differentiate ethnic groups from other groups. At the other end of the spectrum are thoroughgoing constructivist (or instrumentalist) approaches, where ethnic identity is seen as an instrument used by interest groups to achieve more basic political or economic ends. In part, such approaches represent an extreme reaction against the way in which primordial views of ethnicity had been used to undergird unpalatable racial theories such as those adopted by the Nazis.[58] Broadly speaking, however, most theorists tend

---

54. On these aspects, see especially the work of Tajfel and Jenkins: Henri Tajfel, *Human Groups and Social Categories: Studies in Social Psychology* (Cambridge: Cambridge University Press, 1981); Henri Tajfel, ed., *Social Identity and Intergroup Relations*, European Studies in Social Psychology (Cambridge: Cambridge University Press; Paris: Editions de la maison des sciences de l'homme, 1982); Jenkins, *Social Identity*.

55. Barth, *Ethnic Groups and Boundaries*, 13.

56. Barth, *Ethnic Groups and Boundaries*, 21.

57. At this point, social identity theory overlaps considerably with Berger and Luckmann's analysis of the "social construction of reality" (Peter L. Berger and Thomas Luckmann, *The Social Construction of Reality: A Treatise in the Sociology of Knowledge* [Garden City, NY: Doubleday, 1966]), a point observed by Tajfel (*Human Groups and Social Categories*, 255).

58. See the discussions in J. M. Hall, *Ethnic Identity in Greek Antiquity*, 1–13; Werner

to avoid the extremes and to accord some special significance to that set of identity-related raw materials that are used to differentiate ethnic groups from groups more generally. Ethnic identity may be socially constructed, but for the construction to be effective its members need to be able to perceive its foundation in essentialist terms.

A helpful suggestion for how one might mediate between the extremes has been made by Jenkins, whose concept of "primary identifications" might be seen as an elaboration of Barth's idea of a person's "basic, most general identity." Primary identifications are those aspects of personal identity that are formed through the primary socialization that takes place in infancy and childhood, which, Jenkins suggests, "are experienced as more authoritative than those acquired subsequently" and thus "become part of the individual's axiomatic cognitive furniture."[59] The most significant primary identifications have to do with gender, kinship, name, and sense of self. Although ethnic identification emerges somewhat later, Jenkins believes that in many cases it too has the character of a primary identification. Thus, while neither primordial nor immune to change, ethnic identification can nevertheless be seen as one aspect of a fundamental sense of identity, which, he suggests, means that "the notion of primary identification opens up some middle ground" between essentialist and constructivist views.[60] While it remains the case that ethnic identity is a value-added product constructed out of raw materials, some of those materials are foundational for an individual's primary identification and thus can be perceived by members of the group as primordial.

Increasingly, theoretical discourse about ethnicity and social identity is being drawn into the study of nations and groups in antiquity,[61] including the study

---

Sollors, "Foreword: Theories of American Ethnicity," in *Theories of Ethnicity: A Classical Reader*, ed. Werner Sollors (London: Macmillan, 1996), x–xliv. Sollors's foreword also includes a survey of responses to Barth.

59. Jenkins, *Social Identity*, 87. Jenkins prefers "identification" to "identity," since it better captures the idea that identity construction is a dynamic process rather than a static entity.

60. Jenkins, *Social Identity*, 89.

61. For the classical world generally, see, e.g., Greg Woolf, *Tales of the Barbarians: Ethnography and Empire in the Roman West* (Malden, MA: Wiley-Blackwell, 2011); Erich S. Gruen, *Cultural Identity in the Ancient Mediterranean (Issues & Debates)* (Los Angeles: Getty Research Institute, 2011); Daniel S. Richter, *Cosmopolis: Imagining Community in Late Classical Athens and the Early Roman Empire* (Oxford: Oxford University Press, 2011); Ton Derks and Nico Roymans, eds., *Ethnic Constructs in Antiquity: The Role of Power and Tradition*, Amsterdam Archaeological Studies (Amsterdam: Amsterdam University Press, 2009); Richard Hingley, *Globalizing Roman Culture: Unity, Diversity and Empire* (Lon-

of Christian origins.[62] For present purposes, it will be useful at this point to identify several aspects of the discourse that will help to guide the investigation that follows.

As is readily apparent, the role of boundaries in identity construction will be very important. The various uses of *ethnē* cataloged above are shaped by a number of identifiable group boundaries: between Jews and non-Jews generally; between Jewish and non-Jewish members of the early Christian movement; between later (non-Jewish) Christianity and the Jewish community; and between the Christian movement and the larger world of the nations. Some of these boundaries overlap; the whole set of boundaries shifts over time as the Christian movement emerges and develops, and as other changes take place in the wider

---

don: Routledge, 2005); Benjamin H. Isaac, *The Invention of Racism in Classical Antiquity* (Princeton: Princeton University Press, 2004); Jonathan M. Hall, *Hellenicity: Between Ethnicity and Culture* (Chicago: University of Chicago Press, 2002); Simon Goldhill, ed., *Being Greek under Rome: Cultural Identity, the Second Sophistic and the Development of Empire* (Cambridge: Cambridge University Press, 2001); Malkin, *Ancient Perceptions of Greek Ethnicity*; Peter S. Wells, *The Barbarians Speak: How the Conquered Peoples Shaped Roman Europe* (Princeton: Princeton University Press, 1999); J. M. Hall, *Ethnic Identity in Greek Antiquity*; Emma Dench, *From Barbarians to New Men: Greek, Roman, and Modern Perceptions of Peoples of the Central Apennines*, Oxford Classical Monographs (Oxford: Oxford University Press, 1995); Greg Woolf, "Becoming Roman, Staying Greek: Culture, Identity and the Civilizing Process in the Roman East," *Proceedings of the Cambridge Philological Society* 40 (1994): 116–43; Erich S. Gruen, *Culture and National Identity in Republican Rome* (London: Duckworth, 1993); Edith Hall, *Inventing the Barbarian: Greek Self-Definition through Tragedy* (Oxford: Clarendon, 1989); Anthony D. Smith, *The Ethnic Origin of Nations* (Oxford: Blackwell, 1986).

62. See, e.g., Laura Nasrallah and Elisabeth Schüssler Fiorenza, eds., *Prejudice and Christian Beginnings: Investigating Race, Gender, and Ethnicity in Early Christian Studies* (Minneapolis: Fortress, 2009); Love L. Sechrest, *A Former Jew: Paul and the Dialectics of Race* (London: T&T Clark, 2009); Philip A. Harland, *Dynamics of Identity in the World of the Early Christians: Associations, Judeans, and Cultural Minorities* (New York: T&T Clark, 2009); Bengt Holmberg and Mikael Winninge, eds., *Identity Formation in the New Testament* (Tübingen: Mohr Siebeck, 2008); Joseph H. Hellerman, *Jesus and the People of God: Reconfiguring Ethnic Identity* (Sheffield: Sheffield Phoenix, 2007); Caroline Johnson Hodge, *If Sons, Then Heirs: A Study of Kinship and Ethnicity in the Letters of Paul* (Oxford: Oxford University Press, 2007); Buell, *Why This New Race?*; Philip A. Harland, *Associations, Synagogues, and Congregations: Claiming a Place in Ancient Mediterranean Society* (Minneapolis: Fortress, 2003); Philip F. Esler, *Conflict and Identity in Romans: The Social Setting of Paul's Letter* (Minneapolis: Fortress, 2003); Shawn Kelley, *Racializing Jesus: Race, Ideology, and the Formation of Modern Biblical Scholarship* (London: Routledge, 2002); Mark G. Brett, *Ethnicity and the Bible*, Biblical Interpretation Series (Leiden: Brill, 1996).

context. One will necessarily expect, then, to find shifts and developments in the processes of identity construction that take place at these boundaries.

With respect to the nature of group boundaries, Jenkins has cautioned that, in seeking to avoid an essentializing view of "cultural stuff" (to use Barth's phrase), we should not make the opposite mistake of reifying boundaries.[63] Rather, both boundary and identity are caught up together in the same process of identity formation. This process is a dialectical one—an ongoing encounter between a group's internal understanding of its own identity and the external perception of outsiders, the latter in the form both of external reactions to such internal self-definitions and of identities imposed from without.

This leads to a second important aspect, the relationship between external categorization and internal self-definition. Non-Jewish Christ-believers first encountered the category *ethnē* as an identity ascribed to them from without; eventually, at least for many of them, the category became an important part of their own identity.

The distinction between external categorization and internal self-definition arises out of a more general distinction, going back at least as far as Marx, between groups ("a collectivity which identifies itself") and categories ("a collectivity which is identified and defined by others"),[64] or, in Tajfel's terms, between "membership groups" and "reference groups."[65] The distinction is not absolute, however, in that part of a group's process of identifying itself has to do with its response to the categories imposed on its members by others. Social identity theory, then, is interested in the dialectical interaction between external categorization and internal group identification. The external and internal components of the interaction are not to be seen as fixed and static. Rather, they are subject to the process of negotiation across the border, the result of which can be described as an established social identity. Using a fictional example, Jenkins describes the process as

> a cumulative social construction that occurs when people who are identified as, say, Laputans interact with others who are identified differently in any context or setting in which being Laputan matters. In the process the relevant criteria of membership of Laputa—Laputan identity—are rehearsed, presented and developed, as are the consequences of being Laputan.[66]

---

63. A danger to which, in his view, Barth's approach is susceptible; Jenkins, *Social Identity*, 128.
64. Jenkins, *Social Identity*, 45.
65. Tajfel, *Human Groups and Social Categories*, 229.
66. Jenkins, *Social Identity*, 160.

GENTILE CHRISTIAN IDENTITY

One factor affecting the outcome of this cross-border dialectic has to do with the level of correlation between the external category and the internal self-conception. Put differently, one needs to envisage different degrees to which a group might be prepared to internalize an externally ascribed category. Partly, this is conditioned by the desirability of the ascription. A group will naturally be prepared to accept a positive characterization and to resist a negative label or stereotype.[67] However, it is not simply a matter of desirability; a more significant factor is that of relative power. The greater the external group's ability to shape the experienced reality of the group in question, the less successful the group will be in resisting the ascribed identity. In this connection, Jenkins underscores "the centrality of power, and therefore of politics, in identity maintenance and change." He continues: "Asserting, defending, imposing or resisting collective identification are all definitely political."[68]

In our survey of the different occurrences of *ethnē*, we identified two situations in which it functions as an external categorization. One is its use by Jews as a term for outsiders—*ethnē* as the other. Here, except for very special circumstances, we would expect a very small degree of internalization; the term would have little appeal for non-Jews, and Jews generally would have little power to impose it. The situation might differ a little in Judea, however, where Jews were in the majority, or in other situations where non-Jews lived in close association with Jewish communities. This brings us to the second use—*ethnē* as an identity ascribed to non-Jewish Christ-believers by the Jewish Christian majority. Here we are dealing with a situation where those doing the ascribing had greater relative social power. In addition, given that the situation is one in which individuals had freely chosen to associate with the new group, we might expect that non-Jewish believers would be more prepared to assume the new identity—or, at least, not to resist it out of hand.

By the time of Justin Martyr, however, when gentile Christianity had separated itself from its Jewish matrix and was engaged in a concerted effort to find a place for itself within the larger ethnographical map of the Roman Empire, the boundary conditions had shifted considerably. In this context, gentile Christians would have had much more latitude to reject the ascribed identity. Any continued usage of *ethnē* needs to be accounted for on the basis of its internal desirability or usefulness, rather than external ascription. Here a third aspect of social identity theory will be helpful—what Tajfel calls "social comparison," by

---

67. On labeling and stereotyping, see Tajfel, *Human Groups and Social Categories*, ch. 7, and Erving Goffman, *Stigma: Notes on the Management of Spoiled Identity* (Englewood Cliffs, NJ: Prentice-Hall, 1963).

68. Jenkins, *Social Identity*, 45.

which he means the various ways in which a group might attempt to change or alter its relative social location. He is interested in social identity not as a static entity in itself, but as a dynamic factor in processes of social change:

> The concept of social identity ... is not an attempt to describe it for "what it is" in a static sense—a daunting task which has baffled many social scientists of various persuasions and for which one needs a great deal of optimism and temerity. Social identity is understood here as an intervening causal mechanism in situations of "objective" social change—observed, anticipated, feared, desired, or prepared by the individuals involved.[69]

In the course of his analysis, he constructs a typology of various situations of relative power. For present purposes, what is most useful is the type having to do with groups that exist in a situation of relative social deprivation—"groups socially defined and consensually accepted as 'inferior' in some important respects"—but a situation in which group members are also able to envisage the possibility of altering or ameliorating their inferior status. With respect to such groups, he sets out three possible ways in which change might be sought:

1. To become, through action and reinterpretation of group characteristics, more like the superior group.
2. To reinterpret the existing inferior characteristics of the group, so that they do not appear as inferior but acquire a positively-valued distinctiveness from the superior group.
3. To create, through social action and/or diffusion of new "ideologies," new group characteristics which have a positively-valued distinctiveness from the superior group.[70]

The first, then, involves relative assimilation, a strategy followed both by numerous immigrant groups and, in a different way, by colonial subjects. Both the second and the third involve the construction of characteristics that can be perceived as positive, the distinction being that the second has to do with the redefinition and revaluation of already recognized characteristics, while the third involves the construction of new characteristics. To illustrate the former, he uses the example of the revaluation of various cultural indicators (e.g., the use of *black* as a positive identity term among African Americans in the 1960s and '70s). With respect to the latter, he refers to ways in which emerging nation-states

69. Tajfel, *Human Groups and Social Categories*, 276–77.
70. Tajfel, *Human Groups and Social Categories*, 283–84.

attempt to construct commonalities, hitherto latent at best, that might serve to bind different groups or areas into the new nation.⁷¹ These three strategies, as he notes, are not mutually exclusive but can be combined in various ways.

In all three cases, one needs to recognize the important distinction between internal and external perception. It is one thing for a subordinate group to reduce, redefine, or reconstruct the characteristics that differentiate them from the dominant group; it is quite another for these changes to be accepted by the dominant group and to result in real changes in social location. Further, with respect to the second and third strategies, one can imagine differences in intent. Redefining group identity in more positive terms might have the goal of changing the perception of outsiders in a more positive direction. It might, however, be directed instead at members of the group, providing them with a more positive valuation of group characteristics and thus increasing their ability to resist external categorization.

Gentile Christianity existed as a subordinate group attempting to compete with more dominant groups for social space within the larger Greco-Roman world. Tajfel's analysis of identity construction as "an intervening causal mechanism in situations of 'objective' social change" will provide us with useful tools and insights as we explore the role of *ethnē* as an identity term in this ongoing competitive process.

This is perhaps the point to recall the fact that, as we have seen, gentile Christians were prepared to see themselves not only as a transethnic entity—drawn from all the *ethnē*—but also as collectively constituting a new *ethnos*. In the past, the tendency has been to downplay the element of ethnicity inherent in the term and to see it as metaphorical, a kind of rhetorical embroidery on a quite different concept of identity. Often this different concept was contrasted precisely with the ethnic particularity of the Jews. As we noted above in the discussion of the parting of the ways, the key to the success of the Christian movement has often been seen as its abandonment of Jewish particularism, with its basis in ethnic identity, in favor of an all-embracing, non-ethnic universalism.⁷²

---

71. For other seminal studies of identity formation in modern nation-states, see Benedict Anderson, *Imagined Communities: Reflections on the Origin and Spread of Nationalism*, rev. ed. (London: Verso, 2006); Adrian Hastings, *The Construction of Nationhood: Ethnicity, Religion, and Nationalism* (Cambridge: Cambridge University Press, 1997); and, from a quite different perspective, Halvor Moxnes, *Jesus and the Rise of Nationalism: A New Quest for the Nineteenth-Century Historical Jesus* (London: I. B. Taurus, 2012).

72. "Most people—Christian or not—do not think of Christianity as *necessarily* linked with race or ethnicity. Indeed, most historical reconstructions published in the last twenty

More recent constructivist approaches, however, have provided grounds for taking this language of ethnicity more seriously and thus for understanding Christian claims about being a new *ethnos* as part of an attempt to construct an identity for themselves that others would have recognized as ethnic.[73] The world in which these claims were put forward was one in which religious practice was seen as one of the defining elements of an *ethnos*, and where even the notions of kinship and descent were subjects of negotiation. Social identity theory, then, within which ethnicity can be located as a special case, will provide us with a framework for investigating not only the place of "all the nations" in early Christian self-presentation, but also their claims to constitute a new nation or race.

Returning to Tajfel, another aspect of his typology leads us into a further usable aspect of social identity theory. In a situation of relative social deprivation, where a subordinate group is facing difficulties preserving a place for themselves in a social context dominated by others, one option, as we have seen, is social change. Another option, however, is social mobility—that is, where circumstances are conducive, the possibility that individuals simply abandon one group and become part of another. This is one aspect of an issue that is of more general interest to Tajfel—namely, the question of the factors that, in a given social situation, would lead a person to behave or interact with others as a member of a group, on the one hand, or as an individual, on the other. Not that it is a simple either-or, of course; Tajfel sees it rather as an "interpersonal-intergroup continuum,"[74] with the relative importance of each element shifting along the line between the two poles. This raises again the issue of the relationship between individual and social identity, which will be pertinent in several respects.

First, let us return for a moment to the matter of social mobility. In one respect, this is only of peripheral interest; while instances of apostasy exist and are well worth studying,[75] our interest is in group responses on the part of gentile Christians to their social location as a subordinate group within a dominant culture. From another angle, however, individual social mobility is very per-

---

years depict earliest Christianity as an inclusive movement that *rejected* ethnic or racial specificity as a condition of religious identity"; Buell, *Why This New Race?*, 1.

73. Cf. Buell, *Why This New Race?*, 2: "Christians also referred to themselves using other language that their contemporaries would have understood as positioning Christians as comparable to groups such as Jews, Greeks, and Romans: the terms *ethnos, laos, politeia* (Greek), and *genus* and *natio* (Latin) pepper early Christian texts."

74. Tajfel, *Human Groups and Social Categories*, 238; see the whole section "When does inter-individual behaviour become inter-group behaviour?," 228–43.

75. See Stephen G. Wilson, *Leaving the Fold: Apostates and Defectors in Antiquity* (Minneapolis: Fortress, 2004).

tinent to our investigation. The earliest gentile Christ-believers were converts, as was a significant proportion of the gentile Christian community throughout our period of interest. With the concept of social mobility, social identity theory intersects with social-scientific study of conversion.

Seen from one perspective, conversion is a process by which a person is socialized into a new group. Or if this puts it too passively, a convert is one who has decided to take the necessary steps to become part of a new group and, in so doing, has internalized essential aspects of the group's identity. Part of this internalization involves what Snow and Machalek call a "biographical reconstruction," a retrospective version of the convert's own life experience shaped by the "universe of discourse" that embodies the assumptions and values of the new group to which they now belong.[76] Cross-cultural studies of conversion narratives have noted not only the considerable variation among them but also, and more importantly, the extent to which they conform to the respective narrative patterns that characterize the particular groups into which they have converted. In other words, the variations in such narratives are not idiosyncratic but group-specific. In Lewis Rambo's words, "conversion is what a particular group says it is."[77] In turn, what the group "says it is" tends to shape a convert's own account of the process and thus also the new reconstructed identity that has been assumed.[78] Converts, by the very experience of conversion, become inclined and motivated to adopt the identity structures of the group into which they are being incorporated and to reconfigure their previous identity accordingly. This will become significant especially when we examine identity construction among the earliest non-Jewish converts to the movement and how they might have responded to *ethnē* as an ascribed identity.

Further, the question of when a person behaves as a member of a group and when as an individual leads to yet another line of investigation, that of multiple

---

76. David A. Snow and Richard Machalek, "The Convert as a Social Type," in *Sociological Theory*, ed. Randall Collins (San Francisco: Jossey-Bass, 1983), 266-69.

77. Lewis R. Rambo, "The Psychology of Conversion," in *Handbook of Religious Conversion*, ed. H. Newton Malony and Samuel Southard (Birmingham, AL: Religious Education Press, 1992), 160.

78. Brian Taylor, "Recollection and Membership: Converts' Talk and the Ratiocination of Commonality," *Sociology* 12 (1978): 316-24; see also Brian Taylor, "Conversion and Cognition: An Area for Empirical Study in the Micro-Sociology of Religious Knowledge," *Social Compass* 23 (1976): 5-22; Paula Fredriksen, "Paul and Augustine: Conversion Narratives, Orthodox Traditions and the Retrospective Self," *JTS* 37 (1986): 3-34; Beverly Roberts Gaventa, *From Darkness to Light: Aspects of Conversion in the New Testament* (Philadelphia: Fortress, 1986), 5-7; Alan F. Segal, *Paul the Convert: The Apostolate and Apostasy of Saul the Pharisee* (New Haven: Yale University Press, 1990), 27-30.

identities. Christian identity was neither monolithic nor totalizing; it was added to or coexisted with various already-existing identity constructs (ethnic, civic, familial, class, citizenship, etc.). This, of course, was not unique to the Christian movement; most inhabitants of the Roman Empire found themselves negotiating among multiple identities—whether hybrid, nested, overlapping, or operative in different spheres—some of them also transethnic or translocal (e.g., philosophical schools, voluntary associations, religious groups). Thus in investigating the place of *ethnē* in gentile Christian identity construction, we will need to pay attention to the factors that called for and reinforced this aspect of their identity, in contrast to other identity aspects. Here, in addition to Tajfel, John Turner's work on self-categorization theory is helpful, especially the concept of salience, which has to do precisely with the question of which aspect of an individual's constellation of identities comes into play in a given social situation.[79]

Finally, recognizing that the social situation in which early Christian identity construction took place was not simply the Greco-Roman world as a cultural amalgam but the Roman Empire as a political hegemony, we will find it beneficial to supplement the tools of social identity theory with others forged for use within imperial contexts more specifically. Some assistance will be provided by the work of James C. Scott, especially his concepts of *public transcript*—the pattern of interaction, with accompanying rationalization, imposed by the dominant on the subordinate—and *hidden transcript*—the various means by which subordinate groups construct and protect their own social breathing space within an imperial order.[80] Scott's analysis, however, tends to work with a simple binary model, where the line between the dominant and the subordinate is sharp and clear. The line has been blurred considerably—indeed, has given way to a broader, ambiguous, intervening space—by the complex and multifaceted discourse that has been gathered (sometimes reluctantly) under the banner *postcolonialism*.[81] Here the seminal (albeit densely unsystematic) work of Homi Bhabha will be useful.[82]

---

79. John C. Turner and Michael A. Hogg, *Rediscovering the Social Group: A Self-Categorization Theory* (Oxford: Blackwell, 1987). For application of Turner's work to the study of Paul, see Esler, *Conflict and Identity in Romans*; J. Brian Tucker, *You Belong to Christ: Paul and the Formation of Social Identity in 1 Corinthians 1–4* (Eugene, OR: Pickwick, 2010).

80. James C. Scott, *Domination and the Arts of Resistance: Hidden Transcripts* (New Haven: Yale University Press, 1990).

81. For a brief account, with some attention to the reluctance, see Susan B. Abraham, "Critical Perspectives on Postcolonial Theory," in *The Colonized Apostle: Paul through Postcolonial Eyes*, ed. Christopher Stanley (Minneapolis: Fortress, 2011), 24–33.

82. Homi K. Bhabha, *The Location of Culture* (London: Routledge, 2004).

Bhabha's work overlaps with that of Scott in some respects, especially with the concept of *mimicry*, at least at one end of the spectrum. Mimicry has to do with attempts by the colonized to adopt and replicate the culture of the colonizers. To some extent, mimicry can be used as an instrument of resistance, as subalterns, in an exercise of what Bhabha calls "sly civility,"[83] employ the culture of the colonizers to deflect, blunt, or even mock their colonial agenda. Such sly civility bears some resemblance to what Scott identifies as the most benign way in which the hidden transcript of the subordinated comes to expression.[84]

But in Bhabha's analysis, the relationship between the colonizers and the colonized is characterized by much more ambiguity than Scott allows for. In part, the ambivalence emerges in the slippage between the colonizers' ideal of a "reforming, civilizing mission," which seems to have as its goal the effacing of difference and the creation of people who are "just like us," and the colonizing imperative that causes them to shrink back from such equalization and the forces of liberation that it would unleash.[85] This ambivalence has its counterpart among the subalterns, many of whom find aspects of colonial culture attractive, even as they continue to bump up against the limits of assimilation. From either side, colonizers and colonized alike experience the tensions inherent in a situation of "almost the same, but not quite," in Bhabha's repeated phrase. The result of this interplay of civilizing mission and colonial imperative, attraction and resistance, is a hybrid space—and an identity characterized by hybridity.

For groups subjugated to (or emerging within) an imperial power, then, identity construction is shaped by factors of a very specific sort, and Bhabha's concepts of ambivalence, mimicry, and hybridity will provide a helpful sup-

---

83. "[A] subversive strategy of subaltern agency that negotiates its own authority through a process of iterative 'unpicking' and incommensurable, insurgent relinking"; Bhabha, *Location of Culture*, 184.

84. "The safest and most public form of political discourse is that which takes as its basis the flattering self-image of elites. Owing to the rhetorical concessions that this self-image contains, it offers a surprisingly large arena for political conflict that appeals to these concessions and makes use of the room for interpretation within any ideology. For example, even the ideology of white slave owners in the antebellum U. S. South incorporated certain paternalist flourishes about the care, feeding, housing, and clothing of slaves and their religious instruction. Practices, of course, were something else. Slaves were, however, able to make political use of this small rhetorical space to appeal for garden plots, better food, humane treatment, freedom to travel to religious services, and so forth. Thus, some slave interests could find representation in the prevailing ideology without appearing in the least seditious"; Scott, *Domination and the Arts of Resistance*, 18.

85. See Bhabha, *Location of Culture*, 86. Many of Bhabha's examples and case studies stem from British rule in India.

IDENTITY, ETHNICITY, AND POWER IN THE ROMAN EMPIRE

The process of identity construction under investigation here is one in which *ethnē*, initially a Jewish term for the ethnically other, came to be adopted by non-Jewish Christians as a significant term of self-identification, one that they used to negotiate a space for themselves within the multiethnic context of the Roman Empire. Christians, of course, were not the only ones seeking to define themselves and competing for social space. The process of gentile Christian self-definition, then, needs to be located within the larger area of ethnicity and identity construction in the Roman Empire. Later we will look in more detail at the use of *ethnē*, *genos*, and related terms in this larger area. At this preliminary stage, we will take a more general overview. Again, our intent here is to sketch out an area of second-level scholarly discourse rather than to engage in primary-level constructive work.

Awareness of other peoples and groups, curiosity about differences in language and customs, and other manifestations of what might be called rudimentary ethnography seem to have been part of human experience for as long as there have been *ethnē* capable of producing *graphai* (written records). With the emergence of large-scale empires, however, especially those of the Persian, Greek, and Roman periods, contact with other peoples and cultures increased dramatically. Conquest, of course, represented contact of a very direct and particular kind, but conquest was followed by many other forms of interaction, not only with subjugated peoples but also with surrounding nations. Military encampments, colonization, the capture of slaves, strategic intermarriage, embassies, trade, migration, the emergence of diaspora communities, travel for study or other pursuits—the business and bustle of empire brought ethnic groups increasingly into mutual awareness of the other, which in turn generated an increasing desire to describe and understand the bewildering phenomena of human diversity.

The ethnographical tradition goes back at least as far as Herodotus, who, in order to answer the implied question with which he begins ("the reason why they [Greeks and barbarians] warred against each other"; *Histories* 1.1), finds it necessary to describe, in considerable detail, the distinguishing characteristics of barbarians (Persians, Babylonians, Indians, Egyptians, Scythians, and others) and Greeks alike. Ethnographical description continues to be a common feature of historical writing (e.g., Polybius, Diodorus Siculus, Sallust, Livy, Josephus, Tacitus) but can be found as well in works dealing with geography and natural history (Posidonius, Strabo, Pliny), military campaigns (Julius Caesar), medicine (Hippocratic writings, Asclepiades, Galen), architecture (Vitruvius), and mythology (Apollonius Rhodius).

Ancient ethnographers, however, were not content simply to describe, catalog, and classify. They were also concerned to understand and explain. As Woolf notes: "Explanations are clearly important to much ethnographic writing, to judge from the space given to them."[86] The range of explanations stretches all the way from diet to the zodiac, but Woolf helpfully groups them into two broad categories.[87] The first is genealogical—patterns of explanation in which distinctive features of a given group are understood as having been determined by kinship and common descent, often from founding ancestors or ancient heroes, sometimes with intervening stages of ancestral migrations. The other is geographical—explanatory schemes that account for ethnic distinctives on the basis of the land in which a group lives (or, in the case of autochthony, from which its ancestors sprang), its location within larger geographical regions, its climate, and so on. As is demonstrated by the elements of migration (a geographical element within a genealogical explanation) and of autochthonous ancestors (a genealogical within a geographical), the two patterns can readily intertwine and correlate.

In what follows, we will be interested particularly in two broad aspects of ancient ethnographical discourse. The first has to do with what might be described as comparative ethnic historiography—the range of ways in which ethnic groups constructed maps of the nations. Since the purpose of such mapmaking was usually to situate one's own group advantageously, one might just as accurately describe this aspect as competitive ethnic historiography. These maps were historically oriented, in the sense that groups constructed pasts for themselves that could then be correlated in strategic ways with the pasts of other groups. Of course, as Hall reminds us, in these processes of identity construction, "there was no clear division between the historical past and the mythical past."[88] The other broad aspect involves the search for universals—ways of transcending ethnic particularities and arriving at some form of transethnic cosmopolitanism. These two aspects might be seen as moving in opposite directions, the first directed toward the construction of distinct group identities and the second aiming to transcend them. In reality, however, the two were often more dialectically intertwined. While these two aspects of ethnographical discourse took new and distinct forms with the emergence of the Roman Empire, they were well-established phenomena long before Rome arrived on the larger Mediterranean scene.

86. Woolf, *Tales of the Barbarians*, 33.
87. See ch. 2 in Woolf, *Tales of the Barbarians*.
88. J. M. Hall, *Ethnic Identity in Greek Antiquity*, 182.

Positioning the Question

With respect to the first aspect, the most common device used in constructing maps of the nations consisted of ethnic family trees and lines of descent. This genealogical device, however, could function in different ways. Most commonly, ethnic histories functioned to demonstrate the antiquity of a group and thus both its distinct identity and its venerable status with respect to other groups. Josephus, who in his *Antiquities* set out to construct just such an *archaiologia* (*Against Apion* 1.1) on behalf of the Jews, recognized the competitive environment in which he did his work: "each nation endeavors to trace its own institutions back to the remotest date" (2.151). Since unadorned claims to antiquity were not always persuasive, supportive measures were often undertaken. In one such measure, mentioned by Diodorus Siculus, Greeks and barbarians alike buttressed their claims to antiquity by claiming also to be autochthonous in origin, sprung from the earth itself.[89] Alternatively, ethnic origins could be pressed back into the distant past by means of euhemeristic traditions that identified a nation's gods with founder figures or ancient heroes and thus allowed for historicizing interpretations of national myths and sagas.[90] Further, as Diodorus goes on to demonstrate, buttressing could also be sought in claims that one's founding gods or noble ancestors were "the first of all men to discover the things which are of use in life" (*Historical Library* 1.9.3; the *Erfinder* argument), which is usually accompanied by claims that they had taught these elements of common culture (agriculture, crafts, metallurgy, and the like) to others (the *Kulturbringer* argument). Such traditions are well known in Greek mythology (Daedalus, Hephaestus, Hermes), and similar claims are made by Manetho in his history of Egypt, where he presents Egypt to the wider Greek-speaking world as the source of Greek culture and wisdom. With respect to Egypt, Diodorus later catalogs various innovations and inventions that were introduced by Isis and Osiris (1.14–15) and subsequently attributes additional innovations to the legendary Egyptian king Sesostris (1.53–57).

Such *Erfinder* and *Kulturbringer* arguments represent a particular aspect of a larger strategy employed by those engaged in competitive ethnic historiography. Once an ethnic group had established an account of its own origins, usually incorporating historicized interpretations of mythology and saga, the account could readily be used as a subordinating framework within which other groups could be located and their origins explained. While Greek influence and industry

---

89. *Library of History* 1.9.3. See Elias Bickerman, "*Origines Gentium*," *CP* 47 (1952): 76; Jeremy M. Schott, *Christianity, Empire, and the Making of Religion in Late Antiquity* (Philadelphia: University of Pennsylvania Press, 2008), 17. On the Greek claim, see Isocrates, *Panegyric* 24–25.

90. See Schott, *Christianity, Empire, and the Making of Religion*, 17.

helped to ensure that a Homeric framework became dominant, it was just the most successful instance of a much broader phenomenon.[91]

But ethnic histories were used not only to establish difference and separation. As Dench observes, "In the ancient Mediterranean world, . . . it is extremely common to use notions of ancestral kin as a loop to draw peoples in, rather than a fence to keep peoples out."[92] With respect to Greek origins, for example, Hall observes that, at least in the period before the Persian wars, ethnic histories tended to be "aggregative" rather than "oppositional," as various groups in the Greek peninsula used the idea of descent from a common ancestor (Hellen) as a means of banding together as a kin group.[93]

To be sure, the distinction between aggregative and oppositional self-definition was by no means absolute. One of the effects of the Persian wars, for example, was to spur on the "invention of the barbarian,"[94] as the aggregative sense of Greekness that had been emerging in the earlier period was solidified by a new perceived contrast with the alien other. The other was in the first instance Persian (e.g., Aeschylus, *Persians*), but Persians came to be seen at the same time as a particular instantiation of a more categorical other—the barbarians.[95] Of course, such us-them binaries represent an almost instinctive aspect of group identity and were common in the ancient world. At one level, such binaries can be seen as ethnic self-definition in its most basic and primitive form, a rudimentary ethnic map that allows for only two territories (ours and theirs), human diversity being flattened and homogenized accordingly. With the spread of Hellenism, however, both as an imperial force and as a cultural identity that

91. See Bickerman, "*Origines Gentium.*"
92. Emma Dench, *Romulus' Asylum: Roman Identities from the Age of Alexander to the Age of Hadrian* (Oxford: Oxford University Press, 2005), 138. See also Erich S. Gruen, *Rethinking the Other in Antiquity* (Princeton: Princeton University Press, 2011), especially part 2, "Connections with the 'Other.'"
93. J. M. Hall, *Ethnic Identity in Greek Antiquity*, 47. See also Richter, *Cosmopolis*, 118.
94. E. Hall, *Inventing the Barbarian*.
95. Richter draws attention to the fact that Socrates simply assumed a fundamental distinction, rooted in nature itself, between Greek and barbarian: "Socrates maintained that there exists *in nature* a fundamental rift between Greek and barbarian. What is more, he describes this rift in the same language of kinship he had adopted to describe the homogeneity of Kallipolis. Just as the *polis* ought to act and react like a single family, Hellas ought to recognize its own shared kinship as well as the foreignness of the barbarian. . . . Socrates does not attempt to explain why barbarians are the natural enemies of the Greeks. As opposed to almost every other facet of life in the city, we find here the simple assertion of commonplaces rather than systematic argumentation"; *Cosmopolis*, 39.

could be acquired by non-Greeks, this binary came to operate at a much more sophisticated level, allowing for significant travel across the boundary. Various groups were able to use the Greek-barbarian distinction to their own advantage, either aligning themselves with the Greek side of the binary or presenting themselves as significant precursors of the Greeks.[96] Nevertheless, while the binary of Greek and barbarian—and, to a lesser extent, that of Jew and *ethnē*—ended up playing a significant role in the shaping of the ancient world from Alexander to Constantine, they emerged as part of a more widespread part of what we have termed competitive ethnic historiography.

The other aspect of what will be of interest in the discussion of identity construction in the Roman Empire has to do with various ways in which cultural thinkers, imperial apologists, and others searched for ways of transcending ethnic boundaries and of creating more universal, cosmopolitan categories and identities. The primary context in which such transethnic conceptions and developments are to be found, of course, was the Hellenistic world that emerged in the eastern Mediterranean in the wake of Alexander's conquests and the consequent spread of Greek culture and influence.

To be sure, the idealized portrait of Alexander as the enlightened hero who set out to unify the *oikoumenē* by inviting conquered peoples to adopt and embrace Greek culture (*paideia*)—a portrait sketched out by Plutarch and championed in more modern times by writers such as Tarn—has to be set aside.[97] Likewise, Isocrates's definition of Greekness as based not on nature or descent (*genos*) but on education (*paideusis*) and a particular way of thinking cannot be taken as a straightforward throwing open of the doors of membership to all and sundry.[98] In context, the definition was aimed more in direction of restriction than expansion—that is, to identify Athenian culture (rather than birth and ge-

---

96. For the former, see, e.g., Anthony Spawforth's study of Lydia: "Shades of Greekness: A Lydian Case Study," in Malkin, *Ancient Perceptions of Greek Ethnicity*, 375–400. And for the latter, see, e.g., Richter's discussion of how Egyptians and Jews, taking advantage of Herodotus's readiness to see Egypt as the source of some aspects of Greek thought and culture, used this to position themselves advantageously with respect to the Greek-barbarian divide; *Cosmopolis*, 178–84.

97. See, e.g., William W. Tarn, "Alexander the Great and the Unity of Mankind," *Proceedings of the British Academy* 19 (1933): 123–66. The decisive refutation of Tarn was made by Ernst Badian, "Alexander the Great and the Unity of Mankind," *Historia: Zeitschrift für alte Geschichte* 7 (1958): 425–44. For discussion, see further Richter, *Cosmopolis*, 13–16.

98. "And so far has our city distanced the rest of mankind in thought and in speech that her pupils have become the teachers of the rest of the world; and she has brought it about that the name 'Hellenes' suggests no longer a race [*genous*] but an intelligence

nealogical descent) as the standard by which the emerging Greek nation should be defined.[99]

Nevertheless, it is clear that something like this was the result of Alexander's conquests, even if not the intent. While the Greek-barbarian distinction remained intact, the boundary between the two became increasingly permeable. Greekness increasingly became defined in terms of *paideia* rather than *genos*—an identity, based on Greek culture rather than on kinship or descent, that could be acquired by anyone with the means, opportunity, and desire to pursue it. Even in the case of Isocrates, his distinction between *paideusis* and *genos* later provided him with a basis for extending the boundary of Greekness to include Philip of Macedon.[100] Intentionally or not, Philip's son Alexander created a world marked by a new transethnic identity, a world in which "one could 'become Greek' by acculturating oneself through rigorous education and the mimetic practice of Greekness via writing, declamation, and other performances."[101]

At the same time, this new transethnic identity was also positioned as preserving the wisdom of the ancient past. Herodotus is the first of a long line of Greek writers who traveled to Egypt, engaged with their intellectual counterparts, and came away impressed with the wisdom and culture of the Egyptians. In an inverted version of the *Erfinder* motif, Greeks came to see Egypt, along with India, Persia, and other ancient cultures, as the originators of distinctive elements of Greek *paideia*, which were subsequently handed on to the Greeks themselves.[102] Greek culture, then, became a form of uniting people across ethnic boundaries not only because others were invited to acquire it but also because Greek *paideia* itself was said to preserve the best of those venerable cultures generally recognized to be ancient. Of course, as Schott observes, the process of

---

[*dianoias*], and that the title 'Hellenes' is applied rather to those who share our culture [*paideuseōs*] than to those who share a common blood [*physeōs*]" (*Panegyric* 50).

99. See Richter, *Cosmopolis*, 106–7; Dench, *Romulus' Asylum*, 238–39. A similar definition of Greekness, used for somewhat similar ends, can be found several centuries later in a letter attributed to Apollonius of Tyana, in which he reproaches the Ionians for basing their claim to be Greek on kinship and descent (*genē*), when Greek identity is based on "customs, laws, language, and way of life" (*Letters* 71).

100. See Richter, *Cosmopolis*, 107–8.

101. Schott, *Christianity, Empire, and the Making of Religion*, 5. See also J. M. Hall, *Hellenicity*, esp. 172–228; Simon Swain, *Hellenism and Empire: Language, Classicism, and Power in the Greek World, AD 50–250* (Oxford: Oxford University Press, 1996), 67–70.

102. "[F]or centuries, Greeks had located the origins of almost every aspect of civilization in Egypt. Greek intellectuals, from Pythagoras to Cleombrotus, either had actually visited or were reputed to have visited Egypt, talked with the priests of the shrines, and brought the incomparable wisdom of the Nile back to Greece"; Richter, *Cosmopolis*, 194.

transmission and preservation was generally construed in distinctively Greek terms. "Egyptian, Persian, Jewish, or Indian wisdom is valuable only insofar as it can be given an *interpretatio Graeca*" and thus serve to underwrite Greek superiority and to reinscribe the Greek-barbarian distinction.[103]

At the same time, this interest in aligning the *paideia* of the present with the wisdom of the past could serve a competitive purpose within Greek culture itself. For the Stoics in particular, admiration for the wisdom of the past was linked with the belief that the ancients were more in tune with the rational principle (*logos*) that undergirded the natural order, so that the task of philosophy was to recover an original pattern of life that had been dulled and obscured by the trappings of later culture and technology. This leads to another form of transethnic conceptualization that emerged in the Hellenistic era and became a significant aspect of identity construction in the Roman Empire—the cosmic city of the early Stoics. To be sure, Vogt and others have rightly cautioned against an overly anachronistic approach to Stoic cosmopolitanism; for Zeno, Chrysippus, and others of the early Stoa, the cosmic city was not so much a project to be pursued as an already-existing reality to be perceived.[104] Still, they provided conceptual resources for those in the imperial period who were engaged in more deliberate projects of transethnic social construction.[105]

Stoicism was marked by the conviction that the created order is an integrated whole, permeated and animated by a divine rationality (the *logos*). This rational principle serves to bind all human beings—at least to the extent that they are governed by reason—into a single community. More specifically, this community can be understood as a universal cosmic city, of which all rational beings are citizens and whose laws are a kind of natural law dictated by reason itself. To be sure, since citizenship for Zeno was limited to those who were wise, in the sense of being governed by reason, his cosmic city was characterized more by a concern to restrict its membership than to expand its boundaries. Early Stoicism displays little interest in a *cosmopolis* that might become coextensive with the *oikoumenē*. Nevertheless, the fact that citizenship was based not on ethnicity or descent but

---

103. Schott, *Christianity, Empire, and the Making of Religion*, 27.

104. Katja Maria Vogt, *Law, Reason and the Cosmic City: Political Philosophy in the Early Stoa* (Oxford: Oxford University Press, 2008), e.g., 4–6. Richter organizes his study (*Cosmopolis*) around two temporal poles—late-classical Athens and the early Roman Empire—in order to argue that "it was the Roman Stoics . . . who fully developed the sort of cosmopolitanism that both ancients and moderns often associate with Zeno" (p. 63).

105. Richter's goal is to demonstrate "how early imperial intellectuals . . . made use of a late-classical Athenian political-conceptual vocabulary" in "an effort to imagine the unity of the Roman empire" (*Cosmopolis*, 5, 245).

on rationality and wisdom served to make Stoic cosmopolitanism a useful resource for later projects of imperial (or, for that matter, ecclesial) expansion.

Of course, Stoicism was not the only philosophical movement engaged in the search for universals and commonalities. The widespread Greek interest both in the *polis*, its nature and constitution, and in virtue, seen as the necessary foundation of human life, led inevitably to questions about the relative value of descent and *paideia* in the formation of wise and virtuous citizens. The dialogue between Socrates and various interlocutors in Plato's *Meno*, for example, produced answers to such questions that, at least in principle, transcended the boundaries marked out by lines of descent and solidified in ethnic identities.

In addition to the role of philosophy, Richter has drawn our attention to the way in which the pantheon of the gods came to provide a common sacred canopy (to borrow a term from Peter Berger) under which all the peoples of the Mediterranean basin lived their lives. As ethnic groups came into increased contact with each other, they engaged in a kind of syncretistic cross-referencing, by means of which the gods of one's own group were correlated with the gods of other groups. What emerged was the sense that

> all peoples experience the same numinous entities but describe them and act toward them in different ways. Both Greek and Egyptians, to borrow Plutarch's image, sit on the shores of the same Mediterranean Sea; the fact that the Greeks have one name for it and the Egyptians another does not alter the fact that the sea is the same. Similarly, both Greeks and Egyptians "know" the same gods by different names, tell different stories about them, and have different cultic practices.[106]

Thus, just as lines of descent could function aggregatively (as well as oppositionally), so the pantheon could provide means of creating connections and commonalities across ethnic lines. The transethnic potential of comparative theogony and theology was amplified with the emergence of more unitary conceptions of the divine within the philosophical traditions (e.g., the pantheistic *logos* of Stoicism, the ultimate One of Neoplatonism).

Before moving to the Roman imperial period, we should note that resources and models for the transcending of ethnic boundaries existed not only in conceptual forms but in social formations as well. Philosophical schools themselves were translocal and transethnic communities, membership in which was open to all who were appropriately desirous of learning and wisdom. Many of the associations that began to flourish in the Hellenistic period drew members from

---

106. Richter, *Cosmopolis*, 209.

across ethnic lines as well.[107] Likewise, some of the initiatory (or mystery) religions that migrated through the Hellenistic world served to draw initiates from various ethnic groups and to offer shared relationships with deities who were not necessarily bound to specific cities or ethnic groups.

Long before Rome emerged as the dominant power in the Mediterranean world, then, discussions of ethnicity and cosmopolis, the processes of self-definition that fueled them, and the related negotiations for social advantage were well underway. Of course, Roman dominance did not happen overnight, and Rome itself developed within this Hellenistic context. With the accession of Augustus as a new kind of *imperator*, however, the new fact of the empire put these older discussions, processes, and negotiations into a new context and raised pressing questions, for both rulers and ruled alike, of how to conceive of the peoples bound together in this new *imperium*.[108]

The questions, of course, looked different to the ruled than they did to the rulers, which raises a different set of questions for the interpreter. Rome was by no means the last state to enlarge its sphere of geopolitical power and control to such an extent that it could be considered an empire,[109] and imperial realities continue to shape both our contemporary world and the processes of identity construction within it.[110] Investigation of Roman imperial realities has never been an innocent enterprise; any investigator needs both to take account of the ways in which this historical enterprise has been made to serve later agendas and to recognize the ways in which contemporary agendas, commitments, and social locations can exert their own control over the study of the past.

Through the modern period and up until the end of the Second World War, study of the Roman world tended to be shaped by its part in a smooth narrative of progress, one in which the Roman Empire was seen as the means by which

---

107. See now the splendid collection of source material in Richard S. Ascough, Philip A. Harland, and John S. Kloppenborg, eds., *Associations in the Greco-Roman World: A Sourcebook* (Waco, TX: Baylor University Press, 2012).

108. On this term, and its shift in usage from "ruling power" to "territory ruled," see John Richardson, *The Language of Empire: Rome and the Idea of Empire from the Third Century BC to the Second Century AD* (Cambridge: Cambridge University Press, 2008), and further below.

109. For considerations of how to define and identify an empire, see David J. Mattingly, *Imperialism, Power, and Identity: Experiencing the Roman Empire* (Princeton: Princeton University Press, 2011), 6–7; Greg Woolf, *Rome: An Empire's Story* (Oxford: Oxford University Press, 2012), 19–27.

110. See, e.g., Niall Ferguson, *Empire: The Rise and Demise of the British World Order and the Lessons for Global Power* (New York: Basic, 2003).

classical civilization was transmitted to the West. In Hingley's summary of the narrative, civilization

> was successively displaced in time and space from the ancient Near East through "Western" (and democratic) classical Greece and then to Rome. Rome acted as the link to the Christian Middle Ages and then civilization passed through the western European Renaissance and to the modern European imperial powers, finally to form the inheritance of the countries of contemporary Europe and of the USA.[111]

Of course, the role in this narrative played by Christendom and the Christianized Roman Empire varies considerably. In more ecclesiastical versions of the narrative, Christianity is an essential element, classical civilization understood to have been purified and brought to completion through Christian faith.[112] In more secularized versions, Christendom's role is more contingent and temporary, serving as the convenient container within which classical civilization was preserved through the dark ages so that it might be rediscovered in the Renaissance. Once the precious classical cargo was safely delivered, the container could readily be set aside.

In whatever form, this narrative served to draw lines of connection between the modern Western world and two aspects of the Roman Empire. One had to do with Rome's supposed sense of a civilizing mission—the empire as the means by which Greek *paideia* and Roman *humanitas* were transmitted to the barbarians in order that they might become full participants in the civilized world. The other had to do with the legitimization of political power—imperial rule as justified both by the nobility of its civilizing goals and its self-evident success in extending peace and security throughout the *oikoumenē*. Both aspects—the Roman Empire as civilizing pedagogue and as effectively ruling power—were often linked with the concept of Romanization—the spread of Roman culture through the empire and its adoption by the nations and groups within it.[113] With

---

111. Hingley, *Globalizing Roman Culture*, 21.

112. See, e.g., the "confluence model" of the parting of the ways as discussed earlier in the chapter, especially the essay by Inge ("Essay I: Introductory").

113. On the concept of Romanization and recent debates about the term, see Janet Huskinson, "Looking for Culture, Identity and Power," in *Experiencing Rome: Culture, Identity and Power in the Roman Empire*, ed. Janet Huskinson (London: Routledge, 2000), 20–22, together with other essays in the volume; see also Mattingly, *Imperialism, Power, and Identity*, 38; Andrew Wallace-Hadrill, *Rome's Cultural Revolution* (Cambridge: Cambridge University Press, 2008), 9–14; Hingley, *Globalizing Roman Culture*, 15–18.

Positioning the Question

the emergence of European nation-states and their extension through colonial conquest in other parts of the world, Romanization in its dual aspects served as a ready model both to justify and to inspire these later national, colonial, and imperial projects.[114] In return, these projects and the environments in which they flourished served to shape the attitudes and interests of classical scholars. As Mattingly puts it: "Knowledge and admiration of the Roman Empire shaped British policy in its own colonies, while at the same time the modern British imperial experience reinforced a particular view of the Roman world."[115] Indeed, this positive dialectic between modern imperialism and classical studies probably helps account for the popularity of classical studies in the nineteenth and early twentieth centuries.[116]

Since the end of the Second World War, however, this smooth teleological narrative has lost its grip on classical scholarship. The dismemberment of colonial empires, the cultural and political turmoil of the 1960s, the postmodern suspicion of dominant narratives used to mask the realities of power—all have served to cast an unfavorable light on the more benign and optimistic portrayals of the past and to foster the emergence of analyses that are both more critical of the Roman Empire and more interested in the experiences and perceptions of the subject peoples.

The initial manifestations of this shift were shaped by a straightforward anti-imperialistic sensibility. Studies by scholars such as Dahlheim and Harris emphasized the harshness and brutality of Roman warfare, the greed for power and wealth that motivated it, the rapacious looting of cities and enslavement of populations that inevitably followed, and the importance of militaristic expansionism to Roman economy as a whole.[117] In contrast to earlier approaches

---

114. E.g., see Hingley's description of how Theodor Mommsen made strategic alignments between the movement toward German unity in his own day and the Roman unification of Italy as recounted by Appian; *Globalizing Roman Culture*, 32. Dench makes an analogous observation about the mixed ethnic roots of Britain: "according to one strand within the somewhat tortured history of the identification of the British with the Roman empire (within which the undeniable episode of the Roman occupation of ancient Britain threw up particular problems), the greatness of Britain resided in her 'mixed' roots, Romano-British and/or Anglo-Saxon 'just like' the 'mixed' roots of the Roman empire"; *Romulus' Asylum*, 229.

115. Mattingly, *Imperialism, Power, and Identity*, 10.

116. "Classics, as a discipline grew, in particular, out of the Grand Tour of the eighteenth and nineteenth centuries, but it performed a specific role in Britain during the nineteenth and twentieth centuries, to educate future colonial administrators"; Hingley, *Globalizing Roman Culture*, 18.

117. William V. Harris, *War and Imperialism in Republican Rome, 327-70 B. C.* (Oxford:

in which the emergence of the empire was seen as almost accidental—the unintended consequence of various defensive wars—here emphasis is placed on a deliberate and aggressive program of territorial conquest and self-interested rule. In keeping with the binary character of such analyses, most of the attention was given to the conquerors themselves, the conquered appearing primarily in the role of passive victims.

More recently, however, especially under the influence of postcolonial studies, attention has shifted to the experience of subject peoples and their own responses to the Roman reality in which they found themselves.[118] To a certain degree, this question was also taken up within the older Romanization paradigm, where scholars debated the extent to which Romanization was a top-down or a bottom-up enterprise. As Hingley puts it: "Did the Roman administration have an active part in 'Romanizing' the empire" or "did the native elite effectively 'Romanize' themselves under the indirect influence of Rome?"[119] Even so, the linearity of the older model remained intact, the primary category of interest being the degree of progress along a line from native barbarism to Roman *humanitas*. Within this newer approach, however, there is more interest in the variety of interaction and negotiation that took place between native and Roman cultures and thus in the variety of cultural amalgams and hybrid identities that resulted.

Adding to the variety is the fact that, in place of the homogenized figure of the barbarian, this approach gives greater recognition to the distinctive features of

---

Clarendon, 1979); Werner Dahlheim, *Gewalt und Herrschaft: Das provinziale Herrschaftssystem der römischen Republik* (Berlin: de Gruyter, 1977).

118. See especially Jane Webster and Nicholas J. Cooper, *Roman Imperialism: Post-Colonial Perspectives* (Leicester: University of Leicester, 1996); Richard Miles, ed., *Constructing Identities in Late Antiquity* (London: Routledge, 1999); Janet Huskinson, ed., *Experiencing Rome: Culture, Identity and Power in the Roman Empire* (London: Routledge, 2000); Hingley, *Globalizing Roman Culture*; Wallace-Hadrill, *Rome's Cultural Revolution*; Mattingly, *Imperialism, Power, and Identity*; Schott, *Christianity, Empire, and the Making of Religion*, 9; and Woolf, *Rome*, 277. A somewhat dissenting perspective is offered by Ando, who is critical of attempts to view the Roman Empire through the lenses of modern anti-imperialism or postcolonialism, not in the interest of defending an older, more pro-Roman approach, but because he believes that such attempts tend to disregard the differences between modern empires and ancient ones, thus imposing modern agendas and categories on quite different ancient realities; see Clifford Ando, *Imperial Ideology and Provincial Loyalty in the Roman Empire* (Berkeley: University of California Press, 2000), esp. 66–67. For a somewhat similar discussion of the differences between ancient and modern empires, yet combined with a more positive assessment of the potential of postcolonial approaches, see Woolf, *Rome*, 227–29.

119. Hingley, *Globalizing Roman Culture*, 45.

native cultures, which brings with it a greater recognition of regional variations. In place of the older linear model of Romanization, then, recent studies tend to operate within more multidimensional frameworks, with axes that include not only acculturation (the degree to which Roman culture is adopted) but also what might be called accommodation (an axis that stretches from "self-interested collaboration" to "resistance unto death,"[120] as Mattingly puts it), together with local ethnic variation. The social phenomena mapped out within such frameworks—marked by ambivalent allegiances, hybrid identities, subversive mimicry, cultural bricolage, and the like—increasingly serve as the site at which questions about identity construction in the Roman world are being pursued.

One further aspect of this site needs to be noted before we move on. The shift of attention from imperial masters to imperial subjects (from the colonizers to the colonized) has highlighted the degree to which "the formation and contestation of identity are fundamentally about power."[121] Imperial ideology, whose purpose is inevitably to legitimate and reinforce the power structures of the empire, does so in part by constructing and imposing relative identities for the conquerors and the conquered. The extent to which a subordinate group is able to use such an imposed identity to its own advantage, or to reposition itself by establishing a modified or alternative identity, is a measure of its ability to increase its own degree of relative power. To pursue questions about identity construction in the Roman Empire is also to raise questions about how power was exercised, gained, and lost.

No investigation into the development of the Christian movement in the imperial period, then, can remain aloof from the ways in which study of the classical world has intertwined with later cultural, political, and religious agendas. Correspondingly, no investigator can pretend to occupy some neutral outside vantage point from which the classical world can be seen just as it was. While I see no need to engage here in any extended postmodern analysis of my own situatedness,[122] I want to chart a course that avoids pro-Roman narratives of Western civilization and its development, on the one hand, and ideological anti-

---

120. Wallace-Hadrill, *Imperialism, Power, and Identity*, 29. For the concepts of "acculturation" and "accommodation," see John M. G. Barclay, *Jews in the Mediterranean Diaspora: From Alexander to Trajan (323 BCE–117 CE)* (Edinburgh: T&T Clark, 1996), 88–98.

121. As Miles puts it in his introduction to *Constructing Identities in Late Antiquity*, 5. For Schott, postcolonialism "insists that identities are produced and deployed in the context of imperial systems of power and control"; *Christianity, Empire, and the Making of Religion*, 9. See also Mattingly, *Imperialism, Power, and Identity*, xv, 206–7.

122. Pertinent biographical information is readily available: male; white; Canadian, of British and Icelandic stock; Christian, of a more or less conventional sort; coming of

imperialism, on the other. With respect to the study of early Christianity in its Roman imperial context, I have little affinity either for triumphalistic accounts of Christian success in the Roman Empire or for attempts to portray early Christians as thoroughgoing anti-imperialist subversives. All of which is to say that, without wanting to align myself too closely with any specific method or school of interpretation, I find postcolonial approaches to identity construction to be particularly useful and congenial.

To return to the main thread of our discussion, we are interested here in issues of identity construction in the early imperial period, from Augustus through to the end of the Severan dynasty in the early third century CE. Although Augustus made efforts to present himself as a defender of Roman tradition (the *mos maiorum*) and to put a republican patina on his rule, the Roman world was a strikingly different place at the end of its life than it had been when, as Octavian Caesar, he defeated Mark Antony in 31 BCE. Of course, the difference should not be exaggerated: as Cicero and Polybius demonstrate, the belief that Rome had conquered "the whole earth" (*orbis terrarum*) and now ruled "the inhabited world" (*oikoumenē*) was already widespread among Romans and Greeks alike.[123] Nevertheless, his achievements—political, administrative, ideological—consolidated this rule and embedded it in structures that shaped the Mediterranean world through our period of interest. The result was the emergence of not so much a shared sense of identity as the sense of a common territorial and social reality within which identity was to be constructed and negotiated.

This perception of a common imperial reality was shaped by, and came to expression in, a variety of forms. We shall look briefly at several markers—terminological, representational, literary, social—of the changes that were effected in the Augustan period and that continued to shape the Roman world in our period of interest.

We begin with the language of empire, and in particular with the terms *imperium* and *provincia*. In the early republican period, these terms did not have the territorial sense that *empire, province*, and related political terms have in modern usage. Instead, *imperium* had to do with the authorized power or the right to rule that was granted to an official of the state; *provincia* referred to the responsibilities that were entrusted to one who held *imperium*. Of course, as the Roman rule expanded, these terms came to be associated as well with the territory within which such rule was exercised or such responsibilities carried

---

age in the 1960s; moderately left-of-center—all of which has rendered me grateful for the benefits of civilization but wary of power and the structures through which it is wielded.

123. Cicero, *On Behalf of King Deiotarus* 15; Polybius, *Histories* 1.1.5.

out. But as Richardson has demonstrated in his thorough study of these terms,[124] it was with the accession of Augustus, who assumed the supreme *imperium* over Roman affairs and who carried out a full reorganization of the *provinciae*, that the territorial sense came more clearly to the fore: "Whatever may have been the case before Augustus, there was now something which could be described as a Roman Empire in a concrete sense, which was more than the power of the Roman people exercised over a large part of the globe."[125] This new "something" was the awareness of a geographical empire—a territorial domain rather than simply the effective rule of a *dominus*.

Another marker of the new imperial reality was found in visual representations of the empire.[126] The map of the known world initiated by Marcus Agrippa, Augustus's loyal second-in-command, and eventually displayed in the Porticus Vipsania depicted in strikingly visual terms the extent of Roman rule.[127] A similar effect was achieved by means of statues or busts personifying defeated nations or Roman provinces. Pompey erected fourteen of these *similacra gentium* in his theater, the first permanent theater in Rome,[128] and Augustus displayed his own conquests in a similar way in his forum.[129] Although none of these have survived, the portico of the nations in the Sebasteion at Aphrodisias provides an indication of what they might have looked like,[130] doubly interesting in that the Sebasteion

---

124. Richardson, *Language of Empire*.

125. Richardson, *Language of Empire*, 144. For a related study of the developing notions of space and geography in the Roman world, see Claude Nicolet, *Space, Geography, and Politics in the Early Roman Empire* (Ann Arbor: University of Michigan Press, 1991).

126. See especially Paul Zanker, *The Power of Images in the Age of Augustus*, trans. Alan Shapiro (Ann Arbor: University of Michigan Press, 1988).

127. See, e.g., Richardson, *Language of Empire*, 144; Nicolet, *Space, Geography, and Politics in the Early Roman Empire*, 7; and, more generally, O. A. W. Dilke, *Greek and Roman Maps* (Ithaca, NY: Cornell University Press, 1985).

128. See, e.g., Woolf, *Rome*, 147; Dench, *Romulus' Asylum*, 79.

129. Catharine Edwards, "Incorporating the Alien: The Art of Conquest," in *Rome the Cosmopolis*, ed. Catharine Edwards and Greg Woolf (Cambridge: Cambridge University Press, 2003), 65–66; Ando, *Imperial Ideology and Provincial Loyalty*, 277–79. Later, in a different way, Hadrian's villa in Tivoli functioned as a visual display of both the breadth and unity of the empire (Gregg Gardner and Kevin L. Osterloh, "The Significance of Antiquity in Antiquity: An Introduction," in *Antiquity in Antiquity: Jewish and Christian Pasts in the Greco-Roman World*, ed. Gregg Gardner and Kevin L. Osterloh, TSAJ 123 [Tübingen: Mohr Siebeck, 2008], 14).

130. The portico, created before the middle of the first century CE, contained sculpted female figures each personifying a different nation. The surviving remains represent somewhere between nineteen and twenty-four different figures. See R. R. R. Smith, "Sim-

was erected by provincial subjects, not by Romans themselves.[131] The theme of victory over the nations was expressed in imperial sculpture as well, notably in the Prima Porta sculpture of Augustus. In this statue, the emperor is depicted as wearing a cuirass ornamented with a set of reliefs in which his victory over the Parthians is placed in a dual context—Roman rule over subjugated provinces and client states on the earthly plane, and a new harmonious order uniting earth and heaven on the cosmic level.[132]

Similar personifications frequently appear on Roman coinage. In some instances the provinces or nations are depicted in poses of subjection, such as the well-known *Judaea capta* coins issued by the Flavians after the defeat of Judea; in others, the portrayals convey instead the sense of the provinces as "equal and free members of the Roman commonwealth."[133] Another image that appears in both sculpture and coinage is that of the whole world as a globe, again varying between images of conquest and subjection (the globe under the foot of the emperor) and images of benefaction and protection (the globe nestled in his arm).[134] Such images eventually could be found throughout the empire.

Visual representations of empire were also conveyed through spectacle and ceremony. In Rome, the triumphs celebrated by Augustus and his successors functioned not only as expressions of Roman power but also as ethnological displays, providing vivid depictions of the geography, topography, dress, and customs of newly subjugated nations.[135] In the eastern provinces, the emerging emperor

---

ulacra Gentium: The *Ethnē* from the Sebasteion at Aphrodisias," *JRS* 78 (1988): 50–77; Dench, *Romulus' Asylum*, 79–80; Nicolet, *Space, Geography, and Politics in the Early Roman Empire*, 84.

131. See Ando, *Imperial Ideology and Provincial Loyalty*, 304–13. Huskinson describes an analogous depiction, this one a mosaic in an upper-class Tunisian house, in which portraits of six female figures (clearly identified with specific provinces) surround a male figure (Rome); Huskinson, "Looking for Culture, Identity and Power," 3–6.

132. The statue was found in the villa of Livia in Prima Porta and is now in the Braccio Nuovo museum in the Vatican. See the discussion in Zanker, *Power of Images in the Age of Augustus*, 188–92. See also the two-level depiction of imperial order in the Gemma Augustea, discussed in Brigitte Kahl, *Galatians Re-imagined: Reading with the Eyes of the Vanquished* (Minneapolis: Fortress, 2010), 128–29, 144.

133. Niels Hannestad, *Roman Art and Imperial Policy* (Aarhus: Aarhus University Press, 1986), 97. See also Edwards, "Incorporating the Alien," 66–67.

134. Hingley, *Globalizing Roman Culture*, 1; Huskinson, "Looking for Culture, Identity and Power," 8; P. A. Brunt, *Roman Imperial Themes* (Oxford: Oxford University Press, 1990), 438.

135. Dench, *Romulus' Asylum*, 79.

cult smoothly adopted the ritual and rhetoric of the long-established Hellenistic ruler cults and used it to reinforce the perception of Rome as a unifying center, binding the diverse areas of the *orbis terrarum* into a single *cosmopolis*.[136]

Straddling the boundary between material representation and literary depiction are imperial inscriptions of various kinds: treaties, inscribed in stone or bronze and erected both in Rome and in the subject area, such as the one with Judea reproduced in 1 Macc 8:22-32 or another with the people of Callatis (on the Black Sea);[137] edicts, such as the one by Claudius concerning the status of Jews in Alexandria, which, according to Josephus, was to be posted (temporarily) in "the cities and colonies and municipia" throughout the empire (*Jewish Antiquities* 19.290-91); inscriptions on triumphal arches, such as the one concerning the Alpine peoples, reproduced by Pliny (*Natural History* 3.20.136-37); inscriptions in imperial temples, such as the one in Lugdunum (Lyon), recounted by Strabo (*Geography* 4.3.2); or honorary inscriptions dedicated to the people of Rome and set up (in Rome) by provinces or client kings.[138]

Of the inscriptions, the most elaborate is Augustus's *Acts of Augustus* (*Res Gestae*), the lengthy account of his achievements that he left as part of his will, with instructions that it be made public after his death. The fact that the surviving copies were found as far away as Pisidia suggests that it was widely distributed.[139] In Rome it was displayed, in accordance with his wishes, as an inscription attached to his Mausoleum, the family tomb that he had completed in 28 BCE. In the preface, Augustus speaks of his achievements as those "by which he brought the world [*orbem terrarum*] under the empire [*imperio*] of the Roman people."[140] We will have occasion to look again at this remarkable text, but for present purposes two sections are of particular interest, especially in view of its physical location. The first of these, found close to the beginning of the text, describes the erection of Augustus's Altar of Peace (*Ara Pacis*) (12), a monument commemorating the fact that he had "secured peace by land and sea throughout

---

136. Zanker, *Power of Images in the Age of Augustus*, 297.

137. E. H. Warmington, *Archaic Inscriptions*, vol. 4 of *Remains of Old Latin*, LCL 359 (London: W. Heinemann, 1940), 292-95 ("Laws and Other Documents," no. 55).

138. Lycia (*CIL* 1.2.725); Ephesus (*CIL* 1.2.727); Laodicea (*CIL* 1.2.728); Mithridates (*CIL* 1.2.730). Also found in Warmington, *Archaic Inscriptions*, 141-43 (nos. 21, 25, 23, 20 respectively).

139. Nevertheless, it is curious that all three surviving portions were found in Galatia.

140. The translation is that of P. A. Brunt and J. M. Moore, eds. and trans., *Res Gestae Divi Augusti: The Achievements of the Divine Augustus* (London: Oxford University Press, 1967).

the whole empire [*imperium*] of the Roman people" (13). Given that the Altar of Peace stood nearby,[141] anyone reading the *Acts of Augustus* could readily supply a mental image of this symbol of Roman *imperium* to supplement the verbal description. In the second section, the lengthier of the two (25–33), Augustus surveys the territorial extent and demographic areas of the known world in systematic precision, including not only Roman provinces from Spain to Syria,[142] but also peoples as far away as India, who, although "not subject to our government [*imperio*]," nevertheless had sent ambassadors to seek Roman friendship.[143] One can well imagine that, as an observer read this section of the inscription affixed to the Mausoleum, the mental image of Agrippa's map came readily into view.[144] The Porticus Vipsania was also located nearby in the Campus Martius, which means that our observer could well have visited all three material visualizations of the Roman *imperium* in the course of an afternoon's walk.

Moving just across the boundary between the material and the literary, we encounter Virgil's famous description of the shield that Vulcan forges for Aeneas (*Aeneid* 8.626–728), which in symbolic form tells the story of Rome from its founding to the victory of Octavian over Mark Antony at Actium. At the center of the shield is a depiction of the triumphal procession in Rome, celebrating Caesar's victory. In keeping with the theme of the whole work—that Rome was destined "to hold the sea and all lands beneath their sway" and to possess "*imperium* without end" (1.235–36, 278)—the central scene takes the form not simply of the defeat of a rival but of "a world conquest over rivers and peoples of the corners of the earth, with all their variegated costumes and tongues."[145]

The *Aeneid* is no doubt the most significant literary marker of the new imperial reality emerging in the Augustan era, and we will return to it shortly in connection with Roman identity construction.[146] But there were other writers

---

141. While not as close as its current reconstruction (adjacent to the Mausoleum), the Altar of Peace originally stood only 450 meters away.

142. "I extended the territory of all those provinces of the Roman people on whose borders lay peoples [*gentes*] not subject to our government [*imperio*]" (26).

143. *Acts of Augustus* 26, 31. "The *Res Gestae* [*Acts of Augustus*] asserts from the very first line that there was Roman control of the inhabited world (*orbis terrarum*). And it proves this methodically, without symbolism, by using a series of topographic lists that correspond to precise geographical knowledge—knowledge that reflects the science of the times, but that also surpassed the vague beliefs of the common man"; Nicolet, *Space, Geography, and Politics in the Early Roman Empire*, 23.

144. Agrippa himself is mentioned in 8.2.

145. Dench, *Romulus' Asylum*, 79.

146. Of course, Virgil's significance in this connection is not restricted to the *Aeneid*.

in the period who also lauded Augustus's accomplishments and thus helped to establish the Roman *imperium* in public consciousness. Horace's *Hymn for a New Age* was written for the festival celebrating Augustus's declaration of the dawning of a new golden age, and many of his other *Odes* strike similar notes.[147] Vitruvius prefaces his work *On Architecture* by praising the emperor for giving expression to "the majesty of the empire . . . through the eminent dignity of its public buildings" (1.preface.2) and, in keeping with his concern for physical setting, links Rome's moderate climate and central location with its ability "to rule the world" (6.1.10–12). Strabo's *Geography* begins by declaring that geographical knowledge provides essential support for "the needs of states [*politikas*]" and their leaders, especially those "who are able to hold sway over land and sea, and to unite nations and cities under one government" (1.1.16); it ends with a summary of Augustus's division of the empire into provinces (17.3.25). Strabo's geopolitical goals are thus clearly to be seen; his *Geography* accomplishes in literary description what Agrippa's map does in cartographic depiction.[148] Geographers, architects, poets—writers in the Augustan era both reflect the growing awareness of the Roman *imperium* over the *orbis terrarum* and help to reinforce it, at least among the literary elite.

Something similar was accomplished—and in a more generally accessible way—at the social level as well. The *pax Romana* made possible a degree of human mobility that had never before been seen (and would not be seen again until the nineteenth century).[149] In Rome, this resulted in an environment in which the extent of the empire was readily reflected in the faces seen in the forum. Visitors of low rank and high, merchants, philosophers, foreign delegations, hostages, *peregrini*, slaves, members of diaspora communities in the city, travelers passing through—"these people embodied the vastness and diversity of Roman territory, their presence in the heart of the city underlining Rome's power to draw people to itself over distances almost unimaginable, from cultures thrillingly alien."[150] In the provinces, the Roman reality was experienced directly through the presence of governors, soldiers, colonists, and other members of the Roman diaspora, and indirectly through the presence of those from other parts of the empire, visitors and residents alike.

To be sure, the role of direct Roman presence should not be exaggerated. In the early imperial period at least, and unlike some more recent empires, Rome

---

147. See Zanker, *Power of Images in the Age of Augustus*, 167.
148. See Richardson, *Language of Empire*, 137–38; Dench, *Romulus' Asylum*, 262; Nicolet, *Space, Geography, and Politics in the Early Roman Empire*, 47.
149. Woolf, *Rome*, 226–27; Hingley, *Globalizing Roman Culture*, 6.
150. Edwards and Woolf, *Rome the Cosmopolis*, 1.

did not depend on extensive bureaucracy or military occupation to carry out its rule. Instead, the empire operated on the basis of an extensive network of local elites, bound together by "a shared sense of aristocratic culture."[151] In our engagement with Aelius Aristides in the previous chapter, we have already seen a certain example of the type. Rome's embrace of Greek culture—together with the willingness of local elites to acquiesce in Roman rule and to do their part in carrying it out (not to mention enjoying the benefits that came with it)—worked to create something that served both as a structural endoskeleton for the imperial body and as its neural network.[152] For present purposes, the point is that, in city after city, the existence of a Romanized aristocracy served as a visual social indicator and reminder of the larger imperial reality.

Linked with this, of course, was Rome's willingness to grant citizenship not only to local elites but also to allies, freed slaves, retired soldiers, and many others who had rendered service to the empire or who were in a position to further Roman interests.[153] This practice owed something to the spread of Hellenistic identity in the Greek period, the result of Greek willingness to recognize as Greek those who had adopted the language and other characteristic aspects of Greek culture. But by couching such acculturation in the terms of citizenship, which heretofore had been normally associated with the small and local community of a city, Rome was doing something new and distinctive.[154] In the case of Hellenism and the spread of Greek *paideia*, the Greekness that resulted had been kept quite distinct from Athenian citizenship. In this new case, however, the spread of the Roman Empire was accompanied by the spread not only of Romanness but also of citizenship—or at least the realistic expectation of citizenship for those in a position to have realistic expectations. The city of Rome was now, in a sense, becoming coextensive with the empire, its boundaries expanding to incorporate the *orbis terrarum*. The presence of Roman citizens throughout the cities and provinces of the empire, then, served as additional social markers and reminders of the imperial reality.

To a significant extent, the various markers that we have been discussing here

---

151. Woolf, *Rome*, 249. See also (and especially) Ando, *Imperial Ideology and Provincial Loyalty*.

152. On the role of the client-patron system in this integrative network, see Avi Avidov, *Not Reckoned among Nations: The Origins of the So-Called "Jewish Question" in Roman Antiquity*, TSAJ 128 (Tübingen: Mohr Siebeck, 2009), 69–93.

153. See Dench, *Romulus' Asylum*, 93–151; Hingley, *Globalizing Roman Culture*, 56–57; J. P. V. D. Balsdon, *Romans and Aliens* (London: Duckworth, 1979), 82–96. Eventually, under Caracalla (in 212 CE), citizenship was extended to almost everyone in the empire.

154. See Schott, *Christianity, Empire, and the Making of Religion*, 7.

(terminological, representational, literary, and social) constitute what Zanker calls "visual language" or "visual imagery," which he defines as

> the totality of images that a contemporary would have experienced. This includes not only "works of art," buildings, and poetic imagery, but also religious ritual, clothing, state ceremony, the emperor's conduct and forms of social intercourse, insofar as these created a visual impression.[155]

As components of such a visual language, these markers represent more than simply pieces of evidence for a widespread awareness of the imperial reality that reached a new stage with Augustus. Far from being simply inert markers of a reality, most of these elements functioned at the same time as part of an imperial ideology—a deliberate, powerful, self-legitimating discourse by which the empire sought to establish its right to rule and to persuade its subjects to accept it as a foreordained and beneficent reality.[156] We have already caught a glimpse of this in the discussion of Aelius Aristides in chapter 1, where we noted the way in which his *Regarding Rome* served to reflect back to his Roman audience the flattering self-image that Rome presented to its subjects.[157] In a subsequent chapter we will look in more detail at Roman imperial ideology by tracing the place of the nations within it. Here a brief summarizing sketch will suffice.

The bedrock foundation of this imperial ideology was the message of Rome's invincibility. Triumphal processions, coinage, statuary, imperial arches, and columns all proclaimed the irresistible power of Rome's military machine.[158] To be sure, this message was often subordinated to imperial themes that displayed a softer edge. Yet even if it was often muted, it was everywhere implied.

Such an implication was certainly clear in the emphasis on the universality of Roman rule, something proclaimed in the first line of the *Acts of Augustus*.[159] To

---

155. Zanker, *Power of Images in the Age of Augustus*, 3.

156. Zanker continues: "Most importantly, through visual imagery a new mythology of Rome and, for the emperor, a new ritual of power were created. Built on relatively simple foundations, the myth perpetuated itself and transcended the realities of everyday life to project onto future generations the impression that they lived in the best of all possible worlds in the best of all times"; *Power of Images in the Age of Augustus*, 4.

157. To borrow Scott's useful phrase; *Domination and the Arts of Resistance*, 18.

158. A message not lost on Josephus, as can be seen from the speech he puts into the mouth of Agrippa II, the point of which is the absolute futility of any attempt to rebel against Roman might (*Jewish War* 2.342–407).

159. "The *res gestae* of the Divine Augustus, by which he brought the world [*orbem terrarum*] under the empire [*imperio*] of the Roman people." It had already been proclaimed in the first line of Vitruvius's *On Architecture*: "When your Highness's divine mind and

be sure, even Augustus readily acknowledged that there were lands "not subject to our government [*imperio*]" (26). But as Aristides himself demonstrates, this detail could be dismissed as inconsequential—such lands were not worth the bother—and, in any case, did not diminish the universal character of Rome's rule over the *oikoumenē* in any significant way (*Regarding Rome* 29, 34).[160]

But the case for Roman rule was not made on the basis of brute force alone; imperial ideology presented a number of softer edges. Some of these had to do with the beneficial effects of Roman rule. The most loudly trumpeted benefit of Roman rule was the establishment of peace throughout the empire, together with the political stability and economic well-being that came in its wake. Augustus took pride in having secured "peace by land and sea throughout the whole empire of the Roman people" (*Acts of Augustus* 13), a benefit proclaimed both in the text of the *Acts of Augustus* and the fabric of the Altar of Peace, and the refrain was taken up by Romans and provincials alike.[161]

Another, more direct, benefit of Roman rule was imperial benefaction itself. Although much of what Augustus has to say about benefaction in the *Acts of Augustus* pertains primarily to Rome and the cities of Italy (15–23), he does refer to his gifts to temples in the province of Asia (24), and the appendix added to the copy of the *Acts of Augustus* in Ancyra speaks of expenditures "beyond counting" given (*inter alia*) to towns and cities in the provinces (appendix 4).[162] The erection of the Sebasteion in Aphrodisias, with its veneration of Augustus (Greek: *Sebastos*) and the praise of the empire implicit in its gallery of the nations, was no coincidence; Aphrodisias had been amply rewarded for its support of Julius Caesar and his successors, in benefactions and special privileges. And as we have

---

power, Caesar, gained the empire of the world [*orbis terrarum*], Rome gloried in your triumph and victory. For all her enemies were crushed by your invincible courage and all mankind [*omnes gentes*] obeyed your bidding." See also Nicolet, *Space, Geography, and Politics in the Early Roman Empire*, 23.

160. "Nothing escapes [your rule] . . . unless you have condemned it as useless" (*Regarding Rome* 28). Dionysius of Halicarnassus strikes a similar note: "Rome rules every country that is not inaccessible or uninhabited" (*Roman Antiquities* 1.3.3). See Brunt, *Roman Imperial Themes*, 433–38.

161. E.g., "You, Roman, be sure to rule the peoples [*regere imperio populos*]—be these your arts—to crown peace with justice, to spare the vanquished and to crush the proud" (Virgil, *Aeneid* 6.851–53). See Brunt, *Roman Imperial Themes*, 440; Zanker, *Power of Images in the Age of Augustus*, 167. On Plutarch, see Lorna Hardwick, "Concepts of Peace," in *Experiencing Rome: Culture, Identity and Power in the Roman Empire*, ed. Janet Huskinson (London: Routledge, 2000), 349.

162. On the appendix, see Brunt and Moore, *Res Gestae Divi Augusti*, 1–2, 80–81.

seen, by the second century, Aristides can say of Rome that "you have filled your whole empire with cities and adornments" (*Regarding Rome* 92).

Further, the tangible benefits of Roman rule, it was claimed, served as a clear demonstration of Rome's ability to govern. As Ando says, "the Romans came to regard the arts of government as their special skill and boasted of this both at home and abroad," adding that many in the provinces readily "took up this refrain."[163] We have already heard this refrain from Aristides, who credited Rome with the very discovery of how to rule effectively.[164]

Roman rule, of course, was closely connected to Roman law, and some Roman thinkers sought to justify their rule by linking their law with a kind of universal law, recognized (at least ideally) by all civilized people and coming to expression in the laws of civilized states. This was not to say that nations should not have their own distinctive customs and traditions that would come to expression in their own distinctive laws. Cicero, followed by others (e.g., the second-century jurist Gaius), made a distinction between the local law of a specific people (*ius civile*) and a universal natural law (*ius gentium*)—a law "which natural reason establishes among mankind [*omnes homines*] generally" (Gaius, *Institutes* 1.1). While distinct, the two are to be closely connected. Among civilized nations, it should be readily apparent that the local national law, despite its ethnic particularities, contains and is based on the universal international law.[165] The idea of a universal natural law (*ius gentium*), then, enabled Rome to place its own customs and laws within a universal, transethnic frame and thus to provide further legitimization for its imperial rule.

In addition, however, beginning in the late republican period and continuing into the empire, Roman aristocracy increasingly convinced themselves, and proclaimed to others, that their right to rule was grounded in virtue—specifically in their ancestral *mores* and the *humanitas* it engendered.[166] "These concepts were used," says Hingley, "to define the elite as cultivated, enlightened and humane, entirely fitted to rule a wide empire and to lead others by example."[167] *Humanitas* was often aligned with Greek *paideia*, with the result that Rome could present itself as the legitimate heir and defender of classical civilization. At the same time,

---

163. Ando, *Imperial Ideology and Provincial Loyalty*, 6.

164. "Before you the knowledge of how to govern did not yet exist" (*Regarding Rome* 51).

165. "All nations [*omnes populi*] who are governed by laws and customs observe partly their own particular law and partly the law common to all mankind [*omnium hominum*]" (Gaius, *Institutes* 1.1). "The civil law is not necessarily also the universal law; but the universal law ought to be also the civil law" (Cicero, *On Duties* 3.69).

166. On Cicero's thinking in this regard, see Woolf, *Rome*, 148–52.

167. Hingley, *Globalizing Roman Culture*, 62.

however, the one did not fully subsume the other. Roman *humanitas* retained its own distinctive character, not least in its tight connection with the ability—and thus the right—to rule.[168]

Humanitas, however, was not restricted to the ruling Roman elite. Another significant element of imperial ideology was Rome's presentation of itself as a civilizing agent and the empire as a means of spreading *humanitas* throughout the *orbis terrarum*. While there is room for debate about the extent to which imperial conquest was motivated by a deliberate "civilizing mission,"[169] there can be little doubt about either the reality of Romanization or the part it played in the self-legitimating ideology of the empire. To cite Hingley again:

> At the same time that *humanitas* defined an ideal state of being, it also allowed for the idea that others who had not achieved its goals might succeed, given the correct circumstances. *Humanitas* served as an effective element in Roman imperial discourse, since it enabled the empire to absorb into its structure a variety of other peoples from the societies it encountered. It did this by defining its own cultural rules in such a way that they could be adopted by others.[170]

The message was not lost on Aristides: unlike previous conquerors, he says, who had the policy "that no one share in their fortune, but that all be kept apart as far as possible," the Romans, "alone of all people have set out their advantages to be shared like prizes by the best people," and he adds that it does not matter "whether one lives in Europe, Asia, or Africa . . . or whatever place one would mention."[171]

Finally, the capstone of Roman ideology was the claim that the empire was foreordained by the gods, who continued to support it by their favor. Given the geopolitical theology of the day, divine favor could readily be inferred as a straightforward corollary of Roman success and the geographical extent of their rule.[172] In Virgil's *Aeneid*, however, de facto divine approval was transformed

---

168. On the relationship between *humanitas* and *paideia*, see Dench, *Romulus' Asylum*, 65–66; Woolf, *Rome*, 169.

169. On this debate, see Hingley, *Globalizing Roman Culture*, 64–67.

170. Hingley, *Globalizing Roman Culture*, 63. See also Zanker, *Power of Images in the Age of Augustus*, 336.

171. *Panegyric in Cyzicus*, 32.

172. This certainly was the inference drawn by Aristides (*Regarding Rome* 104) and, in his own way, by Josephus (*Jewish War* 2.390; 4.323) as well. See also Ando, *Imperial Ideology and Provincial Loyalty*, 6.

into an imperial narrative of divine foreordination, as "not only the future rule of the Julian house, but the whole history of Rome was portrayed as one of predestined triumph and salvation."[173]

This was the context, then—constituted by the social realities of the Roman Empire and the rhetorical realities of the discourse that sustained it—within which all inhabitants of the empire found it necessary to negotiate an identity for themselves. In what follows, we will look first at the views of the rulers—both Roman conceptions of their own identity and the identities they ascribed to their subjects—and then at the views of the ruled.

As we have seen, identity construction takes place at the boundaries, and the most significant boundary that the Romans needed to take into account was the one imposed by their imperial predecessors—namely, that which divided the world into Greeks and barbarians. Horace's well-known dictum—"Captive Greece took her rough conqueror captive and introduced the arts to rustic Latium" (*Epistles* 2.1.156–57)—captures some of the ambivalence felt by elite Romans as they considered themselves in relation to this Greek map of humanity. On the one hand, they were well aware, as Balsdon has observed, that the Greeks considered their rough and rustic Roman conquerors to be ineradicably "on the wrong side of [the Greek-barbarian] divide."[174] On the other, they generally admired Greek culture, recognized its superiority, and did their best to master it. Without trying simply to do away with the Greek-barbarian map, then (something that would have been difficult in any case), the challenge for Rome was to redraw it so as to locate themselves advantageously within it.

The barbarian side of the problem was the simpler one. A stark contrast between Roman *humanitas* and everything that characterized the barbarian nations was fundamental to Roman self-understanding. "If a Roman looked round the world, he saw *humanitas* in Greece . . . and he found it elsewhere in those who had been properly romanized. . . . These were the children of light; everywhere else was shrouded in the darkness of barbarism."[175] Barbarism and civilization were at opposite poles and, while barbarians might occasionally be admired for their closeness to nature, for the most part this was seen rather as a measure of their distance from civilization (i.e., *humanitas*).[176]

The Greek side of the map was more complex. In their self-presentation, Romans were concerned to combine a close identification with classical Greek culture, on the one hand, and with a claim to represent a distinct and superior

---

173. Zanker, *Power of Images in the Age of Augustus*, 193.
174. Balsdon, *Romans and Aliens*, 30.
175. Balsdon, *Romans and Aliens*, 63–64.
176. Hingley, *Globalizing Roman Culture*, 61.

identity, on the other. The two existed in tension, of course, and in the ongoing negotiations of identity, emphasis came to be placed now on this side and now on that. Still, both need to be kept in view.

On the first side of it, we have already observed how Roman *humanitas* and Greek *paideia* could be closely aligned in Roman discourse—closely aligned, but in a way that was to Rome's advantage. In a letter to Maximus, who was about to take up an official appointment in Achaia, Pliny the Younger urges him to remember, as he carries out his duties, that he is doing so in "that real, genuine Greece where *humanitas*, learning, and even agriculture itself, are supposed to have first arisen." At the same time, however, he makes it clear that what once flourished in Greece has now passed to the Romans; what remains to the Greeks is but a "shadow" of its former glory.[177] This idea that Rome stands in continuity with Greece, inheriting and preserving the glories of Greek *paideia* while at the same time succeeding Greece as the beacon of a civilized culture, was a common theme in Roman self-definition.[178] Sometimes, however, the contrast between past and present was drawn more sharply. Rather than simply being a shadow of its former glorious self, contemporary Greece was often sharply criticized for its softness, vice, decadence, luxurious excess, and debauchery—all of which (it was implied) stood over against both the (Greek) *paideia* of the past and the (Roman) *humanitas* of the present.[179]

But Rome was not content simply to claim the mantle of Greek culture. Although this move was important, there were limits to its usefulness. So we also encounter Roman voices laying claim to a separate identity, one that was both distinct and more ancient. Stories of Aeneas's journey from Troy to Latium enabled subsequent Latins to trace their descent from Trojan heroes and thus to claim an identity that predated the Greeks.[180] While this story was firmly established as a national epic by Virgil in his *Aeneid*, the fact that tales of Aeneas's wanderings had been circulating among the Greeks for centuries provided the

---

177. To Maximus (*Letters* 8.24.1).

178. Richter, *Cosmopolis*, 177–78; Janet Huskinson, "Élite Culture and the Identity of Empire," in Huskinson, *Experiencing Rome*, 98–99; Zanker, *Power of Images in the Age of Augustus*, 336.

179. Huskinson, "Élite Culture and the Identity of Empire," 99; Zanker, *Power of Images in the Age of Augustus*, 239; Balsdon, *Romans and Aliens*, 30–31.

180. Huskinson, "Looking for Culture, Identity and Power," 11–12; Dench, *Romulus' Asylum*, 69–70; Zanker, *Power of Images in the Age of Augustus*, 193; Balsdon, *Romans and Aliens*, 30; Bickerman, "Origines Gentium," 81.

claim with independent credibility.[181] An even stronger genealogical trump card was provided by the various claims, made by the Julians and other aristocratic Roman families, to have descended from the gods themselves.[182]

In using mythological lines of descent to position themselves advantageously with respect to other groups, the Romans were employing a tactic that was widely used in ancient identity politics. Unlike most other groups, however, Rome placed much less emphasis on genealogical descent in its construction of group identity. For Virgil, Livy, and others, there was no place in Rome's identity mythology for the kind of autochthony found in Greek tales or for an insistence on genealogical purity. What we find instead is the idea that, from the times of Romulus on down, the story of Rome was one of the systematic incorporation of heterogenous peoples into its body politic.[183] In one episode of the story, Romulus, in order to populate the city he had just founded, offered asylum to various disenfranchised groups—"political refugees from oppressive regimes, slaves, an immigrant assortment of Latins, Etruscans, Phrygians, and Arcadians."[184] In another, the famous rape of the Sabine women, Roman men sought to populate the city by abducting wives from the nearby Sabine people, resulting eventually in the incorporation of the Sabines into the developing Roman state.

The identity embedded in these episodes comes to expression in a different form in a speech that Tacitus attributes to Claudius. After referring to his own Sabine ancestry, the emperor goes on to say that he employs an incorporative principle in his own administration: "by transferring hither all true excellence, let it be found where it will." He continues:

> For I am not unaware that the Julii came to us from Alba, the Coruncanii from Camerium, the Porcii from Tusculum; that—not to scrutinize antiquity—members were drafted into the senate from Etruria, from Lucania, from the whole of Italy; and that finally Italy itself was extended to the Alps, in order that not individuals merely but countries [*terrae*] and nationalities [*gentes*] should form one body under the name of Romans. (*Annals* 11.24)

---

181. Bickerman, "*Origines Gentium*," 66.
182. Huskinson, "Looking for Culture, Identity and Power," 11–12.
183. See especially Dench, *Romulus' Asylum*. Also: Woolf, *Rome*, 152; Richter, *Cosmopolis*, 113, 132; Schott, *Christianity, Empire, and the Making of Religion*, 7; Catharine Edwards and Greg Woolf, "Cosmopolis: Rome as World City," in Edwards and Woolf, *Rome the Cosmopolis*, 9–10.
184. Dench, *Romulus' Asylum*, 2.

To be sure, he makes the speech to counter arguments made by some senators who were opposing a proposal to fill gaps in senate membership by appointing some new members from Gallia Comata. In other words, there were limits to the incorporative character of the empire, an opinion found also in Juvenal's xenophobic grousing about the "Syrian Orontes" pouring "into the Tiber" (*Satires* 3.62)—that is, about eastern foreigners streaming into Rome. Nevertheless, even where there was opposition, it was based not on blood and descent but on laws and traditions.[185] *Mores* and *leges* undergirded the incorporative character of Roman identity, which in turn came to define the character of the empire itself. It is probably futile to ask which came first—the transnational empire or the incorporative identity. Clearly they both developed in tandem, part of the dialectical process of empire building and identity construction.

Thus by means of both a strategic alignment with Greek culture, on the one hand, and the construction of a distinct identity, on the other, Rome redrew the ethnic map of the world (in the case of Marcus Agrippa, literally as well as figuratively) in order to position itself at the center.

We are interested here not only in Rome's own image of itself as imperial ruler but also in the identities that they ascribed to the nations and peoples subject to their imperial rule. Since the one is largely implicit in the other, all that is needed here are some brief comments to draw a few threads together.

As we have seen, Roman imperial ideology conveyed a dual message: the invincibility of its military might, on the one hand; the benefits bestowed and made available through imperial rule, on the other. Seen from another angle, Rome projected an image of itself both as victor over wild barbarian nations and as civilizing agent within the *orbis terrarum* as a whole. Implicit in this message, then, were two ascribed identities—or better, a single identity with two variable components. Nations within the empire (and, to a certain extent, outside the empire as well) were presented with an image of themselves in which they appeared both as subjugated peoples (or as potentially so) and as (potential) beneficiaries of Rome's civilizing project.

But the proportions of the two components varied from case to case. One end can be seen in the image conveyed by the ongoing series of triumphal processions. Here the slow parade of victory—triumphant general, defeated kings, bound captives, conquering troops, wagons laden with the spoils of war, all processing into Rome through the triumphal gate—imposed on the defeated nation an indelible sense of its total subjugation and (usually) its barbarian otherness. Although the triumphal procession provided some scope for expressions of

---

185. See especially Huskinson, "Looking for Culture, Identity and Power," 12–14.

clemency,[186] the idea that the newly conquered nation might someday become a civilized beneficiary of Roman rule was largely occluded.

At the other end was the image conveyed, for example, by Claudius's speech to the senate, referred to above. For Claudius, the Gauls were part of a whole company of "lands and nations" that had become "blended" with the Romans through "customs, culture, and the ties of marriage" and thus had been incorporated into "one body under the name of Romans."[187] While those taking the opposing position brought up the fact that Gaul had also been conquered by Rome, Claudius appealed to the example of Romulus to present an image in which subjection had been occluded by incorporation: "But the sagacity of our own founder Romulus was such that several times he fought and naturalized [*hostis, dein civis*] a people in the course of the same day." To be sure, despite Claudius's language ("blending"), incorporation was more a constitutional matter than one of full cultural assimilation. People and nations could be Romanized while still retaining aspects of their distinct ethnic identity.[188]

Subjugated enemy (*hostis*) and incorporated citizen (*civis*)—*barbaria* and *humanitas*—were the two poles of the identity that Rome ascribed to the people and nations within the empire. In between, while the proportion of the two components varied along the spectrum, the area in the middle—the dominant identity that people and nations within the empire were encouraged to embrace—had to do with grateful acceptance of the benefits of Roman rule. The resultant identity becomes visible in images constructed by Aristides of the whole inhabited world as a single Roman city with the nations as its citizens, or of the empire as a household, with the emperor as its benevolent *paterfamilias*.[189]

The Greeks, of course, represented a special case. With respect to Greece, the negative pole of the identity ascribed by Rome could not (as it did in other cases) represent subjugated barbarism (though it could include the idea that many Greeks had fallen away from the glories of the classical age into soft self-indulgence). Rather, Roman victory and Greek subjection was to be seen as an indication that Rome had supplanted Greece not only as the ruler of the world but also as the torchbearer and defender of *humanitas*. At the other pole, since

---

186. "As victor I spared the lives of all citizens who asked for mercy" (*Acts of Augustus* 3.1). Some of those spared became the victor's freedmen.

187. Tacitus, *Annals* 11.24.

188. Roman ideology invited "all inhabitants of the Imperium Romanum to participate in the Revival of Classical culture and its ethical values while still preserving their national identity"; Zanker, *Power of Images in the Age of Augustus*, 336. See also Wallace-Hadrill, *Rome's Cultural Revolution*, 3–7.

189. *Regarding Rome* 34, 61–65, 102; see also the discussion of Aristides in ch. 1.

Roman ideology linked *humanitas* with the glories of the classical age, Greeks were thereby invited to see themselves as honored predecessors of their rulers and to shape their identities accordingly.

But what of the ruled themselves? What can be said about the ways in which imperial subjects responded to the identities ascribed to them by the rulers? The question, though crucial for our investigation, is a large one, and here we will have to be content with a sketch, with emphasis on those features that will be particularly important for our investigation of gentile Christian identity construction. As Huskinson has observed, it is only in the case of the Greeks and the Jews that we have substantial evidence of how conquered peoples reformulated their identities in negotiation with the identities ascribed to them in imperial ideology.[190] Fortunately, these two cases are also the most pertinent for our investigation.[191] Even so, there are differences. Most of the Greek material stems from the cultured elite. It is only in the Jewish case that we hear as well from voices from farther down the social scale (the *humiliores* rather than the *honestiores*), reactions that are much less sanguine about Roman rule than those of a Dionysius of Halicarnassus or an Aristides.[192]

We begin with the Greeks.[193] Rome's willingness to align *humanitas* and *paideia*, and to see itself as the successor of the Greeks in a common cosmopolitan project, offered the Greeks a ready-made, advantageous position in the Roman map of the world. Polybius, Dionysius of Halicarnassus, Plutarch, Aelius Aristides, and the Second Sophistic more generally—a succession of Greek authors from the late republican period through to the second century—demonstrated a ready willingness to take up the offer.[194] Of course, even if one sets aside for the moment the fact that this was only one side of Rome's self-presentation, the offer came at a price—namely, the willingness also to acknowledge Rome's

---

190. Huskinson, "Looking for Culture, Identity and Power," 20. See also Woolf, *Rome*, 228–29; Hardwick, "Concepts of Peace," 350–51.

191. At least at the level of the empire as a whole. In addition, one could also inquire into the ways in which the identity held in common among gentile Christians more generally was adapted or refined within specific ethnic areas or Christian subgroups.

192. See Mattingly, *Imperialism, Power, and Identity*, 26.

193. On the topic generally, see Mattingly, *Imperialism, Power, and Identity*; Richter, *Cosmopolis*; Goldhill, *Being Greek under Rome*; Huskinson, *Experiencing Rome*; Swain, *Hellenism and Empire*; Balsdon, *Romans and Aliens*.

194. "One approach to the 'Second Sophistic' is to see it as an attempt by Greek intellectuals in the Roman world to deal with their present subordination to Rome by seeking to revive a glorious Greek tradition from the past"; Richter, *Cosmopolis*, 7. On the significance of the Second Sophistic (Greek writers of the first and second centuries CE) for the issue of identity construction, Richter's work is especially significant.

superior place in the succession of empires. Although such willingness has often been interpreted as unqualified pro-Roman enthusiasm, more recently there has been increasing recognition of the ways in which authors such as these were able to preserve a distinctive Greek identity even as they wrote in praise of Rome.

Polybius, who was particularly liberal in his praise, also provides a ready illustration of how Greek writers negotiated the politics of identity in the imperial context. As with Aristides in a later period, Rome's unprecedented success in bringing "nearly the whole inhabited world" under the rule of a single people (*Histories* 1.1.5) was understood by Polybius as an indication not simply of Roman might but of divine sanction; Rome's success was, almost self-evidently, a state of affairs willed by the gods.[195] Further, by casting his initial question in terms of *politeia* ("by what means and by what system of polity [*politeias*]" did the Romans succeed in "subjecting nearly the whole inhabited world [*oikoumenēn*] under one rule [*archēn*]"), Polybius sets himself up for a very Greek answer: Rome's success resulted from its discovery of how to strike a successful balance among the three types of government that Greeks had been thinking about since the time of Aristotle (monarchy, oligarchy, democracy).[196] As Ando has observed, such an answer also carried with it an independent (and decidedly Greek!) standard by which Roman performance could be measured.[197]

As we have seen, however, there was another side to the coin of Rome's self-presentation. In addition to an alignment with the Greeks, Rome also laid claim to a distinct identity, and this presented Greeks with a different challenge. For his part, Polybius was not prepared either to position Rome fully within the positive side of the Greek-barbarian binary or to subordinate the binary to a Roman map. Rome's distinctive identity, for Polybius, was one that was to be located somewhere in between Greeks and barbarians.[198] While they may have succeeded the Greeks in global influence, they had not thereby supplanted them as the defining exemplars of (nonbarbarian) civilization.

Another strategy, utilized by Dionysius and Plutarch, albeit in different ways, was to turn Romans fully into Greeks. As we have seen, part of Rome's case for a distinctive identity had to do with its stories of origin, not only the peregrinations of Aeneas and his Trojan companions but also the earlier tales of Romulus's asylum, the capture of the Sabine women, and so on. Against those who might

---

195. Dench, *Romulus' Asylum*, 107; Ando, *Imperial Ideology and Provincial Loyalty*, 337.

196. See, e.g., *Histories* 6.2.5 and the discussion that follows. Again, Polybius is followed here by Aristides; see above, ch. 1, n. 11.

197. Ando, *Imperial Ideology and Provincial Loyalty*, 337; see also Dench, *Romulus' Asylum*, 107.

198. Dench, *Romulus' Asylum*, 249.

scoff at these claims to antiquity, Dionysius defended them as fully reliable. As he does so, however, he reads them as a Greek story from beginning to end. Not only are Aeneas and his companions seen as essentially Greek, but even before their arrival, Rome had already been settled by various emigrants from Greece (Arcadia, the Argives, Sparta). His conclusion: "from now on let the reader forever renounce the views of those who make Rome a retreat of barbarians, fugitives and vagabonds, and let him confidently affirm it to be a Greek city" (*Roman Antiquities* 1.89.1). "For Dionysius," Richter observes, "archaic Rome was a panhellenic oasis in a sea of barbarism that over the centuries managed to maintain, for the most part, its Hellenic integrity."[199] Although Dionysius, unlike Polybius, places the Romans fully on the positive side of the Greek-barbarian binary, he does so by subverting Rome's claim to a distinct identity entirely: "one will find no nation that is more ancient or more Greek" (1.89.1).[200]

Like Dionysius, Plutarch also qualifies Rome's claim by Hellenizing essential aspects of Roman identity. But whereas Dionysius's concept of Greekness is based to a considerable extent on descent, in Plutarch's case it is based on culture. Rome can be described as Greek not because it is ancient but only because the Romans have been schooled in Greek *paideia*, divesting themselves of their prior barbarian character in the process.[201] In addition, as Dench observes, there is a retrospective aspect to Plutarch's assimilation of Roman *humanitas* to Greek *paideia*. His presentation of Alexander the Great is such as to suggest that he imposes "onto the figure of Alexander the civilizing 'mission' that became associated with Rome in the imperial period."[202] Where Dionysius rewrites Roman history so as to turn Romans into Greeks, Plutarch reworks Greek history so as to turn a key element of Roman self-presentation (the spread of *humanitas*) into a Greek invention.

While this is admittedly just a brief sketch, these authors provide us with a representative and reliable picture of the strategies for identity negotiation that were utilized by Greek writers in the early imperial period. To be sure, the sketch could be filled in considerably. Richter, for example, has demonstrated how Plutarch, Aristides, and other writers of the Second Sophistic arrived at

---

199. Richter, *Cosmopolis*, 114.

200. On this aspect of Dionysius, see Richter, *Cosmopolis*, 113–15; Dench, *Romulus' Asylum*, 234; Rebecca Preston, "Roman Questions, Greek Answers: Plutarch and the Construction of Identity," in *Being Greek under Rome: Cultural Identity, the Second Sophistic and the Development of Empire*, ed. Simon Goldhill (Cambridge: Cambridge University Press, 2001), 100.

201. See especially Preston, "Roman Questions, Greek Answers," 100–101.

202. Dench, *Romulus' Asylum*, 263.

their distinctive panhellenic conceptions by transposing classical formulations of Greek identity into a more cosmopolitan key. In particular, whereas Isocrates's definition of Greekness (as based not on descent [*genos*] but on *paideia*) functioned restrictively rather than inclusively—that is, for Isocrates true Greekness was to be found within a properly educated subset of the Greek descent group—Aristides and others used Isocrates's formulation to argue "that the possession of Hellenic culture could make a Hellene even out of a barbarian."[203]

With respect to a different area of the sketch, Mattingly and Balsdon have indicated how one might tease out from the evidence how non-elite Greeks responded to Roman ideological claims.[204] For present purposes, however, the sketch will suffice.

But what of Roman subjects who were not Greek? Here the situation is more complicated, in that non-Greeks found it necessary to negotiate among three different identities—Roman, Greek, and their own native culture. True, the situation in the eastern part of the empire, where Hellenization had been widespread long before Rome appeared on the scene, was different from that in the western and northern provinces.[205] Even so, the Roman conquest of Gaul, Spain, and regions beyond inevitably brought Greek realities with it as well. Thus throughout the empire, non-Greeks needed to engage in what Wallace-Hadrill calls "cultural triangulation."[206] As an example of the phenomenon, he cites Favorinus, a second-century-CE native of Gaul, whose level of acculturation enabled him to claim that his life and experience demonstrated to the Greeks "that there is no difference between education and birth," to the Romans that education can result in "high social standing," and to the Celts "that none of the barbarians" need feel that Hellenic culture is out of reach.[207] One might say similar things of Lucian of Samosata (eastern Syria) or Apion (Egypt).[208] Wallace-Hadrill suggests that

---

203. Richter, *Cosmopolis*, 125. Further: "It is the flexibility of Isocrates' cultural and ethnic logic that informs and indeed makes possible the ways in which intellectuals such as Aelius Aristides speak of the Roman empire as the typological fulfillment of the Panhellenic ideal" (p. 111).

204. Mattingly, *Imperialism, Power, and Identity*, 26; Balsdon, *Romans and Aliens*, 161–92. See also Hardwick, "Concepts of Peace," 350–56.

205. On these differences, see especially Woolf, *Tales of the Barbarians*; also James Rives, "Religion in the Roman Empire," in *Experiencing Rome: Culture, Identity and Power in the Roman Empire*, ed. Janet Huskinson (London: Routledge, 2000), 269–71.

206. Wallace-Hadrill, *Rome's Cultural Revolution*, 3–7; the phrase is introduced on p. 5.

207. In a speech recorded by his teacher, Dio of Prusa (*Corinthian Discourse* [*Or.* 37] 26–27).

208. See Richter, *Cosmopolis*, 138–60; and Joseph Geiger, "The Jew and the Other: Doubtful and Multiple Identities in the Roman Empire," in *Jewish Identities in Antiquity:*

the concept of hybridity, while not without its usefulness, is perhaps too binary in nature to serve as an adequate model for this more complex phenomenon.

As has been mentioned, the non-Greek group for which we have the most information is that of the Jews. We will pick this up in the next chapter, where a discussion of Jewish identity negotiation in the competitive context of the Greco-Roman world will provide the groundwork for an analysis of the identity that they in turn ascribed to non-Jewish nations and individuals.

Studies in Memory of Menahem Stern, ed. Lee I. Levine and Daniel R. Schwartz (Tübingen: Mohr Siebeck, 2009), 136–46.

CHAPTER 3

Ethnē *as an Identity Ascribed to Non-Jews: By Jews*

In this chapter and the next, we will be examining the range of identities ascribed to non-Jews by Jews. In chapter 4, we will look specifically at the early Christian movement and the identities ascribed to non-Jewish Christ-believers by Jewish fellow believers. In the present chapter, we are looking at identities ascribed to non-Jews by Jews more generally. In each case, our particular focus will be the term *ethnē* itself, though it will be important to treat it not in isolation but as part of a larger process of identity construction, negotiation, and ascription.

JEWISH IDENTITY CONSTRUCTION IN THE GRECO-ROMAN WORLD

We begin where we left off at the end of chapter 2, in a discussion of how subject peoples responded to the identities ascribed to them by their Roman imperial overlords. As we have observed, these ascribed identities were complex. The Roman Empire developed within a world still heavily imprinted by the Greek sense of superiority over the barbarian nations, and one element of Rome's success was its ability to inscribe a place for itself and its growing empire at the center of this ethnographical map. This revised map, in turn, served to impose corresponding identities on subject peoples, which meant that the Jews, like other non-Greek peoples in the Mediterranean world, found it necessary to negotiate both Roman and Greek realities in order to locate themselves advantageously on the map. The way in which the Jews responded to the identities ascribed to them at these boundaries also served to shape the identities they in turn ascribed to those non-Jews with whom they came in contact.

Of course, like other non-Greek peoples in the eastern Mediterranean world, the Jews had had plenty of experience negotiating Greek realities before the Romans appeared on the scene. Although the arrival of the Romans brought some new challenges, the identity ascribed to them by both the Greeks and the Romans had a similar two-sided character. In the case of the Greeks, the Jews were confronted with a picture of themselves as one of the barbarian nations, on the one hand, and yet, on the other, as people who were invited to "shift over to the Greek way of life" (to use the language of 2 Macc 4:10), with all the enticements that encouraged such voluntary Hellenization (2 Macc 4:13). In the case of the Romans, the Jews saw themselves characterized both as one of the subjugated nations (*gentes devictae*) and as potential members of a transethnic commonwealth of benefaction and *humanitas*. Given the distinctive and sharp-edged character of Jewish identity, both aspects of ascribed identity were especially problematic. On one side, distinctive aspects of Jewish custom (Sabbath observance, circumcision, abstinence from certain foods, rejection of the gods) came in for particular derision from some Greeks and Romans,[1] adding a particular sting to the ignominy of the labels *barbaroi* or *gentes devictae*. On the other, the appeal of Hellenization or Romanization proved to be just as problematic for Jews as was the ignominy of the labels.

Extant Jewish literature provides us with a much broader range of reaction to imperial rule (and cultural imperialism) than is the case with other ethnic groups. To be sure, highly hellenized authors such as Philo, or articulate Roman sympathizers such as Josephus, had their counterparts elsewhere in the empire. At the other end of the spectrum, however, we have a considerable body of information concerning the attitudes and self-definitions displayed by more fervent nationalistic groups. Some of this information comes to us indirectly, especially through the mediation of Josephus's historical accounts; much of it is more direct information, found in literature emerging from the groups themselves.[2] In

---

1. See especially Benjamin H. Isaac, *The Invention of Racism in Classical Antiquity* (Princeton: Princeton University Press, 2004); Peter Schäfer, *Judeophobia: Attitudes toward the Jews in the Ancient World* (Cambridge, MA: Harvard University Press, 1997); Louis H. Feldman, *Jew and Gentile in the Ancient World: Attitudes and Interactions from Alexander to Justinian* (Princeton: Princeton University Press, 1993); John G. Gager, *The Origins of Anti-Semitism* (Oxford: Oxford University Press, 1983); J. N. Sevenster, *The Roots of Pagan Anti-Semitism in the Ancient World*, NovTSup 41 (Leiden: Brill, 1975).

2. Greek period: e.g., Daniel, 1 Enoch, Jubilees, 2 Maccabees. Roman period: e.g., Psalms of Solomon, the War Scroll from Qumran, 4 Ezra, 2 Baruch.

addition, of course, the extant evidence bears witness to a whole range of stances stretched out between (and, in some cases, beyond) the two poles.³

The situation, then, is diverse, and the task of mapping the diversity is complex. Geographically, we can observe significant differences between the situation in Judea and that in the diaspora. Further, within the diaspora, the situation of Jewish communities varies considerably as one moves around the Mediterranean from area to area (Egypt and North Africa; Syria; Asia Minor; the Greek peninsula; Italy). In Judea, the political circumstances of Jewish existence vary from period to period: Greek rule under the Ptolemies and then the Seleucids; independence during the Hasmonean period; Roman rule, direct (under prefects and procurators) and indirect (under Herodian rulers); utter subjection and the dissolution of the Judean state (after the revolt of 66–70 CE).

Further, as we have seen in the discussion of Romanization above (and despite the comments made in the second paragraph before this one), the situation of subject peoples in an imperial context cannot simply be reduced to points between two poles on a one-dimensional axis. At the very least, we would need to think in terms of a grid with two axes—one having to do with acculturation (the degree to which an imperial subject learns and becomes adept in the dominant culture), the other with accommodation (the degree to which a subject either collaborates with or resists imperial rule). In addition, as we have seen in the discussion of postcolonialism toward the end of the previous chapter, one has to reckon with the existence of a considerable degree of ambivalence, hybridity, and (as Wallace-Hadrill suggests) cultural layering within the territory plotted along the two axes.⁴

Nevertheless, despite the diversity, Jewish identity negotiation in the Greco-Roman context took as its starting point a basic sense of inherited identity, passed down through its Scriptures and communal tradition, one that certainly can be described as ethnic. Using the kinds of characteristics that have been in use since the time of Herodotus (with all due recognition of Fredrik Barth's insistence that these are mutable and do not in themselves create ethnic identity), one can say that we are dealing with a named group (Israel, Judeans, Jews), with a sense of common origins and shared kinship (descendants of Abraham and the patriarchs), associated with a homeland or shared territory (the land of Israel, Judea), marked out by a shared history (chronicled in the Torah and Former

---

3. While much of the evidence is literary, archaeological evidence is significant as well.

4. With reference to the Roman world, he speaks of "the complexities of cultural identity, especially the subtle layering of identities in the wake of passages of conquest and colonization"; Andrew Wallace-Hadrill, *Rome's Cultural Revolution* (Cambridge: Cambridge University Press, 2008), 7.

Prophets), and the sense of a common culture and way of life (embodied in the Torah), with common gods (or in Israel's case, God—YHWH) and religious practices (centered on the Jerusalem temple).[5]

Of course, this homogenized definition elides a number of distinctly Jewish formulations of these ethnic characteristics, which worked together to produce a unique sense of inherited identity. Israel's God was not simply one national deity among many, but the supreme God. To be sure, in Israel's tradition, this belief sometimes took the shape more of henotheism (Israel's God is supreme among the gods) or of monolatry (no other gods are to be worshiped) than of monotheism (Israel's God is the only deity, all other so-called gods are subordinate angels, demons, or nonentities).[6] Still, the trend was in the direction of *monotheism* and, in any case, the elevated, universal status of Israel's God inevitably produced and reinforced a more sharply drawn boundary between the Jews and their neighbors than was the case with other nations. Similarly, Israel's sense of shared origins and common descent was expressed in a story of *election*: out of all the nations, the supreme God had chosen Abraham and his descendants to form a special people, separate from the others and under God's own care and supervision. Again, it is true that Israel's election as a divinely chosen people did not necessarily carry with it the negative corollary that other nations were rejected by God in any ultimate sense (though it sometimes did). As Kaminsky has argued, often it was the case that other nations, despite their non-elect status, were nevertheless considered to be "full participants in the divine economy," and that "Israel was to work out her destiny in relation to them, even if in separation from them."[7] Still, the sense of separation remains. This sense of separation was reinforced by the pattern of life set out in the *Torah*, which functioned not merely as a compendium of common customs but as the divinely appointed means of

---

5. For similar descriptions, see Shaye J. D. Cohen, *The Beginnings of Jewishness: Boundaries, Varieties, Uncertainties* (Berkeley: University of California Press, 1999), 6-7; Lee I. Levine, "Jewish Identities in Antiquity: An Introductory Essay," in *Jewish Identities in Antiquity: Studies in Memory of Menahem Stern*, ed. Lee I. Levine and Daniel R. Schwartz (Tübingen: Mohr Siebeck, 2009), 27. The list of ethnic characteristics is similar to that proposed by Anthony D. Smith, *The Ethnic Origin of Nations* (Oxford: Blackwell, 1986).

6. See, e.g., Robert Goldenberg, *The Nations That Know Thee Not: Ancient Jewish Attitudes towards Other Religions* (Sheffield: Sheffield Academic, 1997).

7. Joel S. Kaminsky, "Israel's Election and the Other in Biblical, Second Temple and Rabbinic Thought," in *The "Other" in Second Temple Judaism: Essays in Honor of John J. Collins*, ed. Daniel C. Harlow et al. (Grand Rapids: Eerdmans, 2011), 18. Kaminsky sees a distinction between the "anti-elect" (in effect Israel's perennial enemies) and the "non-elect" (the rest of the nations); see also his longer work *Yet I Loved Jacob: Reclaiming the Biblical Concept of Election* (Nashville: Abingdon, 2007).

preserving Israel's distinct identity. Again, there were nuances. Ways were found to include the sojourner in some aspects of Israel's common life; parts of the Torah were seen as applicable to the rest of the nations as well. Still, it remained apparent to all, outsiders and insiders alike, that the Torah constituted a sharp boundary between them. The uniqueness and universality of Israel's God was mirrored in the existence of a single *temple*, the only place where the full worship of this God could be carried out and thus the center both of the land of Israel and of Israel's common life as a people. In keeping with the universality of the temple, the presence and prayers of the "foreigner, who is not of your people Israel" (1 Kgs 8:41), were expected and welcomed. Nevertheless, the distinction between foreigner and people remained and, at least later in the Second Temple period, was inscribed in the architecture of the temple itself, with its graduated levels of access.[8] Finally, Israel's shared history was not simply accumulated happenstance but was seen instead as the outworking of God's *covenant* with Israel, a relationship between deity and people that contained provisions both for punishment (when Israel was unfaithful) and for blessing, a relationship that would culminate in the future fulfillment of the divine purposes for Israel and its place among the nations. To be sure, this *eschatological fulfillment* of history often contained a promise of blessing for the nations as well. Still, the distinction between Israel and the nations was maintained, even into the projected coming age.

Jewish existence in our period of interest, then, was shaped by a shared sense of inherited identity, one that provided them with the resources both to thrive as a distinct people in a variety of circumstances and—for many of them, at least—to engage in the kind of competitive identity construction that was a characteristic feature of the Greek and Roman eras. Fundamental to this sense of inherited identity was the awareness of an indelible binary between themselves and the other nations of the world. In Gilbert's words:

> Jewish attitudes toward Gentiles start with an understanding that Jews are set apart from Gentiles and that this separation is of divine origin. God selected Israel to be a treasured possession and holy nation. In return Israel is commanded to worship God, and God alone, and not to follow the practices of Gentiles. Gentiles often take on the role of the consummate "other."[9]

---

8. While it was Herod's expansion of the precincts that presumably created the distinct "court of the gentiles," the prohibition of gentile access to the inner courts could not have been an innovation. On gentile access in earlier periods, see Christine Hayes, *Gentile Impurities and Jewish Identities: Intermarriage and Conversion from the Bible to the Talmud* (Oxford: Oxford University Press, 2002), 34–37.

9. Gary Gilbert, "Gentiles, Jewish Attitudes Towards," in *The Eerdmans Dictionary*

In a world defined by the distinction between Greek and barbarian, Jews defined themselves fundamentally in terms of a different binary distinction, that between Jews and non-Jews, between the Jewish people and the non-Jewish nations, between Jews and gentiles. In the basic Jewish map of the world, Greeks, Romans, and barbarians alike were allocated to the single undifferentiated section marked *the nations*; identity distinctions that were often all-consuming in the wider world were, from the perspective of this map, effectively collapsed.[10]

At one corner of the grid, this was all that was needed. For those who produced and read works such as Jubilees, the Testament (Assumption) of Moses, the Apocalypse of Abraham, or, in a modified way, the sectarian literature found at Qumran,[11] the boundary between Jews and non-Jews was high, rigid, and categorical. The attitude toward those on the other side of the boundary was hard-edged, resisting or rejecting any negotiation or accommodation with the other. All those on the other side of the boundary—barbarians, Greeks, or Romans—

---

of Early Judaism, ed. John J. Collins and Daniel C. Harlow (Grand Rapids: Eerdmans, 2010), 670.

10. Ophir and Rosen-Zvi have argued that it is only in the rabbinic period that we encounter such a binary distinction between the Jew and the other; Adi Ophir and Ishay Rosen-Zvi, *Goy: Israel's Others and the Birth of the Gentile* (Oxford: Oxford University Press, 2018). As they describe it, the rabbinic concept of the *gôy* is one in which the distinction between the Jews and the (other) nations has become so categorical, and the distinctions among the other nations has become so inconsequential, that the nature of the non-Jewish other can be represented fully by the *gôy* as an individual. Prior to the rabbis, the term is always plural (*gôyîm*), and Jewish writers are quite prepared to recognize the differences among the nations and the distinctive features that each exhibit. Without wanting to deny either the uniqueness of this rabbinic usage, however, or the evidence for conceptual development, I think that it is still appropriate to speak of a binary distinction between Jews and non-Jews in prerabbinic Judaism. To take one of their examples, it is true that in the Animal Apocalypse (1 Enoch 83–90) "the nations are different from each another, each with its own distinct symbolism: Ishmael is a wild ass, Esau a swine, Egyptians are wolves, and Philistines dogs. The exception of one species does not make all others the same" (p. 94). But this does not negate the fundamental difference in the apocalypse between the "one species" (the Israelite sheep) and all the others. In my opinion, the recognition of difference does not require us to conclude that "this binary representation—Israel and the gentiles— . . . is missing from the apocalypse" (p. 94). To take a parallel example, the fact that Greek writers often show keen interest in the distinctive characteristics of barbarian nations does not negate the basic Greek-barbarian binary. Here the concept of salience is pertinent—that is, the fact that different identity characteristics come into play in different situations.

11. Modified in that the boundary drawn by their distinctive fundamental binary—between the sons of light and the sons of darkness—separated them from fellow Jews as well.

Ethnē as an Identity Ascribed to Non-Jews: By Jews

were seen simply as members of a largely undifferentiated mass of the idolatrous nations. In effect, this segment of the Jewish world simply rejected—or, better, ignored—the binary categorization being imposed on them from outside and replaced it with another.

We will return to this uncompromisingly hard-edged approach to ethnic positioning in a few moments. We begin instead by looking at those Jewish writers and groups who were more sensitive to how they were viewed by others and more prepared to engage in competitive ethnographical discourse. Not surprisingly, most of them were from the diaspora, even though the time is long past when one can assume that cultural distinctions can simply be aligned with geographical location.

Despite their awareness of a sharp separation from the rest of the nations—or, in many cases, precisely because of it—Jews showed themselves to be quite ready to enter the competitive ethnology fray and to jostle for position. For one thing, various aspects of their founding narrative—the first eleven chapters of Genesis,[12] the wanderings of Abraham, the sojourn in Egypt, the exodus—together with the idea of election itself, meant that they could hardly recite their national story without thinking about their position with respect to other nations. Also, widespread recognition of them by outsiders as an ancient people (along with Indians, Egyptians, Greeks, and others),[13] together with the largely positive portraits painted by such early writers as Theophrastus, Hecataeus of Abdera, and Clearchus of Soli,[14] provided them with a ready-made entrée into the arena, even as the scathingly negative accounts of an Apollonius Molon or an Apion made it imperative that they join the fray. Further, as has already been noted, their foundational traditions contained resources that were very amenable to the various aspects of competitive identity construction in the Greco-Roman world.

---

12. Frank Crüsemann notes the uniqueness of the genealogical system of Genesis: "Indeed, a system with the propensity to encompass all of humanity, all neighboring peoples as well as the whole internal structure of one's own people, that is something extraordinary"; "Human Solidarity and Ethnic Identity: Israel's Self-Identification in the Genealogical System of Genesis," in *Ethnicity and the Bible*, ed. Mark G. Brett (Leiden: Brill, 1996), 63.

13. See, e.g., Daniel S. Richter, *Cosmopolis: Imagining Community in Late Classical Athens and the Early Roman Empire* (Oxford: Oxford University Press, 2011), 178-94; Gregg Gardner and Kevin L. Osterloh, "The Significance of Antiquity in Antiquity: An Introduction," in *Antiquity in Antiquity: Jewish and Christian Pasts in the Greco-Roman World*, ed. Gregg Gardner and Kevin L. Osterloh, TSAJ 123 (Tübingen: Mohr Siebeck, 2008), 8-9.

14. Primary texts are collected in Menahem Stern, *Greek and Latin Authors on Jews and Judaism*, 3 vols. (Jerusalem: Israel Academy of Sciences and Humanities, 1974-84).

As we saw in the previous chapter, we can identify two broad approaches to such identity construction: competitive ethnic historiography, the attempt to locate one's own group advantageously on a map of the nations; and the identification of transethnic universals, the attempt to align one's own group with more universal and cosmopolitan categories and identities. We will deal with each in turn.

With respect to the strategies of competitive ethnic historiography, arguments based on antiquity and chronological priority were very amenable to Jewish use. Jewish Scriptures provided considerable material for the argument that the Jews descended from ancient stock and possessed a long and venerable history. As its title suggests, Josephus's *Antiquities* was written precisely to make this point,[15] and his subsequent work, *Against Apion*, represents a lengthy refutation of those who had argued otherwise. While Josephus's work represents the most thoroughgoing exercise in Jewish apologetic historiography,[16] he was following a path that had been laid out by others. The fragments of Hellenistic Jewish writers preserved by Eusebius (who depended on the compilations of Alexander Polyhistor), for example, open a tiny but intriguing window into previous Jewish attempts to present their early history in Greek dress. Included among these writers is Demetrius the Chronographer (third century BCE), who addresses apparent chronological and genealogical problems in order to provide a solid and reliable footing for the biblical account.[17] A century or so later another Jewish writer adapted the Greek literary tradition of the Sibyl to place the (Jewish) "race of most righteous men" (a race that originated in Ur of the Chaldeans; Sibylline Oracles 3.218–19) within a version of world history that stretched from the tower of Babel and the war between Titan and Chronos through a sequence of empires down to the time of Rome (3.97–161).

In a closely related phenomenon, Jewish apologists showed themselves quite ready to give their own spin to *Erfinder* and *Kulturbringer* motifs. Not surprisingly perhaps, they passed up the earliest biblical candidate for the role (Tubal-Cain, "who made all kinds of bronze and iron tools"; Gen 4:22) and focused their attention on more prominent figures, Moses in particular. Artapanus presents Moses as one who "bestowed many useful benefits on mankind" during his time in Egypt, including "boats and devices for stone construction," the organization of Egypt's civil administration, and even (surprisingly) the establishment of Egyp-

---

15. In *Against Apion* 1.1 he calls it the *Archaiologia*.

16. On the genre, see Gregory E. Sterling, *Historiography and Self-Definition: Josephos, Luke-Acts, and Apologetic Historiography*, NovTSup 64 (Leiden: Brill, 1992).

17. The fragments deal primarily with the period from Abraham to Moses (Eusebius, *Preparation for the Gospel* 9.19.4; 9.21.1–19; 9.29.1–3, 15, 16). Eusebius himself devoted a whole treatise to issues of chronology for similar reasons (*Chronicle*).

tian religion.[18] Eupolemus adds to his list of innovations the discovery of the alphabet (which then was transmitted to the Phoenicians and the Greeks).[19] Artapanus also links Moses with the Greeks; the Greeks knew him as Mousaeus, "the teacher of Orpheus."[20] But Moses is by no means unique. Joseph is credited with the discovery of measurements and the introduction of orderly land management;[21] Abraham (again surprisingly) taught astrology to the Egyptian king.[22]

The most significant instance of the phenomenon, however, was the argument that Plato and the other Greek philosophers were taught by Moses or depended in essential ways on his laws.[23] Not only was the law a form of philosophy, equal with that developed by the Greeks;[24] nor was it simply that the law was a superior philosophy, so that those who were instructed by it were thereby able to "far surpass [the philosophers] in attitudes and eloquence."[25] More than this, Moses was the origin of the whole philosophical tradition: "our earliest imitators were the Greek philosophers, who ... in their conduct and philosophy were Moses' disciples."[26]

---

18. Artapanus (frag. 3; preserved in Eusebius, *Preparation for the Gospel* 9.27.4). Moses also taught circumcision to the Ethiopians (9.27.10).

19. Eupolemus (frag. 1; preserved in Eusebius, *Preparation for the Gospel* 9.26.1).

20. Artapanus (frag. 3; preserved in Eusebius, *Preparation for the Gospel* 9.27.3).

21. Artapanus (frag. 2; preserved in Eusebius, *Preparation for the Gospel*, 9.23.2-3).

22. Artapanus (frag. 1; preserved in Eusebius, *Preparation for the Gospel* 9.18.1). In Artapanus's reworking of history, "the Jewish ancestors Abraham, Joseph, and Moses are re-imagined as culture-heroes who bequeath the benefits of civilization to the Egyptians, and correlative riches of cultural capital to the Jews living among the second-century B.C.E. descendants of their Egyptian beneficiaries"; Gardner and Osterloh, "Significance of Antiquity in Antiquity," 8.

23. An argument that resonated in non-Jewish ears: "Moses is among a class of ancient sages whose movements, like those of Pythagoras, Plato, Solon, and others, defined the relationships and hierarchies of groups in the present, and these traditions are best understood in light of one another"; Richter, *Cosmopolis*, 188. See also Erich S. Gruen, "Jews and Greeks as Philosophers: A Challenge to Otherness," in *The "Other" in Second Temple Judaism: Essays in Honor of John J. Collins*, ed. Daniel C. Harlow et al. (Grand Rapids: Eerdmans, 2011), 403.

24. For Josephus, "nearly all the philosophers appear to have held similar views concerning the nature of God" (*Against Apion* 2.168); see also Philo, *On the Virtues* 65.

25. Letter of Aristeas 235; also Philo, *That Every Good Person Is Free* 160; Josephus, *Jewish Antiquities* 1.15-26; *Against Apion* 2.163. Aristobulus makes the point more hesitantly: "It is agreed by all the philosophers that it is necessary to hold holy opinions concerning God, a point our philosophical school makes particularly well" (frag. 4; preserved in Eusebius, *Preparation for the Gospel* 13.12.8).

26. Josephus, *Against Apion* 2.281. The theme also comes to the surface in Philo's work

Since in most cases the role of *Kulturbringer* involved travel, this naturally leads to the theme of migration. In the material just discussed, the journeying of Jewish cultural heroes sometimes comes in for explicit attention. Abraham "came to Egypt" to teach the king and returned to Syria after twenty years; Joseph, to escape the fraternal conspiracy against him, "requested the neighboring Arabs to convey him to Egypt."[27] Here, as with non-Jewish instances of the motif, migration stories are used to forge connections and explain (or create) similarities.[28] More often, however, ancestral journeyings and migrations are used to express and reinforce differences and separation. The story of the exodus, of course, lent itself readily to this theme (e.g., Wis 10:15–11:11). Likewise, Abraham's journey from Ur of the Chaldees to the land of Canaan was also pressed into service. In a variety of writings, his departure from Chaldea is linked with his monotheistic opposition to the idolatry of his ancestors and the related errors of the astrologers. For Josephus, Abraham's departure was occasioned not simply by a call from God but by his pioneering realization "that God, the creator of the universe, is one," an opinion that incited the polytheistic Chaldeans to force him out of the country (*Jewish Antiquities* 1.154–57). In a slightly more allegorical key, Philo interprets Abraham's "migration" (*apoikia*) from Chaldea as a rejection of the polytheistic astrology in which he "had been reared and for a long time remained."[29] In Sibylline Oracles 3, although Abraham's Chaldean origins are used to embed the Jewish story in a broader world history, Chaldean astrology is one of the things explicitly rejected by "the race of most righteous men" (3:218–30).[30]

The theme of migration is also linked with aggregative ethnology—the es-

---

as well; see, e.g., *That Every Good Person Is Free* 57, where "the law-book of the Jews" is described as "the fountain from which Zeno drew" a particular idea. Also Aristobulus (frag. 3; Eusebius, *Preparation for the Gospel* 13.12.1, 4). See further Terence L. Donaldson, *Judaism and the Gentiles: Jewish Patterns of Universalism (to 135 CE)* (Waco, TX: Baylor University Press, 2007), 493–98.

27. Artapanus, frag. 1 (preserved in Eusebius, *Preparation for the Gospel* 9.18.1); frag. 2 (preserved in Eusebius, *Preparation for the Gospel* 9.23.1).

28. Greg Woolf, *Tales of the Barbarians: Ethnography and Empire in the Roman West* (Malden, MA: Wiley-Blackwell, 2011), 44; Jeremy M. Schott, *Christianity, Empire, and the Making of Religion in Late Antiquity* (Philadelphia: University of Pennsylvania Press, 2008), 17; Erich S. Gruen, "Kinship Relations and Jewish Identity," in Levine and Schwartz, *Jewish Identities in Antiquity*, 113–14.

29. Philo, *On the Life of Abraham* 66–71 (here 70); see also *On the Virtues* 210–19.

30. Cf. Apocalypse of Abraham 1–8 and Jubilees 11:14–13:9, which contain highly dramatized accounts of Abraham's opposition to the idolatry of his father Terah, culminating in the fiery destruction of Terah's house along with its gods and Abraham's subsequent migration.

tablishment of genealogical connections in the past that enable alliances and advantageous repositionings in the present. To some extent, Israel's genealogical tradition was better suited for purposes of differentiation and separation than of aggregation and inclusion: Isaac, not Ishmael; Jacob, not Esau; Judea, not Samaria. Still, this is only part of the story. First Maccabees contains a particularly striking example of aggregative ethnology operating as an instrument of political strategy. In an account of attempts made by the Maccabean leader Jonathan to secure his own position, the author includes the text of a letter to the Spartans, in which Jonathan endeavors to forge an alliance with the Spartans on the basis of a supposed common descent from Abraham (1 Macc 12:1–23). To make the case, Jonathan cites a letter purportedly from the Spartan king to the Judeans, in which the Spartans assert that they and the Judeans "are brothers and are of the family [*genous*] of Abraham." The value of the example, of course, does not depend on the historicity of the correspondence.[31]

This, however, is a unique instance. What is more important for our purposes is the way in which the concepts of kinfolk and descent figure into some Jewish discourse about proselytism. The reception of proselytes can certainly be identified as one of the developments in Jewish identity construction that are connected to analogous aspects in the Greco-Roman world. Although the phenomenon is linked with biblical legislation concerning the sojourner or resident alien, only later in the Hellenistic era did this develop into the idea that gentiles who adopted Jewish laws and customs and identified with the Jewish people could thereby become fully and (at least in principle) equally Jewish. While it is difficult to prove, it can hardly be doubted that this development was stimulated by the analogous redefinition of Greekness that we looked at in chapter 2.[32]

What is of particular interest in the present context is the element of kinship and the way in which it becomes a mutable aspect of Jewish identity. In Joseph and Aseneth, for example, Aseneth's conversion is depicted as an alienation from her family and its idolatrous patrimony and an incorporation into the people of Joseph and his fellow Hebrews.[33] In a lengthy prayer of repentance, she appeals

---

31. Of the two, the letter from the Spartans is less likely to be historical than the other; see Lester L. Grabbe, *Judaism from Cyrus to Hadrian* (Minneapolis: Fortress, 1992), 1:264.

32. See, e.g., John North, "The Development of Religious Pluralism," in *The Jews among Pagans and Christians in the Roman Empire*, ed. Judith Lieu, John North, and Tessa Rajak (London: Routledge, 1992), 174–93; Martin Goodman, *Rome and Jerusalem: The Clash of Ancient Civilizations* (New York: Vintage, 2008), 168.

33. The otherness of Aseneth in her pre-conversion state is undercut somewhat by the author's description of her: she "had nothing similar to the virgins of the Egyptians,

to the God of Joseph for refuge "because my father and my mother disowned me and said, 'Aseneth is not our daughter,' because I have destroyed and ground (to pieces) their gods, and have come to hate them."³⁴ On the other side of the process of conversion, Joseph, in his own prayer to God on Aseneth's behalf, calls on God to bless her and to "number her among your people that you have chosen before all (things) came into being" (8:9).

The theme receives considerable emphasis in Philo.³⁵ On the one hand, proselytes are those who have abandoned their own family and patrimony.³⁶ They have left "their country [*patrida*], their kinsfolk [*syngeneis*] and their friends for the sake of virtue and religion" (*On the Special Laws* 1.52); they have "abandon[ed] their kinsfolk [*genean*] by blood, their customs and their temples and images of their gods" (*On the Virtues* 102).³⁷ On the other hand, in making "the passage to piety" (*On the Special Laws* 1.51), they have entered a new commonwealth, home, and kin group. To be sure, although Philo can speak of the "equal rank" (*isotimian, isoteleian*) and "equal privilege" (*isonomian*) of the proselyte (*On the Special Laws* 1.52–53), most of the time he speaks in an imperative rather than an indicative mood. Moses "exhorts the old nobility [*eupatridais*] to honor them . . . with special friendship and with more than ordinary goodwill"; for this reason Philo enjoins his fellow members of the old nobility not to "let them . . . be denied another citizenship or other ties of family and friendship" (*On the Special Laws* 1.52). The fact that he feels a need to exhort suggests that in Philo's world, the biblical/philosophical ideal did not fully translate into social reality. Still, the ideal was one that could be described in terms of incorporation into a kin group: proselytes now "must be held to be our dearest friends and closest kinsmen [*syngenestatous*]" (*On the Virtues* 179).

In one striking passage, Philo presents Abraham as a prototypical proselyte (*On the Virtues* 210–19). Abraham "was a Chaldean by birth, the son of an astrologer, one of those who . . . think that the stars and the whole heaven and universe

---

but she was in every respect similar to the daughters of the Hebrews; and she was as tall as Sarah and handsome as Rebecca and beautiful as Rachel" (1:5).

34. Curiously, this theme appears only in her soliloquies; there is no indication of parental rejection in the narrative itself. For a more thorough discussion of Joseph and Aseneth, see Donaldson, *Judaism and the Gentiles*, 141–51.

35. See also Josephus, *Jewish War* 4.265, where he describes the Idumeans as kinsmen (*syngenōn*; also 278). Also to be mentioned are Jewish texts where converts are described without qualification as Jews (Bel and the Dragon 28; Josephus, *Jewish Antiquities* 13.257–58; 20.38; cf. Epictetus, *Discourses* 2.19.19–21; Cassius Dio, *Roman History* 37.17.1).

36. While Philo uses *prosēlytos* when it appears in a scriptural passage under discussion, his preferred term is *epēlys* (incomer).

37. See also *On the Special Laws* 1.308–9; 4.178; *On the Virtues* 178, 210–19.

are gods." Beginning to perceive the folly of such thinking, he was led "to leave his native country, his race and paternal home [*patrida kai genean kai patrōon oikon*]" in order that he might "discover the One, who alone is eternal and the Father of all things." As a result, this native Chaldean became both "the most ancient member of the Jewish nation [*tou ethnous*]" and "the standard of nobility [i.e., noble birth: *eugeneias*] for all proselytes," those who have abandoned idolatry with its "strange laws and monstrous customs" and have then "come to settle in a better land, in a commonwealth full of true life and vitality." Although Philo does not explicitly call Abraham the father of proselytes, he seems to be suggesting the existence of an alternative, direct line of descent for those who conform to the same "standard of noble birth" as was exhibited by Abraham. Those who imitate Abraham in abandoning their own "native country, race and paternal home," Philo seems to imply, thereby become members "of the Jewish nation" in the same way—and with the same resultant status—as Abraham himself.

The concept of Abraham as the father of proselytes—and thus as the foundation of an alternative, socially constructed line of descent—comes more explicitly into view in one strand of rabbinic tradition.[38] In this strand, Abraham is celebrated as the first and greatest proselyte,[39] and also as one who was engaged in the making of proselytes.[40] Further, God delayed Abraham's circumcision until he was ninety-nine in order to make it clear that the door remained open to proselytes at any age.[41] Abraham's role as father of proselytes comes explicitly into play in the context of a debate about proselyte status. Although it could be said that when a gentile becomes a proselyte "he is deemed to be an Israelite in all respects" (b. Yevamot 47b), a proselyte's status was subject to some qualification and limitation.[42] One debate had to do with whether a proselyte should be permitted to participate in prayers that contain the phrase "the God of our fathers." Although the Mishnah prohibits it (m. Bikkurim 1:4), later rabbinic tradition preserves a tradition in which R. Judah (a second-century Tanna, noted for his positive attitude toward proselytes and sympathetic gentiles [cf. t. Sanhedrin 13:2]) argues the opposite, on the grounds that Scripture identifies Abraham as the "father of a multitude of *gôyîm*" (Gen 17:5).[43] According to the Jerusalem

---

38. Bamberger's treatment of the theme remains useful; Bernard J. Bamberger, *Proselytism in the Talmudic Period* (New York: Ktav, 1968), 175-79.
39. E.g., b. Sukkah 49b; Midrash Exod. 1.36.
40. E.g., Sipre Deut. 32.2 (on Deut 6:5); Midrash Gen. 39.16.
41. Mekilta Nezikin 18 (on Exod 22:20).
42. A theme treated in detail by Gary G. Porton, *The Stranger within Your Gates: Converts and Conversion in Rabbinic Literature* (Chicago: University of Chicago Press, 1994).
43. The tradition is found in y. Bikkurim 1:4 64a. The passage has received extensive

Talmud at least, R. Judah's opinion carried the day. The tradition, of course, is late and thus cannot be used as evidence for our period of interest with any confidence. Nevertheless, at the very least, it does illustrate the pattern of thought to which Philo gives expression.

In addition to competitive ethnic historiography, identity construction in the Greco-Roman world also involved the search for universals—ways of transcending ethnic particularities and arriving at some form of transethnic cosmopolitanism—with which ethnic groups could align themselves in advantageous ways. As we have seen, Greek *paideia*—a complex amalgam of Greek language, culture, and philosophy—offered an entree into a desirable and widely accessible form of social identity for those outsiders with the opportunity and means to acquire it, even as it also created a sharp distinction between these Greeks and those others (barbarians) who did not. Greek philosophical traditions, with their concern for virtue and their search for foundational accounts of reality, provided solid underpinnings for this idea of Hellenism as a universalizing culture. In addition, unitary conceptions of the divine realm in one way (e.g., the pantheistic *logos* of Stoicism, the ultimate One of Neoplatonism) and the pantheon of the gods in another (especially as a means of correlating local gods and incorporating them syncretistically into a single divine company) provided a common sacred canopy first for those in the Hellenistic east and subsequently for those in the Roman Empire as a whole. In its empire, Rome imposed its own form of universality on the human *oikoumenē*, not only through sheer military might but also by positioning itself both as the natural heir of the Greeks (Roman *humanitas* preserving all that was valuable in Greek *paideia*) and as their more capable successors (Rome's long tradition of social incorporation and effective rule making for a much more successful world empire).

Through their long experience under Hellenistic rule, both in Judea and the diaspora, Jews developed relatively sophisticated means of positioning themselves with respect to this transethnic and universalizing discourse. This has already come into view in a limited way, in the discussion about Moses as *Erfinder* and *Kulturbringer*. But these appeals to Moses's achievements were related to a much larger project, whose aim was to align the law of Moses and Jewish monotheism with Greek (and subsequently Roman) cosmopolitanism.

The most significant aspect of this project was what I have described elsewhere as "ethical monotheism"—the attempt to present the torah as a particular (and usually the best) manifestation of a universal natural law, embedded in

---

discussion; see Hayes, *Gentile Impurities and Jewish Identities*, 166–68; Cohen, *Beginnings of Jewishness*, 308–30; Porton, *Stranger within Your Gates*, 7, 77; Bamberger, *Proselytism in the Talmudic Period*, 65–67.

the created order by the divine creator, a law that could, at least in principle, be discovered through educated reason and that, consequently, was also to be seen in the best aspects of Greek philosophy.[44] To be sure, the idea that rational observation of the created order could lead to true knowledge about the creator and the norms for creaturely existence stood in tension with the claim that what was true in the philosophers had been derived from Moses. Even if they were aware of the tension, however, Jewish authors paid little attention to it, concentrating their efforts rather on the argument that the law of Moses and the teachings of the philosophers were parallel articulations of the same underlying monotheistic ethic.[45] Of course, this was anything but self-evident, and the argument was hampered by the many ethnic-specific aspects of the law, some of which (circumcision, Sabbath observance, abstinence from certain foods, rejection of the gods) were seen to be particularly offensive. Jewish writers responded gamely, however, providing allegorical interpretations for various laws or downplaying these aspects of the law in favor of the more universal aspects (monotheistic worship and the pursuit of virtue) that resonated most strongly with Greek *paideia* and Roman *humanitas*. Even the Jerusalem temple, which in many ways seemed to symbolize ethnic particularity and the sharp boundary between Israel and the rest of humankind, could be set into a universalizing frame. Josephus takes great pride in the fact that offerings from non-Jews were welcomed at the temple;[46] more explicitly, Philo frequently declares that the sacrifices and prayers offered in the temple are given both for "the nation in particular and for the whole human race in general."[47] That these responses met with some success seems to be indicated by the existence of a considerable number of proselytes and sympathizers.[48] In the case of sympathizers, perhaps the cause was aided by Jewish readiness to

---

44. Donaldson, *Judaism and the Gentiles*, 493-98. The next few paragraphs draw on material in this section of the book.

45. Much of the pertinent work stems from Alexandria (Philo, Letter of Aristeas, Sibylline Oracles 3, Wisdom of Solomon), but it also comes to expression in Josephus's *Against Apion*. Thoroughgoing discussions of the pertinent material can be found in John J. Collins, *Between Athens and Jerusalem: Jewish Identity in the Hellenistic Diaspora*, 2nd ed. (Grand Rapids: Eerdmans, 2000); John M. G. Barclay, *Jews in the Mediterranean Diaspora: From Alexander to Trajan (323 BCE-117 CE)* (Edinburgh: T&T Clark, 1996).

46. *Jewish War* 2.340-41; 4.181, 275; 5.15-18, 562-64; *Jewish Antiquities* 8.116-17; 11.331-36; 13.78, 242-44; 14.110; 16.14; 18.122; *Against Apion* 2.48.

47. *On the Special Laws* 2.162; he continues: "The reason for this is that the Jewish nation is to the whole inhabited world what the priest is to the State" (the whole section 2.162-68 is significant); see also *On the Life of Abraham* 98; *On the Life of Moses* 1.149; *On the Special Laws* 1.97, 168, 190; 2.188-192; 4.180; *On the Embassy to Gaius* 306.

48. See chs. 10 and 11 in Donaldson, *Judaism and the Gentiles*.

differentiate those aspects of torah that pertained to humankind generally from those that had to do with the Jewish people in particular.[49]

While the more significant aspect of Jewish attempts to align the law of Moses with Greek and Roman ideals had to do with ethics and virtue, another line of argument centered on political constitution. Both Josephus (e.g., *Jewish Antiquities* 1.10) and Philo (e.g., *On the Life of Moses* 2.49–51; *On the Virtues* 108) strove to portray the ancient law of Moses as an ideal constitution, a *politeia* to be emulated by Greeks and Romans alike.[50] It was a particularly bold move, especially as it stood in contrast to the willingness on the part of some Greeks to concede Roman superiority in the art of government.[51] At least in Josephus's case, it also stood out against current discussion about possible forms of government. While Aelius Aristides might have credited Rome with the discovery of an ideal "form of government [*politeian*]," one that took the best elements from the three forms of government already in existence (oligarchy, monarchy, democracy), Josephus credits Moses with the articulation of an additional and superior form ("placing all sovereignty and authority in the hands of God"), for which he coined the term *theocracy* (*theokratia*).[52] Although the portrayal of the torah as an ideal constitution was probably less persuasive than the argument based on ethical monotheism, it nevertheless served to identify the Jews as a civilized nation with an extensive constitution of its own and thus to locate it on a respectable part of the ethnic map.[53]

In various ways and with some success, then, many Jews took their place in the arena of competitive identity construction and marked out an area for themselves on the dominant Greco-Roman map. While they did not fundamentally abandon the sharp binary that was part of the inherited tradition (Israel/

---

49. Cf. the Roman distinction between *ius civile* and *ius gentium*, discussed above (ch. 2).

50. According to Steve Mason, Josephus "offers Judaism as an alternative political constitution and an alternative philosophical system"; "'Should Any Wish to Enquire Further' (*Ant.* 1.25): The Aim and Audience of Josephus' *Judean Antiquities/Life*," in *Understanding Josephus: Seven Perspectives*, ed. Steve Mason, JSPSup 32 (Sheffield: Sheffield Academic, 1998), 80.

51. E.g., Aelius Aristides (e.g., *Regarding Rome* 51, 59, 90–91).

52. Aristides, *Regarding Rome* 90–91; Josephus, *Against Apion* 2.165.

53. "This is a category general enough to make Judeans comparable to other peoples: all nations have their own laws and the Jewish constitution can be compared with others (e.g. Athenian and Spartan), both in its structures and in its specifics"; John M. G. Barclay, "Constructing Judean Identity After 70 CE: A Study of Josephus's *Against Apion*," in *Identity and Interaction in the Ancient Mediterranean: Jews, Christians and Others*, ed. Zeba A. Crook and Philip A. Harland (Sheffield: Sheffield Phoenix, 2007), 107–8.

Ethnē as an Identity Ascribed to Non-Jews: By Jews

the nations; Jews/non-Jews), they certainly softened it and redrew it in ways that enabled it to line up advantageously with the dominant map.[54] In part, this was done by aligning themselves and their tradition with the best elements of the Greek side of the Greek-barbarian binary. In part, it involved rendering the boundary more porous by the willingness to accept proselytes and thus to construct alternatives to genealogical descent as points of entry into group membership. And in part, it involved the construction of some positive enclaves on the other side of the boundary for certain groups of non-Jews (sympathizers and natural-law monotheists).

Nevertheless, there were limits; the boundary was not abandoned. It would be rare to find a Jewish counterpart to Favorinus—that is, a tricultured Jew who felt himself to be fully Roman, fully Greek, and fully Jewish, and who was also accepted as such by other Jews.[55] In Philo's case, for example, even though he, like many other Jews, adopted aspects of Greek and Roman culture, the Jew/non-Jew binary remained fundamental. In a well-known passage (*On the Migration of Abraham* 89–83), Philo describes the position of extreme allegorists, Jews who took the position that since the truth of the Mosaic laws was to be found in their symbolic reference to philosophical "matters belonging to the intellect" (98), the literal observance of the laws concerning circumcision, the Sabbath, the festivals, and so on could readily be dispensed with. Although Philo would have agreed with them that these observances functioned as symbolic pointers to more ultimate truths, he steadfastly resisted their inference: "we must," he insists, "pay heed to the letter of the laws" (93). In another context, faced with mistreatment of the Alexandrian Jews by Flaccus, the Roman governor of Egypt, he declared:

---

54. A measure of the willingness to soften the binary can be seen in an interpretive tradition found in Josephus and Philo. The Greek version of Exod 22:27 (MT 22:28) reads, "You shall not revile (the) gods," rendering the Hebrew *ĕlōhîm* with the plural *theous*. In their references to this piece of Mosaic legislation, Philo (*On the Life of Moses* 2.205; *On the Special Laws* 1.53; *Questions and Answers on Exodus* 2.5) and Josephus (*Jewish Antiquities* 4.207; *Against Apion* 2.237) take advantage of this translational curiosity to portray the torah and the people who adhere to it as respectful toward the gods of their non-Jewish neighbors. Of course, there are limits to this respect, and both Philo and Josephus feel free to engage in polemic that their neighbors could well have perceived as violating the legislation. Nevertheless, the tradition is significant. For discussion, see Goldenberg, *Nations That Know Thee Not*, 66–70.

55. For Favorinus's tricultured identity (Gallic, Greek, Roman), see Wallace-Hadrill, *Rome's Cultural Revolution*, 1–7, and the discussion in ch. 2 above. See also Cavan W. Concannon, *"When You Were Gentiles": Specters of Ethnicity in Roman Corinth and Paul's Corinthian Correspondence* (New Haven: Yale University Press, 2014), 36–47, who compares Favorinus and Paul as examples of what he calls "ethnic malleability."

"He [i.e., Flaccus] knew that both Alexandria and the whole of Egypt had two kinds of inhabitants, us and them."[56] In such a situation of crisis, the nuance readily fell away, and the sharp binary came to the fore.

As another example, the indelible character of the boundary is also on display in the Letter of Aristeas, a fictionalized and entertaining account of the translation of the Torah into Greek. This work contains one of the most generous statements about the character of gentile worship to be found in Second Temple Jewish literature, the generosity only slightly qualified by the fact that the speaker (Aristeas) is a (highly sympathetic) non-Jew. Speaking to the Egyptian king, Aristeas says: "These people [i.e., the Jews] worship God, the overseer and creator of all things, whom all people, ourselves included, O king, also (worship), although naming him differently, Zeus and Dis" (Letter of Aristeas 16). In addition to this stunning alignment of the God of Israel with the head of the Greek pantheon, the author portrays the Jewish high priest Eleazar as valuing Greek learning as highly as Jewish (120–27) and as providing his Egyptian visitors with an allegorical interpretation of the ethnic-specific aspects of the law (143–66). The author also portrays the Egyptian king and his court philosophers, at the series of banquets hosted by the king for the Jewish translators, as being amazed at the ability of their Jewish guests to draw on the Jewish law to express Greek wisdom.

Despite all this, however, the torah-based boundary between Jews and others remains fully intact. In Eleazar's discourse on the Mosaic legislation, he refuses to compromise on the literal significance of the Jewish laws. The various injunctions involving "strict observances connected with meat and drink and touch and hearing and sight" function as "unbroken palisades and iron walls" erected by God to prevent Jews from "mixing with any of the other peoples [*tōn allōn ethnōn*] in any matter" and thus to preserve them "from false [idolatrous] beliefs" (Letter of Aristeas 139). To be sure, a certain degree of mixing does take place in the narrative—the series of banquets that precedes the actual work of translation, for example. Nevertheless, the author is careful to make clear that these palisades remained unbroken: at the banquets, "everything," including the menu (181) and the prayers (184–85), was carried out "in accordance with the customs practiced by all [the king's] visitors from Judea" (184).

Finally, another indication of the indissoluble nature of the boundary is to be seen in the appearance in both Philo and Josephus of what might be called a form of muted national eschatology. Each in his own way, both Philo and Josephus seem to have come to terms with the current political status quo, devoting their energies to the task of defining and defending a place for the Jewish people within the Greek and Roman maps of reality. Yet each of them also retains a

---

56. *Against Flaccus* 43; in the next clause, *us* is identified explicitly as *Ioudaioi*.

certain eschatological reserve, an expectation (even if carefully couched and camouflaged) that eventually the map of reality would be returned to its divinely intended pattern and Israel would be restored to its rightful place among the nations of the world.

In Philo, the key passage appears as the conclusion to the treatise *On Rewards and Punishments*,[57] and thus also as the conclusion to the Exposition, the set of treatises containing his apologetic description and interpretation of the Torah.[58] While the treatise uses the language of blessing and curse in addition to that of reward and punishment,[59] one is not surprised that the discourse centers less on matters of covenantal faithfulness (as in Deut 27–30) than on issues of monotheism (*On Rewards and Punishments* 162) and virtue (164). Be this as it may, the treatise concludes with the expectation of a national restoration that is roundly Deuteronomistic (cf. Deut 30:1–5). When the Jews have been converted "in a body to virtue" (164)—that is, when they have accepted their chastisements and have repented (163) for their departure from "the teaching of their race and of their fathers [*tēs syngenous kai patriou*]" (162)—then

> those who but now were scattered in Greece and the outside world over islands and continents will arise and post from every side with one impulse to the one appointed place, guided in their pilgrimage by a vision divine and superhuman unseen by others but manifest to them as they pass from exile to their home.... When they have arrived, the cities which but now lay in ruins will be cities once more; the desolate land will be inhabited; the barren will change into fruitfulness; all the prosperity of their fathers and ancestors will seem a tiny fragment, so lavish will be the abundant riches in their possession. (165, 168)

---

57. Philo's familiarity with Roman imperial ideology and his ability to use it in defense of the Jewish people is on display in the treatise *On the Embassy to Gaius*; see especially 8–13, 143–47.

58. The discourse in the Exposition is more accessible and less allegorical than the collection of more philosophical works known as the Allegory. The Exposition comprises the treatises *On the Creation of the World, On the Life of Abraham, On the Life of Joseph, On the Decalogue, On the Special Laws, On the Virtues, On Rewards and Punishments*; while *On the Life of Moses* displays similar characteristics, disputes remain about whether it should be fully included. On the grouping of Philo's treatises, see David T. Runia, "Philo and the Gentiles," in *Attitudes to Gentiles in Ancient Judaism and Early Christianity*, ed. David C. Sim and James S. McLaren, LNTS 499 (London: Bloomsbury T&T Clark, 2013), 31–32.

59. Explicitly in 126–27, which functions as the end of a section on blessings and the start of one on curses (127–61). The section on blessings would have started somewhere in the lacuna between 78 and 79.

In what needs to be seen as a related passage (*On the Life of Moses* 2.41-44), Philo anticipates a time when "our nation" experiences "a fresh start . . . to brighter prospects," the result of which will be "that each nation would abandon its peculiar ways, and, throwing overboard their ancestral customs, turn to honoring our laws alone."[60]

While Philo was forced to deal with the hard realities of Jewish existence under Roman imperial rule only toward the end of his life (*Against Flaccus, On the Embassy to Gaius*), Josephus's whole opus was shaped by the shattering collision between Jewish hostility toward the other and the brute force of Roman military power. This is not the place for anything like a thorough discussion of Jewish identity construction by Josephus in response to Roman ideology.[61] Any such discussion would need to take into account the increasing scholarly appreciation of the complexity of his work and the recognition that he cannot be seen simply as a turncoat lackey for his new Roman patrons.[62] For present purposes, I am interested primarily in the element of eschatological reserve.

In his account of the war, Josephus describes his attempt, now as part of Titus's entourage, to persuade the Jewish defenders of Jerusalem to surrender to the superior might of the Romans:

> To scorn meaner masters might, indeed, be legitimate, but not those to whom the universe [*ta panta*] was subject. For what was there that had escaped the Romans, save maybe some spot useless through heat or cold? Fortune, indeed, had from all quarters passed over to them, and God who went the round of the nations [*kata ethnos*; "nation by nation"], bringing to each in turn the rod of empire [*tēn archēn*; imperial sovereignty], now rested over Italy. (*Jewish War* 5.367)

---

60. For further discussion, see Donaldson, *Judaism and the Gentiles*, 231-35. Expectations of an end-time transformation of the non-Jewish nations are found in other Hellenistic Jewish literature as well; see Sibylline Oracles 3:191-95, 556-72, 710-23, 732-33, 762-75; 5:247-80, 420-31, 484-503; Testament of Levi 18:2-9; Testament of Judah 24:4-6; 25:5; Testament of Zebulun 9:8; Testament of Naphtali 8:1-4.

61. Josephus is thoroughly familiar with Roman imperial discourse, as can be seen from the speeches he puts in the mouth of various officials: Petronius (*Jewish War* 2.192-98); Agrippa II (*Jewish War* 2.345-401); Titus (*Jewish War* 6.328-50); Nicolaus of Damascus (*Jewish Antiquities* 16.31-57). But while he presents these speeches with a measure of sympathy, he does not thereby surrender his own Jewish identity and commitments.

62. See, e.g., the accounts of his writings in Steve Mason, *Josephus and the New Testament* (Peabody, MA: Hendrickson, 2003), 55-145; and Barclay, *Jews in the Mediterranean Diaspora*, 346-68. See also Donaldson, *Judaism and the Gentiles*, 279-361.

Ethnē as an Identity Ascribed to Non-Jews: By Jews

At first glance, the passage seems simply to be a parroting of Roman ideology.⁶³ At second glance, one is struck by the reference to God (in context, certainly the God of Israel) as the superior agent of Rome's earthly success. If the statement echoes the ideological theme of Rome's invincibility and the will of the gods, it does so with a decidedly Jewish twist: it is the God of Israel who had delivered the imperial sovereignty to Italy.⁶⁴ This is very much in keeping with Josephus's repeated declaration that Israel's defeat was divine punishment for sin and that Rome's success was in conformity with the divine will.⁶⁵ At third glance, however, one is also struck by the statement that God, who has been making "the round of nations," has "now" come to Italy. The language conveys a certain transitory sense that hints at the possibility that the "rod of empire" might at some point in the future pass on from Rome to another nation.

In two other passages, Josephus strongly implies that the nation of Israel would take its place (as the last in the sequence?) in this succession of empires. The clearer of the two is in his account of Nebuchadnezzar's dream and Daniel's interpretation (*Jewish Antiquities* 10.195–210). After presenting Daniel's description of the dream (the four-part image and the stone that demolished it) and the portion of his interpretation dealing with the four successive empires, Josephus suddenly breaks off, on the grounds that his present purpose concerned "what is past and done" and not "what is to be" (*Jewish Antiquities* 10.210). Nevertheless, anyone who wants "to learn about the hidden things that are to come"—which necessarily would have to do with the destruction of the "iron" empire (commonly understood to be Rome)—could readily do so by reading Daniel.

The second is in Josephus's account of the prophecy of Balaam (*Jewish Antiquities* 4.112–30; Num 22–24), who, though he was hired by the Moabite king Balak to curse Israel, was compelled by Israel's God to bless them. Josephus reads the blessings as prophecies, adding two guarded but highly telling comments. First,

---

63. We have already heard a version of the second sentence on the lips of Aelius Aristides: "Nothing escapes you, neither city, nor nation, nor harbor, nor land, unless you have condemned something as useless"; *Regarding Rome* 28.

64. A lengthier development of the same theme is found earlier, in the speech that Josephus puts into the mouth of the Jewish king Agrippa II, at a point in the narrative where all-out war was not yet inevitable. Agrippa runs through a roll call of the subjected nations in order to demonstrate the futility of any attempt on the part of the Jews to defeat "those to whom the universe [*ta panta*] is subject" (*Jewish War* 2.361), which he concludes by declaring that Roman success was a sign of divine favor: "for, without God's aid, so vast an empire could never have been built up" (*Jewish War* 2.390). On this speech, cf. Clifford Ando, *Imperial Ideology and Provincial Loyalty in the Roman Empire* (Berkeley: University of California Press, 2000), 66.

65. E.g., *Jewish War* 4.323–25; 5.378, 408–12; 6.250–51.

having observed that some of the prophecies had already been fulfilled, including some "within my memory," he added that from these fulfilled prophecies "one may infer what the future has in store" (*Jewish Antiquities* 4.125). A few sentences later, in a parting shot to Balak and the princes of Midian, Balaam declares that, while Israel may experience passing misfortunes at the hands of their enemies, they would eventually "flourish once more to the terror of those who inflicted these injuries upon them" (*Jewish Antiquities* 4.128). While the statement was crafted in such a way as to provide Josephus with plausible deniability, one can readily identify some significant "misfortunes" that the Jews had experienced "within [Josephus's] memory" and thus discern Josephus's expectation that Israel would eventually "flourish," the "rod of empire" passing from Italy to Judea.

Thus while significant elements of the Jewish population were prepared to enter the fray of competitive identity construction, striving to position themselves advantageously with respect to the competing maps of the human world, and while in the process the boundary between Israel and the other nations was modified, softened, and (to some extent) relativized, it was by no means abandoned. While Hellenistic Jewish authors showed themselves to be adept at using the widely accepted strategies of competitive ethnology and cosmopolitan self-alignment, the constraints of Israel's distinctive tradition and the resultant sense of difference from the non-Jewish other produced a form of identity that was also unique in significant respects.

Still, this is only part of the picture. As we observed at the outset, at the opposite corner of the grid, there was a segment of the Jewish population for whom the boundary between Israel and the other nations was sharp, hard-edged, and categorical. The only map that mattered was the one in which the human population was divided simply into Jews and non-Jews, Israel and the nations. Even so, however, as we look more closely at this uncompromisingly hard-edged form of Jewish mapmaking, we can see some analogous elements of competitive identity construction, even if in a negative mode or a pessimistic key.

A fundamental aspect of this hard-edged attitude is the belief that the division between Israel and the other nations was categorical and ordained by God from the beginning. In the retelling of the creation account in Jubilees, for example, on the seventh day of creation, God declares to the accompanying angels that "I shall separate for myself a people from among all the nations; and they will also keep the sabbath" (Jubilees 2:19). A similar note is sounded in the Apocalypse of Abraham, where Abraham has a vision of the creation of the world in which the "great crowd of men and women and children" is divided into two, "those on the right side of the picture" being identified as "the ones I have prepared to be born of you [Abraham] and to be called my people" (21:7–22:4).

In one amplification of this theme, the author of the Testament of Moses declares that, according to God's purpose from the beginning, the world was created for the people of Israel alone (1:11–13). The negative counterpart of this variation on the theme is that the nations have been created for ultimate destruction, a belief clearly on display in Jubilees. Here humankind is divided into two groups, the "sons of the covenant" and the "children of destruction"; the fate of the latter is that they will finally "be destroyed and annihilated from the earth" (Jubilees 15:26). For the author of this work, the only way to please God is to keep the torah in its entirety. Since the torah contains an injunction requiring circumcision on the eighth day, gentiles are in effect condemned to this fate from the outset (15:26).

In some expressions of this hard-edged view, the ultimate destruction of the gentile nations is choreographed by God. According to Jubilees, God "caused spirits to rule [over the nations] so they might lead them astray from following him" (Jubilees 15:31)—a stringently negative rereading of Deut 32:8. For the author of the Testament of Moses, God deliberately withheld from the gentile nations any knowledge of the divine purposes: "the Lord of the world ... created the world on behalf of his people, but he did not make this purpose of creation openly known from the beginning of the world so that the nations might be found guilty" (Testament of Moses 1:11–13).

While the Testament of Moses displays little sensitivity to theodical concerns—guilt or not, the non-Jewish nations were excluded from the "purpose of creation" from the outset—other writers with a generally similar pessimistic outlook felt more obliged to establish the culpability of the gentiles, and thus the ultimate justice of their fate. In Pseudo-Philo's *Biblical Antiquities*, although the law was given as "a light to the world" (11.1), the purpose of this light is simply to silence any gentiles who might protest their condemnation. Likewise for the author of 4 Ezra, the gentiles are justly condemned; they had a real opportunity to repent (7:82), but "[t]hey scorned his Law, and denied his covenants; they have been unfaithful to his statutes and have not performed his works."[66] Even so, 4 Ezra differs from the other Jewish works discussed to this point, in that the author is prepared to open up, even if ever so slightly, the possibility that there might have been one or two individual gentiles here or there "who have kept your commandments" (3:36).[67] Second Baruch is less gloomy than 4 Ezra, envisaging a considerable number of those from the nations "who left behind their vanity and who have fled under your wings," a group described a little later as "those who first did not know life and who later knew it exactly and who mingled with the

---

66. 4 Ezra 7:24; also 7:72–74; 8:55–61; 9:9–12.

67. Of course, 4 Ezra differs from most other Jewish literature from the period, in its pessimism about the ability of Jews to keep the torah to any acceptable extent.

seed of the people" (41:4; 42:5). Still, except for the righteous who keep the law, the "whole multitude" of Adam and Eve's descendants are "going to corruption" (48:43); those "who do not keep the statutes of the Most High" will in the end pass away like smoke (82:6).

This discussion of 4 Ezra and 2 Baruch leads to another element in the hard-edged Jewish view being discussed here—namely, a correspondingly hard-edged view of proselytism. Here the Jew/gentile binary is drawn with particular and categorical sharpness. All non-Jews are on the wrong side of the created order of things and are destined for destruction, except for those (few) who abandon their native identity and "mingle with the seed of the people" Israel. Put differently, the only hope that non-Jews have of pleasing the creator of the world and having a share in the age to come is by becoming a Jewish proselyte in this age. In many cases, this stringent view of proselytism was simply theoretical and theodical—a way of justifying the ultimate destruction of the nations. However, the example of Eleazar—the advisor of King Izates in Adiabene who admonished the king that as long as he hesitated on the wrong side of the line, he was "guilty of the greatest offence against the law and thereby against God" (Josephus, *Jewish Antiquities* 20.44)—suggests that the view was operative in the social sphere as well.

But not every non-Jew had Izates's opportunities to become familiar with the torah. If the ultimate destruction of the nations is to be justified by their rejection of "the statutes of the Most High," how might they have been expected to know them in the first place?[68] In some cases, gentile culpability results simply from the fact that they "did not know my Law" (2 Baruch 48:40) or that "they have not learned my Law" (Pseudo-Philo, *Biblical Antiquities* 11.2). While these statements seem to assume that non-Jews should have known and learned the torah,[69] how this knowledge should have been acquired is left unspecified. Elsewhere in 2 Baruch it is said that non-Jews "despised my Law" (51:4), which implies that they did have at least some awareness of the law's existence. This line of thought is especially prominent in 4 Ezra:

> For God strictly commanded those who came into the world, when they came, what they should do to live, and what they should observe to avoid punishment. Nevertheless, they were not obedient, and spoke against him; they devised for themselves vain thoughts, and proposed to themselves wicked

---

68. Some of the material in the next few paragraphs appears in a different context in Terence L. Donaldson, "Paul, Abraham's Gentile 'Offspring' and the Torah," in *Torah Ethics and Early Christian Identity*, ed. David M. Miller and Susan Wendel (Grand Rapids: Eerdmans, 2016).

69. Given as "a light to the world," according to Pseudo-Philo, *Biblical Antiquities* 11.1.

frauds; they even declared that the Most High does not exist, and they ignored his ways! They scorned his Law, and denied his covenants; they have been unfaithful to his statutes and have not performed his works. (7:20–24; see also 7:72–74; 8:55–61; 9:9–12)

How this strict commandment was communicated, however, and how it was that they "obtained the Law" (7:72) is not made clear, though some of the language (e.g., "who came into the world") is suggestive of a line of thought that is interesting from the perspective of identity construction and competitive ethnography.

According to this line of thought, some basic knowledge of God and of God's commandments is discernible from the created order itself. This theme appears clearly at one point in 2 Baruch (54:13–19). In support of the statement that "those who do not love your Law are justly perishing" (v. 14), Baruch declares: "For his works have not taught you, nor has the artful work of his creation which has existed always persuaded you" (v. 18). The fault, however, lies not with God's "works" but with the "unrighteous ones" themselves, who willfully "rejected the understanding of the Most High" (v. 17).[70] The theme appears as well in the Apocalypse of Abraham. The first eight chapters of this work tell the story of Abraham's recognition of the folly of idolatry, the conflict between Abraham and his father Terah over the nature of Terah's gods, Abraham's discovery of the true God, and his subsequent departure from Chaldea.[71] The example of Abraham, then, demonstrated that it was possible to recognize the folly of idolatry and to perceive from the created order that there was a "God who created all things" (7:10). The gentiles, however, have spurned this opportunity for perception and repentance; as God declares toward the end of the work, "For I waited so that they might come to me, and they did not deign to" (31:6).[72]

What emerges in this latter set of texts, then, is a kind of natural theology in

---

70. In 2 Baruch 48:40, even though the unrighteous did not know God's law, each one nevertheless "knew when he acted unrighteously."

71. A similar account appears in Jubilees 11:14–13:9. Both stories recount the fiery destruction of Terah's house along with its gods. (In Apocalypse of Abraham the house is destroyed by fire from heaven [8:1–6]; in Jubilees the fire is set by Abraham himself [12:12–14].)

72. See also Testament of Moses 1:11–13: "He created the world on behalf of his people, but he did not make this purpose of creation openly known from the beginning of the world so that the nations might be found guilty, indeed that they might abjectly declare themselves guilty by their own . . . discussions." While the sentence is obscure, it could be read as implying that something should have been known about God from the created order.

a pessimistic key. The created order itself bore witness to the creator God and to some fundamental ethical injunctions, which should have led human beings to seek the God who had been revealed more fully in the torah and the covenant. While this did happen in some cases (those "who left behind their vanity and who have fled under your wings"; 2 Baruch 41:4), for the most part the witness of the natural order simply justified the judgment to come. This is a far cry from the kind of ethical monotheism on display in Philo or the Letter of Aristeas. Nevertheless, along with the concern in this more pessimistic literature to locate Israel and the nations more generally within the created order, it does demonstrate the need to engage in competitive ethnology—if even in an unreflective and defensive mode.

Admittedly, this discussion of Jewish identity construction in the Greco-Roman context is far from complete. We have concentrated on two of the extreme segments of the grid, leaving out of account a lot of Jewish literature in between. In addition, more might have been said about attempts to come to terms with the realities of Roman rule—both juridical explanations (God has allowed the Romans to exercise power over Judea specifically as a means of punishing the people of Israel for their sins) and eschatological ones (God may have empowered the Roman Empire as an agent of punishment in the present, but this was just an episode in a longer story that would culminate in a new state of affairs where Israel would be purified, vindicated, and restored to a central place among the nations).[73]

Nevertheless, the preceding discussion provides a sufficient foundation for our primary concern here—to explore the ways in which *ethnē* and related terms were used as ascribed identity terms for non-Jews.

---

73. Psalms of Solomon offers an example of a juridical explanation. Written sometime after Pompey's capture of Jerusalem, it is by turns appalled at Pompey's arrogance and pleased that God has used the Romans to punish the wicked Hasmonean priests and bring their period of dominance to an end (Psalms of Solomon 2, 8). Later, the postwar apocalypses 2 Baruch and 4 Ezra develop the theme that the destruction of Jerusalem was to be seen as divine punishment for Israel's sin, using the first destruction under the Babylonians as a locus for making sense of the second destruction under the Romans. In Josephus's case, although he differed from 2 Baruch and 4 Ezra in his readiness to see Roman success in general as a sign and result of divine favor, we have seen how he too views the outcome of the war as divine punishment.

Staying with this same literature, the eschatological theme is central in Psalms of Solomon 17, and it appears at important junctions in 2 Baruch (e.g., 29–34; 39:1–40:4; 72–74) and (despite its more pessimistic outlook) 4 Ezra (e.g., 11:1–12:39; 13:1–58).

Ethnē and Ascribed Identity

As was discussed in the previous chapter, social identity is negotiated and formed at the significant boundaries, those lines where the "us" becomes aware of itself as distinct from the "not us." Part of the negotiation involves ascribed identities, as those on the other side of the boundary form an image of the group on the basis of their own perceptions and then project the image back over the boundary, where it is experienced as an ascribed identity to which the group itself needs to respond in some way. From this dialectic of perception, projection, and response emerges a constructed self-identification—a social identity—which incorporates within it an image of the other, an ascribed identity in return, which is then projected back across the boundary.[74] Thus the identity that Jews would have ascribed to non-Jewish others was implicit in its own constructed identity—the impress, as it were, of the ring on the sealing wax.

We also need to recall the elements of desirability and of power. The extent to which an undesirable ascribed identity is internalized and incorporated into group identity depends on relative power—the power of the outside agency to impose the ascribed identity and the power of the group itself to resist it. For most Jewish groups in our period of interest, there were not many situations where they were in a position to impose an identity on their non-Jewish neighbors; only in rare situations—Judea during the Hasmonean period, for example—was the identity imposed from a position of power. Nevertheless, non-Jews who came in contact with Jewish groups would become aware, to a greater or lesser extent, of the identity that was being ascribed to them. Where the ascribed identity was perceived as attractive, the attractiveness itself provided its own power.

The identity that Jewish groups projected onto non-Jewish outsiders, then, would have emerged as the reflex of the Jewish identity as discussed above, expressed in a set of distinctive categories (monotheism, election, torah, temple, covenant, eschatology) as these were reshaped and repackaged in the competitive environment of the Greco-Roman world. Of course, one needs to maintain the distinction here between projection and perception. The nature of the perception depends on the lens used to perceive. Only those non-Jews who came into sufficiently close contact with Jewish groups would be able to arrive at a fine-grained perception of the ascribed identities being projected from the Jewish side, and even then the perception would vary according to how much they sympathized with the Jewish world. Someone who would have fallen into Jose-

---

74. This dialectic can also be formalized in terms of external categorization and internal group identification, a central theme in Richard Jenkins's work (as discussed in ch. 2); *Social Identity*, 4th ed. (New York: Routledge, 2014).

phus's category of "those who would enquire further" would have gained a much more accurate and nuanced perception than a Petronius or a Tacitus,[75] with their wildly inaccurate accounts of Jewish beliefs and attitude toward outsiders.[76] Here, however, our present concern has to do more with the ascribed identity itself—or, at least, with the perceptions of non-Jews who were in a position to perceive it accurately.[77]

Like the identities imposed on the other by the Greeks and later the Romans, this ascribed identity had two sides to it. On one side, non-Jews would have perceived themselves to be categorized as the other in an ethnic binary. To be sure, as we have seen, the nature of the boundary varied considerably, from sharp and hard-edged to softer and more porous. Still, the basic distinction between Jews and non-Jews remained. On the other side, non-Jews perceived a range of ways in which they could locate themselves with respect to this binary. The range is considerable. As one moves, say, from Jubilees to Philo, one moves from a map in which the non-Jewish portion is an area of categorical nullification ("children of destruction" destined to be "destroyed and annihilated from the earth"; 15.26) to one in which discerning non-Jews occupy an area equal in status to that of the Jews.[78] In between, one encounters maps where the boundary between Jewish and non-Jewish territories is fitted with gates through which proselytes are invited to enter, together with maps containing a special strip of territory along the non-Jewish side of the border, occupied by various non-Jewish sympathizers, especially those who acknowledge the God of Israel as the one true God and live in conformity with that portion of the torah that pertains to humankind as

---

75. To use Mason's translation of *Jewish Antiquities* 1.25; "'Should Any Wish to Enquire Further.'"

76. Tacitus, in a passage in which he refers on two occasions to the making of proselytes, says of Jews that, "although they are prone to lust, they abstain from intercourse with foreign women; yet among themselves nothing is unlawful" (*Histories* 5.5.1–2). Petronius, who was aware of the circumcision of non-Jews (*Satyricon* 102), describes a Jew as one who "may worship his pig-god" (*Poems* 24).

77. In addition, in this investigation as a whole, we will be interested not so much in the range of perceptions among non-Jews generally, as in the perceptions of identity on the part of some very specific segments of non-Jews (i.e., Christ-believers, both those included in the movement in the early stages when it was primarily Jewish and those at later points who were part of a more identifiable gentile Christian movement).

78. "For what the disciples of the most excellent philosophy gain from its teaching, the Jews gain from their laws, that is, to know highest, the most ancient Cause of all things and reject the delusion of created gods" (*On the Virtues* 65). Such "disciples of the most excellent philosophy" can be found both "in Greek or barbarian lands" (*On the Special Laws* 2.44; also *That Every Good Person Is Free* 72–73).

a whole.⁷⁹ Except for the case of Jubilees and like-minded works, I have carried out an extensive examination of these maps elsewhere (within the framework of what I called "patterns of universalism"), and so I will not attempt to describe and document this phenomenon in more detail here.⁸⁰

Within the broader phenomenon of the various identities that Jews ascribed to the non-Jewish others, we are especially interested in the vocabulary of categorization—the terms in which these ascribed identities are expressed—and, within this vocabulary set, the term *ethnē* in particular. Our interest in this Greek term, of course, is due to its later use in Christian identity construction, though because Jewish and Christian use of *ethnē* has been shaped by prior Hebrew usage, we need to begin here.⁸¹

The identity binary that we have already observed is rooted in Israel's Scriptures, with their contrast between Israel as a people (usually *'am*) and the other nations (usually *gôyîm*). While *gôy* on occasion can be used with reference to Israel (e.g., Gen 12:2; Exod 19:6; Isa 51:4) and *'ammîm* appears with some frequency as a term for the other nations,⁸² the plural *gôyîm* is almost always reserved for the nations other than Israel.⁸³ Indeed, the usage is so standard that the apparently inclusive phrase "all the nations" (*kol-haggôyîm*) almost always excludes the people of Israel,⁸⁴ and the articular form "the nations" (*haggôyîm*), used in

---

79. The plural here (*maps*) is intended to signal the difference between hard-line proselytism (only those non-Jews who become proselytes in this age will share in the age to come) and softer versions in which, while proselytism is welcomed and even encouraged, non-Jews nevertheless can have a share in the divine purposes without becoming Jews.

80. Donaldson, *Judaism and the Gentiles*.

81. We will be interested in Latin equivalents as well, but these do not have much of a bearing on Jewish usage.

82. Often in parallel with *gôyîm*: "Declare his glory among the nations [*gôyîm*], his marvellous works among all the peoples ['*ammîm*]" (1 Chr 16:24; also, e.g., Ps 33:10; Isa 14:6; 33:3; 49:22; Ezek 36:15; Mic 4:3; Hab 2:13; Zech 8:22). Also on its own (e.g., Gen 49:10; Ps 45:5; Isa 14:2; 51:5; Hos 10:10; Mic 1:2; 4:1; Zeph 3:9; Zech 8:20). The nations are denoted by other terms as well: *lə'ummîm* (seventeen times) and the Aramaic *'ummayā'* (seven times).

83. The only clear exception is Ezek 37:22, which refers to the two nations of Judah and Israel; see also Ezek 2:3.

84. Even when the term is used without further qualification: e.g., Deut 29:24; 1 Chr 14:17; 2 Chr 32:23; Ps 59:6; Isa 2:2; 14:26; 34:2; 40:17; 66:20; Jer 3:17; Ezek 39:21; Joel 3:2; Hag 2:7; Zech 14:2. One possible exception is Jer 28:11, 14; the Greek version (= LXX Jer 35:11, 14) will be discussed below, along with other possible inclusive uses of *panta ta ethnē*.

an absolute sense without further qualification, denotes not simply "the nations" but "the nations as distinct from the people Israel."[85]

In addition to *gôyîm*, two other words are consistently (albeit infrequently) used in the plural to refer to nations other than Israel: *lə'ummîm*, appearing primarily in poetic material;[86] and, in the Aramaic material, *'ummayā'*.[87] Also, various forms of *nkr* are used to denote "foreigner(s)" (*nēker, ben-nēker, nokrî*), forms that (unlike *gôyîm*) allow for the possibility of referring to individual non-Jews.[88]

The contrasted pairing of *'am* (Israel) and *gôyîm* (the nations other than Israel) is carried over into the Greek version, though in an even more sharply focused way. While the basic tendency of the translators was to use *ethnos* for *gôy* and *laos* for *'am*, this pattern was subject to significant modifications. For one thing, the Greek version makes a sharper terminological distinction between the people Israel and the (other) nations. In instances where *gôy* appears with reference to Israel, for example, the Greek version often avoids *ethnos*, either using *laos* instead (e.g., Josh 3:17; 4:1; Isa 58:2) or using some alternative expression.[89] On the other side of things, *ethnos* was routinely chosen to render *'am* (sg.) when it denoted a nation other than Israel (e.g., Exod 1:9; 15:14; 21:8; Lev 20:2; Deut 1:28; 2:10, 21). Likewise, *'ammim* is regularly rendered *ethnē* in instances where the Hebrew term denoted peoples other than Israel (e.g., Exod 19:5; 23:27; 33:16; Lev 20:24, 26; Deut 2:25; 4:6; 6:14; 10:15). Further, the range of vocabulary found in the Hebrew Scriptures is reduced in the Greek, with both *ethnos* and *laos* often being chosen as translations of Hebrew words other than *gôy* and *'am*.[90] In short, the Greek version provides evidence for a development in which *laos* and *ethnē*

---

85. A frequent occurrence: e.g., Deut 32:8; 2 Sam 22:50; Ps 2:1, 8; 10:16; 22:8; 115:2; 135:15; Isa 42:1; Jer 46:1; Ezek 5:8; 20:14. The NRSV occasionally uses *other nations*, which seems to imply that Israel might be classed among the nations. In each case, however, *other* is supplied by the translators; the Hebrew is simply a form of *haggôyîm* (1 Sam 8:5, 20; Neh 5:8; Ezek 25:8; also *kā'ammîm* [Hos 9:1]).

86. E.g., Ps 2:1; 44:2; 47:3; Isa 17:13; 34:1; 49:1; Jer 51:58; Hab 2:13.

87. The emphatic plural form of *'ummāh*; Ezra 4:10; Dan 3:4, 7; 4:1 (Aramaic 3:31); 5:19; 7:14.

88. In the singular: e.g., Gen 17:12; Exod 12:43; Ruth 2:10; Isa 56:3; Ezek 44:9; in the plural: e.g., Ps 18:44; 144:7; Isa 56:6; Ezek 44:7.

89. E.g., Josh 5:6, 8; 10:13; Isa 51:4; Ezek 2:3. Exceptions occur, however (e.g., Gen 12:2; Exod 19:6; 2 Sam 7:23).

90. Somewhat surprisingly, however, *ethnos* is rarely used to render forms of *nkr*, for which other words are used (especially *allogenēs, allotrios, allophylos, xenos*). Curiously, in the majority of its appearances in the LXX, *allophylos* is used to denote the Philistines.

Ethnē as an Identity Ascribed to Non-Jews: By Jews

come to function virtually as technical terms for Israel (as God's special people) and the other nations, respectively.

Before moving on, we should note a possible exception to this conclusion, one that has a bearing on some early Christian texts (especially Matt 28:19). It has to do with the phrase "all the nations" (*panta ta ethnē*). In the great majority of its occurrences in the Greek Scriptures (some 115 in total), the phrase denotes the non-Jewish nations. In five passages, however, the phrase might be read in an inclusive sense—that is, "*all* nations [Israel included]." In two passages, the term appears twice, making a total of seven occurrences. The question, then, is whether in these instances the distinction between Israel and the non-Jewish nations has been effaced, so that Israel is seen as just one of the many nations of the world.

Three of these passages (four occurrences)—all of them in Daniel (OG Dan 3:2, 7; 4:37; 6:26)—can be immediately set aside. In each of them, the phrase "all the nations" is either spoken by a gentile king or at least reflects his point of view. In each case, while the Jewish nation is included within "all the *ethnē*" who are subject to the king, the Jewish author is simply replicating the perspective of the non-Jewish character rather than redefining the usual Jewish use of the term. These instances thus have little bearing on the use of the phrase from Jewish perspective.[91]

This leaves us with two other passages (three occurrences): LXX Isa 56:7 and LXX Jer 35:11, 14 (= MT 28:11, 14). The statement in LXX Isa 56:7 has to do with the aliens (*hoi allogeneis*) who, along with others "keep my sabbaths so as not to profane them and hold fast my covenant," will be invited to worship at the temple in Jerusalem, "'for my house shall be called a house of prayer for all the nations [*pasin tois ethnesin*],'[92] said the Lord, who gathers the dispersed of Israel" (vv. 6–8). Certainly this is an inclusive scene: aliens—members of foreign nations—will worship together with reassembled Israel. Logically, then, "all the nations" could have an inclusive sense; members of other nations join with the nation of Israel to worship the Lord. Nevertheless, this is not where the emphasis falls. The clause in question ("for my house shall be called a house of prayer for all the *ethnē*") is subordinate to a main clause that has to do with non-Jews: "I will bring *them* into my holy mountain and make *them* joyful in my house of prayer; *their* whole burnt offerings and *their* sacrifices will be acceptable on my altar." This, coupled with the reference to Israel that follows ("who gathers the dispersed of Israel"), suggests that the distinction between Israel and "all the *ethnē*" remains in place. Further support for this conclusion is provided by the use of *laos* with reference to

---

91. To these we can add Jdt 3:8, the only other possible exception that I have been able to find in postbiblical Jewish literature.

92. Rendering *kāl-hāʿammim*.

Israel in verse 3 and the fact that the other fifteen occurrences of *panta ta ethnē* in Isaiah denote "all the non-Jewish nations." In other words, the thrust of the whole passage is that members of the non-Jewish nations are invited to share in Israel's worship rather than that Israel is being designated as one of the larger group of nations joining together in worship. While the phrase could possibly be read in an inclusive way, the inclusion would be peripheral at best; Israel's special status is by no means dissolved into a homogeneous collection of *ethnē*.

We see a similar case in LXX Jer 35:11–14 (= MT 28:11–14). In the larger context (starting with ch. 34), Jeremiah had placed a wooden yoke around his own neck as a symbolic way of reinforcing his message that God had "given the earth to King Nabouchodonosor of Babylon to be subject to him" and that any nation that did not "put their neck under the yoke of the king of Babylon" would suffer dire consequences (34:6, 8). After crushing Jeremiah's yoke, the false prophet Hananiah declared that within two years God would "crush the yoke of the king of Babylon from the necks of all the nations [*pantōn tōn ethnōn*]" (35:11). Replacing the wooden yoke with a yoke of iron, Jeremiah replied: "Thus did the Lord say, 'I have put an iron yoke on the neck of all the nations [*pantōn tōn ethnōn*] so that they might work for the king of Babylon'" (35:14).[93] The nation of Judah certainly is not excluded from consideration here. Jeremiah urges king Sedekias to submit to the king of Babylon (34:12); anything that he says in general terms about "the nation" that does (34:11) or does not (34:8) submit to Babylon applies to Judah as well. At the same time, however, when he refers to Judah as a whole, he uses *people* rather than *nation*: "I spoke to you and all this people [*panti tō laō toutō*] and the priests" (34:16). Further, when the yoke imagery is first introduced, it is non-Jewish nations that are in view: Jeremiah had first put the yoke around his neck as part of a message that he sent to the kings of surrounding nations (Idumea, Moab, Ammon, Tyre, Sidon; 34:2).[94] In keeping with this, in the message that God instructs Jeremiah to deliver to Hananiah, "all the nations" are then referred to in the third person ("so that they might work for the king of Babylon"; 35:14), which might be taken to imply that the term refers primarily to the other nations. Further, the other six occurrences of the phrase in Jeremiah denote non-Jewish nations. In sum, while what is true of "all the nations" in this passage is true of Judah as well: there is little indication that Judah is being explicitly and deliberately lumped together with Idumea, Moab, and the rest as one of "all the *ethnē*."

Turning to other Jewish literature in the Greek and Roman periods, we are not surprised to find a continuation of the patterns apparent in the Hebrew Scriptures

---

93. In both cases (MT Jer 28:11, 14), the phrase renders *kāl-haggôyîm*.

94. Or does the awkwardly placed phrase *pros Sedekian basilea Iouda* (34:3) stand in parallel somehow with the preceding *pros* phrases?

and their Greek translations. In addition, however, there are several differences that will become significant. One is a development in the use of *ethnē* in which it comes to denote not only the totality of non-Jewish nations but also a multiplicity of non-Jewish individuals. Tannaitic literature takes this one step further, as *gôy* in the singular is frequently used to refer to a single non-Jew. Another striking observation is the almost complete absence of *ethnē* in the sense of the "non-Jewish nations" in a significant body of Greek literature (most notably Philo and Josephus). These aspects will come more fully into view as we proceed.[95]

We begin with the use of "nations" (*ethnē*, *gôyîm*, and various translational equivalents) to denote the non-Jewish other—all nations other than that of Israel. This binary usage, heavily dependent on biblical language, is widespread throughout Second Temple and Tannaitic literature:

> Acknowledge him before the nations [*tōn ethnōn*], O sons of Israel [*hoi huioi Israēl*]; for he has scattered you among them. (Tob 13:3)

> For I did not wish to inquire about the ways above, but about those things which we daily experience: why Israel has been given over to the gentiles [*gentibus*] as a reproach; why the people [*populum*] whom you loved has been given to godless tribes. (4 Ezra 4:23)

> For this will be a time of suffering for Isra[el and a servi]ce of war /against/ all the nations [*hgwyym*]. For God's lot there will be everlasting redemption /2/ and destruction for all the wicked nations [*lkwl gwy rqʻh*]. (1QM XV, 1–2)

> When it says: "It shall be the first month of the year to you" [Exod 12:2], behold, there it tells you that it is commanded only to you and not /38/ to the Gentiles [*lgwyym*].... We thus learn that Israel reckons by the moon and that /40/ the Gentiles [*hgwyym*] reckon by the sun. (Mekilta Tractate Pisha 2.39–40)

In addition to the binary usage in the form "the nations"/"(sons of) Israel,"[96] the Israel side of the binary is also expressed in a variety of other ways:[97] "(the/

---

95. On all these topics, see the pertinent sections in Ophir and Rosen-Zvi, *Goy*.

96. Examples of other instances: *ethnē* (Tob 14:6–7; 1 Macc 1:11, 43; 4:11; 7:23; Jdt 4:12; Testament of Naphtali 8.3–4); *gwyym* (1QM XVI, 1; 4Q372 frag. 1, 4–11; 4Q504 frag. 1–2 III, 2–7; 4Q504 frag. 1–2 V, 9–12; 11QTemple LXIV, 9–11; m. Terumot 8:12; m. ʻErubin 3:5; m. Taʻanit 3:7; m. Ketubot 2:9; m. Nedarim 4:3; t. Peʼah 3:1; t. Demai 1:12–13); other (2 Baruch 72:1–6; Testament of Moses 10:7–8 [*gentes*]).

97. In literature where *ethnē* is used of non-Jews, the singular *ethnos* is sometimes used

God's) people";[98] "(my/our) race";[99] "(your/holy) seed";[100] "Jews";[101] "(God's) son(s)";[102] "we" or "us";[103] "you";[104] contextual references to Zion, Jerusalem, or the temple;[105] various other contextual indicators.[106] With respect to the non-Jewish side of the binary, while the articular or emphatic form ("the nations") is standard, the anarthrous form ("nations") appears occasionally.[107] Also to be noted is the phrase "all the nations," which appears frequently with respect to the totality of non-Jewish nations.[108]

Moving from the level of vocabulary to that of discourse, *gôyîm* and its translational equivalents appear with reference to most of the themes that are familiar from Israel's Scriptures:[109] Israel's election and God's choice of Israel from out

---

of the Jewish nation: e.g., Jdt 9:14; Tob 1:17 (Sinaiticus); 1 Macc 9:29 (and passim); 2 Macc 5:19–20 (and passim); 3 Macc 1:11; 2:27; 2:33; 4 Macc 1:11 (and passim). *Other nations* appears occasionally (2 Macc 6:14; Pseudo-Philo, *Biblical Antiquities* 30.4).

98. E.g., *laos* (1 Macc 1:13; 4:58; 5:19; 2 Macc 13:11; 14:15; Psalms of Solomon 17:34–35); *populus* (Pseudo-Philo, *Biblical Antiquities* 11:1; 20:4; 27:7); *plebs* (Testament of Moses 1:11–13); *'am* (1QpHab V, 3–5; 1QM XIV, 4–5; 1QM XVI, 1; 4Q504 frag. 6, 6–9; 11QTemple LXIV, 9–11).

99. *Genos* (Tob 1:10; 3 Macc 6:13 [of Jacob]; Testament of Levi 14:4).

100. 2 Baruch 72:4 (of Jacob); Jubilees 16:17–18; 18:16; 22:11.

101. 3 Macc 4:1–2; 5:13; 7:3–4; 1 Macc 2:18 (men of Judah).

102. 4Q504 frag. 1–2 III, 2–7

103. Tob 3:4; Sir 36:1; Pr Azar 1:14; 1 Macc 1:11; 2:19; Bar 2:13; Psalms of Solomon 7:3; 17:3; 4Q504 frag. 1–2 III, 2–7.

104. Tob 13:5; Bar 2:29; 4:6; Ep Jer 1:4–5; Testament of Levi 14:1–2, 4; 15:1–2; 4Q394 frag. 3–7 I, 6–11.

105. 1 Macc 1:14–15; 2 Baruch 67:2, 5–6; 68:5–7; Testament of Levi 15:1–2; Psalms of Solomon 1:8; 2:22.

106. 1 Macc 5:43; Ep Jer 1:50–51; Wis 14:11; 15:15; Sir 10:15; 4 Ezra 7.37–38; Jubilees 1:8–10, 13, 15, 19; Lives of the Prophets 1:12–13; CD XII, 6–7; 1QpHab XII, 12–14; 1QpHab XIII, 1–2; 4Q269 frag. 8 II, 1–2; t. Pe'ah 3:1.

107. Wis 14:11; Sir 10:15; 3 Macc 6:13; Psalms of Solomon 2:22; 7:3; 1QM XIV, 4–5.

108. *Panta ta ethnē* (Tob 3:4; 13:5; 14:6; 1 Macc 4:11; 3 Macc 7:4; Sir 36:2; Ep Jer 1:50 [6:51]; Pr Azar 1:14; Testament of Levi 14:1–2, 4; 15:1–2; Psalms of Solomon 17:34–35. *kwl hgwyym* (1QpHab III, 4–6; 1QpHab VIII, 5; 1QM XV, 1–2; 1QM XVI, 1; 1QM XIX, 10; 1Q27 frag. 1 I, 8–9; 4Q378 frag. 3 I, 9; 4Q504 frag. 1–2 III, 2–7; 4Q504 frag. 1–2 IV, 2–12; m. Nedarim 3:11). *Other* (1 Enoch 10:21; 2 Enoch 70:7; 2 Baruch 72:2, 5; Jubilees 12:23; 18:16; 22:11). The phrase also appears occasionally with reference to specific local groups of gentiles (e.g., 1 Macc 1:42; 2:18, 19; 5:43). One instance where "all the nations" might include Israel is Jdt 3:8: the purpose of Holofernes's tour of conquest was "that all the nations should worship Nebuchadnezzar alone."

109. With respect to some of these themes, cf. the categorization in ch. 3 of Ophir and Rosen-Zvi, *Goy*.

of the nations;[110] the nations as those from whom Israel should keep separate and refuse to imitate;[111] the nations as wicked and idolatrous;[112] the nations as enemies;[113] the nations as nevertheless ultimately subject to Israel's God;[114] the nations as divine instruments of punishment;[115] the exile among the nations as one form of punishment;[116] God's action in gathering Israel from all the nations among whom they had been scattered;[117] the nations as witnesses of God's activity with Israel, both in judgment and in salvation;[118] the nations as beneficiaries of Israel's covenantal role;[119] and the eschatological fate of the nations, both in judgment and in salvation.[120]

As was mentioned above, during the Second Temple period *ethnē* and *gôyîm* come to be used not only of non-Jewish nations but also of non-Jewish individuals, a development that became important in early Christian usage as well. The development is curious, both because the basic meaning of *ethnē* has to do with nations or ethnic groups rather than with individuals, and because the term in its singular form always denotes a single nation, rather than a single, non-Jewish individual. In other words, there is no singular equivalent to the plural *ethnē* when used with reference to individuals. We will return to this point presently, but first we will survey the evidence,[121] which suggests that the usage was well established in the Second Temple period.

To begin with, there are frequent occurrences of the usage in 1 and 2 Maccabees. For example, in 1 Macc 4:12–14 we read:

---

110. E.g., Jubilees 2:19; 12:23; 16:17–18; 18:16; Testament of Moses 1:11–13; Pseudo-Philo, *Biblical Antiquities* 11.1; 4Q504 frag. 1–2 III, 2–7.

111. E.g., Tob 1:10; 1 Macc 1:14–15; 2:19; Jubilees 22:16; 30:11–14; 11QTemple^a XLVIII, 6–14; 11QTemple^a LI, 19–21.

112. E.g., 1 Macc 7:23; 2 Macc 6:4; 13:11; Wis 14:11; 15:15; Jubilees 3:31; 22:16; 1QpHab XII, 12–14; 1QpHab XIII, 1–2.

113. E.g., Jdt 4:12; Bar 4:6; 1 Macc 3:52; 2 Macc 8:16; Lives of the Prophets 1:12–13; Apocalypse of Abraham 27:1; Jubilees 1:19; Pseudo-Philo, *Biblical Antiquities* 27.7.

114. E.g., Sir 10:15; 17:17; 3 Macc 5:13; 6:13; Psalms of Solomon 17:3.

115. E.g., Tob 3:4; Bar 4:6; Psalms of Solomon 2:22; 7:3.

116. E.g., Tob 3:4; 13:3; Bar 2:13, 29; Testament of Levi 15:1–2; Jubilees 1:13; 4Q372 frag. 1, 4–11.

117. E.g., Tob 13:5; Jubilees 1:15; 4Q504 frag. 1–2 V, 9–12.

118. E.g., 1 Macc 4:11; Ep Jer 1:50–51; Testament of Levi 14:1–4; Testament of Naphtali 8:3–6.

119. Testament of Levi 14:4; Jubilees 12:23; 18:16.

120. E.g., Tob 14:6–7; 1 Enoch 10:21; 2 Baruch 72:1–6; Psalms of Solomon 17:34–35; 4 Ezra 7:37–38; Testament of Moses 11:1–13; 1QM XIV, 4–5; XV, 1–2.

121. We will postpone an examination of early rabbinic usage until a little later.

GENTILE CHRISTIAN IDENTITY

> When the foreigners [*hoi allophyloi*] looked up and saw them coming against them, they went out from their camp to battle. Then the men with Judas blew their trumpets and engaged in battle; *ta ethnē* were crushed, and fled into the plain.

The context is a battle between Judas and his company of three thousand men (*andrasin*; 4:6) and the "five thousand infantry and one thousand picked cavalry" led by Gorgias (4:1). In the passage just quoted, *ta ethnē* stands in parallel with *hoi allophyloi* ("foreigners"—a plurality of foreign individuals) and thus serves to identify those who "were crushed and fled into the plain" as a group, not of nations, but of non-Jewish soldiers. Similarly, the result of another battle was that Simon and his troops "pursued them to the gate of Ptolemais; as many as three thousand of the *ethnē* fell, and he despoiled them" (5:22). Again, soldiers, not nations.[122]

Turning to 2 Maccabees, in 2 Macc 6:4 we read: "For the temple was filled with debauchery and reveling by the *ethnē*, who dallied with prostitutes and had intercourse with women within the sacred precincts, and besides brought in things for sacrifice that were unfit." Clearly those who were dallying with the prostitutes were individuals and not nations. Individuals are also in view in 2 Macc 14:14: "And the *ethnē* throughout Judea, who had fled before Judas, flocked to join Nicanor, thinking that the misfortunes and calamities of the Jews would mean prosperity for themselves."[123]

Instances of this usage are by no means restricted to 1 and 2 Maccabees. Third Maccabees contains an account of a letter written by King Ptolemy Philopator to his Egyptian subjects, announcing harsh measures against the Jewish residents in Egypt. The announcement was greeted with great joy by the local non-Jewish residents: "In every place, then, where this decree arrived, a feast at public expense was arranged for the *ethnē* with shouts and gladness" (3 Macc 4:1). In the Psalms of Solomon, the psalmist laments the incursion of Pompey and his soldiers into Jerusalem and the temple: "Foreign *ethnē* went up to your place of sacrifice; they arrogantly trampled [it] with their sandals"; "*ethnē* insulted Jerusalem, trampling her down"; "let it be enough, Lord, to make your hand heavy on Jerusalem by bringing *ethnē* [upon her]" (2:2, 19, 22).[124] In each case, *ethnē* denotes groups of non-Jewish individuals, not nations.[125]

---

122. For other instances, see 1 Macc 3:10, 25, 52, 58; 5:9-10; 14:36.

123. The use of the masculine article with the neuter noun *ethnē* (*hoi de ... ethnē*) underlines the fact that individuals are in view. Other instances of the usage appear in 2 Macc 8:9, 16; 12:13.

124. A curious use of the singular appears in Psalms of Solomon 7:6: "While your name lives among us, ... *ethnos* will not overcome us."

125. Although the Apocalypse of Abraham is extant only in Old Slavonic, it is plausible

Several other instances have to do with sexual activity. The *Biblical Antiquities* of Pseudo-Philo contains an account of Tamar's pregnancy in which her motivation is explained in this way: "For her intent was not fornication, but being unwilling to separate from the sons of Israel she reflected and said, 'It is better for me to die for having intercourse with my father-in-law than to have intercourse with gentiles [*gentibus*]'" (9.5). In a description of end-time woes found in the Testament of Moses, among the calamities to be expected are these: "And their wives will be divided among the gentiles [*gentibus*] and their young sons will be cut by physicians to bring forward their foreskins" (8.3).[126]

Sexual intercourse with non-Jews is the focus of an extended passage in Jubilees (30:1-17). The statement of particular interest here appears after the account of Dinah and the men of Shechem, as the angel of the presence instructs Moses: "And you, Moses, command the children of Israel and exhort them not to give any of their daughters to the gentiles [Latin: *gentibus*], and not to take for their sons any of the daughters of the gentiles [Latin: *gentium*] because that is contemptible before the Lord" (Jubilees 30:11). While it is possible that the second use of *gentes* in this sentence is to be read as nations rather than individuals ("daughters of non-Jewish nations"; also vv. 13-14), individuals are decidedly in view in the first clause (where *gentes* stands in parallel with "daughters"). The same is to be said of another passage dealing with separation from non-Jews, this time in terms of social rather than sexual intercourse: "Separate yourself from the gentiles [Latin: *gentibus*], and do not eat with them, and do not perform deeds like theirs. And do not become associates of theirs. Because their deeds are defiled, and all of their ways are contaminated, and despicable, and abominable" (Jubilees 22:16).[127]

---

that *gôyîm* stood in the original of 27:1: "And from its left side [i.e., of the visual depiction seen by Abraham] a crowd of heathens ran out and they captured men, women, and children who were on its right side [i.e., the side representing Abraham's descendants]."

126. This is the probable reading. The Latin MS reads *diisdonare*, which *Old Testament Pseudepigrapha* translator Priest (apparently) interprets as *diis donare* (to give to the gods); thus "And their wives will be given to the gods of the nations." Although this reading cannot be dismissed entirely, it seems to require the genitive (*gentium* rather than *gentibus*). The reading preferred here follows Tromp, who has argued persuasively for *disdonare*, understood as a synonym for *didare* (to divide). See Johannes Tromp, *The Assumption of Moses: A Critical Edition with Commentary*, SVTP 10 (Leiden: Brill, 1993), 218-19.

127. In literature that is extant only in translation, one cannot always be sure of the original lying behind a word such as *gentes*. Given the midrashic character of Jubilees, however, one can be reasonably certain that *gentes* renders the Hebrew *gôyîm*. Jubilees 12:22-23, which contains the statement "all the nations of the earth will bless themselves by you," clearly is a repetition of Gen 12:1-3. Although the Latin version of this passage

GENTILE CHRISTIAN IDENTITY

Three of the seven or eight instances of the usage in the Qumran literature have to do with social separation from the *gôyîm*, seen as individuals. Two of these appear in the Damascus Document: "No one <should stay> in a place close to *gôyîm* [*lgwyym*] on the sabbath" (CD XI, 14-15); "No one should sell clean animals or birds to *gôyîm* [*lgwyym*] lest they sacrifice them" (CD XII, 8-9). The third (4Q271 frag. 5 I, 9) repeats the injunction in CD XI, 14-15. 4QIsaiah Pesher interprets Isa 10:33-34 as follows: "Its interpretation concerns the] Kittim, wh[o] will be pla[ced] in the hands of Israel, and the meek [of the earth . . .] all the *gôyîm* [*kwl hgwyym*] and soldiers [*gbwrym*] will weaken and [their] he[art] will melt" (4Q161 frag. 8-10, 1-4). Here the parallelism between *gôyîm* and "soldiers" suggests strongly that the *gôyîm* are also to be seen as a plurality of individuals. In the case of 4Q159, while the manuscript is quite fragmentary, the fact that it seems to rework Lev 25:47-55, which deals with an impoverished Israelite selling himself into slavery, suggests that *gôyîm* refers to individuals: "And if [. . . to a] foreigner [*gr*] or the descendant of a [foreign] fam[ily . . .] in the presence of Is[rael.] They are [no]t to serve gentiles [*hgwyym*]; with . . . [. . . from the land of] Egypt and commanded them not be sold for the price of a slave" (4Q159 frag. 2-4, 1-3).[128] Finally, there are two passages in the Temple Scroll in which members are commanded not to behave as the *gôyîm* behave: "And you shall not do as the *gôyîm* [*hgwyym*] do: they bury their dead in every place, they even bury them in the middle of their houses; instead you shall keep places apart within your land where you shall bury your dead" (11QTemple[a] XLVIII, 11-13); "You shall not behave in your land as the *gôyîm* [*hgwyym*] behave; in every place they sacrifice, and plant asheroth for themselves, and set up for themselves stelae, and place hewn stones in order to bow down before them, and build for themselves" (11QTemple[a] LI, 19-21). In both cases, although there is a representational character to the usage—that is, this is how the *gôyîm* behave; these actions typify the nations as a whole—the actions of the *gôyîm* nevertheless are carried out by individuals (e.g., burying the dead in the middle of their houses; constructing various things for themselves).

This representational overtone to the use of *gôyîm* with reference to individuals, which is apparent as well in one or two of the texts already cited,[129]

---

is not extant (unlike Jubilees 30), the Ethiopic term for nations is the same as in Jubilees 22:16 and 30:11; see the text in James C. VanderKam, *The Book of Jubilees: English and Ethiopic*, CSCO 510-511 (Leuven: Peeters, 1989).

128. 4Q228 frag. 1 II, 1-2 is probably too fragmentary to include here: "[. . .] flesh and not the race of the nation[s] [*mšpḥt hgwyym*]." Is this a race made up of non-Jewish individuals?

129. Especially Jubilees 22:16: "Separate yourself from the gentiles (*gentibus*), and do

is thrown into sharper relief by some additional passages where one finds not simply representational overtones but a more clearly representational usage. In these passages, *nations*, usually articular and without modification, is used in very specific contexts, most often with reference to a very specific event involving a restricted number of people. One instance appears already in Israel's Scriptures; in Lam 1:10, the prophet speaks of the desecration of the temple as the work of "the nations" (*gôyîm*, *ethnē*). Although those who "invaded her sanctuary" were a group of Babylonian soldiers, the author sees it as the work of "the nations," categorically considered. Likewise, in 1 Macc 2:12 Mattathias laments: "And see, our holy place, our beauty, and our glory have been laid waste; the *ethnē* have profaned them." The temple was profaned by a specific group, the agents of Antiochus IV; the text seems to view them, however, as representatives of the nations in general. A little later, after the recapture of the temple, Judas and his companions, deliberating over what to do with the altar, "thought it best to tear it down, so that it would not be a lasting shame to them that the *ethnē* had defiled it" (1 Macc 4:45). Again, the actions of a very specific group of non-Jews is probably being portrayed as the work of the nations as a whole. The Epistle of Jeremiah provides another case in point: "Now in Babylon you will see gods made of silver and gold and wood, which people carry and which cause the *ethnē* to fear" (Ep Jer 1:4).[130]

To be sure, it is sometimes difficult to draw a sharp line between this set of representational texts and those that clearly refer to a collectivity of individuals. Even in the latter, the representational element is not entirely absent. Those *ethnē* who consorted with prostitutes in the Jerusalem temple (2 Macc 6:4), for example, or who "trampled [the sanctuary] with their sandals" (Psalms of Solomon 2:2) were not simply foreigners, they were typical representatives of the nations—the ethnic other from whom Israel was to remain separate and whose ways Israel was to shun. Rather than making a sharp distinction, then, between representative and individual usage, it is probably more appropriate to recognize the presence of both individual and representative elements in all these passages,

---

not eat with them, and do not perform deeds like theirs. And do not become associates of theirs. Because their deeds are defiled, and all of their ways are contaminated, and despicable, and abominable" (Jubilees 22:16); perhaps also Psalms of Solomon 2:22.

130. Literally, "which, being carried on shoulders, cause the *ethnē* to fear." Other instances of the representational use of the term appear in 1 Macc 2:40, 44; 4:7, 54, 60; 6:53; 14:36; 3 Macc 6:9; 4 Baruch 6:19; 7:37. In a related but distinguishable category, 1 Macc 1:14 speaks of the gymnasium in Jerusalem as having been constructed "according to the customs of the *ethnē*," even though the custom in question pertained to a single ethnic group, the Greeks.

with the balance shifting from case to case as we move from, say, 2 Macc 6:4 (specific activity pertaining to non-Jewish individuals) to 11QTemple^a XLVIII, 11–13 (typical gentile behavior) to 1 Macc 4:45 (activity pertaining to individual non-Jews seen as representatives of the nations as a whole).

These nuances notwithstanding, the basic development—one in which a word that in its singular form denoted a nation came to be used in the plural to denote a set of individuals (rather than nations)—is curious and requires some explanation. It is not as if there were no alternatives; both Hebrew and Greek already provided other ways of denoting the non-Jewish other (Heb. *nokrî, bennēkār*; Gk. *allophylos, allogenēs*, etc.). Why did *gôyîm* and *ethnē* come to denote collectivities of non-Jewish individuals when other terms were already available for the purpose? Further, these other terms had the advantage of referring to individuals in their basic sense and thus of being able to denote not only non-Jews in the plural but also individual non-Jews. *Ethnē* is quite awkward in this respect; in its singular form, the term always denotes a single nation rather than a single, non-Jewish individual. In other words, there is no singular equivalent to the plural *ethnē* when used with reference to individuals.[131]

Two observations can be made about this development. First, the fact that the usage was able to establish itself despite these obstacles seems to suggest that *gôyîm* and *ethnē* had crystallized as categorical terms for the non-Jewish other to such an extent that generic terms for foreigners simply were not adequate to express the covenantal binary. By denoting individual non-Jews as *gôyîm* or *ethnē*, these texts characterize them as members of the (non-Jewish) nations. What this choice of designation accomplished was to link these groups of non-Jewish individuals with that scriptural category—the nations (*haggôyîm, ta ethnē*)—that, more than any other, served to give Israel its distinct identity.

The second observation has to do with the process of development. Although it would be difficult to prove conclusively, it seems plausible to suggest that the fully representational use—actions of a group of non-Jewish individuals portrayed as actions carried out, in a representational sense, by the non-Jewish nations as a whole—is to be seen as an intermediate step in the process. In that it uses the term *nations* with respect to individuals only indirectly, this usage can be seen both as a more natural extension of the term's semantic range and as providing a plausible basis for a further extension to individuals directly. The fact that

---

131. The same can be said of *gôyîm* in the prerabbinic period. To be sure, references to a non-Jew in the singular are rare in our literature (except for rabbinic literature, on which see below): *allogenēs* (Psalms of Solomon 17:28; Luke 17:18); *allophylos* (Acts 10:28); *ethnikos* (Matt 18:17). In Gal 2:14, Paul resorts to a circumlocution with *ethnikōs*.

evidence for (primarily) representational use (Lam 1:10) predates any evidence for (primarily) individual use is at least consistent with this explanation.

This brings us to rabbinic literature and a further stage in the development. As with earlier Jewish literature, *gôyîm* is used in Tannaitic literature to denote not only nations—especially *haggôyîm*,[132] the non-Jewish nations as a whole—but also pluralities of non-Jewish individuals. Several examples: "A man stipulates concerning his *erub* and says, 'If gentiles [*gôyîm*] come from the east, my *erub* is at the west. [If they come] from the west, my *erub* is at the east'" (m. Eruvin 3:5). "A city in which Israelites and gentiles [*gôyîm*] live—the collectors of funds for the support of the poor collect equally from Israelites and from gentiles [*gôyîm*], for the sake of peace" (t. Gittin 3:13–14).[133] In addition, however, the Tannaim take the development one step further, as they frequently use the singular *gôy* to denote an individual non-Jew. The well-known injunction of R. Judah is a case in point: "A man must recite three benedictions every day," the first of which is "Praised [be Thou, O Lord ...] who did not make me a gentile [*gôy*]" (t. Berakhot 6:18). Another is a comment on Exod 12:43 in the Mekilta, where "There shall no alien [*ben-nēkār*] eat thereof" is explained as "meaning both an apostate Jew and a Gentile [*gôy*]" (Mekilta Pisha 15.19–20). This use of *gôy*—which, of course, is familiar to modern ears, given its currency in contemporary English—is common in rabbinic literature.[134]

Given that the more significant extension of the semantic range had already taken place with the use of the plural *gôyîm* to refer to individuals, this further extension to the singular is readily understandable as a logical additional step. Still, it should not be simply taken for granted. To refer to individual foreigners both in the plural and the singular, the rabbis had other terms at their disposal, both drawn from Scripture (*nokrî, nokrîth, ben-nēkār*) and formulations of their own devising.[135] Again one gets the sense that generic terms for *foreigner* did not

---

132. For examples, see above.

133. Also, e.g., m. Pe'ah 2:7; m. Terumot 8:12; m. Ta'anit 3:7; m. Nedarim 4:3; t. Demai 1:12–13; t. Eruvin 3:8; 5:19; t. Pesahim 2:5; t. Ketubbot 3:2; Mekilta Pisha 2.35–50.

134. Other Tannaitic examples: m. Demai 6:10; m. Shabbat 23:4; m. Yevamot 16:5; t. Berakhot 5:31; t. Pe'ah 2:9–11; t. Demai 4:25–27; 6:12, 13; t. Pesahim 2:12; t. Sheqalim 3:11; t. Megillah 2:16; t. Yevamot 14:7; Mekilta Pisha 9.34–37.

135. Especially *'bd kwkbym* (servant of stars; e.g., m. Pe'ah 4:6; m. Demai 3:4) and *'bd glwlym* (servant of idols; e.g., m. Shabbat 1:8; m. Bava Metzi'a 5:6). Somewhat surprisingly, several standard treatments of the gentiles in rabbinic literature pay little attention to the range of terms by which non-Jews are denoted, using the term *gentiles* as the English equivalent for all of them; e.g., Hayes, *Gentile Impurities and Jewish Identities*; Gary G. Porton, *Goyim: Gentiles and Israelites in Mishnah-Tosefta*, BJS 155 (Atlanta: Scholars Press, 1988).

fully capture the fundamental and categorical distinction between us and them that was conveyed by the biblical language of Israel and the nations.

In this connection, it is striking to note that *yiśraēl* (Israel) is often used, in binary constructions with *gôy*, to denote an individual Israelite. To cite just one example, here is a Tosefta passage having to do with laws concerning harvesting and the poor: "[As regards] a gentile [*gôy*] who sold his standing [crop] to an Israelite [literally, "to Israel": *yiśraēl*] for harvesting—[the produce that the Israelite harvests] is subject to designation as *peʾah*" (t. Peʾah 2:9).¹³⁶ Equally striking is that *yiśraēl* can be used in tandem with *gôyîm* to denote Israelites in the plural. We have already seen an example: "A city in which Israelites [*yśrʾl*] and gentiles [*gwyym*] live . . ." (t. Gittin 3:13). In both cases, the representational character of the usage is fully in view: Whenever some Jews live in a city or a Jew has dealings with a non-Jew, Israel—conceived of as a distinct category of human existence—is present. The significance of this for present purposes is that this use of *yiśraēl* serves to underscore the analogous representational use of *gôy*. As with Israel, so with *gôy* and *gôyîm*: the latter have also come to designate a category of human existence sufficiently distinct and fundamental that whenever one or more non-Jews live in a city with Jews or have dealings with them, one can say that the human category itself is present.¹³⁷ While this does not mean that such non-Jews are perceived or portrayed any less as individuals, the usage serves to highlight their membership in a particular class and thus to ascribe to them a distinctive (non-Jewish) identity. This combination of representative and individual elements in the rabbinic use of *yiśraēl* and *gôy* adds further plausibility to the suggestion that the emergence of a primarily representational sense of *gôyîm* and *ethnē* (e.g., Lam 1:10) paved the way for the two further developments that we have been tracing—first, the use of *gôyîm* and *ethnē* to denote pluralities of non-Jews, and then the rabbinic use of *gôy* to denote an individual non-Jew (with distinct connotations in each case).

As was mentioned above, however, these distinctive uses of *gôyîm* and *ethnē* with reference to the non-Jewish nations—both the original scriptural usage and the later developments—are almost completely absent from a significant body of

---

136. Other examples: m. Shevi'it 5:7; m. Shabbat 23:4; t. Berakhot 5:31; t. Demai 6:13; t. Pesahim 2:12; t. Sheqalim 3:11; t. Yevamot 14:7; Mekilta Pisha 15.19. The same use of *yiśraēl* is found with other terms for the non-Jew: e.g., m. Demai 5:9; 6:1; m. Bava Qamma 4:3.

137. This point is well made, and in much more detail, by Rosen-Zvi and Ophir in their significant monograph, *Goy*, which was preceded by several pioneering essays: "Goy: Toward a Genealogy," *Diné Israel* 28 (2011): 69–122; "Paul and the Invention of the Gentiles," *JQR* 105 (2015): 1–41.

Jewish literature composed in Greek. To be sure, the usage does appear in some Hellenistic Jewish literature, notably Wisdom and the Testaments of the Twelve Patriarchs.[138] It is virtually absent, however, from Philo, Josephus, the Jewish Sibyllines (Sibylline Oracles 3, 4, and 5), and the Letter of Aristeas.[139] The cases of Philo and Josephus are particularly striking, given that extensive components of their writings are directly related to Scripture.

As we have seen, this literature represents one end of the spectrum of Jewish ethnography—marked by apologetic rather than polemic, presenting a softer-edged boundary between the Jewish people and the rest of the human race, preserving the binary distinction between Jews and non-Jews while relativizing it beneath a more universal canopy of ethical monotheism, all in the attempt to negotiate a place for Israel and the Jewish people on the ethnographical maps of the Greco-Roman world. The absence of the distinctive biblical vocabulary for this binary distinction (i.e., Israel/the nations) needs to be seen within this context.[140]

Looking a little more closely at vocabulary usage, we note first that, in contrast to the tendency in the LXX, Israel is frequently designated as a nation (*ethnos*).[141]

---

138. Wis 10:5; 12:12; 14:11; 15:15; Testament of Levi 14:1-4; 15:1; Testament of Judah 24:6; Testament of Zebulun 9:8; Testament of Naphtali 8:3-6.

139. The possible exceptions are very few and do not require detailed examination here. In Philo, they are restricted to the more esoteric, allegorical portion of his work (*On the Posterity of Cain* 89-93; *On the Migration of Abraham* 53-61; *Questions and Answers on Genesis* 3.60; *Questions and Answers on Exodus* 2.22), where they echo the language of the biblical text under discussion; see Runia, "Philo and the Gentiles." In the case of Josephus, the clearest possibility comes in his description of Agrippa I, who "made it a point of honour to be high-minded towards *ethnē*" (*Jewish Antiquities* 19.328). Feldman's LCL rendering ("gentiles") seems plausible. The other possible exception is *Jewish Antiquities* 13.200, where Simon declares his confidence that, with God's help, he will be able to take Judas's place as leader, to defeat Israel's enemies, and to preserve the temple, adding: "for I see that the nations [*ta ethnē*] hold you in contempt as being without a leader, and are eager to make war." While specific nations are in view, the articular and unmodified form is at least consistent with the more categorical biblical usage.

140. For the depiction of Israel and the Jews in Philo and Josephus, see especially Ellen Birnbaum, *The Place of Judaism in Philo's Thought: Israel, Jews, and Proselytes* (Atlanta: Scholars Press, 1996); Paul Spilsbury, *The Image of the Jew in Flavius Josephus' Paraphrase of the Bible*, TSAJ 69 (Tübingen: Mohr Siebeck, 1998).

141. Philo: e.g., *Who Is the Heir?* 174, 278-79; *On Flight and Finding* 185; *On the Change of Names* 191; *On Dreams* 1.167; *On the Life of Abraham* 56, 98; *On the Life of Moses* 1.4, 7, 8, 34, 71, 73, 86, 123 ; *On the Special Laws* 1.54, 78; 2.162, 163, 166, 167, 188, 190; 4.179; *On the Virtues* 107; 226; *On Rewards and Punishments* 77; *Against Flaccus* 170; *On the Embassy to*

GENTILE CHRISTIAN IDENTITY

Other terms appear (especially *genos* and *laos*), but *ethnos* is very common.[142] This designation is also implied in a number of instances in which outsiders are referred to as "the other nations,"[143] the implication being that Israel is also one of the nations. On the other side, to designate non-Jewish nations, Philo and Josephus regularly use generic terms for foreigners (*allogenē, alloethnē,* and *allophyloi*).[144] When they use *ethnē* with reference to non-Jewish nations, this is always clearly indicated in the context.

More generally, this literature tends to accept and work within the more widely accepted maps of the human race as a whole. The distinction between Greeks and barbarians,[145] the concepts of the whole inhabited world (*oikoumenē*) and of the human race (usually *to tōn anthrōpōn genos*)—this is the universal conceptual framework within which the Jewish apologists want to locate themselves and the Jewish people.[146] In his exposition of the *Special Laws*, for

---

Gaius 119, 194, 214, 279, 351. Josephus: e.g., *Jewish War* 5.233; 7.423; *Jewish Antiquities* 6.32; 8.120; 10.271, 275, 276; 11.3, 138, 184, 185, 303, 326; 12.7; 13.419; *Against Apion* 1.172; 2.220. In addition, of course, Philo also interprets *ethnos* allegorically, usually with reference to the soul and its characteristics (e.g., *That God Is Unchangeable* 148; *On the Migration of Abraham* 60; *On the Change of Names* 148–50; *On the Life of Moses* 189; *On the Decalogue* 37; *On the Virtues* 186).

142. For *genos*, see, e.g., Letter of Aristeas 6; Philo, *On the Sacrifices of Cain and Abel* 7 (here *genos* is superior to *laos*); *That God Is Unchangeable* 144; *Who Is the Heir?* 272, 278; *On the Life of Abraham* 56; Josephus, *Jewish War* 2.397; *Jewish Antiquities* 2.215–216; 10.183; 11.207, 211; *Against Apion* 1.1, 59. And for *laos*, see, e.g., Philo, *On the Posterity of Cain* 89; *On Planting* 59; *On the Life of Moses* 1.87, 139, 278; 2.165, 225, 271; *On the Virtues* 184–85; *On Rewards and Punishments* 123; Josephus, *Jewish Antiquities* 11.19.

143. Philo, *On the Life of Moses* 1.278; Letter of Aristeas 139. Frequent usages of the term appear in Philo, *On the Life of Joseph* 242; *On the Special Laws* 1.2; 2.123; 3.110; *On the Virtues* 147; and Josephus, *Jewish War* 2.397; *Jewish Antiquities* 5.98; 6.130; 11.285; 12.269.

144. For *allogenē*, see Philo, *Dreams* 1.161; *On the Special Laws* 1.124; *On the Virtues* 147; Josephus, *Jewish War* 2.417. For *alloethnē*, see Philo, *On the Special Laws* 3.29; *On the Embassy to Gaius* 183 (also *heteroethnē*: *On the Special Laws* 4.19; *On the Virtues* 147); Josephus, *Jewish Antiquities* 11.140–152; 12.241; 15.417; 19.330. And for *allophyloi*, see Philo, *On the Special Laws* 1.56; *On the Virtues* 160, 222; *On the Embassy to Gaius* 200, 211; Josephus, *Jewish War* 2.85–86, 412; 3.41; 4.261–62, 397; 5.563; 6.102; 7.351; *Jewish Antiquities* 13.200; 16.2; 18.345; 19.329; 20.256; *Against Apion* 2.122, 209.

145. See, e.g., Philo, *On the Life of Joseph* 56, 134; *On the Special Laws* 1.211; 2.165; *That Every Good Person Is Free* 72–74.

146. For *oikoumenē*, see, e.g., Letter of Aristeas 9; Philo, *On the Life of Abraham* 226; *On the Life of Joseph* 19, 56, 135; *On the Life of Moses* 1.2, 195; 2.205; *On the Special Laws* 2.163; 3.8; Josephus, *Jewish War* 2.362, 364, 382; 4.261–62; 6.442; *Jewish Antiquities* 4.114–16; 8.116; 11.3; 14.110. And for *to tōn anthrōpōn genos*, see, e.g., Letter of Aristeas 190–91, 208,

example, as Philo discusses the laws pertaining to firstfruits, he characterizes the firstfruit offering as something pertaining both to "the land which has been given to the nation to dwell in" and to "the whole earth," and then he draws out its anthropological significance:

> so that it serves that purpose both to the nation [*tou ethnous*] in particular and for the whole human race [*hapantos anthrōpōn genous*] in general. The reason of this is that the Jewish nation [*to Ioudaiōn ethnos*] is to the whole inhabited world [*tēn oikoumenēn*] what the priest is to the State. (*On the Special Laws* 2.162–63)

The idea that the Jewish nation plays a special representative role on behalf of the whole human race or inhabited world comes up frequently in Philo's work.[147] Further, as with the Jewish nation, so with its lawgiver and his laws. Not only is Moses "the best of all lawgivers," surpassing "any that have ever arisen among either the Greeks or the barbarians," but his laws "attract and win the attention of all, of barbarians, of Greeks, of dwellers on the mainland and islands, of nations of the east and the west, of Europe and Asia, of the whole inhabited world [*tēn oikoumenēn*] from end to end."[148] In contrast, say, to Jubilees, where the distinction between the torah and the ways of the nations is qualitative, categorical, and dualistic, here it is quantitative; to say that Moses is "the best of all lawgivers" is to say that Moses and the other lawgivers can be ranged on the same scale, measured according to a common standard.[149]

257, 259; Philo, *On Dreams* 2.230; *On the Life of Moses* 2.25–28; *On the Decalogue* 153; *On the Special Laws* 1.303; *On Rewards and Punishments* 14; *On the Embassy to Gaius* 144; Josephus, *Jewish War* 3.402; *Jewish Antiquities* 3.23; 4.262; 6.61, 342; 8.120; 16.36.

147. See above, n. 47.

148. *On the Life of Moses* 2.12, 17–21. On one occasion, Philo was prepared to locate the Jews on the barbarian side; when speaking of the translation of the Torah into Greek, he says that up to that point, the law was found "in one half only of the human race, the barbarians" (i.e., the Jews; *On the Life of Moses* 2.27). But this is an exception. Katell Berthelot has demonstrated that Philo consistently locates the Jews on the Greek side of the binary; "Grecs, Barbares et Juifs dans l'oeuvre de Philon," in *Philon d'Alexandrie: un penseur à l'intersection des cultures gréco-romaine, orientale, juive et chrétienne*, ed. Baudouin Decharneux and Sabrina Inowlocki (Turnhout: Brepols, 2011), 47–61. Most of Philo's prodigious energy was directed toward the goal of uniting (the Jewish) Moses and (the Greek) Plato and thus of bringing Israel into alignment with the Greek side of the binary.

149. Josephus's presentation of Moses's legislation as an ideal constitution (*politeia*), incorporating "the best of all models" (*Jewish Antiquities* 1.19), moves in this direction as well.

The conviction that the story of the Jewish people belongs within the established frameworks of Greco-Roman discourse is present in Josephus as well. The phrase "Greeks or/and barbarians," for example, often serves as Josephus's way of denoting humanity as a whole: Korah's rebellion against Moses was a sedition with "no parallel whether among Greeks or barbarians."[150] In his paraphrase of Deuteronomy, where Moses warned Israel that if they strayed from the covenant, "the Lord will scatter you among all the nations" (*pasin tois ethnesin*; LXX Deut 4:27), Josephus has Moses declare: "dispersed through the habitable world [*oikoumenēs*], you will fill every land and sea with your servitude" (*Jewish Antiquities* 4.190). Likewise, in his repackaging of Balaam's prophecy, where the biblical narrative spoke in terms of "a people living alone and not reckoning itself among the nations," but "devour[ing] the nations that are its foes" (Num 23:9; 24:8), Josephus's Balaam declares that for Israel "the habitable world [*oikoumenēn*] . . . lies before you as an eternal habitation, and your multitudes shall find abode on islands and from continent to continent, more numerous even than the stars in heaven" (*Jewish Antiquities* 4.116).

Still, as has been noted already, absence of the terminology does not mean absence of the conception. All of this literature retains the clear distinction between Israel and the other nations of the world, a point that requires little justification but can nevertheless be illustrated. According to Philo (as we have seen), "Alexandria and the whole of Egypt had two kinds of inhabitants, us and them" (*Against Flaccus* 43). Abraham had to depart from his native land because God planned to make him the founder of "another race [*genous*] and nation [*ethnous*]," which Philo also describes as a "new race and nation" (*Who Is the Heir?* 278). In Philo's account of the story of Balaam and Balak, Balaam describes the "Hebrews" as a people "not reckoned among other nations [*heterois ethnesin*] . . . because in virtue of the distinction of their peculiar customs they do not mix with others to depart from the way of their fathers" (*On the Life of Moses* 1.278). Tellingly, Philo uses "other nations" to formulate the distinction, even though the biblical account he is following speaks more categorically of the nations (Num 23:9); distinction there may be, but it is not expressed in a binary formulation with the nations.[151] For his part, Josephus also speaks of Abraham's

---

150. *Jewish Antiquities* 4.12; also *Jewish War* 6.199; *Jewish Antiquities* 1.107; 8.284; 11.299; 15.136; 16.177. Of course, this could be read in the sense either that "Greeks and barbarians" constitutes the sum of the non-Jewish nations or that the Jewish people belongs to one or the other (or both). Josephus seems content to leave this ambiguity unresolved.

151. To be sure, he does add the (biblical) term *laos* to the account. In addition, on rare occasions, he reproduces the binary language when he is citing or paraphrasing Scripture—for example, the citation of Deut 32:7-9 in *On Planting* 59.

race (*genos*) as not "mixing with the others" (*Jewish Antiquities* 1.192),[152] and he sums up his work in the *Antiquities* with the declaration "that no one else, either Jew or foreigner [*allophylos*], would have been equal to the task" (*Jewish Antiquities* 20.262). The pairing of *Jews* and *foreigners* appears a number of times in the *Jewish War*, albeit in an ironic way, as Josephus contrasts the impieties of the Jewish rebels with the reverence of the foreigners (*Jewish War* 4.261-62; 5.563-64; 6.102).

In his study of Philo's attitude to the gentiles, Runia observes that, "although the binary opposition of Jew and non-Jew is central to his thinking in the religious, political and cultural domains, he has not developed a clear and constant terminology to express it."[153] While not disagreeing with Runia, for present purposes I would prefer to say that Philo and those like him deliberately avoided the "clear and constant terminology" that was readily available in the biblical tradition.[154]

Why was this so? In part, no doubt, it was because the biblical usage was in-house language. The distinctive Jewish use of *the nations* took a common term and assigned a meaning that would have struck outsiders as odd (one might even say foreign). Such in-house antilanguage might be useful in maintaining a stout boundary between us and them,[155] but it would pose a significant obstacle for those with an interest in negotiating a place for themselves in social space shared with others.[156] The other side of this coin is that, regardless of whether the ethnological terminology of Greco-Roman discourse met the criterion for being "clear and constant," it could hardly be avoided. Anyone attempting to engage in the kind of apologetic projects that we find in the massive works of Philo

---

152. Here with specific reference to circumcision. Also worth mentioning here are the statements about the prohibition of marriage to foreigners (*allophylos, alloethnēs*; *Jewish Antiquities* 11.140-41, 145, 151-52; 18.345). A similar concern with separation from outsiders is present in Letter of Aristeas 139: God "surrounded us with unbroken palisades and iron walls to prevent our mixing with any of the other nations [*tōn allōn ethnōn*] in any matter."

153. Runia, "Philo and the Gentiles," 43.

154. To be sure, Runia is fully cognizant of this; his previous sentence reads: "There is no equivalent in his writings for the opposition *'am/gôyîm* in the Hebrew Bible or the opposition Jew/Gentile in the New Testament." My concern with terminology here is a little different from his.

155. For the term *antilanguage*, see Michael A. K. Halliday, *Language as Social Semiotic: The Social Interpretation of Language and Meaning* (London: Edward Arnold, 1978).

156. Indeed, as Runia notes, in situations of social tension and conflict (as did break out in Alexandria), such language could exacerbate the situation; "Philo and the Gentiles," 44.

and Josephus would necessarily need to use this terminology and the category structures undergirding them.

Of course, any non-Jews who associated closely with a Jewish community—the "multitude of Greeks," say, who were attracted to Jewish "religious ceremonies" in Antioch (*Jewish War* 7.45), or the "multitudes of others" who joined Jews in an annual celebration of the giving of the law in Alexandria (*On the Life of Moses* 2.41–42)—would necessarily become familiar with the distinctive biblical usage. It is difficult to keep in-house language to yourself when you invite others into the house. One wonders what the houseguests would have thought of it.

This question is important for its own sake, and we will return to it in chapter 6. Our primary interest in that chapter will have to do with a more particular subset of non-Jews—those who became Christ-believers, especially in the early stages of the movement—and with their perception of the identity ascribed to them as *ethnē* by Jewish Christ-believers. Even so, as we consider their perception of this ascribed identity, it will be helpful to give some consideration to the question of what non-Jews more generally thought about *ethnē* as an identity term.

As the next step, however, we turn our attention to the early Jewish Christ-believers—to their conceptions of how non-Jews might become Christ-believers as well and thus to the identity (or range of identities) that they constructed for those non-Jews who were prepared to do so.

CHAPTER 4

Ethnē *as an Identity Ascribed to Non-Jews:*
By Jewish Christ-Believers

The discussion carried out in the previous chapter provides the broad contours of the identity ascribed to non-Jewish Christ-believers by means of the term *ethnē*. This identity was filtered, however, through the more specific lens represented by the self-definitional frameworks of the Jewish Christ-believers and the various ways in which they conceived of the inclusion of gentile members. In this chapter, then, we continue our investigation of identity ascription, with the goal of identifying the range of identities ascribed by Jewish Christ-believers to gentile believers, paying particular attention to the term *ethnē*. Given these specific purposes, this is not the place to attempt anything like a thoroughgoing history of the Jewish Christ-movement—an enterprise that is at least conceivable up to the Judean revolt against Rome (a period for which Paul's letters and the Acts of the Apostles provide some source material), but which becomes much more difficult after that point.[1] Nevertheless, in order to construct a detailed picture of the range of ascribed identities, it will first be necessary to describe, at least in broad strokes, the emergence of the movement, the dynamics of its identity construction with respect to the larger Jewish community, the beginnings of a gentile mission, and the debates surrounding it. Then we will go on to construct a typology of the various ways in which Jewish Christ-groups conceived of their relationship to the rest of the Jewish world and the terms on which gentiles might be included. Our emphasis here will be placed on periods

---

1. A difficulty compounded by the fact that Josephus's narrative ends at this point as well.

151

and situations in which Jewish Christ-believers were in a position of sufficient strength that they were able effectively to ascribe identity to gentile believers. We will conclude with a few additional observations on the usage of *ethnē* and related terms in the pertinent literature.

Earliest Jewish Christ-Communities and the Gentiles

Of course, to embark on such an enterprise is to find oneself confronted immediately by the problem of sources. Our two most pertinent sources for the period are also highly problematic.[2] While Paul represents our earliest source, he provides us with a very partial picture (in both senses of the term) of early Jewish Christ-believers and their communities. He was clearly an outsider to the Christ-communities in Jerusalem and Judea, a situation reinforced both by his prior activity as a zealous "persecutor of the *ekklēsia*" (Phil 3:6; cf. Gal 1:13–14) and his subsequent career as a self-proclaimed "apostle to the *ethnē*" (Rom 11:13). His relationships with "those who were already apostles before [him]" (Gal 1:17) were evidently strained, at least in part as a result of his own insistence on equal apostolic status (1 Cor 9:1; 15:8–11) and his less than deferential attitude toward them (Gal 2:6; 1 Cor 15:10). And while he was able to come to some sort of working relationship with the Jerusalem apostles (Gal 2:1–10), the terms on which he carried out his mission to the *ethnē* were vigorously resisted by a segment of the Jerusalem *ekklēsia* (Gal 2:3–5) that he referred to as "false brothers" (2:4) and (probably) "the circumcision group" (*tous ek peritomēs*; 2:12). In addition, while he does provide us with essential information on the earliest communities of Jewish Christ-believers (on which more in a moment), this information is piecemeal and often allusive.

At first glance, Acts seems to provide us with what is lacking in Paul's letters—a continuous and sequential narrative of the beginnings, growth, and expansion of the movement, with a particular interest in the inclusion of non-Jews and the emergence of gentile Christianity. A closer examination, however, reveals that the narrative is substantially episodic, the impression of continuity and comprehensiveness being provided in major part by the recurring summary statements and speeches that serve to tie the individual episodes together.[3] Pre-

---

2. Of course, sources in addition to Paul's letters and the Acts of the Apostles need to be kept in view as well, especially the Gospels, which are each shaped by the later contexts in which they were written and contain elements that point beyond the time period covered by the narratives themselves.

3. Summary statements especially in the first half of the narrative (2:43–47; 4:32–35;

sumably this episodic character is due at least in some measure to the limitations of the author's sources. In addition, however, Luke devotes the second half of the narrative (from ch. 13 to the end) almost entirely to Paul's missionary activity, with the result that the story of the movement elsewhere is left largely in the shadows.[4] Although Luke clearly wants to make the point that the decisive opening to the gentile world was firmly established prior to and apart from Paul's own mission,[5] his interest in these other manifestations of Christ-belief among non-Jews tends to fall away once Paul appears fully on the scene. We hear nothing at all of the ongoing results of the apparently successful mission to Samaria (8:5-25), a silence that is both surprising and disappointing—surprising, in view of the position of Samaria as an intervening step between Jerusalem and "the ends of the earth" in the mission sequence set out in Acts 1:8, and disappointing, in view of the fact that the inclusion of Samaritans must have necessitated some consideration of their status as (semi-)outsiders.[6] Likewise, the evangelization of the Ethiopian eunuch (8:26-39), which also raises questions of status (not to mention curiosity about the spread of the faith to North Africa), receives no narrative follow-up.[7] We hear very little about the travels and activity of Peter

---

5:12-16, 42; 6:7; 9:31; 12:24), and speeches appearing in significant portions of chs. 2, 3, 7, 10, 11, 13, 17, 20, 22, 26.

4. I use the traditional name *Luke* for convenience. On the gentile identity of the author, see below.

5. Especially through the experience of Peter (10:1-11:18).

6. While the district of Samaria contained many non-Jews (especially the city of Samaria, renamed Sebaste by Herod), it is probable that ethnic Samaritans are in view here. The issue is complicated somewhat by a textual variant in Acts 8:5 (involving the presence of the definite article: "*the* city of Samaria"), which might be taken as a reference to the city itself; for details and discussion, see C. K. Barrett, *A Critical and Exegetical Commentary on the Acts of the Apostles*, ICC (Edinburgh: T&T Clark, 1994-98), 1:396, 401-3. But the emphasis on the story of Cornelius as the point at which the door is opened to gentiles makes it highly unlikely that the narrative has to do with non-Jewish residents of Samaria (though see the next note). On the question of status, in comparison to gentiles, neither circumcision nor torah observance would have presented a fundamental issue. Still, despite Luke's silence, one wonders whether some Jewish Christ-believers would have insisted that Samaritans display allegiance to the Jerusalem temple rather than to Mount Gerizim as a condition of membership (cf. John 4:19-21). On Luke's particular interest in Samaritans (Luke 9:52-55; 10:30-37; 17:11-19; Acts 8:4-25) and Samaria (Acts 1:8; 8:1; 9:31; 15:3), see Reinhard Pummer, *The Samaritans: A Profile* (Grand Rapids: Eerdmans, 2016), 37-41.

7. Despite the eunuch's evident attachment to Judaism (having traveled to Jerusalem in order to worship and possessing a scroll of Isaiah), Luke clearly portrays him as a

after his departure from Jerusalem (12:17), nor are we given much information on how it was that James came to have the level of authority in the Jerusalem community that is simply assumed in chapter 15 (cf. 1:14; 12:17). Although Barnabas plays an important leadership role in the ethnically mixed church in Antioch (11:23–26) and in the mission activity that it commissioned (13:1–14:28), after his break with Paul (15:36–41) he disappears completely from view. Despite the important role played by the Jerusalem church in validating and overseeing the gentile mission (Acts 11:1, 18, 19–26), it comes into the picture again only when it is part of Paul's story (ch. 15; 18:22; chs. 21–23). And despite the importance of the church in Antioch to this point, it disappears from view as well, except on one occasion when Paul's itinerary took him through the city (18:22–23). On the origins or nature of the Christ-communities in Damascus (9:10–22), Galilee (9:31), Puteoli (28:13–14), or Rome (28:15) we are given no information at all.

Further, it is readily apparent that Luke's account has been shaped by discernible emphases, some of which stand in considerable tension with impressions conveyed by Paul's letters. The account in Acts tends to emphasize peaceful concord among the early Jewish believers; the centrality of the Jerusalem community in the supervision of the growing movement, a role that is generally recognized and accepted; and the smooth progression of the apostolic witness from Jerusalem, through all Judea and Samaria, and to the ends of the earth (cf. 1:8).

The distinctiveness of these Lukan themes can be seen in his account of Paul's (Saul's) early years as a Christ-believer. According to Luke, the purpose of Paul's first visit to Jerusalem (Acts 9:26–30) was to "join the disciples" (v. 26). After some resistance on the part of the whole community ("they were all afraid of him"), his acceptance into the community was facilitated by Barnabas, a member of the Jerusalem community (cf. 4:36–37), who from this point took Paul under his wing as a kind of protégé. After a period of active preaching both within the community ("he went in and out among them in Jerusalem"; 9:28) and outside it

---

gentile; a Jewish resident of Ethiopia would not be identified simply as an Ethiopian (*anēr Aithiops*). But Luke also seems to see Cornelius as the first gentile convert (11:18). Might the Ethiopian have been a proselyte? If so, one would have expected Luke to mention it (cf. 6:5). Further, if *eunochos* is taken literally (a castrated person) rather than as a court title (which is possible), he could not have been a proselyte; according to Deut 23:1, eunuchs are not to be "admitted to the assembly of the Lord" (cf. Isa 56:3–5). Perhaps the story of gentile conversion reflected by Luke's sources is much less linear than the Acts account implies. For a thorough discussion of these issues (together with an argument that Luke does see the Ethiopian as a gentile, foreshadowing the progress of the gospel to "the ends of the earth" [1:8]), see Craig S. Keener, *Acts: An Exegetical Commentary* (Grand Rapids: Baker Academic, 2012–15), 2:1541–71.

with Hellenistic Jews (9:29), he departed Jerusalem for Tarsus. When the church in Antioch began a deliberate program of evangelizing non-Jews, the Jerusalem church commissioned Barnabas to assess the development on its behalf. After granting his approval, Barnabas sought out Paul to help with the new development (11:19-26). When the church in Antioch decided to sponsor a similar evangelizing program elsewhere, it in turn commissioned "Barnabas and Saul" (13:2) to carry it out. It is during the account of this missionary venture that Luke's focus shifts to Paul ("Paul and his companions" [13:13]; "Paul and Barnabas" [13:42]), who now emerges as the dominant figure.[8] Even so, when controversy breaks out over whether gentile believers needed to become circumcised and the decisive meeting takes place in Jerusalem, Paul recedes into the background; while "Barnabas and Paul" have an opportunity to recount "all the signs and wonders that God had done through them among the *ethnē*" (15:12), it is Peter who proves to be the decisive witness and James who makes the decision.[9]

The contrasts with Paul's own account are striking. In the substantial biographical narrative in his letter to the Galatians (1:13-2:14), he minimizes his contacts with the Jerusalem church, emphasizes his independence as an apostle, and downplays his relationship with Barnabas. Whereas Luke speaks of the interval between Paul's Damascus experience and his trip to Jerusalem in terms of days (albeit "a considerable number" of them [*hēmerai hikanai*]; Acts 9:23), Paul not only speaks in terms of years ("after three years"; Gal 1:18) but also adds that he deliberately stayed away from Jerusalem, choosing to go into Arabia and return to Damascus (1:17) rather than to go up to Jerusalem to meet with "those who were already apostles before [him]." Further, he presents his eventual first visit to Jerusalem as a private one—meeting only with Peter and James, and remaining "unknown by sight to the churches of Judea" (1:18-24). While he mentions that Barnabas was present with him on his second visit (2:1),[10] his own role is emphasized: "I went up in response to a revelation" (2:2); "I laid before them . . . the gospel that I proclaim among the *ethnē*" (2:2); "they saw that I had been entrusted with the gospel for the circumcised" (2:7). Although "James and Cephas and John . . . gave to me and Barnabas the right hand of fellowship,"[11] it was because they had "recognized the grace that had been given to me" (2:9). The final account in Paul's narrative is a situation of conflict in Antioch where Paul

---

8. And, not coincidentally, that he shifts from *Saul* to *Paul* in referring to him (13:9).

9. Peter speaks first (15:7-11), and it is his account to which James refers ("Simeon has related . . ."; 15:14) in making his decision ("I have decided . . ."; 15:19).

10. It is not necessary here to raise the question of how the two visits referred to in Galatians might relate to the first three visits in Acts (9:26; 11:29-30; 15:2).

11. The NRSV inexplicably inverts the order ("Barnabas and me").

found himself in sharp opposition with Peter, a delegation from James (and thus indirectly with James himself), and even Barnabas (2:11–14). The closest that Acts gets to a scene such as this is a "sharp disagreement" between Paul and Barnabas that developed not over "the truth of the gospel" (Gal 2:14) but simply over the suitability of John Mark as a mission assistant (Acts 15:36–41).

Of course, a recognition of the distinct thematic characteristics of Acts and of the striking differences with information derived from Paul's letters goes back at least as far as the work of F. C. Baur and his students in the mid-nineteenth century,[12] and discussion of the usefulness of Acts as a historical source has been an ongoing issue in the study of Christian origins since then.[13] For present purposes, we need not tarry unduly over the issue, a discussion of which would take us too far afield. There is general recognition that Luke has access to independent information on the first generation of the Christ-movement. While it is probably not possible to identify written sources with any precision,[14] we are justified in thinking more generally of several bodies of traditional source material (especially one associated with Peter, and another with Antioch).[15] While we need to recognize Luke's distinctive themes, biases, and purposes, we are in a much better position than were Baur and his scholarly contemporaries to recognize that, when read in the light of ancient historiographical standards and practices, Luke's stated intention to write a historical narrative (cf. Luke 1:1–4) is not necessarily nullified by his apologetic concerns.[16] Interpreted critically and with caution, Acts can be used, along with other sources, to provide at least a general picture of early Jewish Christ-believers and the inclusion of gentiles.

Part of the critical use of Acts involves a recognition that Paul's letters need

---

12. See the introductory chapter of F. C. Baur, *Paul: The Apostle of Jesus Christ* (London: Williams & Norgate, 1876), translated from the 2nd German edition (*Paulus, Der Apostel Jesu Christi* [Stuttgart: Becher & Müller, 1845]) by A. Menzies. His approach to Acts was worked out more thoroughly by his students Matthias Schneckenburger and Eduard Zeller.

13. See the pertinent sections in William Baird, *History of New Testament Research* (Minneapolis: Fortress, 1992–2003).

14. Harnack's treatment continues to be a point of reference; see Adolf Harnack, *The Acts of the Apostles*, trans. J. R. Wilkinson (London: Williams & Norgate, 1909), 162–202.

15. On Luke's sources more generally, together with thorough discussions of Acts and history, see Barrett, *Acts of the Apostles*, 1:30–56; 2:xxiv–lxii; James D. G. Dunn, *Beginning from Jerusalem*, vol. 2 of *Christianity in the Making* (Grand Rapids: Eerdmans, 2009), 64–98.

16. On Luke-Acts as apologetic history, see Gregory E. Sterling, *Historiography and Self-Definition: Josephos, Luke-Acts, and Apologetic Historiography*, NovTSup 64 (Leiden: Brill, 1992).

Ethnē as an Identity Ascribed to Non-Jews: By Jewish Christ-Believers

to be given a certain measure of priority.[17] Not only do his letters represent our earliest sources, but they also provide first-person accounts relating to the Christ-movement that go back to the earliest days. Paul's Damascus experience,[18] which was preceded by a period of persecuting activity, probably took place not more than three or four years after the crucifixion.[19] Since his persecuting activity implies at least some familiarity with those being persecuted, his knowledge of the Christ-movement must go back in some form to its very earliest period. And while he does not let us know where his persecuting activity took place, at the very least he does tell us that his familiarity with the Jerusalem apostles begins at an early stage as well ("after three years"; Gal 1:18). This is not to disregard the fact that Paul's letters, no less than the Acts of the Apostles, are shaped by the distinctive perspective and commitments of their author. One can well imagine that James or Peter would have provided quite different accounts of the events narrated in Gal 1 and 2. Still, Acts needs to be interpreted in conjunction with Paul's letters, and the letters need to be given some interpretive control.

This is not the place to attempt any comprehensive discussion about what Paul has to say about Jewish Christ-groups in the first generation of the movement, but it will nevertheless be useful to provide a brief survey of pertinent material.[20] With respect to foundational beliefs, Paul claims that his central belief in a crucified and resurrected Christ is one that was shared by Jewish believers from the beginning (1 Cor 15:3-7). This belief was formulated in a proclamation (gospel) that, according to what he says was a traditional rendering (1 Cor 15:3), contained these elements: the figure of Christ; Christ's death, burial, and resurrection; that his death and resurrection were "according to the scriptures"; that his death was "for our sins"; that the risen Christ "appeared" to the earliest believers (Cephas, the Twelve, James, the apostles, together with five hundred unnamed others). Elsewhere Paul presents an account of the Last Supper as a tradition that he had received (1 Cor 11:23-25), and his letters contain a number

---

17. As was seen by Baur himself: in comparison to Paul's letters, "the Acts must fill a secondary place"; Baur, *Paul*, 1:5.

18. I recognize that the term "Damascus experience" might be seen as conceding too much to the Acts account, since it is Luke who says explicitly (and repeatedly: 9:3; 22:6; 26:12) that Paul's experience took place in the vicinity of Damascus. Still, the fact that Paul speaks of returning (*hypestrepsa*) to Damascus (Gal 1:17), the term is not inappropriate in this context.

19. For a discussion of chronology, see Jerome Murphy-O'Connor, *Paul: A Critical Life* (Oxford: Clarendon, 1996), 1-31.

20. For a more thorough treatment, see Larry W. Hurtado, *Lord Jesus Christ: Devotion to Jesus in Earliest Christianity* (Grand Rapids: Eerdmans, 2003), 155-76.

of other formulations that have often been seen as reflecting traditional material originating from Jewish Christ-groups.[21]

Paul also makes frequent reference to various Jewish believers who evidently played leadership roles. Some of the persons mentioned in the summary of the gospel in 1 Cor 15:3-7 appear elsewhere as well: Cephas/Peter (1 Cor 1:12; 9:5; Gal 1:18; 2:7, 9, 11–14);[22] James (Gal 1:19; 2:12); apostles (1 Cor 9:1; 2 Cor 11:5, 21–23; 12:11; Gal 1:17–19); Barnabas (1 Cor 9:6; Gal 2:1, 9, 13). In addition, he mentions John (Gal 2:9) and the "brothers of the Lord" (1 Cor 9:5), together with Apollos (1 Cor 1:12; 3:4, 5, 6, 22; 4:6; 16:12) and several others who are probably to be identified with Jewish believers appearing in Acts (Mark [Phlm 24]; Silvanus [1 Thess 1:1]).[23]

As has already been noted, the centrality of the Jerusalem community is readily apparent in Paul's letters. In recounting his activity immediately after his Damascus experience, he simply takes it for granted that Jerusalem was where the apostles were to be found (Gal 1:17). In addition, while part of his purpose in this biographical section (Gal 1:13–2:10) was to emphasize his independence of Jerusalem, this nevertheless has the ironic effect of underlining Jerusalem's central place and role. Later, his project to collect a financial gift from his gentile churches for "the saints at Jerusalem" (Rom 15:26) serves to demonstrate the continuing significance of the Jerusalem community.[24] And despite his assertions of independence, when summing up his work in the eastern Mediterranean, he anchors it in Jerusalem: "from Jerusalem and as far around as Illyricum I have fully proclaimed the good news of Christ" (Rom 15:19). In addition to Jerusalem, however, Paul's letters make reference to Jewish communities in other locales: "the churches of Judea" (Gal 1:22; 1 Thess 2:15); the ethnically mixed community in Antioch (Gal 2:11–14).[25] The role of Peter in the geographical spread of Christ-groups from Jerusalem to Antioch can be inferred from his presence in both cities and from his identity as the "apostle for the circumcised" (Gal 2:7–8). Perhaps this can also be turned the other way around: Peter's identity as

---

21. Especially Rom 1:3–4; 3:25; 8:15; 10:8–9; 1 Cor 12:3; 16:22; 1 Thess 1:9–10.

22. Paul prefers the Aramaic form *Cephas*, using *Peter* only in Gal 2:7–8, where his usage may reflect the language of the agreement narrated in the passage; see J. Louis Martyn, *Galatians: A New Translation with Introduction and Commentary*, AB (New York: Doubleday, 1997), 202–3.

23. Additional references to some of these figures appear in the disputed letters as well.

24. The collection project comes into view in 1 Cor 16:1–4; 2 Cor 8 and 9; Rom 15:25–29; and (possibly) Gal 2:10.

25. It is possible that his reference to Damascus (Gal 1:17) implies that the movement had spread that far, but this is not explicit.

Ethnē as an Identity Ascribed to Non-Jews: By Jewish Christ-Believers

the "apostle for the circumcised" indicates the existence of a concerted effort (a mission) to spread Christ-belief outside Jerusalem itself.

Another element that comes into view in Paul's letters with respect to Jewish Christ-groups is opposition from other Jews. Of course, Paul's own activity as a persecutor ("violently persecuting the church of God and trying to destroy it"; Gal 1:13; also Gal 1:22-23; 1 Cor 15:9; Phil 3:6) is important here.[26] But other references to persecution in Judea (1 Thess 2:14-16; Rom 15:31) indicate that the phenomenon was more widespread and ongoing. Paul's description of his persecuting activity as an exhibition of "zeal" (Phil 3:6), together with his reference to persecution in conjunction with his self-identification as a "zealot [$z\bar{e}l\bar{o}t\bar{e}s$] for the traditions of [his] ancestors" (Gal 1:13-14), serves to locate this phenomenon within a Jewish tradition of zeal, which can be described as a readiness to use force to defend the torah, the temple, and the Jewish way of life from perceived threats.[27]

As is well known, Paul's letters indicate a certain level of conflict between himself and elements in the Jerusalem community. But his accounts of these conflicts also indicate a degree of diversity among other Jewish leaders and groups themselves. These conflicts were mostly focused on the issue of the terms on which gentile believers might be included and the lines of division differed somewhat depending on the issue (circumcision and table fellowship), but they probably reflect broader constellations of views. In his epistle to the Galatians, Paul recounts two separate incidents (2:1-10, in Jerusalem; 2:11-14, in Antioch). In both of them, the conflict is sharpest between Paul and a group within the Jerusalem church that he labels "false brothers" (2:4) or "the circumcision group" (literally, "those of circumcision" [$tous\ ek\ peritom\bar{e}s$]; 2:12). In between, distinct shades of opinion seem to be represented by James (and a delegation sent by him to Antioch; 2:12), Peter, and Barnabas; while all three of them side with Paul on the issue of gentile circumcision, they differ with him in varying degrees of intensity on the issue of table fellowship between Jewish and gentile believers.[28]

---

26. For the argument that "violently" (NRSV) is an overtranslation of *kath' hyperbolēn* that has been unduly influenced by the Acts account, see Murphy-O'Connor, *Paul*, 67.

27. For a concise account of this tradition, see James D. G. Dunn, *The Theology of Paul the Apostle* (Grand Rapids: Eerdmans, 1998), 350-53.

28. Scholarly discussion of these accounts has been voluminous, and there is no need here to add to the volume. I take the position that "those of circumcision" (2:12) refers to a group of Jerusalem Christ-believers who insist that gentiles need to become full proselytes to Judaism in order to be accepted, and thus they are to be linked with the "false brothers" of 2:4 (in contrast to opinions that the term refers to hostile Jewish outsiders in Jerusalem, as is argued by Richard N. Longenecker, *Galatians*, WBC 41 [Waco, TX: Word,

Finally, and following on from this, Paul provides us with some information—albeit not as much as we might like—about the existence of gentile Christ-believers and the early stages of a mission to gentiles. Despite Paul's claims that his Damascus experience was a call "to proclaim [Christ] among the *ethnē*" (Gal 1:16) and that he "had been entrusted with the gospel for the uncircumcised" (Gal 2:7), he does not make the stronger claim that this gospel and proclamation originated with him. In other words, gentiles were becoming believers prior to and apart from his own missionary activity. Some have argued that this was taking place even before his Damascus experience—indeed, that the inclusion of gentiles as gentiles was one of the reasons for his persecuting activity.[29] While this is certainly possible, what supporting evidence there might be is too scant and allusive to build anything on the suggestion.[30] Nevertheless, there is solid evidence for independent evangelization of gentiles not long after his Damascus experience. Although he was active in the mixed-ethnic community in Antioch, he clearly did not found it, and several more senior Jewish believers (Barnabas, Peter, James) played authoritative roles. In addition to Barnabas, during the course of his ministry Paul became associated with other Jewish believers who were already engaged in gentile evangelization (Apollos; Prisca and Aquila). Further, the mixed-ethnic community in Rome, which seems to have been established long before Paul's letter ("for many years"; 15:23), was not founded by him. What about Jerusalem itself? While the circumcision group had a definite position on the conditions under which gentiles could be included, Paul provides little evidence to suggest that they took any initiative to seek out gentiles. They may have been playing more of a gatekeeping role than one of evangelization.

1990], 73-74, or that it refers to the delegation from James, the position of, e.g., Ernest de Witt Burton, *A Critical and Exegetical Commentary on the Epistle to the Galatians*, ICC [Edinburgh: T&T Clark, 1921], 107).

29. This has been suggested by many, among them: Rudolf Bultmann, "Paul," in *Existence and Faith*, trans. Schubert M. Ogden (New York: Meridian, 1960), 113; John Knox, *Chapters in a Life of Paul*, 2nd ed. (Macon, GA: Mercer University Press, 1987), 76; J. Christiaan Beker, *Paul the Apostle: The Triumph of God in Life and Thought* (Philadelphia: Fortress, 1980), 143-44; Jürgen Becker, *Paul: Apostle to the Gentiles* (Louisville: Westminster John Knox, 1993), 65-66; Heikki Räisänen, "Paul's Conversion and the Development of His View of the Law," *NTS* 33 (1987): 406; James D. G. Dunn, *The Partings of the Ways between Christianity and Judaism and Their Significance for the Character of Christianity* (Philadelphia: Trinity Press International, 1991), 122.

30. Paul's statement in 1 Thess 2:14-16 about Jewish persecution, in which he links persecution of the churches in Judea with opposition to the gentile mission, is at least consistent with the suggestion, as is his claim in Gal 6:12 that those who are urging gentile believers to be circumcised are doing so to escape persecution.

Further, the gates in question may have all been in the diaspora; Paul provides no information to suggest that there were any non-Jews among "the saints at Jerusalem" (Rom 15:26).[31]

Although Paul's letters and Acts are the most pertinent sources, we are not solely dependent on them for information about the earliest Jewish Christ-communities. In particular, while the canonical Gospels in their final forms stem from a later period,[32] they incorporate traditional material, much of which took shape in the earlier period and some of which pertains directly to matters concerning mission and gentile inclusion. The Gospels are layered documents, and each of the discernible layers—the redactional composition of the Evangelists, reflecting situations and outlooks in their own day; the sources and traditions that they utilized, formed in prior times and situations; and the remembrances of the speech and activity of Jesus himself—will come into our investigations at different points. For present purposes, it is the middle layer that will be most germane, though Jesus's own attitudes toward non-Jews will have some part to play as well.

As we have already had occasion to observe, Judaism in our period of interest was marked by considerable diversity, and the earliest community of Jewish Christ-believers can readily be seen as another manifestation of this larger phenomenon. As with other groups—from stable and enduring groups such as the Qumran community or the Pharisees, to the less sharply defined groups addressed in works such as the Testament (Assumption) of Moses, to the various short-lived prophetic or messianic movements described by Josephus—the earliest Jewish Christ-group was characterized by a distinctive subidentity within the larger identity structures of the Jewish people as a whole. Common to most of these groups was the sense of an inside track on what it meant to be the people of Israel. This inside track, in turn, became the organizing center around which the subidentity was constructed, the nub of the distinctive version of Jewish identity that characterized the group.

The distinctive subidentity of the earliest group of Jewish Christ-believers was rooted in the mission of Jesus (which, in turn was rooted in that of John the Baptist, though with distinctive variations)—an itinerant mission of preaching,

---

31. Indeed, his sharp contrast between the Jerusalem believers and "the Gentiles" (Rom 15:26-27) seems to suggest the opposite. As for Acts, the only gentile who appears as part of the Jerusalem *ekklēsia* is a certain Nicolaus, "a proselyte of Antioch," who evidently had become a proselyte before becoming a Christ-believer.

32. Although the Gospel of Thomas probably contains some sayings of Jesus that have been preserved independently of the canonical Gospels, it has very little light to shed either on gentile believers or on the ascription of identity by Jewish believers.

teaching, and healing, centered on a call directed toward Israel to prepare for the imminent appearance of the reign of God. The nature of this mission meant necessarily that the Jesus-movement was marked by a dialectical sense of identity with respect to Israel as a whole—bearing a message that had to do with the culmination of Israel's hopes and history, while at the same time differentiated, because of that message, from the greater portion of Israel that was untouched or unmoved by it.[33] Christ-belief was characterized by a significant additional element, however—the belief that God had identified Jesus as Israel's expected Messiah by raising him from the dead. This new belief generated a movement that differed in significant ways from the movement that gathered around Jesus during his lifetime. Put differently, the Christ-movement did not see itself as simply carrying on the mission of a now-dead pioneer; the belief that the dead leader had been raised produced a different self-identifying center and dynamic.

To be sure, this way of describing it runs the risk of setting *Christ-belief* and *Jesus-movement* over against each other in too sharp and clearly defined a manner. For one thing, there was an essential continuity between the two, in terms of both the key leaders and the centrality of Jesus himself. For another, as we have already noted and will continue to see, the implications of a belief in a resurrected Messiah were developed in a range of ways, producing considerable diversity among Christ-believers. Indeed, despite Luke's portrayal of a unified movement with a unitary origin, the picture was probably more complex and diverse from the beginning.[34] One aspect of this diversity may well have involved the continuation of groups shaped more by the mission and self-understanding of the Jesus-movement than by the cross-and-resurrection kerygma of the Christ-movement. Evidence for such a possibility comes from the conjectural document Q, which has plausibly been postulated as a written source held in common by the authors of Matthew and Luke. As it has been reconstructed, the document displays a coherent structure and outlook.[35] A collection of mostly sayings material, dealing with the mission of Jesus and the life of discipleship, the document is evidently aware of Jesus's death but assigns no salvific significance to

---

33. I use *Jesus-movement* (or *Jesus-group[s]*) to refer to followers of Jesus during his lifetime, and also to any who simply carried on his mission after his death, in contrast to those who subsequently proclaimed a message having to do with his postmortem resurrection and its eschatological-salvific significance (*Christ-groups*, *Christ-believers*, etc.).

34. On this point, see Dunn, *Beginning from Jerusalem*, 133–37.

35. For the standard reconstruction, see James M. Robinson, Paul Hoffmann, and John S. Kloppenborg, eds., *The Critical Edition of Q*, Hermeneia (Minneapolis: Fortress, 2000).

Ethnē *as an Identity Ascribed to Non-Jews: By Jewish Christ-Believers*

it and says nothing about his resurrection.³⁶ While one needs to exercise caution in using a conjectural source to reconstruct a historical group, the reconstruction is not simply to be dismissed for that reason; one can well expect that there were followers of Jesus, in Galilee or elsewhere, who remained outside the influence of the new Jerusalem-centered belief and who continued to proclaim his message and pursue his mission.³⁷

Nevertheless, even if such a nonkerygmatic group of Jesus-followers continued to exist,³⁸ it would not have a significant bearing on our study.³⁹ While Q contains a couple of references to non-Jews that will be pertinent to our question,⁴⁰ there is very little evidence to suggest that such a group might have attracted gentile adherents in any substantial way, and especially that *ethnē* was ascribed

---

36. For a thorough discussion of the death and resurrection of Jesus with respect to Q, see John S. Kloppenborg Verbin, *Excavating Q: The History and Setting of the Sayings Gospel* (Minneapolis: Fortress, 2000), 363-79. While there is no reference to resurrection, Q does identify Jesus with the Son of Man (Q 7:34; 9:58), who is also expected to come in the future (Q 12:40; 17:24-30). Daniel A. Smith has argued that this postmortem existence of Jesus as Son of Man is to be understood in terms of assumption rather than of resurrection; *The Post Mortem Vindication of Jesus in the Sayings Gospel Q*, LNTS 338 (London: T&T Clark, 2006).

37. Cautious critiques of such reconstructions include those of Hurtado, *Lord Jesus Christ*, 217-57; and Arland J. Hultgren, *The Rise of Normative Christianity* (Minneapolis: Fortress, 1994), 31-41.

38. For continuities and connections with the epistle of James, see Patrick J. Hartin, *James and the Q Sayings of Jesus*, JSNTSup 47 (Sheffield: JSOT Press, 1990); and with the Gospel of Thomas, see James M. Robinson, "LOGOI SOPHON: On the Gattung of Q," in *Trajectories through Early Christianity*, ed. James M. Robinson and Helmut Koester (Philadelphia: Fortress, 1971), 71-113.

39. For more thoroughgoing reconstructions of Christian origins that dispense with Acts, which argue that the resurrection-centered Christ-group was simply one of several early groups and thus marginalize the place of resurrection belief in Christian origins, see Burton L. Mack, *A Myth of Innocence: Mark and Christian Origins* (Philadelphia: Fortress, 1988); *The Christian Myth: Origins, Logic, and Legacy* (New York: Continuum, 2001); Ron Cameron and Merrill P. Miller, eds., *Redescribing Christian Origins*, SBL Symposium Series (Atlanta: Society of Biblical Literature, 2004). While I recognize both the heuristic value of the project and the fact that our understanding of Christian origins would be immensely enriched if there had been more than one attempt "to set down an orderly account of the events that have been fulfilled among us" in the postcrucifixion period (cf. Luke 1:1), I think that critical analysis of Acts can put us in touch with early traditions and therefore that Acts needs to be included in any description of Christian origins.

40. Q 12:30; 13:29, 28; possibly 6:34.

as an identity term. The phenomenon of gentile Christianity that is of interest to us here is one that develops out of the Jerusalem Christ-believing movement.

To pick up the thread of the discussion, this movement was characterized by the belief that God had raised Jesus from death, thus identifying him as Israel's expected Messiah (Christ). As Meyer has put it: "The disciples who made up the core of the first Christian community interpreted their Easter experience as follows: God raised Jesus from the dead . . . , so exalting him as Messiah and Lord."[41] This is generally recognized and does not require much in the way of demonstration or defense. The title appears in 1 Cor 15:3-7, in Paul's summary of the shared gospel ("Christ died . . . and was buried . . . and was raised"), and while Paul often is seen as using the term more as a name than as a title,[42] the fact that 1 Cor 15:3-7 is a piece of inherited tradition indicates that the titular sense of *Christos* was part of the traditional formulation.[43] In Acts, the message that God has "raised up Jesus" and has "made him both Lord and Messiah" (2:32, 36) is a common theme in the early sermons. While the speeches of Acts are certainly Lukan compositions, the variations among them may be taken as an indication that Luke was at least attempting to provide informed accounts of distinctive earlier viewpoints.[44]

---

41. Ben F. Meyer, *The Early Christians: Their World Mission and Self-Discovery* (Wilmington, DE: Michael Glazier, 1986), 37.

42. See Nils A. Dahl's influential article, "The Messiahship of Jesus in Paul," in *The Crucified Messiah, and Other Essays* (Minneapolis: Augsburg, 1974), 37-47. But see now Matthew V. Novenson, *Christ among the Messiahs: Christ Language in Paul and Messiah Language in Ancient Judaism* (New York: Oxford University Press, 2012).

43. Paul is certainly aware of the titular sense (Rom 9:5), and his almost exclusive use of *Christos* in his subsequent discourse on the resurrection of Jesus (twelve occurrences in 1 Cor 15:12-28; one additional reference to "the Son" [v. 28]) suggests that he is aware of the tradition here. On the traditional character of 1 Cor 15:3-7 (i.e., that it goes back to the earliest Jerusalem Christ-group), see Hurtado, *Lord Jesus Christ*, 168-69, and the literature cited there.

44. One variation appears when comparing Peter's speech in Acts 3:12-26 with Stephen's speech. In the former, Jesus is the promised prophet like Moses (vv. 22-24), and Peter's hearers are both Moses's "brothers" (v. 22) and "the descendants of the prophets and of the covenant that God gave to your ancestors" (v. 25). In the speech of Stephen (7:2-53), Jesus is also the Moses-like prophet (v. 37), but Stephen's hearers are the descendants of those who rejected Moses (v. 39) and persecuted the prophets ("Which of the prophets did your ancestors not persecute?" [vv. 51-53]).

On the speeches of Acts and *prosōpopoiia* (i.e., the practice of writing "speeches in character"), see David E. Aune, *The New Testament in Its Literary Environment* (Philadelphia: Westminster, 1987), 124-28. On the speeches more generally, see Marion L. Soards,

Ethnē as an Identity Ascribed to Non-Jews: By Jewish Christ-Believers

Both the identification of Jesus as Messiah and the claim of resurrection serve to locate the early message within the sphere of Jewish eschatology.[45] The eschatological character of early Christ-belief is also evidenced by the Jerusalem locale of the movement. While messianism was not an essential element in Jewish eschatology—eschatological scenarios often contain no messianic figure or no agent other than God (e.g., Isa 2:2–4; Tob 13:11–17; 14:5–7; 1 Enoch 90.6–39; Sibylline Oracles 3.667–795)—Jerusalem and the temple are central, as is clearly evidenced in the passages just cited.[46] Why did a movement that had first gathered around an itinerant Galilean prophet decide to settle in Jerusalem after his death? "Why Jerusalem?" as Meyer has asked. Clearly, the central role played by Jerusalem in Jewish eschatology is an important part of the answer. Zion eschatology, together with the belief that the messianic agent of the end-time restoration had been revealed through his resurrection in Jerusalem, led the Galilean disciples (some of them, at least) to remain in Jerusalem in anticipation of the fulfillment of Jesus's messianic mission.[47] Seen from another angle, the Jerusalem orientation of the earliest Christ-movement serves to identify and highlight the eschatological context within which the movement understood itself. The community gathered in the name of the recently revealed Messiah of Israel was, by virtue of their relationship with him, the portion of Israel that was most closely aligned with the restoration yet to come.

As has been noted, this sense of existing as a distinct subgroup within Israel—indeed, as embodying the identity that should characterize Israel as a whole—produced a two-sided sense of the relationship between the Christ-group and the rest of Israel. On the one hand, they had a message that (they believed) was of intrinsic interest to Israel as a whole; all Israel should join them in rejoicing that the Messiah had appeared and in awaiting the imminent restoration of all things. On the other hand, to the extent that this message was resisted or ignored, it served to accentuate the line of differentiation between them and the

---

The Speeches in Acts: Their Content, Context, and Concerns (Louisville: Westminster John Knox, 1994).

45. Belief in resurrection was not universal in Second Temple Judaism, but, where it was present, it was an element of end-time expectation.

46. Admittedly, the "snow-white cow" of 1 Enoch 90.37 has frequently been seen as a messianic figure; even so, however, he appears only after the final judgment and the end-time restoration of Israel and the temple has been fully accomplished.

47. Meyer, *Early Christians*, 53–66; also Ferdinand Hahn, *Mission in the New Testament* (London: SCM, 1965), 47–48; Seán Freyne, *The Jesus Movement and Its Expansion: Meaning and Mission* (Grand Rapids: Eerdmans, 2014), 201–5; Martin Hengel, *Between Jesus and Paul: Studies in the Earliest History of Christianity*, trans. John Bowden (Philadelphia: Fortress, 1983), 12, 59.

rest of Israel; those failing to respond were, by their lack of response, putting themselves outside the sphere of Israel's messianic restoration. The Jerusalem community, then, had the marks both of a renewal group and of a remnant group—renewal, in that they were charged with a task aimed at transforming the rest of Israel; remnant, in that they and those willing to join them constituted the Israel destined for messianic restoration. Put differently, the nature of their message created two different possibilities for their stance toward the rest of Israel—or, perhaps better, a range of possibilities between two poles—one characterized by solidarity, continuity, and identification; the other by separation, discontinuity, and opposition.

The actualization of these possibilities is reflected to a certain extent in a sequence of events recounted in Acts 6:1–8:8—the disagreement between groups that Luke describes as the Hebrews and the Hellenists, the subsequent martyrdom of Stephen, the persecution of the Jerusalem Christ-groups, and the expulsion of many of their members. Strictly speaking, the terms *Hebraioi* and *Hellēnistai* differentiate the groups simply on the basis of their primary language (Aramaic and Greek, respectively), which almost certainly means that the Hellenists are to be seen as diaspora Jews who had taken up residence in Jerusalem. But the speech that Luke attributes to Stephen, one of the leaders of the Hellenists, reflects an attitude toward the temple cult and the established Jewish authorities that is significantly different from that exhibited either in the earlier chapters of Acts or the ongoing descriptions of the Jerusalem Christ-community in the period after the expulsion (e.g., 9:26–30; 11:1–3; 15:1–2). This has widely and traditionally been taken to suggest that the Hellenists are to be seen as a distinct group or party within the early Jerusalem Christ-community, characterized by a lax and liberal attitude toward the Jewish law and cult, and an affinity for a more cosmopolitan and universal outlook.[48]

However, in reflecting on what we might learn from this account about the history of the movement, we need to exercise a measure of caution. Scholars from F. C. Baur to the present have been tempted to construct an idea of "Hellenistic Jewish Christianity" that outruns the evidence but then is used as an explanatory device for elaborate interpretive enterprises.[49] But it is probably not with-

---

48. For a historical survey of this line of interpretation, with critical assessment, see Craig C. Hill, *Hellenists and Hebrews: Reappraising Division within the Earliest Church* (Minneapolis: Fortress, 1992).

49. While Hengel is critical of approaches that construct Hellenistic Jewish Christianity in terms of "syncretism, paganism and antinomianism" (*Between Jesus and Paul*, 14), his linguistically based construction is nevertheless used to carry an inordinate amount of theological and historical freight.

out significance that Luke does not use *Hellēnistai* to refer to any well-defined theological or ideological party within the early Jewish Christ-movement.⁵⁰ It cannot simply be assumed on linguistic grounds that Greek-speaking Jews would necessarily be more inclined to adopt gentile patterns of thought or to feel alienated from Jewish ways of life. If anything, the fact that these Hellenistic Jews had relocated to Jerusalem says something about their commitment to Jewish distinctives.⁵¹ Realistically, we probably need to expect a range of diversity among them—and among the Hebrews as well—with respect to their assumptions and allegiances.⁵² For one thing, the message proclaimed by the early Christ-believers was not intrinsically aligned with any of the already-existing lines of division within Judean society. Since eschatological expectation belonged to the common stock of Jewish tradition and expectation, we can well imagine that it might have been of interest to a certain cross-section of the Jewish populace. Without wanting to build anything on Luke's specific details, the diverse collection of members that appears in his account—a Levite from Cyprus (Acts 5:36), a proselyte from Antioch (6:5), "a great many of the priests" (6:7), "believers from the sect of the Pharisees" (15:5), not to mention the disciples from Galilee (2:7; 13:31)—no doubt reflects some of the demographic diversity of the early movement.

Still, Luke does present us with two broad tendencies in his account of the early Jewish Christ-movement: one that seems content to take its place within the established boundaries and institutions of Judean life, and the other that adopts a more critical stance toward Jewish leadership and Jerusalem-based institutions. Certainly Luke cannot be taken at face value in his statement that, as a result of the persecution, "all but the apostles were scattered throughout the countryside of Judea and Samaria" (Acts 8:1). It is clear that the group that remained represented the first tendency, with James emerging as the dominant leader,⁵³ and that those who were scattered reflected the second. While we cannot look to Paul to confirm the details of the Acts account here, Luke's picture of two broad tendencies is certainly not inconsistent with the situation reflected in Paul's letters.

---

50. On this point, see Barrett, *Acts of the Apostles*, 1:309.

51. Hengel suggests that they might have experienced the same sort of disillusionment with the realities of Jerusalem as Luther experienced in his pilgrimage to Rome; *Between Jesus and Paul*, 28, 57. But this would hardly be true of the Hellenists as a linguistic class.

52. Again, see Barrett, *Acts of the Apostles*, 1:308.

53. Note especially the description of the Jerusalem community given later in the narrative by James: it consisted of "many thousands of [Jewish] believers, . . . and they are all zealots [*zēlōtēs*] for the law" and upset about reports that Paul teaches "all the Jews living among the Gentiles to forsake Moses and . . . not to circumcise their children or observe the customs" (21:20–21).

GENTILE CHRISTIAN IDENTITY

Be that as it may, it is not central to my purpose here to trace the development of distinct parties and groups within the early Christ-movement. I am interested in identity ascription rather than in the identification of groups per se. Ultimately, my goal in this chapter is to identify the range of identities that Jewish Christ-believers came to ascribe to gentiles who adopted the same beliefs. Such ascribed identities, however, were not stand-alone constructions but were extensions of the various senses of identity that Jewish Christ-believers had of themselves—as Jews who had come to believe that God had identified Jesus as Israel's expected Messiah by raising him from the dead. In other words, the identities that Jewish Christ-groups constructed for themselves constitute a necessary penultimate goal of our investigation here. While a range of such identity constructions can be identified, they do not necessarily map onto distinct subgroups. Groups themselves can comprise members with different senses of identity, and as we will see, the same can be true of individual pieces or bodies of literature.

For our purposes, then, Luke's account of the Hebrews and Hellenists is of interest not because it has been seen as providing evidence for the existence of two ideologically distinct and nameable groups but because it draws our attention more generally to the possibility of a range of stances on the part of Jewish Christ-believers with respect to the traditions and social structures of Judaism—that is, a range of ways in which these believers constructed their specific identity with respect to the larger Jewish community. In order to explore this further, we need to look more closely at the nature of early Jewish Christ-belief and the processes of conceptual development that emerged from it.

The message proclaimed to Israel by the earliest Jewish Christ-believers contained within it significant elements of dynamic tension and issues of logical coherence. It provoked questions that needed to be addressed, paradoxes or contradictions that needed to be resolved, and options that needed to be explored, if the message was to be comprehensible to outsiders and to provide believers with a stable foundation for communal existence. Among these, the most pertinent had to do with what, for convenience, might be described as Christology (including messianism), eschatology, soteriology, and ecclesiology. While the terms are perhaps anachronistic, they nevertheless refer to questions that emerged naturally and necessarily from the message itself.

The first element to be mentioned, having to do with Christology (suffering and messiahship), provides a clear example of logical tension. Put simply, the message of a suffering and dying messiah would have appeared as a contradiction in terms. This is captured well by the statement that Luke puts on the lips of the disciples on the road to Emmaus: "we had hoped that *he* was the one who would redeem Israel" (Luke 24:21). The *he* is emphatic (*autos estin*); the implication is "but obviously we were wrong about him." Almost by definition, messiahs do not die; they triumph over evil, they defeat Israel's enemies, they act as God's powerful agents to inaugurate and establish God's reign. Despite its diversity, Jewish eschatological expectation contained no real notion of an age to come that would be brought about by a suffering, dying, and rising messiah. The early Christ-believers, convinced nevertheless that the crucified Jesus had been raised from death by God, thereby identifying him as Israel's Messiah, reread the Scriptures in light of the cross, in order to demonstrate that the sufferings of "God's Christ" were foretold by God through "the mouth of the prophets" (Acts 3:18).[54] This theme was not to be found in those passages that traditionally were seen as messianic (e.g., 2 Sam 7; Ps 2; Isa 9:1–7; 11:1–9; Mic 5:1–5).[55] But in addition to these texts, the early Christ-believers took over and applied to Jesus a collection of passages dealing with suffering (e.g., Pss 22; 69; the Servant Songs of Isaiah) that formerly had not been seen as messianic at all.[56] This led to a christocentric hermeneutic, not recognized by those other Jews who did not share their basic kerygmatic convictions. While this hermeneutical enterprise did not necessarily contribute to a diversity of identity constructions among Jewish Christ-believers themselves, it did serve to accentuate the more fundamental line of demarcation between themselves and the rest of the Jewish world.

In addition to this basic messianic issue, there were developments in christological thinking among early Jewish Christ-believers that did have more of a bearing on identity diversity. It is probable that the earliest form of Christ-belief was one that fit rather smoothly with traditional Jewish messianic and eschatological expectation. To expand on what has already been said about the shape of early Christ-belief, the immediate corollary of the belief that God had identified Jesus as Israel's expected Messiah by raising him from the dead was that this Messiah would appear in the near future to bring the prophetic promises to completion, to redeem Israel, and to usher in the messianic age. It might be going too far to say that in the present, Jesus was seen simply as the Messiah-designate. Nevertheless, the emphasis remained on the future—on what the expected Messiah would accomplish when he should come in full messianic glory.[57]

---

54. The theme appears twice in the tradition cited by Paul in 1 Cor 15:3–7, and frequently in the Acts sermons.

55. For a thorough and reliable account of Jewish messianism, see John J. Collins, *The Scepter and the Star: Messianism in Light of the Dead Sea Scrolls* (Grand Rapids: Eerdmans, 2010).

56. In a classic and still-instructive work, C. H. Dodd describes the result as "the substructure of New Testament theology"; *According to the Scriptures: The Sub-structure of New Testament Theology* (London: James Nisbet, 1952).

57. See, e.g., Adolf von Harnack, *The Mission and Expansion of Christianity in the First*

Such a scenario seems to be reflected in parts of Peter's sermon in Acts 3:12–26, especially vv. 19–21. Here Jesus is "the Messiah appointed for you, ... who must remain in heaven until the time of restoration of all things that God announced long ago through his holy prophets." Jesus has been "appointed" (*prokecheirismenon*) as Messiah, made "ready to act in a particular way,"[58] and he will play his appointed role when the time comes for the "restoration of all things"; but nothing is said about his status and role in the present except that it is a period of waiting ("remain in heaven"). With respect to those who are bearing witness (v. 15) to this reality, the present is a time to call Israel to repentance: "Men, Israelites" (v. 12); "you are the descendants of the prophets and of the covenant that God gave to your ancestors" (v. 25). "Repent, therefore, ... so that ... the Lord may send the Messiah appointed for you" (v. 20).[59]

While little is said here about the specific shape of the "restoration of all things," we might supplement the picture by turning to the hymns of Luke's infancy account, which are widely understood to preserve traditions stemming from early Jewish Christ-groups.[60] Here, especially in the Magnificat and the Song of Zechariah, both John and Jesus are introduced in terms that are resonant with traditional Jewish expectations about the messiah and the restoration of Israel: "He has helped his servant Israel ... according to the promise he made to our ancestors, to Abraham and to his descendants forever" (Luke 1:54-55); "He has raised up a mighty salvation for us in the house of his servant David ... and has remembered his holy covenant, the oath that he swore to our ancestor Abraham" (1:72-73). In keeping with the theme, Luke introduces Simeon as one who was "looking forward to the consolation of Israel" (2:25) and Anna as one of those "who were looking for the redemption of Jerusalem" (2:38).[61]

In this early form of Christ-belief, then, the conviction that Jesus had been identified as the coming Messiah was smoothly combined with traditional Jewish expectations about the role of the messiah and the shape of the expected

---

Three Centuries, trans. James Moffatt (London: Williams & Norgate, 1908), 45.

58. Barrett, *Acts of the Apostles*, 1:204.

59. On this passage and its Christology, see especially John A. T. Robinson, "The Most Primitive Christology of All?" *JTS* 7 (1956): 177–89; also Reginald H. Fuller, *The Foundations of New Testament Christology* (New York: Scribner, 1965), 165–67; Barrett, *Acts of the Apostles*, 1:203–7.

60. See especially Raymond E. Brown, *The Birth of the Messiah: A Commentary on the Infancy Narratives in the Gospels of Matthew and Luke*, Anchor Bible Reference Library (New York: Doubleday, 1993), 346–55.

61. Luke seems to give voice to a similar expectation with the words he puts on the lips of the disciples in the account of the ascension: "Lord, is this the time when you will restore the kingdom to Israel?" (Acts 1:6).

messianic deliverance. Consequently, Christ-believers of this type could readily continue to live within the boundaries, institutions, and traditions of Israel. But christological developments took place, evidently at a fairly early date, which had the effect of placing more emphasis on the newness of the present situation and thus of introducing more tension between Christ-belief and the established patterns of Jewish life.

One of these early developments has to do with the present status of the risen Jesus and the belief that his resurrection was also an exaltation to a position of cosmic authority. Eventually, reflections on Christ's status developed into ideas of his preexistence and divine identity. For present purposes, however, we need not get into the question of how early this took place.[62] The point here has to do with the concept of exaltation, and thus with a focus on the present role and rule of the heavenly Messiah. Evidence from Paul's letters, both traditional formulations incorporated by Paul and aspects of his own christological discourse, indicates that the link between resurrection and exaltation was quite early.

Traditional material incorporated into Paul's letters ascribes elevated titles to Christ on the basis of the resurrection. Romans 1:3-4 is of particular interest in its juxtaposition of traditional messianic and exalted christological descriptors: "who was from the seed of David according to the flesh and was declared to be Son of God with power . . . by the resurrection of the dead." Subsequently, Paul grounds the confession "Jesus is Lord" on the belief "that God raised him from the dead" (Rom 10:9).[63] Given the widespread use of Ps 110:1 ("The Lord said to my Lord, 'Sit at my right hand until I put your enemies under your feet'") with reference to Christ, Paul's allusion to this verse in Rom 8:34 ("Christ Jesus, who died, yes, who was raised, who is at the right hand of God") can be seen as traditional as well.[64] While there is no reference to the resurrection in 1 Cor 16:22, the Aramaic formulation (*maranatha*), probably to be rendered "our Lord, come" (*marana tha*), indicates that the title *Mar* (Lord) was being ascribed to Jesus by the early Aramaic-speaking believers. Paul himself asserts on several occasions that Christ's resurrection was also an exaltation—for example, in his commentary on the resurrection in 1 Cor 15:24-28 ("For he [God] has put all

---

62. For an early development, see, e.g., Hurtado, *Lord Jesus Christ*; Richard Bauckham, *Jesus and the God of Israel: God Crucified and Other Studies on the New Testament's Christology of Divine Identity* (Grand Rapids: Eerdmans, 2008); for a later development, see James D. G. Dunn, *Christology in the Making: A New Testament Inquiry into the Origins of the Doctrine of the Incarnation*, 2nd ed. (London: SCM, 1989).

63. The confession "Jesus is Lord" (Rom 10:9) appears elsewhere in Paul as well (1 Cor 12:3; 2 Cor 4:5; Phil 2:11).

64. See Mark 12:36; Matt 22:44; Luke 20:42-43; Acts 2:33-35; 5:31; Heb 1:13.

things in subjection under his feet," citing Ps 2:7) and his paraenetical statement in Rom 14:9 ("For to this end Christ died and lived again, so that he might be Lord both of the dead and the living").

In addition to such specific links between resurrection and exaltation, exaltation Christology, both by title and by theme, is widespread in Paul's letters. This is well known and does not need to be documented here.[65] What is to be noted in addition, however, is that while some aspects of Paul's preaching and practice were sharply criticized by other Jewish Christ-believers, nothing suggests that his Christology was subject to critique.[66] This, together with the pre-Pauline tradition discussed above, serves to indicate that, from a fairly early date, the significance of Christ's resurrection was not simply that God had thereby identified him as the coming Messiah but, in addition, that God had also exalted him to an elevated status of sovereign lordship. This shift from purely future expectation to present sovereignty carried with it the possibility that Christ's present sovereignty might be seen to clash with the current institutional structures of Jewish life, thus complicating the question of how those who acknowledged his lordship were to understand their relationship to the rest of the Jewish people who did not.

The second area in which the message of the earliest Christ-believers presented inherent tensions and precipitated conceptual development had to do with eschatology and its relationship with the present. The basic belief—that God had identified Jesus as the expected Messiah—was, of course, thoroughly eschatological. The Messiah was a figure of the end time and his role was to establish the anticipated era of salvation, the reign of God. At the outset, as we have observed, the emphasis in the message seemed to be placed on the future. The resurrection identified Jesus as the Messiah who was to come; the expected eschatological scenario would unfold when he did (Acts 3:19-21). This is not to say that the present moment was simply seen as dead time—a brief period of waiting for the other eschatological shoe to drop, as it were. The idea of a mis-

---

65. For thorough treatments, see Dunn, *Theology of Paul the Apostle*, 234-65, and Hurtado, *Lord Jesus Christ*, 79-153.

66. "[A]mong the disagreements with other Jewish Christians registered in Paul's letters, there is a conspicuous lack of evidence of specifically christological matters, for example about the person of Jesus, his status, or the reverence due him"; Hurtado, *Lord Jesus Christ*, 165; for the argument more generally, see pp. 165-77. For what it is worth, most of the kerygmatic sermons that Luke puts on Peter's lips contain the theme of post-resurrection exaltation: Acts 2:33-35 ("exalted at the right hand of God"); 4:11 ("the stone that was rejected . . . has become the cornerstone"); 5:31 ("God exalted him at his right hand as Leader and Savior"); 10:42 ("the one ordained by God as judge of the living and the dead," though this statement might pertain more to the future than the present). The exception, perhaps significantly, is the speech in Acts 3:12-26.

sion to Israel seems to have been present from a very early point (Acts 3:19; Gal 2:7–8). Even so, Luke apparently felt that there were grounds for believing that the earliest postresurrection community expected an immediate appearance of the kingdom (Acts 1:6). If a present mission to Israel quickly came to be seen as a necessary implication of the basic belief, it was still conceived of as occupying a brief period of time—a last-minute summons to Israel in advance of the imminent coming (parousia) of the Messiah.

Evidence for the expectation of an imminent parousia appears frequently in New Testament material. In his letter to the *ekklēsia* in Thessalonica, Paul counts himself as belonging to those who would be alive at the coming of Christ ("we who are alive, who are left until the coming of the Lord"; 1 Thess 4:15). Evidently the Thessalonian believers did too, since they were unsettled by the death of some members. In a letter to the Corinthians, he expresses a similar belief ("we shall not all die"; 1 Cor 15:51) and counsels unmarried believers to remain in this state since the "appointed time" remaining before "the present form of this world" comes to an end is so short (1 Cor 7:29–31). Similar expectations punctuate the Gospels as well: "some standing here will not taste death" (Mark 9:1 // Matt 16:28 // Luke 9:27); "this generation will not pass away" (Mark 13:30 // Matt 24:34 // Luke 21:32); "they supposed that the kingdom was to appear immediately" (Luke 19:11); "the rumor . . . that this disciple would not die [before Jesus comes]" (John 21:22–23). The significance of this for present purposes is that the expectation of an imminent parousia tended to focus attention on the future as the time of Christ's messianic and saving activity, rather than the present. Such a focus on the future is reflected in Paul's recollection of how the Thessalonian believers "turned to God from idols, to serve a living and true God and to wait for [God's] Son from heaven, whom he raised from the dead—Jesus, who rescues us from the wrath that is coming" (1 Thess 1:10).

However, forces were also at work in the experience of the early Christ-believers that led to an increasing emphasis on the eschatological significance of the present interim period. In part, this was driven by tensions within the basic message itself. The idea of a suffering and dying Messiah was not the only aspect of the message that stood in tension with traditional Jewish messianic expectations. As has been mentioned, a messiah figure was not an essential element of Jewish eschatological expectation; Jewish expectation placed more emphasis on the coming age than on any human agent who would help to bring it about. Thus a message that had to do with a Messiah who had appeared but without the arrival of the messianic age could also be perceived as paradoxical or even self-contradictory. The longer the interim period was extended, the greater the perceived tension.

To be sure, the significance of the delay of the parousia has often been over-

GENTILE CHRISTIAN IDENTITY

estimated in the history of New Testament scholarship.[67] The early message contained not one but two temporal foci—both the Messiah who is to come and the Messiah who has been raised. From the beginning, the message had to do at least as much with a decisive event that had already taken place as with an expected event that was yet to occur. Still, the longer the interim period was extended, the greater was the need to reflect on the eschatological significance of this unanticipated period between the resurrection and the parousia.

This brings us to another aspect of the experience of the early Christ-groups that also seems to have been present from the beginning. It is readily apparent and generally recognized that the early Christ-believers felt themselves to be characterized and bound together by the powerful presence of God's Holy Spirit.[68] Paul simply takes it for granted that the experience of the Spirit was a universal and shared aspect of Christ-belief.[69] The Thessalonians "received the word with joy inspired by the Holy Spirit" (1 Thess 1:6; cf. 4:8); the Corinthians were "baptized into one body" "in the one Spirit" (1 Cor 12:13; cf. 2:4; 3:16). In his admonition of the Galatians, he can use their initial reception of the Spirit as the premise for an argument (Gal 3:1-5); later, in language that might echo an early Aramaic baptismal liturgy, he links the experience of the Spirit with the ecstatic utterance "Abba, father" (Gal 4:6).[70] In writing to the Romans—a community he had not visited—he can assume that they would agree with the statement that "God's love has been poured into our hearts through the Holy Spirit that has been given to us" (Rom 5:5) and that he could therefore engage in an extended exposition of the role of the Spirit in the life of the believer (Rom 8:1-27). In Acts, the shared experience of the Holy Spirit seems to be a pervasive theme in the traditions Luke draws on for his account of the Jerusalem Christ-believers (Acts 2:16-22, 33, 38; 5:32), even if he uses it for his own programmatic conception of history.[71] More generally, Dunn points to the pervasive use of Spirit language (especially having to do with "giving and receiving the Spirit") throughout New

---

67. See Christopher Rowland, *Christian Origins: An Account of the Setting and Character of the Most Important Messianic Sect of Judaism*, 2nd ed. (London: SPCK, 2002), 287-96.

68. See especially Hahn, *Mission in the New Testament*, 50-52; Meyer, *Early Christians*, 76, 175-76; Hengel, *Between Jesus and Paul*, 22-24. While Hengel deals with the theme in connection with the Hellenists, the significance of the Spirit cannot be restricted to one portion of the early movement.

69. Dunn, *Theology of Paul the Apostle*, 419.

70. On the connection with baptismal liturgy, see Martyn, *Galatians*, 392.

71. The postresurrection era conceived of as a distinct period, "set by [the Father's] own authority" and characterized by Spirit-empowered witness "in Jerusalem, in all Judea and Samaria, and to the ends of the earth" (Acts 1:7-8).

Testament material as evidence that the early Christ-movement "was evidently marked out within first-century Judaism by its claim to have been given the Spirit of God in a new and exceptional way."[72]

The early experience of the Spirit readily lent itself to an eschatological interpretation. In Galatians, Paul describes it as the fulfillment of a "promise," linking it with the blessing promised to Abraham (Gal 3:14). More explicitly, Luke depicts Peter as proclaiming that it is a fulfillment of the prophet Joel's prophecy of an outpouring of God's Spirit "in the last days" (Acts 2:16–21). Taken together, both the experience itself and the perception of its eschatological character led to the idea that the present period was not simply a time of preparation for the parousia and the future age but instead already manifested some of the realities of that age. Thus Paul can speak of the Spirit as the "firstfruits" of the coming age of redemptive glory (Rom 8:23).[73] In a related image, he elsewhere describes the Spirit as "first installment" (*arrabōn*) of the coming state of affairs ("God's promises" [2 Cor 1:20–22]; the resurrection body [2 Cor 5:5]). More generally, he can characterize Christ-believers as those "on whom the ends of the ages have come" (1 Cor 10:11).[74] While these images bear a distinctly Pauline stamp, they give expression to a more widespread conception—the idea that through the resurrection of Christ and the giving of the Holy Spirit, the age to come was breaking into the present in a preliminary yet powerful way.

To return to a point already made, the emergence of this conception is not to be accounted for solely on the basis of the delay of the parousia, as if it were simply a compensation for a failed expectation. Rather, the basic Christ-message contained within it the potential for different characterizations of the period between the resurrection and the parousia. At one end, it could be seen as a period marked more by what was yet to come (the parousia and the arrival of the promised reign of God); at the other, as a period marked more by what had already taken place (the decisive event of the resurrection and the experience of the Spirit). The delay of the parousia served to encourage the development of the latter.

A third area where the message of the earliest Christ-believers contained the potential for development and shifts in emphasis had to do with soteriology—

---

72. Dunn, *Theology of Paul the Apostle*, 417.

73. He uses the same image of the resurrected Christ in 1 Cor 15:23. But whereas in this usage the emphasis remains on the future as far as believers are concerned ("then at his coming those who belong to Christ"), when it is used of the Spirit, the emphasis shifts to present experience.

74. Cf. Heb 6:5, where believers are those who "have tasted the . . . powers of the age to come."

that is, salvation. In proclaiming that God had revealed the coming Messiah by raising Jesus from the dead, the early Christ-believers were identifying Jesus as the coming agent of salvation. As the appointed Messiah whom God would send, Jesus would bring into effect "the time of universal restoration that God announced long ago through his holy prophets" (Acts 3:20–21). It is probable that, as this passage suggests, the earliest preaching located salvation in the eschatological future: at his parousia, the Messiah would (in keeping with traditional expectations) judge the wicked, vindicate the righteous, and usher in the age of peace, blessing, and redemption.

In the traditional summary of the gospel that Paul cites in 1 Cor 15:3–8, however, we find early evidence of soteriological significance being attached to Christ's death: "Christ died for our sins, according to the scriptures" (1 Cor 15:3). While Luke's account of the early Jewish Christ-movement ascribes no saving significance to his death, repentance and forgiveness are commonly linked to Jesus in other ways: "repent in the name of Jesus so that your sins might be forgiven" (Acts 2:38); "God exalted him at his right hand as Leader and Savior that he might give repentance to Israel and forgiveness of sins" (5:31); "everyone who believes in him receives forgiveness of sins through his name" (10:43).[75] It lies beyond my purposes here to explore earliest thinking about the significance of Jesus's death, though we have already observed that the idea of a dying Messiah presented early Christ-believers with a challenge, one that they met by appealing to various suffering figures in Israel's Scriptures.[76] More generally, however, this early development in which forgiveness of sins is said to have been made possible by Jesus's death, or was at least somehow made available through him, had the potential to raise questions about the status of the temple and its system of sacrifice and atonement and thus about the relationship of Christ-believers and the central institution of Jewish life.

The fourth and final area where the early message presented ambiguities and the potential for diversity of development is one that might be termed ecclesiology, since it has to do with the nature and identity of the community of Jewish Christ-believers. Actually, we touched on this already at the outset, where we observed that implicit in the basic message was a distinction between those proclaiming it (who were identified by their allegiance to Jesus and their belief

---

75. In Acts 3:19 the link is with God rather than Jesus: "Repent, therefore, and turn to God so that your sins may be wiped out." The difference is probably significant.

76. The phrase "for our sins" (*hyper tōn hamartiōn hēmōn*) in 1 Cor 15:3 probably echoes language in Isa 53; see, e.g., Hans Conzelmann, *1 Corinthians: A Commentary on the First Epistle to the Corinthians*, trans. James W. Leitch, Hermeneia (Philadelphia: Fortress, 1975), 253–55.

about his messianic identity) and the rest of Israel. There we noted that, while this message was one that could be proclaimed in a spirit of solidarity with the rest of Israel (the Christ-group as a renewal movement identifying fully with the rest of Israel), the fact that the message served to identify the Christ-believers as a distinct group also carried with it the possibility of a relationship of separation and discontinuity (the Christ-group as a remnant or even as a sectarian group, standing over against the rest of Israel). This possibility became greater whenever Christ-belief was proclaimed as essential—that is, whenever it was proclaimed that, in order to share in the messianic blessings that would come in the future, it was necessary to recognize Jesus as the Messiah in the present.

Further, each of the areas of conceptual development that we have discussed—having to do with Christology, eschatology, and soteriology—has had ecclesiological implications; that is, they have produced additional options along several lines of development that had implications for identity construction among early Christ-believers.[77] As we have seen, each of these could be formulated in ways that would fit rather smoothly with the identity structures of Israel as a whole. Nevertheless, each of them also contained ambiguities and tensions, or otherwise raised questions requiring attention, that produced lines of development with greater potential for differentiation and tension between the Christ-believing subgroup and the larger group.

More specifically, the line of development for each of these areas had a certain temporal aspect to it. On the one hand, each of them could be formulated in such a way as to place the emphasis on the future: Jesus as the Messiah-designate, whom God would send in the future to usher in the messianic age of redemption (Christology); the end of the age as imminent, but not yet present (eschatology); salvation as the state of existence in the age to come and thus something that the Messiah would accomplish at his future coming (soteriology). But on the other hand, as we have also seen, both the internal dynamics of the message and the external circumstances of the early Jewish Christ-believers led to developments that served to place greater emphases on the present age: the risen Messiah as the exalted Lord of all, presently exercising sovereignty "at God's right hand"; the age to come, breaking into the present age in a powerful way, as experienced in the activity of the Holy Spirit; salvation as a present experience, accomplished by the death (and resurrection) of the Messiah and made effective through the presence of the Spirit. Each of these developments could well have had the effect of sharpening the differentiation between the Jewish Christ-groups and the Jewish people as a whole, thus necessitating further developments in the area of

---

77. These four areas of conceptual development might be presented in question form: Who is he? What time is it? What has he accomplished—and how? Who are we?

identity construction and self-definition. Even here, however, we need to recognize a further distinction with respect to this sort of shift from future expectation to present experience—between developments that simply corresponded to what any Jewish person might have expected to occur with the arrival of the end times (e.g., a heightened experience of the Spirit) and those that would have represented a decisive break with Jewish tradition and expectation (e.g., the practice—if the accusation were true—of teaching "all the Jews living among the Gentiles to forsake Moses and . . . not to circumcise their children or observe the customs"; Acts 21:21).[78]

None of this is to suggest that the process of development should be conceived as simply linear and progressive. That is, it was certainly not the case that once a particular development had taken place, earlier formulations and positions disappeared. We need to think here in terms of a range of positions along several axes—and thus of an increasing potential for diversity—rather than of unitary developmental trajectories.

But what about the gentiles and their place in the new community of Christ-believers? From the preceding discussion, it is apparent that the earliest Christ-community was focused on Israel and on the future—the imminent fulfillment of the end-time promises to Israel.[79] In keeping with this, there seems to have been no conception of a mission to non-Jews at the beginning. Nevertheless, the first generation of the Christ-movement saw a development that led to the inclusion of non-Jews in significant numbers and the emergence of a concerted gentile mission. This development needs to be seen as one of the most significant social developments within the early Christ-movement, both depending on and then substantially reshaping the communal self-understandings of the movement in its various manifestations and stages of development.[80] Before we can recognize and describe the various forms of identity that were ascribed to gentile Christ-believers by Jewish Christ-groups, we need to complete our present discussion of the earliest Jewish Christ-communities by looking more closely at the origins of these developments.

To be sure, in itself the attraction of non-Jews and their inclusion within early Jewish Christ-groups was not remarkable. As we have seen in chapter 3, throughout the Second Temple period there were gentile sympathizers who attached themselves to local synagogue communities and paid homage to the God

---

78. Hengel, who tends to see Jewish tradition as a barrier to be transcended, sees the experience of the Spirit itself as effecting this sort of break; *Between Jesus and Paul*, 23.

79. In addition, see Freyne, *Jesus Movement and Its Expansion*, 209–13.

80. A "momentous" development (Dunn, *Beginning from Jerusalem*, 50); "a pivotal moment" (Meyer, *Early Christians*, 13).

Ethnē as an Identity Ascribed to Non-Jews: By Jewish Christ-Believers

of Israel at the Jerusalem temple; some of them took the necessary additional steps to become proselytes and thus to become more fully incorporated into the Jewish people. This was met on the Jewish side with conceptual developments by which Jews made space for others on their covenant-centered map of the human world—the conception of proselytism itself, of course (including the hard-edged view that only by becoming proselytes in this age could gentiles hope to have a place in the age to come), but also conceptions in which gentiles as gentiles could relate positively to the God of Israel and Creator of all, by adhering to that part of the torah that applied to gentiles as well or by discerning that form of universal ethical monotheism of which the torah was a particular instantiation. In addition, many Jews expected that in the eschatological future—"the time of universal restoration that God announced long ago through his holy prophets" (to quote Acts 3:21)—gentiles would abandon their sinful ways, recognize the God of Israel, and share in the blessings of the new age.

The story of the early Christ-movement and the beginnings of the gentile mission is often constructed on the assumption that the inclusion of gentiles represented ipso facto a turning away from the Jewish world and the (at least incipient) abandonment of Jewish identity—as if an openness to gentiles on the part of a Jewish group is something in need of explanation.[81] On the contrary, in their attitudes toward non-Jews, early Christ-believers were very much part of their Jewish environment. Once gentiles began to show an interest in their communities, their reception of non-Jews did not differ in essential ways from synagogue reception more generally. To be sure, there were differences among them—sharp conflicts even—over the terms on which non-Jews were to be included within the Christ-movement. And some participants in the conflicts may have eventually taken positions that went beyond the bounds of Jewish patterns of inclusion.[82] But for the most part, the range of opinions in the disputes over

---

81. Several representative examples: "Stephen, then, seems to have been the first Christian to realize that Christianity meant the end of Jewish privilege, and the first to open the way for a mission to the Gentiles" (G. B. Caird, *The Apostolic Age* [London: Duckworth, 1955], 86). "The real mission to the Gentiles in the full sense of the word may only have begun in Antioch (Acts 11.19ff.). . . . Its detachment from Judaism then led this early Hellenistic community, following the LXX, to give itself the name *ekklesia* and in this way to proclaim its eschatologically conditioned difference from the Jewish synagogue communities" (Hengel, *Between Jesus and Paul*, 58). "Whatever it was that set them [the *hellēnistai*] apart from the *hebraioi* at this level, it appears to have found expression in hostility to Torah and temple (Acts 6:14) and in openness to Samaritans (Acts 7:5) and gentiles (Acts 11:20)" (Meyer, *Early Christians*, 68). See further the discussion of the parting of the ways in ch. 2.

82. Some of Paul's statements—for example, that Jewish Christ-believers should be

terms of inclusion reflected the range of opinions in the wider Jewish population. In itself, the openness to non-Jews on the part of the early Christ-believers requires no special explanation. The beginnings of (what developed into) the gentile mission were a fully natural reflection of the Jewish character of the early Christ-movement.

Within the first generation of the movement, however, we do witness the emergence of something quite new—a vigorous expansion of the movement among non-Jews, the development of mixed-ethnic or even largely gentile Christ-groups around the Mediterranean basin and the accompanying conception of a universal mission to all the nations. While we do not need to account in any special way for the attraction of non-Jews to the Christ-movement or for the willingness of Jewish Christ-believers to receive them in accordance with established patterns of inclusion, these new developments mark the Christ-movement as distinct and thus do require some explanation.

Several lines of interpretation probably need to be set aside at the outset, even if they have to be taken into account at a secondary level. One of these, which appeals to the Jewish environment in an even stronger way, holds that Jews were already engaged in a thoroughgoing mission to attract sympathizers and make converts and that the Christ-centered mission can be accounted for simply as a continuation of this mission on modified terms. This position, which in effect minimizes the element of newness in the Christ-centered mission, was championed by Harnack and has continued to receive support.[83] But while the existence of the Jewish diaspora was undoubtedly an essential factor in the spread of the Christ-movement, it seems clear that one cannot speak of an analogous Jewish mission, either in external form or internal conceptualization.[84]

Other lines of approach to be set aside are those that would account for the mission by straightforward appeals to Jesus himself—either that Jesus initiated or prepared for a gentile mission in his earthly activity or that a mission to all

---

prepared to live "in a Gentile, not a Jewish, manner" (*ethnikōs kai ouxi Ioudaikōs*; Gal 2:14), or that uncircumcised Christ-believers were not only part of the "nations" (*ethnē*) who would be blessed in Abraham (Gal 3:8, citing Gen 12:3), but were part of that "seed" (*sperma*; Gal 3:29; Rom 4:13, 16–17) of Abraham for which circumcision was a sine qua non (Gen 17:9–14)—would understandably have been seen in this way.

83. Harnack, *Mission and Expansion*, 1–18. For a discussion of the issue, see my *Judaism and the Gentiles: Jewish Patterns of Universalism (to 135 CE)* (Waco, TX: Baylor University Press, 2007), 5–6, together with the literature cited there.

84. See especially Scot McKnight, *A Light among the Gentiles: Jewish Missionary Activity in the Second Temple Period* (Minneapolis: Fortress, 1991), and Martin Goodman, *Mission and Conversion: Proselytizing in the Religious History of the Roman Empire* (Oxford: Clarendon, 1994).

Ethnē as an Identity Ascribed to Non-Jews: By Jewish Christ-Believers

the nations was commanded by the risen Christ. Against such appeals, we need to recognize that, while both the mission of Jesus and the resurrection experiences of the disciples have a part to play, they do not by themselves provide an adequate explanation for the emergence of the early mission to the gentiles. Two considerations are crucial here. First, as has already been noted, the earliest Christ-believers do not seem to have had any conception of a mission that would go beyond the boundaries of the Jewish world; the earliest mission centered entirely on Israel. Second, when the inclusion of non-Jews did become a live issue, there was a significant lack of agreement on the conditions of admission. Both considerations make it difficult to believe that, through their presence with Jesus or their resurrection experiences, the disciples had been given any clear indication of a commission to evangelize the gentiles and of the terms in which it would take place.

Nevertheless, these phenomena—gentile attraction to Jewish religious life, the mission of Jesus, and the experiences of the early disciples that were understood as encounters with the risen Jesus—were part of the environment in which the gentile mission emerged and thus were component elements of the larger process of development. Let us look at the elements of this process in a little more detail.

Although it is unlikely that Jesus initiated the gentile mission in any direct way, his own mission, together with his attitude toward the gentiles, played an important preparatory role. Rooted in the prior mission of John the Baptist, the mission of Jesus—an urgent and itinerant enterprise, calling Israel to prepare for the imminent inbreaking of God's reign—represented the substantive context in which the relationship between Jesus and his disciples was formed. Disciples were called to follow him in his itinerant mission (e.g., Mark 1:16-20) and were sent out to extend it on their own (Mark 3:13-19; Luke 10:1-16). The sense of a mission to Israel, which characterized the earliest Jewish Christ-believers, was rooted in the experience of the disciples with Jesus and his mission.

But what of Jesus and the gentiles? While a detailed treatment of the question would take us too far afield here, we can note several pertinent undisputed aspects of Jesus's activity and sayings.[85] First, Jesus's mission was directed pri-

---

85. For helpful surveys of scholarship, see Hahn, *Mission in the New Testament*, 26-28, and Michael F. Bird, *Jesus and the Origins of the Gentile Mission*, LNTS 331 (London: T&T Clark, 2006), 1-23. The topic is treated in full-scale monographs (e.g., in addition to Bird, Friedrich Spitta, *Jesus und die Heidenmission* [Giessen: Alfred Töpelmann, 1909]; Joachim Jeremias, *Jesus' Promise to the Nations*, SBT 24 [London: SCM, 1958]); studies of the historical Jesus (e.g., Albert Schweitzer, *The Mystery of the Kingdom of God: the Secret of Jesus' Messiahship and Passion* [New York: Dodd, Mead, 1914], 117-18 and passim; E. P. Sanders,

marily at Israel, especially at "the lost sheep of the house of Israel" (the poor, the marginalized, the deprived; Matt 10:6). Even if the saying preserved in Matt 10:5-6, with its sharp prohibitions, has been preserved and shaped within a particularistic circle of Christ-believers, it is consistent with the general theme of Jesus's preaching and the contours of his activity.[86] Second, this Israel-focus notwithstanding, but in keeping nevertheless with his concern for the marginalized, Jesus also demonstrated an openness toward those outside the Jewish boundaries—especially gentile supplicants who sought him out (the Syrophoenician woman of Mark 7:24-30; the gentile centurion of Matt 8:5-13 and Luke 7:1-10).[87] This openness suggests that Jesus viewed gentiles as capable of relating positively to the God of Israel in the present age. Third, Jesus seems to have expected that some gentiles would share in the eschatological blessings of the coming reign of God.[88] Such an expectation certainly comes to expression in the so-called parable of the sheep and the goats in Matt 25:31-45. The statement about those who will "come from east and west, from north and south, and will eat in the kingdom of God" (Luke 13:28-29; also Matt 8:12-13) almost certainly should be read in the same way.[89]

Jesus and Judaism [Philadelphia: Fortress, 1985], 212-21); and studies of early Christian mission (Harnack, *Mission and Expansion*, 36-43; Hahn, *Mission in the New Testament*, 26-36; David J. Bosch, *Transforming Mission: Paradigm Shifts in Theology of Mission*, American Society of Missiology Series 16 [Maryknoll, NY: Orbis, 2011], ch. 1; Eckhard J. Schnabel, *Early Christian Mission* [Downers Grove, IL: InterVarsity, 2004], 1:207-386).

86. "Go nowhere among the Gentiles, and enter no town of the Samaritans, but go rather to the lost sheep of the house of Israel."

87. The openness toward Samaritans, on view in Jesus's parable of the exemplary Samaritan (Luke 10:30-37), represents an intermediate case.

88. Meyer summarizes it this way: "Contrary to a stubborn misconception, Jesus was no 'universalist,' nor did he envisage a world mission. The nations were indeed invited to the banquet of salvation, but in the post-historical future, and by their own coming 'from east and west' to share it (Matt 8:11; par. Luke 13:29)"; *Early Christians*, 58-59. See also Freyne, *Jesus Movement and Its Expansion*, 144-46.

89. Taken by itself, the statement in Matt 8:11 ("many will come from east and west . . .") could refer to the incoming of the Jewish diaspora rather than an influx of gentiles. Sanders considers it possible that the subsequent statement ("but the sons of the kingdom will be cast out") is inauthentic (*Jesus and Judaism*, 219-20), which would mean that the incoming group is not necessarily gentile. But in Luke, the incoming group is also set over against a group of Jews ("you yourselves" [Luke 13:28], i.e., Jesus's hearers in the towns and villages in which he taught on his way to Jerusalem), which makes it more likely that the contrast between included gentiles and excluded Jews is authentic. If so, the statement of Jesus combines two themes that are present in Jewish eschatological expectation—the

Ethnē as an Identity Ascribed to Non-Jews: By Jewish Christ-Believers

While this is a rough sketch that certainly deserves a more detailed elaboration, it is sufficient for present purposes. In their experience with the earthly Jesus, the disciples were drawn into a mission whose aim was to prepare Israel for the imminent arrival of the kingdom of God, an eschatological state of affairs in which gentiles would also have an opportunity to share.

The next element in the process of development was the set of experiences through which the disciples came to believe that God had raised Jesus from the dead and had poured out the divine Spirit in an unprecedented way. The immediate impact of these experiences was to intensify the sense of mission that the disciples had inherited from Jesus. What they had experienced—that God had identified Jesus as Israel's Messiah by raising him from the dead—added fresh energy and urgency to the message that Jesus had sent them to proclaim during his own ministry. In Hahn's words, the experiences

> meant that the shattered community was restored again, and it meant further that the Kingdom of God, which, as Jesus proclaimed, had drawn near, was realized still more intensively, for indeed the event of Easter was for the earliest Christians merely an anticipation of the events of the end. From this it followed that Jesus' message must continue to be proclaimed, and that the commission that he had entrusted to his disciples, far from being cancelled, was confirmed.[90]

It is probable that the concept of apostleship, in the distinctive sense that apostles were authoritative witnesses to the risen Christ who took the lead in the mission, goes back to the early days of the Jerusalem Christ-group. The association with James in the early summary of the message (1 Cor 15:7) points in this direction. More tellingly, Paul's evident concern to claim the title for himself as the one entrusted with the mission to the gentiles (Gal 1:1; 1 Cor 9:1–2; 15:8–11; 2 Cor 12:11–12) indicates that it had already been established as the recognized title for those engaged in mission to Jews.

But while the resurrection experiences confirmed and intensified the disciples' sense of mission, they did not effect any change with respect to the gentiles. As we have seen, the earliest Christ-message was directed exclusively at Israel; if it had implications for the gentiles, this would come with the "time of universal

---

pilgrimage of the gentiles and the judgment of sinners within Israel (on which see Mark Adam Elliott, *The Survivors of Israel: A Reconsideration of the Theology of Pre-Christian Judaism* [Grand Rapids: Eerdmans, 2000], 57–113)—but that are not often juxtaposed.

90. Hahn, *Mission in the New Testament*, 47.

restoration" (Acts 3:21) that would soon arrive.[91] Here it might be mentioned in passing that the traditions anticipating the redemption of the gentiles in the end times contained little to suggest that this would involve a mission. For the most part, the role of Israel would be passive rather than active; it is God's salvation of Israel that would prompt the gentiles to seek Israel's God. The motion is centripetal rather than centrifugal—gentiles streaming to Zion rather than Jewish emissaries spreading out to summon the gentiles.[92]

Gentiles did begin to come into contact with the Jewish Christ-movement, however, and eventually to express an interest in it, especially as the movement spread outward from Jerusalem into the hellenized cities of Judea (e.g., Caesarea Maritima) and the diaspora (e.g., Antioch). The available evidence seems to suggest that this contact and interest occurred spontaneously and naturally—that is, in a manner consistent with already-established patterns of gentile attraction to Judaism.

Some of this evidence has to do with Jerusalem. The Acts account contains two references to gentiles who had traveled to the city for the purposes of worship, thereby coming into contact with Christ-believers—the proselytes from Rome who came to Jerusalem for the Festival of Weeks, where they heard Peter's Pentecost discourse (Acts 2:10),[93] and the Ethiopian official who encountered Philip on his way home from Jerusalem (Acts 8:26-39). In addition, Nicolaus, a proselyte from Antioch, is listed as one of the leaders of the Hellenists in the Jerusalem *ekklēsia*, though nothing is said about how he came to reside in Jerusalem.

---

91. Might there be a hint of this in v. 26? The statement that God sent his servant (*pais*) "first [*prōton*] to you," that is, "the seed of Abraham" (v. 25), seems to suggest a subsequent sending of the servant to "all the families of the earth" (v. 25). Both the primitive christological term *servant* (together with other indications of an early tradition; see, e.g., Dunn, *Beginning from Jerusalem*, 92-93) and the fact that it was the servant himself who would be sent subsequently might suggest the presence of eschatological pilgrimage patterns of thought.

92. For a survey of prophetic material in Israel's Scriptures, see Schnabel, *Early Christian Mission*, 1:76-91. While Schnabel has a particular interest in the idea of a centrifugal mission, he recognizes that "Is 66:19 is the only passage in the Old Testament, excepting the Servant Songs, that refers to a proclamation to Gentiles by human emissaries" (p. 85). For material in Second Temple Jewish literature, see Donaldson, *Judaism and the Gentiles*.

93. If "Rome" in Acts 2:10 had stood at the end of the list, the phrase "both Jews and proselytes" could be taken as applying to all the nations mentioned. But while it seems odd to mention proselytes only in connection with Rome (surely it was just as likely for there to have been proselytes from Asia or Egypt), this seems to be the meaning of the text as it stands (with "Cretans and Arabs" rounding out the list).

Ethnē as an Identity Ascribed to Non-Jews: By Jewish Christ-Believers

Moving outward from Jerusalem, the Acts account makes reference to evangelizing activity in the mixed-ethnic areas of Samaria, Gaza, Azotus (Ashdod), and Caesarea (in connection with Philip), of Joppa and Caesarea (in connection with Peter), and of Phoenicia, Cyprus, and Antioch (in connection with the founding of the *ekklēsia* in Antioch). Although Luke would have it that, before the developments in Antioch, "the word" was spoken "to no one except Jews" (Acts 11:19), his sources tell a different tale, especially with respect to Cornelius, the Godfearing centurion who initiates a meeting with Peter in Caesarea, and to the Ethiopian official who meets with Philip on his return journey. In addition, given the realities of life in densely packed cities and the phenomenon of gentile sympathizers associated with the synagogues, it probably was the case that any word being spoken to Jews would necessarily have been heard by non-Jews as well. Although we need to give due attention to the distinction between gentile attraction to a Jewish message and a Jewish mission directed at gentiles specifically, it was no doubt the case that non-Jews were hearing and, to a certain extent, responding positively to the Jewish message more or less from the beginning.[94]

This element of the process of development, then, can be seen as a Christ-centered version of the more general Jewish phenomenon—of gentiles being attracted to Jewish groups and Jewish beliefs, and of their being allowed to associate with these groups in what were felt to be appropriate ways. For the Jerusalem Christ-believers, at least, this seems to have meant either proselytism or some acceptable form of Godfearing. To be sure, we do not have much evidence to rely on here, but the positions staked out at a later point in the Jerusalem Council seem to reflect these options.[95]

The next element to be mentioned in the emergence of the idea of a concerted

---

94. On this point, and on the development of the early mission more generally, see Paula Fredriksen, *Paul: The Pagans' Apostle* (New Haven: Yale University Press, 2017), 77–80.

95. It is not necessary for my purposes here to enter into the tangled discussion of the Jerusalem Council and of how to reconstruct the sequence of events on the basis of Acts and Galatians, though it seems likely that the Acts account conflates the results of several events into a single meeting. Here I am interested in what we can discern about the attitudes toward interested non-Jews on the part of Jewish Christ-believers in the early stage of the movement, and Luke's account seems to reflect the concerns of the Jerusalem *ekklēsia*. Nor is it necessary to resolve the question whether the terms of the apostolic decree (Acts 15:29; 21:25) are to be aligned with the Noachian decrees or the regulations governing resident aliens living in the land (Lev 17:8–14; cf. 18:26); see Dunn, *Beginning from Jerusalem*, 465–67; Barrett, *Acts of the Apostles*, 2:733–35. While a distinction can be made between the diaspora and the land with respect to the setting in which Jews

gentile mission probably has to do with the surprising degree of positive response on the part of gentiles themselves. The importance of Antioch in this regard cannot be doubted, given its prominence in both Acts and Galatians. To be sure, it is quite probable that analogous developments were to be found in Caesarea, Damascus, and other cities with mixed Jewish-gentile population. Still, the only substantial early evidence we have pertains to the situation in Antioch.

According to the Acts account, the new development in Antioch was that, instead of speaking "the word to no one except Jews," some began to "proclaim the Lord Jesus" to non-Jews as well.[96] As we have already observed, it is to be expected that, in a diaspora situation, any proclamation to Jews would inevitably have come to the attention of non-Jews as well. In all probability, the innovation here was an initiative to proclaim the message to non-Jews directly. As Dunn has observed, we should not necessarily think here of "a change of venue," a transition away from the Jewish community into the non-Jewish world. Given the situation in Antioch as described by Josephus—the Jews "were constantly attracting to their religious ceremonies multitudes of Greeks, and these they had in some measure incorporated with themselves" (*Jewish War* 7.45; also 2.463[97])—one can readily envisage a situation where a surprisingly positive level of interest on the part of these gentile sympathizers led some of the Jewish Christ-believers to focus their evangelizing activity on non-Jews directly. The transition, then, was one in which a mission to Jews, with gentile attraction as a kind of by-product, was supplemented by a mission to non-Jews.[98] A further step in consolidating the idea of a gentile mission was represented by the decision on the part of the Antioch *ekklēsia* to support Barnabas and Saul in an initiative to replicate the Antioch situation elsewhere in the diaspora. While Paul puts his own complexion on things, his references to "the gospel I proclaim among the *ethnē*" (Gal 2:2), a proclamation in company with Barnabas (Gal 2:1, 9) and with Antioch as a kind

---

encounter non-Jews, it is not clear that a sharp distinction can be made with respect to the specific terms on which appropriate relations were regulated.

96. The most probable reading here (*hellēnistas*; cf. *hellēnas*, found in P[74] ℵ[2] A D*) raises a problem, in that elsewhere in Acts, *hellēnistai* is used of Greek-speaking Jews. Nevertheless, the contrast with *Ioudaiois* makes it virtually certain that non-Jews are in view here.

97. Thackeray's LCL rendering ("attracting") is overly passive; Josephus's statement implies a more active role on the part of the Jewish community: they were "leading [non-Jews] to" (*prosagomenoi*) their religious observances.

98. "The dispersed Hellenists preached the good news of Jesus in the Antioch synagogue(s) and found, perhaps somewhat to their own surprise, that the God-fearing Gentile adherents found their message most compelling"; Dunn, *Beginning from Jerusalem*, 299.

of center (2:11; cf. 1:21 ["Syria and Cilicia"]), testifies also to the early appearance of a mission directed at non-Jews in and around Antioch.

From the accounts of subsequent attempts to compel these gentile converts to accept circumcision (in the case of males) and to undertake full adherence to the law of Moses (Acts 15:1-2; Gal 2:11-14), it is clear that this had not been a requirement of admission on the part of the nascent gentile mission.[99] While this has often been seen as a significant departure from Jewish practice,[100] in itself it probably did not differ very much from the practice of the wider Jewish community in Antioch (as described by Josephus). Still, there were differences in the social dynamics in these ethnically mixed Christ-communities. In contrast to the situation of gentile sympathizers more generally, gentile participation in the Christ-groups was marked by practices and commitments that served more to unite them with Jewish members than to mark them as ethnically distinct. Belief in Christ, baptism, experience of the Spirit, participation in the Lord's meal—all of these were held in common and could readily have been perceived as more prominent and more significant than the distinction between Jew and non-Jew. In the case of Christ-communities that were totally Jewish, these practices and commitments served to mark them out as subgroups or sectarian groups. But when such communities welcomed non-Jews without requiring that they become proselytes, the distinction between sympathizers and full members was inevitably blurred. To be sure, belief in Christ meant acceptance of a Jewish savior-figure; the Lord's meal carried with it overtones of the Jewish Passover; it also carried with it the potential for tensions concerning Jewish food laws. Gentile participants in a Christ-group could hardly be unaware of its Jewish foundations and character. Still, the practices and commitments of the group were such as to foster a situation in which the things that were shared by all participants could come to overshadow differences in ethnic identity.

Of course, given the Jewish foundations of the Christ-movement, such a sit-

---

99. Though Paul's description of it is harsh and caustic, it seems that this initiative to insist on full proselytism for gentile converts developed into a distinct torah-centered form of gentile mission itself (Galatians; Phil 2:2-3); see Raymond E. Brown, "Not Jewish Christianity and Gentile Christianity, but Types of Jewish/Gentile Christianity," *CBQ* 45 (1983): 74-79, esp. 77.

100. E.g., "For the *hellēnistai* the eschaton had been inaugurated by the enthronement of the crucified Messiah at God's right hand. The economy of temple and Torah had thus been brought to an end. . . . In accord with the resultant missionary perspectives and policies of the Antioch community, it was taken for granted that gentiles would 'come in' to present fellowship and future glory without 'coming in' to a religious economy already obsolete"; Meyer, *Early Christians*, 97-98; also Hengel, *Between Jesus and Paul*, 58.

uation could also (and did!) evoke initiatives to reinforce Jew-gentile distinctions, either by insisting on full proselytism or by defining the terms on which non-Jews could participate in Christ-groups. But here demographics soon became a consideration. The greater the proportion of non-Jews in these mixed Christ-groups, the greater the pressure exerted by the things held in common. The impact of such pressure might be seen in the idea that the inclusion of the gentiles represented something new—a "mystery" that had not been revealed before (Rom 11:25),[101] a new revelation of divine impartiality ("God has shown me that I should not call anyone profane or unclean"; Acts 10:28; also 10:34–35).

At this point, the discussion of the development of a specific mission to gentiles joins up with our previous discussion about conceptual and theological developments. As we have seen, conceptual developments in the areas of Christology, soteriology, and eschatology served to shift the focus and emphasis of the Christ-message from the future (God has revealed Jesus as the coming Messiah by raising him from the dead) to the present. Jesus is not simply the coming Messiah but is the presently reigning Lord of all. Salvation is not simply something that the Messiah will accomplish in the future but is available in anticipatory forms through the death and resurrection of Christ and the coming of the Spirit. The age to come is not simply a state of affairs that will come but is already breaking into the present in a powerful way through the activity of the Spirit. As we have also seen in a preliminary way, these conceptual developments had implications for the place of non-Jews in the new Christ-centered state of affairs (the ecclesiological outworkings of the Christ-message).

To carry this forward, there were two broad ways in which the emerging concept of a gentile mission could be constructed with respect to the Christ-message. On the one hand, it could be formulated in a way that would fit more or less smoothly with the identity structures of Israel. The Scriptures anticipated that in the latter days the nations would abandon their idols and worship the God of Israel alone; with the death and resurrection of the Messiah (it could be argued), these days have begun to dawn; thus the time is here for the expected influx of the gentiles. James's appeal to Amos 9:11–12 (Acts 15:15–17) might be seen as a reflection of this straightforward pattern of thought. To be sure, since scriptural expectations were rather ambiguous about the status of such end-time gentile believers, it was not surprising that debates broke out over the issue of circumcision and torah observance. But both options on the table from the perspective of the Jerusalem Christ-believers—full proselytism or a kind of reduced set of torah observances for gentiles—fell within the established patterns of Second Temple Judaism.

---

101. Further developed in deutero-Pauline material (Rom 16:25–27; Eph 1:9–13; 3:1–9).

Ethnē *as an Identity Ascribed to Non-Jews: By Jewish Christ-Believers*

On the other hand, the unexpected nature of the eschatological fulfillment proclaimed in the Christ-message, especially when combined with the forces at work in the gentile mission that favored gospel commonalities over ethnic distinctions, led to formulations that in some cases went beyond traditional patterns of Jewish identity and expectation. I will leave until later in the chapter any attempt to describe or document these more precisely. But patterns of thought in which the defining institutions of Israel (torah, temple, sacrifice, circumcision, etc.) were seen as outmoded or transcended; or that ascribed the titles, prerogatives, or identity of Israel to uncircumcised gentiles; or that saw the teachings of Jesus as a new torah transcending the old—all of these could be seen as discontinuous with the main body of Jewish expectations about how non-Jews might relate to the God of Israel in the coming age of fulfillment. Even so, one needs to remain alert to the possibility of a distinction between formulations that represent modifications of Jewish expectation that might be understandable in view of the basic Christ-message and formulations that are significantly discontinuous.[102]

The final element to be considered here is the emergence of a concept of universal mission—that is, not simply that the gospel should be preached to gentiles as well as Jews, but that such preaching was part of a mission "to all the nations," "to the ends of the earth," "in the whole world," or equivalent formulations. Such formulations appear in two broad streams of tradition—one associated with Paul, the other with Peter and the Twelve (or Eleven). Perhaps not surprisingly, the leading figure or figures in each stream tend to be presented as the recipient of divine commissioning and the originator of the mission.

Paul's sense of having received an apostolic commission from God for a mission to the gentiles is fully on display in his letters, Galatians and Romans especially. The material is well known and there is no need to survey it here;[103] a few observations about its universal scope will suffice.[104] In Galatians, the first two pertinent references speak simply about a proclamation "among the *ethnē*": the

---

102. With respect to the former, I am thinking, for example, of attempts (such as that of W. D. Davies) to portray Paul's formulation of the status and role of the torah as what would be produced by a Jew of a particular type, who also believed that the Messiah had come.

103. On his own role as apostle to the *ethnē*, see especially Rom 1:5, 13; 11:13; 15:16-18; Gal 1:16; 2:1-10; 1 Thess 2:16; and, in the disputed epistles, Eph 3:1-9; Col 1:25-28; 1 Tim 2:7.

104. On the scope of his mission, see also Terence L. Donaldson, "'The Field God Has Assigned': Geography and Mission in Paul," in *Religious Rivalries in the Early Roman Empire and the Rise of Christianity*, ed. Leif Vaage, ESCJ 18 (Waterloo, ON: Wilfrid Laurier University Press, 2006), 109-37.

purpose of Paul's call was that he "might proclaim him [God's Son] among the *ethnē*" (1:16); to the Jerusalem leaders, Paul laid out "the gospel that I proclaim among the *ethnē*" (2:2). As he continues with the account of the meeting in Jerusalem, however, he sets his proclamation within a more explicit ethnic binary: "the gospel for the uncircumcised ... the gospel for the circumcised" (2:7); "the *ethnē* ... the circumcised" (2:9). Then a little later he aligns "the gospel" with the promise made to Abraham: "All the *ethnē* [*panta ta ethnē*] will be blessed in you" (3:8).

In Romans, the universal scope of the gentile mission is more pronounced. Paul begins by speaking of having received "grace and apostleship to bring about the obedience of faith among all the *ethnē* [*panta ta ethnē*]" (1:5). He returns to his apostolic role in 11:13, speaking of himself as "the [or "an"] apostle to the *ethnē* [*ethnōn apostolos*]," and this just after a passage in which *ethnē* has been set over against *Israel* in binary fashion (11:7–12).[105] The universal sense of *ethnē* is also in view in 11:25 ("the fullness of the *ethnē*"), in the binary of "the circumcised ... the *ethnē*" in 15:8–9, and in the catena of scriptural citations that follows (15:9–12, including "all the *ethnē*" in v. 10).[106] Also significant is the progress of Paul's mission as he sets it out in 15:19–29—"from Jerusalem and as far around as Illyricum" (v. 19), and then on to Rome and Spain.[107]

Turning to the other stream of tradition, we have already noted the accounts in Acts, which probably draw on traditions associated with Peter, in which Peter appears as the one who initiates a new opening toward the gentiles. In Luke's account of the Jerusalem Council, he attributes this summary to Peter: "My brothers, you are well aware that from early days God made his choice among you that through my mouth the *ethnē* would hear the word of the gospel and believe" (Acts 15:7). A related set of traditions is represented by the postresurrection commissioning scenes, in which the risen Christ commissions the disciples to carry out a universal mission: "Go and make disciples of all the *ethnē* [*panta ta ethnē*]" (Matt 28:19–20); "repentance and forgiveness of sins is to be proclaimed in his name to all the *ethnē* [*panta ta ethnē*], beginning from Jerusalem" (Luke 24:47); "and you will be my witnesses in Jerusalem, in all Judea and Samaria,

---

105. Since the article is often omitted with predicate nouns following a form of *einai*, the definite form "the apostle" is at least possible; further, given Paul's self-conception (note the first-person singular forms in Gal 2:7–8), it may well be probable.

106. In Romans, *ethnē* frequently appears in a binary with "Jews" (3:29; 9:24), "Israel" (9:30; 11:11, 12), and related terms (God's "people" [15:10]; "the saints at Jerusalem" [15:26–27]).

107. For a related sense of territorial progression with corresponding jurisdiction, see Paul's discourse about "the field that God has assigned to us" in 2 Cor 10:13–16.

and to the ends of the earth [*heōs eschatou tēs gēs*]" (Acts 1:8).¹⁰⁸ It is probable that, while these each have been shaped and formulated in accordance with the redactional interests of their authors, they draw on a stock of preexisting tradition.¹⁰⁹ In addition, a mission to "all the *ethnē*" appears in the apocalyptic discourse of Mark 13 (Mark 13:10; cf. Matt 10:18; 24:14), which also makes use of preexisting material.¹¹⁰

How are we to understand the origin of the idea of a universal mission and its twofold development? Here we need to be brief. Probably the earliest factor had to do with contingent realities—the surprising spread of the movement in the first few decades of its existence. By mid-century, Christ-groups were well established even as far afield as Rome, something that served to place the movement in at least an empire-wide frame of reference. Another factor was undoubtedly the christocentric rereading of Israel's Scripture, which seems to have been a characteristic feature of the movement from the beginning. The universal sovereignty of Jesus as Lord was bolstered by references to royal psalms (especially Pss 2 and 110 [LXX 109]) and the Danielic son of man (Dan 7:13-14),¹¹¹ texts that made explicit reference to the "nations."¹¹² The rereading of the suffering servant passages of

---

108. It is at least possible that Mark 16:15 is to be included here as well: "Go into all the world [*eis ton kosmon hapanta*] and proclaim the good news to the whole creation [*pasē tē ktisei*]." The longer ending of Mark (16:9-20), of course, was not part of the original Gospel; as is readily apparent, much of it simply recycles details found elsewhere in canonical material. Nevertheless, distinctive aspects of vv. 14-16 have been taken to suggest that the author was drawing on an independent version of a postresurrection commissioning scene. See, e.g., Reginald H. Fuller, *The Formation of the Resurrection Narratives* (New York: Macmillan, 1971), 155-57; Benjamin J. Hubbard, *The Matthean Redaction of a Primitive Apostolic Commissioning: An Exegesis of Matthew 28:16-20*, SBLDS 19 (Missoula, MT: Society of Biblical Literature, 1974), 137-49; cf. Adela Yarbro Collins, *Mark: A Commentary*, Hermeneia (Minneapolis: Fortress, 2007), 806-18.

109. Included in this material is the tradition underlying the commissioning scene in John 20:19-23, though here the sense of a universal mission is at best implicit. On the tradition history generally, see again Fuller, *Formation of the Resurrection Narratives*; Hubbard, *Matthean Redaction of a Primitive Apostolic Commissioning*; and, more recently, James D. G. Dunn, *Jesus Remembered*, vol. 1 of *Christianity in the Making* (Grand Rapids: Eerdmans, 2003), 841-66, esp. 859.

110. For a survey of the discussion on Mark's sources, see Collins, *Mark*, 594-600.

111. For Ps 2, see Acts 4:25-26; 13:33; Mark 1:11 and parr. For Ps 110, see Acts 2:34-35; Mark 12:36 and parr.; 14:62 and parr. For Dan 7:13-14, see Mark 13:26 and parr.; 14:62 and parr.; Matt 28:18.

112. To be sure, the references to the nations have to do more with subservience than with blessing (Ps 2:8-9; 110:5-6; Dan 7:14).

GENTILE CHRISTIAN IDENTITY

Deutero-Isaiah served to identify Jesus as the one who would be "a light to the nations" (Isa 42:6; 49:6) with the result that God's salvation would "reach to the end of the earth" (Isa 49:6).[113] The patriarchal narratives, which naturally would come into view for a group that saw itself as participating in the fulfillment of the story of Israel, promised a blessing not only for Abraham's seed but also for "all the families [*pasai hai phylai*]" (Gen 12:3) or "all the nations [*panta ta ethnē*]" (Gen 22:18) of the earth.[114] While the statement might be retrospective, Luke has certainly captured something of the early interpretive dynamic, when (in a passage to which we will return in a moment) he said that the risen Jesus "opened their minds to understand the scriptures . . . that repentance and forgiveness of sins is to be proclaimed in his name to all the nations" (Luke 24:45–47). A third factor undoubtedly was the forceful set of claims that Paul made about his own activity. He was an apostle, standing on equal ground with "those who were already apostles before [him]" (Gal 1:17; also Gal 1:1; 1 Cor 15:8–11). But within this apostolic group, he had a unique role: he had been entrusted with "the gospel for the uncircumcised" (Gal 2:7) and thus could describe himself as "apostle to the *ethnē*" (Rom 11:13).[115] Further, as we have already seen, this apostolic mission had universal dimensions—an "apostleship to bring about the obedience of faith among all the *ethnē*" (Rom 1:5). This forceful claim on Paul's part was eventually matched by an equally forceful claim on the part of those who identified with the original apostles. Reshaping the early resurrection accounts in light of later developments, they produced commissioning narratives in which the mission to "all the nations" is entrusted to the original (eleven) apostles.[116]

Before moving on to the issue of ascribed identity, one remaining question

---

113. In Acts 13:47, Isa 49:6 is cited with respect to Paul's mission. Also, in Paul's account of his own call (Gal 1:15), he seems to echo the call of the Servant in Isa 49:1. Isa 42:1–3 is cited in Matt 12:18–20.

114. See Acts 3:25 (citing Gen 22:18); Gal 3:8 (Gen 12:3); Rom 4:17 (Gen 17:5).

115. It has often been observed that while Paul uses the title *apostle* with respect to Peter in Gal 2, he seems to avoid using it of himself ("entrusted with the gospel for the uncircumcised" [v. 7]; "sending me to the *ethnē*" [v. 8]). Given the forceful claim to apostleship with which the epistle begins, this reticence is surprising. It may well be that Paul's narration here reflects the language used in the agreement itself; see Hans Dieter Betz, *Galatians: A Commentary on Paul's Letter to the Churches in Galatia*, Hermeneia (Philadelphia: Fortress, 1979), 95–99.

116. Luke is content to combine the two. The commission is given originally to the Eleven (Luke 24:46–48 [cf. v. 33]; Acts 1:8]) and is initiated in a decisive way through Peter (Acts 10–11). While Luke is reticent to see Paul as an apostle in the full sense of the term (see Acts 1:21–22 for the criteria; cf. Acts 14:4, 14), he does include several references to Paul's special commission (Acts 9:15; 13:47; 22:14–15, 21; 26:17–28).

about the universal mission needs to be flagged for later reference. In the earliest account of a discourse about a mission to non-Jews (i.e., Gal 2:1–10), two distinct missions seem to be in view—one to "the circumcised," the other to "the uncircumcised" or "the *ethnē*." A related distinction seems to be present in the idea of Jewish priority—that the Jewish "children" are to be fed first (Mark 7:27); that the gospel "should be spoken first" to "the Jews," and only then to "the *ethnē*" (Acts 13:46); and that salvation comes to everyone who has faith, "to the Jew first and also to the Greek" (Rom 1:16; 2:9–10). While this sense of priority might have been eschatologically determined in the beginning—the Jews in the period between the resurrection and the parousia, then the gentiles when the Messiah appears to restore all things—in the passages just cited, it seems to refer to a distinction in the present-day mission. In some of the later statements, however, the ethnic distinction seems to recede behind the vision of a single universal mission: "witnesses in Jerusalem, in all Judea and Samaria, and to the ends of the earth" (Acts 1:8); "wherever the good news is proclaimed in the whole world" (Mark 14:9); "go into the whole world and proclaim the good news to the whole creation" (Mark 16:15); "repentance and forgiveness of sins is to be proclaimed in his name to all the *ethnē*, beginning from Jerusalem" (Luke 24:47).

This final passage is notable in that "all the *ethnē*" seems to include the Jewish nation explicitly ("beginning from Jerusalem"). Elsewhere in Luke-Acts, *ta ethnē* by itself denotes non-Jews (nations or individuals); but here the addition of *panta* apparently indicates that Israel is included among the *ethnē*. The phrase "all the *ethnē*" appears in related material as well (Matt 28:19; Mark 13:10), and it has been commonly assumed that here too it has a universalized sense—"all the nations," inclusive of Israel, rather than "all the gentiles." The issue is complex and a universalized reading of the phrase is certainly possible (as Luke 24:47 demonstrates). However, such a reading would represent a significant departure from normal Jewish usage. Of the 125 or so occurrences of the phrase *panta ta ethnē* in Jewish literature, virtually all of them refer to non-Jews.[117] Six possible exceptions can be identified, but as we have seen in chapter 3, in none of them is Israel's character as a distinctive nation simply merged into a generic mass of "nations."[118] We will need to return to this issue at pertinent points in the next section.

---

117. Occurrences as a stand-alone phrase (i.e., without modifiers or qualifiers): LXX (one hundred); Apocrypha (nine); other Second Temple Jewish literature (twenty or so, though all but three are in translations other than Greek).

118. LXX Isa 56:7; LXX Jer 35:11, 14 (= MT 28:11, 14); OG Dan 3:2, 7; 4:37c; 6:26; Jdt 3:8.

Ascribed Identities

We are now in a position to look more directly at the identities ascribed to gentile Christ-believers by Jewish Christ-groups. In the previous section, it was not my purpose to describe in any comprehensive way the history of the Christ-movement in its earliest stage. Instead, the goal was to set out some of the self-definitional dynamics at work in the movement, especially as Jewish believers attempted to spell out the implications of their new convictions about Jesus and to make sense of the unanticipated and ever-extending interval between resurrection and parousia. For these purposes, it was not necessary to define the period precisely, though the period of interest certainly came to an end with the Jewish revolt (66–70 CE). As long as the Jerusalem community continued, it served as a touchstone and gravitational center for the movement. With its disappearance, the framework within which Jewish and gentile Christ-believers related to each other was altered significantly.

In this section, while our area of interest will include the first generation of the movement and the material discussed to this point, it will also extend beyond the destruction of Jerusalem. However, the area will be determined not so much temporally as situationally. We are primarily interested in those social situations where the relationship between Jewish and gentile Christ-believers or groups was such that the identity ascribed by the one was a significant factor in the construction of identity by the other. This means that as gentile groups expanded and became more independent, the ascription of identity by Jewish groups becomes less significant as a factor in their own identity construction.

Our investigation will proceed in several steps. First, since the material we have to work with is primarily documentary, we will begin by identifying writings that provide evidence for such identity ascription—writings that were probably produced by Jewish Christ-believers or at least that would have had a role in conveying Jewish ascriptions to gentile readers. Second, we will carry out a preliminary survey of the use of *ethnē* (and related terminology) in the pertinent literature, looking at its semantic range and other aspects of usage. Finally, we will identify and describe the range of identities ascribed to gentile Christ-believers by Jewish believers, noting especially the use made of *ethnē* and taking into account the related array of identity constructions produced by Jewish believers for themselves.

Literature pertinent to our investigation falls into several categories, to be used with different levels of confidence. Outside the seven undisputed letters of Paul, we are hard-pressed to identify pertinent writings that were certainly written by Jewish authors.[119] For the most part, we have to be content with

---

119. It is striking how often in standard reference works one encounters lengthy dis-

probabilities. In addition, however, since our final concern has to do with gentile identity construction, the question of authorship is not ultimate: literature that probably drew on Jewish Christ-tradition and that would have been perceived by its readers as ascribing identity to non-Jewish Christ-believers is also pertinent to our investigation.

The highest level of confidence, then, certainly includes the seven undisputed letters of Paul. As with many things pertaining to Paul, however, these letters represent a special case, in that they were addressed to communities whose membership was largely non-Jewish and were written by a "Hebrew of the Hebrews" (as he describes himself in Phil 3:5; cf. 2 Cor 11:22) who also claimed a special status as "apostle to the *ethnē*." While Paul's letters are invaluable, we nevertheless need to guard against allowing them to overshadow literature emerging from other Jewish Christ-circles.

With respect to the latter, we will include the following within the first group: the document Q;[120] other probable pre-Gospels traditions;[121] traditions utilized in the Acts of the Apostles; the Gospel of Mark; the Gospel of Matthew;[122] the

---

cussions of authorship that are content to conclude in favor of pseudonymity or anonymity but that then have nothing to say about the ethnic identity of the actual author.

120. For my present purposes, it is not necessary to engage with the many issues associated with and arising from the Q hypothesis; see Kloppenborg Verbin, *Excavating Q*, for a comprehensive discussion. I take it as highly probable that there was a Greek document underlying non-Markan material held in common by Matthew and Luke and that its probable contents are fairly represented by Robinson, Hoffmann, and Kloppenborg, *Critical Edition of Q*. Q is pertinent especially because of its reflection of a mission to Israel (involving both prophecy of judgment and proclamation of the kingdom of God) and its statements about non-Jews.

121. For present purposes, I will not attempt any thoroughgoing reconstruction of pre-Gospels tradition history. It is sufficient to take note of apparently traditional material that reflects postresurrection attitudes of Jewish Christ-believers toward non-Jews (especially the apocalyptic discourses, passion narratives, and postresurrection commissioning scenes).

122. While some have argued that the final layer of Matthean redaction reflects a "Gentile bias" and probably a gentile author (e.g., Kenneth W. Clark, "The Gentile Bias in Matthew," *JBL* 66 [1947]: 165–72; Rolf Walker, *Die Heilsgeschichte im ersten Evangelium*, FRLANT 91 [Göttingen: Vandenhoeck & Ruprecht, 1967]; Lloyd Gaston, "The Messiah of Israel as Teacher of the Gentiles: The Setting of Matthew's Christology," *Int* 29 [1975]: 24–40), this remains a minority view. For recent and convincing readings of Matthew as a Jewish Gospel, see Matthias Konradt, *Israel, Church, and the Gentiles in the Gospel of Matthew*, trans. Kathleen Ess, Baylor-Mohr Siebeck Studies in Early Christianity (Waco, TX: Baylor University Press, 2014), Anders Runesson, *Divine Wrath and Salvation in Matthew*:

Didache;¹²³ the Gospel of John;¹²⁴ the Epistle to the Hebrews;¹²⁵ and the book of Revelation. All of these can be identified, with varying degrees of high probability, as stemming from Jewish circles; all of them contain references in some form or other to non-Jews and their status; and all of them were accessible to gentile readers and thus would have had an effect on identity construction. Since neither John nor Hebrews contains the term *ethnē* as an explicit designation of non-Jews, however, these two writings will play a secondary role in what follows.¹²⁶ Further, while the Gospel of Mark does use the term *ethnē* (10:33, 42; 11:17; 13:10) and while non-Jewish characters occasionally appear in a positive light (the Syrophoenician woman [7:24–30]; the centurion at the cross [15:39]), Mark does not display the same sort of reflection on the place of the *ethnē* in the ongoing movement as is found in other literature under discussion here. For our purposes, then, Mark will be used more as a source of earlier tradition (and as a

---

The Narrative World of the First Gospel (Minneapolis: Fortress, 2016), and John Kampen, *Matthew within Sectarian Judaism*, AYBRL (New Haven: Yale University Press, 2019).

123. The Jewish character of the Didache is widely recognized, together with its close affinity with Matthew. Further, much of it can be understood as providing catechetical instruction for gentiles; see, e.g., Jonathan A. Draper, "'You Shall Not Give What Is Holy to the Dogs' (*Didache* 9.5): The Attitude of the *Didache* to the Gentiles," in *Attitudes to Gentiles in Ancient Judaism and Early Christianity*, ed. David C. Sim and James S. McLaren, LNTS 499 (London: Bloomsbury T&T Clark, 2013), 242–58.

124. Despite the harsh polemic against "the Jews" in the Fourth Gospel, there is little indication that this functioned to privilege the gentiles; *ethnē* does not appear at all, and it is Jewish concerns and traditions that fill the Johannine horizon. John seems to reflect the attitudes of a disaffected sectarian Jewish Christ-group that was forced out of the synagogue (9:22; 12:42–43), that subsequently relocated to the diaspora (cf. 7:35), and that came to refer to the antagonists it had left behind as "the Judeans." At the same time, an interest in gentiles as potential Christ-believers seems to be reflected in references to certain "Greeks" (7:35; 12:20–21), to "other sheep that do not belong to this fold" (10:16), and probably to the "scattered children of God" who are set over against "the nation" in 11:52.

125. The relevance of Hebrews is not entirely clear in that, although its Jewish character is readily apparent, there are no clear references to non-Jewish believers. Perhaps a universal outlook is present in statements such as 2:9: "so that . . . [Christ] might taste death for everyone [*hyper pantos*]." This, together with the reference to "our brother Timothy" in 13:23 (presumably the associate of Paul), might indicate that the writing was intended for an audience that included gentiles. Since this is a possibility, we will include Hebrews in the first group.

126. The closest we get in the Johannine literature is the use of *ethnikos* (*ethnōn* in Byzantine MSS) as a designation for outsiders in 3 John 7.

conveyor of that tradition to Matthew) than as a case of sustained reflection on that element of the tradition.[127]

A second group, to be used in a supplementary way, consists of three writings that contain material pertinent to our purposes and whose Jewish character is probable. Two of these, Colossians and Ephesians, are letters bearing Paul's name. While they are widely seen as deutero-Pauline—written by an associate, successor, or later admirer of Paul—both of them reflect a social situation where Jew and gentile continue to be significant categories, and both of them address gentile readers from the perspective of a Jewish Christ-believer.[128] The third, 1 Peter, displays similar characteristics.[129]

Finally, we will include within our purview some of the literature produced by the distinctively Jewish Christ-groups that continued to exist outside the

---

127. To be sure, Mark is capable of narrative subtlety (especially in his juxtaposition of material), which might suggest that there is more here than meets the eye; see, e.g., Ian J. Elmer, "Fishing the Other Side: The Gentile Mission in Mark's Gospel," in Sim and McLaren, *Attitudes to Gentiles in Ancient Judaism and Early Christianity*, 154–72. Still, the term *ethnē* does not seem to be drawn into any such narrative pattern.

128. This perspective is clearer in Ephesians: "you *ethnē* . . . were . . . aliens from the commonwealth of Israel, and strangers to the covenants of promise" (2:11–12); "I Paul am a prisoner of Christ Jesus for the sake of you *ethnē*" (3:1). In Col 1:25–27, while the syntax is not entirely clear, there seems to be a distinction between the "saints" (the author apparently included), to whom God has revealed the mystery of the significance of Christ for the *ethnē*, and "you" (who clearly are part of the gentiles). Admittedly, the Jewish perspective of the author in each case may have been a posture adopted for rhetorical purposes. But the result, as far as identity ascription is concerned, could well have been the same; that is, the epistles functioned to convey Jewish identity ascription to gentile readers. While I am inclined to think that Colossians was written by Paul, for present purposes it is enough to observe the Jewish orientation of the epistle.

129. The statement in 1:18—"you were ransomed from the futile ways inherited from your ancestors"—serves both to identify the intended readers as gentiles (even though *ethnē* is an identity that they gave up when they became Christ-believers [4:3; cf. 2:12]) and to establish an ethnic distinction between them and the author. The location of the author in Babylon (i.e., Rome) suggests strongly that the letter was written after the destruction of the temple and thus after Peter's death. Still, the author who writes in Peter's name shares (or possibly adopts) his ethnic identity.

Of the remaining NT material, I take Luke-Acts to have been written by a gentile. Two of the Pastoral Epistles make reference to the *ethnē* (1 Tim 2:7; 3:16; 2 Tim 4:17), but neither epistle contains any compelling evidence of Jewish perspectives or concerns. In the remaining NT writings, the issue of the gentiles and their status does not come into view at all.

boundaries of the emerging proto-orthodox church in the second century and beyond.[130] This material will be pertinent in two ways. First, and more importantly, given the probable continuities with earlier Jewish Christ-groups, this material will provide both corroborative evidence for earlier attitudes and some indication of how those attitudes developed. In other words, it will help us to see earlier attitudes as part of a longer trajectory. Second, to the extent that these later groups included or, at least, were in contact with gentile Christ-believers, this material played a role at a later point in the ascription of identity to gentile believers.[131] The material to be included here is as follows: among the Jewish gospels, the gospel known to Epiphanius (often identified with the Gospel of the Ebionites)[132] and the Hebrew Gospel of Matthew;[133] Jewish Christian material discernible in the Pseudo-Clementine *Recognitions* and *Homilies*;[134] and Jewish

---

130. The material is cataloged and discussed in part 3 ("The Literary Heritage of Jewish Believers") of Oskar Skarsaune and Reidar Hvalvik, eds., *Jewish Believers in Jesus: The Early Centuries* (Peabody, MA: Hendrickson, 2007). In addition, Skarsaune makes the case that, in his arguments from Scripture, Justin Martyr drew on several bodies of interpretive tradition, one of which originated among Jewish Christ-believers; see *The Proof from Prophecy: A Study in Justin Martyr's Proof-Text Tradition: Text-Type, Provenance, Theological Profile*, NovTSup 56 (Leiden: Brill, 1987).

131. The boundaries between gentile Christ-believers, Jewish Christ-groups, and Jewish communities more generally were more porous and less well defined than has often been supposed—an idea that is central to the work of Adam H. Becker and Annette Yoshiko Reed, eds., *The Ways That Never Parted: Jews and Christians in Late Antiquity and the Early Middle Ages* (Minneapolis: Fortress, 2007).

132. Surveyed in Craig A. Evans, "The Jewish Christian Gospel Tradition," in Skarsaune and Hvalvik, *Jewish Believers in Jesus*, 241-77. Until recently, it was believed that the Jewish gospels excerpted and discussed by patristic writers could be identified with three Jewish Christian gospels (Gospel of the Hebrews, Gospel of the Ebionites, and Gospel of the Nazarenes); see, e.g., A. F. J. Klijn, *Jewish-Christian Gospel Tradition*, VCSup 17 (Leiden: Brill, 1992). More recently, this neat pattern has been called into question; Evans suggests that until further clarification is forthcoming, it is more prudent to refer to this material by means of the patristic writer in which it appears.

133. Preserved in a fourteenth-century treatise by Shem Tob, in which the cited text is supplemented by a running refutation. While George Howard's argument that the Hebrew version is "primitive" (*The Gospel of Matthew according to a Primitive Hebrew Text* [Macon, GA: Mercer University Press, 1987]) has been subjected to criticism, some aspects of it may reflect earlier (second-century?) tradition; see the discussion (with full bibliography) in Evans, "Jewish Christian Gospel Tradition," 267-70. Even so, it will not be given much weight in what follows.

134. While these writings probably date from the fourth century CE, it is possible to

Ethnē as an Identity Ascribed to Non-Jews: By Jewish Christ-Believers

Christian editing of Jewish pseudepigrapha (especially Lives of the Prophets, Testimony of the Twelve Patriarchs, 4 Baruch [Paraleipomena Jeremiou] and Apocalypse of Abraham).[135]

Our goal, then, is to use this material, in conjunction with the discussion in the first part of this chapter, to identify and describe the range of conceptions among Jewish Christ-believers of the ways in which gentiles could enter into the new realities opened up by and through Christ. Further, we are particularly interested in these conceptions where the Jewish believers who held them were in a position to shape the self-definition of gentile believers. In other words, we are interested in these conceptions as ascribed identities. In all this, we will pay special attention to the use of *ethnē* as an identity term. While the most pertinent occurrences of the term will come into our discussion as we proceed, we will begin with a brief survey of the term as it appears in this literature, considering its semantic range and other aspects of usage.

There are well over one hundred pertinent occurrences of the term in the literature listed above—most commonly *ta ethnē*, but *ethnē* and *panta ta ethnē* appear as well.[136] Some fourteen of these appear in scriptural citations.[137] As

---

discern earlier sources (including a *Grundschrift* drawn on by both); see the discussion in Graham Stanton, "Jewish Christian Elements in the Pseudo-Clementine Writings," in Skarsaune and Hvalvik, *Jewish Believers in Jesus*, 305-24. Of interest for our purposes are what Stanton calls "An Apologia for Jewish Believers in Jesus" (*Recognitions* 1.27-71) and material underlying *Recognitions* 4.5.5-9 and *Homilies* 8.6.1-8.7.5.

135. See Torleif Elgvin, "Jewish Christian Editing of the Old Testament Pseudepigrapha," in Skarsaune and Hvalvik, *Jewish Believers in Jesus*, 278-304. On the reception and transmission of Jewish pseudepigrapha by Christ-believers more generally, see James R. Davila, *The Provenance of the Pseudepigrapha: Jewish, Christian, or Other?* JSJSup 105 (Leiden: Brill, 2005); Richard Bauckham, "The Continuing Quest for the Provenance of the Old Testament Pseudepigrapha," in *The Pseudepigrapha and Christian Origins: Essays from the Studiorum Novi Testamenti Societas*, ed. Gerbern S. Oegema and James H. Charlesworth (London: T&T Clark, 2008), 9-29.

136. *Ethnē*: Matt 10:5; 12:21; Luke 2:32; Acts 4:25, 27; 9:15; 15:14; Rom 2:14; 3:29; 9:24, 30; 11:12, 13; 15:9, 10, 12, 18; 1 Cor 1:23; 12:2; 2 Cor 11:26; Gal 2:15; Rev 17:15; Testament of Benjamin 3.8.

Panta ta ethnē: Matt 24:9, 14; 25:32; 28:19; Mark 11:17; Acts 15:17; Rom 1:5; 15:11; Gal 3:8; Rev 12:5; 14:8; 15:4; 18:3, 23; Lives of the Prophets (Jeremiah) 2.12; Testament of Simeon 7.2; Testament of Judah 22.2; Testament of Asher 7.3; Testament of Zebulun 9.8; Testament of Joseph 19.11.

137. Rom 2:24 (Isa 52:5); Rom 4:17 (Gen 17:5); Rom 15:9 (Ps 18:49); Rom 15:10 (Deut 32:43); Rom 15:11 (Ps 116[117]:1); Rom 15:12 (twice; Isa 11:10); Gal 3:8 (Gen 12:3; 18:18); Matt

GENTILE CHRISTIAN IDENTITY

with Jewish usage more generally, the term almost always refers to non-Jews. This is most clearly the case where *ethnē* stands in a binary relationship with some other term. One common pairing is with *Israel*—three occurrences in the undisputed letters of Paul, one in Luke's infancy hymns, and several in the Christianized sections of the Testaments of the Twelve Patriarchs.[138] Elsewhere in Paul, *ethnē* is paired with "Jews" (five occurrences),[139] "the circumcision" (four, plus a further occurrence in Ephesians),[140] and several other individual terms.[141] In many other instances, the contrast with Israel or the Jews is implicit in the larger context; quite a few of these will come into view in what follows.

As is the case in postbiblical Jewish literature more generally, *ethnē* is used to denote not only non-Jewish nations but also non-Jews as individuals. In Paul's letters, individuals are necessarily in view in Gal 2:12; one can hardly imagine Peter eating with nations. Individuals are also in view in places where Paul addresses his readers directly as *ethnē*: "I am speaking to you *ethnē*" (Rom 11:13)—that is, to the non-Jews among his intended readership.[142] Although the issue is debated, as we will see, Jesus's command to "make disciples of all the *ethnē*"

4:15 (Isa 9:1-2); Matt 12:18, 21 (Isa 42:1, 4); Acts 4:25 (Ps 2:1); Acts 15:17 (Amos 9:11-12); Didache 14.3 (Mal 1:11, 14).

138. In Rom 11:25, e.g., "a hardening has come upon part of Israel, until the fullness of the *ethnē* has come in." Also Rom 9:30-31 and 11:11 (where the pronoun *autous* refers back to "Israel" in v. 7). In Luke 2:32, "A light for revelation to the *ethnē*, and for glory to your people Israel." And in Testament of Simeon 7.2, e.g., "For the Lord will raise up from Levi someone as high priest and from Judah someone as king, God and man. He will save all the *ethnē* and the tribe [*genos*] of Israel." Also Testament of Asher 7.3; Testament of Benjamin 3.8. Testament of Judah 22.2 has a similar construction with "Jacob."

139. Rom 3:29; 9:24; 1 Cor 1:23; Gal 2:15; 1 Thess 2:14-16. In an additional occurrence, *ta ethnē* is paired with the verb *ioudaizein*: "how can you compel the *ethnē* to Judaize?" (Gal 2:14).

140. Rom 15:8-9; Gal 2:8, 9, 12; Eph 2:11. The use of *peritomē* ("circumcision") and *akrobystia* ("foreskin, uncircumcision") with reference to people groups ("those who are circumcised/uncircumcised") is without explicit parallel outside Pauline literature. Joel Marcus has suggested that this usage originated in intergroup slander, Jews and non-Jews using the respective terms as insulting epithets for the other; see "The Circumcision and the Uncircumcision in Rome," *NTS* 35 (1989): 67-81.

141. Three other binary pairs with *ethnē* appear in Romans: with "my flesh," in the sense of "my kinfolk" (11:13-14); with "his [God's] people" (15:10); and with the "saints who are in Jerusalem" (15:26-27). One other is found in 2 Corinthians: with *genos*, evidently in the sense of "my [Paul's] race" (11:26).

142. Also Rom 1:13 and 1 Cor 12:2.

Ethnē as an Identity Ascribed to Non-Jews: By Jewish Christ-Believers

(Matt 28:18–20) probably has to do with individuals; baptism, teaching, and becoming disciples are activities that more naturally pertain to individuals than to nations. Also to be included are the statements mentioned above in which *ethnē* stands in a binary construction with groups of Jewish individuals—for example, "Jews" or "the saints at Jerusalem" (Rom 15:27)—together with other statements concerning individual activity.[143]

On the other hand, nations or ethnic people groups are probably being referred to in those statements in which *ethnē* is paired with *Israel* or with other terms denoting Israel as a national entity.[144] In Revelation, where the imperial rule of Babylon over the nations is a dominant theme and where *ethnē* often appears in phrases such as "peoples and tribes and languages and nations" (11:9; also 10:11; 17:15), *ethnē* refers to national entities in probably every occurrence.[145] With respect to the remaining occurrences of *ethnē* throughout this material, it is often difficult to say whether the term refers to national groups or non-Jewish individuals. Given the basic meaning of the term and the fundamental binary that underlies the distinctive Jewish usage, however, even where it refers to individuals, national connotations ("members of non-Jewish nations") are generally present.

As has been mentioned, in the overwhelming majority of its occurrences, *ethnē* denotes non-Jews (individuals or nations). But there are a few instances where Israel might be included among the *ethnē*. For the most part, these involve the phrase *panta ta ethnē*, where in a few occurrences the addition of the adjective might generate an inclusive sense: *all* the nations, Israel included. All four of the Matthean occurrences (24:9, 14; 25:32; 28:19) have been read in this way, though as we shall see, the reading is debated. Mark 11:17, in which Jesus cites Isa 56:7 ("My house shall be called a house of prayer for *panta ta ethnē*"), might be mentioned here as well. In Revelation, where the phrase occurs five times, there is a puzzling ambiguity in the use of *ta ethnē* throughout the work. On the one hand, in Rev 11:1–2, where the term stands in contrast to "the holy city" and the "temple of God," and at the end of the book, where it contrasts with the new Jerusalem (21:24, 26; 22:2), *ethnē* seems to carry its distinctive

---

143. Doing what the law requires (Rom 2:14); exercising obedience (Rom 15:18) or self-control (1 Thess 4:5); responding to Paul's message (1 Thess 2:16). See also Eph 3:6; 1 Pet 2:12; 4:3.

144. "[God's] people [*laos*]" (Luke 2:32; Rom 15:10); "the circumcision" (Rom 15:9 [twice]; Gal 2:9); Paul's own "race" (*genos*; 2 Cor 11:26).

145. The fact that an equivalent phrase also appears in the singular—"every nation and tribe and language and people" (14:6; also 5:9; 7:9; 13:7)—provides a further indication of this reading. See also the discussion in the next paragraph.

Jewish sense (the non-Jewish nations). Elsewhere, however, the term appears in several variations of a phrase containing "peoples [*laoi*] and nations [*ethnē*] and languages [*glōssai*]" (also including "kings" [10:11], "tribes" [*phyloi*; 11:9], or "multitudes" [*ochloi*; 17:15]), a formulation that seems to have a more universal reference. This impression seems to be confirmed by the use of a similar phrase in the singular: "every nation and tribe and language and people" (14:6; also, with variations, 5:9; 7:9; 13:7).[146] In both the singular form and the plural, there is no compelling reason to exclude Israel from the group. Added to this is the fact, already mentioned, that the book is centrally concerned with the rule of Rome (in its guise as Babylon) over the nations of the world, which would naturally include the nation of the Jews as well. It is possible, then, that in at least some of these passages in Revelation, Israel is seen as included among the *ethnē*. We will not attempt to sort out any of these ambiguities here; they will come up for further discussion in due course.

Turning to other aspects of usage, in some instances, the *ethnē* appear simply as examples of sinful behavior to be avoided. A passage in Mark's Gospel, also taken over by Matthew, presents Jesus as warning his disciples not to imitate gentile patterns of domination: "You know that among the *ethnē* those whom they recognize as their rulers lord it over them, and their great ones are tyrants over them" (Mark 10:42). In a Q passage, speaking of excessive concern for the necessities of life, Jesus says to his disciples: "For it is the *ethnē* who strive for all these things; and indeed your heavenly Father knows that you need all these things" (Matt 6:32; cf. Luke 12:30). Echoing Matthean language, the Didache begins its exposition of the "way of life" with this admonition: "For why is it so great to love those who love you? Do the *ethnē* not do this as well?" (Didache 1.3).[147] All of these statements can be understood as addressing an entirely Jewish audience, at least in their original form.

Moving along the spectrum in a more positive direction, we find many texts in which gentiles are referred to as targets of mission: "[God] was pleased to reveal his Son to me, so that I might proclaim him among the *ethnē*" (Gal 1:16); "speaking to the *ethnē* that they may be saved" (1 Thess 2:15); "the good news must first be proclaimed to *panta ta ethnē*" (Mark 13:10); "Go and make disciples of *panta ta ethnē*" (Matt 28:19); "God made a choice among you, that I should be the one through whom the *ethnē* would hear the message of the good news" (Acts 15:7); "This grace was given to me to bring to the *ethnē* the news of the boundless riches of Christ" (Eph 3:8).

---

146. A unique variation in Rev 7:9, in that *ethnos* is singular while the other terms are plural.

147. Matthew has similar formulations with *ethnikoi* rather than *ethnē* (5:47; 6:7).

Ethnē as an Identity Ascribed to Non-Jews: By Jewish Christ-Believers

Once gentiles have become Christ-believers, in some of this material they continue to be identified as gentiles. In other words, *ethnē* functions as a continuing identity. This is clearly the case in some of the epistles, where readers are addressed directly as such: "I am speaking to you *ethnē*," Paul says at one point in his letter to the believers in Rome (Rom 11:13). A similar direct ascription of the term is at least implicit in Rom 1:5–6 ("among all the *ethnē*, . . . including yourselves") and Rom 1:13 ("among you as . . . the rest of the *ethnē*"). The author of Ephesians speaks in similar terms: "I, Paul, a prisoner of Christ Jesus for the sake of you *ethnē*" (Eph 3:1). In addition, *ethnē* is often used more generally with reference to believers: "When Cephas came to Antioch, . . . he used to eat with the *ethnē*" (Gal 2:11–12); "Now the apostles and the believers who were in Judea heard that the *ethnē* had also accepted the word of God" (Acts 11:1); "the *ethnē* have become fellow heirs, members in the same body, and sharers in the promise in Christ Jesus" (Eph 3:6); "But since it was necessary for the *ethnē* to be called in the place of those who remained unbelievers so that the number that was shown to Abraham might be filled, the saving proclamation of the kingdom of God was sent out into the whole world" (Pseudo-Clement, *Recognitions* 1.42.1). In all these instances, non-Jews who have become Christ-believers continue to be identified as *ethnē*. Also to be included here are references to non-Jewish Christ-believers as being "from the *ethnē*." Paul speaks of those "whom he [God] has called, not from the Jews only but also from the Gentiles [*ex ethnōn*]" (Rom 9:24). Additional instances are found in the account of the Jerusalem Council in Acts 15. In his summary speech, James speaks of God as having taken "from the *ethnē* [*ex ethnōn*] a people for his name" (15:14); the subsequent letter is addressed "to the brothers who are from the *ethnē* [*ex ethnōn*] in Antioch and Syria and Cilicia" (15:23).

At the same time, however, *ethnē* can be used to refer to those outside the Christ-community.[148] Addressing an egregious instance of sexual misbehavior in Corinth, Paul expresses his displeasure as follows: "It is actually reported that there is sexual immorality among you, and of a kind that is not found even among the *ethnē*" (1 Cor 5:1). First Peter also uses *ethnē* as a term for unbelieving outsiders: "Conduct yourselves honorably among the *ethnē*, so that, though they malign you as evildoers, they may see your honorable deeds and glorify God when he comes to judge" (1 Pet 2:12). The regulations for church order in Matt 18 contain this instruction for a situation where a wayward member of the com-

---

148. For a fine survey of *ethnē* as a term for outsiders, see Paul R. Trebilco, *Outsider Designations and Boundary Construction in the New Testament: Early Christian Communities and the Formation of Group Identity* (Cambridge: Cambridge University Press, 2017), 150–76.

munity refuses to repent (using *ethnikos* as an ersatz singular form of *ethnē*): "if the offender refuses to listen even to the *ekklēsia*, let such a one be to you as an *ethnikos* and a tax collector" (Matt 18:17).

From here it is just a short step to a situation where *ethnē* designates an identity that non-Jews leave behind when they become followers of Christ. Staying with 1 Peter, later in the letter, the author reminds his readers of what they used to be: "You have already spent enough time in doing what the *ethnē* like to do, living in licentiousness, passions, drunkenness, revels, carousing, and lawless idolatry" (1 Pet 4:3). A similar note is struck in Eph 4:17: "you must no longer live as the *ethnē* live, in the futility of their minds." Paul is even more explicit in 1 Cor 12:2: "You know that when you were *ethnē*, you were enticed and led astray to idols that could not speak." Here *ethnē* clearly denotes an identity that was abandoned, what Paul's converts used to be before they came to believe in Christ.[149]

As used with respect to non-Jewish Christ-believers, then, *ethnē* could function as an ascribed identity in two different ways. On the one hand, it could denote an ongoing aspect of identity: non-Jews who had come to believe in Christ continued to be *ethnē*. To use Paul's language in Galatians, once they were "sinners from the *ethnē*," but now they are *ethnē* "in Christ" (2:15; 3:15). On the other hand, it could refer to an identity that they left behind: "when you were *ethnē*" (1 Cor 12:2). But even in the latter case, it nevertheless remained an essential element of the new identity ascribed to them. For in taking on their new identity as followers of Christ, they were at the same time enjoined to reconstrue their former identity: before turning to Christ they had been *ethnē*. And even now this former identity continued to define them: the fact that they used to be *ethnē* in the past meant that they continued to be differentiated from Jewish Christ-believers in the present.

Further, the fact that Paul can use the term in both senses—"you *ethnē*" (Rom 11:13); "when you were *ethnē*" (1 Cor 12:2)—suggests that we should not view the two usages simply as mutually exclusive alternatives. Seen from one angle, there is a clear distinction between gentile Christ-believers and the *ethnē*-group to which they previously belonged; by virtue of their new faith in Christ, they are no longer *ethnē* in that sense. But seen from the perspective of the new community of Christ-believers, there is a clear distinction between them as believers from the *ethnē* and those believers who were "Jews by birth" (*physei Ioudaioi*),

---

149. While it is possible that the phrase "believers from the *ethnē*" (as discussed above) could be understood as implying that such believers are *ethnē* no longer, this is probably not the case in the Jewish material being discussed here. In Gal 2:15, for example, when Paul speaks of "sinners from the *ethnē* [*ex ethnōn*]," his use of the phrase certainly does not negate the fact that such sinners are *ethnē*.

Ethnē as an Identity Ascribed to Non-Jews: By Jewish Christ-Believers

to use Paul's phrase in Gal 2:15. The new factor of Christ-identity has complicated the previous simple binary of Jews and *ethnē*. Put differently, it has created new boundaries across which the Jew-gentile distinction is to be negotiated. Depending on the nature of the identity negotiations at these boundaries, one or other of these alternatives—"you *ethnē*"; "when you were *ethnē*"—might be more salient.[150] In some cases it might be more useful to stress difference from gentile outsiders and similarity with Jewish believers; in others, similarity with other gentiles and difference from Jews might be more pertinent.[151]

But what can be said about the larger patterns of thought and self-definition within which these various occurrences of *ethnē* find their place? In a constructive article published some time ago, Raymond Brown argued that instead of speaking simply about "Jewish Christianity" and "Gentile Christianity," we need to recognize that there were "different types of Jewish/Gentile Christianity," which came into being when "Jewish Christians of different persuasions converted Gentiles who shared the respective theology of their missionaries."[152] He proceeded to identify four such types, differentiated on the basis of their stance toward the structures of Judaism and the terms on which gentiles were admitted to the group. My goal in what follows is to construct a similar—but more thorough and nuanced—typology of Jewish conceptions, though I will move beyond Brown's work by drawing on an identity typology that I developed elsewhere in the context of a discussion of early Christian identity more generally.[153] That typology dealt with gentile conceptions, as well as Jewish, and took into account a larger range of identity issues, related to three sets of variables: (1) a range of conceptions concerning the nature and purpose of scriptural Israel and its religion, as understood in relation with new beliefs about Christ and his significance; (2) a range of conceptions concerning the place and status of the continuing Jewish people and their religion; and (3) a range of conceptions concerning the place and status of Jewish and gentile believers within groups

---

150. On the concept of salience, which has to do with the question of which aspect of an individual's constellation of identities comes into play in a given social situation, see the work of John C. Turner and Michael A. Hogg, *Rediscovering the Social Group: A Self-Categorization Theory* (Oxford: Blackwell, 1987).

151. In English usage, the choice of "gentiles" or "heathen" as renderings of *ethnē* provides a way of indicating this distinction. Cf. Fredriksen's discussion of the different nuances captured by "gentiles" and "pagans" as alternative renderings of *ethnē*; *Paul*, 34–35.

152. Brown, "Not Jewish Christianity and Gentile Christianity," 76.

153. The article dealt with the issue of supersessionism and the need for a more nuanced typology when considering Christ-groups in the first and second centuries; see Terence L. Donaldson, "Supersessionism and Early Christian Self-Definition," *JJMJS* 3 (2016): 1–32.

of Christ-believers of varying ethnic composition. While (1) and (2) will have a part to play in the typology developed below, our particular interest in (3) means that the two typologies will not correspond exactly.[154]

Work done in the previous section provides us with a starting point for discerning these ranges of conceptions. There I made a case for the view, on the one hand, that the earliest Christ-movement (at least in its dominant form) was characterized by the conviction that God had revealed the identity of the coming Messiah by raising Jesus from the dead and, on the other, that this message contained within it significant elements of dynamic tension and issues of logical coherence that compelled the early believers to engage in a process of reflection, elaboration, and conceptual development. The result of this process was a spectrum of opinion and outlook. One end of the spectrum could be characterized as the covenantal status quo, with the additional conviction that the risen Jesus was to be the coming Messiah. Moving along the spectrum, we observed a greater emphasis on the perception of a new state of affairs in the present (Jesus as the exalted and reigning Lord; the Spirit as bringing the realities of the age to come into present experience). Moving farther along the spectrum, this new state of affairs appears not simply as the realization in the present of what was expected for the eschatological future but as an unexpected reality that necessitated a reinterpretation not only of eschatological expectation but also of inherited covenantal tradition. This suggests a typology comprising three broad identity types or models.

Before turning to the typology, however, a few additional comments are in order, having to do with the fact that our primary interest here concerns gentile perception and identity construction among gentile Christ-believers. This means, for one thing, that I am not attempting here to engage in a thorough history of identity construction among Jewish Christ-believers. It is sufficient for our purposes that I identify the various Jewish conceptions of how non-Jews might share in Christ-belief, which, in turn, formed the basis for the identities ascribed by the one to the other. This means as well that it is not necessary here to carry out a full discussion of each piece of primary literature with respect to the issue of gentile inclusion. I am using this literature to identify the range of ascribed identity patterns that circulated among early mixed-ethnic Christ-groups, rather than to discern the distinctives and commonalities of the individual texts themselves.[155] Finally, in some cases, the evidence that I appeal to for any given position is subject to different interpretations. In such cases, it is not

---

154. Nevertheless, I have drawn on some material from that article for the discussion in this section.

155. Or further, to trace their subsequent reception and influence as individual texts.

essential to identify the most probable intended meaning; indeed, it probably is not even desirable. If a text is sufficiently ambiguous that modern readers differ in their interpretations, the inherent ambiguities would probably have generated different perceptions among gentile readers as well. Within certain limits, the potential for differing interpretations will be useful for our analysis.[156] Thus it will be sufficient for present purposes that a given interpretation has been suggested and plausibly defended.

The typology comprises three major identity types, with several subtypes.

1. Christ as the Messiah appointed for Israel; believing gentiles brought into relationship with Israel as a whole in accordance with already-existing patterns

In this type, Jewish Christ-believers are differentiated from their Jewish compatriots by their belief that Jesus has been appointed to be the coming Messiah and by their determination to call on Israel as a whole to recognize Jesus as well. Israel's covenantal identity continues to be based on temple worship and torah observance, which are understood in traditional terms and have not been redefined by Christ-belief in any fundamental way, and on the expectation of God's promised deliverance. Thus they can be seen as a remnant or renewal group within Israel, standing in solidarity (albeit sometimes strained) with Israel as God's covenant people. Given what we can know about Jesus's attitudes toward the gentiles, most would have anticipated a significant influx of non-Jews in the eschatological future, at the parousia of Jesus in his full messianic role. This expectation, together with the identity of the Jewish Christ-believers as a messianic renewal group within the larger Jewish community, probably represented their dominant initial attitude toward non-Jews. But just as the larger Jewish community had developed ways of accommodating gentiles in the present era, this initial attitude was supplemented by assumptions about ways in which interested gentiles could be included in the present. That is, they could be incorporated into Israel as proselytes (1.1) or associated with Israel by adhering to patterns of righteousness appropriate for gentiles (1.2).[157] Still, this type differs from the ones

---

156. In this chapter, we are interested primarily in the range of identities ascribed by Jewish Christ-believers. In many cases, later gentile believers used received material to construct identities that would have been unthinkable for earlier Jewish believers (e.g., identities based on ethnic supersessionism). While such interpretations will be of interest in later chapters, here they fall outside the limits of what is pertinent for present purposes.

157. What I designate as (1.1) is somewhat similar to Brown's first type: "Jewish Christians and their Gentile converts who practiced full observance of the Mosaic Law, includ-

to follow in that it lacks a similar commitment to seek out gentile converts and to engage in a gentile mission in the present.

Most of the comprehensive evidence for this identity type is found in the traditions utilized in Acts, together with Paul's accounts of his conflicts, debates, and agreements with members of the Jerusalem community. This evidence suggests that the earliest Jerusalem community directed their mission energies only at fellow Jews, but that when the phenomenon of gentile Christ-believers presented itself, they responded either by insisting on circumcision and full torah observance or by devising a form of righteous behavior appropriate for non-Jews. This material has been discussed above and need not be revisited here.

This evidence can be supplemented, however, with texts reflecting the ongoing existence of Jewish Christ-groups that understood themselves as differing from the rest of Israel only in their convictions about Jesus, that concentrated on a mission restricted to other Jews in the present, and that expected an influx of non-Jews in the eschatological future. In the Q document, while the *ethnē* in the present era are characterized as the negative other,[158] there is an expectation that in the future "many will come from east and west and recline with Abraham and Isaac and Jacob in the kingdom of God" (Q 13:29, 28).[159] In other pre-Synoptic tradition, material in Matthew's Mission Discourse bears witness to the expectation that a mission restricted to Israel (10:5-6) would last until the parousia of the Son of Man (Matt 10:23). The idea of a mission restricted to (or focused on) Israel reappears in material produced by later Jewish Christ-groups. In the gospel known to Epiphanius, usually identified with the Gospel of the Ebionites, Jesus, speaking to his disciples "in the house of Simon, surnamed Peter," declared: "According to my intention you shall be twelve apostles for a testimony to Israel."[160] Likewise, in the Hebrew Gospel of Matthew, the concluding commission makes

---

ing circumcision, as necessary for receiving the fullness of the salvation brought by Jesus Christ. This movement, which originated in Jerusalem, had some success in Galatia and Philippi, and perhaps elsewhere"; "Not Jewish Christianity and Gentile Christianity," 77. However, while (1.2) shares some similarities with Brown's second type, his first two types assume more of a commitment to a gentile mission than does my first type.

158. "For all these the *ethnē* seek; for your Father knows that you need them all" (Q 12:30 [= Luke 12:30]); probably also the Q text underlying Matt 5:47 "Do not even the *ethnikoi* do the same?" (The *telōnai* and *ethnikoi* of Matt 5:46, 47, are probably to be preferred to Luke's *hamartōloi*.)

159. Translation (slightly adapted) from Robinson, Hoffmann, and Kloppenborg, *Critical Edition of Q*, 416.

160. Epiphanius, *Panarion against Heresies* 30.13 (trans. J. K. Elliott, ed., *The Apocryphal New Testament: A Collection of Apocryphal Christian Literature in an English Translation* [Oxford: Clarendon, 1993], 15). Curiously, only eight disciples are named.

Ethnē as an Identity Ascribed to Non-Jews: By Jewish Christ-Believers

no reference whatsoever to the *ethnē*, with the result that the restriction to "the lost sheep of the house of Israel" (10:5–6) remains fully in place.[161] And while the source preserved in the Pseudo-Clementine *Recognitions* 1.27–71 will be more pertinent for the next type, here we can note a statement that occurs several times in a section where Peter is informing Clement of the emergence of "the church of God established in Jerusalem" (*Recognitions* 1.43.3).[162] Recounting discussions between the apostles and the priests about the identity of Jesus and the legitimacy of the new movement, Peter declares that "only in this regard [i.e., the identification of Jesus as "the prophet whom Moses predicted"] does there seem to be a difference between us who believe in Jesus and the unbelieving Jews."[163] As the narrative continues, this mission to Israel showed signs of being successful, until the intervention of "a certain hostile person" (1.70.1)—subsequently identified as Saul/Paul—turned the tide in the direction of violence and persecution.[164]

2. Christ as inaugurating a new era of fulfillment for (a remnant within) Israel, which gentiles are invited to share

The distinguishing features of this identity type are (1) a positive attitude toward gentile inclusion and a commitment to a gentile mission; (2) a continued commitment on the part of Jewish Christ-believers to traditional, covenant-centered identity markers (circumcision, food laws, Sabbath observance, temple

---

161. The commission simply states that the disciples are to "teach them to carry out all the things that I have commanded you forever." See the discussion in Evans, "Jewish Christian Gospel Tradition," 267–70.

162. *Recognitions* 1.27–71 contains a survey of history from the creation down to the appearance of Jesus (the "true prophet" promised by Moses) and the early Jerusalem Christ-movement. Stanton labels it "An Apologia for Jewish Believers in Jesus"; Stanton, "Jewish Christian Elements in the Pseudo-Clementine Writings," 317–23. See also F. Stanley Jones, *An Ancient Jewish Christian Source on the History of Christianity: Pseudo-Clementine Recognitions 1.27–71*, Texts and Translations (Atlanta: Scholars Press, 1995).

163. *Recognitions* 1.43.2. Also 1.50.5–6: "Therefore the Jews have erred about the first coming of the Lord. Between them and us there is discord about this matter alone. For even they know and expect that Christ is coming. But they do not know that he has already come in humility, namely, the one called Jesus." The translation is that of Jones, *Ancient Jewish Christian Source*.

164. This person "had received a commission from Caiaphas the high priest to persecute all who believed in Jesus, and to go to Damascus with his letters so that even there, when he had gained the help of the nonbelievers, he might bring destruction on the believers" (*Recognitions* 1.71.3–4).

worship,¹⁶⁵ etc.); and (3) the expectation that gentile believers would respect the distinctiveness of Jewish identity and accommodate themselves in appropriate ways to the Jewish character of Christ-belief. As we have observed already in previous discussion, the commitment to a gentile mission is generally coordinated with a greater emphasis on the present experience of eschatological realities and on the exalted status and role that Christ is already occupying. The inclusion of the gentiles, then, is generally seen as an aspect of the new era of fulfillment inaugurated by Christ, and their experience of salvation is thus to be seen as a participation in the messianic blessings being bestowed on Israel.

Although Jewish expectations of end-time redemption for the gentiles left open the possibility that they would fully embrace the torah, for the most part the expectation in this type is that gentiles would commit themselves to a pattern of behavior appropriate for gentiles.¹⁶⁶ Within the land of Judea, this pattern of behavior tended to be seen as adherence to that part of the torah that pertained to the gentiles; in the diaspora, it was often thought of more with reference to a universal natural law that undergirded the written torah and to which it pointed. However, the distinction between the two cannot be sharply drawn, and in any case, the resultant patterns of behavior turn out to be much the same. In this identity type, then, the distinction between Jews and gentiles is clearly maintained. Gentiles are included as gentiles, and the Christ-movement consists of a body of gentile believers adjoined to the foundational core of Jewish believers.

As we will see when we look more closely at the evidence, two subtypes can be discerned within this identity type, both having to do with the relationship between the body of gentile Christ-believers and the Jewish people as a whole. The first of these (2.1), probably earlier than the other, emphasizes inclusion and participation, thus highlighting the positive aspects of the relationship. In this subtype, gentile believers are seen as having been drawn near to share with Israel—or, at least, with the Christ-believing remnant of Israel—in the promised blessings now being accomplished for Israel by its Messiah. In the second type (2.2), the emphasis falls not on the believing remnant but on that part of Israel that failed to recognize Jesus as the expected Messiah. Here the conception is that gentile believers have come in to replace that portion of Israel that had failed to respond, or more generally, it is that their opportunity for salvation has somehow

---

165. At least while the temple was still standing.

166. While these two options (proselytism or righteous gentiles) could also be associated with the first type, what differentiates the two is the belief that a new era of gentile salvation had been opened up by Christ in the present, together with a commitment to a vigorous gentile mission.

been made possible by that failure.[167] While these two subtypes are not mutually exclusive, there is a clear difference in emphasis.

As with the first type, evidence for this type has already come into view in our discussions of the traditions underlying the Acts account, together with Paul's accounts of his sometimes stormy relationship with the Jerusalem Christ-believers. The legitimacy of the gentile mission and the terms on which gentile Christ-believers might be included in the movement were the primary issues on the agenda of the Jerusalem Council (Acts 15; Gal 2). According to both accounts, the gathering rejected the argument that it was necessary for (male) gentiles to be "circumcised according to the custom of Moses" (Acts 15:1); according to the Acts account, the gathering also decided to impose certain obligations on "those from the *ethnē* who are turning to God" (15:19). While the terms of the decree are in line with Jewish expectations for proper gentile behavior,[168] it is interesting to note that an additional rationale is attributed to James—namely, that the inclusion of non-Jews is in keeping with the expectation of "the prophets" for an end-time turning of "the rest of humankind . . . even all the *ethnē*," to the God of Israel.[169] While the position attributed to James represents more one of simple approval rather than of active engagement in a mission to non-Jews, it nevertheless goes beyond the first type in the sense that in "look[ing] favorably on the *ethnē*, to take from among them a people for his name" (15:14), God was doing a new thing, albeit something that was also anticipated by the prophets. At the same time, nothing indicates that this new thing brought with it any change in the status of the torah or other covenantal identity markers for Jewish Christ-believers.[170] This "people from the *ethnē*" and the Christ-believing remnant of

---

167. Of course, this concept of replacement is a central feature of the supersessionist theology of later gentile Christianity. Nevertheless, the evidence suggests that it existed previously in a Jewish form.

168. For a thorough canvass of the possible backgrounds of the apostolic decree, see Keener, *Acts*, 3:2260-69.

169. The fact that the citation of Amos 9:11-12 in Acts 15:16-17 is drawn from the LXX, which differs considerably from the Hebrew, has generated considerable discussion. For present purposes, it is not necessary to resolve the question whether James of Jerusalem would have cited a Greek text (see, e.g., Barrett, *Acts of the Apostles*, 2:724-29). It is sufficient to note that such an argument was present in the traditional account of the meeting that Luke had at his disposal.

170. Despite Paul's consternation at the behavior of Peter and Barnabas in Antioch after the arrival of a delegation from James (Gal 1:11-14), it is likely that the latter were motivated, at least in part, by a recognition that Jewish Christ-believers should be able to live in conformity with their Jewish identity.

GENTILE CHRISTIAN IDENTITY

Israel stood alongside each other as distinct groups, even though they were also bound together by their common faith in God and confession of Christ.

That Paul's letters are "hard to understand" (2 Pet 3:16) is something that has been recognized from the beginning, and they contain a variety of statements that might be cited in support of several types and subtypes. While we will need to leave the most characteristic aspects of his discourse for our discussion of the third identity type, some aspects can be mentioned with profit here. Two things are of interest: (1) discourses in which gentiles are presented as sharing in the end-time blessings that have already been bestowed on Jewish Christ-believers (i.e., 2.1); and (2) discourses suggesting that gentile salvation has somehow been made possible by the (relative) lack of Jewish response to Christ (i.e., 2.2). As with all the material discussed in this section of the chapter, we need to be brief.

Toward the end of his epistle to the believers in Rome, Paul makes a striking statement about the collection for "the saints" in Jerusalem (Rom 15:25), a project that had occupied a considerable portion of his attention in the years leading up to this point. While the project was ostensibly a relief effort for those in need ("the poor among the saints in Jerusalem"; Rom 15:26; cf. 2 Cor 8:14–15; Gal 2:10), he goes on to locate it within a relationship of benefaction and obligation, describing it as an appropriate response on the part of gentiles to the spiritual blessings that have been shared with them by the Jews. After saying that the churches of Macedonia and Achaia "were pleased" to participate in the collection, he continues: "and indeed they owe it to them; for if the *ethnē* have come to share in their spiritual blessings [*tois pneumatikois*], they ought also to be of service to them in material things [*tois sarkikois*]" (15:27).[171] Here the prior existence of the Jewish Christ-believing "saints" is the essential foundation for the subsequent existence of the gentile Christ-groups. The two groups are united by their common share in "the blessing of Christ" (15:29), but this spiritual reality belongs in the first instance to the Jewish "saints"; the relationship of each to this commonality is not symmetrical. What comes into view here is a model in which Jews and gentiles represent two distinct groups of Christ-believers, the Jewish group not only prior to the gentile but also the (penultimate) source of the blessings that are both properly theirs in the first place and that also bind the two groups together.

A similar model—where gentile salvation is dependent on and made possible by the blessings bestowed on Jewish believers—comes into view in several other passages. A little earlier in Romans, Paul states that "Christ became a servant to the circumcised . . . in order that he might confirm the promises given to the

---

171. Though for a different take on their degree of pleasure in participating, see 2 Cor 8 and 9!

patriarchs, and in order that the *ethnē* might glorify God for his mercy" (15:8-9). While the syntax is difficult, the extension of divine mercy to the *ethnē* seems to be one of the goals of Christ's ministry to the circumcised.[172] Likewise, in Gal 3:13-14, the redemption of the Jews ("Christ redeemed us . . .") had as its goal that "the blessing of Abraham might come to the *ethnē*."[173] In these cases as well, the salvation of the gentiles has been made possible by Christ's saving activity among the Jews, resulting in the existence of a bipartite community of Christ-believers — a foundational group of Jews, experiencing the promised endtime blessings, and an adjoining community of the *ethnē*, invited in to share in these blessings.

At the same time, however, Paul's letters also contain material suggesting that gentile salvation is somehow dependent on the failure of Christ's ministry "to the circumcised." The clearest instances of such a view are found in a formulation that appears several times in Rom 11:11-15. The passage begins with the declaration that "through their [i.e., all but "the elect" of Israel; v. 7] stumbling [*paraptōmati*] salvation has come to the *ethnē*" (v. 11b) — an idea that is repeated (in various terms) three times in conditional form: "if their stumbling means riches for the world [*kosmou*]" (v. 12); "if their defeat [*hēttēma*] means riches for the *ethnē*" (v. 12); "if their rejection [*apobolē*] is the reconciliation of the world" (v. 15). It is important to note that this stumbling/defeat/rejection is only temporary. The whole passage begins with a rejection of the proposition that "they have stumbled so as to fall" (v. 11a); the apodosis of each conditional sentence goes on to talk about "their full inclusion [*plērōma*]" (v. 12) or "their acceptance [*proslēmpsis*]" (v. 15). This means that it is not appropriate to speak here of replacement. What is needed apparently for the salvation of the *ethnē* is not space but time. Eventually "all Israel will be saved" (11:26); there will be plenty of space on the olive tree for the Jewish branches to be grafted back in (11:23-24). In the meantime, Israel's "stumbling" has opened up a period of time for "the fullness [*plērōma*] of the *ethnē*" to come in (11:25).[174]

To be sure, in the next section Paul does give expression to the idea of re-

---

172. I have discussed the syntax in some detail in Terence L. Donaldson, *Paul and the Gentiles: Remapping the Apostle's Convictional World* (Minneapolis: Fortress, 1997), 95-100, 240.

173. Again, for more detailed discussion, see Donaldson, *Paul and the Gentiles*, 180-82, 240, and the literature cited there.

174. For my attempt to discern the convictional logic at work here, see Terence L. Donaldson, "'Riches for the Gentiles' (Rom 11:12): Israel's Rejection and Paul's Gentile Mission," *JBL* 112 (1993): 81-98, an argument taken up in Donaldson, *Paul and the Gentiles*, 215-26.

placement. Imagining a gentile response to his olive-tree analogy, he says: "You will say, 'Branches were broken off so that I might be grafted in'" (11:19). According to a common interpretation, Paul states this gentile proposition in order to agree with it. He begins his comment on the proposition with the single word *kalōs* ("well"; v. 20a), which the NRSV renders as "That is true." This, however, is probably an over-translation of the more ambiguous *kalōs*.[175] For one thing, Paul immediately goes on to deny any direct replacement causality.[176] For another, Paul's own statement in v. 17 places the emphasis on inclusion rather than replacement: "you, a wild olive shoot, were grafted in *among them* [*en autois*]"—that is, among the natural branches that remain—"and have *become a partner* [*synkoinōnos*] in the rich root of the olive tree."[177] The whole section (i.e., 11:7–24), then, should be seen as an example of how subtypes 2.1 (gentiles coming in to share the promised blessings with Jewish Christ-believers) and 2.2 (gentile salvation made possible by the failure of Israel to respond) could be combined in a single discourse.

While the author of Matthew's Gospel seems to take as his model a "scribe trained for the kingdom of heaven," one who is deftly able to combine "what is new and what is old" (13:52), the result of his exercise in combination is a narrative characterized by recurring contrasts and tensions. This is especially true with respect to the gentiles and their place in the story. On one side of things, the *ethnē* (6:32; 20:25) or *ethnikoi* (5:47; 6:7) appear as negative outsiders, marked by attitudes and actions not to be emulated. Further, according to two categorical statements, they are outside the sphere of Jesus's ministry: "Go nowhere among the *ethnē* . . . but go rather to the lost sheep of the house of Israel," he says to his disciples on sending them out (10:5–6); "I was sent only to the lost sheep of the house of Israel," he says to a Canaanite supplicant (15:24).

On the other side of the ledger, gentiles are also capable of behavior that puts

---

175. While *kalōs* can be used to signal agreement (e.g., Plato, *Republic* 5.21 [477]), it can also be used as an ironic agreement (Lucian, *Demonax* 38.4), a more noncommittal introduction to the speaker's real response (Aristophanes, *Women of the Assembly* 1092), or even a polite refusal (Aristophanes, *Frogs* 888).

176. "They were broken off because of their unbelief, but you stand only through faith. So do not become proud, but stand in awe. For if God did not spare the natural branches, perhaps he will not spare you" (11:20b–21).

177. In keeping with its reading of v. 20a, the NRSV renders *en autois* (which clearly means "in" or "among them") as "in their place" (i.e., in place of the branches that were broken off), thus importing replacement ideas into a sentence having to do with inclusion. For the rendering "among them," see, e.g., Ernst Käsemann, *Commentary on Romans*, trans. and ed. Geoffrey W. Bromiley (Grand Rapids: Eerdmans, 1980), 308; James D. G. Dunn, *Romans 9–16*, WBC (Dallas, TX: Word, 1988), 673.

Jews to shame (Matt 8:10; 12:41–42). Similarly, despite Jesus's restriction of his mission to Israel, he responds positively to demonstrations of exemplary faith on the part of gentiles, healing the centurion's servant (8:5–13) and the Canaanite woman's daughter (15:21–28). Further, without annulling the restrictions in the present, the Gospel anticipates a future in which gentiles would be included in mission (24:14) and in the blessings of salvation (8:11–12; 12:18, 21; 25:32).

These tensions between positive and negative attitudes toward the gentiles seem to be resolved in the commissioning scene with which the Gospel ends, in which the risen Jesus sends the eleven disciples out to "make disciples of all the *ethnē*" (28:18–20). With these words, the missional restriction of 10:5–6 is lifted, and the way is cleared for a more universal mission.

But the narrative logic by which this change has taken place is anything but clear. The issue turns, in part, on the question of how to render *panta ta ethnē* in v. 19. Does the phrase refer to "all the nations" including Israel? Or does *ta ethnē* here retain its usual Jewish sense of "all the non-Jewish nations (or individuals)"? The question, which has been at the center of an ongoing debate, has significant implications for our reading of Matthew and is not easy to resolve.[178]

Until recently, it has been assumed that the reading "all the Gentiles" would imply what Clark called a "Gentile bias" on the part of Matthew. In this reading, despite the apparent Jewishness of the Gospel, the overall thrust of the narrative is that by their definitive rejection of Jesus ("All the people [*pas ho laos*] answered, 'His blood be on us and on our children'"; Matt 27:25), the people of Israel forfeited their place in the kingdom and were replaced by a new community of disciples drawn from "all the Gentiles."[179] The mission to Israel (10:5–6; 15:24) has come to an end; in its place is a mission to the gentiles. If this reading is valid, the Gospel (at least in its final redaction) would necessarily represent a gentile outlook and thus would need to be left for a subsequent chapter.[180]

---

178. It was precipitated by Clark, "Gentile Bias in Matthew," and was subsequently highlighted in a pair of articles in the *Catholic Biblical Quarterly*: Douglas R. A. Hare and Daniel J. Harrington, "'Make Disciples of All the Gentiles' (Mt 28:19)," *CBQ* 37 (1975): 359–69, and John P. Meier, "Nations or Gentiles in Matthew 28:19?," *CBQ* 39 (1977): 94–102. For a thorough recent discussion, with extensive bibliography on both sides of the debate, see Konradt, *Israel, Church, and the Gentiles*, 311–23.

179. For Walker, Matthew sees Israel as a *massa perditionis* that has been rejected by God and replaced by a gentile church; *Heilsgeschichte im ersten Evangelium*, 10. See also Gaston, "Messiah of Israel as Teacher of the Gentiles."

180. Often in this view, the community for which the Gospel was written had made the transition from a mixed community with a Jewish core into one that was largely gentile, with more Jewish tradition being retained out of loyalty to the past but nevertheless subordinated to an overarching story of ethnic rejection and replacement.

If the phrase is to be rendered inclusively, however—"all the nations," Israel included—the mission mandate with which the Gospel ends can be read not as a replacement of the mission "to the lost sheep of the house of Israel" but as an expansion, so that it now includes the gentiles as well. Even so, however, this expansion would also be accompanied by a certain redefinition of the status of Israel. In Meier's words,

> In Matt's eyes they no longer enjoy the former privileged status of the chosen people of God (21:43). But they do qualify in Matt's vocabulary as an *ethnos* (24:7). And so they do fall under the mandate of the risen Jesus to make disciples of *panta ta ethnē* (28:19).[181]

In other words, in this reading the distinction between Israel and the non-Jewish nations has been transcended, and the ongoing community of Jesus's disciples is a new community characterized by baptism and the teaching of Jesus rather than by ethnic identity. To the extent that an inclusive reading of *panta ta ethnē* can be combined with a Jewish-centered provenance for the Gospel, this interpretation of Matthew would belong in the third identity type.

More recently, however, a number of studies have appeared with an interpretation of Matthew that does belong in this second identity type. These studies are part of a recent resurgence in *intra muros* interpretations of Matthew—that is, interpretations in which Matthew's community is understood as still located "within the walls" of the Jewish community, existing as a kind of sect or subgroup within the larger world of Judaism.[182] Of particular significance is the work of several scholars within this group who read *panta ta ethnē* in Matt 28:19 as "all the Gentiles" (or scholars, like Matthias Konradt, who are open to the reading) but who do not take this to imply a rejection of Israel and an exclusive turning to the gentile world.[183] While there are some variations among them, they agree

---

181. Meier, "Nations or Gentiles in Matthew 28:19?," 102.

182. For earlier examples of this resurgence, see Amy-Jill Levine, *The Social and Ethnic Dimensions of Matthean Salvation History*, Studies in the Bible and Early Christianity 14 (Lewiston, NY: Edwin Mellen, 1988), 2, 185–97; J. Andrew Overman, *Matthew's Gospel and Formative Judaism: The Social World of the Matthean Community* (Minneapolis: Fortress, 1990); Anthony J. Saldarini, *Matthew's Christian-Jewish Community* (Chicago: University of Chicago Press, 1994); and David C. Sim, *The Gospel of Matthew and Christian Judaism: The History and Social Setting of the Matthean Community* (Edinburgh: T&T Clark, 1998).

183. A strong case can be made for this reading on two grounds. First, in Jewish usage the exclusive sense of the term is found in the overwhelming majority of instances (see the discussion in ch. 3 above). Second, it is likely that individuals rather than nations are in view in 28:18–20; baptism, teaching, and observing commandments pertain much more

that for Matthew the already-initiated mission to "the lost sheep of the house of Israel" remains in place and will continue until the parousia (Matt 10:23) but that, with Jesus's new postresurrection status of universal authority, this continuing Jewish mission is now supplemented by a distinct mission to "all the Gentiles." Jewish believers continue to represent the (no longer lost) "sheep of the house of Israel," identified in traditional covenantal terms, but there is a difference of opinion about gentiles. For some, the combination of Jesus's instruction in v. 20 ("teaching them to observe *everything that I have commanded you*") and his command in 5:19 (that no one teach others to break "one of the least of these commandments") means that gentile disciples need to observe the whole law; that is, they are to become proselytes to Judaism as well as disciples of Jesus.[184] On the other hand, the nature of Jesus's actual "commands" and teaching about the law in Matthew—for example, his prioritization of the weightier ethical aspects of the law over the minutiae of tithing (23:23) or over (ethnic-specific) cultic worship (9:13; 12:7), his summation of the law in ethical-monotheistic commandments (22:34-40) or moral maxims (7:12)—has led others to believe that non-Jewish disciples are to observe instead those aspects of the law that are universally binding.[185] In either case, the elements in Matthew that have been used to support a gentile-bias reading of the Gospel—especially the statement in 8:11-12 contrasting the "sons of the kingdom" with those who "will come

---

readily to individuals than to nations. But it is only with reference to non-Jews that *ethnē* can denote individuals. See Konradt, *Israel, Church, and the Gentiles*, esp. 311-17; Axel von Dobbeler, "Die Restitution Israels und die Bekehrung der Heiden: Das Verhältnis von Mt 10,5b-6 und Mt 28,18-20 unter dem Aspekt der Komplementarität; Erwägungen zum Standort des Matthausevangeliums," *ZNW* 91 (2000): 18-44; Runesson, *Divine Wrath and Salvation in Matthew*, esp. 379, n. 97. Of the earlier scholars, Levine is the only one who reads 28:19 in this way. Overman does not have much to say about the issue, while both Saldarini and Sim read 28:19 inclusively, i.e., as signaling an expansion of the earlier Jewish mission so that it now encompasses "all the nations"; Saldarini, *Matthew's Christian-Jewish Community*, 81-82; Sim, *Gospel of Matthew and Christian Judaism*, 41-44.

184. Especially Sim, *Gospel of Matthew and Christian Judaism*, 251-54; Benjamin L. White, "The Eschatological Conversion of 'All the Nations' in Matthew 28.19-20: (Mis) Reading Matthew through Paul," *JSNT* 36 (2014): 353-82, esp. 357, 367-71. Also, with some qualifications, Levine, *Social and Ethnic Dimensions of Matthean Salvation History*, 183-84; Runesson, *Divine Wrath and Salvation in Matthew*, 350, n. 16, 380; see also Runesson's references on p. 372, n. 80.

185. Saldarini, for example, appeals both to the phenomenon of Godfearers and to Jewish writings that emphasize ethical monotheism, in his discussion of gentile disciples; *Matthew's Christian-Jewish Community*, 157-60. Konradt also rejects the idea that gentile disciples are to be circumcised; *Israel, Church, and the Gentiles*, 321-23.

GENTILE CHRISTIAN IDENTITY

from east and west"—tend to favor the idea that the gentile disciples replace the sinners within Israel (subtype 2.2) rather than that they share the blessings with the Jewish "sheep" (subtype 2.1), though the two are not mutually exclusive.

Standing in some apparent relationship with Matthew is the late first- or early second-century-CE document known as the Didache. The longer of the two titles appearing in the only extant manuscript introduces the work as "The teaching of the Lord through the twelve apostles to the nations [*ethnesin*]." While the titles are probably later additions, there are solid reasons to believe that the work, which stands in some relationship to Matthew, originated in a Jewish-centered community of Christ-believers and that one of the particular concerns of the work has to do with the terms on which non-Jews might be included.[186]

The Didache contains three or four distinct sections, each of which may well have had an independent, prior existence; if so, here they have been worked together into a composite set of instructions on church life.[187] The document as a whole is marked by a strongly Jewish flavor: the two-ways teaching, which (except for ch. 1) contains no explicit Christian material and is similar to Jewish two-ways traditions;[188] within the two-ways section, an emphasis on the "commandments of the Lord" (Didache 4.13); phraseology such as the "holy vine of David" (9.2) and "Hosanna to the God of David" (10.6); echoes of the Birkat Hamazon, the prayer recited after a meal;[189] the concern for purity (14.1, 3); and so on.

At the same time, however, even in material that suggests a certain connection with the larger Jewish world, the text addresses a distinct community standing at a certain distance from that world. They and their leaders are assumed to be "Christian" (Didache 12.4). The "high priests" who are to receive the firstfruits (*aparchēn*) of the community are in actuality the community's prophets (13.3). The "pure sacrifice" offered by the community is the Eucharist (14.1-3). Their

---

186. On the titles as later additions, see Kurt Niederwimmer, *The Didache: A Commentary*, trans. Linda M. Maloney, Hermeneia (Minneapolis: Fortress, 1998), 56-57.

187. Ethical teaching on the "two ways" (chs. 1-6); instructions concerning baptism, prayer and fasting, and the Eucharist (chs. 7-10); instructions concerning itinerant and settled teachers (chs. 11-15); an apocalypse (ch. 16, abruptly broken off at v. 8). While some interpreters prefer to see chs. 7-15 as a single manual of instruction for church life and order, the two sections stand on their own quite readily.

188. Probably drawing on the two choices—blessings and life; curses and death—presented to Israel by Moses in Deut 30. See especially the Testament of Asher (and the Testaments of the Twelve Patriarchs more generally); and the Rule of the Community from Qumran (especially 1QS III, 17–IV, 26). For thorough discussion, see Niederwimmer, *Didache*, 30–41.

189. See Niederwimmer, *Didache*, 155–61.

practice of regular fasting differs from that of the "hypocrites" in a manner that—while trivial at one level (a matter of schedule: Wednesdays and Fridays rather than Tuesdays and Thursdays; 8.1)—nevertheless serves to reinforce a significant boundary between the two groups. The community apparently is concerned both to define itself in characteristically Jewish terms and to maintain a distinct identity within—or at least with respect to—the larger Jewish world.[190]

In this connection, the appropriation of Matthean tradition for the purposes of community formation is of particular interest. The term *hypocrites* is distinctively Matthean, as is the concern to differentiate the community's practices of fasting from those of the hypocrites (cf. Matt 6:16–18).[191] As with Matt 6:5–18, where prayer and fasting are treated together (though in reverse order), Didache 8 then enjoins his readers not to "pray like the hypocrites" and continues: "but [pray] as the Lord commanded in his gospel [*euangeliō*]," quoting the prayer in its longer, distinctively Matthean form (Didache 8.2).[192] These are not the first echoes of Matthean tradition in the Didache, however. After introducing the theme of the "two ways, one of life and one of death," at the outset of the work (1.1) but before taking up the Jewish form of the theme ("the second commandment of the teaching"; 2.1), the author provides a first description of "the way of life" in the form of a pastiche of Jesus sayings, almost all of them highly reminiscent of Matthew's Gospel. For present purposes, we do not need to decide on the precise nature of the relationship between Matthew and the Didache—whether

---

190. On the sectarian nature of the Didache community, see, e.g., Peter Tomson, "The Halakhic Evidence of *Didache* 8 and Matthew 6 and the *Didache* Community's Relationship to Judaism," in *Matthew and the Didache: Two Documents from the Same Jewish-Christian Milieu?*, ed. Huub van de Sandt (Assen: Royal Van Gorcum; Minneapolis: Fortress, 2005), 131–41; Jürgen K. Zangenberg, "Reconstructing the Social and Religious Milieu of the Didache: Observations and Possible Results," in *Matthew, James, and Didache: Three Related Documents in Their Jewish and Christian Settings*, ed. Huub van de Sandt and Jürgen K. Zangenberg, SBL Symposium Series 45 (Atlanta: Society of Biblical Literature, 2008), 43–69; Jonathan A. Draper, "Do the Didache and Matthew Reflect an 'Irrevocable Parting of the Ways' with Judaism?," in van de Sandt, *Matthew and the Didache*, 217–41.

191. Fourteen occurrences; elsewhere in the Gospels it is found only three times in Luke, two of which are Q passages shared with Matthew.

192. With some minor changes in wording. Older scholarship tended to take *euangelion* as referring to a written gospel, usually that of Matthew. More recently, however, emphasis has been placed on oral tradition and performance. For discussions of the issue, see Taras Khomych, "Another Gospel: Exploring Early Christian Diversity with Paul and the Didache," in *The Didache: A Missing Piece of the Puzzle in Early Christianity*, ed. Jonathan A. Draper and Clayton N. Jefford, ECL 14 (Atlanta: Society of Biblical Literature, 2015), 469–73; Niederwimmer, *Didache*, 134–36, esp. n. 10.

the Didache draws on Matthew directly or on traditions that were also incorporated into Matthew, and whether the communities reflected in the respective works were related in any direct way.[193] We are interested in the presence and status of gentile Christ-believers within the purview of the Didache, and here Matthew provides us with a useful comparator.

The term *ethnē* appears twice in the Didache, once at the outset (1.3) and again near the end (14.3). In both instances, *ethnē* appears in traditional material incorporated into the text; nevertheless, the use of the term probably yields some information about the identity and viewpoint projected by the text. The first of these evokes Matt 5:43–47: "For why is it so great to love those who love you. Do the *ethnē* not do this as well?" (Didache 1.3). As with Matthew, here the *ethnē* are outsiders who appear in a somewhat negative light—as examples of a minimal standard of behavior that those on the "path of life" should greatly surpass.

The second appears in a section dealing with the Eucharist (Didache 14), which the author identifies as "the sacrifice mentioned by the Lord" in Mal 1:11: "In every place and time, bring me a pure sacrifice. For I am a great King, says the Lord, and my name is considered marvelous among the *ethnē*" (14.3).[194] As we will see in subsequent chapters, this text from Malachi was frequently cited by gentile Christians as a prophecy of their own existence. By contrast, in the Didache it is cited in support of the author's concern with the need for purity in eucharistic practice;[195] indeed, the version cited here replaces the indicative of the LXX ("in every place incense is brought to my name, and a pure offering"; also the MT) with the imperative ("bring me a pure sacrifice"). Nevertheless, even though the point about purity was established by the first sentence, the author nevertheless considered it pertinent that this pure sacrifice was enhancing the reputation of the Lord's name "among the *ethnē*." At the very least, this suggests not only that the community addressed in the Didache was located in the diaspora but also that they desired to evoke praise for God "among the *ethnē*."

In addition to these explicit references to the *ethnē*, it is also to be noted that some of the two-ways teaching specifically addresses gentile practices (e.g., pederasty, the practice of magic, enchanted potions, infanticide, incantations, astrology; Didache 2.2; 3.4). While it is not impossible that such admonitions were addressed to an exclusively Jewish readership, simply reinforcing the boundary

---

193. See, e.g., the chapters in part 3 of Draper and Jefford, *The Didache*, together with Draper's concluding chapter; "Missing Pieces or Wild Goose Chase? A Retrospect and Prospect," 529–43.

194. The second sentence incorporates some language from Mal 1:14.

195. On this point, see Niederwimmer, *Didache*, 198–99.

Ethnē *as an Identity Ascribed to Non-Jews: By Jewish Christ-Believers*

between them and the *ethnē*, the admonitions more probably should be taken as an indication that the community included non-Jews as well. Indeed, much of the two-ways material in chapters 2–6 is similar to Jewish traditions of ethical instructions for non-Jews. Since the instructions for baptism in chapter 7 begin with the statement "Having said all these things in advance," the whole two-ways section (chs. 1–6) can be seen as prebaptismal instruction for converts, including those from the *ethnē* who had come to recognize that the "name of the Lord" was "marvelous."

If gentiles are included within the horizon of the Didache, the question of how to categorize the terms of their inclusion comes to a focus with the discussion of Didache 6.2: "For if you can bear the entire yoke of the Lord, you will be perfect; but if you cannot, do as much as you can." What is meant by "the entire yoke of the Lord"? The range of this discussion is analogous in some ways to the discussion of "everything I have commanded you" in Matt 28:20. Those who see the Didache community as still located within the wider Jewish world tend to see the "yoke of the Lord" as a reference to the torah as a whole. On the basis of this reading, it is argued that, while full proselytism was held out as an ideal, gentile converts were nevertheless acceptable on the basis of baptism and adherence to the level of torah observance appropriate for gentiles, such as was summarized in the two-ways section.[196] Gentile believers, then, represented a distinct group that had been accepted into a community of Jewish Christ-believers, a community that continued to be identified in traditional covenantal terms. On the basis of such an interpretation, the Didache can be seen as another example of the second identity type being discussed here.

Others, however, understand "the entire yoke of the Lord" as referring not to the Mosaic torah directly but to the pattern of teaching set out in the preceding chapters. One argument in support of such a reading is that, unless one envisages the document as addressing gentiles exclusively, the admonitions in chapter 6, together with the concession of v. 2b, seem to be addressed to the community as a whole, without ethnic distinction. Further support has been sought in the lack of attention, in the work as a whole, to explicit Jewish identity markers—circumcision, cultic purity, temple sacrifice, the land of Israel, the hope for Israel's restoration, and so on. This has been taken as an indication that the Jewish features of the Didache have been given an "abstract and symbolic" character and have been absorbed into a new universal Christian identity.[197] In this reading, the Didache falls into the third identity type, to be developed below.

---

196. See, e.g., Draper, "'You Shall Not Give What Is Holy to the Dogs' (*Didache* 9.5)."

197. "The Didache asserts a Christian identity, even while it holds on to an increas-

The book of Revelation is distinctive among early Christian literature in many ways, among which is its central concern to place the story of Jesus and his followers in the context of a sweeping panorama of God's dealings with "every nation and tribe and language and people" (14:6). Revelation is also bewilderingly complex, stubbornly resisting attempts to arrive at consistent readings of its various themes, sections, and elements. Among these is what we might call its demography—the identities of Jesus's followers and the nations, and their respective places in the complex narrative that unfolds in the book.

Variations of the phrase "every nation and tribe and language and people" appear on seven occasions, three in the singular (5:9; 13:7; 14:6), three in the plural (10:11; 11:9; 17:15), and one in a mixed form (7:9, where *ethnos* appears in the singular and the other terms in the plural).[198] Elsewhere *ethnos* appears on its own in the plural (sixteen occurrences), usually as a stand-alone phrase (*ta ethnē*) or with *panta*.[199]

Looking at this set of occurrences in their literary context, readers are struck with a certain level of ambiguity in the relationship of the Jewish nation to these national groups. On the one hand, especially with the plural forms (*ta ethnē*, *panta ta ethnē*), the author's usage seems to be consistent with typical Jewish patterns. To begin with, in several instances, *ta ethnē* clearly seems to indicate non-Jewish nations. In Rev 11:1–2, where the seer is commanded to "measure the temple of God and the altar and those who worship there," the courtyard outside the temple is excluded, because "it has been given over to the *ethnē*, and

---

ingly abstract and symbolic Jewish identity"; Stephen Finlan, "Identity in the *Didache* Community," in Draper and Jefford, *The Didache*, 31. See also Huub van de Sandt, "Was the Didache Community a Group within Judaism? An Assessment on the Basis of Its Eucharistic Prayers," in *A Holy People: Jewish and Christian Perspectives on Religious Communal Identity*, ed. Marcel Poorthuis and Joshua Schwartz, JCP 12 (Leiden: Brill, 2006), 85–107.

198. In the four occurrences where *ethnos* is singular, the terms are modified by a form of *pan* (5:9; 7:9; 13:7; 14:6). Curiously, no two occurrences are identical. (In 7:9 the shift from the singular to the plural makes for an odd phrase: "every nation and tribes and peoples and tongues.") On the variations, see Allan J. McNicol, *The Conversion of the Nations in Revelation*, LNTS 438 (London: T&T Clark, 2011), 18; Richard Bauckham, *The Climax of Prophecy: Studies on the Book of Revelation* (Edinburgh: T&T Clark, 1993), 327; Nils A. Dahl, "Nations in the New Testament," in *New Testament Christianity for Africa and the World: Essays in Honour of Harry Sawyerr*, ed. Mark E. Glasswell and Edward W. Fasholé-Luke (London: SPCK, 1974), 66.

199. *Ta ethnē* (2:26; 11:2, 18; 15:3, 4; 16:19; 19:15; 20:3; 21:24, 26; 22:2); *panta ta ethnē* (12:5; 14:8; 18:3, 23). The single exception is 20:8, where the term is modified ("the nations at the four corners of the earth, Gog and Magog").

Ethnē as an Identity Ascribed to Non-Jews: By Jewish Christ-Believers

they will trample over the holy city for forty-two months." Subsequently, the city is identified as the place "where their Lord was crucified" (11:8).[200] At the end of the book, the "holy city" (now in the form of the new Jerusalem [21:2]) and the *ethnē* appear again, this time in a much more positive context: the *ethnē* walk in its light (21:24); "the glory and the honor of the *ethnē*" are brought into the city (21:26); and the tree of life produces leaves that "are for the healing of the *ethnē*" (22:2).

Taken together, these two passages epitomize the twofold aspect of the *ethnē* in Revelation, both of them also reflective of Jewish usage.[201] On the negative side of the tableau, the nations are the ungodly other—raging against God and destined for judgment (Rev 11:18); deceived by Babylon (18:23) or by the devil (20:3, 8); participating in Babylon's debauchery and fall (14:8; 16:19; 18:3); destined to be ruled by Christ with a rod of iron (12:5; 19:15; cf. 2:26).[202] On the positive side, at least some of the *ethnē* will participate in the final messianic blessings. In addition to the passages in chapters 21 and 22, the final blessing of the nations is anticipated in 15:4: "Lord, who will not fear and glorify your name? . . . All the nations [*panta ta ethnē*] will come and worship before you, for your judgments have been revealed." While these positive expectations for the destiny of the *ethnē* might seem surprising in light of the scenes of their wholesale destruction, the two-sided depiction is common in biblical and later apocalyptic tradition and is an essential part of the book.[203] In Bauckham's words, "the question of the conversion of the nations—not only whether it will take place but also how it will take place—is at the center of the prophetic message of Revelation."[204]

In this connection, the striking scene in chapter 7 can be drawn into the

---

200. Several puzzling aspects of the passage (e.g., the city is also called "the great city" [11:8], a term elsewhere used of Rome/Babylon [17:18; 18:10, 16, 18, 19, 21], and the fact that this is the only place where the earthly Jerusalem temple is mentioned) suggest that it might have been a piece of tradition that was incorporated awkwardly into the text; see the discussion in David E. Aune, *Revelation 6-16*, WBC (Nashville: Thomas Nelson, 1998), 593-98.

201. McNicol has drawn attention to "the deep tension in the narrative between the destructive defeat of the kings of the nations in Revelation 19.15-21 and the joyous welcome extended to them in 21.24-26" and "of contrasting accounts of the extermination and ingathering of the nations"; *Conversion of the Nations in Revelation*, xiii, 2.

202. On whether the "great city" in 16:19 is Jerusalem or Babylon, see Aune, *Revelation 6-16*, 900-901. In either case, the association of "the cities of the *ethnē*" with Babylon is clear.

203. For a prime example, see the concluding section of the Animal Apocalypse (1 Enoch 90:13-39). See also ch. 4 of McNicol, *Conversion of the Nations in Revelation*.

204. Bauckham, *Climax of Prophecy*, 238.

discussion. Here, in an interlude between the opening of the sixth and seventh seals, the prophet describes two groups of people: first, the 144,000 who were "sealed," twelve thousand out of "every tribe of the people of Israel"; second, "a great multitude that no one could count, from every nation, from all tribes and peoples and languages, standing before the throne and before the Lamb" (7:9). There is clearly a temporal distinction between the two groups; the first group is sealed as a form of protection for the ordeal that is about to take place (see especially 9:4); the second group has "come out of the great ordeal" (7:14) and are now praising God and the Lamb in heaven (7:9-12). The first scene takes place in the earthly present, the second in the eschatological future.[205]

As we will see, there has been considerable discussion about the identity of the two groups and how they are to be correlated.[206] For present purposes, it is enough to note that the prima facie sense of the text is that the first group comprises a symbolically significant number from the whole people of Israel, while the second group either consists of gentiles entirely or, if Israel is to be included as an *ethnos*, contains a substantial number from the gentile nations.[207] But even if the second group contains people drawn from the Jewish nation as well, the contrast between a present group drawn from "every tribe of the people of Israel," who remain faithful through the time of woes that precede the future reign of God, and a future multitude redeemed "from every nation" necessarily calls to mind the Jewish expectations that the *ethnē* would have a share in the end-time redemption of Israel. This impression is further confirmed by the reappearance of the 144,000 in chapter 14, where they are described as "firstfruits [*aparchē*] for God and for the Lamb" (14:4) and by the proclamation (in the next sentence) of an "eternal gospel . . . to every nation and tribe and language and people"

---

205. "Revelation 7 is composed of two parts: 7:1-8 and 7:9-17. The first section tells about the sealing, in the face of divine judgment, of 144,000 who were chosen from all the tribes of the sons of Israel. The second section describes the eschatological completion of the community of salvation out of all nations, tribes, peoples, and tongues"; Peter Hirschberg, "Jewish Believers in Asia Minor According to the Book of Revelation and the Gospel of John," in Skarsaune and Hvalvik, *Jewish Believers in Jesus*, 224.

206. For the alternatives, see Aune, *Revelation 6-16*, 445-48.

207. If the phrase were *panta ta ethnē* rather than *pan ethnos*, a gentile multitude would probably be in view. But since there is no evidence that *ethnos* in the singular form is ever used exclusively—i.e., to denote a non-Jewish nation—it is at least possible that the "great multitude" includes people from the Jewish nation. For instances of *ethnos* used with reference to the Jewish nation in literature that also uses the plural *ethnē* in its distinctive exclusive sense, see, e.g., Jdt 9:14; 1 Macc 9:29; 10:20; 11:21, 25; 12:3, 6; 13:6; 14:4, 6, 28, 29, 30, 32, 35; 16:3; 2 Macc 5:19, 20; 6:14, 31; 7:37; 10:8; 11:27; 14:34; 3 Macc 1:11; 2:27; 2:33.

Ethnē as an Identity Ascribed to Non-Jews: By Jewish Christ-Believers

(14:6)—a hint of the full harvest yet to come. As Hirschberg has put it: "[The author] adheres to a priority of the salvation history of the Jewish people and differentiates between Israel and the Gentiles by letting the movement flow—in a good biblical manner—from Israel to the Gentiles."[208]

On the other hand, some factors have led many readers to believe that the distinction between the two poles of this movement is not as clear as it might appear on the surface. A certain slippage away from a purely ethnic construal of the two is apparent even in the first occurrence of the phrase in question. In the heavenly hymn to the Lamb in Rev 5:9-10, those who have been "ransomed for God from every tribe and language and people and nation" are then said to have been made "a kingdom and priests for our God." The language clearly echoes Exod 19:5-6, where God declares to Israel: "you shall be my treasured possession out of all the peoples [MT: *hā-'ammim*; LXX: *pantōn tōn ethnōn*] ... you shall be for me a priestly kingdom and a holy nation."[209] Here a term that originally was an important indicator of Israel's special identity in contrast to "all the *ethnē*" is transferred to a new multiethnic collective identified by their allegiance to the Lamb. Further, the statement in Revelation that this new people has been ransomed "out of" (*ek*) every nation is probably to be seen as a reinterpretation of the statement in Exod 19:5 that from all the nations (MT: *mikkol hā-'ammim*; LXX: *apo pantōn tōn ethnōn*), God has chosen Israel as a special possession. What was originally a selection of one nation out of the multitude of nations has become here a selection of a new collection of redeemed individuals from the various nations of the world.

This has led many interpreters to a less ethnic-specific and more symbolic reading of the 144,000 in chapter 7. Given the fact that Revelation as a whole is addressed to seven churches in Asia Minor, and thus that it was written in a context where Jewish and gentile Christ-believers coexisted, many interpreters have found it unlikely that it would be only Jewish believers who would receive a protective seal in advance of the great ordeal. Further, when the 144,000 appear later in the work (Rev 14:1-5), they are identified as "firstfruits" from humankind as a whole (*apo tōn anthrōpōn*; 14:4) rather than from the tribes of Israel. This has reinforced the belief on the part of many that the 144,000 is to be seen as a symbolic Israel, the identity of Israel as a whole having been transferred to a new royal and priestly people drawn from all the nations of the world. In this

---

208. Hirschberg, "Jewish Believers in Asia Minor," 225.

209. See David E. Aune, *Revelation 1-5*, WBC (Nashville: Thomas Nelson, 1997), 47-49, 362; Bauckham, *Climax of Prophecy*, 327. A similar description appears at the outset of the work ("a kingdom, priests for [Christ's] God and father"; 1:6), where the author applies it to himself and his readers.

reading, while a certain biblical "flow ... from Israel to the Gentiles" remains—that is, in the scenario in which the redemption of Israel in the present is the precursor to the more complete redemption of the nations in the eschatological future—the role of Israel is played by the multiethnic church in the (author's) present day.[210]

To this one might add that, despite the dense interweaving of biblical material and Israel-centered symbols in Revelation, the author displays very little positive interest in the usual elements of Jewish identity (torah, circumcision, food and purity laws, Judea, etc.). In the few places where specific references appear (synagogue [2:9; 3:9]; Jerusalem temple [11:1-2]), they are put into a negative light.[211]

Again, what we are ultimately interested in here are the possible perceptions that gentile readers might have had concerning the identity of gentile Christ-believers and their place in the narrative. Therefore we can leave to one side questions of the most probable reading or of the author's intended meaning. With respect to our typology of the identities ascribed to gentile Christ-believers by their Jewish counterparts, the first reading set out above—which highlights the Jewish patterns of ethnic distinction and gentile salvation—is clearly an instance of the second type being discussed in this section. The latter reading—where ethnic distinctions are blurred to a certain extent and the new people drawn from every nation takes on an Israel identity—belongs to the third type, to be taken up below.

Finally, some of the material reflecting the views of later Jewish Christ-believers belongs in this second identity type. While this material emerges in the second century CE, it provides us with a retrospective point of reference

---

210. "John, a prophet schooled in the traditions and thought categories of the sectarian Jewish world of the second temple period was well equipped to make a grim assessment of Rome's ultimate destiny. He places the conflict between Rome and the church in the context of the conflict between Israel (the people of God) and Babylon historically anchored in the exilic period. Of course, this choice for his biblical framework has an overlay of a set of beliefs whereby he transforms Israel into a people who see their history linked to the coming of Jesus, the Christ"; McNicol, *Conversion of the Nations in Revelation*, 82-83.

211. If those targeted in Rev 2:9 and 3:9 are synagogue Jews ("those who say that they are Jews and are not, but are a synagogue of Satan"; 2:9), the reference is extremely negative. For the argument that those in view are actually gentile Christian Judaizers, see Michele Murray, *Playing a Jewish Game: Gentile Christian Judaizing in the First and Second Centuries CE*, ESCJ 13 (Waterloo, ON: Wilfrid Laurier University Press, 2004), 73-81. The reference to the temple in Jerusalem is more mixed. On the one hand, Jerusalem is the "holy city" (11:2) and the reference to "those who worship" at the temple is matter of fact (11:1). On the other, Jerusalem is subsequently identified as a "great city" that is "spiritually [*pneumatikōs*] called Sodom and Egypt" (11:8). For a discussion of the probable use of preexisting tradition here, see Aune, *Revelation 6-16*, 588-603.

Ethnē as an Identity Ascribed to Non-Jews: By Jewish Christ-Believers

for the views of Jewish Christ-believers in the earlier period. We will look first at the Testaments of the Twelve Patriarchs, a Jewish work containing a number of later interpolations and revisions.[212] One set of these simply speak of Christ as accomplishing salvation for Jews and gentiles, without much in the way of further elaboration. For example, Testament of Simeon 7.2 reads: "For the Lord will raise up from Levi someone as high priest and from Judah someone as king, God and man. He will save all the gentiles and the tribe of Israel [*panta ta ethnē kai tou genos tou Israēl*]." Testament of Joseph 19.10-11 strikes a similar note: "You, therefore, my children, keep the Lord's commandments; honor Levi and Judah, because from their seed will arise the Lamb of God who will take away the sin of the world, and will save all the nations [*panta ta ethnē*], as well as Israel." In these and similar passages, we simply encounter two groups — all the nations and Israel — with no indication of how the salvation of the one relates to that of the other.[213]

In other passages, however, we get glimpses of a more elaborate picture. Here the coming of Christ precipitates a division within Israel. The partial failure of Israel to respond creates the possibility of salvation for the gentiles. This failure, however, is only temporary; ultimately, Israel will return and be restored. Most of this picture is present in Testament of Benjamin 9.2-3. The passage begins with a typical expression of Zion eschatology but then continues with an explicit reference to Christ ("the unique prophet"), his mistreatment, and the turning to the nations:

> But in your allotted place will be the temple of God, and the latter temple will exceed the former in glory. The twelve tribes shall be gathered there and all the nations [*panta ta ethnē*], until such time as the Most High shall send forth

---

212. See especially Elgvin, "Jewish Christian Editing of the Old Testament Pseudepigrapha," 286-92. Some of the references to gentiles are clear Christian interpolations; others seem to be part of the Jewish original. For my attempt at differentiating the two, see Donaldson, *Judaism and the Gentiles*, 123-26. For the Greek text, see Marinus de Jonge, *The Testaments of the Twelve Patriarchs: A Critical Edition of the Greek Text* (Leiden: Brill, 1978). In addition, Skarsaune argues that Justin Martyr drew on an exegetical tradition developed by Jewish Christ-believers, which shows affinities with the interpolations and revisions in the Testaments; *Proof from Prophecy*, together with discussion in subsequent chapters.

213. Also Testament of Levi 2.10-11 ("the one who is about to redeem Israel" and "saving every race of humankind [*pan genos anthrōpōn*]); Testament of Asher 7.3 ("he will save Israel and all the nations"); Testament of Benjamin 3.8 ("the salvation of the gentiles and of Israel"); 11.2-5 ("enlightening all the nations with new knowledge" and "the light of knowledge will mount up in Israel for her salvation").

his salvation through the ministration of the unique prophet. He shall enter the first temple, and there the Lord will be abused and will be raised up on wood. And the temple curtain shall be torn, and the spirit of God will move on to the nations as a fire is poured out. And he shall ascend from Hades and shall pass on from earth to heaven.

Here the mistreatment of Christ leads to the pouring out of God's Spirit on "the nations." Although the Christ-centered addition does not go on to speak of the future restoration of Israel, this theme is present elsewhere in the Testaments. In Testament of Levi 16.3-5, after a reference to the plot to kill the one "who by the power of the Most High renews the Law" and the resultant "dispersion among the nations," the passage continues: "until he will again have regard for you and will take you back in compassion." A similar sequence appears in Testament of Zebulun 9.8-9: "He will turn all the nations [*panta ta ethnē*] to being zealous for him. And you shall see God in a human form, he whom the Lord will choose: Jerusalem is his name. You will provoke him to wrath by the wickedness of your works, and you will be rejected until the time of the end."

Most of these elements are also present in the Apocalypse of Abraham, in a section (29.3-13) of Abraham's vision of human history and the created order that has been heavily reworked from a Christ-perspective. Here Christ ("the man whom you [Abraham] saw insulted and beaten and again worshiped") is presented as a descendant of Abraham ("this man from your tribe" [29.9]) and as the one who is destined to be "the liberation from the heathen for the people who will be (born) from you" (29.8).[214] He receives a mixed reception from Israel ("those of your seed . . . some insulting him, some beating him, and others worshiping him" [29.12]) but is also worshiped by "many of the heathen" (29.11). In what was probably part of the original Jewish apocalypse, the passage goes on to describe the ultimate restoration of the "righteous men" from Abraham's "seed" (29.17-19).

To round out the picture, we can look briefly at the Pseudo-Clementine literature, in particular the "Apologia for Jewish Believers in Jesus" preserved in

---

214. The interpretation of the passage is complicated by the fact that the "man" is first presented as emerging from the heathen side of the vision that Abraham was seeing ("a man going out from the left, the heathen side" [29.4]). While the passage is jumbled, Elgvin suggests that it is to be seen as "a christological reworking of a Jewish vision originally criticizing the imperial cult"; "Jewish Christian Editing of the Old Testament Pseudepigrapha," 302. For a different view, see John J. Collins, *The Apocalyptic Imagination: An Introduction to Jewish Apocalyptic Literature*, 2nd ed. (Grand Rapids: Eerdmans, 1998), 230.

Ethnē as an Identity Ascribed to Non-Jews: By Jewish Christ-Believers

Recognitions 1.27–71.[215] Among other things, this work contains an account of the early Jerusalem church, in which Peter provides Clement with what amounts to a counterversion of the story found in Acts. While Peter states that the only point of difference "between us who believe in Jesus and the unbelieving Jews" is whether Jesus is the prophet like Moses whom Moses himself had predicted (1.43.1–2), the differences were somewhat more substantial. In Peter's view, Moses had instituted the system of temple sacrifice only because the practice of sacrificing to idols (which the people had become accustomed to in Egypt) was too deeply ingrained in them to be eradicated all at once. Sacrifice to God alone was thus a first step; the second step—the full eradication of sacrifice—would be accomplished by the coming prophet (1.36.1–2). The preaching of the apostles about the appearance of the expected prophet in the person of Jesus led to mixed results—popular reception by a growing proportion of the Jewish people accompanied by increasing repression by the priestly leaders.[216] As with some of the material surveyed above, these mixed results—the lack of full acceptance on the part of the people of Israel—led to the inclusion of the gentiles: "But since it was necessary for the nations to be called in the place of those who remained unbelievers so that the number that was shown to Abraham might be filled, the saving proclamation of the kingdom of God was sent out into the whole world" (1.42.1).[217]

This material from later Jewish Christ-groups, then, represents further instances of this second type. In all this material, the distinction between Jewish and gentile believers is maintained. In much of it, the inclusion of the gentiles is linked to the lack of full acceptance of Christ on the part of Israel (i.e., type 2.2). What Elgvin has to say about the Testaments of the Twelve Patriarchs can be applied to the rest of this material as well:

> The main theological issue . . . is the future of Israel. Earlier prophecies by the patriarchs about Israel's disobedience, judgment, and future salvation are

---

215. Stanton's title for the source; see "Jewish Christian Elements in the Pseudo-Clementine Writings," 317–23. For a full study, including a translation of the Syriac and Latin versions and the Armenian fragments, see Jones, *Ancient Jewish Christian Source*.

216. "Thus the priests eventually became afraid lest to their confusion by the providence of God the entire people should come to our faith" (1.43.1). As was noted above, the opposition was led by someone who "had received a commission from Caiaphas the high priest to persecute all who believed in Jesus, and to go to Damascus with his letters" (i.e., Paul; 1.71.3–4).

217. Curiously, the account of Abraham (1.32.1–1.34.1) contains no mention of the number of promised descendants (cf. "exceedingly numerous" [Gen 17:2]; "as numerous as the stars of heaven" [Gen 22:17]; etc.).

reinterpreted by relating them to Christ. Israel's sin and disobedience are now seen to be its lack of faith in Jesus. Its judgment is only temporal. Torah obedience and belief in Christ together will bring Israel future salvation. In the meantime, salvation has been given to the Gentiles. All Israel, the twelve-tribe people, will be saved.[218]

3. Christ as inaugurating a new era of fulfillment, bringing into being a new people that both comprises Jews and gentiles without distinction and stands in essential continuity with scriptural Israel

The distinctive characteristics of the third identity type move in two directions. On the one hand, (1) there are no distinctions in membership requirements for Jewish and gentile believers. Unlike the previous type, Jew and gentile do not have ongoing foundational significance as identity categories within the community of Christ-believers. In keeping with this, (2) the community of Christ-believers is seen as constituting a new people, with a new and distinct identity. On the other hand, however, (3) this new identity has been constructed (and ascribed) by believers who are self-consciously Jewish. Although ethnic distinctions no longer have foundational significance, they have not lost their meaning entirely. The new people is one in which both Jewish and gentile members are aware that the foundational members were Jewish, that gentiles have been welcomed into a larger community whose core members continue to be Jewish, and that the new shared identity is one that has been constructed by Jewish believers. Consequently, (4) this new people sees itself as standing in some form of continuity with scriptural Israel and as bearing an identity that is grounded on that of Israel. On this point, there is some similarity to the claim, present in the first two types, that Jewish Christ-believers represent the continuing remnant of Israel, though points (1) and (2) would make it difficult to make the case in any convincing way.

Picking up on observations made near the outset of this chapter, this third identity type can be associated with those strands of early Jewish Christ-belief that emphasize themes of newness and fulfillment—the present exaltation of Christ, the inbreaking of the eschatological age, the experience of the Spirit, and so on—and of the ways in which all of this represents a set of developments that transcend and redefine traditional Jewish expectations of what is to come. In this third type, the emphasis on fulfillment and newness is accompanied by a redefinition of covenantal institutions—the idea of a new law, a new temple, a new

---

218. Elgvin, "Jewish Christian Editing of the Old Testament Pseudepigrapha," 287.

circumcision, the crucifixion as an ultimate paschal sacrifice, and so on. Covenantal institutions and identity markers that were part of the old era are seen to have been transcended, and in some cases their original purpose is rethought in the light of Christ. This leads to two subtypes, though it is sometimes difficult to draw a sharp line between them. In one of these (3.1), the Mosaic covenant is seen to have had a legitimate preparatory purpose as it was traditionally understood and practiced, though this purpose has now been brought to completion in Christ. In the other (3.2), the nature and purpose of the Mosaic covenant itself is reworked and reinterpreted on the basis of the new belief in Christ.

Material that might be seen to represent this type is well known, which means that we do not need to engage in lengthy exposition here. The goal in what follows will be more to evoke what is commonly known than to provide detailed description. What will be important, however, is the Jewish character of the type, as indicated in (3) above—that is, the identity in question has been constructed by Jewish believers and it pertains to a group that, while including non-Jews, is nevertheless identifiably Jewish in its foundation and core membership.

Some of the pertinent material has come into view already. In the discussion of the second type above, we noted the presence in Matthew, the Didache, and Revelation of ambiguities that have led interpreters to read these texts in quite different ways. In each case, in addition to readings that conformed to the second identity type, we noted alternative readings that aligned them with the third type (probably the first subtype, i.e., 3.1). Without repeating the more detailed survey of the evidence that was carried out above, here I will look at each of these more briefly in turn.

The issue in Matthew turns on the interpretation of the key phrase *panta ta ethnē* in 28:19—in particular, whether *ta ethnē* is to be taken in its typical Jewish sense, so that the phrase denotes "all the gentiles," or whether the addition of *panta* has the effect of overriding the usual Jewish usage and giving the phrase a universal sense, "all the nations, Israel included." Appearing as it does in the commissioning scene with which the Gospel concludes, the phrase plays a crucial role in the interpretation of the Gospel as a whole. As we have already observed, up until this point, the position of the gentiles with respect to Jesus's mission has been decidedly ambiguous. On the one hand, Jesus seems to have categorically excluded them, restricting his own mission (15:24) and that of his disciples (10:5–6) to the "lost sheep of the house of Israel" and prohibiting his disciples from going to the *ethnē*. On the other hand, he anticipates the presence of gentiles at the eschatological banquet in the future (8:11) and responds positively to gentiles who exhibit faith in him and his mission in the present (8:5–13; 15:21–28). With the concluding commission, however, this ambiguity is resolved. However one interprets the key phrase, the previous restriction is now definitely lifted, and the invitation to become disciples is henceforth to be offered to the gentiles.

If *panta ta ethnē* is taken in an inclusive sense, then the Matthean narrative is one in which the covenantal distinction between Israel and the nations is transcended in the end, and the new community of disciples is one in which Jews and non-Jews are included without distinction. The same set of requirements—baptism and observance of Jesus's commands—applies to all members of the community. Some interpreters understand this as involving a demotion for Israel, a kind of national leveling in which Israel loses its special status and is simply absorbed into the larger plurality of nations without distinction.[219] While this is possible, it is equally possible to read the narrative as one in which Israel's special status is opened up to the rest of the nations, so that they can also benefit from the blessings brought into being by Israel's Messiah. As we have observed in chapter 3, in the few occurrences in Jewish material where the phrase "all the nations" (MT: *kol hā-'ammim*; LXX: *panta ta ethnē*) might have an inclusive sense, the special status of Israel is by no means occluded or set aside. Further, since in Matthew the mission to "the lost sheep of the house of Israel" (10:6) is to continue until the parousia (10:23), the special identity of Israel necessarily continues until the end as well. An inclusive reading of *panta ta ethnē* in Matt 28:19—"all the nations, Israel included"—can be understood in terms not of a loss of status for Israel but of an opening up of Israel's special status to include disciples from the gentiles as well.[220] Either way, however, the inclusive sense of the term leads to readings of the Gospel that correspond to

---

219. E.g., Ulrich Luz: "the risen Jesus abolishes the privileged position of his nation of Israel in salvation history and regards the previously chosen people as simply one among other ἔθνη." He adds, "The mission command of the Lord of heaven and earth—that is, of the whole world—is, in my judgment, *fundamentally* universal and is for all nations"; *Matthew 21–28: A Commentary*, trans. Wilhelm C. Linss, Hermeneia (Minneapolis: Fortress, 2005), 630, 631.

220. This, of course, opens up the perennial question of Matthew and the torah. Some have argued that the commands that disciples are to observe include the whole torah. See especially Sim, *Gospel of Matthew and Christian Judaism*, 251–54; also, with some qualifications, Levine, *Social and Ethnic Dimensions of Matthean Salvation History*, 183–84; Runesson, *Divine Wrath and Salvation in Matthew*, 350, n. 16, 380; see also Runesson's references on p. 372, n. 80. For the purposes of this type, however, emphasis is probably to be placed on statements (commands) of Jesus that lead more in the direction of a "new law"—his prioritization of the ethical aspects of the law over the minutiae of tithing (23:23) or over (ethnic-specific) cultic worship (9:13; 12:7), his summation of the law in ethical-monotheistic commandments (22:34–40) or moral maxims (7:12), and related material, together with his harsh criticism of proselytism (23:15).

this third identity type. In addition, some of the elements that have often been adduced as evidence of Matthew's Jewishness—Jesus's statement that even "the least" of the commandments in the law are to be observed (5:19); the assumption that disciples would offer sacrifices at the temple (5:23–24); the endorsement (with qualifications) of the laws of tithing (23:23);[221] and so on—suggest at the very least that the traditional terms of the covenant were seen as valid. In other words, the Gospel of Matthew would reflect the first subtype (3.1).

With respect to the Didache, the interpretive crux is found in 6.2: "For if you can bear the entire yoke of the Lord, you will be perfect; but if you cannot, do as much as you can." As we have seen, many readers have taken the "entire yoke of the Lord" to be a reference to the full Mosaic torah and have understood the intended audience here (evidently being prepared for baptism; 7.1) as gentile converts in particular. In such a reading, the Didache can be aligned with the second identity type. It is also possible, however, that "the entire yoke of the Lord" refers more specifically to the teaching about the "way of life" contained in Didache 1–4 and that the admonition is addressed to new converts more generally, Jews as well as gentiles. In this case, the Didache might be seen as drawing on what Finlan calls "an increasingly abstract and symbolic Jewish identity" in order to construct a new pan-ethnic "Christian identity," which would be more in keeping with the third identity type (specifically, 3.1).[222]

In the book of Revelation, we again encounter a tension between material that suggests a clear contrast between Israel and the non-Jewish *ethnē* and material that seems to assign a "symbolic Jewish identity" to an *ekklēsia* consisting of Jewish and gentile believers. On the one hand, we find what appears to be a clear ethnic distinction within the community of the redeemed in chapter 7 (between the twelve tribes of the people of Israel and a "great multitude . . . from every nation") and chapters 21 and 22 (between the new Jerusalem and the *ethnē*; 21:24, 26; 22:2). On the other hand, the recurring phrase "every tribe and language and people and nation" suggests that Israel is seen simply as one nation among many;[223] language that echoes a phrase used in Israel's Scriptures to characterize Israel ("a priestly kingdom and a holy nation" [Exod 19:6]) is used on several occasions with reference to the community of those ransomed "from every tribe and language and people and nation" (5:9–10; cf. 1:6); and, given the situation presupposed in the work as a whole, it is difficult to imagine the group of those who received the protective "seal" (7:3–4) as consisting exclusively of

---

221. While the emphasis falls on "the weightier matters of the law: justice and mercy and faith," "the others" (including those to do with tithing) are not to be neglected.

222. Finlan, "Identity in the *Didache* Community," 31.

223. 5:9, with variant forms in 7:9; 10:11; 11:9; 13:7; 14:6; and 17:15.

ethnic Jews. This has led many interpreters to believe that, while Revelation retains a certain distinction between the people of God and the nations, the people of God consists of an *ekklēsia* drawn from all the nations of the world, and the identity previously born by the nation of Israel itself has now passed over to this new multiethnic community. In this reading, Revelation belongs to the third identity type.

In our discussion of the second identity type, we noted a number of elements in the letters of Paul where a distinction between Jews and gentiles seems to be fundamental and where gentile participation in salvation is said to be dependent on Jewish action—both negatively (the failure of many Jews to respond positively to Christ has brought "riches to the *ethnē*" [Rom 11:12-15]) and positively (the Jewish remnant have shared their spiritual riches with the *ethnē* [Rom 15:27]). Indeed, not only has this bivalent relationship opened up the possibility of gentile salvation but the incoming of "the fullness of the *ethnē*" will also lead in turn to the salvation of "all Israel" (Rom 11:25-26). At the same time, however, many of the more distinctive elements in Paul's discourse—elements that have loomed large in Pauline interpretation—are characterized by what might be called a universalistic frame of reference. These universalistic elements have been taken to imply that ethnic distinctions play a secondary role in Paul's thought and that his more fundamental category is generic humanity, humankind as a whole.

This material is well known to readers of Paul and so can be described briefly.[224] In one set of pertinent references, Paul asserts that there is no distinction between Jews and non-Jews. The assertion appears explicitly in Rom 3:22 ("There is no distinction [*diastolē*]") and 10:12 ("There is no distinction [*diastolē*] between Jew and Greek"). In 3:22-24 the absence of distinction pertains both to plight ("since all have sinned and fall short of the glory of God") and salvation ("they are now justified by God's grace as a gift, through the redemption that is in Christ Jesus"). The passage is flanked by two related assertions: "we have already charged that all, both Jews and Greeks, are under sin" (3:9); "Or is God the God of Jews only? Is he not the God of Gentiles also?" (3:29). In chapter 10 the absence of distinction also has to do with salvation; the passage continues: "the same Lord is Lord of all and is generous to all who call on him." An analogous assertion appears in a different form in Gal 3:28: "There is no longer Jew or Greek ... for all of you are one in Christ Jesus" (cf. 1 Cor 12:13).

In another set of pertinent passages, Paul uses universal or generic language (*pas* [all]; *anthrōpos* [man, human being]) in the context of substantive theological discourse, where for other Jewish Christ-believers distinctions between

---

224. I have discussed it more thoroughly in ch. 5 ("Generic Humanity") of my *Paul and the Gentiles*.

Jews and gentiles might have been pertinent. Several relevant occurrences of the term *all* were mentioned already in the previous paragraph ("all have sinned"; "all, both Jews and Greeks"; "Lord of all"; "all of you are one in Christ Jesus"). Examples can be readily multiplied: "[Christ] died for all" (2 Cor 5:14–15); "so that at the name of Jesus every knee should bend" (Phil 2:10). Elsewhere the universal significance of Christ is conveyed with the use of *anthrōpos*: "on the day when, according to my gospel, God, through Jesus Christ, will judge the secret thoughts of human beings" (*anthrōpōn*; Rom 2:16); "for we hold that a human being [*anthrōpos*] is justified by faith apart from works prescribed by the law" (Rom 3:28); "yet we know that a human being [*anthrōpos*] is justified not by the works of the law but through faith in Jesus Christ" (Gal 2:16). Both terms appear together in passages contrasting Adam and Christ, though here *anthrōpos* denotes Adam and Christ specifically: "just as one man's trespass led to condemnation for all, so one man's act of righteousness leads to justification and life for all" (Rom 5:18); "for as all die in Adam, so all will be made alive in Christ" (1 Cor 15:22). This use of the term to contrast Adam and Christ is central to Rom 5:12–21 as a whole ("for just as by the disobedience of the one *anthrōpos* the many were made sinners, so by the obedience of the one *anthrōpos* the many will be made righteous" [5:19; also vv. 12, 15]) and is found also in 1 Cor 15, where Paul is discussing the significance of Christ's resurrection ("for since death came through one *anthrōpos*, the resurrection of the dead has also come through an *anthrōpos*" [v. 21; cf. vv. 22, 45]). Alongside this binary contrast between Adam and Christ, *anthrōpos* appears also in the context of binary depictions of human existence (in Christ and apart from Christ): "our old *anthrōpos*" (which implies a new *anthrōpos*; Rom 6:6); "our outer *anthrōpos* . . . our inner *anthrōpos*" (2 Cor 4:16; also Rom 7:22; cf. 1 Cor 2:14).

As can be seen from the passages cited, the universal language under discussion is used in the context of significant aspects of Paul's theological discourse: the identity and role of Christ; the reality of sin; the redemption in Christ; and righteousness and justification by faith. Turning to the nature of the *ekklēsia*, his discourse moves in two directions. On one side, he can speak of the *ekklēsia* as a kind of third entity. Addressing the believers in Corinth, he exhorts them: "Give no offense to Jews or to Greeks or to the *ekklēsia* of God" (1 Cor 10:32). His discourse about those who are "in Christ Jesus" as constituting a community that somehow transcends the categories of "Jew" and "Greek" (Gal 3:28) moves in the same direction.

At the same time, however—and sometimes even in the same breath—Paul can speak of this new community as bearing the identity of Israel. In the following verse (Gal 3:29), he goes on to say: "And if you are Christ's, then you are Abraham's seed [*sperma*], heirs according to the promise." Similar language of

235

GENTILE CHRISTIAN IDENTITY

fictive ethnicity appears in Rom 4:13-16. Here those "who believe without being circumcised" (4:11) are by virtue of this faith said to belong to the category of Abraham's "seed [*sperma*]" and "heirs." The language of *sperma* here clearly echoes Gen 17, where God commands circumcision as the identifying mark of the line of Abraham's covenantal descendants, which God will establish through Isaac.[225] Paul is fully aware of the passage (Gen 17:4), as he cites it in Rom 4:17. Here we will not pause to consider the oddness of Paul's attempt to characterize uncircumcised gentile believers as part of Abraham's *sperma*, despite the fact that in Gen 17 circumcision is essential for all members of Abraham's *sperma*. Rather, the point is that Paul is prepared to take an identity term that pertains specifically to Israel and to transfer it to the mixed-ethnic community of Christ-believers. Or perhaps it would be better to say that he redefines an Israel identity term so that it can be opened up to include gentiles. The inclusion of gentile believers within Israel's heritage seems to be implied also by Paul's reference to "our fathers" in his letter to the gentile believers in Corinth (1 Cor 11:1).[226] A similar kind of redefinition and expansion may be at work in Paul's use of the term "the Israel of God" in Gal 6:16. While some have argued that the term here refers specifically to Jewish Christ-believers rather than to Christ-believers more generally, the fact that it appears in the same epistle as Gal 3:28 makes it understandable that many would see it as an inclusive term.[227]

In significant sections of his letters, then, Paul seems to be portraying the *ekklēsia* as a new human community that, on the one hand, transcends the old distinctions between Jews and gentiles and that, on the other, can be said to bear the identity of Israel. Further, it has appeared to many readers of this ma-

---

225. The issue of who will be Abraham's heir is central to the account in Gen 15.

226. The fact that he goes on to say, with reference to the exodus and wilderness experience, that these things serve "as examples for us" (1 Cor 10:6-11) clearly indicates that Paul is using "our fathers" in an inclusive sense — i.e., including the Corinthian gentile Christ-believers — rather than exclusively — i.e., Paul and his fellow Jews (or Jewish Christ-believers), exclusive of his gentile readers.

227. The issue hinges on whether *kai* (in the phrase *kai epi ton Israēl tou theou*) should be rendered "and" — in which case "the Israel of God" is a distinct Jewish group existing alongside "those who follow this rule" — or whether it has an epexegetical sense ("even") — so that only one group is in view ("those who follow this rule," who can also be designated as "the Israel of God"). The latter rendering is more common; see, e.g., Martyn, *Galatians*, 567, 574-77, and the literature cited there. For a strong defense of the former, see Peter Richardson, *Israel in the Apostolic Church*, SNTSMS 10 (Cambridge: Cambridge University Press, 1969), 74-84; Richardson makes the observation that, this statement aside, the title *Israel* is never applied to the (mixed-ethnic or fully gentile) *ekklēsia* until Justin Martyr.

terial that Paul assigns little positive significance to Israel and its covenantal distinctives as they would have been understood by most Jews before and apart from Christ. With respect to the law, while it might promise life (Rom 7:10) and righteousness (Rom 2:13) to those who adhere to it, in reality the promise cannot be fulfilled (Rom 7:10), and it is totally ineffective in producing a righteously distinctive people (Rom 3:20; Gal 2:21; 3:11). The primary function of the law is a negative one: to reveal sin (Rom 3:20; 7:7) and even to aid and abet the power of sin (Rom 5:20; 7:5, 8, 11). With respect to the temple, while most Jews would have understood it as the means by which atonement could be made, God's forgiveness received, and righteousness maintained, for Paul these were possible only through Christ (Gal 2:21; Rom 3:21–26). Indeed, Paul studiously avoids any discussion of the role of the temple entirely.[228]

All of this is simply to acknowledge aspects of Paul's letters that are well known and that could be (and frequently have been!) described and explored at great length. For present purposes, the point is simply that this aspect of Paul's discourse could easily be understood as reflecting a radical Christ-centered reinterpretation of Israel's covenantal distinctives, producing a view of the Mosaic covenant that contrasted sharply with the way it was traditionally understood and practiced. In other words, this aspect of Paul's discourse can be seen as representing the second subtype of the third identity type (3.2).

Turning to the deutero-Pauline literature, the pertinent material in Colossians and Ephesians overlaps to a significant extent with the material we have just looked at, though with some distinctive features. As we have observed, while there is widespread doubt that these letters were written by Paul directly, if they were not, at least it can be said that they probably emerged from a wider Pauline circle that shared and developed his patterns of thought. In both epistles, we encounter a clear distinction between Jews and gentiles, with the intended readers being addressed as gentiles and the author clearly addressing them from a Jewish perspective.[229]

---

228. Perhaps there is an allusion in Rom 3:25 ("in his divine forbearance, [God] had passed over the sins previously committed"). The more striking thing to observe, however, is that even though the passage seems to raise the question of temple sacrifice, Paul says nothing about it. See E. P. Sanders, *Paul and Palestinian Judaism* (Philadelphia: Fortress, 1977), 499–500.

229. Passages showing the gentile identity of the readers include the following: "I became its [the church's] servant according to God's commission that was given to me for you, to make the word of God fully known ... to make known how great among the *ethnē* are the riches of the glory of this mystery, which is Christ in you, the hope of glory" (Col 1:25–26); "So then, remember that at one time you *ethnē* by birth, called 'the uncircum-

As with some material in the undisputed epistles, both Colossians and Ephesians put the work of Christ and its significance for Jews and gentiles in a decidedly universal framework.

Each letter begins with a thanksgiving prayer, along with a related benediction (Eph 1:3–14) and hymnic section (Col 1:15–20), which set the *ekklēsia* and the gospel within the cosmic outworking of a divine plan.[230] While neither letter treats Israel and the *ethnē* as insignificant categories, this plan is one that transcends these categories and brings a new entity into being, one that in Ephesians is even identified as a "new humanity" (*kainos anthrōpos*; 2:15).

This new entity has been brought about by the overcoming of the distinction between Jew and gentile. In a statement that echoes Gal 3:28 (though with a greater emphasis on ethnic distinctions), Col 3:11 declares: "there is no longer Greek and Jew, circumcised and uncircumcised, barbarian, Scythian, slave and free, but Christ is all and in all." In Ephesians, the abolition of the distinction between the two is developed at considerable length (2:11–22):

> For [Christ] is our peace; in his flesh he has made both groups [*ethnē* and Israel; the uncircumcised and the circumcised (vv. 11–12)] into one and has broken down the dividing wall, that is, the hostility between us. He has abolished [*katargēsas*] the law with its commandments and ordinances, that he might create in himself one new *anthrōpos* in place of the two. (vv. 14–15)

That which had served to differentiate Jew and gentile has been abolished, making it possible for the two groups to be joined into one, a new entity that is described as "one body" (v. 16) and "one new *anthrōpos*" (v. 15). The term "new

---

cision' by those who are called 'the circumcision'" (Eph 2:11); "I Paul am a prisoner of Christ Jesus for the sake of you *ethnē*" (Eph 3:1).

The Jewish perspective of the author is implicit both in the identification of the readers as "you *ethnē*" (Eph 2:11; 3:1; also, though not as concisely, in Col 1:27) and in the assumption that the readers would be familiar with Paul the apostle, the one who had received a commission from God "for you *ethnē*" (Eph 3:1–6; Col 1:25–27).

230. Colossians: Christ is "the firstborn of all creation" (1:15); "all things have been created through him and for him" (1:16); "through him God was pleased to reconcile to himself all things" (1:20); "the gospel . . . which has been proclaimed to every creature under heaven" (1:23); the gospel that "is bearing fruit in the whole world" (1:6). Ephesians: God's "plan for the fullness of time, to gather up all things in [Christ], things in heaven and things on earth" (1:10); God placed Christ "far above all rule and authority and power and dominion, and above every name that is named, not only in this age but also in the age to come. And he has put all things under his feet and has made him the head over all things for the church, which is his body, the fullness of him who fills all in all" (1:21–23).

anthrōpos" is at least implicit in Paul's reference to "our old *anthrōpos*" (Rom 6:6), and the discourse beginning with Rom 5:12 contains enough of a corporate emphasis to suggest that "our old *anthrōpos*" does not refer simply to an aspect of individual human existence.[231] However, the discourse in Eph 2:11–22 takes this a significant step further. The positive term appears explicitly and with an explicit corporate sense. What Christ has brought into existence is a new humanity, in which the old distinctions between "the *ethnē*" and "the commonwealth [*politeia*] of Israel" have been transcended and a new humanity is now becoming apparent in "the church, which is [Christ's] body, the fullness of him who fills all in all" (Eph 1:22–23).

In both epistles, however, this incorporation of Jews and gentiles into one new entity does not entail the complete effacing of Israel's identity. Part of the plight from which "you *ethnē*" (Eph 2:11) were delivered was the fact that they had been "foreigners and sojourners" (*xenoi kai paroikoi*; v. 19), "aliens [*apēllotriōmenoi*] from the commonwealth of Israel, and strangers [*xenoi*] to the covenants of promise" (v. 12). Now those who "once were far off have been brought near" (v. 13) and have been incorporated into a body that not only represents a new humanity but also carries marks of Israel's identity: the gentiles are "fellow citizens [*sympolitai*]" with the [Jewish] "saints" (v. 19); together they constitute a "holy temple" (v. 21); in some sense, they are now no longer *ethnē* ("you must no longer live as the *ethnē* live"; 4:17).

On the one hand, then, the *ekklēsia* is a new entity—a new humanity made possible by the abolition of those "commandments and ordinances of the law" that had served as a boundary marker between Jew and gentile. On the other, this new entity carries the identity of Israel; Israel's identity has been redefined in Christ so that it can now include the *ethnē*. While this construction is not as fully articulated in Colossians, it is at least adumbrated: the *ethnē* once were "estranged [*apēllotriōmenous*] and hostile in mind" (1:21); they have now become part of a new entity in which "there is no longer Greek and Jew" (3:11); in so doing they have "stripped off the old *anthrōpos* and have clothed [themselves] with the new" (3:9–10); while they once were "dead in trespasses and in the circumcision of [their] flesh," by means of their baptism into Christ, they have received a "circumcision not made with hands" (2:11–12).

This construction, of course, could readily become supersessionistic once it was taken over by a fully gentile church. Both epistles, however, are marked by what could readily be perceived as a Jewish self-consciousness—the perspective of Jewish believers in Christ who had welcomed non-Jews into a new corporate

---

231. So, e.g., James D. G. Dunn, *Romans 1–8*, WBC (Dallas, TX: Word, 1988), 318–19.

body in which old distinctions had been transcended but in which the (now transcended) ethnic origins of its members were nevertheless readily apparent.

Both epistles, then, represent clear examples of the third identity type under discussion. While for both of them the coming of Christ has brought into being a new reality that represented a substantial reinterpretation of Jewish eschatological expectation, there is little to suggest that Israel's history and covenantal identity in the past has been devalued or radically reinterpreted from a christocentric position. The new reality is "a mystery" that "in former generations was not made known to humankind [*tois hyiois tōn anthrōpōn*]" (Eph 3:3-6; also Eph 1:9; 3:9; Col 1:26-27). The "commonwealth of Israel" and "the covenants of promise" are presented as positive entities (Eph 2:12) to which the gentiles now have access. In other words, Ephesians and Colossians are probably to be seen as exemplifying the first subtype (3.1).

The final piece of literature to be discussed here is 1 Peter.[232] The intended

---

232. As mentioned above, while both the Gospel of John and the Epistle to the Hebrews can be taken as reflecting the perspectives of distinct groups of Jewish Christ-believers, the fact that neither uses *ethnē* as a designation of non-Jews means that they are not as significant for our purposes here—especially since our purposes have to do with identifying a set of types rather than with a full exploration of literature produced by Jewish Christ-believers. Both of them, however, can certainly be taken as examples of the third identity type.

I have discussed issues of identity and self-definition in John's Gospel at some length elsewhere (see ch. 4 of *Jews and Anti-Judaism in the New Testament: Decision Points and Divergent Interpretations* [London: SPCK; Waco, TX: Baylor University Press, 2010]). Here I will simply observe several things briefly. (1) The Fourth Gospel represents a thoroughgoing christological reinterpretation of Israel's Scriptures, history, and covenantal identity. (2) The use of the blanket term "the Jews" (often in a sharply pejorative way) is an odd and puzzling feature of the Gospel, especially as it is sometimes used to refer to distinct subgroups of Jews. It has often been taken as an indication of the non-Jewish perspective of the Gospel. (3) Nevertheless, the Gospel retains a definitely Jewish center of gravity (albeit sectarian and alienated), even though the intended readership of the Gospel probably included non-Jews. (4) Where non-Jewish believers do (probably) come into view (see the discussion of pertinent passages [7:35; 10:16; 11:52; and 12:20-21] in n. 124, above), they are incorporated into a group of Jewish believers that bears Israel identity markers. Thus the Gospel can be taken as an example of the third identity type, subtype one (i.e., 3.1).

With respect to Hebrews, the idea that Christ has inaugurated a new era is certainly a central theme. Jesus is the "mediator of a new covenant" (9:15), one that has rendered the first covenant "obsolete" (8:13). The old covenant, together with the law, was simply "a shadow of the good things to come and not the true form of those realities" (10:1). To establish the point, the author asserts the superiority of Jesus, and the new reality that

Ethnē as an Identity Ascribed to Non-Jews: By Jewish Christ-Believers

readers of this letter are clearly identified as non-Jewish. Addressing them directly, the author declares that before they came to believe in the "God who raised [Jesus] from the dead" (1:21), they were characterized by "desires that [they] formerly had in ignorance" (1:14) and lived in "the futile ways inherited from [their] ancestors" (1:18)—descriptions that would not have been applicable to Jews. During this time, they did "what the *ethnē* like to do, living in licentiousness, passions, drunkenness, revels, carousing, and lawless idolatry" (4:3). In short, they were gentiles—or at least they used to be. The author implies that this is an identity that they left behind in coming to Christ: "conduct yourselves honorably among the *ethnē*" (2:12).

Further, this is an identity that the author does not seem to share. Of course, on the surface of it, this might seem obvious: the author identifies himself as Peter, apostle (1 Pet 1:1) and "witness of the sufferings of Christ" (5:1). Most interpreters, however, believe that the letter was written after the death of Peter and thus was written by someone else in his name.[233] Nevertheless, other aspects of

---

has come into being through him, with respect to various persons, elements, and aspects of the old era: the angels (2:1–2), Moses (3:1–6), Joshua (4:8), the high priest (5:1–10), the sabbath rest (4:8–10), the sanctuary (9:6–12), and the temple sacrifices (9:25–26). But what about the Jewish people? Is Israel itself another one of the shadow entities that have given way to a new reality—specifically, a new people containing non-Jews as well? The question comes to a focus with the statement in 2:16, where "the people" who are redeemed by Christ are identified as "the descendants [*sperma*] of Abraham." It is quite possible that this "people" includes gentiles. Even in the immediate context (2:10–18), the "descendants of Abraham" are set over against "the angels" and are characterized by their shared "flesh and blood," which might suggest that a broader humanity is in view (also: Jesus tasted death "for everyone" [2:9]: "it is appointed for human beings [*anthrōpoi*] to die" [9:27]). Many interpreters hold this view (see, e.g., Ole Jakob Filtvedt, *The Identity of God's People and the Paradox of Hebrews*, WUNT 2.400 [Tübingen: Mohr Siebeck, 2015], 66–70; Stephen G. Wilson, *Related Strangers: Jews and Christians, 70–170 C.E.* [Minneapolis: Fortress, 1995], 110–27). If so, Hebrews is another example of the third identity type (probably 3.1). However, the idea of descent from Abraham also comes up in 7:5–6 ("from the loins [*osphyos*] of Abraham"), in a context where ethnic descent is clearly in view. This, together with the absence of any explicit reference to non-Jews, means that it is possible to give the statement in 2:16 its full and literal force—i.e., that gentiles are not in view at all. (See especially Richard B. Hays, "'Here We Have No Lasting City': New Covenantalism in Hebrews," in *The Epistle to the Hebrews and Christian Theology*, ed. Richard Bauckham et al. [Grand Rapids: Eerdmans, 2009], 151–73). In this case, Hebrews would not have a direct bearing on the issue of gentile identity.

233. The reference to "Babylon" (5:13), almost certainly an allusion to Rome, indicates a date after Rome's destruction of the Jerusalem temple in 70 CE, seen as a repetition of the Babylonian destruction centuries earlier.

the letter indicate that the author was writing not only in the name of Peter but also from a self-consciously Jewish perspective. For one thing, this is implied by the term *ethnē* itself, a Jewish designation for non-Jews. In addition, the author describes the former lifestyle of his readers in terms that exclude himself; note the use of the second-person plural throughout: "your ancestors" (1:18), "the desires that you formerly had in ignorance" (1:14), "you spent time in doing what the *ethnē* like to do" (4:3). One might also mention the way in which the author reaches almost instinctively to biblical material for purposes of illustration and embellishment: the whimsical picture of the inquisitive prophets (1:10–12); the depiction of believing women as "daughters of Sarah" (3:6); the story of Noah (4:18–20).

Such instinctive and casual use of biblical material is also pertinent for the question of identity ascription. If the intended readers are no longer identified as *ethnē*, what have they become? For one thing, these former *ethnē* have become a new *ethnos*; having been called "out of darkness into [God's] marvelous light," they are now "a chosen race [*genos*], a royal priesthood, a holy nation [*ethnos*], a people for [God's] possession [*laos eis peripoiēsin*]" (1 Pet 2:9).[234] More specifically, this new nation is one that lives in exile (1:1–2) as a community of sojourners and resident aliens (2:11–12). While the ethnoracial character of this new identity is not to be overlooked, what is more important for present purposes is that much of this language resonates with biblical descriptions of Israel's own identity.[235] The language of 2:9 is drawn explicitly from depictions of Israel in LXX Exod 19:6 ("you shall be for me a royal priesthood and a holy nation") and LXX Isa 43:20–21 ("my chosen people, the people whom I formed for myself [*laon mou hon periepoiēsamēn*]"). Further, while "sojourners and resident aliens" is commonly used in Israel's Scriptures with reference to non-Israelites, the term "exiles of the diaspora" (1:1) is highly evocative of Israel.[236]

In a casual and unreflective way, then, the author picks up biblical language that characteristically denoted Israel's identity and applied it to an *ethnos*, brought into being by God's action in Christ, to which *ethnē* now belong. While the letter seems to have been written from the perspective of a Jewish Christ-believer, it does not display any interest in questions of how Israel and the nations might fit into the larger divine purposes, or on the relative status of Jews and gentiles within this new race, people, and nation. Indeed, the term *new* does not appear

234. They are also identified as "Christians" (4:16).
235. David G. Horrell has drawn attention to the explicitly ethnoracial terms in which this new identity is expressed; "'Race', 'Nation', 'People': Ethnic Identity-Construction in 1 Peter 2:9," *NTS* 58 (2011): 123–43.
236. E.g., for *diaspora*, see LXX Deut 28:25; 30:4; Neh 1:9; Ps 146:2; Isa 49:6.

at all. Nevertheless, despite the unreflective character of the discourse, 1 Peter can also be taken as an example of the third identity type.

If we were primarily interested in Jewish Christ-believers and the nature and development of their thinking about the place of non-Jews in the new realities effected through Christ, we would need to subject this literature to a much more fine-grained analysis than we have been able to carry out here. But for our purposes—identity construction among Christ-believing *ethnē*—this is sufficient. We have been able to discern three broad identity types (each with several subtypes), and these together represent a range of identities that Jewish Christ-believers ascribed to Christ-believing *ethnē*. While some of the material reflected later situations in which Jewish believers were no longer in a position to ascribe identity with any power or effectiveness, all of it provides a reliable picture of the identity possibilities that were handed on to gentile believers.

Before looking at what non-Jews made of this range of ascribed identity, however, we need to return to the issue of ethnicity in the Greco-Roman world, with special attention to the collective term *ethnē* and related Latin terms. As we will see in detail, these terms also figured prominently in the competitive ethnographical discourse carried on among Romans, Greeks, and barbarians throughout the Roman Mediterranean. This discourse would already have shaped the perceptual filters through which gentile Christ-believers would have heard and received these ascriptions of identity.

CHAPTER 5

The Nations in Roman Imperial Discourse

The world that Rome inhabited was a world constituted in large measure by nations. In the self-identifying narratives that Rome constructed for itself, in the versions of these narratives that it projected onto its subject peoples, and in the ways in which the subject peoples appropriated, revised, or resisted these narratives, the nations of the inhabited world (*orbis terrarum, oikoumenē*) occupied a prominent place.

To describe the Roman world in this way, of course, is to say that it was a product of social construction, which indeed it was. At the same time, however, it was not constructed out of thin air. The German nation (*gens*) of the Suebi, described at some length by Julius Caesar in his account of the Gallic wars (*Gallic War* 4.1–3), may well have been puzzled or amused by some of the details in Caesar's description of their diet, dress, land-use customs, behavior in war, and so on;[1] their neighbors the Ubii may well have had their own version of the character of the Suebi and their place among the Germanic nations.[2] But there can be no doubt that both the Suebi and the Ubii—not to mention the Romans themselves—thought of themselves as distinct people groups characterized by just the kind of elements itemized by Herodotus in his well-known account of Greekness.[3]

1. A description based to some extent on reported information (*dicuntur*; 4.1, 3).
2. While Caesar describes them as "the largest ... nation [*gens*] among the Germans" (*Gallic War* 4.1), in Tacitus's depiction the term *Suebi* denotes a larger entity comprising a number of nations or people groups (*Germany* 38–41).
3. *Histories* 8.144.

The Nations in Roman Imperial Discourse

Both aspects of the Roman world—the symbolic world of the rulers, embedded in imperial ideology and projected in the various textual and material accoutrements of imperial rule, and the experienced world of the ruled, as they negotiated and defined their own space within this imposed world—were populated by ethnic people groups, or nations. And *nations* not simply in an abstract or conceptual sense, but *nations* in explicit linguistic denotation: *gentes, nationes, populi, ethnē, laoi*. As we will see, the language of peoplehood that so clearly marked the spread of Christ-belief into the non-Jewish world—the world of the gentile *ethnē*—was already densely present in the Roman world. Before attempting, then, to explore the question of what sense non-Jewish Christ-believers might have made of *ethnē* as an ascribed identity, we need to become better attuned to the place of *ethnē* and related terms in the Roman world—a world consisting of many *ethnē*, a world in which non-Jews existed as members of this *ethnos* or that.

In the latter part of chapter 2, we examined pertinent aspects of identity construction in the Roman world, looking specifically at ethnology and ethnological negotiation in the ancient world generally, Roman imperial ideology and the means by which it was conveyed and imposed, the responses on the part of the subject peoples to this imposed ideology, and the ascribed identity that came with it. In the present chapter, we will retrace our steps, looking specifically at *ethnē* and related terms, the language of ethnic peoplehood. We begin with some general observations about vocabulary and usage, before looking in more detail at usage in the Roman imperial context. With respect to the latter, we will focus on Roman imperial ideology, but we will also have occasion to observe aspects of Rome's self-positioning with respect to barbarians and Greeks, and ways in which Greeks attempted to negotiate a favorable position for themselves on the Roman map of the world.[4]

VOCABULARY AND USAGE: GENERAL CONSIDERATIONS

Given our interest in gentiles, our exploration of usage will necessarily center on the Greek term *ethnē* (sg. *ethnos*), together with Latin equivalents. *Ethnos*, most commonly rendered as "nation," is one of a set of terms used to denote specific people groups, a set that includes *laos* (people), *phylē* (also *phylon*: tribe), *patria* (family, clan), and *genos* (race, kind)—to use the most common translation equivalents for these terms. While these terms differ in etymology and in some of their uses and aspects, they overlap considerably in the usage most pertinent to our discussion—that is, to denote people groups characterized by typical ethnic

---

4. And to a certain extent Jews, though this has been examined already in ch. 3.

245

markers (descent, language, land, worship, custom, name).⁵ Because of our particular interest in *ethnē* itself, we do not need to concern ourselves unduly with the distinctions among these terms, though it can be noted that *ethnos* appears with greater frequency and denotes ethnic people groups in broader terms than any of the others.⁶

In Latin, the terms that correspond most closely are *gens* (pl. *gentes*: clan, nation), *natio* (nation), *populus* (people), *tribus* (tribe), and *genus* (race, descendants). Although two of these (*gens*, *natio*) overlap considerably with *ethnos*, *gens* will be much more significant for our purposes.⁷ For one thing, it appears with much greater frequency than does *natio*.⁸ For another, some evidence suggests a closer correlation in usage between *ethnos* and *gens*. This can be seen quite clearly in bilingual or translated texts, where *ethnos* seems to be the preferred equivalent for *gens*. To take one prominent example, *gens* (or *gentes*) appears on eight occasions in the *Acts of Augustus*, in each case with reference to a foreign nation or nations; all of these are rendered by *ethnos* (or *ethnē*) in the Greek version, and *natio* does not appear at all.⁹ Further, although it is not exactly a situation of

---

5. *Genos* can also be used of animals, plants, and inanimate "kinds"; *laos* (usually in the plural) can be used of unrelated aggregations of human beings (soldiers, assemblies); *patria* highlights descent from a common father and thus shared heritage; *ethnos*, which can also be used of animals (flocks) or insects (swarms), when referring to people groups perhaps highlights the presence of common customs (cf. *ethos*). See the pertinent entries in *LSJ*; on the possible semantic connection between *ethnos* and *ethos*, see *TDNT* 2:369.

6. On the basis of the statistical information available on the Perseus Digital Library (http://www.perseus.tufts.edu). Although the Perseus figures are not precise (the software cannot disambiguate forms that derive from more than one lexicon entry; the Perseus site thus provides maximum and minimum figures), there is no ambiguity with *ethnos*, which means that the relative frequency is readily apparent in this case.

7. In addition to this broader denotation, both *gens* and *natio* can refer to more restricted groups. *Gens* commonly denotes families or clans within the Roman population (such as the Julii, the Claudii, the Cornelii). *Natio* can also be used of human subgroups, as in Cicero's rejection of the term when used by his opponents as a contemptuous term of abuse for Publius Sestius and other members of the aristocratic elite (which Gardner rendered "breed"; *In Defense of Sestius* 132 [LCL]).

8. Again using the Perseus statistics and comparing the figures for a selection of Latin authors who are important here (Cicero, Livy, Pliny the Elder, Sallust, Seneca, Suetonius, Tacitus, Virgil, Vitruvius), we find that *gens* appears somewhere between 1019 and 2270 times, while *natio* is found in only 311 instances. (On the maximum and minimum figures, see note 6.)

9. *Acts of Augustus* 3, 26 (twice), 27, 30 (twice), 32, 33. Six occurrences are in the plural, two in the singular.

translation, we can consider the reliefs of personified nations in the Sebasteion in Aphrodisias, each one of which is identified as an *ethnos* (e.g., *ethnos Ioudaiōn*) in the accompanying inscription.[10] Since this set of figures was "almost certainly based on a particular model in Rome, most likely the figures of the *gentes* in the Portico of the Nations" in Augustus's forum,[11] and since the Roman models (including those of the fourteen conquered nations in Pompey's theater) are consistently described as representations of the *gentes*,[12] it is probable that the Sebasteion provides further evidence for the translational correspondence between *gens* and *ethnos*. More generally, we can note the definite preference for *gens/gentes* and *ethnos/ethnē* in unilingual inscriptions.[13]

Nevertheless, given the nature of the case, we should not restrict our attention

---

10. At least three islands are also included. See R. R. R. Smith, "*Simulacra Gentium*: The *Ethnē* from the Sebasteion at Aphrodisias," *Journal of Roman Studies* 78 (1988): 55.

11. Catharine Edwards, "Incorporating the Alien: The Art of Conquest," in *Rome the Cosmopolis*, ed. Catharine Edwards and Greg Woolf (Cambridge: Cambridge University Press, 2003), 66.

12. The "*gentes* whose names adorn his Forum" (Velleius Paterculus, *Compendium of Roman History* 2.39.2); "the *simulacris gentium* which had been dedicated in Pompey's theatre" (Suetonius, *Nero* 6.46.1).

13. *Gens/gentes*: on the arch erected by the city of Pisa after the death of Gaius, who defeated or received into loyalty "the most warlike and greatest nations [*bellicosissimis ac maxsimis gentibus*]" (*ILS* 140); an inscription honoring Claudius, who received the surrender of "British kings and barbarian nations [*gentesque*] across the Ocean" (*ILS* 216); an inscription reportedly commemorating Titus, who "conquered the nation [*gentes*] of the Jews and the city of Jerusalem," which "all the leaders, kings, nations before him [*omnibus ante se ducibus regibus gentibus*]" had not been able to do (*ILS* 264); an inscription honoring Marcus Aurelius, who "either annihilated or subdued the most warlike nations [*bellicosissimis gentibus*]" (*ILS* 374); a second-century-CE inscription concerning Claudius Pollio, the "prefect of nations [*gentium*] in Africa" (*ILS* 1418).

Evidence for *ethnos/ethnē* is present in several literary reports of inscriptions: Diodorus Siculus's account of the victory inscription set up by Pompey after his campaigns in the east, in which the list of those conquered includes a number of named groups, certain tribes (*ta phyla*) and "*panta ta ethnē* that dwell between the Pontic and the Red Seas" (*Library of History* 40.4); Strabo's report of a temple to Augustus in Lugdunum, whose altar bore "an inscription of the names of the nations [*ethnōn*], sixty in number," each with an accompanying image (*Geography* 4.3.2); Josephus's report of Claudius's edict concerning Jewish civic rights in Alexandria, which also enjoined the Jews to respect "the beliefs about the gods held by other nations [*tōn allōn ethnōn*]" (*Jewish Antiquities* 19.290–91); the treaty recorded in 1 Macc 8:22–32 between Rome and the "nation of the Judeans [*to ethnos tōn Ioudaiōn*]," a phrase used three times (vv. 23, 25, 27). For inscriptional material, see, e.g., *IG* IX,1² 2:241; *SEG* 20:324; IKnidos I 31, Dlph; *OGIS* 533.

to the term *gens/gentes*. While on the Greek side we are interested primarily in a specific term, on the Latin side our interest has to do more with a particular denotation. *Natio/nationes* will also be important,[14] as will other terms (*populus, genus*) when they serve to denote ethnic people groups in a similar way.[15] When they are used in this way, these terms tend to be more or less synonymous. It is difficult to discern any significant differentiation in usage; in instances where more than one term appears in the same passage, any differentiation between them usually can be attributed to contextual or stylistic convenience.

Looking first at *gens* and *natio*, the degree of overlap can be discerned from the curiously conflicting descriptions of usage in the lexicon of Lewis and Short. Speaking of *gens* when used to denote "a race, nation, people," the entry continues: "sometimes more restricted than *natio* and *populus*, and sometimes put for them." But speaking of *natio* when used in the same sense ("a race of people, nation, people"), the lexicon contains an almost identical (and hence opposite) comparative description: "used commonly in a more limited sense than *gens*, and sometimes as identical with it." This inadvertent affirmation of interchangeability is borne out in the texts themselves. In an account of strife among groups in Gaul, for example, Tacitus refers to them as *gentes* in one sentence and *nationes*

---

14. To take one example from inscriptional material, a law initiated by Gaius Gracchus (having to do with cases of extortion) speaks of "any person who is one of the allies or the Latin name or any foreign people [*exterarumve nationum*]" (*CIL* 1.2.583); the text and translation is also found in the chapter "Laws and Other Documents," in *Archaic Inscriptions*, trans. E. H Warmington, vol. 4 of *Remains of Old Latin*, LCL 359 (London: W. Heinemann, 1940), no. 59, section 1.

15. *Populus* is the preferred term for the Roman people, which perhaps tends to limit its use for other peoples. Perhaps for related reasons, it also appears with reference to people groups associated with cities: inscriptional evidence collected in Warmington, *Archaic Inscriptions* (in the chapter "Laws and Other Documents"), includes a lengthy treaty between Rome and the city of Callatis (on the Black Sea), which refers to "the *populus* of Rome" and "the *populus* of Callatis" throughout (no. 55); and a law that touches on "land which is situated in Africa," which speaks of "the free peoples [*populorum leiberorum*] of Utica, Hadrumetum, Tampsus, Leptis, Aquilla, Usalis and Teudalis" (no. 60, section 79; *CIL* 1.2.585). Nevertheless, *populus* is also used of ethnic people groups more generally. (*Tribus* denotes a subdivision [originally one-third] within the Roman people and thus is usually used as an intra-Roman term.)

Where it is used of human groups, *genus* often denotes the human race (*genus humanum*) more generally (e.g., Cicero, *On the Laws* 2.8; Horace, *Odes* 1.12.49–50; Livy, *History of Rome* 36.17.16; Pliny the Elder, *Natural History* 7.6; Tacitus, *Annals* 3.59; Florus, *Epitome of Roman History* 1.introduction.2), though some references to specific people groups do appear (e.g., Rome: Cicero, *Philippic* 4.13; Virgil, *Aeneid* 12.838).

The Nations in Roman Imperial Discourse

in the next.[16] Likewise, Velleius Paterculus speaks in one place of "the *gentes* of the Pannonians and the *nationes* of the Dalmatians"; when he picks up the account a little later, however, the latter have become "Dalmatia and all the races [*gentibus*] of that region."[17] Such parallel or interchangeable use of *gens* and *natio* is widespread.[18]

To be sure, in some instances, there might appear to be a degree of differentiation between the terms. In his discussion of the ethnic groups in Germany, for example, Tacitus introduces one of the German *gentes* living on the shore of the Rhine as the Frisii. This *gens*, he says, comprises two *nationes*, who "are called the Greater or Lesser Frisii according to the measure of their strength" (*Germany* 34). A little later, however, he describes an apparently similar situation—an ethnic people group (the Suebi) that contains within it a number of smaller distinct ethnic groups—but with a considerable measure of terminological fluidity. He begins the discussion by using *gens*, not *natio*, to speak of smaller distinct subgroups: "Now I must treat of the Suebi, in whom are comprised not one tribe [*gens*] only, as with the Chatti and the Tencteri" (38). Here, in contrast to the case of the Frisii, the subgroups are seen as *gentes*, which might seem to imply that the Suebi constitute something other than a *gens*. But as the discussion continues, the categories shift again; the groups that make up the Suebi are designated as *nationes*, and the Suebi as a totality constitute a *gens*:

16. "[F]or, now that the Romans had withdrawn and the foreign menace was removed, the tribes [*gentis*]—obedient to the national custom, and embittered in this case by their rivalry in prestige—had turned their weapons against each other. The power of the clans [*nationum*] and the prowess of their leaders were upon a level; but while his kingly title rendered Maroboduus unpopular with his countrymen, Arminius aroused enthusiasm as the champion of liberty" (*Annals* 2.44). Similarly, in a description of Germany: "So much in general we have ascertained concerning the origin of the undivided Germans and their customs. I shall now set forth the habits and customs of the several races [*gentium*], and the extent to which they differ from each other; and explain what tribes [*nationes*] have migrated from Germany to the Gallic provinces" (*Germany* 27).

17. "In another place I shall describe the tribes [*gentes*] of the Pannonians and the races [*nationes*] of Dalmatians, the situation of their country [*regionum*] and its rivers, the number and extent of their forces, and the many glorious victories won in the course of this war by this great commander [Tiberius]" (*Compendium of Roman History* 2.92.2–3). "[A]ll Pannonia, grown arrogant through the blessings of a long peace and now at the maturity of her power, suddenly took up arms, bringing Dalmatia and all the races [*gentibus*] of that region into her alliance" (*Compendium of Roman History* 2.110.2).

18. E.g., Cicero, *Philippic* 7.3; *Concerning the Consular Provinces* 33; Vitruvius, *On Architecture* 6.1.9; Velleius, *Compendium of Roman History* 2.106.1; Tacitus, *Agricola* 12; *Germany* 34, 38.

for they [the totality of subgroups] occupy the greater part of Germany, and are still distinguished by special national names [*nationibus nominibusque*], though styled in general Suebi. One mark of the race [*gentis*; i.e., the Suebi] is to comb the hair back over the side of the face and tie it low in a knot behind: this distinguishes the Suebi from other Germans and the free-born of the Suebi from the slave. (38)

In both cases, Tacitus is dealing with real distinctions. But while he uses *gens* and *natio* to express them, the way he does so indicates that the distinctions do not inhere in the terms themselves.

In view of this, before proceeding any further, a word about English equivalents is appropriate. Given the degree of semantic overlap between *gens* and *natio*—and thus the degree of correspondence with *ethnos*—from this point on, I will render *gens* as "nation" and *natio* as "national group."[19] This rendering is meant both to signal the synonymity of usage and to differentiate the two Latin words. Likewise, I will render *ethnos* as "nation."[20] Of course, in our use of these terms, we need to guard against allowing modern notions of nation-states to creep into our interpretations of ancient phenomena. In many cases, for example, these terms are used of groups that we might rather refer to as "tribes." Still, as we will see in more detail shortly, the semantic range of these terms is quite broad. This, together with the close association in scholarly discussion between nations and gentiles, provides some justification for the rendering I have adopted.

In addition to this semantic overlap, the two terms (*gentes*, *nationes*) are frequently found either paired or as part of a longer sequence of nouns, where the intent is clearly to express a kind of totality rather than differentiation. Quintilian, for example, makes reference to "the linguistic diversity of the nations and national groups [*gentes nationesque*] of the world," a phrase that he places in parallel with "the human race" (*omnium hominum*).[21] Similarly, Velleius speaks of his intention "to give a brief synopsis of the nations and national groups which [*quae gens ac natio*, literally, "which nation and national group"] were reduced to provinces and made tributary to Rome" (*Compendium of Roman History* 2.38.1). Cicero is especially partial to longer concatenations in which *gentes* and *nationes*

---

19. Similarly, *populus* will be rendered as "people" and *genus* as "race." All other translations follow the Loeb editions, except where otherwise indicated.

20. In addition, when citing Greek material in English translation, I will on occasion leave *ethnē* untranslated, though in such cases I will use the nominative form in place of any inflected form in the original.

21. To use Russell's LCL rendition (*The Orator's Education* 11.3.87); more literally, "all humankind."

The Nations in Roman Imperial Discourse

are part of larger totalities: "kings, nations and national groups" (*regum, gentium, nationum*); "all nations, national groups, provinces and kingdoms" (*omnes gentes, nationes, provincias, regna*)"; and (speaking of Pompey's victories) "our bitterest enemies, mighty national groups, kings, savage and hitherto unknown nations [*qui maximas nationes, qui reges, qui gentes feras atque inauditas*], countless hordes of pirates and a band of slaves as well."[22] In all these instances, whether *gentes* and *nationes* appear by themselves or as part of a longer list, the point is that they are used together to signal a totality of ethnic people groups—"all people groups, whatever we might like to call them," as it were—rather than distinct and differentiated entities.[23]

With respect to *populus*, in addition to its (frequent) use in reference to the Roman people, it also appears from time to time in conjunction with *gens*. Sometimes the terms are paired or form part of a longer list, in a manner similar to the cases with *natio* just discussed. Martial, for example, speaks of the "peoples and nations [*populi gentesque*]" of the Roman Empire (*Epigrams* 12.6), Cicero of "all kingdoms, peoples [*populi*] and nations [*gentes*]" (*Laws* 2.33). Here, as in the previous case, the terms are used more or less synonymously, to express a kind of human totality. In other instances, however, the terms appear to be used with a certain element of differentiation. In his description of Thrace, for example, Pliny the Elder describes it as "one of the most powerful nations [*gentes*] of Europe" and then goes on to talk about the "peoples [*populorum*]" that it contains (*Natural History* 4.40). Similarly, Tacitus speaks of the Batavi, one of the German "races [*gentium*]" on the west bank of the Rhine, who "were once a people [*populus*] of the Chatti" on the other side, before crossing the river and coming to live in Roman territory (*Germany* 29). In both cases, a *populus* is depicted as forming part of a larger *gens*. But as with the analogous situation with *gens* and *natio* discussed above, it would be rash to conclude that such a distinction was inherent in the terms themselves. To be sure, the distinctions were perceived as real; later we will see how Greek and Latin authors were well aware of the complexities and fluidities of ethnic identities and spent some time puzzling over them. As they reflected on the distinctions, they made convenient use of the terms that were at their disposal. But the distinctions did not become embedded semantically in the terms themselves in any stable or substantial way.

To sum up: Our discussion of pertinent Latin literature will center on the

---

22. Respectively: *In Defense of Sestius* 51; *On the Agrarian Law* 2.39; *In Defense of Sestius* 67. See also *On Behalf of Fonteius* 35: "foreign national groups and nations" (*exteris nationibus et gentibus*).

23. Something akin to the "peoples and tribes and languages and nations" in Revelation (11:9; also 10:11; 17:15).

terms *gens/gentes* and *natio/nationes* (with some attention given to *populus* and *genus*, where appropriate). Both *gentes* and *nationes* correspond closely to *ethnē* as denotations of ethnic people groups and thus in the meanings and usage that interest us. Further, in the bilingual milieu of the Roman Empire, there is clear evidence that the correspondence between *gentes* and *ethnē* was clearly recognized and well established.

Before moving on, two additional aspects of semantics and usage require attention. The first has to do with humankind as a whole, the whole human race. The second has to do with the "other"—ways in which nations other than one's own and members of other ethnic groups were designated. In each case, other terms come into play in both Greek and Latin; but in each case, we are interested primarily in *ethnē* (Greek) and related Latin terms.

We can deal with the first aspect briefly. Greek speakers had a variety of ways of referring to the whole human race: *oikoumenē* (inhabited world), which referred to the inhabitants as well as to the inhabited territory; *pantes anthrōpoi* (all men, all human beings); *to anthrōpōn genos* (the race of human beings, the human race); *panta tōn anthrōpōn genē* (all races of human beings); and so on. Of particular interest are instances where *panta ta ethnē* has a universal denotation. In Dio Chrysostom's oration on the deity, for example, he speaks of an idea that "has been exceedingly potent and persistent since the beginning of time, and has arisen among all nations [*pasi tois ethnesin*] and still remains, being, one may almost say, a common and general endowment of rational beings [*tou logikou genous*]" (*Man's First Conception of God* [*Or.* 12] 39.5). Similarly, after describing "the first generation of the universe" and their development of language, Diodorus Siculus goes on to say that this explains "the present existence of every conceivable kind of language, and, furthermore, out of these first groups to be formed came all the original nations [*tōn hapanta ethnōn*] of the world" (*Library of History* 1.8.4).

The picture in the Latin world is similar. Here the terms for the whole of humankind include *genus humanum* (the human race), *gens humana* (the human nation), *omnes homines* (all human beings), *omnes populi* (all people), and (like *oikoumenē*, combining inhabitants with territory) *orbis terrarum* (the circle of the earth). In addition, there are formulations with *gentes*. Livy, describing the final meeting between Hannibal and Scipio, describes the two of them as "being not only the greatest of their own age, but equal to any of the kings or commanders of all nations [*omnium gentium*] in all history before their time" (*History of Rome* 30.30.1). In addition, in contexts where the idea of universality is already present, *gentes* by itself can denote the whole human race. Horace, speaking of the origin of fire, uses "human race" and "the nations" in parallel: "The human species [*gens humana*], audacious enough to endure anything, plunges into forbidden sacrilege. The audacious son of Iapetus [*Iapeti genus*] by an act of criminal deception brought fire to the nations [*gentibus*]" (*Odes* 1.3.25–28). Something similar appears in Pliny the Elder's work: "And about the human race [*generis humani*] as a whole we have in large part spoken in our account of the various nations [*gentium*]" (*Natural History* 7.6). A striking collection of parallel terms, including *omnes gentes*, is found in the opening chapter of Gaius's *Institutes*:

> All nations [*omnes populi*] who are governed by laws and customs observe partly their own particular law and partly the law common to all mankind [*omnium hominum*]. For that law which any people [*populus*] establishes for itself is its own proper law, and is called *jus civile*, being the peculiar law of that state [*civitatis*]; but that which natural reason establishes among mankind [*omnes homines*] generally is uniformly observed by all people [*omnes populos*], and is called *jus gentium*, as that law which all nations [*omnes gentes*] observe. Thus the Roman people use partly their own peculiar law, partly that law which is common to all men [*omnium hominum*]; each of which we will treat of in its proper place. (*Institutes* 1.1)

Turning to the second aspect—ways of denoting the "other"—as we have already seen in our discussion of Hellenistic Jewish material in chapter 3, there are several Greek formulations with *allo-* that were used to denote foreign nations or individuals. The most significant of these are *alloethnēs*, *allogenēs*, and *allophylos*, adjectives that were also used substantively. These appear from time to time in non-Jewish writings as well—for example, "dangers from foreign nations [*alloethnōn*]"; "the pronunciation of all alien nations [*alloethnōn*] . . . I mean of those that were not Greek"; "an alien [*allophylos*] soldier"; "against foreign or barbarous nations [*allophyla ē barbara ethnē*]."[24] This last example, of course, also contains the most widely established us-them formulation in the ancient world, the Greek distinction between themselves and the barbarians. As this example demonstrates, *barbarian* can be used adjectivally (here with *ethnē*), though it most often appears as a substantive.[25]

---

24. Respectively: Dionysius of Halicarnassus, *Roman Antiquities* 6.63; Strabo, *Geography* 14.2.28; Diodorus Siculus, *Library of History* 21.21.9; Appian, *Civil Wars* 4.137; see also IKnidos I 31 (*ta ektos ethnē*); *IG* XII,4 1:266 (*tōn alloethnōn*). By contrast, *allogenēs* is found primarily in Hellenistic Jewish material. In addition, *heteroethnēs* appears occasionally: e.g., "Many nations [*ethnē*] occupy these mountains, all Celtic except the Ligurians; but while these Ligurians belong to a different race [*heteroethnēs*], still they are similar to the Celts in their modes of life" (Strabo, *Geography* 2.5.28).

25. Strabo provides another example of an adjectival use: "Passing to the poet, Apol-

But what about *ethnē* itself? The entry on *ethnos* in the standard Greek lexicon (*LSJ*) states, in a subsection under "nation, people," that the plural *ta ethnē* was used in the post-Homeric period to denote "foreign, barbarous nations." The documentation that follows contains references to classical as well as later Jewish and Christian material. While the entry has been widely cited in support of the idea that there was in the Greek world an already-existing analog to the Jewish usage,[26] the documentation itself does not bear it out. The distinctive feature of the Jewish usage is that the plural noun, used with an article (*ta ethnē*) but without any further modification, denotes "the other, non-Jewish nations" in and of itself. The references in *LSJ*, however, all contain further modification. The passage from Aristotle's *Politics* (1324b) is rendered as follows in LCL:

> and also among all the non-Hellenic nations [*en tois ethnesi pasi*] that are strong enough to expand at the expense of others, military strength has been held in honor, for example, among the Scythians, Persians, Thracians and Celts.

The phrase in question is simply "among all the nations" (*en tois ethnesi pasi*); "non-Hellenic" has been supplied by the translator. The rendering is probably not inappropriate: while Aristotle is speaking in general terms here, it is clear from the context that the specific nations under discussion—nations "that are strong enough to expand at the expense of others"—are non-Greek.[27] However, the ethnicity of the nations under discussion is indicated by the modifying clause in the larger context of the passage; it is not conveyed by the phrase *tois ethnesi pasi* itself. The passage provides no support at all for the assertion that *ta ethnē* as a stand-alone phrase was used in the post-Homeric period to denote "foreign, barbarous nations."

Likewise, in the inscriptional material that is then cited, *ethnē* in each case is modified, and the identification of the nations in view as "foreign, barbarous nations" is effected by the modifier: the "nomadic nations" (*ethnē nomadōn*) of Bedouin;[28] the Thracian association that was the only one of "the other na-

---

lodorus rightly says that much confusion of the barbarian nations [*tōn barbarōn ethnōn*] has taken place from the Trojan times to the present" (*Geography* 14.5.27).

26. E.g., "Since the time of Aristotle, there was a propensity to use *ethnē* for the 'nations' other than the Greeks"; James M. Scott, *Paul and the Nations*, WUNT 84 (Tübingen: Mohr Siebeck, 1995), 58, n. 7; also Carolyn Osiek, *Shepherd of Hermas: A Commentary*, Hermeneia (Minneapolis: Fortress, 1999), 50, n. 21.

27. The topic has to do with the ideal constitution (*politeia*) and the relative place of the contemplative life and the political life within it.

28. Philippe Le Bas and W. H. Wadding, *Voyage archéologique en Grèce et en Asie Mineure* (Paris: Firmin-Didot, 1888), #2203.

tions" (*tōn allōn ethnōn*) that had been granted certain rights by the people of Athens (in *IG2* 1283).[29] In each case, *ta ethnē* is not used in an absolute way but is further modified; in each case, one can infer from the modifiers, together with the wider context, that the nations are non-Hellenic; but in no case is this denotation carried by the term itself. In short, the *LSJ* entry cannot be used to support the idea that *ethnē* was used to denote "foreign, barbarous nations," and I am not aware of any other instance in Hellenistic usage in which the term in an absolute (unmodified) form refers to "the other nations" in contrast to one's own.

The situation, however, is somewhat different in the Roman period. Among Roman and pro-Roman writers in the period of the late republic and early empire, especially in contexts where the Roman Empire is in view, *ethnē* and the related Latin terms (*gentes, nationes*) are commonly used to denote nations other than Rome. Often, what this amounts to is simply that Rome considered its empire to be constituted by nations—nations as the basic building block of the empire. We will be looking at this aspect of the usage in more detail in the next section. Here, however, we look more briefly at instances in which a distinction is made, or at least implied, between the *populi Romani* and the nations. This distinction is more prevalent in Latin material, though Greek material contains a pertinent but more limited use of *ethnē* that is of particular interest.

Let us look first at Latin usage. Several adjectives were available to denote foreigners and foreign nations, of which *exterus* is most pertinent.[30] *Exterae gentes* is sometimes used to denote all "foreign nations" as distinct from Rome,[31] though it can also refer to nations outside the empire, in contrast to provinces and client kingdoms.[32] Here, however, we are more interested in cases in which the idea of non-Roman nations adheres to *gentes* itself. A number of these are

29. For a translation of the inscription, see Richard S. Ascough, Philip A. Harland, and John S. Kloppenborg, eds., *Associations in the Greco-Roman World: A Sourcebook* (Waco, TX: Baylor University Press, 2012), 26–28 (no. 18).

30. *Peregrinus* was more commonly used of individuals (though see Quintilian, *An Orator's Education* 1.5.55). While *barbarus* was used in conjunction with *gens* (e.g., *Rhetoric for Herennius* 4.13; Cicero, *Against Piso* 16.38; Pliny the Younger, *Panegyric* 56.4), Romans would have used it only of nonhellenized nations, not of all other nations.

31. E.g., "the Roman people and foreign nations [*populus Romanus et exterae gentes*]" (Cicero, *In Defense of Cluentius* 134; also *On Behalf of Fonteius* 35; *Philippic* 5.12); "the Roman people [*populi Romani*] . . . foreign nations [*exterasque gentis*]" (Livy, *History of Rome* 26.49.8).

32. E.g., "You [Trajan] have held a second consulship, I know, but the armies, the provinces, even foreign nations [*exteris gentibus*] can be said to have benefited from it, not any of us" (Pliny the Younger, *Panegyric* 59.3).

found in the writings of Cicero, who often uses *omnes gentes* (all the nations) in this way. In his oration supporting Pompey's command of the war against Mithridates, for example, he referred to the popular support that Pompey enjoyed at the time of the naval war: "that great day on which the entire Roman People [*universus populus Romanus*], thronging into the Forum and filling every temple that commands a view of this platform, demanded the appointment of Gnaeus Pompeius alone to be their general in a war against all the nations [*omnium gentium bellum*]" (*On the Manilian Law* 44). While the phrase is hyperbolic (the war against piracy was not exactly a war against *all* nations), it nevertheless signals a distinction between the "Roman people" and "their general," on one side, and "the nations" with whom they engaged in battle, on the other. In another instance, also speaking of Pompey, he describes him as "a man . . . whose exploits, crowned by glorious victory on land and sea had compassed all nations [*omnis gentis*], whose three triumphs were a witness that the whole world [*totum orbem terrarum*] was subject to our Empire, whom the Roman people had invested with unexampled and outstanding honors" (*In Defense of Balbus* 6.16). Here again, we find a distinction between the Roman people and the empire, on one side, and "all nations," on the other.[33] Similar instances are found in Vitruvius and Livy.[34] In addition, on several occasions, *gentes* by itself (i.e., without *omnes*) serves to denote the non-Roman nations. In Tacitus's *Germany*, after describing a situation in which one of the enemy nations had been destroyed by another, he adds this comment: "Long may it last, I pray, and persist among the nations [*gentibus*], this—if not love for us—at least hatred for each other: since now that the destinies of the Empire have passed their zenith, Fortune can guarantee us nothing better than discord among our foes" (*Germany* 33). In the entry on *gens* in the standard Latin dictionary (Lewis and Short), this passage is cited as one of the rare instances in which *gentes* denotes "foreign nations, foreigners" in contrast to Romans. Also to be included here is Martial's encomium on Nerva:

33. Also: "not only among our own people . . . but upon the lips and in the minds of all nations [*omnium gentium*]" (*Against Catilina* 4.22); "Pompeius, the vanquisher of all nations [*omnium gentium victore*]" (*Against Piso* 16); "not this state alone, but all nations" (*On Behalf of Milo* 19); "the Roman people, the conqueror of all nations [*populo romano, victori omnium gentium*]" (*Philippic* 4.15).

34. "When your Highness's divine mind and power, Caesar, gained the empire of the world [*orbis terrarum*], Rome gloried in your triumph and victory. For all her enemies were crushed by your invincible courage and all nations [*gentes omnes*] obeyed your bidding" (Vitruvius, *On Architecture* 1.preface.1). "Nevertheless, although he [Scipio] had victory almost within his grasp, he was not rejecting a peace, in order that all nations [*omnes gentes*] might know that the Roman people [*populum Romanum*] acted fairly both in beginning and ending wars" (Livy, *History of Rome* 30.16.9).

"The terrors that were with us so long have taken flight. Loyal Rome, the prayer of your people and nations [*populi gentesque tuae*] is this: may your Leader ever be such as he, and long be he" (*Epigrams* 12.6).³⁵

Turning to Greek usage in the Roman period, as we will see in the next section, Roman and pro-Roman authors writing in Greek also saw nations (*ethnē*) as the basic constituent element of the empire.³⁶ In contrast to Latin literature, however, *ethnē* does not appear in explicit contrast with the Roman people to the same extent as is the case with *gentes*.³⁷ Nevertheless, the instances where something like this is present are of particular interest since, in these cases, *ethnē* is used to denote administrative units within the empire and even Roman provinces themselves.

The more formal Greek equivalent to the Latin *provincia* was *eparcheia*, as can be seen in the bilingual *Acts of Augustus* (25, 26, 27 [twice]).³⁸ But the place of nations as the constituent element of the empire, together with the territorial dimension of ethnic identity, makes it not surprising that *ethnos* could come to be used, at least informally, with reference to Roman provinces.³⁹ Indeed, the close association of the two is apparent in the *Acts of Augustus* itself: "I extended the borders of all the provinces [*provinciarum/eparcheiōn*] of the Roman people which neighbored nations [*gentes/ethnē*] not subject to our rule" (26). The im-

---

35. LCL renders *populi* as a plural: "your peoples and nations." However, since *populi* is commonly used of the Roman people (*populi Romani*) and *populus* is rarely used of other nations, it is more probable that the phrase is to be understood as making a distinction between the Roman people and the non-Roman nations within the empire.

36. E.g., "the empire of so many and such great nations [*ethnōn*]" (Appian, *Roman History* preface.6).

37. In inscriptions, where a distinction is made between the Roman people and the *ethnē*, the term is generally accompanied by further modification: e.g., "the citizens of Rome . . . the outside nations [*ta te ektos ethnē*], who are in friendship with the people of the Romans" (IK Knidos I 31, Dlph Caria; also IK Knidos I 31, Kn Caria; Knidos 18 Caria [twice]). In addition, *alloethnos* appears on occasion: "the magistracy of the Roman people or of the foreign nations [*tōn alloethnōn*]" (*IG* XII,4 1:266 Cos and Calymna); "the one administering justice between Romans and members of other nations [*alloethn(ōn)*]" (*Ephesos* 4*5 Ionia).

38. See also John Richardson, *The Language of Empire: Rome and the Idea of Empire from the Third Century BC to the Second Century AD* (Cambridge: Cambridge University Press, 2008), 105.

39. By the first century, the sense of *provincia*, which originally denoted the governing authority that was given to an individual, had shifted in the direction of the territory over which a governor had jurisdiction. For a thorough examination of the shift in meaning, see Richardson, *Language of Empire*.

plication of this statement—that is, that nations who are subject to Roman rule thereby become provinces—becomes explicit in a slightly later text, in which Velleius Paterculus speaks of "the plan which I have set before me in my work to give a brief synopsis of the nations and national groups [*gens ac natio*] which were reduced to provinces [*provinciae*], and made tributary to Rome, and by what generals" (*Compendium of Roman History* 2.38). In Latin usage, a *gens* (or a group of *gentes*) can take on the status of a Roman *provincia*;[40] in Greek, by contrast, the province itself can be denoted by *ethnos*.

Early evidence for this development is found in Josephus's *Jewish War*, where on two occasions he uses *ethnos* with respect to Galilee (a name that in no way identified an ethnic group) as a jurisdictional area under Roman rule. The first of these has to do with Cestius, the Roman governor of Syria, just after the outbreak of the Jewish revolt: "To Galilee he sent Caesennius Gallus, commander of the twelfth legion, with such forces as he considered sufficient for the reduction of that *ethnos*" (*Jewish War* 2.510). While Galilee was not exactly a province (in 44 CE it ceased being part of a client kingdom and was incorporated into the province of Judea), *ethnos* here clearly denotes a distinct portion of a province. A similar instance appears a little later in the narrative: "it appeared to him [Vespasian] that the loss of Sepphoris would be a hazard gravely affecting the impending campaign, as it was the largest city of Galilee, a fortress in an exceptionally strong position in the enemy's territory [*chōriō*], and adapted to keep guard over the entire *ethnos*" (*Jewish War* 3.34). Here the territorial sense (*chōrion*) of *ethnos* is explicit.[41]

The use of *ethnos* to denote jurisdictional territories corresponding to Roman provinces becomes more clearly evident in the second century, as can be seen from Appian's widespread use of the term.[42] Appian often uses the term

---

40. In cases of a group of *gentes*, the name of the province often is that of the dominant nation (e.g., Germany, Galatia); on the perceived artificiality of Illyria, see Appian, *Roman History* 10.6 (discussed further below). On provincial names and ethnic groups, see Smith, "*Simulacra Gentium*," 57.

41. Another example appears later in his *Antiquities*: "Quirinius . . . arrived in Syria, dispatched by Caesar to be governor of the *ethnos* [*tou ethnous*]" (*Jewish Antiquities* 18.1). LCL renders it "governor of the nation," but the reference is clearly to the administrative area.

42. References to *ethnē* appear also, at least as administrative units, in several inscriptions: "I [Hadrian] wrote also to the councils of the *ethnē* . . ." (Petzl and Schwetheim, *Hadrian* 8/16 Troas); "And these many *ethnē* and all the rulers of the *ethnē* that are from every region [*merous*] . . ." (*IK Estremo oriente* 261); ". . . and in the other *ethnē* province by province [*kat' eparchion*] where there were colonies . . ." (*SEG* 20:324); perhaps also *Ephesos* 1497.

The Nations in Roman Imperial Discourse

in contexts where provinces are clearly in view. A few examples will suffice. In his account of the end of Hannibal's invasion of Italy, for example, he has this to say about a certain group that was excluded from a more general amnesty because of their continuing allegiance to Hannibal: "They were also forbidden to be enrolled in the military forces thereafter, as being not even free persons, but were required to attend as servants upon the consuls and praetors, when they went to govern their *ethnē* [*es tas tōn ethnōn hēgemonias*]" (*Roman History* 7.61). A similar reference to the governance of provinces appears in a passage that describes an agreement among the first triumvirate:

> All things were now possible to Caesar by reason of his large army, his great riches, and his readiness to oblige everybody. Pompey and Crassus, his partners in the triumvirate, came also. In their conference it was decided that Pompey and Crassus should be elected consuls again and that Caesar's governorship [*hēgemonian*] over his *ethnē* should be extended for five years more.[43] (*Civil Wars* 2.17)

More generally, in the preface to his work, Appian describes its major divisions this way:

> Thus, the foreign wars have been divided into books according to the *ethnē*, and the civil wars according to the chief commanders. The last book will show the present military force of the Romans, the revenues they collect from each *ethnos*, what they spend for the naval service, and other things of that kind. (*Roman History*, preface.15)

The collection of revenue clearly indicates that provinces are in view.[44] Subsequent to the work of Appian, evidence that *ethnos* was used to denote Roman provinces can be found in Aelius Aristides, Cassius Dio, and the Christian apologist Athenagoras.[45]

---

43. For further references to governors of *ethnē*, see, e.g.: "He [Caesar] appointed or changed the governors of the *ethnē* according to his own pleasure" (*Civil Wars* 2.48); "He [Caesar] pardoned his enemies and forthwith advanced many of those who had fought against him to the yearly magistracies, or to the command of *ethnē* and armies" (*Civil Wars* 2.107).

44. For other evidence from Appian, see, e.g., *Roman History* preface.12; 6.38; *Civil Wars* 2.13; 2.18; 2.27; 2.106.

45. In Aristides, e.g., "Thus the cities are free of garrisons; cohorts and cavalry troops are sufficient to guard whole *ethnē*, and not even many of these are quartered throughout

259

GENTILE CHRISTIAN IDENTITY

In various ways, then, the Greek and Latin terms of interest to us (especially *gentes* and *ethnē*) came to be used of other nations, nations as distinct from Rome. The distinction is not absolute. Rome itself is sometimes described as a nation, as when Cassius Dio depicts Augustus as accusing men who remained unmarried and childless of being "bent upon destroying and bringing to an end the entire Roman nation [*pan to Rōmaiōn ethnos*]," or when Suetonius said that Claudius "allowed the people of Ilium perpetual exemption from tribute, on the ground that they were the founders of the Roman nation [*Romanae gentis*]."[46] Further, as we have already seen, Rome is included among the nations when the term is used with reference to humankind as a whole. Roman use of *the nations* as a way of referring to the other nations is by no means as thoroughgoing as is *ta ethnē* or *haggôyîm* in Jewish usage. The usage did not function as a fundamental aspect of Roman identity; Roman identity was too inclusive and aggregative for that. Nevertheless, in that Rome could differentiate themselves as a people from the subject or non-Roman nations, there was a certain measure of overlap.[47]

---

the cities of each race, but . . . they are scattered in the countryside, so that many *ethnē* do not know where their garrison is" (*Regarding Rome* 67). Cassius Dio speaks of Augustus's arrangement for the rule of the empire: "In this way he had his supremacy ratified by the senate and by the people as well. But as he wished even so to be thought democratic, while he accepted all the care and oversight of the public business, on the ground that it required some attention on his part, yet he declared he would not personally govern all the *ethnē*, and that in the case of such provinces [supplied] as he should govern he would not do so indefinitely" (*Roman History* 53.12.1; see also 48.28.4; 51.18.1; 52.19.1-3; 52.27.1; 53.4.3; 53.5.4; 53.9.6; 53.12.8; 53.13.1; 53.15.1-4). And in Athenagoras's apology (addressed to Marcus Aurelius and Commodus), he speaks of "the governors of the *ethnē* [*tous . . . hēgemonas tōn ethnōn*] sent by you" (*Embassy for the Christians* 34).

46. Cassius Dio, *Roman History* 56.4.4; Suetonius, *Claudius* 5.25.3. See also Virgil, *Aeneid* 6.788-89 ("Turn hither now your two-eyed gaze, and behold this nation [*gentem*], the Romans that are yours"); Ovid, *Fasti* 2.683-84 ("The land of other nations [*gentibus aliis*] has a fixed boundary: the circuit of Rome is the circuit of the world"). Also, in contrast to many other Latin authors, Virgil readily uses *populi* of other nations (e.g., *Aeneid* 1.33; 6.788) and *gens* of Rome (e.g., 1.261; 2.282; 8.327). The inclusion of Rome within *the nations* is also apparent in discussion concerning the relationship between the civil law (*ius civile*), the law of a particular people, and the "law of the nations" (*ius gentium*), the universal law (e.g., Cicero, *On Duties* 3.69; *The Republic* 3.33; Gaius, *Institutes* 1.1).

47. There is one passage where, at least in the LCL rendering, *gentes* might appear to denote a group of individuals rather than of ethnic people groups (which would represent an overlap with the Jewish use of *ethnē* to denote individuals): "The full number of the races and tribes which had rebelled [*Gentium nationumque, quae rebellaverant, omnis numerus*] reached a total of more than eight hundred thousand" (Velleius, *Compendium of Roman History* 2.110.3). Since it is difficult to imagine that Tiberius and his army were

Moving on from matters of vocabulary and translational correspondence, let us look more closely at Greek and Latin discourse and at the place of ethnic people groups within it. How was ethnic identity perceived and understood? How were these terms used in the expression of such perceptions and understandings?

We begin by picking up something that has been observed already, the appearance of nationhood terms (*ethnē gentes, nationes*) in the context of longer lists of human groups. In addition to the examples just mentioned, we find other instances where one or other of these terms is part of a structured sequence that, in its most complete formulation, stretches from individuals, at one end, to the whole human race, at the other. One such instance appears in Polybius's account of the fall of Carthage, in which the victorious general Scipio reflects on the fate that governs human existence: "After being wrapped in thought for long, and realizing that all cities, nations, and empires [*kai poleis kai ethnē kai archas hapasas*] must, like men [*anthrōpous*], meet their doom..."[48] Scipio's reflections range over four categories of human groupings, in increasing order of size—individual human beings, cities, nations, empires. In his *On the Agrarian Law*, Cicero has a longer sequence, here of entities under Roman rule: "cities, national groups [*nationes*], provinces, free peoples [*liberos populos*], kings, in fact, the whole world [*terrarum orbem*]."[49] In this case, four entities appear between cities and the "whole world." All four of them represent ethnic people groups of one sort or another ("kings" implying the existence of kingdoms). Since the latter three (provinces, free peoples, kingdoms) refer to distinct political configurations of people groups within the Roman Empire, the more generic term *nationes* (ethnic people groups in general) probably serves to introduce the more specific forms of national existence that follow. Dio Chrysostom's list, by contrast, contains only

---

engaged in battle with "more than eight hundred thousand nations and national groups," one might wonder whether *gentium nationumque* denotes individuals rather than nations. This, however, is certainly to be ruled out. No evidence suggests that *gentes* or *nationes* ever has this sense. Further, even if there were evidence, the conjunction of the two (i.e., *gentium nationumque*) would make it highly unlikely. I suggest instead that the phrase should be rendered in a partitive way: "Of the nations and peoples that rebelled, the full number [i.e., of individuals drawn from "the nations and peoples that rebelled"] reached a total of more than eight hundred thousand."

48. *Histories* 38.22 (preserved in Appian, *Roman History* 8.1.132). The translation of *archas* as "empires" appears in the LCL version of Appian; the LCL edition of Polybius renders it "authorities." But given that Scipio goes on to talk of Assyria, Media, Persia, and Macedonia, "empires" is to be preferred.

49. *On the Agrarian Law* 2.98. Actually, Cicero is accusing his opponents here (led by Servilius Rullus) of attempting to construct a rival city in place of Rome.

three categories: "a city, or a number of nations [*ethnōn*], or the whole world [*hē sympantōn anthrōpōn*]" (*Kingship 3* [*Or.* 3] 45). Other variations of the form appear, but in each case, *nation* represents a fundamental category, occupying the space in between city and empire, or city and the human race as a whole.[50]

The importance of nation as a fundamental category is also apparent in a number of texts in which the human race as a whole is conceived of as an entity made up of nations. Cicero, for example, speaks of "the whole world [*orbis terrarum*] and all nations [*gentium omnium*] in it" (*On the Agrarian Law* 2.33). Pliny, as he moves from his geographical survey of the nations to a discussion of human diversity, declares: "And about the human race [*generis humani*] as a whole we have in large part spoken in our account of the various nations [*gentium*]" (*Natural History* 7.6). To give an account of the various *gentes* is to say all that needs to be said about the *genus humanum* as a whole.[51] And Quintilian, in a section where he deals with the importance of the hands in rhetorical delivery, contrasts "the linguistic diversity of the nations and national groups of the world [*omnis gentes nationesque*]" with the universality of hand gestures, "the common language of the human race [*omnium hominum*]" (*An Orator's Education* 11.3.87). In each case, nations (*gentes*, *nationes*) are seen as fundamental building blocks of the whole human race.

Looking at the ordered sequence in the other direction, it is also to be noted that cities are embedded in nations just as nations are embedded in the human race as a whole. Speaking of the peaceful character of Roman rule, Aelius Aristides declares: "Thus the cities are free of garrisons; cohorts and cavalry troops are sufficient to guard whole nations [*ethnōn*]," with the result that "many nations" (*polla tōn ethnōn*) do not even know where the nearest garrison is located.[52] The close association of nations and cities is also apparent in Vitruvius's

---

50. Or between city and other forms of multination realms, as is frequently the case in Dio Chrysostom: e.g., "those, however, who rule over many cities and nations [*ethnōn*] and over a boundless territory, as the Persian king does" (*On Tyranny* [*Or.* 6] 56); "and others make themselves emperors and absolute rulers of cities and nations [*ethnōn*]" (*Retirement* [*Or.* 20] 17); "a city, or a nation [*ethnous*], or still larger aggregations of mankind [*kai pleionōn anthrōpōn*]" (*Refusal of the Office of Archon* [*Or.* 49] 1). See also Aelius Aristides, *Regarding Rome* 88: "one man [the emperor], whose authority is all pervasive and who oversees everything, nations [*ethnē*], cities, legions, the generals themselves, and end with one man who commands four or two, for we have omitted everything in between." Cf. *Ephesos* 4*5 Ionia, an inscription (75 BCE, with additions in 62 CE) having to do with the Roman port tax in Asia ("... free cities or *ethnē* or peoples [*dēmōn*] ...").

51. Also, at the start of this book: "The above is a description of the world [*mundus*] and of the lands, nations [*gentes*], seas, important rivers, islands and cities that it contains" (Pliny the Elder, *Natural History* 7.1).

52. *Regarding Rome* 67. Behr renders *ethnē* here as "provinces"—quite rightly, in that

reference to Berosus of Babylon: "Berosus, who sprang from the Chaldaean city, or rather national group [*natione*]" (*On Architecture* 9.2.1).

The ethnographical map that was operative in the Roman Mediterranean world, then, was one in which nations formed part of a tightly connected, ordered sequence ranging from individuals and cities to empires and the whole human race. The ordering on the basis of increasing size appears explicitly in Strabo's argument for the significance of geographical knowledge for the practice of statecraft. Speaking of the "greatest generals" as those who are able "to unite nations and cities [*ethnē kai poleis*] under one government and political administration," he links this with the geographical size of the lesser and greater jurisdictions:

> The scene [*chōra*: space, region] is small when the activities are of small importance, and large when they are of large importance; and the largest is the scene that embraces all the rest (which we call by the special name of "the inhabited world" [*oikoumenēn*]) and this, therefore, would be the scene of activities of the largest importance. (*Geography* 1.1.16)

But this conception of a nation as part of a structured sequence of human group categories is only part of the picture. On the other side of things, ancient observers were well aware of ethnic diversity, of the considerable range in the size and character of the human groups to which the term was applied, and of the fluidity and mutability of ethnic boundaries. We have already noted instances in which observers struggled to describe and denote larger associations of related nations. The structured category may have been fixed and stable; the entities that might be so categorized were diverse and subject to change.

Strabo, whose *Geography* includes substantial elements of ethnographical description, comments several times on the difficulties in arriving at clear accounts of ethnic groups. Part of the problem, in his view, has to do with confusion on the part of ethnographical observers: "These writers, however, on account of the continual migrations, changes of political administrations, and intermixture of tribes, seem to have confused both the names and the nations [*ethnōn*], so that they sometimes present difficult questions for the writers of today" (*Geography* 9.5.21). Or in another place: "Passing to the poet, Apollodorus rightly says that much confusion of the barbarian nations [*tōn barbarōn ethnōn*] has taken place from the Trojan times to the present because of the changes, for some of them have been added to, others have vanished, others have been dispersed, and oth-

---

Aristides has provinces particularly in view; see Charles A. Behr, *P. Aelius Aristides: The Complete Works: Orations XVII–LIII* (Leiden: Brill, 1981).

ers have been combined into one" (*Geography* 14.5.27). But as these passages clearly indicate, the underlying problem is the complexity and changeability of things on the ground:[53] "And so it comes to pass, as I have said before, that the boundaries and the political organizations of nations [*tōn ethnōn*] and places are always undergoing changes" (*Geography* 9.5.8).[54]

Strabo's awareness of ethnographical complexity was widely shared, and several dimensions of the phenomenon can be identified. One has to do with the changes that take place over time—through migration, intermarriage, conflict, conquest, and the like. Strabo himself provides a further example—that of the Cataonians, who were described by earlier writers as distinct from the Cappadocians (both referred to as *ethnē*) but who now do not differ from them either in language or custom, so that "it is remarkable how utterly all signs of their being a different nation [*tēs alloethnias*] have disappeared" (*Geography* 12.1.2). We have also seen another instance of this in Tacitus's account of the Batavi, a nation (one of the German *gentes*) that was "once a people [*populus*] of the Chatti" but that subsequently separated itself because of local conflicts (*Germany* 29). Despite this instance of change, however, Tacitus is more struck by the fact that "the peoples of Germany" (*Germaniae populos*) as a whole remain "untainted by intermarriage with other national groups [*aliarum nationum*], a peculiar nation [*gentem*] and pure, like no one but themselves" (*Germany* 4). Even so, Tacitus's expression of praise implies that such ethnic purity was rare. Livy gives expression to a similar opinion, though in a negative key, in his expression of disdain for the Gauls of his own day: "those forefathers of ours had to do with true Gauls, born in their own land; these now are degenerates, of mixed race [*mixti*], and really Gallogrecians, as they are named."[55] (This, of course, stands in contrast

---

53. However, he can level a charge of simple ignorance when he thinks it is warranted. Speaking of the compound ethnic terms *Celtiberians* and *Celtiscythians*, he adds the comment: "the several nations [*ethnōn*] being classed under one name through ignorance of the facts" (*Geography* 1.2.27).

54. Also: "Now ancient tradition suggests some such position of the nations [*tōn ethnōn*] as this, but the present differences are the result of numerous changes, since different rulers have been in control at different times, and have confounded together some tribes and sundered others" (*Geography* 12.4.6).

55. The passage continues: "just as, in the case of plants and animals, the seeds have less power to maintain their natural quality than the character of the soil and climate in which they live has power to change it. The Macedonians who hold Alexandria in Egypt, who hold Seleucia and Babylonia and other colonies scattered throughout the world, have degenerated into Syrians, Parthians, Egyptians; Massilia, situated among the Gauls, has acquired something of the disposition of its neighbours; what have the Tarentines retained of that stern and dreadful Spartan discipline? Whatever grows in its own soil, has

The Nations in Roman Imperial Discourse

to Rome's own vaunted traditions of an origin through ethnic blending.[56]) Admiration for nations that are ethnically unmixed and that continue to inhabit their own land is closely linked to the idea of autochthonous nations, nations descended from ancestors produced spontaneously by the land itself. Diodorus Siculus admires India on this basis: "Now India as a whole, being of a vast extent, is inhabited, as we are told, by many nations [*ethnē*] of every description, and not one of them had its first origin in a foreign land, but all of them are thought to be autochthonous" (*Library of History* 2.38.1). At the other end of the temporal axis, Strabo gives some thought to a change of a different sort—that of extinction, which, he says, can be of two different kinds: "either the people [*tōn anthrōpōn*] vanished and their country has become utterly deserted, or else merely their national name [*onomatos tou ethnikou*] no longer exists and their political organization no longer remains what it was" (*Geography* 9.5.12).

A second area of recognized complexity has to do with situations where smaller nations are encompassed by, or are nested within, a larger national group.[57] What is in view here are situations involving similar or closely related nations, rather than those in which a number of nations are under the hegemony of a different and stronger nation or are part of a larger empire. Of particular interest are instances in which both the smaller and larger people groups are identified as nations. We have seen some such instances already, as we discussed the denotations and semantic ranges of *gentes*, *nationes*, and other Latin terms. Tacitus's characterization of Germany as a nation (*gentem*) that contains a number of "peoples" (*populos*) is one such example (*Germany* 4). Staying with Tac-

---

greater excellence; transplanted to a soil alien to it, its nature changes and it degenerates towards that in which it is nurtured" (*History of Rome* 38.17.8–12). Livy's disdain also carries over to ethnically mixed armies: e.g., "a mixture of the offscourings of all nations [*gentium*]" (*History of Rome* 28.12.3; also 30.34.2; 30.35.7; 37.38.3).

56. E.g., Sallust: "The city of Rome, as I have learned, was at the outset founded and inhabited by Trojans, who were wandering in exile, without any fixed abodes, under the leadership of Aeneas; their cofounders were the Aborigines, a rustic folk, without laws, without government, free and unrestrained. After these two peoples [supplied], different in race [*genere*], unlike in speech and living according to different customs, came together within the same walls, it is unbelievable to relate how easily they merged, so quickly did harmony change a heterogeneous and roving throng into a body of citizens" (*The War with Catiline* 6.1–2). See further below.

57. On differences in size, see, e.g., Diodorus: "Gaul is inhabited by many nations [*pollōn ethnōn*] of different size; for the largest number some two hundred thousand men, and the smallest fifty thousand" (*Library of History* 5.25.1). While we cannot put much confidence in the population figures themselves, the perception of size differences is worth noting.

265

itus's *Germany* for a moment, he elsewhere refers to the various people groups that constituted the Germans and describes how the name *German*, originally referring to a single *natio*, came to apply to the whole set.[58] Velleius, who also refers to Germany as a single nation (*gens*) on several occasions (*Compendium of Roman History* 2.97.3–4; 2.106.2), describes Spain in a similar nations-within-a-nation way. Elsewhere in the work, he speaks of "all the nations [*gentibus*]" of Spain (2.5.1) but somewhat later of Spain itself as a nation ("Spain and the other nations [*gentes*] whose names adorn his [Augustus's] Forum"; 2.39.2). In addition to Germany, a number of other larger entities, well known as encompassing other smaller nations, are themselves described as nations: Greece; Achaia; Gaul; India; Rome itself; and others.[59]

A third area of complexity, closely related to the second, has to do with similarities and connections among ethnic people groups, with resultant ambiguities

---

58. *Germany* 2 (*natio*); 27 (*gentium, nationes*).

59. "The national group of the Greeks [*Graecorum natio*]" (Cicero, *On the Making of an Orator* 2.18). Speaking of the Peloponnesian nations, for example, Dionysius of Halicarnassus recounts how "the Arcadian, the Ionian and many other nations [*ethnē*]" came to be called Achaia, "after one of the nations [*ethnōn*] that inhabited it, namely the Achaean" (*Roman Antiquities* 1.25.5). Cf. the use of *ethnos* as a designation for the Achaean "Confederacy" or "League" (e.g., Polybius, *Histories* 38.9.6–8 and passim). "Of all the nations [*gentium*] who inhabit Asia, the Gauls stand first in reputation for war" (Livy, *History of Rome* 38.17.2); "Thracians and Gauls, the most warlike of all nations [*gentium*]" (Livy, *History of Rome* 42.52.10); cf. Strabo, *Geography* 4.4.2: "the whole race [*to de sympan phylon*] which is now called both 'Gallic' and 'Galactic' is war-mad, and both high-spirited and quick for battle, although otherwise simple and not ill-mannered." "India, indeed, has been well-defined in many ways, by a mountain, a river, a sea, and by a single term, as of a single nation [*hōs henos ethnous*]—so that Eratosthenes rightly calls it four-sided and rhomboidal" (Strabo, *Geography* 2.1.31). "So vast was the effort to found the Roman nation [*Romanam gentem*]" (Virgil, *Aeneid* 1.32–33)."[Tigranes] would not have submitted himself to the alliance of any man but Gnaeus Pompeius, whether Roman or of any other nation [*ullius gentis*]" (Velleius, *Compendium of Roman History* 2.37.4); "He [Claudius] allowed the people of Ilium perpetual exemption from tribute, on the ground that they were the founders of the Roman nation [*gentis*]" (Suetonius, *Claudius* 5.25.3); "others said that the Romans were, generally speaking, a civilized nation [*politikon . . . ethnos*]" (Polybius, *Histories* 36.9.9). Livy classes Thrace with Gaul as "the most warlike of all nations [*gentium*]" (*History of Rome* 42.52.11). Pliny the Elder also refers to Thrace as a nation: "Next comes Thrace, one of the most powerful nations [*gentes*] of Europe" (*Natural History* 4.40). Dionysius of Halicarnassus speaks of Tyrrhenia as the contemporary name of a group of nations: "the several nations of which it was composed having lost their distinctive appellations [*tas kata to ethnos onomosias*]" (*Roman Antiquities* 1.25.2). With respect to the Ethiopians, Scythians, and Celts, see Strabo, *Geography* 2.3.1.

The Nations in Roman Imperial Discourse

about the classification of nations according to affinity groups. The ancients were well aware that the assemblage of characteristics that gave nations their distinct identities could also be found in certain measure in other groups, those living in the same geographical area or sharing overlapping histories. In a passage that we have already looked at from another angle, Tacitus describes one distinguishing feature of the Suebi: "One mark of the nation [*gentis*] is to comb the hair back over the side of the face and tie it low in a knot behind: this distinguishes the Suebi from other Germans, and the free-born of the Suebi from the slave." Then he continues: "In other nations [*gentibus*], whether from some relationship to the Suebi, or, as often happens, from imitation, the same thing may be found" (*Germany* 38). Strabo for his part has this to say about "the nation [*to ethnos*] of the Armenians and that of the Syrians and Arabians":

> [They] betray a close affinity, not only in their language, but in their mode of life and in their bodily build, and particularly wherever they live as close neighbors. Mesopotamia, which is inhabited by these three nations [*tōn triōn ethnōn*], gives proof of this, for in the case of these nations the similarity is particularly noticeable. (*Geography* 1.2.34)

But similarities can be ambiguous, and ancient observers puzzled over their implications. Tacitus, for example, expresses uncertainty over how to classify several of the German nations:

> As for the national groups [*nationes*] of the Peucini, Venedi, and Fenni, I am in doubt whether to count them as Germans or Sarmatians. Though the Peucini, whom some men call Bastarnae, in language, culture, fixity of habitation, and house-building, conduct themselves as Germans, all are dirty and lethargic: the faces of the chiefs, too, owing to intermarriage, wear to some extent the degraded aspect of Sarmatians: while the Venedi have contracted many Sarmatian habits. (*Germany* 46)

For Dionysius of Halicarnassus, mistakes of ethnic classification were often made simply because observers were too far removed from the groups in question to recognize the differences:

> But in my opinion all who take the Tyrrhenians and the Pelasgians to be one and the same nation [*to auto ethnos*] are mistaken. It is no wonder they were sometimes called by one another's names, since the same thing has happened to certain other nations [*ethnē*] also, both Greeks and barbarians,—for example, to the Trojans and Phrygians, who lived near each other (indeed, many

267

have thought that those two nations were but one [*genos hen*], differing in name only, not in fact). And the nations [*ta ethnē*] in Italy have been confused under a common name quite as often as any nations anywhere. For there was a time when the Latins, the Umbrians, the Ausonians and many others were all called Tyrrhenians by the Greeks, the remoteness of the countries inhabited by these nations [*tōn ethnōn*] making their exact distinctions obscure to those who lived at a distance. (*Roman Antiquities* 1.29.1–2).

And Diodorus seeks to clear up a similar misconception, this one involving the Celts:

And now it will be useful to draw a distinction which is unknown to many: The peoples [supplied] who dwell in the interior above Massalia, those on the slopes of the Alps, and those on this side the Pyrenees mountains are called Celts [*Keltous*], whereas the peoples who are established above this land of Celtica in the parts which stretch to the north, both along the ocean and along the Hercynian Mountain, and all the peoples who come after these, as far as Scythia, are known as Gauls [*Galatas*].[60]

As Diodorus continues, however, he makes an observation that leads into a further area of complexity: "the Romans, however, include all these nations [*panta tauta ta ethnē*] together under a single name, calling them one and all Gauls." A persistent aspect of ethnological discourse in antiquity was that ethnic people groups (*gentes, nationes, ethnē*) were named entities. But as this example illustrates, there were uncertainties and disagreements over the process of naming. While these groups are "called Celts" or "known as Gauls"—presumably by themselves and their neighbors—the Romans call them "one and all Gauls." In this case, it is not a matter of simple uncertainty over a name; since it is the Romans who are doing the naming, the text draws our attention to the role of power in the ascription of names. Rome is also the naming agent in this text from Appian:

These peoples, and also the Pannonians, the Rhaetians, the Noricans, the Mysians of Europe, and the other neighboring tribes who inhabited the right

---

60. *Library of History* 5.32.1. Strabo is also confident about his ability to differentiate Celtic nations from others with similar characteristics: "Many nations [*ethnē*] occupy these mountains, all Celtic except the Ligurians; but while these Ligurians belong to a different nation [*heteroethneis*], still they are similar to the Celts in their modes of life [*tois biois*]" (*Geography* 2.5.28).

bank of the Danube, the Romans distinguish from one another just as the various Greek peoples are distinguished from each other, and they call each by its own name, but they consider the whole of Illyria as embraced under a common designation. Whence this idea took its start I have not been able to find out, but it continues to this day, for they farm the tax of all the nations [*tōn ethnōn*] from the source of the Danube to the Euxine Sea under one head, and call it the Illyrian tax. (*Roman History* 10.6)

However, in a passage touched on already, it is the nation itself that chooses the name and makes it stick:

The first tribes [supplied] in fact to cross the Rhine and expel the Gauls, though now called Tungri, were then styled Germans: so little by little the name—the name of a national group, not of a nation [*nationis nomen, non gentis*]—prevailed, until the whole people [*omnes*] were called by the artificial name of "Germans," first only by the victorious tribe [supplied] in order to intimidate the Gauls, but afterwards among themselves also. (Tacitus, *Germany* 2)

For present purposes, these texts serve to illustrate the fact that ethnic names represented another area of complexity and ambiguity in ancient ethnographical discourse. At the same time, however, they also remind us that ethnic identity in the Roman world was not simply a fixed (albeit complex) aspect of human existence, but it was something to be negotiated and thus was dependent on relationships of power.

The ethnographical discourse that is of interest to us, then, was carried on in between two poles. At one end is the concept of a nation as a fixed category in an ascending sequence of human groupings—individuals, cities, nations, empires (and related multiethnic hegemonies), the whole human race. At the other is the fluid set of ethnic realities on the ground—nations in an ongoing process of change, division, realignment, and evolution; nations as contained within larger affinity groups, shared territories, and political structures (imposed or accepted); nations as both linked and differentiated by factors of language, custom, genealogy, and the like; nations as identified by names chosen, ascribed, or negotiated.

In chapter 2 we looked at this ethnographical discourse in a preliminary way, first discussing ethnic identity in the Greco-Roman world in general terms and then sketching out the more particular dynamics of identity construction in the context of Roman imperial ideology. The literature that was touched on in chapter 2 and that has come into clearer view in this chapter has included history

(Livy, Velleius Paterculus, Tacitus, Polybius, Diodorus Siculus, Cassius Dio), military accounts (Julius Caesar), geography (Pliny the Elder, Strabo), architecture (Vitruvius), orations (Cicero, Dio Chrysostom), poetry (Virgil, Horace), and imperial inscriptions of various kinds (e.g., *Acts of Augustus*). To this point in the chapter, we have been interested primarily in preliminary issues of semantics and basic usage; the material that we have looked at has also created the impression that the Greco-Roman world was marked by a lively interest in ethnic people groups and that the resultant ethnographical discourse was carried out on the basis of the vocabulary that is of interest to us. Before turning more directly to the Roman imperial context, it is appropriate to underline these impressions and explore them a little further.

It is striking how much of this literature has a programmatic interest in ethnological description and how central these vocabulary items are to this description.[61] In a number of these writings, ethnological interests are signaled from the outset, in the introductory setup of the work as a whole. To begin with Julius Caesar's account of the *Gallic War*, after his famous opening clause "Gaul is a whole divided into three parts," he continues by identifying the parts in terms of the ethnic groups that inhabit them: "one of which is inhabited by the Belgae, another by the Aquitani, and a third by a people [supplied] called in their own tongue Celtae, in the Latin Galli. All these are different one from another in language, institutions, and laws" (*Gallic War* 1.1). Although ethnic vocabulary does not appear here, when he later returns to the topic of the differences in "language, institutions and laws," it is in explicitly ethnic terms: "Since I have arrived at this point, it would seem to be not inappropriate to set forth the customs of Gaul and of Germany, and the difference between these nations [*nationes*]" (*Gallic War* 6.11).

Tacitus's treatise on Germany, which has come into view a number of times already, provides us with another case in point. He begins by describing the surrounding nations from which Germany is to be distinguished: "Germany as a whole is separated from the Gauls and from Raetians and Pannonians by the rivers Rhine and Danube: from the Sarmatians and Dacians by mutual misgivings

---

61. This is true as well for fanciful reports of ethnic characteristics, what Diodorus calls "manners of life which men consider astonishing" (*Library of History* 3.35.1): e.g., "nations [*gentes*] of people without noses, their whole face being perfectly flat, and other tribes that have no upper lip and others no tongues" (Pliny the Elder, *Natural History* 6.187–88); the nation (*ethnos*) of the female Amazons, who "mutilated both the legs and the arms of the male [children], incapacitating them in this way for the demands of war, and in the case of the females they seared the right breast that it might not project when their bodies matured and be in the way" (Diodorus, *Library of History* 2.45.3).

or mountains...." Then he adds that it was because "war has lifted the curtain" that "some of [these] nations [*gentibus*] and their kings have but recently become known to us" (*Germany* 1).

Diodorus Siculus provides us with another, more elaborate example. After an opening discourse on the importance of history—"the profit which history affords its readers lies in its embracing a vast number and variety of circumstances"—he contrasts his own project with what has gone before: while "most writers have recorded no more than isolated wars waged by a single nation [*ethnous*] or a single city [*poleōs*]," he is one of the few who "have undertaken, beginning with the earliest times and coming down to their own day, to record the events held in common by all [*tas koinas praxeis*]." The goal he set for himself was to "record ... the affairs of the entire world [*tou sympantas kosmou*] down to his own day, so far as they have been handed down to memory, as though they were the affairs of some single city" (*Library of History* 1.3.2). Accordingly, at key points in the work that follows, he signals transitions from one section to the next by referring to the nations that had been or were to be discussed: "Now that we have discussed the peoples [supplied] who dwell on the coast from Babylonia to the Arabian Gulf, we shall describe the nations [*ethnōn*] who live next to them" (3.23.1);[62] "And now that we have discussed the principal facts concerning the nations [*tōn ethnōn*] and the manners of life which men consider astonishing, we shall speak in turn of the wild animals of the countries which we are considering" (3.35.1); "Now in the three preceding Books we have recorded the deeds of mythological times which are found among other nations [*tois allois ethnesi*], ... and in the present Book we shall set forth what the Greeks in their histories of the ancient periods tell" of themselves (4.1.5–6).

Polybius begins his history of the Roman rise to power by comparing the Roman Empire with those that went before, differentiating them on the basis of the territorial extent of their respective domains and "the nations" (*tōn ethnōn*) that they contained (*Histories* 1.2.1–8). Later, looking back on his project, he contrasts his work with that of historians more interested in what he calls "genealogical" matters: "The genealogical side appeals to those who are fond of a story, and the account of colonies, the foundation of cities, and their ties of kindred, ... while the statesman is interested in the doings of nations [*ethnē*], cities, and monarchs." His "whole work," he declares, has been "confined ... strictly to these last matters."[63]

---

62. Cf. *Library of History* 3.14.6: "the nations [*tōn ethnōn*] which inhabit the coast of the Arabian Gulf."

63. *Histories* 9.1.3–5. To be sure, the terms in which he draws the contrast indicates that genealogical historians were equally interested in matters having to do with *ethnē*.

For his part, Strabo begins his *Geography* by asserting the importance of geographical knowledge for "the activity of commanders," the greatest of which are those "who are able to hold sway over land and sea, and to unite nations [*ethnē*] and cities under one government and political administration" (*Geography* 1.1.16). More generally, in their prefaces, Vitruvius, Livy, and Pliny the Elder position their diverse works with respect to the dominant status of Rome among the nations. Addressing Augustus as the one who had "gained the empire of the world [*orbis terrarum*]" and the one whom "all nations" (*gentes omnes*) now obeyed, Vitruvius declared that it was the emperor's interest in public architecture that prompted him to publish his own architectural treatise (*On Architecture* 1.preface.1–2). As Livy begins his account of "the achievements of the Roman people [*populi*] from the foundation of the city" (*History of Rome* 1.preface.1), he says that he does not care either "to affirm or to refute" the "poetic legends" about the origins of the Roman people. Still, he continues,

> if any people ought to be allowed to consecrate their origins and refer them to a divine source, so great is the military glory of the Roman People [*populo Romano*] that when they profess that their Father and the Father of their Founder was none other than Mars, the nations of the earth [*gentes humanae*] may well submit to this also with as good a grace as they submit to Rome's dominion. (*History of Rome* 1.preface.7–8)

Pliny the Elder, in his flowery opening address to Vespasian, declares (in effect) that he has written his *Natural History* "for the glory of the people victorious over the nations [*populi gentium victoris*] and of the Roman name."[64] Later, when he first turns his attention to terrestrial geography, he returns to the theme: "To begin then with Europe, nurse of the people that has conquered all the nations [*victoris omnium gentium populi*], and by far the loveliest portion of the earth."[65]

This brings us close to the point where we can turn our attention more directly to Roman imperial ideology and the place of the nations within it. But before we do, a few final observations are in order about ethnological discourse in antiquity more generally. One has to do with the concept of a nation itself. Despite the importance of nations as a category in this discourse—the thematic and structural role of *gentes/nationes/ethnē* in some of the literature, the lively in-

---

64. Actually, he uses the phrase with reference to Livy, setting his own work alongside his (*Natural History* preface.16).
65. *Natural History* 3.5. Book 1 sketches out the contents of the work as a whole; book 2 deals with the universe.

The Nations in Roman Imperial Discourse

terest in distinct national characteristics—and despite the awareness on the part of the authors of the inherent complexities, little direct attention is given to the category itself. That is, what constitutes a nation—what makes it possible for both the Germans as a whole and an obscure German group such as the Dulgubnii to be classified alike as *gentes*—seems simply to be taken for granted.[66] Or to put this in more positive terms: despite the lack of explicit attention to the category in general, what is taken for granted is that nations (*gentes, nationes, ethnē*) can be identified as such on the basis of the kinds of identifying indices first found in Herodotus:[67] kinship and genealogical descent;[68] a common language;[69] a

---

66. See Tacitus, *Germany* 34: "The Angrivarii and Chamavi are closed to the south by the Dulgubnii and the Chasuarii and other nations [*gentes*] not so well known to history." For Germany itself as a *gens*, see *Germany* 4 (also Velleius, *Compendium of Roman History* 2.97.3–4; 2.106.2).

67. Herodotus's indices are found in the context of an Athenian response to the proposition that they come to terms with the Persians: "For there are many great reasons why we should not do this, even if we so desired; first and chiefest, the burning and destruction of the adornments and temples of our gods, whom we are constrained to avenge to the uttermost rather than make covenants with the doer of these things, and next the kinship of all Greeks [*to Hellēnikon*] in blood and speech, and the shrines of gods and the sacrifices that we have in common, and the likeness of our way of life" (*Histories* 8.144). Analogous lists are found in the later literature under discussion here: e.g., "an army [Hannibal's] not made up of his own citizens but a mixture of the offscourings of all nations [*omnium gentium*], men who had in common no law, no custom, no language, differing from each other in bearing, in garb, in their arms, differing as to religious rites, sacred observances, one might almost say as to their gods" (Livy, *History of Rome* 28.12.2–4).

68. E.g., "in the peoples [*populos*] of Germany there has been given to the world a race untainted by intermarriage with other national groups [*aliarum nationum*], a peculiar nation [*gentem*] and pure, like no one but themselves" (Tacitus, *Germany* 4); "[Poseidonius] derives an etymology of the words from the kinship of the nations [*tēs tōn ethnōn syngeneias*] and their common characteristics. For the nation of the Armenians and that of the Syrians and Arabians betray a close affinity, not only in their language, but in their mode of life and in their bodily build, and particularly wherever they live as close neighbours" (Strabo, *Geography* 1.2.34); "Autarieus had a son Pannonius, or Paeon, and the latter had sons, Scordiscus and Triballus, from whom also nations [*ethnē*] bearing similar names were derived" (Appian, *Roman History* 10.3).

69. E.g., "Foreign words, just like people and indeed many institutions, have come to us from almost every nation [*gentibus*]" (Quintilian, *An Orator's Education* 1.5.55); "Amid all the linguistic diversity of the nations and national groups [*gentes nationesque*] of the world" (Quintilian, *An Orator's Education* 11.3.87); "I am persuaded, therefore, that these nations [*tois ethnesi*] changed their name along with their place of abode, but

homeland or shared territory;[70] common religious practices;[71] a shared history;[72]

---

cannot believe that they both had a common origin, for this reason, among many others, that their languages are different and preserve not the least resemblance to one another" (Dionysius of Halicarnassus, *Roman Antiquities* 1.29.1–2).

70. E.g., "Now India as a whole, being of a vast extent, is inhabited, as we are told, by many nations [*ethnē*] of every description, and not one of them had its first origin in a foreign land, but all of them are thought to be autochthonous" (Diodorus Siculus, *Library of History* 2.38.1); "This was the course of events at that time in Palestine; for this is the name that has been given from of old to the whole nation [*to sympasan ethnos*] extending from Phoenicia to Egypt along the inner sea. They have also another name that they have acquired: the country [*chōra*] has been named Judaea, and the people themselves Jews" (Cassius Dio, *Roman History* 37.16.5). Cf. "And those forefathers of ours had to do with true Gauls, born in their own land; these now are degenerates, of mixed race [*mixti*], and really Gallogrecians, as they are named; just as, in the case of plants and animals, the seeds have less power to maintain their natural quality than the character of the soil and climate in which they live has power to change it.... Whatever grows in its own soil, has greater excellence; transplanted to a soil alien to it, its nature changes and it degenerates towards that in which it is nurture" (Livy, *History of Rome* 38.17.9, 12).

71. E.g., "the whole nation [*natio . . . omnis*] of the Gauls is greatly devoted to ritual observances" (Julius Caesar, *Gallic War* 6.16); "a mixture of the offscourings of all nations [*omnium gentium*] . . . differing as to religious rites, sacred observances, one might almost say as to their gods" (Livy, *History of Rome* 28.12.3); "Now in the three preceding Books we have recorded the deeds of mythological times which are found among other nations [*tois allois ethnesi*] and what their histories relate about the gods, also the topography of the land in every case" (Diodorus Siculus, *Library of History* 4.1.5); "They [the *ethnos* of the Jews] are distinguished from the rest of mankind [*tōn loipōn anthrōpōn*] in practically every detail of life, and especially by the fact that they do not honour any of the usual gods, but show extreme reverence for one particular divinity" (Cassius Dio, *Roman History* 37.17.2).

72. This is harder to illustrate succinctly, but it is readily apparent in the writing of history generally and in the place of national history in ethnological discourse. With respect to the latter, see, e.g., the largely historical way in which Julius Caesar establishes "the difference between [the] nations [*nationes*]" of Gaul and Germany (*Gallic War* 6.11–28), or Tacitus's treatise on Germany, which deals, in part, with the way in which a collection of tribes became a "nation [*gentis*] . . . called by the artificial name of 'Germans'" (*Germany* 2). See also the discussion of ethnic change and fluidity above.

The Nations in Roman Imperial Discourse

common customs and way of life;[73] an identifying name;[74] and so on. All of this is quite evident from the discussion to this point; documentary evidence could be extended indefinitely. While more modern theorization has demonstrated how the use of such indices can be clarified, refined, and systematized, it has not in any fundamental way supplanted the implicit notion of what constitutes an ethnic people group that was present in ancient ethnographical discourse.

In our discussion of this discourse in chapter 2, we noted several further elements in addition to simple description. Two of these—the use of ethnic historiography to situate one's own group advantageously in the world of the nations, and the search for universals that would undergird transethnic differences—do not require much more examination here, though the first will come into view from time to time. Here, however, we will draw this section to a close by looking briefly at another element—the interest in explaining ethnic differences, rather than simply describing them.

One explanatory device was to account for the present characteristics of a

---

73. E.g., "the customs of Gaul and of Germany, and the difference between these nations [*nationes*]" (Julius Caesar, *Gallic War* 6.11); "At the height of the public grief a throng from foreign nations [*exterarum gentium multitudo*] went about lamenting each after the fashion of his country" (Suetonius, *Divus Julius* 84.5); "nations [*nationes*] with customs the reverse of our own" (Tacitus, *Annals* 14.44); "So much in general we have ascertained concerning the origin of the undivided Germans and their customs. I shall now set forth the habits and customs of the several nations [*gentium*], and the extent to which they differ from each other" (Tacitus, *Germany* 27); "Moreover, men differ with one another in everything—in dress and apparel, in food and sexual pleasures, in honour and dishonor—according to nations [*ethnē*] and cities" (Dio Chrysostom, *Opinion* [*Or.* 68] 4).

74. The literature is replete with names of *gentes*, *nationes*, and *ethnē*, many of them obscure and long-forgotten, sometimes in lengthy lists, as in the imperial inscription reproduced by Pliny the Elder, with its list of some forty-five Alpine *gentes* (*Natural History* 3.20.136), or the list of "all the nations [*omnes gentes*]" that had formerly been under Macedonian rule, in Livy's account of the Roman victory (*History of Rome* 33.32.4–6). In some cases, it is simply assumed that nations have names: "distinguished by special national names [*nationibus nominibusque*]" (Tacitus, *Germany* 38); "It is no wonder they were sometimes called by one another's names, since the same thing has happened to certain other nations [*ethnē*]" (Dionysius of Halicarnassus, *Roman Antiquities* 1.29.1–2); "they call each [of the *ethnōn*] by its own name" (Appian, *Roman History* 10.6). National names are generally the plural form of a name designating an individual member: e.g., "the nation of the Colchi [*nationem Colchorum*]" (Vitruvius, *On Architecture* 2.1.4) "Alpine races conquered [*gentes alpinae devictae*]—the Triupilini, Camunni, Fenostes..." (Pliny the Elder, *Natural History* 3.20.136). Alternatively, with well-known nations, an adjectival form might be used: "the Greek nation [*Graecorum natio*]" (Cicero, *On the Making of an Orator* 2.18).

people group by tracing ethnic genealogies and lines of descent. This has been touched on already, for example, in Diodorus's account of the autochthonous character of the Indian *ethnē* (*Library of History* 2.38.1), in Tacitus's praise of the pure genealogical lineage of the German nation (*gens*; *Germany* 4), and in Livy's negative account of the way in which the Gauls, by leaving their own land, degenerated into "Gallogrecians" (*History of Rome* 38.17.9–12). A more expansive example is found in Vitruvius's treatise on architecture, in which he explains the origin of building by means of a whimsical account of the development of nations from a primordial existence (in which "men [*homines*] . . . were born like animals in forests and caves and woods, and passed their life feeding on the food of the fields"; *On Architecture* 2.1.1), through the discovery of fire and language, to the construction of rudimentary huts and ultimately to the emergence of civilized nations:

> When, therefore, these matters were so first ordained and Nature had not only equipped the nations [*gentes*] with perceptions like other animals, but also had armed their minds with ideas and purposes, and had put the other animals under their power, then from the construction of buildings they progressed by degrees to other crafts and disciplines, and they led the way from a savage and rustic life to a peaceful civilization [*humanitatem*]. (*On Architecture* 2.1.6)

Later in his treatise, Vitruvius develops another line of explanation, having to do with geography and climate (*On Architecture* 6.1.5–11). He divides the earth into three zones—the south, the middle, and the north—that differ in atmosphere, temperature, and climate. These differences produce differences among the nations (mostly referred to as *nationes*, though *gentes* appears as well). One set of differences concerns vocal pitch; as one moves from south to north, "the national groups [*nationes*]" are characterized by voices that move from "thin and very shrill" to those of "deeper tones." While Vitruvius does not seem to pass any value judgment on this difference, in the next set of differences, the middle section of the earth provides the optimum environment for human development and ability. Southern nations are more mentally acute: "Southern national groups [*nationes*] also, owing to the rarity of the atmosphere, with minds rendered acute by the heat, are more readily and swiftly moved to the imagination of expedients." However, they lack endurance: "they give way when courage is demanded because their strength is drained away by the sun." By contrast, the cold climate renders the northern nations (*gentes*) courageous but sluggish: "those who are born in colder regions, by their fearless courage are better equipped for the clash of arms, yet by their slowness of mind they rush on without reflection, and through lack of tactics are balked of their purpose." In between the two, of course, is Italy. Unlike all these other national groups (*omnes nationes*) with their "unbalanced temperament," the inhabitants of Italy "are exactly tempered in either direction" and thus occupy "the true mean within the space of all the world [*orbis terrarum*] and the regions of the earth." He concludes: "Thus the divine mind has allotted to the Roman people [*populi Romani*] an excellent and temperate region in order to rule the world [*orbis terrarum imperii*]."[75]

ROMAN IMPERIAL IDEOLOGY AND THE NATIONS

With Vitruvius's confident declaration of Rome's divinely ordained destiny "to rule the world," we move from general matters of semantics and usage to the place of the nations in Roman imperial ideology and related discourse. For the most part, we will concentrate on the main themes of Roman ideology itself, though we will pay attention to ways in which these themes link up with the broader aspects of competitive ethnology—both Rome's own endeavors to locate itself centrally with respect to Greeks and barbarians on an ethnic map of the world, and corresponding endeavors on the part of the subject nations to preserve or create a meaningful place for themselves.

We have had several opportunities already to explore Roman imperial ideology and to identify its characteristic themes.[76] Here we will build on this work by looking at the significant place of the nations in these themes, thus arriving at a richer understanding of *gentes*, *nationes*, and *ethnē* as identity terms and instruments of identity construction in the Roman world. Since Roman conceptions are more directly in view in this section, we will begin with Latin material and then move to the Greek.[77] With respect to the latter, while we are primarily interested in material in which Greek writers reproduce Roman ideology, we will also remain alert to the kind of strategic reserve that we have already noted

---

75. Pliny the Elder provides another example of an appeal to climate and geography to explain ethnic characteristics: "For it is beyond question that the Ethiopians are burnt by the heat of the heavenly body near them, and are born with a scorched appearance, with curly beard and hair, and that in the opposite region of the world the nations [*gentes*] have white frosty skins, with yellow hair that hangs straight; while the latter are fierce owing to the rigidity of their climate but the former wise because of the mobility of theirs" (*Natural History* 2.189).

76. Once at the outset, in our discussion of Aelius Aristides's *Regarding Rome* (ch. 1), and again in our more detailed examination of identity, ethnicity, and power in the Roman empire (ch. 2).

77. In each case, we will also begin with earlier material and proceed more or less chronologically.

in our initial discussion of Aelius Aristides's *Regarding Rome*, who praises Rome by echoing the Romans' own congratulatory self-presentation but in ways that preserve a place for Greek priority and areas of Greek superiority.

The first thing to observe, however, is not so much a theme of Roman imperial ideology as it is a presupposition of the ideology as a whole. In the previous section, where we observed how nations functioned as a fundamental element in any discussion of the habitable world, we had occasion to note in passing that nations functioned as a fundamental component of empires as well, including the Roman Empire. Here we will look more closely at the way in which nations appear as a fundamental constituent element of the Roman Empire. This is not to deny that other things could be included; cities, kingdoms, lands, seas, and other human or natural entities also came into view.[78] Nevertheless, the most common conception of the Roman *imperium* was that it was constituted by rule over the nations—even of "all the nations." While the point will continue to emerge from our discussion of primary sources in other contexts, here we will look particularly at places where the language of empire—in word (*imperium, imperator, dominus; archē, hēgemonia, autokratōr*; etc.) or visual symbol (e.g., official inscriptions)—is in view.

To begin with an early example—a remarkable statement that can almost be seen as a condensed version of imperial ideology as a whole—the unknown author of the *Rhetoric for Herennius* speaks of "that sovereignty over the whole world [*imperium orbis terrae*] which all nations, kings, and national groups [*omnes gentes, reges, nationes*] have accepted, in part compelled by force, in part of their own will, when conquered either by the arms of Rome or by her generosity" (4.13). The LCL translator attempts to differentiate *gentes* and *nationes* ("civilized peoples ... barbarous nations"), but nothing suggests that this was the author's intention; the use of synonymous terms simply underlines the point: sovereignty over the "whole world" (*orbis terrae*) is sovereignty over all the nations (and, in some cases, their kings).

Many other examples can be adduced. Cicero, in a treatise on rhetoric, speaks in passing about our "empire of all the nations" (*imperio omnium gentium*) and the peace that accompanied it (*On the Making of an Orator* 1.14). Sallust records

---

78. E.g., "cities, national groups [*nationes*], provinces, free peoples [*liberos populos*], kings, in fact, the whole world" (Cicero, *On the Agrarian Law* 2.98); "national groups [*nationes*], cities, peoples, kings, tetrarchs, rulers, ... voiceless tracts, remotest lands, seas, harbours, islands, coasts" (Cicero, *In Defense of Balbus* 5.13); "nations [*gentibus*] ... men and cities" (Velleius, *Compendium of Roman History* 2.5.1); "land and sea, nations [*ethnē*] and cities" (Strabo, *Geography* 1.1.1); "neither city, nor nation [*ethnos*], nor harbor, nor land" (Aelius Aristides, *Regarding Rome* 28).

a speech given by Gaius Memmius to a popular assembly in which, in the course of a denunciation of the nobles for the their treatment of Jugurtha, he addresses his hearers ("you, that is to say the Roman people") as "unconquered by your enemies, rulers of all nations [*imperatores omnium gentium*]" (Sallust, *The War with Jugurtha* 31.20). Vitruvius's treatise on architecture begins with an address to Augustus in which Rome's world empire is equated with the obedience of all nations: "When your Highness's divine mind and power, Caesar, gained the empire of the world [*imperio . . . orbis terrarum*], Rome gloried in your triumph and victory. For all her enemies were crushed by your invincible courage and all nations [*gentes omnes*] obeyed your bidding" (*On Architecture* 1.preface.1). As we have seen, Livy strikes a similar chord in a preface of his own: "so great is the military glory of the Roman people that when they profess that their Father and the Father of their Founder was none other than Mars, the nations of the earth [*gentes humanae*] may well submit to this also with as good a grace as they submit to Rome's dominion [*imperium*]" (*History of Rome* 1.preface.8). Livy also links Rome's imperium with the nations in his description of Rome as "a people that was destined presently to rule the nations [*populi gentibus mox imperaturi factum*]" (5.48.8). In his abridged history, Florus describes an encounter between Marcus Crassus and the leader of the Moessian army (*Epitome of Roman History* 2.26). When asked "Who are you?" Crassus replied: "We are Romans, lords of the nations [*gentium domini*]." To which the Moessian replied, "So you will be, if you conquer us." Crassus, it is to be noted, got the last word—on the battlefield.

In addition to these (and other) passages that make reference to the universality of Roman rule (on which more below), it is just as important to note that statements in which nations are assumed to represent the basic constituent element of the empire appear in more limited contexts as well. The *Acts of Augustus*, with its multiple references to *gens* or *gentes*, is a telling example.[79] Another is provided by Pliny the Elder, who makes reference to the triumphal arch erected to commemorate Tiberius's victories in the Alps, by means of which "all the Alpine nations [*gentes Alpinae omnes*] stretching from the Adriatic Sea to the Mediterranean were brought under the dominion [*imperium*] of the Roman people" (*Natural History* 3.20.136). A similar assumption is present in this statement of Suetonius about Augustus: "he never made war on any nation [*genti*] without just and due cause, and he was so far from desiring to increase his dominion [*imperium*] or his military glory at any cost, that he forced the chiefs of certain barbarians to take oath in the temple of Mars the Avenger that they would faithfully keep the peace for which they asked" (*Augustus* 2.21.1). For Suetonius, in-

---

79. *Acts of Augustus* 3, 26 (twice), 27, 30 (twice).

creasing the *imperium* consists in bringing yet another *gens* under Roman rule.[80] Also to be noted is Virgil's use of *populi* with reference to the subjects of Roman rule: "You, Roman, be sure to rule the peoples [*regere imperio populos*]—be these your arts—to crown peace with justice, to spare the vanquished [*subiectis*] and to crush the proud" (*Aeneid* 6.851–53).

The idea that nations represent the fundamental building block of the empire is present in Greek material as well. Dionysius of Halicarnassus declares early in his *Roman Antiquities* that Rome's ambition to rule the world was present "from the time that she mastered the whole of Italy," and that now, in his own day, Rome continues "to hold sway [*archonta*] over every region of the world, and there is no nation [*ethnos*] ... that disputes her universal dominion [*tēs koinēs hēgemonias*] or protests against being ruled [*archesthai*] by her" (1.3.5). Rome's *hēgemonia* consists precisely of rule over *ethnē*. In a passage that we will look at in more detail a little later on, Josephus speaks of "the might of the Roman empire [*tēn Rōmaiōn hēgemonian*]" and the fact that (as he says in effect) this empire consists of defeated *ethnē* "throughout the whole known world [*tēs oikoumenēs*]" (*Jewish War* 2.362). This is not to overlook the fact that imperial sovereignty can occasionally be expressed in terms of domains other than (or in addition to) nations, as in Aristides's observation about "the boundaries of your empire [*tēs archēs*]": "Nothing escapes you, neither city, nor nation [*ethnos*], nor harbor, nor land."[81] Nevertheless, the basic and perennial building block is the nation.

As was the case with Latin material, in addition to passages such as these that make explicit reference to the universality of Roman rule over the nations, other Greek passages, more limited in scope, also take it for granted that the Roman Empire is composed of nations. Appian, for example, speaks of the nearly two hundred years of imperial rule as a time when "some nations [*tois ethnesin*] have been added to the empire [*tēn hēgemonian*] by these emperors," going on to say that they have also refused to incorporate others ("poverty-stricken and profitless barbarian nations [*barbara ethnē*]") (*Roman History* preface.7). Aristides refers to "the rulers who are sent to the cities and the nations [*ta ethnē*]" and the small number of troops that "are sufficient to guard whole nations [*ethnē*]."[82] That nations constituted a basic building block of the empire was apparent as well in references to *ethnē* in official public inscriptions: the treaty between "the

---

80. Also, e.g., Cicero, *Philippic* 4.13; Tacitus, *Annals* 14.44.

81. *Regarding Rome* 29. Also, e.g., Cassius Dio, quoting Augustus: "I, who am supreme over the entire sea within the Pillars of Hercules, ... I who possess both cities and nations [*ethnē*] in every continent ..." (*Roman History* 53.8.1).

82. Aristides, *Regarding Rome* 31, 67. Also, e.g., Appian, *Roman History* preface.1, 6; *Civil Wars* 1.5; Cassius Dio, *Roman History* 52.22.1.

Romans and . . . the nation of the Jews [*tō ethnei Ioudaiōn*]" in the Maccabean era, erected on bronze tablets in Jerusalem (1 Macc 8:22–32); the temple in Lugdunum, dedicated to Augustus by the Gauls, with an altar "bearing an inscription of the names of the nations [*tōn ethnōn*], sixty in number," along with images of each tribe (Strabo, *Geography* 4.3.2); Claudius's edict concerning Jewish civic rights in Alexandria, which granted to the Jews the right to observe their ancestral customs, while enjoining them also "not to set at nought the beliefs about the gods held by other nations [*tōn allōn ethnōn*]" (Josephus, *Jewish Antiquities* 19.290–91); and the reliefs of personified nations in the Sebasteion in Aphrodisias, each one identified as an *ethnos*.[83]

Turning more directly to the characteristic themes of imperial ideology, we note first that Romans took considerable pride in their reputation as being victorious over the nations or as conquerors of nations. In a phrase that takes on the character of an epithet, Cicero on several occasions refers to "the Roman people, the conqueror of all nations," as in one of his orations against Mark Antony: "So, Men of Rome, the whole conflict lies between the Roman people, the conqueror of all nations [*victori omnium gentium*], and an assassin, a bandit, a Spartacus" (*Philippic* 4.15)."[84] Similar phraseology ("the people, victor of the nations") is used both by Pliny the Elder and by his nephew, Pliny the Younger.[85] Elsewhere, individual generals are described as victors over nations or as having defeated nations. Cicero, for example, describes Pompey as "that hero, who by the valour of his victorious [*victoria*] arms had conquered [*domuisset*] our most

---

83. Smith, "*Simulacra Gentium*." Nicolet sees some connections between the Aphrodisias Sebasteion and the *Acts of Augustus*, particularly in "the choice of the countries and especially of the *gentes* represented"; Claude Nicolet, *Space, Geography, and Politics in the Early Roman Empire* (Ann Arbor: University of Michigan Press, 1991), 76. On the personification of nations more generally, see Emma Dench, *Romulus' Asylum: Roman Identities from the Age of Alexander to the Age of Hadrian* (Oxford: Oxford University Press, 2005), 79–80.

84. Also *On the Making of an Orator* 2.76. An expanded version—"the Roman people, conqueror and lord of all nations [*victoris dominique omnium gentium*]"—is used in *Philippic* 6.12.

85. "For assuredly he [Livy] ought to have composed his history for the glory of the people, victor of the nations [*populi gentium victoris*] and of the Roman name, not for his own" (Pliny the Elder, *Natural History* preface.16). "To begin then with Europe, nurse of the race that has conquered all the nations [*victoris omnium gentium*]" (Pliny the Elder, *Natural History* 3.5). "Elsewhere the vast façade of the Circus rivals the beauty of the temples, a fitting place for a people which has conquered the nations [*populo victore gentium*], a sight to be seen on its own account as well as for the spectacles there to be displayed" (Pliny the Younger, *Panegyric* 51.3).

impious citizens, our bitterest enemies, mighty national groups, kings, savage and hitherto unknown nations [*qui maximas nationes, qui reges, qui gentes feras atque inauditas*], countless hordes of pirates and a band of slaves as well" (*In Defense of Sestius* 1.67).[86] Later, after Caesar's defeat of Pompey, Cicero (having quickly adjusted to the shifting political winds) praises Caesar as having "subdued [*domuisti*] nations [*gentis*] barbarous in their brutality, innumerable in their multitude, infinite in their extent, and abounding in every description of resource," going on to say that "the honors you have won in war shall indeed be acclaimed by the literature and the eloquence not only of our own but of well-nigh all nations [*paene omnium gentium*]" (*On Behalf of Marcellus* 8–9). Elsewhere he describes Caesar as "the fairest light of all nations [*omnium gentium*]" and "the vanquisher of the world [*victorem orbis terrarum*]" (*On Behalf of King Deiotarus* 15). Caesar himself, in his account of the war with the forces of Pompey, praises the conduct of his own troops in a difficult situation: "They remembered that after suffering great scarcity at Alesia, and even more at Avaricum, they had left the field as conquerors [*victores*] of supremely great nations [*maximarum ... gentium*]" (*Civil War* 3.47.5). Similar language of victory is also used by Pliny the Younger (of Trajan), Tacitus (of Tiberius), Velleius (of Pompey and Tiberius), and Florus (of Crassus).[87]

---

86. Also speaking of Pompey: "whose exploits, crowned by glorious victory [*victoria*] on land and sea had compassed all peoples [*omnis gentis*]" (*In Defense of Balbus* 6.16).

87. Speaking in laudatory terms of Trajan's consulship, Pliny says that it was "held not in the tranquil atmosphere of the city deep in the embrace of peace, but in the face of savage nations [*barbaras gentes*], like those heroes of old who changed the toga of office for a soldier's cloak and carried victory [*victoria*] to lands unknown" (*Panegyric* 56.4). Tacitus: "First eulogizing the victors in an address, the Caesar raised a pile of weapons, with a legend boasting that 'the army of Tiberius Caesar, after subduing [*debellatis*] the national groups [*nationibus*] between the Rhine and the Elbe, had consecrated that memorial to Mars, to Jupiter, and to Augustus'" (Tacitus, *Annals* 2.22). Velleius: "Then, after conquering all the races in his path [*victor omnium ... gentium*], Pompey returned to Italy" (Velleius, *Compendium of Roman History* 2.40.2); "Ye Heavens, how large a volume could be filled with the tale of our achievements in the following summer under the generalship of Tiberius Caesar! All Germany was traversed by our armies, nations were conquered [*victae gentes*] hitherto almost unknown, even by name ... after proving victorious over many nations [*plurimarum gentium victoria*] ..." (2.106.1, 3); "Victorious over all the nations and countries [*victor omnium gentium locorumque*] ... Caesar led his legions back to winter quarters" (2.107.3). Florus: In a passage cited above, in which, to Crassus's claim that the Romans are "lords of the nations [*gentium domini*]," the leader of the Moesians replies: "So you will be ... if you conquer [*vinceritis*] us" (Florus, *Epitome of Roman History* 2.26).

The Nations in Roman Imperial Discourse

Obversely, Rome's character as victor is also conveyed by a presentation of the nations as vanquished, the linguistic equivalent of the typical depiction in coin and sculpture where the defeated nation appears as a kneeling figure.[88] Of particular interest here are phrases such as "defeated nations," which commonly appear in connection with triumphs or other commemorations of victories. Pride of place here belongs to Virgil's description of Augustus's triumphs, as famously depicted on Aeneas's shield: "He [Augustus] himself, seated at the snowy threshold of shining Phoebus, reviews the gifts of peoples [*populorum*] and hangs them on the proud portals. The conquered nations [*victae... gentes*] move in long array, as diverse in fashion of dress and arms as in tongues" (*Aeneid* 8.720–23).[89] With respect to Augustus's successor, we have already noted Pliny the Elder's description of the triumphal arch erected after Tiberius's campaign in the Alps and the portion of the inscription declaring that "all the Alpine races [*gentes Alpinae omnes*] stretching from the Adriatic Sea to the Mediterranean were brought under the dominion [*imperium*] of the Roman people." The passage continues with a list of some four dozen ethnic groups, under the heading: "Alpine nations conquered [*gentes Alpinae devictae*]" (*Natural History* 3.20.136). With respect to a different triumphal arch, this one commemorating Domitian's victories in Germany, Martial describes the emperor's triumph in Rome, noting the triumphal arch that "stands exultant over subjugated nations [*domitis gentibus*]" (*Epigrams* 8.65). In his account of Trajan's triumph after the First Dacian War, after a description of the captured enemies and their arms, Pliny the Younger continues: "then, close behind the conquered nations [*domitarum gentium*] your own self standing high in your chariot, before which are the shields pierced by your own hand" (*Panegyric* 17.2).[90] Several other passages describe situations where victorious generals are given the names of conquered nations as *cognomina*. Speaking of Scipio and Mummius, Velleius states: "The

---

88. And in architecture as well: "Spain and other nations [*gentes*] whose names adorn his [Augustus's] Forum" (Velleius, *Compendium of Roman History* 2.39.2); "the statues of the nations [*simulacris gentium*]" erected in Pompey's theater (and coming frighteningly to life in Nero's dream; Suetonius, *Nero* 6.46.1).

89. Also *Aeneid* 6.851–53: "You, Roman, be sure to rule the peoples [*regere imperio populos*]—be these your arts—to crown peace with justice, to spare the vanquished [*subiectis*] and to crush the proud."

90. Similar phraseology appears in verbal formulations: "the most warlike nations having been subdued [*bellicosissimis gentibus devictis*]" (Julius Caesar, *Gallic War* 8.24); "As for the nations [*gentes/ethnē*] of the Pannonians, ... [w]hen they were conquered [*devictas/ēssēthenta*] through Tiberius" (*Acts of Augustus* 30); "the nations [*gentes*] that ... are nowadays vanquished [*vincantur*] by the Roman people" (Pliny the Elder, *Natural History* 16.5).

two conquerors [*uterque imperator*] were honored by the names of the conquered races [*devictae... gentis*]. The one was surnamed Africanus, the other Achaicus. Before Mummius no new man earned for himself a cognomen won by military glory" (*Compendium of Roman History* 1.13.2). In a more lyrical mode, Ovid says of Julius Caesar: "Did Caesar take his titles from the vanquished [nations] [*victis*], then must he assume as many names as there are nations [*gentes*] in the whole world" (*Fasti* 1.599-600).

The twin themes of victor and vanquished are well represented in Greek literature as well. Caesar's victories in Gaul come up twice in Plutarch's *Lives*, once in *Caesar* ("he took by storm more than eight hundred cities, subdued [*echeirōsato*] three hundred nations [*ethnē*] ..."; 15.3) and, in very similar terms, in *Pompey* 67.6. The language of victory is particularly prominent in Appian's account of Pompey's defeat of King Mithridates. After a survey of the nations that came under Roman rule with the victory, including those that "were gained by the impetus of the victory [*tēn nikēn*] over him" (i.e., indirectly), he continues:

> For these reasons especially I think they considered this a great war and called the victory which ended it the Great Victory [*tēn ... nikēn megalēn kalein*], and gave the title of Great (in Latin Magnus) to Pompey who gained it for them (by which appellation he is called to this day); on account of the great number of nations [*ethnōn*] recovered or added to their dominion, the length of time (forty years) that the war had lasted, and the courage and endurance of Mithridates, who had shown himself capable of meeting all emergencies. (Appian, *Roman History* 12.118)

Cassius Dio, for his part, speaks of the astonishment of the people in Rome at the news of Caesar's accomplishments in Gaul and the fact "that he had seized so many nations [*ethnē*], whose names they had known but imperfectly before." In his account of Augustus's funeral, he also mentions that included in the funeral procession was "an image of Pompey the Great, ... and all the nations [*ta ethnē*] he had acquired, each represented by a likeness which bore some local characteristic."[91]

Closely related to the theme of Rome as conqueror is that of Roman invincibility. Rome has not only conquered the nations; Rome remains unconquered and therefore invincible. We have already noted Sallust's description of the Roman people as "rulers of all nations" (*imperatores omnium gentium*); here what merits attention is the phrase that precedes: "unconquered [*invicti*] by your enemies" (*The War with Jugurtha* 31.20). In another passage that has already come

---

91. Cassius Dio, *Roman History* 39.5.1; 56.34.1-2.

into view, Vitruvius praises Augustus as embodying Roman invincibility in his own person: "Rome gloried in your triumph and victory. For all her enemies were crushed by your invincible [*invicta*] courage and all nations [*gentes omnes*] obeyed your bidding" (*On Architecture* 1.preface.1). Livy, engaging in a bit of contrafactual history, speculated that if Alexander had attempted to conquer Rome, he would have been unsuccessful: "These factors, whether viewed separately or conjointly, afford a ready assurance, that, even as against other princes and nations [*regibus gentibusque*], so also against this one [i.e., Alexander] the might of Rome would have proved invincible [*invictum*]" (*History of Rome* 9.17.3). Florus, dealing with the period before the war between Julius and Pompey, describes Rome as "a people that was sovereign over the nations [*principi gentium populo*]" and speaks of Roman invincibility in these terms: "Almost the whole world having been now subjugated [*pacato*], the Roman Empire was too strong to be overcome by any foreign power" (*Epitome of Roman History* 2.13). An inscription honoring Titus's conquest of Judea gives expression to Roman invincibility by proclaiming (with a significant measure of exaggeration, if not outright falsehood) that Titus had accomplished what no other nation had been able to do: "He [Titus] conquered the nation [*gentem*] of the Jews and the city of Jerusalem, either attacked in vain or not attempted at all by all the leaders, kings, nations [*ducibus regibus gentibus*] before him, he destroyed."[92]

The theme is less pronounced in Greek literature, but a particularly forceful portrayal of Roman invincibility with respect to the nations is given by someone who had experienced it firsthand. In his account of the Judean War, Josephus presents a lengthy speech by the Jewish king Agrippa II, whose territories did not include Judea but who had a certain proprietary interest in Jewish affairs.[93] Addressing a Jewish audience at a point when war seemed imminent, Agrippa attempted to dissuade his hearers from continuing in their present course of action:

> Will you shut your eyes to the might of the Roman empire [*tēn Rōmaiōn hēgemonian*] and refuse to take the measure of your own weakness? Have not our forces been constantly defeated even by the neighboring nations [*tōn*

---

92. *ILS* 264. This inscription has been preserved only in a later account (which also says that it was affixed to the Circus Maximus): see Steve Mason, *A History of the Jewish War, A.D. 66–74* (Cambridge: Cambridge University Press, 2016), 4.

93. *Jewish War* 2.345–401. For a discussion of the speech in its Roman imperial context, see David A. Kaden, "Flavius Josephus and the *Gentes Devictae* in Roman Imperial Discourse: Hybridity, Mimicry, and Irony in the Agrippa II Speech (*Judean War* 2.345–402)," *Journal for the Study of Judaism* 42 (2011): 481–507.

prosoikōn ethnōn], while theirs have never met with a reverse throughout the whole known world [*tēs oikoumenēs*]? (*Jewish War* 2.362)

Thereupon he embarks on a roll call of the "myriads of other nations [*alla ethnē myria*]" who have been unable to withstand Roman military might, treating the more prominent of them systematically one by one. He then concludes:

> There may be some who imagine that the war will be fought under special terms, and that the Romans, when victorious, will treat you with consideration; on the contrary, to make you an example to the rest of the nations [*tōn allōn ethnōn*], they will burn the holy city to the ground and exterminate your race. Even the survivors will find no place of refuge, since all the peoples of the earth either have, or dread the thought of having, the Romans for their masters. (*Jewish War* 2.397)

While Josephus is not the Roman toady that he is often thought to be, here he presents (or has Agrippa present) a full-throated and hard-line version of Roman imperial ideology, with an emphasis on Roman invincibility.[94]

Another theme of Roman imperial ideology, already apparent in some of the preceding references, is the universality of the empire. It is not simply that the Roman people have been victorious in battle with the nations; they are "the conquerors of all the nations" (*victor omnium gentium*). In addition to passages that have already come into view,[95] the idea that the Roman Empire encompassed all nations also appears in contexts in which the theme of victory is not explicit. Again Cicero is a significant source. Speaking to the senate after Pompey's defeat of the pirates, he said that, because of Pompey's victories, "you seemed at last in very truth to be holding empire over all nations and national groups [*omnibus gentibus ac nationibus*] by land and sea" (*On the Manilian Law* 56). In quite a different context, he links the desire for oratorical fame (presumably speaking in part of himself) with the establishment of the empire: "For as soon

---

94. See the discussion in ch. 3, with the literature cited there (n. 62).

95. As discussed above: Cicero, *Philippic* 4.15; 6.12; *On the Making of an Orator* 2.76; Florus, *Epitome of Roman History* 2.26. Of course, the universality of the empire was also expressed in terms that did not include *gentes* or *nationes*: e.g., *orbis terrarum* (Cicero, *In Defense of Balbus* 28.64; *Philippic* 2.15; 7.19; 8.10; Sallust, *Histories* 4.17; Velleius, *Compendium of Roman History* 1.12.7; Florus, *Epitome of Roman History* 1.introduction.1–2); *genus humanum* (Tacitus, *Annals* 3.59); boundaries coextensive with the known world (Cicero, *In Defense of Balbus* 16.39; Livy, *History of Rome* 36.17.13–16); *imperium sine fine* (Virgil, *Aeneid* 1.277–87).

as our empire of all nations [*imperium omnium gentium*] had been established, and an enduring peace had assured us leisure, there was hardly a youth, athirst for fame, who did not deem it his duty to strive with might and main after eloquence" (*On the Making of an Orator* 1.14). In his speech against the agrarian law proposed by Rullus, he speaks on several occasions of the universal harm it could cause—"throughout the whole world and all nations in it [*orbis terrarum gentiumque omnium*]" and to "all nations, national groups, provinces and kingdoms [*omnes gentes, nationes, provincias, regna*]" (*On the Agrarian Law* 2.33, 39). Elsewhere in the speech, he speaks of Rome and its temple of Jupiter as the "citadel of all nations [*arcem omnium gentium*]" (*On the Agrarian Law* 1.18). In addition to Cicero, the idea that Rome's empire encompassed all nations has appeared in passages that have already come into view: the reference in *Rhetoric for Herennius* to "that sovereignty over the whole world [*imperium orbis terrae*] which all nations, kings and national groups [*omnes gentes, reges, nationes*] have accepted" (4.13); Vitruvius's address to Augustus as the one who had "gained the empire of the world [*orbis terrarum*]" and the one whom "all nations [*gentes omnes*] obeyed" (*On Architecture* 1.preface.1); Sallust's description of "the Roman people" as "unconquered by your enemies, rulers of all nations [*imperatores omnium gentium*]" (Sallust, *The War with Jugurtha* 31.20); and Livy's characterization of Rome as "a people that was destined presently to rule the nations [*gentibus*]" (*History of Rome* 5.48.8). In addition, Velleius speaks of Augustus as the one "who was destined by his greatness to overshadow men of all nations [*omnium gentium viris*]" (*Compendium of Roman History* 2.36.1).[96]

The universal extent of Rome's rule over the nations comes to expression in other ways as well. Cicero again: by means of his victories over "mighty national groups, kings, savage and hitherto unknown nations [*qui maximas nationes, qui reges, qui gentes feras atque inauditas*], countless hordes of pirates and a band of slaves as well," Pompey "had set the boundary of the empire of the Roman people at the limits of the world [*imperium populi Romani orbis terrarum terminis*]" (*In Defense of Sestius* 67). A similar idea is expressed poetically by Ovid: "The land of other nations [*gentibus . . . aliis*] has a fixed boundary: the circuit of Rome is the circuit of the world" (*Fasti* 2.683–84). Both Virgil and Livy present Rome and Carthage as rivals in the struggle for universal rule. According to the *Aeneid*, Juno loved Carthage "above all other lands," and her "aim and cherished hope" was that "here should be the capital of the nations [*regnum . . . gentibus*]." Nev-

---

96. See also Calpurnius Siculus's poem in praise of the new emperor Nero: "Let all the nations [*quaecumque notum gens*: "whatever known nation"] rejoice, whether they dwell furthest down in the low south or in the uplifted north, whether they face the east or west or burn beneath the central zone" (*Eclogue* 1.74–76).

ertheless, "in truth she had heard" that Carthage would fall to "a race [that] was springing from Trojan blood" (*Aeneid* 1.12–22). In Livy's more soberly historical account: "Whether Rome or Carthage should give laws to the nations [*iura gentibus*] they would know the next day before nightfall. For not Africa, they said, or Italy but the whole world [*orbem terrarum*] would be the reward of victory" (*History of Rome* 30.32.2).

In some places, to be sure, such hyperbolic claims to universal rule were tempered with a measure of qualification. For one thing, as was recognized explicitly on occasion, it was not the case that all nations within the empire were there because they had been conquered. Some of the "nations, kings and national groups" (*gentes, reges, nationes*) had accepted Rome's "sovereignty over the whole world" (*imperium orbis terrae*) "of their own will," having been drawn by Rome's generosity (*liberalitate*) (*Rhetoric for Herennius* 4.13).[97] In one uncharacteristically restrained passage, Cicero goes a step further, presenting universal renown not as a reality but as something to be hoped for: "we Romans, though confined to a scanty portion of it [the earth] and entirely unknown to many nations [*plurimis . . . gentibus*], hope nevertheless that our name will be borne abroad on wings and will spread to the ends of the earth [*latissime*]" (*The Republic* 1.26). Florus, speaking of the Augustan era, recognizes that there were nations "not under the rule of the empire" who nevertheless "felt the greatness of Rome and revered its people as the conqueror of all nations [*victorem gentium omnium*]" and thus sought "friendship" (*amicitiam*) with the Romans (Florus, *Epitome of Roman History* 2.34). Also speaking of Augustus, Suetonius sees the fact that there were nations that remained outside the boundaries of the empire as a reflection of the emperor's good judgment: "But he never made war on any nation [*genti*] without just and due cause, and he was so far from desiring to increase his dominion [*imperium*] or his military glory at any cost, that he forced the chiefs of certain barbarians to take oath in the temple of Mars the Avenger that they would faithfully keep the peace for which they asked" (*Augustus* 2.21.2).[98] In

---

97. LCL renders the phrase "in part compelled by force, in part of their own will, when conquered either by the arms of Rome or by her generosity." While this rendering expresses the free-will acceptance as a form of conquest, the verb is not *vincere* but *superare*.

98. In his very helpful study of the way in which conceptions of the empire as a geographical and spatial entity developed during the Augustan era, Nicolet begins with a question about Augustus's military restraint: "why did the Roman conquest seem to come to a standstill at precisely the time when this transition [i.e., from republic to empire] took place with the reign of the first 'emperor'? Augustus—rightly or wrongly—is not perceived as one of the conquerors who helped the empire make spectacular advancements (like Pompey or Caesar, and later Trajan). On the contrary, he is credited with a foreign policy

some instances, then, authors remain content simply to affirm the great extent of the empire. Cicero, for example, exults in the fact that Caesar's conquest of the nations (*gentes*) and national groups (*nationes*) of Gaul means that "the limits [*extremum*] of our empire and of those lands are one and the same," but without attempting to extend the limits of the empire to the world as a whole (*Concerning the Consular Provinces* 33).[99]

Turning to Greek material, the universality of Roman rule over the nations is a common theme as well, though perhaps with less hyperbole than appears in Latin writings. In a passage in which he compares "the Roman dominion [*hyperochēn*]" with "the most famous empires [*tōn dynasteiōn*] of the past," Polybius observes that "the Romans have subjected to their rule not portions, but the whole of the world [*pasan . . . tēn oikoumenēn*]," a world comprising named and unnamed nations (*tōn ethnōn*).[100] Diodorus Siculus, speaking of Rome's "pursuit of world empire [*tēs tōn holōn hēgemonias*]," says that "because of their surpassing humanity . . . kings, cities and nations [*ta ethnē*] went over to the Roman standard," so that "they held sway over virtually the whole inhabited world [*pasēs tēs oikoumenēs*]."[101] A little later on, he reproduces the content of an inscription that Pompey erected to commemorate his accomplishments in Asia, which lists all the conquered tribes (*ta phyla*) and nations (*panta ta ethnē*) and then declares that the frontiers of the empire were thus extended "to the limits of the earth [*tois horiois tēs gēs*]."[102]

Like Diodorus, Dionysius of Halicarnassus speaks of Rome's aspiration "to govern all mankind [*epi tēn hapantōn . . . archēn*]," the outcome of which is that "there is no nation [*ethnos*] . . . that disputes her universal dominion [*tēs koinēs hēgemonias*] or protests against being ruled by her" (*Roman Antiquities* 1.3.5). Strabo, for his part, praises the Roman ability to supplement force with reason, so that "from the time that they began to have dealings with more civilized nations and tribes [*ethnē kai phyla*]," they were able to establish themselves "as

---

that was one of caution, if not of inertia, as the historian Florus would later state"; *Space, Geography, and Politics in the Early Roman Empire*, 1.

99. Cf. Florus, in a statement that does not refer explicitly to nations: "The Roman people during the seven hundred years, from the time of King Romulus down to that of Caesar Augustus, achieved so much in peace and war that, if a man were to compare the greatness of their empire with its years, he would consider its size as out of all proportion to its age" (*Epitome of Roman History* 1.introduction.1).

100. Polybius, *Histories* 1.2.1–8.

101. Diodorus Siculus, *Library of History* 32.4.4–5. He goes on to criticize the Romans, however, for using terror and destruction to consolidate their power.

102. Diodorus Siculus, *Library of History* 40.4.

lords of all [*pantōn kyrioi*]" (*Geography* 9.2.2). In his account of the embassy of Alexandrian Jews to Gaius, Philo contrasts the present troubles with the more idyllic early phase of Gaius's reign. When he had "succeeded to the sovereignty [*tēn hēgemonian*] of the whole earth and sea," "a dominion extending... from the rising to the setting sun both within the ocean and beyond it," the peace and prosperity were such as to bring "joy to the Roman people and all Italy and the nations [*ta... ethnē*] of Europe and Asia" (*On the Embassy to Gaius* 8–10).[103]

As with Latin writers, we can find among Greek writers a recognition that Roman rule was not exactly universal in the full sense of the term. Of particular interest is the apparent desire to rationalize the limitation. For Appian, some nations were simply more bother than they were worth; after speaking of the nations (*ethnē*) that were added to the empire since Augustus, he continues:

> Possessing the best part of the earth and sea they have, on the whole, aimed to preserve their empire by the exercise of prudence, rather than to extend their sway indefinitely over poverty-stricken and profitless nations of barbarians [*barbara ethnē*], some of whom I have seen at Rome offering themselves, by their ambassadors, as its subjects, but the emperor would not accept them because they would be of no use to him. They give kings to a great many other nations [*ethnesi allois*] whom they do not wish to have under their own government. (*Roman History* preface.7)

Aristides strikes a similar note: After declaring that "nothing escapes you, neither city, nor nation [*ethnos*], nor harbor, nor land," he adds the qualification: "unless you have condemned something as useless" (*Regarding Rome* 28)—a qualification that reflects positively on Roman shrewdness rather than negatively on the limits to their power. Something similar is accomplished in passages that simply speak of the extent of the empire without any claim of universality, as in Appian's comment that, with Augustus's conquest of Egypt, he had added "the only [country] wanting to complete the Roman empire as it now stands," going on to speak of the emperor's authority "over the fatherland and the nations subject to it [*tē patridi kai tois hyp' autēn ethnesin*]" (*Civil Wars* 1.5).

---

103. Of course, the universal scope of Roman rule could be expressed without explicit reference to the nations that it comprised. Polybius, for example, says that he begins his history of Rome as far back as he does so that "it may be clear to readers that they had quite adequate grounds for conceiving the ambition of a world empire [*tēs tōn holōn archēs kai dynasteias*] and adequate means for achieving their purpose" (*Histories* 1.3.8–10). In the same passage, he speaks of "that enterprise which has made them lords [*enkrateis*] over land and sea."

The Nations in Roman Imperial Discourse

In addition, Greek writers often emphasized the great extent of the Roman Empire in comparison with empires that went before. While the theme of universality can be present, or at least hinted at, the emphasis falls on comparative size. To take an early example, Polybius sets out to demonstrate "how striking and grand is the spectacle presented by the [Roman] period" by "compar[ing] with the Roman dominion [*hyperochēn*] the most famous empires [*tōn dynasteiōn*] of the past," notably those of the Persians, Greeks, and Macedonians. Unlike these empires, which "left the larger part of the inhabited world [*tēs oikoumenēs*] as yet outside its boundaries," including "the most warlike nations [*ethnōn*]," "the Romans have subjected to their rule not portions, but the whole of the world [*tēn oikoumenēn*]" (*Histories* 1.2.1–8). Writing several centuries later, Appian declares that "no empire [*archē*] down to the present time ever attained to such size and duration" as that of the Romans, going on to speak of "the nations of Europe" and "the Asiatic nations" (*tōn ethnōn* in both cases) now part of an empire "whose boundaries extend from the setting of the sun and the Western ocean to Mount Caucasus and the river Euphrates, and through Egypt up country to Ethiopia and through Arabia as far as the Eastern ocean" (*Roman History* preface.8–9). Returning to a passage that has already drawn our attention, Aristides compares the Roman Empire with that of the Persians in these terms: "Proceeding westward from the point where the limit of the Persian empire was then fixed, the remainder of your empire is much greater than the whole of that one. Nothing escapes you, neither city, nor nation [*ethnos*], nor harbor, nor land, unless you have condemned something as useless." He continues by saying that places considered by the Persians to stand "at the ends of the earth" (such as the Nile) are for the Romans simply "the fence of courtyard" (*Regarding Rome* 28).

Victory, invincibility, and mastery over a universal empire (or, at least, one unparalleled in its extent) were the central themes in Roman imperial ideology. But the hard edge of this aggressive and triumphalistic self-presentation was softened somewhat by Roman attempts to present these aspects of empire as means to loftier and more humane ends. Clemency in victory, benevolence in rule, and the worldwide spread of civilization (*humanitas*, enlightened *politeia*) were the lineaments of the flattering self-portrait that Rome attempted to superimpose over the primary militaristic image.

We begin with clemency in victory. The theme comes to expression, with specific reference to the nations, several times in Cicero's work. In one place, he sees it as a characteristic of Roman military action in the past (going on to lament that it has fallen by the wayside since the time of Sulla): "as long as the empire of the Roman people maintained itself by acts of service, not of oppression, wars were waged in the interest of our allies or to safeguard our supremacy; the end of our wars was marked by acts of clemency or by only a necessary degree of severity; the senate was a haven of refuge for kings, tribes, and nations [*regum, populorum, nationum*]" (*On Duties* 2.26-27). After Caesar's defeat of Pompey, however, Cicero was prepared to recognize a similar (but post-Sulla) form of clemency in Caesar's treatment of his opponents: "to conquer the will, to curb the anger, and to moderate the triumph—not merely to uplift from the dust the foe whose rank, genius, and merit were pre-eminent, but even to enhance his previous greatness"—is an "act of mercy, of kindliness, of justice, of moderation, and of wisdom" that is worthy of acclaim from "all the nations [*omnium gentium*]" (*On Behalf of Marcellus* 8-9).

The theme of clemency also appears in two of the primary texts of the Augustan era. Virgil's *Aeneid* contains a scene in which Aeneas encounters his father Anchises in the underworld. In the course of this encounter, Anchises provides his son with a vision of Rome's future, in the course of which he declares: "You, Roman, be sure to rule the peoples [*regere imperio populos*]—be these your arts—to crown peace with justice, to spare the vanquished [*subiectis*] and to crush the proud" (*Aeneid* 6.851-53). Augustus, the Roman *imperator* who inspired Virgil's work, while summing up his own life's work in the *Acts of Augustus*, declares: "Wars, both civil and foreign, I undertook throughout the world, on sea and land, and when victorious I spared all citizens who sued for pardon. The foreign nations [*externas gentes/ta ethnē*] which could with safety be pardoned I preferred to save rather than to destroy" (*Acts of Augustus* 3).

The theme is picked up by Greek writers as well. In a passage that will come up for consideration again, Diodorus Siculus expresses it in these terms:

> In more recent times the Romans, when they went in pursuit of world empire [*tēs tōn holōn hēgemonias*], brought it into being by the valour of their arms, then extended its influence far and wide by the kindest possible treatment of the vanquished. So far, indeed, did they abstain from cruelty and revenge on those subjected to them that they appeared to treat them not as enemies, but as if they were benefactors and friends. Whereas the conquered, as former foes, expected to be visited with fearful reprisals, the conquerors left no room for anyone to surpass them in clemency.

He goes on to say that, partly for this reason, "kings, cities and nations [*ta ethnē*]" readily accepted Roman rule.[104] One nation that did not readily accept Roman rule, however, was that of the Jews. In Josephus's account of the Jewish war with

---

104. *Library of History* 32.4.4-5. Like Cicero, however, he goes on to say that in more recent times, Rome has fallen away from this ideal, using victory instead as an opportunity for "terrorism and . . . destruction."

The Nations in Roman Imperial Discourse

Rome, he presents a scene in which the victorious general Titus, son of the new emperor Vespasian, addresses the leaders of the defeated Jewish rebels. In the speech, Titus contrasts the rebelliousness and hostility of the Jews with both the response of other nations to the news of Vespasian's accession and with the humanity and clemency of his father:

> But by you his humanity [*to philanthrōpon*] was taken for weakness, and upon our clemency [*praotētos*] you nursed your audacity. On Nero's decease, you acted like the basest scoundrels. Emboldened by our intestine troubles, when I and my father had departed for Egypt, you abused your opportunities by preparing for hostilities, and were not ashamed to harass those, now made emperors, whose humanity [*philanthrōpous*] as generals you had experienced. Thus, when the empire [*tēs hēgemonias*] found refuge in us, when throughout its length was universal tranquility, and foreign nations [*tōn exōthen ethnōn*] were sending embassies of congratulation, once again the Jews were in arms. (*Jewish War* 6.340–42)

For present purposes, it matters not that the themes expressed in the speech are probably to be attributed to Josephus rather than to Titus. Josephus is simply picking up an element that was part of Rome's own flattering self-presentation.

The theme of clemency in victory leads naturally to a larger theme, having to do with the benevolent character of Roman rule. A little later we will look at the actual benefits that were experienced and appreciated by the subjects of Roman rule—or, at least, that Romans themselves thought were being (or should be) appreciated. Here we are highlighting the character and intentions of Roman rule (benevolence: the desire for the good) rather than the experienced results (benefits). Again, in all this, we are dealing with what Scott calls the public transcript, the flattering self-image that Rome wanted to project toward its subject nations and that they in turn were invited to accept and admire.[105]

The image appears in the poetic form of a polished cameo in Anchises's charge to Aeneas, which has come into view several times already: "You, Roman, be sure to rule the peoples [*regere imperio populos*]—be these your arts—to crown peace with justice, to spare the vanquished and to crush the proud" (*Aeneid* 6.851–53). When we looked at the passage a moment ago, we were interested in the theme of clemency. But clemency for the vanquished here is just one aspect of a larger picture, in which it stands alongside the desire for peace, justice, and the overthrow of the haughty, as the set of imperial arts with which Rome is to rule the

---

105. James C. Scott, *Domination and the Arts of Resistance: Hidden Transcripts* (New Haven: Yale University Press, 1990).

GENTILE CHRISTIAN IDENTITY

peoples. Prior to the Augustan era, the image is fully on display in the work of Cicero, not least in a letter to his brother Quintus while the latter was governor of the province of Asia. In this letter, which reads almost as a handbook on the art of governing, Cicero praises Quintus's "ability, discretion, and self-restraint." He goes on to express the fact—or perhaps the hope—that Quintus's virtues would not be

> hidden away in some dark corner but placed in the full light of Asia, for the most brilliant of provinces to see and for all nations and national groups [*omnium gentium ac nationum*] to hear tell of: how no man is afraid of your progresses or put to crushing expense or disturbed by your arrival; how there is hearty rejoicing in public and private wherever you go, for you enter a city as a protector, not a tyrant, and a house as a guest, not a looter. (*Letters to Quintus* 1.9–10)

Further on in the letter, Cicero says that even if Quintus had been assigned the governance of "savage, barbarous national groups [*immanibus ac barbaris nationibus*] in Africa or Spain or Gaul," it would still be incumbent on him "as a civilized man [*humanitatis tuae*] . . . to think of their interests and devote yourself to their needs and welfare." But since he is governing Greeks—"the race from which civilization [*humanitas*] is believed to have passed to others," "those very people whose precepts have rescued us from barbarism"—Quintus is doubly bound to rule well (1.27–28). This idea—that Roman *humanitas* is something that they have taken over from the Greeks and now have an obligation to exhibit and defend—is one of the strategies by which Rome attempted to justify the empire and to position themselves in the Hellenistic world that they had inherited.[106]

Staying with Cicero for a moment, in a passage that we have also looked at in connection with Roman clemency, he goes on characterize Roman rule (at least in its ideal past) in this way:

> the senate was a haven of refuge for kings, peoples, and national groups [*regum, populorum, nationum*]; and the highest ambition of our magistrates and generals was to defend our provinces and allies with justice and honor.

---

106. Not that this prevented Cicero from adopting a position of cultural superiority with respect to Greeks in the present. For example, when it is a matter of "morality, rules of life, family and household economy," and indeed all "natural gifts apart from book-learning," Romans are "above comparison with the Greeks or any other nation [*gente*]" (*Tusculan Disputations* 1.2).

And so our government could be called more accurately a protectorate of the world than a dominion. (*On Duties* 2.26–27)[107]

This striking image of Rome as a "haven of refuge" for the nations appears a number of times in various forms in Cicero's works: Rome as "the light of the whole world and the fortress of all the nations [*lucem orbis terrarum atque arcem omnium gentium*]" (*Against Catilina* 4.11); the senate house as "the fount of security for all the nations [*summum auxilium omnium gentium*]" (*Against Catilina* 4.2) or as "the haven of all the nations [*portum omnium gentium*]" (*On Behalf of Milo* 90); the temple of Jupiter as the "citadel of all the nations [*arcem omnium gentium*]" (*On the Agrarian Law* 1.18).[108] It is a striking image indeed—Rome as the benevolent center of a world of nations that lived under its protection and illumination.

Rome's benevolent rule of the nations is also on display in Augustus's own *Acts of Augustus*. Augustus takes evident pride in declaring that peace was established in Gaul, Spain, Germany, and the Alps, "with no unjust war waged against any nation [*genti/ethnei*]" (26). Rather than imposing direct Roman rule, he granted the privilege of rule by native kings to the nation (*gentem/to ethnos*) of Armenia and the "nations [*gentes/ethnē*] of the Parthians and Medes" (27, 33). In addition to the many kings who sent their sons to be raised in Rome as a token of friendship, "many other nations [*gentes/ethnē*] experienced the fidelity [*fides*] of the Roman people, of whom nothing had previously existed of embassies or interchange of friendship with the Roman people" (32).

A few other examples will suffice to underline the point. Speaking of Augustus's alliances with the kings of "foreign nations [*alienigenis*]," Suetonius said that "he never failed to treat them all with consideration as integral parts of the empire [*membra partisque imperii*]" (*Augustus* 48.1). In Livy's account of Scipio's treatment of some Spanish hostages liberated from the Carthaginians, he says that the Roman general "bade them all to be of good cheer; for they had come into the power of the Roman people, which prefers to bind men by favor rather than by fear, and to keep foreign nations [*exterasque gentis*] linked by loyalty and alliance, rather than reduced to a harsh slavery" (*History of Rome* 26.49.7–9).

---

107. And even with respect to his own day, Cicero can declare (in 56 BCE) that "wars abroad with kings, peoples, and tribes [*regum, gentium, nationum*] have long ago so completely ceased, that our relations with those whom we treat as pacified dependants are excellent" (*In Defense of Sestius* 51).

108. Cf. his comment on a failed assassination plot against Pompey: "had he ... fallen, not this state alone, but all nations [*gentes omnes*], would have lain in the dust" (*On Behalf of Milo* 19).

Despite the disgust that Tacitus expresses elsewhere at the presence of foreign people and influences in Rome, he relates with apparent positive amusement an incident involving some German envoys who, while touring "the usual places shown to barbarians," came to Pompey's theater. Spotting a few evident foreigners sitting in seats reserved for senators, they were told that "this was a compliment paid to the envoys of nations [*gentium*] distinguished for their courage and for friendship to Rome." The Germans—proudly declaring that, where "arms or loyalty" were concerned, they did not need to take a back seat to anyone—promptly "went down and took their seats among the Fathers" (*Annals* 13.54).

The benevolent character of Roman rule is also a recurring theme among Greek writers, and the fact that this rule was exercised over nations comes to expression as well. We have already noted a passage in which Diodorus Siculus observes that, while the Romans won their empire by military conquest, they maintained it through their clemency, treating those whom they had conquered "not as enemies, but as if they were benefactors and friends." He continues:

> Some they enrolled as fellow citizens, to some they granted rights of intermarriage, to others they restored their independence, and in no case did they nurse a resentment that was unduly severe. Because of their surpassing humanity [*hēmerotētos*: gentleness], therefore, the kings, the cities and, in short, the nations [*ta ethnē*] went over to the Roman standard. (*Library of History* 32.4.4–5)

Dionysius of Halicarnassus credits Rome's rise to prominence—"from the smallest nation [*ethnos*] to the greatest and from the most obscure to the most illustrious"—to "their humane [*philanthrōpō*] reception of those who sought a home among them," their granting of citizenship to those who had been conquered and to their own slaves, and to the fact that they "disdain[ed] no condition of men from whom the commonwealth might reap an advantage." More important than these factors was "their form of government [*politeumatos*], which they fashioned out of their many experiences, always extracting something useful from every occasion" (*Roman Antiquities* 1.9.4). In addition, it is part of Dionysius's purpose to root Rome's benevolent character in the present in the fact that they were Greeks from the beginning: "the nations [*ta . . . ethnē*] which joined in founding the city of Rome were Greek colonies sent out from the most famous places, and not, as some believe, barbarians and vagabonds" (*Roman Antiquities* 7.70.1).

Strabo also highlights Rome's readiness to progress in their exercise of rule, supplementing brute force with more enlightened governmental arts. After observing that, while "force is stronger than reason in dealing with the barbarians," things such as learning and peaceful interchange with other people "are particularly useful in dealing with Greeks," he continues: "And the Romans too, in ancient times, when carrying on war with savage tribes, needed no training of this kind, but from the time that they began to have dealings with more civilized nations and tribes [*hēmerōtera ethnē kai phyla*], they applied themselves to this training also, and so established themselves as lords of all" (*Geography* 9.2.2). As a native of Pontus, the distinction between civilized and barbarian nations was evidently one that Strabo wanted to press; as a Greek, he also had an interest in attributing Roman benevolence to its interactions with the Greeks and other civilized nations.

Rome's flattering self-portrait is also in view in Philo's *On the Embassy to Gaius*, in a passage that we have already looked at in connection with the universality of Roman rule. Here our attention is drawn by what Philo has to say about the benevolent character of Roman rule. The passage appears near the beginning of the work, where he is describing the idyllic conditions surrounding Gaius's accession to power and the first seven months of his reign, before he goes on to contrast it with the emperor's subsequent mistreatment of the Jews in Alexandria and Jerusalem. The passage recounts the admiration, astonishment, and joy that filled the whole Roman Empire during this period, an empire comprising both the inhabited world (*oikoumenē*), including "the nations [*ta . . . ethnē*] of Europe and Asia," and "all the more brutish nations [*ethnē*]" lying outside. These idyllic conditions—"all parts, east, west, south, north, harmoniously adjusted, the Greek in full agreement with the barbarian, the civil with the military, to enjoy and participate in peace"—were made possible by the orderly exercise of Roman law, the fact that Gaius's "sovereignty of the whole earth and sea" was "not gained by faction but established by law" (8–10). Philo puts forward this idealized picture, of course, not to praise Rome but to call the empire to live up to the ideals embedded in its own official self-portrait.[109]

The benevolent character of Roman rule is also a major theme in Aelius Aristides's *Regarding Rome*. We have already had occasion to look at this remarkable oration (in ch. 1), with its full-orbed version of Roman imperial ideology, noting also in passing the ways in which it was refracted through the competing loyalties and sensibilities of this particular Anatolian Greek subject of the empire. The

---

109. In Scott's analysis of the "arts of resistance" exercised by subject peoples, the kind of approach taken here by Philo, "which takes as its basis the flattering self-image of elites," represents "[t]he safest and most public form" of resistance. He continues: "Owing to the rhetorical concessions that this self-image contains, it offers a surprisingly large arena for political conflict that appeals to these concessions and makes use of the room for interpretation within any ideology;" *Domination and the Arts of Resistance*, 18.

Roman Empire surpassed the empires that had gone before not only in territorial extent but also in their governing ability. Those who went before simply "did not know how to rule" (23). The blame for this previous state of affairs is not to be shifted onto their subjects: "it is impossible to be good subjects whenever the rulers rule badly" (23). The Romans, however, "have discovered a form of government [*politeian*] which no one had before, and have imposed unvarying law and order on all" (91).[110] Still, Aristides attempts to preserve some space for the Greeks. His praise of the Romans should not be taken as an "indictment of the Greeks," he declares, going on to argue (rather unpersuasively) that prior to the Romans "the knowledge of how to govern did not yet exist"—for if it did "it would have been found among the Greeks, who certainly far excelled all others in knowledge" (51).

Closely related to the theme of Rome's enlightened and benevolent mode of governing is that Roman rule brought significant benefits to the subject nations. Indeed, several of these benefits of Roman rule have come into view in the preceding section. The most prominent of these is peace, a theme widely encountered elsewhere as well, but others have also come into view (e.g., protection, citizenship).[111] Here we will note various aspects of the theme as they

---

110. A *politeia* consisting of a judicious combination of the three forms of government that were already in existence (tyranny/oligarchy, kingship/aristocracy, democracy)—"a mixture of all the constitutions [*politeiōn*] without the inferior side of each" (*Regarding Rome* 90).

111. The theme of peace as a benefit is at least implicit in this declaration of Cicero: "Wars abroad with kings, nations, and national groups [*regum, gentium, nationum*] have long ago so completely ceased, that our relations with those whom we treat as pacified dependants are excellent" (*In Defense of Sestius* 51). In the *Acts of Augustus*, Augustus takes pride in the fact that the doors of the temple of Janus, "which our ancestors ordered to be closed whenever there was peace, secured by victory, throughout the whole domain of the Roman people on land and sea," were closed on three occasions during his reign, something that had happened only twice before (13). While the statement contains no explicit reference to the nations, the fact that "the whole domain of the Roman people on land and sea" was constituted primarily by nations (*gentes/ethnē*) is clear from the work as a whole. Calpurnius Siculus sums up his *Eclogue* on the "untroubled peace" (a second "Golden Age") that existed in the time of Nero by calling on "all the nations [*quaecumque notum gens*: "whatever known nation"]" to rejoice (*Eclogue* 1.74–76). Writing somewhat later, Florus provides his own account of the closing of the temple of Janus in the time of Augustus:

Now that all the nations [*omnibus . . . gentibus*] of the west and south were subjugated [*pacatis*], and also the races of the north, those at least between the Rhine and the Danube, and of the east between the Cyrus and Euphrates, the other na-

appear in individual authors, rather than attempting to separate them out and treat them individually.

The theme appears in very general terms in *Rhetoric for Herennius*, in which the unknown author speaks of the "generosity" (*liberalitate*) that has induced some of "the nations, kings and national groups [*gentes, reges, nationes*]" to freely accept Roman sovereignty (the others were compelled by force) (4.13). Not surprisingly, given what we have seen already about Roman imperial ideology in Cicero's writings, he has more to say about the benefits of Roman rule. In addition to peace itself, he praises Rome for its readiness to grant citizenship to members of other nations and for its universal benefaction.[112]

In his account of the Roman victory over Philip V of Macedonia, Livy presents Rome not primarily as a victor but as a great liberating force, bringing freedom to formerly enslaved peoples. The announcement that "all the nations [*omnes gentes*] that had been under King Philip's rule" were "to be free, exempt from taxes and living under their own laws" was met with a sense of "elation [that] was too great for people to take it in all at once," since "of all possible blessings none is more welcome to the masses than freedom" (*History of Rome* 33.32.5–7). Speaking as an omniscient narrator, Livy sums up the thoughts of the people in these terms:

> There was, then, some nation [*gentem*] on earth that waged war for the freedom of others, at its own expense and itself assuming the hardship and danger; and it did so not just for its neighbors or for people geographically close or on the same landmass, but it actually crossed seas to prevent an unjust empire

---

tions too, who were not under the rule of the empire, yet felt the greatness of Rome and revered its people as the conqueror of the nations [*victorem gentium populum Romanum*]. . . . Thus everywhere throughout the inhabited world [*totius generis humani*] there was firmly established and uninterrupted peace or truce, and Caesar Augustus ventured at last, in the seven hundredth year since the foundation of the city, to close the double doors of the temple of Janus, which had previously been shut on two occasions only, in the reign of Numa and after the first defeat of Carthage. (*Epitome of Roman History* 2.34)

112. "Through his [Romulus's] authority and example our forefathers never ceased to grant and to bestow citizenship. And so, many members of towns, the inhabitants of Tusculum and of Lanuvium for instance, and from other stocks whole nations [*gentes universae*], such as the Sabines, the Volscians and the Hernicans, were admitted to citizenship" (*In Defense of Balbus* 13.31). In his overly effusive praise for Milo: "Titus Annius stands unrivalled as the greatest public benefactor [*rei publica profuisse*] in history, who has shed joy unparalleled upon the Roman people, all Italy, and all national groups [*nationes*]" (*On Behalf of Milo* 77).

existing anywhere in the world and to ensure that right, divine justice, and law should be paramount everywhere. (33.4–6)

Later he returns to the same theme: "First of all it was voted that the Macedonians and Illyrians should be given their independence, so that it should be clear to all nations [*omnibus gentibus*] that the forces of the Roman people brought not slavery to free peoples, but on the contrary, freedom to the enslaved" (45.18.1). In all this, Livy is especially interested in presenting the Romans as the liberators and protectors of the Greeks and thus as their natural successors. In particular, we can look at the speech he puts on the lips of the leader of a delegation from Rhodes (37.54.15–28), who, addressing the Roman senate, speaks of the Rhodian alliance with the Romans and "of the services rendered by the Rhodians first in the war against Philip and then in that against Antiochus." He presents the Rhodians as an "ancient nation [*gentis*]," no less Greek than the "cities which are on the ancient [Greek] soil," but who now have come "under your [i.e., Roman] protection and guardianship." Once the Greeks themselves "possessed empire, as a result of their own might." But now that power has passed to the Romans, they "hope that empire may abide for ever where it now resides; they hold it sufficient to maintain liberty through your arms since they cannot through their own."

In his oration in praise of Trajan, Pliny the Younger develops the theme that, by being part of the empire, the nations share in benefits made possible by the freedom of travel and trade, a degree of mobility that has itself been made possible by the existence of a single sovereign. Like Pompey before him, Trajan "has opened roads, built harbors, created routes overland, let the sea into the shore and moved the shore out to sea, and linked far distant nations [*diversas gentes*] by trade so that natural products in any place now seem to belong to all" (*Panegyric* 29.1). As a result, the emperor is in a position to "switch earth's bounty here and there, as occasion and necessity require, bringing aid and nourishment to a nation [*gentem*] cut off by the sea as if its people were numbered among the humbler citizens of Rome" (32.1). The emperor "can so join East and West by convoys that those nations [*gentes*] who offer and those who need supplies can learn and appreciate in their turn, after experiencing licence and discord, how much they gain from having one master to serve" (32.2).

The idea that the nations enjoy a range of benefits by virtue of their submission to Roman rule also comes to expression in Greek writings. As with Latin literature, some of these benefits have already appeared, in passages having to do with the admirable quality of Roman rule. Both Diodorus Siculus and Dionysius of Halicarnassus draw attention to the granting of citizenship, Diodorus adding the right of intermarriage and (in some cases) the restoration of independence. Diodorus even takes the theme of benefaction one step further, in his

The Nations in Roman Imperial Discourse

observation that Rome was ready to treat conquered nations as if these nations themselves were "benefactors [*euergetais*] and friends."[113] We have also noted how Strabo praises the Romans for learning how to supplement the exercise of sheer force with more civilized forms of rule once they had come into contact with more civilized nations (*Geography* 9.2.2). Elsewhere, while not using *ethnē* specifically, he notes the civilizing effects of Roman rule among specific barbarian nations.[114]

Turning to Jewish writers, we have also observed Philo's (strategically exaggerated) account of the idyllic conditions enjoyed by both "the nations [*ta . . . ethnē*] of Europe and Asia" and "all the more brutish nations [*ethnē*]" lying outside. In the passage, he goes on to list the "good things public and private" that were enjoyed by Roman subjects throughout the empire.[115] Later in the treatise, he recalls the benefits brought to "the nations" (*tōn . . . ethnōn*) of the habitable world by Augustus,

> who reclaimed every state to liberty, who led disorder into order and brought gentle manners and harmony to all unsociable and brutish nations [*ethnē*], who enlarged Hellas by many a new Hellas and hellenized the outside world in its most important regions, the guardian of the peace, who dispensed their dues to each and all, who did not hoard his favors but gave them to be common property, who kept nothing good and excellent hidden throughout his life. (*On the Embassy to Gaius* 144–47)

---

113. Dionysius of Halicarnassus, *Roman Antiquities* 1.9.4.

114. The Turdetanians "have completely changed over to the Roman mode of life," with the result that they have taken on "the qualities of both gentleness and civility [*to hēmeron kai to politikon*]" (*Geography* 3.2.15). Because of the Roman presence established by Augustus and Tiberius, various Iberian nations have become "not only peaceable but civilized [*politikous*] as well" (3.3.8). Nearby, "on account of the overmastery of the Romans, the barbarians who are situated beyond the Massiliotes became more and more subdued as time went on, and instead of carrying on war have already turned to civic life [*politeias*] and farming" (4.1.5).

115. "Thus nothing was to be seen throughout the cities but altars, oblations, sacrifices, men in white robes and crowned with garlands, bright and smart, their cheery faces beaming with goodwill, feasts, assemblages, musical contests, horse races, revels, nightlong frolics with harp and flutes, jollification, unrestraint, holiday-keeping, every kind of pleasure ministered by every sense. In these days the rich had no precedence over the poor, nor the distinguished over the obscure, creditors were not above debtors, nor masters above slaves, the times giving equality before the law" (*On the Embassy to Gaius* 12–13).

With respect to Josephus, we have already had occasion to consider the speech that he puts on the lips of the victorious Titus, who highlights the humanity (*philanthrōpia*) of the Roman generals in their past dealings with Judea, and the fact that the Jewish revolt took place precisely at the point "when the empire [*tēs hēgemonias*] found refuge in us [i.e., Titus's father Vespasian], when throughout its length was universal tranquility, and foreign nations [*tōn esōthen ethnōn*] were sending embassies of congratulation" (*Jewish War* 6.341–42). Elsewhere, Josephus reports a happier speech, this one addressed to Marcus Agrippa on behalf of the Jewish community in Ionia by Nicolas of Damascus, in which he speaks of "the happiness that the whole human race now enjoys, thanks to you," enjoyed especially in "the fact that it is possible for people in every country to live and prosper while respecting their own (traditions)." A little later Nicolas continues with some rhetorical questions: "Is there any people or city or common nation of human beings [*koinon ethnos anthrōpōn*] for which the protection of your empire and the power of the Romans have not come to be the greatest of blessings? Or would anyone want to revoke the favors coming from you?" Answering his own questions, he declares that everyone has been able to share in these blessings and favors, both "privately and publicly" (*Jewish Antiquities* 16.36, 39).

Elsewhere, Appian speaks of Rome's willingness to spend more on the *ethnē* within the empire than they receive from them; Cassius Dio recounts Pompey's activity in organizing "most of the nations [*ta te pleiō ethnē*] in the continent of Asia . . . with their own laws and constitutions"; and so on.[116]

The most thoroughgoing Greek account of Roman benefaction, however, is found in Aelius Aristides's encomium *Regarding Rome*. We have already looked at this striking oration, from several different angles; here we look in a little more detail at his account of the benefits enjoyed by imperial subjects. The section of particular interest (92–104) begins with a comparison of Rome and previous rulers: "Now I think that one would not be wrong in saying that all former men,

---

116. Appian, *Roman History* preface.7; Cassius Dio, *Roman History* 37.20.2. Here we can also mention the inscription found in the temple to Roma and Augustus in Ancyra (*OGIS* 533), which lists benefactions made by a succession of priests in the imperial cult. Some of the benefactions took the form of public banquets. In several of the cases, the recipients of the banquets were identified; among these were three banquets for groups of *ethnē* ("for the three *ethnē*"; "for the two *ethnē*"; and again, "for the two *ethnē*"). Presumably these were identifiable ethnic groups in Roman Galatia. It is worth noting as well that a copy of the *Acts of Augustus* (with Greek translation) was also attached to the walls of the cult temple, reinforcing the link between the local benefaction and the ultimate imperial benefactor. For a discussion of this inscription with reference to Paul's letter to the Galatians, see Brigitte Kahl, *Galatians Re-imagined: Reading with the Eyes of the Vanquished* (Minneapolis: Fortress, 2010), 192–99.

even those who ruled the largest portions of the earth, ruled over, as it were, only the naked bodies of their nations [*autōn tōn ethnōn*], but you have filled your whole empire with cities and adornments" (92).[117] With this, Aelius embarks on a lengthy description of the metaphorical clothing with which the nations of the empire had been adorned:

> Now all of the Greek cities flourish under you, and the offerings in them, the arts, and all their adornments bring honor to you, as an adornment in a suburb. (94)
>
> Iona, much fought over, freed of its garrisons and satraps, is set forth for all as a model of beauty, having now surpassed herself to the extent that she formerly seemed to exceed the other races [*tōn allōn genōn*] in grace and adornment. The proud and great city of Alexander in Egypt has become an ornament of your empire, like a necklace or bracelet of a rich lady among many other possessions. (95)
>
> You continually care for the Greeks as if they were your foster fathers, protecting them and, as it were, resurrecting them, giving freedom and self-rule to the best of them, who were of old rulers, while guiding the others with moderation and with great consideration and care, and educating the barbarians gently or harshly depending on the nature of each people. (96)

---

117. The shift from "nations" to "cities" is not without significance; perhaps because of his Greek identity, Aristides tends to think more in terms of cities than of nations. Indeed, he conceives of the empire as a universal city, of which all nations and races have become citizens; as he says earlier: "What a city is to its boundaries and its territories, so this city is to the whole inhabited world, as if it had been designated its common town" (61). Consequently, "the government [*tēn politeian*] is universal and like that of a single city," which means that "the governors with good reason rule not foreigners, but, as it were, their own people [*oikeiōn*]" (65). In the present passage, this shift reappears in the next paragraph; even though previous rulers "ruled the same lands as you," the character of the rule and the experience of the ruled differed considerably: "to the nation [*ethnei*] which then existed there can be counterpoised the city which now exists among them. And one would say that those men had been kings, as it were, of deserts and garrisons, but that you alone are rulers of cities" (93). Nevertheless, as we have seen in ch. 1, the language of nation and race is found throughout the work, which probably reflects the central place of the nations in the imperial ideology that Aristides is reflecting back to his Roman audience. This serves to indicate that, although *ethnē* does not appear again in the section of interest here, it is not inappropriate to place the account of Roman benefaction that follows within the framework of Aristides's conception of the Roman Empire as an incorporation of the *ethnē* into a universal *polis*.

303

> And the whole inhabited world, as it were attending a national festival [*panēgourizousa*], has laid aside its old dress, the carrying of weapons, and has turned, with full authority to do so, to adornments and all kinds of pleasures. . . . Everything is full of gymnasiums, fountains, gateways, temples, handicrafts, and schools. (97)

Peace, freedom and self-rule, architectural benefactions, the spread of learning, and the enjoyment of culture—such were the benefits bestowed by Rome on the nations of the inhabited world. Aristides concludes in these terms: "And it seems that the gods, watching from above, in their benevolence join with you in making your empire successful and that they confirm your possession of it" (104).

This reference to the gods leads to the final element of Roman imperial ideology—the claim that Rome's rise to power over all the nations was willed and foreordained by the gods and that the rule of the empire was exercised under divine favor. Again we can begin with Cicero: "It is against divine law for the Roman people to be enslaved, since the immortal gods willed that they rule over all nations [*omnibus gentibus*]" (*Philippic* 6.19). Elsewhere he compares Rome with other nations, declaring that, while other nations may have excelled in other things, Rome has "excelled every nation and national group" (*omnes gentes nationisque*) "in piety, in devotion to religion [*pietas et religio*] and in that special wisdom which consists in the recognition of the truth that the world is swayed and directed by the disposal of the gods" (*The Speech concerning the Response of the Soothsayers* 19).

To be sure, the gods were sometimes not all of one mind, as is apparent at the start of the *Aeneid*, where Virgil tells us that Juno loved Carthage instead and desired "that here should be the capital of the nations [*regnum gentibus*]" (1.15–18). Still, Juno's desires in the matter had to give way to those of Jupiter. Jupiter, we learn a little later, had already decreed that the "empire without end" (*imperium sine fine*) would be given instead to the Romans, the "lords of the world and the nation [*gentem*] of the toga" (1.277–82), through a process that would begin with Aeneas, who "shall wage a great war in Italy [and] shall crush proud peoples [*populos*]" (1.261–64), and would culminate with "[Augustus] Caesar, who shall extend his empire to the ocean, his glory to the stars" (1.286–87). Later in the work, the unfolding of this divinely ordained history is portrayed on the shield forged by Vulcan, a portrayal that reaches its climax in Augustus's triumph after the battle of Actium: "He himself, seated at the snowy threshold of shining Phoebus, reviews the gifts of peoples [*populorum*] and hangs them on the proud portals. The conquered nations [*gentes*] move in long array, as diverse in fashion of dress and arms as in tongues" (7.720–23). Rome, then, was no latter-day imperial upstart, at risk of being overshadowed by the empires of the past. The origins of Roman *imperium* go back not only to the journeys of Aeneas in the aftermath of the Trojan war but, farther back than that, to a divine decree by Jupiter himself.

As another Latin example of the theme, we can turn to Velleius Paterculus, who ends his *Compendium of Roman History* with a prayer to Jupiter "and all other divinities who have exalted this great empire of Rome to the highest point yet reached on earth" (*Compendium of Roman History* 2.131.1–2). A little earlier he provides an account of King Tigranes's surrender to Pompey. The king declares "that he would not have submitted himself to the alliance of any man but Gnaeus Pompeius, whether Roman or of any other nation [*gentis*] ... [for] there was no disgrace in being beaten by one whom it would be a sin against the gods to defeat" (2.37.3–4).

Perhaps the most lyrical and expansive account, however, is found in this paean of Roman self-praise by Pliny the Elder, which sets the theme of divine providence in the context of a full proclamation of imperial ideology:

> [Rome] is at once the nursling and the mother of all other lands, chosen by the providence of the gods to make heaven itself more glorious, to unite scattered empires [*imperia*], to make manners gentle, to draw together in converse by community of language the jarring and uncouth tongues of so many peoples [*populorum*], to give humanity civilization [*humanitatem humani*], and in a word to become throughout the world the single fatherland of all the nations [*una cunctarum gentium in toto orbe patria*]. (*Natural History* 3.39)

Among the Greek writers, in addition to Aristides, the theme of divine supervision of Rome's rise to power is developed by Plutarch in his treatise *The Fortune of the Romans*, in which he maintains "that the progress of Rome's sovereignty was not brought about by the handiwork and urging of human beings, but was speeded on its way by divine escort and the fair wind of Fortune" (11). To be sure, this divine supervision was not a simple, uncomplicated thing; Plutarch's sub-theme is the question whether Virtue or Fortune was responsible for the creation of "such a mighty power" (1). He concludes that it was, in fact, a joint effort: "it is likely that they [Virtue and Fortune] suspended hostilities and joined forces; and by joining forces they co-operated in completing this most beautiful of human works" (1). More precisely, those whom Fortune used to advance Roman rule were those in whom "Virtue in every form was inborn" (2).[118] It is to be noted in passing that when Plutarch speaks of Virtue, he understands it particularly in

---

118. A little later he can turn the sequence around, with Virtue finishing what Fortune had started: "who would not at once declare touching the birth, the preservation, the

terms of Greek *paideia*, which Rome eventually acquired through contact with the Greeks.[119] For our purposes, we note in particular the place of the nations in his account of the beneficial competition between Fortune and Virtue that resulted in the Roman Empire. Human affairs were marked by strife and disorder "until such time as Rome acquired strength and growth, and had attached to herself not only the nations and peoples [*ethnē kai dēmous*] within her own borders, but also royal dominions of foreign tribes [*allophylous*] beyond the seas," with the result that "the affairs of this vast empire gained stability and security, since the supreme government, which never knew reverse, was brought within an orderly and single cycle of peace" (*The Fortune of the Romans* 2). The measure of Rome's victories was given "not by the multitude of corpses and spoils, but by captive kingdoms, by nations [*ethnesi*] enslaved, by islands and continents added to their mighty realm" (11).

Finally, we return to a passage from Josephus that we encountered already in chapter 3. Josephus at this point has already surrendered to Titus and is now trying to persuade the Jewish defenders of Jerusalem to surrender as well. He declares:

> To scorn meaner masters might, indeed, be legitimate, but not those to whom the universe [*ta panta*] was subject. For what was there that had escaped the Romans, save maybe some spot useless through heat or cold? Fortune, indeed, had from all quarters passed over to them, and God who went the round of

---

nurture, the development of Romulus, that Fortune laid the foundations, and that Virtue finished the building?" (8).

119. In his oration on Marcellus, for example, he describes him as "modest, humane, and so far a lover of Greek learning and discipline as to honour and admire those who excelled therein, although he himself was prevented by his occupations from achieving a knowledge and proficiency here which corresponded to his desires" (*Marcellus* 1). A little later he describes the Romans as a people that "have no barbarous or unnatural practices, but cherish towards their deities those mild and reverent sentiments which especially characterize Greek thought" (*Marcellus* 3). In his *Roman Questions*, he asks, "Why do they suppose Janus to have been two-faced and so represent him in painting and sculpture?" and provides two forms of a Greek answer. While he considers the possibility that Janus was originally a Greek god who "had crossed to Italy and had settled among the savages [*tois barbarois*] there" and who had "changed both his speech and his habits," his second answer is more in keeping with his own views: Janus "changed the people of Italy to another manner and form of life by persuading a people which had formerly made use of wild plants and lawless customs to till the soil and to live under organized government" (22).

The Nations in Roman Imperial Discourse

the nations [*kata ethnos*: "nation by nation"], bringing to each in turn the rod of empire [*tēn archēn*], now rested over Italy. (*Jewish War* 5.367)

While several other elements of imperial ideology come to expression here, what is of particular interest is the idea that Rome now exercised the "rod of empire" through divine choice and agency.[120] Josephus's identification of the agent as Fortune (*tēn tychēn*) serves to reinforce the echoes of imperial themes. At the same time, however, one can perceive an element of reservation, a desire to qualify the Roman claim in a significant, albeit muted, way. Not only is the God who has granted imperial power to the Romans the God of the Jews, but Rome is just one of a sequence of nations to whom God has granted this "rod of empire," each in its turn.[121] To say that God's favor "now" rests on Italy is to take a much more limited position than, say, Virgil's "empire without end." Indeed, as we have already noted, Josephus makes it clear elsewhere that he still anticipates a time when the expectations of Daniel and the other prophets will be realized and when God's favor will rest, fully and finally, on the Jews.[122] Josephus may not reject the Roman map of the nations outright, but he does redraw it in a way that preserves an advantageous position for his own nation.

While this survey of Roman imperial discourse has not been exhaustive, it has been sufficiently detailed to substantiate the claim made at the beginning of this section—namely, that this discourse is thoroughly permeated by the language of the nations. Both as a conceptual category and as a set of living realities, the nations represented a basic element of the Roman Empire and of the ways in which the empire was perceived by Romans and subject peoples alike. By *Roman imperial discourse*, I mean both the basic themes of Roman ideology itself and the enterprise of competitive ethnology, by means of which Romans and subject peoples alike attempted to position themselves in advantageous ways on the map of the populated world and to defend their position against counterclaims and counterversions of the map.

The major portion of this section has consisted of an examination of texts in which the language of nations (especially *gentes*, *nationes*, and *ethnē*) has appeared in articulations of the main themes of Roman imperial ideology:[123] Rome as conqueror; Roman military might as invincible; the universality of the

---

120. Among those other elements, e.g., is the virtual universality of the empire, only the useless territories being excluded.

121. As is clear not only from the work as a whole but also in the recitation of Israel's history that follows (*Jewish War* 5.376–419).

122. See the discussion of *Jewish Antiquities* 4.112–30 and 10.195–210 in ch. 3.

123. Because of this linguistic focus, I have not overburdened this chapter with ref-

empire; Roman clemency in victory; the enlightened, effective, and benevolent character of Roman rule; the various benefits of Roman rule (peace, liberty, material benefactions, the spread of civilization [*humanitas, paideia*]); the empire as willed and foreordained by the gods. Along the way, we have also noted the ways in which Roman writers endeavored to position themselves with respect to the already prevalent map that divided the world into Greeks and barbarians. On the one hand, they presented themselves as inheritors and defenders of Greek tradition and culture, engaged in the spread of Greek *paideia* among the nations; on the other, they conceived of themselves as a distinct people, a people with an ancient history predating that of the Greeks and characterized from the beginning by a willingness to incorporate other nations into a new entity. We have also noted the ways in which Greek authors reflected these self-portraits back to the Romans, but in ways that sometimes retained a privileged position for the Greeks. To the extent to which Rome depicted itself as the successor to the Greeks, this was simple and straightforward: as Greeks, they were the originators, the ones whose *paideia* became Roman *humanitas* (e.g., Plutarch). To the extent to which Rome emphasized distinctive origins and character, these origins could be presented as thoroughly Greek (Polybius). And as we have seen in chapter 3, the Jews had their own ways of claiming a space for themselves on Greek and Roman maps alike.

My approach in this section has been broad and synthetic. While there is certainly a place for a more fine-grained analysis of individual works or authors in order to identify distinctive features of each, I have approached these writings more as individual points of access to a widespread and common discourse—a window opening onto a set of shared assertions and assumptions, claims and counterclaims—about Rome and the nations. This discourse formed part of the environment in which groups of gentile Christ-believers first came into being and then worked to construct a new identity for themselves.

We are now in a position to turn our attention more directly to this process of identity construction and, in particular, to the question of what gentile Christ-believers did with the specific identity—*ethnē*, members of the non-Jewish nations—that was ascribed to them by Jews who were Christ-believers before them. In light of what we have seen in this chapter, a few concluding observations are in order before we do.

First, this ascription of identity did not take place in a vacuum; *ethnē*, along with its singular *ethnos*, was already a lively part of identity discourse in the Roman world of which they were a part. This discourse inevitably helped to shape

---

erences to scholarly discussions of Roman imperial discourse. For this I refer the reader to ch. 2.

the perceptual filters through which they received the more particular identity being ascribed to them. Further, all gentile Christ-believers, actual or potential, belonged to one or other of the *ethnē* that made up the Roman world. Not only was membership in an *ethnos* part of the basic identity structure of each of them, but also these individual ethnic identities were gathered up into the collectivity of *ethnē* that constituted the Roman Empire. More specifically, Roman imperial ideology had identity implications for the nations within the empire. As we have noted in chapter 2, Rome's dual self-presentation—as victor over uncivilized barbarian nations and as civilizing agent conveying *humanitas* to the barbarians—carried with it a range of ascribed identities spread out between two poles: as conquered and subjugated nations, at one end, and as beneficiaries of Rome's civilizing project, at the other.[124] Finally, each *ethnos*, including those from which the various gentile Christ-believers were drawn, had had some degree of experience in competitive ethnology—the attempt to negotiate a recognized and favorable position for themselves on the Roman imperial map.

---

124. While Lopez has done valuable work in highlighting the imperial overtones in Paul's use of the term *ethnē* with respect to his mission, depicting them primarily as conquered nations limits these overtones to an overly restricted set of notes on the scale; see Davina C. Lopez, *Apostle to the Conquered: Reimagining Paul's Mission* (Minneapolis: Fortress, 2008).

CHAPTER 6

Ethnē *and Gentile Christian Identity (Before 135 CE)*

Non-Jews who became Christ-believers in the formative period of the movement found themselves in a social world in which the binary distinction between Jews and non-Jews (*ethnē*: "gentiles") functioned as a foundational element in the discourses of identity. More to the point, they found themselves in a situation where they were identified as belonging to the non-Jewish half of this binary. Jewish believers, those who represented the continuing core of the movement, considered them as *ethnē* and assumed that they would accept this designation (a form of benevolent othering) as part of their basic identity as Christ-believers. To be sure, there were variations (as we have seen) in the way in which this ascribed identity was understood. In situations where it was important to emphasize the difference between gentile Christ-believers and the larger gentile world, *ethnē* could denote an identity that was left behind with their new allegiance to Christ (e.g., "when you were *ethnē*"; 1 Cor 12:2). But this did not erase their basic identity as *ethnē*; while they no longer were part of "the *ethnē* who do not know God" (1 Thess 4:5), from the perspective of Jewish Christ-believers, they were "the *ethnē* who were turning to God" (Acts 15:19). In either case, *ethnē* was an essential element of the new identity ascribed to them.

A lot of scholarly time and energy has been spent on questions having to do with the origins and development of the movement and the place of the gentiles within it. But very little attention has been given to the perceptions of non-Jews themselves.[1] What did non-Jewish Christ-believers think of the identity term?

1. An important recent exception is Cavan W. Concannon, *"When You Were Gentiles":*

Ethnē and Gentile Christian Identity (Before 135 CE)

What did it mean for them? To what extent did they resist the designation? Alternatively, were they prepared to assume it as part of their new identity? If so, how and on what terms? Such questions have undergirded our discussion to this point, and we are now in a position to address them directly.

SETTING UP THE QUESTIONS

At this point, it will be useful to recall briefly some of the discussion carried out in chapter 4; we will look first at the emergence and development of Christ-belief among non-Jews and then at the place of *ethnē* in the identity ascribed to such believers by their Jewish fellow believers.

As we observed in chapter 4, the movement first took shape in the form of a messianic advance party or renewal movement, self-consciously locating itself within the Jewish people as a whole, centered in Jerusalem but appearing as well in other Jewish cities and centers in Judea and environs.[2] While non-Jews soon began to show an interest in the movement and its message, this did not in itself represent any significant departure from patterns found in other Jewish groups and communities. The phenomenon of gentile attraction to Judaism—with resultant groups of sympathizers and, in some cases, proselytes—was apparently a typical feature of Jewish life, and one should not be surprised if Josephus's description of the Jewish community in Antioch—"they were constantly attracting to their religious ceremonies multitudes of Greeks, and these they had in some measure incorporated with themselves" (*Jewish War* 7.45)—was also applicable to Jewish Christ-groups in Antioch and elsewhere. With the emergence of a deliberate and energetic appeal to gentiles more directly, however, and the eventual conception of a universal mission to all the *ethnē*, the Christ-movement began to display a distinctive profile that set it apart from other Jewish groups.

After an initial stage, then, when the movement consisted exclusively of

---

Specters of Ethnicity in Roman Corinth and Paul's Corinthian Correspondence (New Haven: Yale University Press, 2014). Still, he addresses his attention more to ethnic discourse in general than to *ethnē* specifically; see further below.

2. Cf. Shaye J. D. Cohen's description: "After his [Jesus's] death his followers, all of whom were Jews like Jesus himself, constituted a Jewish movement, perhaps a sect, meeting and praying regularly in the Temple of Jerusalem and interacting with other Jewish worshipers. (At least this is the story in the opening chapters of Acts.)"; "The Ways That Parted: Jews, Christians, and Jewish-Christians, ca. 100–150 CE," in *Jews and Christians in the First and Second Centuries: The Interbellum 70–132 CE*, ed. Joshua Schwartz and Peter J. Tomson, CRINT 15 (Leiden: Brill, 2018), 307–39, here 307.

Jewish Christ-groups (especially in Jerusalem),[3] the phenomenon of gentile Christ-belief developed in several forms and configurations: the inclusion of some gentiles within largely Jewish Christ-communities (e.g., Antioch); a more substantial proportion of gentiles within mixed-ethnic communities (e.g., probably Rome, the Matthean church); predominantly gentile communities, but still within a Jerusalem-centered movement (many of Paul's communities). Not discussed directly in chapter 4, but certainly within the scope of our study, are the various forms of distinctively gentile groups that come into view in the second century—proto-orthodox gentile Christianity, the network of Marcionite communities, the various groups traditionally lumped together as Gnosticism, and other variations and subgroups. While there is a certain temporal progression to these developments, one is not to imagine a smooth linear chronological process, especially one in which each stage fades away with the emergence of the next. The point, rather, is that what has traditionally been called "gentile Christianity" existed in several distinct and temporally overlapping forms.

Nevertheless, this reference to temporal progression raises the issue of the parting of the ways, discussed in general terms in chapter 2. While I do not want to constrain this investigation of identity construction among gentile Christ-believers by pressing it into any particular position on the issue, it is nevertheless the case that the two issues are related and thus that any discussion of gentile Christian identity needs to be carried out in conversation with the parting-of-the-ways discussion. For one thing, the eventual emergence of proto-orthodox gentile Christianity as the dominant form of the movement represents one of the two endpoints of the process that parting-of-the-ways theories seek to explain. Even if this two-ways bifurcation is a misleading oversimplification of a much more complex and multistrand process, the emergence of gentile forms of Christ-belief remains a significant aspect and outcome of the process. In addition, however one weighs the various factors that might have contributed to the process (the effect of the Jewish revolts, the theological ideology of the Christ-groups and the exegetical arguments that supported it, and so on), the dramatic geographical spread of gentile forms of the movement and the demographic shift that this represents have to be seen not simply as an aspect and outcome of the process but as significant factors as well.[4]

Without wanting to overestimate the significance of the Jewish revolts,[5] for

---

3. And even then we need to make room for a figure such as Nicolaus (Acts 6:5), a proselyte incorporated into the larger Jewish community in Antioch who subsequently became a member of the Jerusalem Christ-community.

4. On all this, see ch. 2 above.

5. For a caution in this regard, see James Carleton Paget, "Jewish Revolts and Jewish-

purposes of convenience, I will proceed with the discussion of gentile identity construction in three chronological periods.[6] We will deal with the first two in this chapter, leaving the third for chapter 7. (1) Up to the end of the first Jewish revolt (i.e., 70 CE). In this period, the Christ-movement was marked by a clear Jewish center of gravity, both in the role of the Jerusalem church and in the Jewish identity of the leaders. While there is no clearly identifiable gentile literature from this period, the Jewish material (primarily the undisputed letters of Paul and the traditions underlying Acts) provide invaluable, albeit partial, information concerning the origins of the movement, including the inclusion of non-Jews and the use of *ethnē* as an ascribed identity, together with some muffled echoes of what the non-Jews might have thought of the term.[7] (2) Between the destruction of Jerusalem and the Bar Kokhba revolt (i.e., 70–135 CE). This period witnesses the continuation of Jewish and mixed-ethnic forms of the movement, an apparent increase in the number of gentile believers and groups, and the emergence of gentile leaders and literature. Although the sources do not provide much by way of historical information, literature of Jewish provenance provides further evidence for the ways in which gentile inclusion is understood and the use of *ethnē* as an identity term, while gentile literature provides us with glimpses into various gentile Christ-groups and some indication of gentile responses to the use of *ethnē* as an ascribed identity.[8] To a certain extent, the choice of the revolt as a terminus ad quem is a matter of convenience. For our purposes, the significant difference has to do with *ethnē* as an identity term: in contrast to the gentile Christian literature that begins to appear toward the middle of the second century, material from the earlier period (roughly the latter third of the first century and the first third of the second) displays much less interest in the term.[9] While the Bar Kokhba revolt may have been one of the factors contributing to the shift, nothing in the following analysis of the material depends on any assumptions about a causal connection. (3) From Justin to

---

Christian Relations," in Schwartz and Tomson, *Jews and Christians in the First and Second Centuries*, 276–306. He is primarily interested, however, in the extent to which the revolts might have led gentile Christ-believers to distance themselves more emphatically from Jews and the Jewish roots of the movement. The impact on Jewish Christ-believers is a separate matter (partially, at least).

6. Uncertainties about dating in some instances mean that the boundaries between the three periods are not to be drawn too sharply.

7. On the nature and use of this material, see the discussion in ch. 4.

8. For a discussion of Jewish material, see ch. 4. Pertinent gentile material will be identified and discussed later in this chapter.

9. For the most part; Luke-Acts is a prominent exception.

the early third century. This period is marked by the emergence or increasing dominance of several competing forms of distinctly gentile Christ-belief—the followers of Marcion; those groups commonly labeled as Gnostic, associated with teachers such as Basilides, Valentinus, and others; and the proto-orthodox Christians, precursors of the orthodox form of Christianity that later became normative.[10] Marcion shows some interest in the binary distinction between the Jews and the other nations, though discerning his attitude toward the term *ethnē* itself is problematic, given the indirect nature of our evidence. Most of our attention in this period will be given to proto-orthodox literature, which is marked by its more more deliberate engagement with the Greco-Roman world and its thought forms, and to the use of *ethnē* (along with *gentes* and *nationes*) in the context of this engagement.

In chapter 4 we also looked at the term *ethnē* in extant literature produced by Jewish Christ-believers through our periods of interest, with particular attention to its use as an ascribed identity. As we observed, some of the pertinent material simply corresponds to existing Jewish conceptions and attitudes, especially those texts that present the *ethnē* as non-Jewish outsiders, whose practices are sinful and whose way of life is to be avoided.[11] In other material, the *ethnē* appear as objects of mission—disciples in the making (Matt 28:19) and potential Christ-believers to whom the gospel is to be proclaimed.[12] In the case of those non-Jews who respond positively to the mission, we noted two different ways in which *ethnē* functioned as an identity term. On the one hand, it was a continuing aspect of their identity as Christ-believers—"you *ethnē*," as Paul says to the non-Jewish Christ-believers in Rome (Rom 11:13); "to the believers of the *ethnē*," as the Jerusalem apostles wrote in the apostolic decree (Acts 15:23).[13] On the other, it was an identity that was left behind when they became Christ-believers—"when you were *ethnē*," as Paul can also say to his readers in Corinth (1 Cor 12:2).[14] The fact that Paul can use both identity designations with respect to his converts (albeit in different letters) suggests that we need to expect a certain fluidity in the use of *ethnē* as an identity term.

---

10. Among these proto-orthodox groups, both the increased use of *Christian* and *Christianity*, as identity terms, and the normative trajectory of which these groups were a part justify the use of these terms when discussing this period.

11. E.g., Mark 10:42; Matt 6:32; 18:17; Rev 11:2; Didache 1.3.

12. E.g., Rom 1:5; Gal 1:16; 1 Thess 2:16; Mark 13:10; Acts 15:7.

13. Also Rom 1:5–6, 13; Gal 2:11–12; Acts 11:1; Eph 3:1, 6; Pseudo-Clementine *Recognitions* 1.42.1.

14. Also 1 Pet 4:3; Eph 4:17. More generally, in some texts addressed to non-Jewish believers, those outside the *ekklēsia* can be described as *ethnē* (1 Cor 5:1; 1 Pet 2:12).

Ethnē *and Gentile Christian Identity (Before 135 CE)*

Further, we attempted to set this material within some larger patterns of identity construction, by proposing a typology of ways in which Jewish Christ-believers construed their place with respect to Israel as a whole and the terms on which non-Jews were to be included. In constructing this typology, we interpreted the pertinent textual evidence on the basis of the ways in which it might have been read and understood by gentile Christ-believers. That is, we were not concerned to arrive at a single, most probable, originally intended meaning. The resultant typology consisted of three primary types, with several subtypes:

1. Christ as the Messiah appointed for Israel; believing gentiles brought into relationship with Israel as a whole in accordance with already-existing patterns

    1.1 Gentiles as incorporated into Israel as proselytes

    1.2 Gentiles as associated with Israel by adhering to patterns of righteousness appropriate for gentiles

2. Christ as inaugurating a new era of fulfillment for (a remnant within) Israel, which gentiles are invited to share

    2.1 Gentile believers as having been drawn in to share with Israel—or, at least, with the Christ-believing remnant of Israel—in the promised blessings now being accomplished for Israel by its Messiah

    2.2 Gentile believers as having come in to replace that portion of Israel that had failed to respond, or, more generally, as having an opportunity for salvation that has somehow been made possible by that failure

3. Christ as inaugurating a new era and a new Jewish-centered people, in which the traditional distinction between Jews and gentiles has been transcended or overshadowed (though not eliminated)

    3.1 The Mosaic covenant as having had a legitimate preparatory purpose as it was traditionally understood and practiced, though this purpose has now been brought to completion in Christ

    3.2 The nature and purpose of the Mosaic covenant itself as reworked and reinterpreted on the basis of the new belief in Christ

Without repeating the full analysis and descriptions presented in chapter 4, we can provide a brief summary of the distinguishing features of each main type by looking at their different approaches to a number of key elements. In type 1, Christ's role as Messiah is seen primarily as having to do with the future; Jesus is the "messiah appointed for [Israel]" (cf. Acts 3:20), who will carry out his messianic activity at the parousia. The other two types place more emphasis on the present—on the exalted status that Christ is already occupying and the saving role that he is already carrying out.

Related to this are different approaches to the fulfillment of Jewish eschatological expectation. Type 1 is of a piece with other Jewish expectations about "the time of universal restoration that God announced beforehand through his holy prophets" (Acts 3:21), the primary difference being the belief that God has disclosed the identity of the Messiah ahead of time by raising Jesus from the dead.[15] Types 2 and 3 place more emphasis on the present experience of eschatological realities, though type 2 remains closer to traditional expectations of what those realities look like.

With respect to the relationship between Jewish Christ-believers and Israel, in type 1 they function as heralds of the coming Messiah, and thus as a Jewish renewal group standing in full solidarity with Israel as God's covenant people. While type 2 is characterized by more of a remnant stance with respect to Israel as a whole, it is nevertheless marked by a continuing commitment on the part of Jewish Christ-believers to the traditional, covenant-centered identity markers and practice and thus to a continuing distinction from gentile Christ-believers. In type 3, the emphasis falls more on the existence of a new people, consisting of Jewish and gentile believers alike, marked by a new common identity. While this new people is understood to stand in some form of essential continuity with Israel, the emphasis on newness effects and reflects a greater distance from the continuing Jewish people.

Picking up on one aspect of the preceding point, types 1 and 2 both attach ongoing significance to the traditional identity markers and practice of the Mosaic covenant, whereas in type 3, these have been superseded in one way or another by the new realities brought into being through Christ.[16]

Types 2 and 3 are characterized by a commitment to an active mission to non-Jews as an element of the present age of fulfillment, and a willingness to accept them as fellow Christ-believers without requiring them to become full

---

15. This is not to disregard the diverse ways in which this eschatological fulfillment was understood and depicted in Jewish tradition.

16. Type 3 is readily susceptible to the idea of ethnic supersessionism, though a distinction needs to be made between type 3 as a form of identity constructed by Jewish Christ-believers and the transformation that is effected when it is taken over by gentile Christians.

Ethnē and Gentile Christian Identity (Before 135 CE)

torah-observers. In type 1, there was probably the expectation of a significant influx of non-Jews at the time of eschatological fulfillment at the parousia, but this was accompanied by a willingness to accept gentile Christ-believers in the present on the basis of terms and patterns already established within the Jewish community.

Finally, types 1 and 2 maintain a distinction between Jewish and gentile Christ-believers, seeing the community of Jewish believers as standing in an essential relationship with larger Israel and (with the exception of full proselytes) viewing gentile Christ-believers as having come to share in blessings that belonged properly and first of all to Israel. In type 3, the distinctions between Jews and gentiles have been transcended by the new state of affairs brought into being by Christ, which results in a new people consisting of Jews and gentiles on an equal basis. Nevertheless, this new people sees itself as standing in some form of continuity with scriptural Israel and as bearing an identity that is grounded in that of Israel.

In each of these types and subtypes, *ethnē* appears as an aspect of the identities ascribed to non-Jews who come to believe in Christ. In our investigation of how they responded to *ethnē* as an identity term, we need to pay attention not only to the use of the term narrowly considered—in particular, whether it denoted an ongoing identity or an identity left behind—but also to these larger identity structures within which the term was used.

Before turning to the textual evidence directly, however, it will be useful to engage in some preliminary considerations about gentile responses to *ethnē* as an identity term. Here it would be helpful to know something about how non-Jews more generally perceived this ascribed identity. Unfortunately, explicit evidence is lacking. Of course, there is a considerable body of material dealing with Greek and Roman perceptions of Jews and Judaism, most of it made readily accessible by Menahem Stern in his indispensable collection.[17] But while this material touches on many aspects of Jewish life and practice, with a mixture of scorn and admiration,[18] no notice is taken of the distinctively Jewish use of *ethnē* as a term for non-Jewish nations and individuals.[19] To be sure, evidence for proselytes and

---

17. Menahem Stern, *Greek and Latin Authors on Jews and Judaism*, 3 vols. (Jerusalem: Israel Academy of Sciences and Humanities, 1974–84).

18. For detailed studies, see especially John G. Gager, *The Origins of Anti-Semitism* (Oxford: Oxford University Press, 1983); Louis H. Feldman, *Jew and Gentile in the Ancient World: Attitudes and Interactions from Alexander to Justinian* (Princeton: Princeton University Press, 1993); Peter Schäfer, *Judeophobia: Attitudes toward the Jews in the Ancient World* (Cambridge, MA: Harvard University Press, 1997); Benjamin H. Isaac, *The Invention of Racism in Classical Antiquity* (Princeton: Princeton University Press, 2004).

19. Nothing appears in Stern's collection, and I have not discovered anything else in my research into the use of the pertinent terms (*ethnē, gentes, nationes,* etc.).

sympathizers indicates that a considerable number of non-Jews not only became aware of the usage but also were able to come to some sort of terms with it. To go further, however, and to ask about how they did this or what awareness of the term there might have been among non-Jews more generally would take us beyond the available evidence.

Despite the lack of evidence, however, it will be useful to engage in some a priori considerations about gentile responses to *ethnē* as an identity term. On the one hand, we can take it as probable that non-Jews would have found the term off-putting and would have been reluctant to accept it as an ascribed identity. Being identified as some different group's other is not something that is readily embraced. As a Jewish designation for outsiders, the descriptor *ethnē* would have had little more natural appeal for non-Jews than *barbarian* would have had for non-Greeks.

In addition, in contrast to *barbaros*, this use of *ethnē* would have struck non-Jews as quite odd. Unlike *barbaros*, a univocal term originally coined for the purpose of denoting non-Greeks, *ethnē* and its singular *ethnos* were common everyday terms, used to denote ethnic people groups. The use of *ethnē* to denote every ethnic people group but one would have gone against the linguistic grain.[20]

Further, as we have already observed, by the first century CE, the usage had undergone a further stage of development in that it came to denote not only non-Jewish people groups (nations) but also multiplicities of non-Jewish individuals. This development produced an odd disjunction between the singular *ethnos* and the plural *ethnē*. Since *ethnos* in its basic sense referred to an ethnic people group, this in-group use of the plural to denote individuals would have struck outsiders as curious at best. If Peter was customarily eating with *ethnē* in Antioch (Gal 2:12), how would one describe a situation where he was eating with one of them? While *ethnē* functioned as the plural of *ethnos* when ethnic people groups were in view, *ethnos* could hardly serve as the singular of *ethnē* when it denoted a group of non-Jewish individuals.[21] The oddness of the term would no doubt have been off-putting for many non-Jews.

---

20. Justin acknowledges the oddness in his *First Apology* when, after claiming that "the Gentile Christians [*tous ex ethnōn . . . Christianous*] are more numerous and true than those from among the Jews and the Samaritans," he adds a word of explanation: "For all the other human races are called Gentiles [*ethnē*] by the prophetic Spirit, but the Jewish and Samaritan [races] are called the tribe [*phylon*] of Israel and the house of Jacob" (53). I have not been able to find any analogous evidence among earlier Christian or Greco-Roman sources, but the usage would have struck most outsiders as odd.

21. To be sure, there were work-arounds—e.g., *allophylos* (Acts 10:28); *ethnikos* (Matt 18:17); *Hēllēn* (Gal 2:3). But these simply underlined the oddness of the plural.

Ethnē and Gentile Christian Identity (Before 135 CE)

On the other hand, however, and thinking more directly of potential converts, these considerations would not necessarily have been determinative. Any non-Jews who had become proselytes to Judaism or members of Christ-groups had, in so doing, already demonstrated a willingness to undertake a significant reconfiguration of their identities. Despite the oddness of the term *ethnē*, and even if it might have had an initially alienating effect, it is not unreasonable to expect that they would have been predisposed to accept this new identity as something that came with the territory.

We can find some additional support for this reasonable expectation from contemporary social-scientific studies of conversion.[22] Seen from one perspective, conversion is a process by which a person is socialized into a new group. Or if this puts it too passively, a convert is one who has decided to take the necessary steps to become part of a new group and, in so doing, has internalized essential aspects of the group's identity. Part of this internalization involves what Snow and Machalek call a "biographical reconstruction," a retrospective version of the convert's own life experience shaped by the "universe of discourse" that embodies the assumptions and values of the new group to which they now belong.[23] Cross-cultural studies of conversion narratives have noted not only the considerable variation among them but also, and more importantly, the extent to which they conform to the narrative patterns characteristic of the particular groups into which they have converted. In other words, the variations in such narratives are not idiosyncratic but group-specific. In Lewis Rambo's words, "conversion is what a particular group says it is."[24] In turn, what the group "says it is" tends to shape a convert's own account of the process and thus also the new

---

22. For a significant full-length treatment, see Lewis R. Rambo, *Understanding Religious Conversion* (New Haven: Yale University Press, 1993); see also John Lofland and Rodney Stark, "Becoming a World-Saver: A Theory of Conversion to a Deviant Perspective," *American Sociological Review* 30 (1965): 862–75; David A. Snow and Cynthia L. Phillips, "The Lofland-Stark Conversion Model: A Critical Reassessment," *Social Problems* 27 (1980): 430–47; David A. Snow and Richard Machalek, "The Convert as a Social Type," in *Sociological Theory*, ed. Randall Collins (San Francisco: Jossey-Bass, 1983), 259–89; Snow and Machalek, "The Sociology of Conversion," *Annual Review of Sociology* 10 (1984): 167–90. Despite its specifically Christian orientation, helpful surveys can be found in H. Newton Malony and Samuel Southard, eds., *Handbook of Religious Conversion* (Birmingham, AL: Religious Education Press, 1992), especially Lewis R. Rambo, "The Psychology of Conversion," 159–77, and William Sims Bainbridge, "The Sociology of Conversion," 178–91.

23. Snow and Machalek, "Convert as a Social Type," 266–69.

24. Rambo, "Psychology of Conversion," 160.

reconstructed identity that has been assumed.[25] Converts, by the very experience of conversion, become inclined and motivated to adopt the identity structures of the group into which they are being incorporated and to reconfigure their previous identity accordingly.

With respect to non-Jewish converts in the early stages of the movement, then, we can reasonably expect that they would have been prepared to accept the characterization of them as *ethnē* and to incorporate this ascribed identity, in some manner, into the new version of themselves that they had come to accept. To be sure, there was an element of fluidity in the manner in which the ascribed identity was formulated: an identity that had been left behind in the turn to Christ, in one formulation, and an identity that continued to define them as (a distinct group of) Christ-believers, in another. However, even in the first case, *ethnē* constitutes an enduring aspect—albeit in a negative form—of the new identity taken on in the turn to Christ. It is also worth noting in passing that this new identity did not displace anyone's primary ethnic identity; non-Jewish believers continued to be identified as Cyreneans, Galatians, Macedonians, Bithynians, and so on. As with *barbaros*, *ethnē* functioned as a kind of transethnic or hyperethnic category.

We can buttress and amplify this insight from the study of conversion by placing it within the larger discussion of social identity that was summarized in chapter 2. There we began with the seminal work of Fredrik Barth on ethnicity and his argument—now widely accepted—that ethnic identity needs to be seen more as the negotiated result of a process of social construction than as an objective reality produced naturally by a set of contributing factors (genealogical descent, language, land, way of life, religious practice, political organization, shared history).[26] To be sure, group members often perceive or portray their ethnic identity as fixed and immutable, but studies of the ways in which these

---

25. Brian Taylor, "Recollection and Membership: Converts' Talk and the Ratiocination of Commonality," *Sociology* 12 (1978): 316–24; see also Taylor, "Conversion and Cognition: An Area for Empirical Study in the Micro-Sociology of Religious Knowledge," *Social Compass* 23 (1976): 5–22; Paula Fredriksen, "Paul and Augustine: Conversion Narratives, Orthodox Traditions and the Retrospective Self," *JTS* 37 (1986): 3–34; Beverly Roberts Gaventa, *From Darkness to Light: Aspects of Conversion in the New Testament* (Philadelphia: Fortress, 1986), 5–7; Alan F. Segal, *Paul the Convert: The Apostolate and Apostasy of Saul the Pharisee* (New Haven: Yale University Press, 1990), 27–30.

26. The key conceptions were set out in the introductory chapter of Fredrik Barth, ed., *Ethnic Groups and Boundaries: The Social Organization of Culture Difference* (Boston: Little, Brown, 1969), and developed in subsequent work; see Fredrik Barth, *Process and Form in Social Life: Selected Essays of Fredrik Barth* (London: Routledge & Kegan Paul, 1981).

Ethnē and Gentile Christian Identity (Before 135 CE)

factors shift and undergo redefinition over time betray the extent to which such perceptions or portrayals themselves are part of the process by which such identity is constructed and maintained.

Then we noted how this understanding of ethnicity connected with the study of social identity more generally, looking in particular at the work of Richard Jenkins.[27] One useful aspect of his work has to do with externally imposed identities. Drawing on Marx's distinction between "groups" and "categories," Jenkins makes a distinction between "categorization," identities ascribed from without, and "group identification," internally constructed self-definitions.[28] Part of the process of self-definition involves the extent to which group members are willing to internalize the externally ascribed categories. If the categories are negative, the effectiveness of the ascription depends on the power of those doing the ascribing and the extent to which the category corresponds to the social realities of the recipients.[29] But Jenkins observes that the theory can be applied to positive instances as well. In such cases—which would include the ascription of the category *ethnē* to non-Jewish Christ-believers—the willingness of recipients to internalize such categories would depend on the degree of authority they were prepared to grant to those doing the ascribing and on the degree to which the category corresponded with aspects of their own social realities. In the early stages of the movement, both factors were such as to foster a willingness on the part of non-Jewish converts to accept and internalize the ascribed identity.

However, while this might have been the case in the early stages of the movement, when Jewish Christ-believers constituted the great majority and were thus in a position to shape the new identities being assumed by (the relatively few) non-Jewish Christ-believers, this was not the only demographic configuration during our period of interest. In the early stages, *ethnē* as an ascribed identity could simply be taken for granted; it was simply a given part of the identity transformation that a non-Jew underwent in becoming part of a Christ-group.

---

27. Especially in his book *Social Identity*, now in a fourth edition: Richard Jenkins, *Social Identity*, 4th ed. (New York: Routledge, 2014).

28. See Jenkins, *Social Identity*, 45–47, and ch. 9 ("Groups and Categories").

29. Jenkins makes use of social deviance theory here: "Internalisation may occur if an individual is authoritatively labelled within an appropriate institutional setting.... The capacity of authoritatively applied identification to constitute or influence individual experience affects whether or not individuals internalise the label(s) concerned. This is a matter of whose definition of the situation *counts* (put crudely, power). Identification by others has *consequences*"; *Social Identity*, 44–45.

But what about situations where gentiles constituted a significant proportion of a group or where a group was predominantly or completely gentile? To draw in another aspect of social identity theory, what about situations where the primary boundary experienced by gentile Christ-believers was not the one differentiating themselves from Jews and Jewish Christ-believers but the one between them and the wider Greco-Roman world?[30]

In such situations, *ethnē* in its distinctively Jewish sense could well lose much of its taken-for-granted force. More in control of their own identity negotiation, gentile Christians might be prepared to let it fall into disuse or, at least, to prefer other more salient terms, unless there were specific reasons to retain it. Usefulness, rather than givenness, might become the determining factor. Here is where the use of the term in the wider Greco-Roman world, especially in Roman imperial discourse, will become important. As we have already seen in our preliminary foray into the work of Eusebius (ch. 1), *ethnē* became very useful as an identity term as gentile Christianity negotiated social space for itself in the Greco-Roman world. We will explore this in more detail as we proceed (especially in ch. 7).

At this point, we turn from a priori and theoretical considerations to the textual evidence itself. What we might expect to have been the case is one thing, evidence is quite another. Still, social-scientific models can help us look at the evidence we do have in new ways and, perhaps, wring new information from it.

ETHNĒ AND IDENTITY: UP TO 70 CE

In the first stage of our investigation, from the beginnings of the movement up to the Jewish revolt and the destruction of the Jerusalem temple in 70 CE, what evidence we have that pertains to non-Jewish Christ-believers is indirect, stemming from Jewish sources. Of the Jewish material identified in chapter 4, we can have a good measure of confidence in assigning the following to this period: the undisputed letters of Paul; the document Q; other pre-Gospels traditions; the Gospel of Mark (in approximate terms); and the traditions utilized in Acts.[31] Of

---

30. As Jenkins puts it, "the internal and external moments of the process of collective identification [i.e., respectively, "group identification" and "categorisation"] ... take place most definitively—although not only—at the boundaries of identification"; *Social Identity*, 160. It is when a group is confronted with a boundary between itself and some significant other that issues of identity become pressing and need to be negotiated.

31. The Gospel of Mark is usually dated to a few years on either side of 70 CE.

this list, while the material pertaining to the Gospels indicates that *ethnē* was used by Jewish Christ-believers with reference to non-Jews, it contains nothing that might reflect gentile attitudes toward *ethnē* as an ascribed identity and thus is of little help. Gentile Christ-believers and groups do come into view, however, in the Pauline epistles and the traditional material in Acts, which thus provide us with some material to go on. Even so, they do not offer any direct access to the perceptions of the gentile believers themselves. The best we can do is to listen in on the conversations reflected in the letters and in the narrative material, with one ear attuned to the muffled sounds that might be audible from the other end, and with the other to the range of ways in which Jewish Christ-believers conceived of the terms on which non-Jews were to be included.

This exercise can draw some inspiration from a number of other investigations that have attempted, through creative listening, to discern and recover what Concannon calls the "spectral voices" that speak only faintly from the margins of our texts.[32] Such investigations usually draw on available literary, inscriptional, and archaeological material to reconstruct the social environments assumed and addressed by the texts, and then use these reconstructions as a means of amplifying these faintly heard voices.[33] While such approaches have been pioneered by feminist scholars,[34] several more recent studies have focused on issues of ethnicity and identity.[35] Some of this work, however, is deliberately speculative—using imaginative reconstructions of possible alternative voices to produce thicker and more layered understandings of a particular text or to decenter the normative voice of the text.[36] While such reconstructions can have a certain heuristic value, our specific focus here—on what the texts can reveal about the identity

---

32. Concannon, *"When You Were Gentiles"*, e.g., xii.

33. E.g., Peter S. Oakes, *Reading Romans in Pompeii: Paul's Letter at Ground Level* (Minneapolis: Fortress, 2009).

34. Especially Elisabeth Schüssler Fiorenza, *In Memory of Her: A Feminist Theological Reconstruction of Early Christian Beginnings* (New York: Crossroad, 1983), and, on a more focused topic, Antoinette Clark Wire, *The Corinthian Women Prophets: A Reconstruction through Paul's Rhetoric* (Minneapolis: Fortress, 1990).

35. In addition to Concannon (*"When You Were Gentiles"*), see Davina C. Lopez, *Apostle to the Conquered: Reimagining Paul's Mission* (Minneapolis: Fortress, 2008), and Brigitte Kahl, *Galatians Re-imagined: Reading with the Eyes of the Vanquished* (Minneapolis: Fortress, 2010).

36. "I make no presumptions that these conjurings were the 'real' Corinthians.... The Corinthians whom I have sought to conjure in this book are possibilities that may have been and might yet be, possibilities that beg to be given even spectral bodies as some kind of existence. It is my hope that what amounts to a number of séances might have conjured for the reader new ways of thinking of what might have been, what could be,

perceptions of non-Jewish Christ-believers—requires us rather to look for the probable than to imagine the possible. We will concentrate, then, on material that provides us with more probable indications of how gentile Christ-believers responded to *ethnē* as an identity term.

As we proceed, two clusters of material will be of particular interest. One of these is focused on Paul's rebuke of apparently protosupersessionistic attitudes among those whom he addresses as "you *ethnē*" (Rom 11:13–32). The other has to do with indications (from Galatians especially) that some gentile believers were attracted by the invitation to undergo circumcision and thus to cross over the line dividing the *ethnē* from the Jews. Between them, they provide evidence for two quite different responses to the ascribed identity. By so doing, they also alert us to the possibility of other responses lying in between the two.

Before looking at these two cases directly, however, we can begin with some more general observations. First, Paul clearly assumes that his gentile readers are familiar with the term *ethnē* in its distinctively Jewish sense and are prepared to accept it as part of their new identity. This plural form appears some forty-one times in the seven undisputed letters: Romans (twenty-five times);[37] 1 Corinthians (three); 2 Corinthians (one); Galatians (ten); 1 Thessalonians (two). The matter-of-fact way in which he uses it suggests strongly that it was a familiar element of their new vocabulary as Christ-believers. In the autobiographical section of his epistle to the Galatians, for example, Paul not only uses *ethnē* with respect to his apostolic call ("God . . . called me . . . so that I might proclaim [his Son] among the *ethnē*"; 1:15–16) and preaching ("the gospel that I proclaim among the *ethnē*"; 2:2), with the evident assumption that the term was familiar, but he also assumes that his readers would understand themselves to be the recipients of this proclamation ("so that the truth of the gospel might always remain with you"; 2:5). His usage here and elsewhere implies that he had used the term freely in his initial preaching and his ongoing face-to-face encounters with the new believers.

In addition, Paul's letters indicate that *ethnē* was common currency in *ekklēsiai* founded by others. In Galatians, the account of his interactions with James, John, and Peter in Jerusalem (2:1–10), and with Peter and Barnabas in Antioch (2:11–14), suggests strongly that the term was already used among the communities in Jerusalem and Antioch. Further, his letter to the Romans, which contains more occurrences of *ethnē* than any of the other letters that bear his name, was

---

and what should be different in how we tell our histories of earliest Christianity, of Paul, and of the Corinthians"; Concannon, *"When You Were Gentiles"*, 172.

37. This figure excludes the occurrence in Rom 16:26, which is probably part of a later non-Pauline addendum.

Ethnē and Gentile Christian Identity (Before 135 CE)

addressed to a group that was not founded by him and that he had not yet visited. Not only does *ethnē* feature prominently in the argument of the letter, but he also addresses his readers directly as "you *ethnē*" in 11:13 and, by implication, in 1:5-6 and 1:13 as well. Clearly, he assumes that the believers in Rome are also familiar with the term. Further, eight of the occurrences of *ethnē* are in scriptural quotations, which indicates that he assumes an awareness of Israel's Scriptures as well. While he has not had direct experience of the community, he apparently knows enough about it (as suggested by his list of greetings in ch. 16) that we can take his assumptions as well founded. In other words, the epistle to the Romans adds to the evidence suggesting that the term was known and used more widely among non-Jewish Christ-groups.

Further, there is no hint in any of Paul's letters that the term was controversial or that the ascribed identity was resisted. Nowhere does Paul give any indication that he needs to explain the term or defend its use. Not only was the term familiar among gentile Christ-believers, but it seems to have been acceptable as an identity term as well.

Turning to the Acts of the Apostles, here the evidence is less compelling, partly because we cannot be certain of the nature and extent of its pre-70 CE sources;[38] for the most part, Acts will come into our discussion as a piece of post-70 gentile literature. Still, there are two narrative passages to be considered, each of which portrays Jewish Christ-believers as using *ethnē* in the context of an address to non-Jews, with some indication of a positive gentile response.[39]

One of these has to do with the visit of Paul and Barnabas to Pisidian Antioch, a visit that involved an initial sermon to a mixed synagogue audience ("Israelites and those who fear God"; 13:16) and a subsequent encounter the following Sabbath. In this second incident (13:44-52), after experiencing opposition from Jewish members of the synagogue, Paul declares that since they had rejected "the word of God," "we are now turning to the *ethnē*," punctuating the declaration with a quotation of Isa 49:6 ("I have set you to be a light for the *ethnē*"). The narrative continues: "When the *ethnē* heard this, they were glad and praised the word of the Lord" (13:48).[40] It would be rash, however, to build anything on this narrative detail. For one thing, the enthusiastic response of the

---

38. See the discussion in ch. 4 above.

39. In the account of Cornelius's encounter with Peter (Acts 10), although *ethnē* is present in the narrator's discourse (10:45), it is absent from the dialogue among the characters themselves.

40. At the beginning of the narrative, the non-Jews are identified as "those who fear [*hoi phoboumenoi*] God" (13:16); at the end of the first sermon, they are described instead as "devout proselytes [*tōn sebomenōn prosēlytōn*]" (13:43). For a discussion of this puzzling

non-Jewish hearers would tell us little about their attitude toward the term itself. But more importantly, the sequence that plays out in the narrative—preaching to Jews, opposition, turning to the *ethnē*—is a characteristic Lukan pattern (cf. 18:5–6; 28:17–28) and thus cannot be attributed to traditional material with any confidence.

We might be on more solid ground, however, with the account of the apostolic decree—the letter written by the Jerusalem apostles and elders to the "brothers from the *ethnē* in Antioch and Syria and Cilicia" (Acts 15:23), conveying the decision that was made concerning gentile believers, circumcision, and the law of Moses. Aspects of the letter as it is found here (15:23–29) suggest that it was drawn, in whole or in part, from traditional material.[41] Again, we probably cannot build anything on Luke's description of the reception of the letter by the Antioch believers ("they rejoiced at the exhortation"; 15:31). However, if Luke's account draws on traditional material, this might suggest that an original letter was preserved by the congregations addressed, which could imply a general acceptance of *ethnē* as an identity term.

At a general level, then, we are justified in expecting a broad, low-level acceptance of the term by non-Jewish believers as an aspect of their identity. This is suggested by studies of the phenomenon of conversion itself and is probably confirmed by the material we have examined from Paul's letters and Acts.

In addition to this basic, low-level acceptance of the term, Paul's letters contain material that enables us to hear, in a muffled sort of way, the voices of some gentile believers themselves, as they speak about their own identity with respect to Jewish Christ-believers. What emerges is evidence for two more specific—and quite different—responses to *ethnē* as an identity term.

The first set of voices belongs to those in Galatia who were being encouraged by rival teachers to allow themselves to be circumcised and thus to become full members of Abraham's family of descendants. In other words, they were being encouraged to become proselytes. While the related account in Acts 15 helps put the Galatian situation into the context of a larger enterprise and debate, what sets Galatians apart is the indication that some were finding the arguments per-

---

shift, see Terence L. Donaldson, *Judaism and the Gentiles: Jewish Patterns of Universalism (to 135 CE)* (Waco, TX: Baylor University Press, 2007), 426–29.

41. E.g., the address (Antioch, Syria, Cilicia), which, on the one hand, does not correspond well with the geography of the narrative to this point and which, on the other, is much more limited in scope than Luke's universal vision (cf. "the ends of the earth"; Acts 1:8); the specific requirements of the decree (15:29), which are not thematized by Luke elsewhere. See the discussion in C. K. Barrett, *A Critical and Exegetical Commentary on the Acts of the Apostles*, ICC (Edinburgh: T&T Clark, 1994–98), 2:709–11.

Ethnē *and Gentile Christian Identity (Before 135 CE)*

suasive. In Acts, the "teaching" that was brought by "certain individuals from Judea" (15:1) is presented simply as a burdensome imposition.[42] That the gentile believers in Antioch did not respond positively to this teaching (at least in the view of the author) can be inferred from the statement that they "rejoiced" at the (less burdensome) news contained in the letter from the Jerusalem apostles and elders (15:31).[43] In Galatians, by contrast, although the gentile believers have not yet fully succumbed to the arguments of the rival teachers—they have not yet "let [themselves] be circumcised" (5:2)—it is clear that the prospect is appealing,[44] that they desire to take this step,[45] and that they are already turning in that direction.[46]

---

42. Cf. "a yoke that neither our ancestors nor we have been able to bear" (v. 10); "to impose on you no further burden than these essentials" (v. 28).

43. Cf. 15:28, where the letter conveys the decision "to impose on you no further burden than these essentials."

44. For an illuminating reconstruction of the perspective of the rival teachers and of the place of the *ethnē* in their own version of the gospel (with particular attention to the universal role of the torah and the significance of Abraham as the first proselyte), see J. Louis Martyn, *Galatians: A New Translation with Introduction and Commentary*, AB (New York: Doubleday, 1997), 120–26.

Fredriksen has shed light on one aspect of this appeal to become circumcised, by delineating the ambiguous situation in which gentile Christ-believers found themselves. From the beginning, gentiles who wanted to become Christ-believers were required to dissociate themselves from the worship of the array of pagan gods. Such worship was widely regarded as an essential aspect of human existence and ethnic identity, and such atheistic refusal to honor the gods was viewed with deep suspicion. The only exception were the Jews, with their exclusive devotion to their own ethnic god—an exception that was eventually accepted by outsiders as a tolerable aspect of ancestral tradition. Proselytism—"a pagan's 'becoming' a Jew"—also came to be "tolerated, if resented, because Judaism itself was a familiar point on the urban landscape." But in becoming Christ-believers, non-Jews adopted a similar anomalous religious exclusiveness while remaining non-Jews—a practice that both disrupted the social order and threatened to arouse the anger of the gods. In such a situation, identifying fully with the Jewish people could readily become an attractive option. See Paula Fredriksen, *Paul: The Pagans' Apostle* (New Haven: Yale University Press, 2017), 88–93 and passim; the quotations are from p. 90. See also James B. Rives, "Animal Sacrifice and Political Identity in Rome and Judea," in *Jews and Christians in the First and Second Centuries: How to Write Their History*, ed. Peter J. Tomson and Joshua Schwartz, CRINT 13 (Leiden: Brill, 2014), 105–25.

45. "You want [*thelete*] to be enslaved [to the elemental spirits] again?" (4:9); "you who desire [*thelontes*] to be subject to the law" (4:21).

46. "You are deserting the one who called you ... and are turning to a different gospel" (1:6); "Who has bewitched you?" (3:1); "Having started with the Spirit, are you now

As he attempts to dissuade them from taking this decisive step, Paul frames his argument in terms of the sharp binary between Jews and gentiles. The term *ethnē* appears ten times in the first three chapters, half of the time in explicit contrast with one Jewish identity term or another.[47] In other words, Paul frames their contemplated action as a desire to abandon one identity (as *ethnē*) for another (as *Ioudaioi*). Since it is almost certain that the Galatian Christ-believers had become familiar with the binary from the outset of their relationship with Paul, there is every reason to expect that they would have already understood their situation in these terms. That is, even in their desire to Judaize and thus to abandon their identity as *ethnē*, they had accepted and internalized the ascribed identity.

The other case to be considered here comes into view in Rom 11, where Paul, addressing himself to "you *ethnē* (11:13)," rebukes some of them for what could be described as protosupersessionistic attitudes. After he has introduced the image of Israel as an olive tree, with some natural (Jewish) branches broken off and a wild (gentile) olive shoot having been grafted in, he gives voice to a gentile interlocutor: "You will say, 'Branches were broken off so that I might be grafted in'" (11:13).[48] We have already had occasion to look at this passage, in our attempt to construct a typology of the different ways in which Jewish Christ-believers conceived of the inclusion of non-Jews within the new movement.[49] There is no need to repeat what was said there about Paul's rebuke of the position or of his own understanding concerning the connection between the breaking off of some branches and the ingrafting of another. What is important here is that he can conceive of someone, speaking on behalf of gentile believers as a whole, as adopting an attitude of superiority toward Jewish outsiders and as holding to a rejection-replacement understanding of their own position as gentile Christ-believers.

It is not necessary to see this position as something developed in toto in a non-Jewish context. As we observed as part of the typology developed in chapter 4, it is probable that some Jewish Christ-believers, seeing themselves as constituting a remnant within Israel (in distinction from other Jews who had refused to listen to the promised prophet like Moses [cf. Acts 3:22–24]), also saw gentile Christ-believers as constituting a replacement for those within Israel who had

---

ending with the flesh?" (3:3); "how can you turn back again to the weak and beggarly elemental spirits?" (4:9).

47. "The circumcised" (2:8, 9); "those of the circumcised" (2:12); "Jews" (2:14, 15). In 2:14 the adverb *ethnikōs* is thrown in for good measure.

48. Here in contrast to the plural of v. 13 ("you *ethnē*"), we encounter the singular (*ereis*, "You will say"); cf. the singular, "you [*sy*], a wild olive shoot," in v. 17.

49. See ch. 4 above.

Ethnē and Gentile Christian Identity (Before 135 CE)

failed to believe. An important element of this type, however, was the essential role assigned to Jewish Christ-believers as the remnant of Israel for whom the messianic promises were being fulfilled. What is new in Rom 11 is the evidence that this model was being adopted enthusiastically by non-Jews who were also giving it an arrogant, anti-Jewish spin, a harbinger of the exclusively gentile Christian form of supersessionism that developed later.

To be sure, it is Paul himself who identifies those who hold this position as *ethnē*; the passage does not provide us with explicit evidence that they would have formulated the position in these terms. Further, we cannot be certain that this position was actually held by a group of non-Jewish Christ-believers in Rome. Nevertheless, for his argument to be effective, the profile of the non-Jewish interlocutor must at least have been recognizable to his intended readers. What the passage does suggest, then, is that his readers were aware of non-Jewish Christ-believers who perceived themselves as constituting a distinct group in contrast to the Jews. The most readily available term for such a self-perception was *ethnē*.

Paul's letters, then, provide us with evidence for two quite contrasting responses on the part of gentile Christ-believers to *ethnē* as an ascribed identity—one in which the term was enthusiastically adopted, together with a degree of arrogant superiority toward (unbelieving) Jews, and another in which the identity category was accepted, but with a desire to leave it behind in favor of a fully Jewish identity. While we may well wish that more gentile voices had been preserved from this early period, the fact that those to which we do have access represent such contrasting positions is valuable in itself. If the extremes were present, we can be fairly confident that intervening positions were represented as well.

Ethnē and Identity: Between the Destruction of Jerusalem and the Bar Kokhba Revolt

This period witnesses the continuation of Jewish and mixed-ethnic forms of the movement, an apparent increase in the number of gentile believers and groups, and the emergence of gentile leaders and literature. In examining the literature that can be dated to this period (with varying levels of confidence), it is not always an easy task to identify the ethnicity of the authors—that is, whether authors are Jewish or non-Jewish. Indeed, in some cases (especially the Pastoral Epistles), it is striking to note how often standard reference works contain lengthy discussions of authorship that decide in favor of pseudonymity, but that then have nothing to say about the ethnic identity of the actual author. In any case, literature that, in my opinion, probably emanated from gentile circles during this period and that uses the term *ethnē* in pertinent ways is represented primarily by the following: Luke-Acts, 1 Timothy, 2 Timothy, 1 Clement, 2 Clement, the letters of Ignatius, the letter of Polycarp to the Philippians, the Epistle of Barnabas, the Shepherd of Hermas, and the Apology of Aristides.

Here we are interested in the use of *ethnē*—especially in its particular sense as a denotation for non-Jewish nations—in connection with questions of gentile Christian self-definition. How did gentile Christ-believers understand their emergence as a distinct entity, in relation to scriptural Israel, on the one hand, and present-day Jews (including Jewish Christ-believers), on the other, and what use did they make of the identifier *ethnē*?[50] Speaking in broad and general terms, with the exception of Luke-Acts, this literature for the most part does not display very much in the way of sustained, thematic interest in *ethnē* as an identity term, especially as an aspect of Christian identity. Still, in none of the occurrences is *ethnē* used in simply trivial or inconsequential ways. In each case, we can discern some connection to the themes and identity concerns of the texts and, in varying degrees, to questions concerning gentile Christian identity.

The details will emerge as we look at the pieces of literature one by one. While the writings do not fall into any readily apparent sequence, the usage that appears in the greatest number of texts (six) is that of an identity term for outsiders.[51] We will begin here, dealing with the writings in a rough order of increasing interest in the identity questions that concern us.[52] Then we will go on to the remaining writings, in the same order.[53]

---

50. This is a briefer and more gentile-specific version of the identity indices set out in ch. 4, which were formulated as follows: (1) a range of conceptions concerning the nature and purpose of scriptural Israel and its religion, as understood in relation with new beliefs about Christ and his significance; (2) a range of conceptions concerning the place and status of the continuing Jewish people and their religion; and (3) a range of conceptions concerning the place and status of Jewish and gentile believers within groups of Christ-believers of varying ethnic composition.

51. In many instances, for example, it is difficult to date the material with any confidence and, in any case, any attempt to trace lines of development would take us too far afield.

52. We begin with two writings in which *ethnē* is used only with reference to outsiders (Polycarp, *To the Philippians*, 2 Clement) and then go on to those in which the term is used in more than one way (Shepherd of Hermas, Ignatius, 1 Clement, Epistle of Barnabas). In addition to these writings, *ethnikos* appears once in the Johannine epistles (3 John 7) as a term for outsiders. The striking lack of interest in Jewish issues, which contrasts sharply with the Fourth Gospel, might suggest gentile authorship for the epistles. But since *ethnē* does not appear, and since 3 John 7 would not add much to the discussion here, it will be left out of account.

53. 1 Timothy, 2 Timothy, Apology of Aristides, Luke-Acts.

Ethnē and Gentile Christian Identity (Before 135 CE)

We begin with Polycarp and his letter *To the Philippians*. Unlike some of the other authors whose work we will examine here, we have a considerable body of information about Polycarp, including his letter to the church in Philippi, a letter to him by Ignatius, an account of his martyrdom written under the aegis of his own church in Smyrna, and various comments by other early writers (Ignatius, Irenaeus, Tertullian, Eusebius).[54] While this material contains no explicit indication of his ethnic origins, there is nothing at all to suggest that he might have been a Jewish Christ-believer. The picture that emerges in the Martyrdom of Polycarp—where Polycarp and his followers are identified as "Christians," in sharp contradistinction both to "the Jews" and to the polytheistic *ethnē*—no doubt provides us with an accurate picture of his social location and sense of identity.[55] As bishop of Smyrna, with a much wider sphere of influence, Polycarp was firmly embedded in the emerging proto-orthodox form of gentile Christianity.

Polycarp's letter to the Philippian church falls into two parts, in two different ways. Linguistically, all of the extant Greek manuscripts end abruptly at the end of chapter 9.[56] The remainder of the letter is available in a Latin version, itself a translation of the Greek. With respect to content, the letter as it has survived seems to represent the conflation of two separate letters to the Philippian church, written by Polycarp at different times. In chapter 9, Polycarp includes Ignatius in a list of those (including "Paul himself and the other apostles") who have suffered and died and who are now "in the place they deserved, with the Lord, with whom they also suffered" (9.2). In chapter 13, however, Ignatius is apparently still alive. Polycarp has received a letter from him, in which he requests that Polycarp take charge of sending on to Syria what he (Ignatius) had written to the Philippians (13.1). After discussing this request, Polycarp goes on to ask whether they can provide him with any news "about Ignatius and those who are with him" (13.2), which implies that Ignatius was still alive or, at least, that Polycarp assumed this to be the case.

Since the pioneering work of Harrison in 1936, the dominant scholarly opinion has been that the extant form of the text contains two epistles—one (chs. 13–14) written while Ignatius was still on his way to Rome (ca. 110 CE), the

---

54. For a comprehensive listing of material, see Paul Hartog, ed., *Polycarp's Epistle to the Philippians and the Martyrdom of Polycarp: Introduction, Text, and Commentary*, OAF (Oxford: Oxford University Press), 1–9.

55. See Martyrdom of Polycarp 9.2; 12.2; 13.1; 17.2; 18.1; 19.1.

56. All nine of them continue with the text of the Epistle of Barnabas, beginning at 5.7, which implies dependency on a single textual ancestor. In addition, Eusebius quotes two portions of the letter (all of ch. 9; most of ch. 13).

other (chs. 1–12) written after his death, some time later (130–140?)—though other positions continue to find supporters.[57] The letter contains two passages of interest (10.2; 11.2)—both in the Latin section and, if the theory of two letters holds, both in the (chronologically) later letter. In both, *gentes* appears as a term denoting outsiders.

Near the beginning of his epistle, Polycarp says that he is "writing these things about righteousness" (*To the Philippians* 3.1), and this is as good a characterization as any of the epistle in its overall thrust. Most of the first six chapters consists of exhortations addressed to various segments of the community (wives, widows, deacons, young men, virgins, presbyters), in which he encourages them to "walk in the commandment of the Lord" (4.1), a blanket term for standard Christian ethical teaching. In chapter 7, he turns briefly to theology, warning his readers against false teaching, especially the denial "that Jesus Christ has come in the flesh" (7.1). But this quickly moves into an exhortation to imitate Christ in his suffering (ch. 8), with Ignatius, Paul, and others being held up as models (ch. 9).

As Polycarp sums up his exhortations in chapter 10, he introduces the idea of maintaining a good reputation among outsiders, urging his readers to keep "your interactions with the outsiders [*in gentibus*] above reproach, that by your good works you may receive praise and the Lord not be blasphemed because of you" (*To the Philippians* 10.2). The theme appears elsewhere (e.g., 2 Clement 13.1-3; Justin, *Dialogue with Trypho* 17.2; cf. Rom 2:24), in each case with a citation of LXX Isa 52:5. Although there is no explicit citation of Scripture here, the influence of Isa 52:5 is readily apparent in the reference to blasphemy.

In chapter 11, he turns from general exhortation to discussion of a particular case of misbehavior. The case concerned a certain Valens, formerly a presbyter in the Philippian church, who had abused his office through some form of financial impropriety ("the love of money") and was thus deposed. In discussing the case, he makes a general statement about such persons: "Anyone who cannot avoid

---

57. See P. N. Harrison, *Polycarp's Two Epistles to the Philippians* (Cambridge: Cambridge University Press, 1936). The primary alternative is that the letter can be understood as a unity, written on a single occasion; so, originally, J. B. Lightfoot, *The Apostolic Fathers: Clement, Ignatius, and Polycarp: Revised Texts with Introductions, Notes, Dissertations and Translations*, part 2 (Peabody, MA: Hendrickson, 1989), 1:588-89, followed (with some hesitation or qualification) by others; e.g., Michael W. Holmes, *The Apostolic Fathers* (Grand Rapids: Baker, 2006), 132–33; and Hartog, *Polycarp's Epistle to the Philippians*, who also provides an up-to-date survey of the discussion (pp. 33–40). In addition, some have argued for a later interpolation, an argument tied up with older debates about the authenticity of the epistles of Ignatius; see Thomas Lechner, *Ignatius adversus Valentinianos? Chronologische und theologiegeschichtliche Studien zu den Briefen des Ignatius von Antiochien*, VCSup 47 (Leiden: Brill, 1999).

Ethnē and Gentile Christian Identity (Before 135 CE)

the love of money ... will be judged as if among the outsiders [*inter gentes*] who know nothing about the judgment of the Lord" (11.2).

In both cases, then, *gentes* functions as a term for outsiders, one side of an identity binary, with members of Polycarp's group—variously designated as "the church of God," "the saints," "the brotherhood," and so on—on the other side. In both cases, individuals rather than national people groups are clearly in view. While the Greek has not survived, there can be little doubt that *gentes* renders an original *ethnē* in each case. Given the profile of this usage (i.e., outsiders, individuals), it must have developed in some way under the influence of the range of identities ascribed by Jewish Christ-believers that we examined in chapter 4. Unlike some other literature to be studied here, however, Polycarp's letter provides us with virtually no information on how he might understand the identity of "the church of God" in relationship with scriptural Israel, the earliest Jewish Christ-believers, or local Jewish communities in his own day. While his letter is peppered with quotations from and allusions to apostolic writings, the echo of Isa 52:5 that was noted above is the closest we get to any use of Israel's Scriptures.[58] In one other passage, he does make mention of "the prophets" but in a thoroughly Christianized way: "the apostles who proclaimed the gospel to us and the prophets who preached, in advance, the coming of our Lord" (6.3). In view of this lack of apparent interest in the Jewish origins of "the gospel" and its "Lord," we probably should view the use of *gentes* (= *ethnē*) with reference to outsiders simply as a residue of an identity discourse that has ceased to be relevant or useful.

Despite the title under which it has been preserved—the Second Epistle of Clement to the Corinthians—2 Clement is not a letter, nor was it written by the author of 1 Clement.[59] Epistolary features are absent, and the general consensus is that it should be seen as a homily or sermon.[60] To be sure, the reference in 19.1

---

58. He appears to acknowledge his lack of knowledge of the Scriptures in 12.1.

59. The designation Second Epistle of Clement to the Corinthians is a composite of the titles that appear in the three surviving manuscripts—Alexandrinus ("Epistle of Clement B"); Hierosolymitanus ("Clement to the Corinthians B"); Syriac ("Of the same Clement to the Corinthians B"); for details, see Wilhelm Pratscher, *Der zweite Clemensbrief*, Kommentar zu den Apostolischen Väter 3 (Göttingen: Vandenhoeck & Ruprecht, 2007), 9–11.

Stylistically, the two writings (neither of which bears the name of Clement) are quite distinct. Nevertheless, the fact that 2 Clement follows 1 Clement in the three manuscripts that contain 2 Clement may suggest some connection between the two (e.g., a Roman or Corinthian provenance).

60. So, e.g., Lightfoot, *Apostolic Fathers*, part 1, 2:194–97; Pratscher, *Der zweite Clemensbrief*, 25–27; Alistair Stewart-Sykes, *From Prophecy to Preaching: A Search for the Origins of the Christian Homily*, VCSup 59 (Leiden: Brill, 2001), 174–87.

GENTILE CHRISTIAN IDENTITY

to a "reader" who is "reading you a request to pay attention to what has been written" sits awkwardly with the homiletical material that precedes and raises the possibility that chapters 19–20 stem from a different author.[61] Since the two instances of *ethnē* appear earlier, however, we can safely leave this question to one side and examine the use of the term within the framework of chapters 1–18. There is general agreement that the document was written sometime in the second quarter of the second century.[62] While Rome, Corinth, Syria, and Egypt have each been suggested as the place of origin, what is more important for our purposes is that it clearly stems from a gentile Christian environment.[63] Near the beginning of the homily, in a section where he is extolling the magnitude of God's gift of salvation, the author describes their former state in these terms: "We were maimed in our understanding, worshiping stones and pieces of wood and gold and silver and copper—all of them made by humans" (1.6). A similar depiction of typical polytheistic identity appears in 3.1.

The themes of the sermon are simple and straightforward—an appeal for righteous living, steadfast obedience to God's commands and resistance to the attractions of this age, with the promise that those who heed the appeal would thereby attain the blessings of the age to come. This statement in chapter 5 provides a convenient summary:

> You should realize, brothers, that our visit in this realm of the flesh is brief and short-lived, but the promise of Christ is great and astounding—namely, a rest in the coming kingdom and eternal life. What then must we do to obtain these things, except conduct ourselves in a holy and upright way and consider these worldly affairs foreign to us, and not yearn after them?" (2 Clement 5.5–6)

For 2 Clement, the foreignness (*allotria*) of "these worldly affairs [*kosmika tauta*]" is rooted in a sharply drawn eschatological duality: "this age and the

---

61. Regardless of whether "what is written" refers to Scripture (so Lightfoot, *Apostolic Fathers*, part 1, 2:195), the most plausible understanding of the "request" (or appeal; *enteuxis*) that is being read is that it has to do with the sermon that precedes (so Karl Paul Donfried, *The Setting of Second Clement in Early Christianity*, SupNovT 38 [Leiden: Brill, 1974], 14–15; Wilhelm Pratscher, "The Second Epistle of Clement," in *The Apostolic Fathers: An Introduction*, ed. Wilhelm Pratscher [Waco, TX: Baylor University Press, 2010], 72–73). But it seems odd that the person who has spoken directly and personally to his audience through chs. 1–18 would then refer to himself in 19:1 as "the one who is your reader." It is more likely that the "I" of chs. 1–18 and the "I" of chs. 19–20 are distinct.

62. See, e.g., Bart D. Ehrman, ed. and trans., *The Apostolic Fathers*, LCL (Cambridge, MA: Harvard University Press, 2003), 1:159–60.

63. On the place of origin, see Pratscher, *Der zweite Clemensbrief*, 59–61.

age to come are two enemies" (6.3).⁶⁴ This characterization of the present age as foreign provides a connection with the first occurrence of *ethnē*.

In chapter 13, the author shifts his appeal for righteous living onto new ground—the opinion of outsiders: "We should not be crowd-pleasers nor wish to please only ourselves, but through our righteous activity we should be pleasing as well to those outside the fold"—literally, "the persons outside [*tois exō anthrōpois*]" (2 Clement 13.1). He is primarily concerned, however, not with positive effects but with the other side of the coin, the effect on outsiders of unrighteous behavior. He continues: "so that the name not be blasphemed because of us," underlining this with a citation of LXX Isa 52:5:⁶⁵ "For the Lord says, 'My name is constantly blasphemed among all the *ethnē*'" (13.2).⁶⁶ As he continues with the theme, he does so in the language of the citation: "For when the *ethnē* hear the sayings of God from our mouths, they are astonished at their beauty and greatness. Then when they discover that our actions do not match our words, they turn from astonishment to blasphemy, saying that our faith is some kind of myth and error" (13.3).

This use of *ethnē* is similar to the passage in Polycarp's letter discussed above (*To the Philippians* 10.2–3). The first thing to note here is that, as with Polycarp, a gentile Christ-believer writing to other gentile believers is using *ethnē* as a term for outsiders, those not belonging to the group. The parallel with "the persons outside [*tois exō anthrōpois*]" makes it clear that individuals are in view. Since the author presents both himself and his readers as former polytheists (2 Clement 1.6; 3.1), *ethnē* could also function as an identity left behind when they came to "know the Father of truth" (3.2), though this remains implicit at best. As with Polycarp, *To the Philippians* 10.1–3, the usage stands in some line of development that goes back to the use of *ethnē* in the identity discourse among early Jewish Christ-believers. But 2 Clement provides us with a little more information on how this ascribed identity was being understood and interpreted.

The next thing to note is that LXX Isa 52:5, which in its original context was addressed to Israel, is read here in a simple and straightforward way as an address to the author's community of gentile Christ-believers. This is not an

---

64. On the foreignness of the present age, cf. 5.5: "our visit in this world of the flesh [*en tō kosmō toutō tēs sarkos tautēs*]."

65. To which he adds another citation of unknown origin: "And again he says, 'Woe to the one who causes my name to be blasphemed.'" A similar woe formulation appears in Polycarp, *To the Philippians* 10.2–3.

66. This last phrase appears in the LXX but not in the MT. The Greek version also contains the phrase "because of you [*di' hymas*]," which is reflected in the phrase in the sentence before the citation ("because of us").

isolated occurrence, as similar appropriations of passages from Israel's Scripture are found elsewhere in the work.[67] What are we to make of this? Is the author aware of their Jewish origins, so that his reading of these texts is undergirded by some considered reflection on the relationship between the gentile church and the Israel of Scripture (or the Jews of his own day)? Or does he simply assume without further ado that these texts are Christian Scripture and, as such, that they can be applied to his readers in a straightforward and simpleminded way?

While 2 Clement does not provide us with a great deal to go on, one passage early in the work deserves some comment. We have already noted how the homily begins with a description of their former plight ("our entire life was nothing other than death"; 1.6) and subsequent salvation ("he graciously bestowed light upon us; . . . while we were perishing, he saved us"; 1.4), a passage in which the author characterizes himself and his readers as former polytheists and thus as gentiles. As he continues, he expatiates on this creation of life out of death by citing a passage from Isaiah: "Be jubilant, you who are infertile and who do not bear children! Let your voice burst forth and cry out, you who experience no pains of labor! For the one who has been deserted has more children than the one who has a husband" (Isa 54:1).[68] As we might expect, he understands this passage as referring to the church: "Now when it says, 'Be jubilant, you who are infertile and who do not bear children,' it is referring to us. For our church [*ekklēsia*] was infertile before children were given to it." Further: "And when it says, 'For the one who has been deserted has more children than the one who has a husband,' it is because our people [*ho laos hēmōn*] appeared to be deserted by God, but now that we believe we have become more numerous than those who appear to have God" (2.3). The contrast between "our people," identified a few verses earlier as former polytheists, and "those who appear to have God" is striking. The simplest and most probable interpretation is that the contrast is between the gentile church and the Jewish people.[69]

If this is so, then the combination of (1) the assumption that Israel's Scriptures speak directly to the church and (2) the assertion that the gentile church is greater than the Jewish people, a people who moreover only "*appear* to have God," suggests a thinned-out form of supersessionism or replacement theology. To be sure, the statement that "our church was infertile before children were given to it" strikes the reader as odd: How could the church have existed (even in a barren state) before there were any believers? One might be tempted to see

---

67. See 2.1–2 (Isa 54:1); 7.6 (Isa 66:24); 14.1 (Jer 7:11); 15.3 (Isa 58:9); cf. 11.1–4.

68. 2 Clement 2.1. Some see Isa 54:1 as the text on which the whole sermon is based; see, e.g., Holmes, *Apostolic Fathers*, 73.

69. So Lightfoot, *Apostolic Fathers*, part 1, 2:214–15; followed by others.

the statement simply as driven by the language of Isa 54:1—especially in view of the contrasting statement that appears just prior to the citation: God "called us while we did not exist, and he wished us to come into being from nonbeing" (2 Clement 1.8). However, later in the homily, we encounter the idea of a preexistent spiritual church—"the first church, the spiritual church, the church that was created before the sun and moon" (14.1)—a church created at the outset both as the "body of Christ" and as the female counterpart to the male Christ.[70] So the statement in 2.1 can be read in these terms (i.e., a primordial spiritual church that later becomes physically manifest on earth).

All of this is complex and rather muddled, and we need not explore it any further. The main thing to observe is that, while the author seems to acknowledge the existence of Israel—the children of "the one who has a husband"—he shows little interest in them or their possible significance. While they occupy a position in between the primordial creation of the spiritual *ekklēsia* and the latter appearance of the earthly body of Christ, they remain overshadowed by both and of little apparent interest. At most, we can detect some evidence of a replacement theology—that the earthly *ekklēsia* has displaced the previous "children" and now possesses their Scriptures.

The apparent implication that the members of the *ekklēsia* used to be part of the polytheistic *ethnē* gives this replacement theology an ethnic character: Jewish "children" displaced by a greater group of "children" drawn from the non-Jewish *ethnē*. But the theme remains thin and undeveloped; perhaps we are to see this as the attenuated remnants of previous identity struggles that have ceased to be pressing and are now no longer relevant.

The other occurrence of *ethnē* can be treated more briefly. In chapter 17 we encounter once again a call to repentance and perseverance (especially vv. 1–3), undergirded by a reminder of eschatological judgment:

> For the Lord said, "I am coming to gather all the nations [*panta ta ethnē*], tribes and tongues." And this is what he calls the "day of his appearance," when he comes to redeem each of us, according to our deeds. And the unbelievers [*hoi apistoi*] will see his glory and power and be shocked when they see that the rulership of this world has been given to Jesus. (2 Clement 17.4–5)

---

70. "But I cannot imagine that you do not realize that the living church is the body of Christ. For the Scripture says, 'God made the human male and female.' The male is Christ, the female the church. And, as you know, the Bible [Or: the books] and the apostles indicate that the church has not come into being just now, but has existed from the beginning" (14.2). On this primordial syzygy, see Pratscher, *Apostolic Fathers*, 79–80.

GENTILE CHRISTIAN IDENTITY

The citation, including the phrase *panta ta ethnē*, is drawn primarily from Isa 66:18, though incorporating some language found in Dan 3:2, 7. The author does not pick up the term, and so we can only speculate on how he would have understood it. But since, in what follows, the end-time gathering includes both members of the church ("each of us"; also v. 7) and "the unbelievers" (also vv. 5–6), it is probable that *panta ta ethnē* is understood here as a reference to humankind in its totality. In other words, with the addition of *panta*, the special sense of *ta ethnē* that appeared in 13.1–3—that is, as a reference to (polytheistic) outsiders—has fallen away.

The Shepherd of Hermas is a lengthy, rambling first-person account of a series of visions and revelations experienced by Hermas, who introduces himself at the outset as the former slave of a certain woman of Rome named Rhoda.[71] As the story begins, Hermas has become reacquainted with her and, as he puts it, "began to love her as a sister." Somehow he had an opportunity to see "her bathing in the Tiber river" and thus to "observe her beauty" as he helped her out of the water. She, apparently, did not interpret the event in a sisterly way at all, as she subsequently accused him "before the Lord" of allowing "the desire for evil [to] rise up in your heart."[72]

This interaction leads quickly into the first of the five visions with which the book begins. Shaken by the accusation, Hermas has a vision of "an elderly woman, . . . dressed in radiant clothes and holding a book in her hands" (Visions 1.2.2). Although she is thoroughly familiar with Hermas and has a message for him from God, she does not show much concern about the accusation of sexual impropriety. Instead, she informs Hermas that he has displeased God by the problems that he has tolerated in his own family. He has been lax with his children; their resultant "sins and lawless acts," together with his own lack of attention, has brought him "to ruin," which, as we learn later, involved financial loss;[73] and his wife has compounded the problem by her inability to "restrain her tongue."[74] In the second vision, the woman is identified as a personification of the church in its heavenly ideal form (2.4.1), and the problems in Hermas's family begin to merge with problems that he is also warned about in the earthly church of his own experience.[75]

---

71. The Shepherd of Hermas is normally seen as comprising three sections—Visions, Mandates, and Similitudes. See further below.

72. These details are all found in Visions 1.1.1–9 (using the traditional system of citation).

73. "When you were wealthy, you were of no use; but now you are useful and helpful in life" (Visions 3.7.7).

74. These problems are introduced in Visions 1.3.1–3 and repeated with further detail in 2.2.2–3 and 2.3.1.

75. Note how the woman's admonition about the sins of Hermas's children (Visions

Ethnē and Gentile Christian Identity (Before 135 CE)

Hermas then encounters the heavenly woman in two further visions.[76] The third has to do with the construction of a great stone tower, which the heavenly woman identifies as an image of the (earthly) church (Visions 3.3.3). In the fourth vision, Hermas sees "an enormous wild beast," which he learns is "a foreshadowing of the great affliction that is coming" (4.2.4–5).

After Hermas has encountered the heavenly woman in these four visions, he has a fifth vision in which a different heavenly figure appears—"an eminent looking man . . . dressed in shepherd's clothing" (Visions 5.1), who introduces himself as "the shepherd to whom you have been entrusted" (5.3) and who subsequently is identified as the "angel of repentance."[77] The remainder of the work consists of the shepherd's message to Hermas, which the shepherd describes as "the commandments and parables" (5.6).

The work as a whole, then, consists of three interconnected sections: five Visions, twelve commandments (or Mandates), and ten parables (or Similitudes). The Mandates contain ethical instructions of various kinds, some of which relate to issues that have already surfaced in the Visions (family relations, sexual propriety, the dangers of wealth, the need for repentance) and others that reflect early Christian moral teaching more generally (including material that echoes the kind of two-ways teaching found in the Didache and the Epistle of Barnabas).[78] The Similitudes continue to deal with the central themes of the work in the form of allegorical discourses on a series of parabolic images. The longest and most significant of these are the eighth and the ninth, each of which returns to the image of the tower (first seen in the third Vision) and the construction of the repentant and purified church.

In older discussions of the Shepherd of Hermas, attention tended to be focused on its distinctive approach to postbaptismal sin and repentance. Unlike some of the more rigorist strands in the early Christian movement that denied any possibility for repentance in the case of a believer who willfully sinned and fell away (e.g., Heb 6:4–6; 10:26–29), the position taken in the Shepherd of Hermas is that such repentance is possible—but only once: "the one who sins and repents must be accepted back. But not many times. For there is but one repentance given to the slaves of God" (Mandates 4.1.8). Indeed, it seems that the rev-

---

2.2.4) shifts smoothly into an admonition that "those who lead the church" need to "make their paths straight in righteousness" as well (2.2.6).

76. In the first three, she is elderly; in the fourth she appears as "a young woman . . . clothed as if coming from a bridal chamber" (Visions 4.2.1). In all four, however, she represents the church in its heavenly glory.

77. Visions 5.7; Mandates 12.4.7; Similitudes 9.1.1; 9.14.3; 9.23.5; 9.24.4.

78. "A person has two angels, one of righteousness and the other of wickedness" (Mandates 6.2.1).

elation to Hermas is to play a dual role in this regard—both making known the possibility of repentance and establishing "the day" beyond which no further sin will be forgiven (Visions 2.2.4–6). This aspect of the Shepherd of Hermas has led interpreters of a previous era to read the work primarily as part of a developing discourse within the early church on penitential theology.[79]

Such a reading, however, slides over another obvious and significant theme, that of "rich and poor in the Shepherd of Hermas."[80] The dangers that accompany the search for wealth and the resultant entanglement in business affairs; the problems experienced by those whose allegiance is split between the world and the church; the enervating effect on the church of such dual allegiance or "double-mindedness" (*dipsychia*);[81] the obligations of the rich believers toward those who are poor—it is increasingly being recognized that such social and economic factors represent an important part of the context within which the Shepherd of Hermas's concern for repentance and ecclesiastical purity is to be located and understood.[82] We will return to this theme presently when we look at the place of *ethnē* in the work.

For present purposes, we do not need to spend much time on the usual questions of critical introduction. Formally, given its narrative shape—a first-person narrative account of revelatory experiences in which divine knowledge is communicated to Hermas through visions and their interpretations by heavenly intermediaries—the Shepherd of Hermas can be classified as an apocalypse,[83] even though a number of elements that often are associated with the genre are

---

79. For discussions of such earlier approaches, see, e.g., Carolyn Osiek, *Shepherd of Hermas: A Commentary*, Hermeneia (Minneapolis: Fortress, 1999), 28–29, esp. n. 219; Harry O. Maier, *The Social Setting of the Ministry as Reflected in the Writings of Hermas, Clement, and Ignatius* (Waterloo, ON: Wilfrid Laurier University Press, 1991), 58–59; David Hellholm, "The Shepherd of Hermas," in Pratscher, *Apostolic Fathers*, 225–26.

80. To borrow the title of Carolyn Osiek's pioneering work: *Rich and Poor in the Shepherd of Hermas: An Exegetical-Social Investigation*, CBQMS 15 (Washington, DC: Catholic Biblical Association of America, 1983). See pp. 39–45 of her work for a survey of the pertinent vocabulary and a catalog of key texts.

81. The word-group occurs some fifty-five times in the work; see Osiek, *Shepherd of Hermas*, 30–31.

82. In addition to Osiek and Maier (cited above), see, e.g., Peter Lampe, *From Paul to Valentinus: Christians at Rome in the First Two Centuries*, trans. Michael Steinhauser, ed. Marshall D. Johnson (London: T&T Clark, 2003), 90–93.

83. Compare this description of the narrative shape of the Shepherd of Hermas with the widely accepted description of apocalypse as a literary genre, in John J. Collins, ed., *Apocalypse: The Morphology of a Genre*, Semeia 14 (Missoula, MT: Scholars Press, 1979), 9.

absent.⁸⁴ With respect to provenance, while we should not assume that the biographical details associated with Hermas can be taken as transparent historical information about the actual author and his circumstances,⁸⁵ they probably do provide a general reflection of the social situation surrounding the work: a socially stratified Christian community in an urban setting, probably Rome, whose wealthy members were probably upwardly mobile members of the lower classes (freedmen, artisans, and the like) rather than part of the social elite.⁸⁶ The question of date has been complicated, perhaps unnecessarily, by suggestions, on the one hand, that the work in its final form incorporates discrete writings by different authors and,⁸⁷ on the other, by attempts to build too much on incidental personal references.⁸⁸ While, in view of its length, it is probable that it was written over a period of time, the fact that it was so widely known by the end of the second century suggests that it appeared in its final form sometime well before the middle of the century.⁸⁹

Ethnē appears in the Shepherd of Hermas a total of sixteen times, functioning in two distinct ways: as a designation for outsiders or unbelievers (twelve times, plus one occurrence of *ethnikos*) and, in one extended passage, in a construction referring to humankind as a whole (four occurrences). We will deal with each in turn.

The first appearance of *ethnē* occurs early in the work, in the context of the first vision. The elderly woman has just read two portions of a book (presumably "the books of the living"; Visions 1.3.2), the first of which Hermas experienced as "terrifying," while the second was "beneficial . . . and gentle" (1.3.3). In response,

---

84. E.g., the periodization of history leading up to the end; the closest analog in the Shepherd of Hermas is the elaborate categorizations of the different types of people (with respect to the mixture of sin and repentance) in several of the Similitudes (especially the eighth and ninth). One apocalyptic feature that is not often highlighted is the concern that the revelations be written in books and disseminated (Visions 2.4.3). On the Shepherd of Hermas as an apocalypse, see the discussion in Osiek, *Shepherd of Hermas*, 10–12.

85. See the helpful discussion in Mark Grundeken, *Community Building in the Shepherd of Hermas: A Critical Study of Some Key Aspects*, VCSup 131 (Leiden: Brill, 2015), 1–22.

86. Osiek, *Rich and Poor in the* Shepherd of Hermas, 91–135; Maier, *Social Setting of the Ministry*, 59–65; Lampe, *From Paul to Valentinus*, 90–99, 234–36.

87. See, e.g., Hellholm, "Shepherd of Hermas"; for a brief history of the theories of multiple authorship, see Osiek, *Shepherd of Hermas*, 9–10.

88. Specifically, the reference to a "Hermas" in Rom 16:14; the reference to a "Clement" in Visions 2.4.3; and the statement in the Muratorian Canon that Hermas wrote the Shepherd of Hermas "while his brother Pius was sitting as bishop" in Rome.

89. Irenaeus, Clement of Alexandria, Tertullian, Origen, and (if it is a second-century document) the Muratorian Canon; for details, see Osiek, *Shepherd of Hermas*, 4–7.

the woman explains the difference between the two: "These last words are for those who are upright [*tois dikaiois*], but the former are for the outsiders [*tois ethnesin*] and apostates [*tois apostatais*]" (1.4.2). The parallel between *ethnē* and "apostates" indicates that individuals are in view. In the woman's explanation, *ethnē* appears without introduction or explanation; the author simply takes it for granted that his readers will recognize it as a designation for those who are outside the community of the righteous (or "the elect" [1.3.4]).

As the narrative progresses, *ethnē* continues to function as the primary term for outsiders (sinners, unbelievers).[90] Used in this way, it appears in connection with the central themes of the work. Despite the fact that *ethnē* face the prospect of final judgment and destruction,[91] repentance remains a possibility; indeed, in contrast to the situation of sinful believers, the possibility of repentance remains open for the *ethnē* until the end:

> For the Master swore by his own glory to his chosen ones: "If there is any more sinning once this day has been appointed, they will not find salvation. For there is a limit to repentance for those who are upright [*tois dikaiois*], and the days of repentance for all the saints are complete. But the *ethnē* will be able to repent until the final day." (Visions 2.2.5)

In the meantime, however, unrepentant *ethnē* continue to represent a danger for the believers. The first similitude contains the warning that believers are not to "participate in the extravagance sought by the *ethnē*; for it is of no profit for you who are slaves of God" (Similitudes 1.10). This warning comes at the end of a discourse in which the shepherd describes believers as living in a foreign city that is a long way from their own. They cannot have it both ways, he warns. They cannot continue to set down economic roots in this city and at the same time expect to be able to live according to the laws of their own city. Eventually "the ruler [*ho kyrios*] of the country" will say: "Either live by my laws or leave my country" (1.1.4). Clearly the similitude is only partly metaphorical; the readers after all are living in the city of Rome. The contrast between the *ethnē*, who are at home in the city of this lord (*kyrios*), and the "slaves of God," who are citizens

---

90. Other occurrences of a general nature: Mandates 4.1.9 ("whoever behaves like the *ethnē* commits adultery"); Similitudes 9.28.8 ("If the *ethnē* punish their slaves for denying their own lord, what do you suppose the Lord who has authority over all things will do to you?").

91. The *ethnē* "will be burned like withered trees and shown for what they are, because they did what was evil in their lifetimes . . . the *ethnē* will be burned for not knowing the one who created them" (Similitudes 4.4).

Ethnē and Gentile Christian Identity (Before 135 CE)

of God's city, begins to hint at a counterimperial construction of identity, even if it remains undeveloped.[92]

A similar warning appears in the eighth similitude, which uses the image of a willow tree to categorize the various types of believers according to their degree of adherence to "the law of God that has been given to the whole world" (Similitudes 8.3.2),[93] the likelihood of their repentance (where necessary) and whether they will ultimately be allowed to enter the tower:

> Those who handed over sticks that were two parts withered and the third part green are those who have been faithful, but who also have grown wealthy and maintained a high standing among the *ethnē*. These have clothed themselves with great arrogance and become conceited; they have abandoned the truth and do not cling to those who are upright, but live with the *ethnē*. And this path has become very sweet to them. (8.9.1)

While these have not yet fallen away completely ("they have not fallen away from God, but have remained in the faith, even though they do not do the works of faith"), there are others who have crossed the line into apostasy: "But others have taken up residence, once and for all, with the *ethnē*. These have fallen away from God by being borne along by the vanities of the outsiders and acting like them. And so these are counted among the *ethnē*" (8.9.3).[94]

There is a considerable element of fluidity, then, in the spiritual demography of the Shepherd of Hermas. Some among "those who have been called by the name of the Lord" will fall away and be "counted among the *ethnē*"; some among the *ethnē* will take advantage of the opportunity for repentance and thus be admitted eventually into the tower. Nevertheless, the category is clear; those who are found outside, either now or in the "final day," constitute the *ethnē*. While

---

92. Similar warnings have already appeared in Mandates 10 and 11. Those who "become mixed up with business affairs and wealth and friendships with outsiders [*philiais ethnikais*] and many other matters that pertain to this age" run the risk of becoming corrupt and "barren in spirit" (10.1.4). Such double-mindedness can result in the adoption of the ways of the *ethnē*: "But all those who are of two minds and who are constantly changing their minds, consult the oracle as do even the *ethnē*" (11.1.4).

93. The believers are characterized as "those who have been called by the name of the Lord [and have come] under the shadow of the willow" (Similitudes 8.1.1).

94. The two categories (*ethnē* and believers who have completely fallen away) appear together in Visions 1.4.2 ("the *ethnē* and the apostates [*apostatais*]") and Similitudes 4.1.4 ("the *ethnē* and the sinners").

the use of the term has elicited little comment from interpreters, it is clear that it is Jewish in origin.[95]

In addition to this use as a designation for outsiders, *ethnē* appears in the ninth similitude with reference to humankind as a whole. By far the longest single section of the work, the ninth similitude represents a much more elaborate version of the account in the third vision, in which the development of the church is portrayed through the image of the construction of a tower. As with the eighth similitude, the author is especially concerned to categorize the various types of believers—in this case represented by different types of stones—and their ultimate destinies as the church undergoes a process of purification.

In this version, the construction of the tower takes place on a "great plain, with twelve mountains surrounding the plain, each having its own appearance" (Similitudes 9.1.4). Here we are particularly interested in the stones that are used to construct the tower. One set of stones came up "out of a great depth" and was used to build a foundation in four layers—ten, twenty-five, thirty-five, and forty stones, respectively (9.3.3; 9.4.2-3). We will return to these a little later. The other stones were drawn from the twelve mountains. Though they were originally of various colors, when they "were placed in the building, they changed their former colors and all alike became white" (9.4.5). When the tower was close to completion, the Lord of the tower came to examine it and found that a number of the stones had become discolored or faulty and needed to be replaced. Even so, the faulty stones were stored nearby in case they could yet be salvaged for use in the tower.

As the shepherd explains the vision to Hermas, we learn (as we may well have suspected) that it has to do with postbaptismal sin, the possibility and necessity of repentance, and the ultimate purity of the church. More importantly, we also learn that the twelve mountains from which the building blocks were hewn are "twelve tribes [*phylai*] that inhabit the entire earth" or "twelve *ethnē*" or "all the *ethnē* that dwell under the sky." When, through the preaching of the "apostles,"[96] they first "believed in the name of the Son of God," they were transformed into

---

95. Presumably as mediated by Jewish Christ-believers. Unlike most commentators, who simply translate the term as "heathen" or "outsiders," Osiek stops to give it some attention. However, depending on BADG, she treats the term as a generic, transcultural term for "outsider": "for Greeks, non-Greeks; for Romans, non-Italians; for Jews, Gentiles; for Christians, pagans" (Osiek, *Shepherd of Hermas*, 50, n. 21; see also Osiek, *Rich and Poor in the* Shepherd of Hermas, 124, n. 118). As we have seen, however, there is no solid evidence that *ta ethnē* as a stand-alone, unmodified term was used to denote the other anywhere but in Jewish contexts.

96. Later we learn that "the believers from the eighth mountain, where there were many

white stones, but later "some of them defiled themselves and were cast out from the race of the upright [*ek tou genous tōn dikaiōn*], and they again became as they were formerly, only somewhat worse."[97] Presumably those who believed and thus became part of the "race" (*genos*) of the righteous thereby ceased to belong to the *ethnē*.

This use of *ethnē* presents us with a puzzle that is also characteristic of the Shepherd of Hermas as a whole. On the surface of it, the phrase "twelve tribes" seems to represent a clear echo of biblical language concerning Israel. But these twelve tribes are also described as "twelve *ethnē*"—decidedly unbiblical language for Israel—and they are equated with humankind as a whole: they "inhabit the entire earth"; they are "all the *ethnē* that dwell under the sky." While there has been some attempt to see this language as governed by an Israel ecclesiology—the church drawn from all the *ethnē* as the new or true Israel—there is virtually nothing in the ninth similitude to suggest any interest at all in the people or history of Israel, or the Jewish roots of the church.[98] The closest one gets is the account of the other set of stones—those emerging from the depths rather than drawn from the mountains. In response to Hermas's question, the shepherd identifies them as "the first generation" (the first ten stones), "the second generation of upright men" (the twenty-five), "the prophets and ministers of God" (the thirty-five), and "the apostles and teachers who proclaim the Son of God" (the forty) (Similitudes 9.15.4). While the first three groups could have been identified with the patriarchs and prophets of Israel, the author shows no inclination to do so.[99] As the passage continues, it is clear that his primary concern instead is to provide a way for righteous individuals, from the time prior to the proclamation of the Son of God, to be included in the church.[100]

---

springs that provided drink to all the creatures of the Lord, . . . are apostles and teachers who proclaimed their message throughout the whole world" (Similitudes 9.25.1-2).

97. Quoted material from Similitudes 9.17.1, 2, 4, 5.

98. For such an attempt, see, e.g., Graydon F. Snyder, *The Shepherd of Hermas*, vol. 6 of *The Apostolic Fathers: A New Translation and Commentary* (Camden, NJ: Thomas Nelson, 1967), 14, 147.

99. See Grundeken, *Community Building*, 44-45.

100. Their ascent through the watery depths providing an equivalent to the seal of baptism: "Through these people [i.e., the apostles and teachers], therefore, they were made alive and came to know the name of the Son of God. For this reason also they rose up with them and were fit together with them into the building of the tower; and without being hewed they were put into the building together. For they died in righteousness and great purity—only they did not have this seal" (Similitudes 9.16.7). This interest in those who are righteous but unbaptized parallels the more extensive interest in those who have been baptized but become (or remain) unrighteous; see Osiek, *Shepherd of Hermas*, 238.

As with the ninth similitude, so with the Shepherd of Hermas as a whole. Some of its themes and elements seem to reflect origins within Jewish forms of Christ-belief: the apocalyptic character of the work; the concern with the law and commandments of God; the echoes of two-ways material; the reference to the Book of Eldad and Modat (Visions 2.3.4);[101] angels (symbolized by men and shepherds); and so on.[102] To this list we can add *ethnē* as a designation for outsiders and *panta ta ethnē* as the sphere of apostolic proclamation. But these seem to be little more than residue from the past; as Hvalvik has observed: "a most conspicuous feature in the Shepherd is total silence about Jews and Judaism."[103] Nowhere in the Shepherd of Hermas do we find a living concern with the people or Scriptures of Israel, or the Jewish origins of the church. There is no mention of Jewish rites or institutions, no interest in the Son of God as Messiah (or as the earthly Jesus of Nazareth, for that matter), and no indication that keeping the law and commandments was ever a source of controversy in the church. While the twofold use of *ethnē* in the work clearly has roots in the ascription of *ethnē* as an identity term in the first generation of the movement, the Shepherd of Hermas displays little interest in (or even awareness of) the Jewish origins of the term.

The letters of Ignatius were written while Ignatius, bishop of Antioch in Syria, was being transported to Rome, where he would be executed. He was well aware of his impending martyrdom; indeed, one of the purposes of his letters was to forestall any attempts on the part of other Christians (especially those in Rome) to prevent it. Four of the letters were written from Smyrna, where he had the opportunity to meet not only with members of the church there, including its bishop Polycarp, but also with members of several nearby churches. He sent letters to three of these (Ephesus, Magnesia, Tralles); the fourth went to Rome. A little later he had an opportunity for further communication during a stop in Troas, where he wrote letters to the church in Smyrna, to Polycarp, and also to the church in Philadelphia.

This, at least, is the most widely accepted interpretation of the Ignatian material, which in the manuscript tradition has come down to us in three discernible recensions: a longer recension, containing these seven letters in a longer form, together with a number of additional letters; a shorter recension, preserved in a Syriac manuscript, containing only three letters (to Poly-

---

101. An apocryphal work (named after two prophets mentioned in Num 11:26-30) that circulated in early Christian circles but has not survived.

102. Snyder places a lot of weight on such Jewish features; *Shepherd of Hermas*, 16-17.

103. Reidar Hvalvik, "Jewish Believers and Jewish Influence in the Roman Church until the Early Second Century," in *Jewish Believers in Jesus: The Early Centuries*, ed. Oskar Skarsaune and Reidar Hvalvik (Peabody, MA: Hendrickson, 2007), 214-15.

Ethnē and Gentile Christian Identity (Before 135 CE)

carp, Ephesus, and Rome) in a much shorter form; and, in between, a middle recension of the seven letters as described above.[104] The work of Zahn and Lightfoot in the latter part of the nineteenth century served to create a broad consensus concerning both the originality and the authenticity of the middle recension—that is, that the middle recension represents the earliest form of the letters and that the letters were written by Ignatius.[105] While dissenting voices continue to be heard, they remain minority opinions.[106] There is also a general consensus that the letters were written during the time of Trajan or Hadrian; while the former is perhaps more probable, it is not necessary for our purposes to be more precise.

Although the letters are distinct, a number of shared themes reappear.[107] We have already noted Ignatius's desire for martyrdom; as he says to the Ephesians, it is only by fighting the beasts in Rome that he will "be able to be a disciple"; until he has been "perfected" in this way, he has "merely begun to be a disciple" (*To the Ephesians* 1.2; 3.1). Another well-known theme is his vigorous and uncompromising assertion of the essential role of the bishop for the existence and unity of the church, and of the bishop's overriding local authority. A third theme has to do with the situation of the church he has left behind in Antioch. The repeated requests for prayer on behalf of the Syrian church in the earlier letters betray a level of anxiety that comes into greater focus in the later letters, where we learn that he has received reports that the church there has "found peace" and that "their own corporate body has been restored to them," and where he requests that churches send delegates to help celebrate the restoration.[108] Evidently Ignatius's arrest had coincided with some situation of conflict and disunity, a situation that later was resolved. A previous generation of scholarship tended to understand the problem simply as one of external persecution. What is more likely, however,

---

104. Eusebius speaks of letters to these seven recipients (*Ecclesiastical History* 3.36.1–11).

105. Theodor Zahn, *Ignatius von Antiochien* (Gotha: F. A. Perthes, 1873); Lightfoot, *Apostolic Fathers*, part 2, vol. 1.

106. For surveys of the issues and discussion, see William R. Schoedel, *Ignatius of Antioch: A Commentary on the Letters of Ignatius of Antioch*, Hermeneia (Philadelphia: Fortress, 1985), 1–7; Hermut Löhr, "The Epistles of Ignatius of Antioch," in Pratscher, *Apostolic Fathers*, 91–115; Thomas A. Robinson, *Ignatius of Antioch and the Parting of the Ways: Early Jewish-Christian Relations* (Peabody, MA: Hendrickson, 2009).

107. See Mikael Isacson, *To Each Their Own Letter: Structure, Themes, and Rhetorical Strategies in the Letters of Ignatius of Antioch*, ConBNT 42 (Stockholm: Almqvist & Wiksell, 2004).

108. In the earlier letters, see, e.g., *To the Ephesians* 21.2; *To the Magnesians* 14; *To the Trallians* 13; *To the Romans* 9.1–3. And in the later ones, see *To the Smyrnaeans* 11.1–3; *To the Philadelphians* 10.1; the quoted material is from *To the Smyrnaeans* 11.2.

is that internal dissension had broken out—perhaps even centered on the bishop himself—spilling out beyond the community itself and attracting unwanted attention from the civic authorities.[109]

Two other recurring themes to be mentioned are more theological in nature, or at least have to do with theological diversity. One is docetism, that form of hyperexalted Christology in which Christ is seen as only appearing to be human. Especially in his letters to Tralles and Smyrna, Ignatius inveighs against those who say that Christ "only appeared to suffer" (*To the Trallians* 10), emphasizing instead that "he was truly from the family of David according to the flesh" and "was truly nailed for us in the flesh" (*To the Smyrnaeans* 1.1–2). The other, which concerns us more directly, has to do with Ignatius's opposition to Judaizers and with the more general relationship between what he calls "Judaism" and "Christianity."[110]

We will turn to this in a moment, but first we might note two additional questions that have been discussed with respect to these theological themes. One has to do with the suggestion that docetism and Judaizing were closely linked; that is, that Ignatius was confronting a single deviant group, in which Jewish and proto-Gnostic elements were combined. There is little evidence, however, of such a combination in the letters themselves.[111] It is more probable that we should see these polemical themes as directed at two distinct movements or tendencies.[112] The other question concerns location. Was Ignatius simply fighting Syrian battles on Asian soil, or did his attacks on docetism and Judaizing also reflect situations in the churches addressed in the letters? Since his knowledge of the churches in Asia was limited, there can be little doubt that he was viewing the situation there through the lens of his experience in Syria. Nevertheless, both phenomena

---

109. On the situation in Antioch and the related issue of the reasons for Ignatius's arrest, see Schoedel, *Ignatius of Antioch*, 10–11; Christine Trevett, *A Study of Ignatius of Antioch in Syria and Asia*, Studies in the Bible and Early Christianity 29 (Lewiston, NY: Edwin Mellen, 1992), 52–66.

110. As Schoedel observes, this is "the first appearance of the proper noun 'Christianity' in Christian literature"; *Ignatius of Antioch*, 126, n. 1. More generally, see Judith M. Lieu, *Christian Identity in the Jewish and Graeco-Roman World* (Oxford: Oxford University Press, 2004), 250–59.

111. As Ehrman points out, Ignatius addresses the two issues in different letters, Judaizing in the letters to Magnesia and Philadelphia, docetism in those to Tralles and Smyrna; *Apostolic Fathers*, 1:206.

112. The theory of "a kind of judaizing Gnosticism" (Ehrman, *Apostolic Fathers*, 1:206) was advocated by Zahn and Lightfoot, among others. For the position that Ignatius was addressing distinct groups, see (in addition to Ehrman) especially Trevett, *Study of Ignatius of Antioch*, 147–93.

were present in Asia as well,[113] and so it is probable that he was reacting, at least in part, to things that he had observed and experienced in his encounters with Asian Christians.[114]

Ignatius uses *ethnē* on two occasions, the first of which has to do with outsiders. In a manner similar to passages that have come up for discussion already (Polycarp, *To the Philippians* 10.2–3; 2 Clement 13.2), Ignatius exhorts his readers not to engage in behavior that would give the church a bad reputation among outsiders: "Let none of you hold a grudge against your neighbor. Give no occasion to the *ethnē* lest on account of a few foolish persons the entire congregation in God be slandered" (*To the Trallians* 8.2).[115] As with these other passages, the reproach is followed by a statement of woe: "For woe to that one through whom my name is slandered in vain by some." As with the other passages, it is clear that the statement is based on Isa 52:5, even though (unlike 2 Clement 13.2) the text is not cited explicitly. And like the others, an admonition initially addressed to Israel is here addressed to the church. Clearly we are dealing here with a widely used exegetical tradition.[116]

An exegetical tradition may also underlie the other occurrence of *ethnē*, where it clearly denotes non-Jewish believers. In the doxology with which Ignatius begins his letter to the church in Smyrna, at the end of a quasi-creedal and antidocetic section, he declares that the purpose of Christ's resurrection was that "he might eternally lift up the standard for his holy and faithful ones, whether among Jews or *ethnē*, in the one body of his church" (*To the Smyrnaeans* 1.2). The idea of raising (*airō*) a standard (*syssēmon*) clearly echoes Isaianic language (LXX Isa 5:26; 49:22; 62:10); in all three passages, the standard is raised for the *ethnē*. In this doxology, then, the language of Greek Isaiah has been reworked christologically to describe the union of the "holy and faithful ones," Jews and non-Jews alike, in one church. As Schoedel observes, such a union of Jews and

113. On Judaizing, see, e.g., Rev 2:9; 3:9.

114. For a reference to actual encounters, see *To the Philadelphians* 8.2: "For I heard some saying...."

115. Although the behavior in question is described in general terms (literally, "have anything against your neighbor"), the admonition is sandwiched in between passages having to do with divisions caused by heretical teachings and lack of submission to the bishop and other ministers (*To the Trallians* 6–10). Trevett suggests that Ignatius's concern here about the effect of internal disunity on the opinion of outsiders may reflect his own experience in Antioch; see *Study of Ignatius of Antioch*, 61, 88.

116. For a discussion, see Schoedel, *Ignatius of Antioch*, 150. Schoedel observes that Isa 52:5 was used in two ways in the early church: in-group admonition, as here; and polemical denunciations of Jews for their supposed failings (e.g., Rom 2:24; Justin, *Dialogue with Trypho* 17.2).

GENTILE CHRISTIAN IDENTITY

gentiles is "not characteristic of Ignatius," who places the emphasis instead on the distinction between "Judaism" and "Christianity." This, he suggests, is one of the reasons for discerning dependence on tradition here.[117] While this is certainly correct, Ignatius's reuse of traditional material here suggests that he was able to accept at some level the idea that "the one body of [Christ's] church" included Jews and gentiles.

To explore this further, we need to return to the issue of Judaizing. The key passages are as follows:

> Do not be deceived by false opinions or old fables that are of no use. For if we have lived according to Judaism until now, we admit that we have not received God's gracious gift. (*To the Magnesians* 8.1)

> It is outlandish to proclaim Jesus Christ and practice Judaism. For Christianity did not believe in Judaism, but Judaism in Christianity—in which every tongue that believes in God has been gathered together. (*To the Magnesians* 10.3)

> But if anyone should interpret Judaism to you, do not hear him. For it is better to hear Christianity from a man who is circumcised than Judaism from one who is uncircumcised. (*To the Philadelphians* 6.1)

The statements are puzzling in a number of respects, but at least two things are clear. First, Ignatius warns his readers to beware of certain persons who believed in Christ but also practiced some aspects of Judaism and encouraged others to do the same. These people were deceptively propagating "false opinions" and "old fables" that involved "liv[ing] according to Judaism"; they were "proclaim[ing] Jesus Christ and practic[ing] Judaism"; they were attempting to "interpret Judaism" to those who were already Christians. At least some of these were non-Jews: he warns the church in Philadelphia not "to hear . . . Judaism from one who is uncircumcised."[118]

Second, the terms on which he denounces such interpretive initiatives indicate that his objection to Judaization is based on a fundamental conviction that Christianity and Judaism were distinct and mutually exclusive ways of life. That is, what he objects to is not simply a situation where non-Jews are encouraged to adopt Jewish practices by Jewish or gentile Christians, but the very idea that

---

117. Schoedel, *Ignatius of Antioch*, 223.
118. On this group, see Stephen G. Wilson, *Related Strangers: Jews and Christians, 70–170 C.E.* (Minneapolis: Fortress, 1995), 163–65.

Ethnē and Gentile Christian Identity (Before 135 CE)

Christian proclamation and Jewish practice could be combined at all, even for Jews. It is totally out of place (*atopon*) "to proclaim Jesus Christ and practice Judaism." Any Christians, Jews included, who are also living "according to Judaism" are attempting to straddle an unbridgeable gap and thus "have not received God's gracious gift" (*To the Magnesians* 8.1). A little later in his letter to the Magnesians, he holds up the example of Jews who, in coming to believe in Christ, abandoned their old Jewish way of life: "And so those who lived according to the old ways came to a new hope, no longer keeping the Sabbath but living according to the Lord's day" (9.1). While Schoedel is probably right in seeing this statement as referring primarily to the Jewish believers in the days of the apostles—those "who once lived as Jews (by observing the Sabbath) but came to live as Christians (by observing Sunday)"—it is also open to a more general application.[119] Jews who want to believe in Christ need to abandon their "old [Jewish] ways" and take on a new (Christian) identity.

But the opposition between the two seems to be even more fundamental. Ignatius is apparently not prepared to grant any positive aspect of a life "according to Judaism" (cf. *To the Magnesians* 8.1) even prior to Christ. As he continues: "For the most divine prophets lived according to Jesus Christ. For this reason also they were persecuted" (8.2). The prophets in a sense were Christians before Christ, persecuted precisely because they "lived according to Jesus Christ" and not "according to Judaism."[120] To be sure, he acknowledges elsewhere that there is "something distinct" about the gospel; what the prophets could only anticipate, the gospel events have actually accomplished. Even so, it is this fully conscious anticipation, rather than anything to do with a Jewish way of life, that matters; Christ is the "door ... through which Abraham and Isaac and the prophets and the apostles and the church enter" into the "unity of God" (*To the Philadelphians* 9.1-2). This is probably the sense in which we are to understand the enigmatic statement in *To the Magnesians* 10.3: "For Christianity did not believe in Judaism, but Judaism in Christianity." Christianity, for Ignatius, does not base its faith on Judaism,[121] in the sense that it is the new Israel, or the fulfillment of the Jewish story, or the like.[122]

---

119. Schoedel, *Ignatius of Antioch*, 123.

120. See also *To the Philadelphians* 5.2: "And we should also love the prophets, because their proclamation anticipated the gospel and they hoped in him and awaited him. And they were saved by believing in him."

121. Trevett's helpful rendition of the phrase; following Corwin, she believes that Ignatius is echoing a slogan of the Judaizers (viz., "Christianity bases its faith on Judaism"); *Study of Ignatius of Antioch*, 172.

122. Ignatius displays little interest in christological readings of the Scriptures or of positioning the gospel with respect to the story of Israel. In response to those who did

Rather, the only value to be found in Judaism is that the patriarchs, prophets, and priests were actually "Christians-in-waiting."[123] When the apostles and other early believers, who had been living "according to the old ways," recognized the truth of the gospel, they "came to a new hope," abandoned their Jewish ways for Christian ways (*To the Magnesians* 9.1), and—in the most probable interpretation of *To the Philadelphians* 6.1 ("it is better to hear Christianity from a man who is circumcised")—began to proclaim Christianity to the gentiles.

All of this provides the framework within which Ignatius is able to speak of the presence of Jews and gentiles "in the one body of his church" (*To the Smyrnaeans* 1.2). In the founding generation of the church, Jewish apostles proclaimed the gospel to Jews and gentiles alike, drawing them into the new unified body of Christ's church. But while the tradition on which he drew may have assigned a more positive significance to the initial Jewish component, Ignatius leaves no space for the idea of a Jewish foundation, core, or remnant. In responding to the gospel, Jews and gentiles alike became Christians, a new identity that superseded, or at least completely overshadowed, their prior identities.

In addition, it should be noted that Ignatius finds little that is positive in the gentile side of things either. He draws a sharp contrast between believers and the world: "there are two kinds of coin, one from God and the other from the world, and each of them has its own stamp set upon it: the unbelievers the stamp of this world and the believers the stamp of God the Father, in love, through Jesus Christ" (*To the Magnesians* 5.2). Although he is heading to Rome, the imperial center of the Mediterranean world, he displays little interest in the Roman Empire in and of itself. As part of the unbelieving world, however—what he elsewhere calls the evil "ancient realm" (*palaia basileia*)—it has already been "destroyed and ... brought to ruin" through the birth, death, and resurrection of Christ, three decisive events

---

(those whom he heard saying, "If I do not find it in the ancient records, I do not believe in the gospel"), he simply replaced "the ancient records" (which at least included Israel's Scriptures) with Christ: "But for me, Jesus Christ is the ancient records; the sacred ancient records are his cross and death, and his resurrection, and the faith that comes through him" (*To the Philadelphians* 8.2). Trevett suggests that this reflects not simply a lack of interest but a lack of scriptural knowledge, especially in comparison with the Judaizers; see *Study of Ignatius of Antioch*, 99.

123. A phrase borrowed from Robinson: "Ignatius presents the Hebrew prophets more as Christians-in-waiting than as Jews (Ign. *Magn.* 8.2–9.2)"; *Ignatius of Antioch*, 210, n. 26. See also Schoedel: "'Judaism,' then, is not granted even a historically limited role in the unfolding of God's plan. Consequently Ignatius radically Christianizes the 'prophets' ... and elsewhere also the 'law' (*Sm.* 5.1). Thus the negative view of Judaism is more emphatic in Ignatius than in the Pastorals and approaches the extreme position of Barnabas"; *Ignatius of Antioch*, 119.

Ethnē and Gentile Christian Identity (Before 135 CE)

that had been accompanied by celestial signs, even though they had "escaped the notice of the ruler of this age" (*To the Ephesians* 19.1–3).

In contrast to the four writings considered to this point, 1 Clement is steeped in Scripture, primarily in the form of quotations from the Scriptures of Israel (in Greek) but also in the use of Septuagintal language and turns of phrase and in allusions to material that was eventually included in the New Testament.[124] By one count, 1 Clement contains some seventy-five quotations, amounting to one-quarter of the text as a whole.[125] Partly for this reason, *ethnē* appears in a richer array of uses than was the case in these other writings.

Unlike 2 Clement, 1 Clement is indeed a letter, sent from "the church of God that sojourns in Rome" to the church in Corinth. The letter begins with a reference to "the matters causing disputes among you" (1.1), a factional insurrection (*stasis*) in which "the dishonorable rose up against the honorable, ... the young against the elders [*presbyterous*]" (3.3). However, it is not until much later in the epistle that the author returns to the topic and provides more explicit details about the matter: despite the apostles' foresight in planning for an orderly succession of leadership, the Corinthians "have deposed some [of the presbyters] from the ministry held blamelessly in honor among them" (44.6). The purpose of the letter, then, is to denounce what has been done, to call for repentance on the part of the perpetrators, and to exhort the church to restore the presbyters to their rightful position.[126] The material in between chapters 3 and 42 serve this overall purpose, much of it by pointing to examples of righteous people who had been attacked unjustly but who had remained faithful and were ultimately vindicated by God, and by the models of order and harmony that can be found in the created order, in a well-organized army, in a healthy body, and in the sacrificial system of the Jerusalem temple. Scholars have observed that both in its vocabulary and its themes, 1 Clement resembles Greco-Roman political rhetoric whose purpose was to denounce unrest and insurrection (*stasis*), to encourage order, peace, and concord (*taxis, eirēnē, homonia*), and thus to defend the constitution (*politeia*) of a well-ordered city-state.[127]

---

124. E.g., the prayer in 59.3–61.3; see Robert M. Grant and Holt H. Graham, *First and Second Clement*, vol. 2 of *The Apostolic Fathers: A New Translation and Commentary* (New York: Thomas Nelson, 1965), 92–96; Andreas Lindemann, *Die Clemensbriefe*, HNT 17, Die Apostolischen Väter 1 (Tübingen: Mohr Siebeck, 1992), 162–76.

125. Donald Alfred Hagner, *The Use of the Old and New Testaments in Clement of Rome*, NovTSup 34 (Leiden: Brill, 1973), 21–23.

126. And the letter probably also calls for self-exile: "Let that one say, 'If I am the cause of faction, strife, and schisms, I will depart; I will go wherever you wish ...'" (54.2).

127. All these words and related terms appear frequently in 1 Clement. See Ehrman,

Concerning authorship, tradition going back to Dionysius of Corinth (ca. 170 CE) has attributed the letter to Clement, a leader in the church of Rome during the reign of Domitian.[128] While the tradition gains some indirect support from the reference in the Shepherd of Hermas to a Clement who was responsible for communicating with other churches on behalf of the church in Rome (Visions 2.4.3), discussions about the author's identity remain inconclusive. Here, however, we are more interested in the author's ethnicity than in his individual identity. As has already been observed, the author was thoroughly conversant with the Scriptures of Israel, and this has led some to conclude that he must have been Jewish.[129] The conclusion does not necessarily follow, however; as we will see, the way in which he reads what Christians later call the Old Testament makes it almost certain that he was not.[130] With respect to date, while older attempts to date the epistle on the grounds of a supposed persecution in the time of Domitian have been rightly abandoned, a date around the turn of the century remains probable on other grounds.[131]

The term *ethnē* appears eight times in 1 Clement, three of these in scriptural citations.[132] We will begin with the one instance in which it is used explicitly of outsiders (55.1). The passage appears just after the author has encouraged the schismatics to repent and depart for the good of the "flock of Christ" (ch. 54) and within a longer section (chs. 53–55) in which he provides a series of examples of noble leaders who were prepared to suffer themselves in order to protect the well-

---

Apostolic Fathers, 1:19–20; David G. Horrell, *The Social Ethos of the Corinthian Correspondence: Interests and Ideology from 1 Corinthians to 1 Clement* (Edinburgh: T&T Clark, 1996), 251–57; Barbara Ellen Bowe, *A Church in Crisis: Ecclesiology and Paraenesis in Clement of Rome*, HDR 23 (Minneapolis: Fortress, 1988), 86–87.

128. Tradition cited by Eusebius (*Ecclesiastical History* 4.23.9–13).

129. So Lightfoot, *Apostolic Fathers*, part 1, 1:59–61, in the context of a discussion about whether Clement was actually the consul Flavius Clemens; Hagner, *Use of the Old and New Testaments in Clement of Rome*, 6–7, following Lightfoot.

130. See especially Hvalvik, "Jewish Believers and Jewish Influence," 211–12; also Adolf von Harnack, *Einführung in die alte Kirchengeschiche: Das Schreiben der Römischen Kirche an die Korinthische aus der Zeit Domitians* (Leipzig: Hinrichs, 1929), lxiii; Lampe, *From Paul to Valentinus*, 75–76.

131. E.g., the statement that the deaths of Peter and Paul took place "in our own generation" (5.1), together with the statement that some who brought the letter from Rome to Corinth had been members of the church "from youth to old age" (63.3). See Lindemann, *Die Clemensbriefe*, 12–13; Ehrman, *Apostolic Fathers*, 1:23–25.

132. In one of the other instances (6.4), the term is used generically ("Jealousy and strife overturned great cities and uprooted great *ethnē*") and thus requires no further comment here.

Ethnē and Gentile Christian Identity (Before 135 CE)

being of the larger community. (That the examples do not exactly correspond to the situation at hand does not seem to have caught the author's attention.) He begins with Moses, who was prepared to be blotted out with the people of Israel if God was not willing to "forgive the sin of this people" (53.4). After urging the insurrectionists to leave and allow the original presbyters to be reinstated, he continues: "but we should bring in examples from the *ethnē* as well" (55.1). The examples are vague and quickly dealt with: "many kings and rulers" who accepted death "in order to deliver their fellow citizens"; "many" who "left their own cities to avoid creating more factions."[133] Then he turns from the *ethnē* to "ourselves" (55.2). Again he lists some anonymous examples: "many among us [*en hēmin*]" who accepted prison or even slavery for the benefit of others; "many women" whom God empowered to perform masculine deeds. This latter example leads into a longer recitation of the deeds of "the blessed Judith," because of her love for "the homeland [*tēs patridos*] and the people [*tou laou*]," and of Esther, on behalf of "the twelve tribes of Israel who were about to perish" (55.5-6).

Two things are to be noted here. First, the author makes a clear distinction between the *ethnē* and "us." As with the other writings considered to this point, *ethnē* is used to denote outsiders, those who are not Christ-believers. Second, the author includes in his own group both Judith and Esther (and probably the "people" or "twelve tribes of Israel" associated with them as well). Taken in isolation, the passage might appear to suggest that the author and his group are part of the people of Israel—that is, that they are Jewish Christ-believers. But since it appears in a letter addressed to the church in Corinth—a church founded by Paul, a "herald [*kērux*] in both East and West" who "taught righteousness to the whole world [*holon ton kosmon*]" (1 Clement 5.6-7), a church that contained non-Jews from the very beginning—such a reading is clearly out of the question. Here we need to turn to other instances of *ethnē* in the letter.

In 1 Clement 29.1, the author sums up the exhortations of the previous chapters by encouraging his readers to give undivided devotion to "our gentle and kind-hearted Father, who made us his own chosen portion [*meros*]." This leads into a citation of the well-known passage in Deut 32:8-9 about the choice of Israel out of all the nations as God's special portion:

> For so it is written: When the Most High divided the *ethnē* and scattered the descendants of Adam, he established the boundaries of the *ethnē* according to the number of the angels of God. His people [*laos*], Jacob, became the portion [*meris*] for the Lord; Israel became the allotment of his inheritance. (29.2)

---

133. For a discussion of specific instances that the author might have had in mind, see Lindemann, *Die Clemensbriefe*, 154-55.

After punctuating this citation with his own pastiche of phrases drawn from several scriptural passages—"See, the Lord takes from himself an *ethnos* from among the *ethnē*"—he continues with an exhortation to Christians: "Since then we are a holy portion [*meris*], we should do everything that pertains to holiness" (30.1).[134]

This reading of the scriptural text is striking in its naive immediacy. The author identifies himself, his readers, and Christians in general with the "people" that he encounters in Israel's Scriptures. The people that, alone of all the *ethnē*, became God's portion is identified in a simple and straightforward way as the church. He simply takes it for granted that Christians now bear Israel's identity. Indeed, to say "now" is perhaps to say too much; the time between the "then" of the text and the "now" of the contemporary situation seems to have collapsed completely. In Skarsaune's words: "So directly is the Old Testament applied to the Church, that the author betrays no awareness of a radical new beginning, a new covenant established by Christ; no awareness of the deep disruption between the Christian community and the Jewish people."[135]

This form of naive appropriation of Israel's identity appears elsewhere in the letter as well, not only in casual language about "our father Abraham" (1 Clement 31.2) but also in a similar scriptural pastiche found in the prayer with which the letter moves toward its conclusion (59.3–61.3).[136] Here the author prays that "the eyes of our heart" might be opened that we may recognize" God as the one who (among many other things) "destroys the reasonings of the *ethnē* . . . who multiplies the *ethnē* upon the earth and who from them all has chosen those who love you through Jesus Christ" (59.3). Here the language of Deut 32:8–9 is simply appropriated as a straightforward statement about the church.[137] The prayer continues with a similar statement about the church in the scriptural language about Israel: "Let all the *ethnē* know you, that you alone are God, that

---

134. While he introduces it as a citation found "in another place," it combines parts of several verses (Deut 4:34; Num 18:27; Exod 22:29[28]).

135. Oskar Skarsaune, "The Development of Scriptural Interpretation in the Second and Third Centuries—Except Clement and Origen," in *From the Beginnings to the Middle Ages (Until 1300)*, vol. 1 of *Hebrew Bible/Old Testament: The History of Its Interpretation*, ed. Magne Saebø (Göttingen: Vandenhoeck & Ruprecht, 1996), 381–82.

136. Note also 32.2–4, with its smooth and continuous chain from Jacob to "the priests and all the Levites who minister at the altar of God," to "the kings, rulers and leaders in the line of Judah," to "the Lord Jesus according to the flesh," to us "too who have been called through his will in Christ Jesus"—all of whom "God has made . . . upright, from the beginning of the ages."

137. There is little reason to believe that *ethnē* here is to be understood as denoting the non-Jewish nations exclusively.

Jesus Christ is your child, and that we are your people [*laos*] and the sheep of your pasture" (59.4).

The one remaining occurrence of *ethnē* requires little comment. In 1 Clement 36.4, the author cites Ps 2:7–8, in the context of a larger passage that echoes Heb 1: "But the Master says this about his Son: 'You are my Son, today I have given you birth. Ask from me, and I will give you the *ethnē* as your inheritance, and the ends of the earth as your possession.'" While the passage might have been used as an opportunity to say something about the *ethnē* and Christ the Son, the author simply passes it by.

Three final observations need to be made before we move on. The first has to do with the author's identity. The easy assumption that believers in Jesus are simply part of the same people who appear in the Scriptures, with no complicating concerns about the historical identity of Israel or the relations between the church and contemporary Jews, speaks strongly in favor of a gentile author. As Hvalvik has observed, "Clement's lack of interest in Israel's salvation-historical uniqueness" makes it "difficult to imagine that Clement himself was a Jewish believer in Jesus. . . . His teachers may have been Jewish believers, but his own naive approach to the Jewish traditions seems more characteristic of a third generation Gentile believer."[138]

Second, and somewhat surprisingly, 1 Clement is virtually devoid of *adversus Judaeos* tendencies. His "lack of interest in Israel's salvation-historical uniqueness" seems to be accompanied by the absence of any need to validate the church's identity as God's chosen portion by denigrating Israel or the Jews. Scriptural passages critical of Israel that, in other hands, might have been used to demonstrate the disobedience and desolation of the Jews are instead used to encourage the readers to turn to God.[139] The Jerusalem cult is introduced as an example of divinely appointed orderliness rather than as an opportunity to contrast carnal and spiritual interpretation (ch. 41). While the author makes some reference to people in Scripture who were persecuted or cast out, and makes it clear that those responsible were "lawless," "unholy," and "transgressors of the law," the only example he gives is that of Daniel and those (officials of the Medes and Persians) who had him "cast into the lions' den" (45.2–5). In sum, passages that others might have used to denounce the Jews as people who capped their long history of persecuting the prophets by betraying and murdering the Righteous One (cf. Acts 7:52) are here used instead for internal critique and hoped-for restoration.

---

138. Hvalvik, "Jewish Believers and Jewish Influence," 212.

139. See especially the catena of passages in ch. 15 and the lengthy citation of Isa 53 in ch. 16.

Finally, we have already noted how 1 Clement tends to deal with problems of communal organization in Corinth by treating the church as if it were a city-state whose "peace and harmony" and common life (*politeia*) were being threatened by internal insurrection (*stasis*). Many of these themes come up one final time in the prayer with which the letter moves to its conclusion (59.3–61.3). With reference to this prayer, scholars have noted in addition the extent to which it displays a positive attitude toward the state, which in view of the circumstances of the letter means not simply the state in general but the Roman Empire in particular. The prayer asks for "harmony and peace" not only for "us" but also for "all those who inhabit the earth," and it acknowledges that God has given "to those who rule and lead us here on earth . . . the authority of rulership [*basileias*]" (60.4; 61.1). As Horrell has observed: "Clement's model for behavior in the church and the household is also his model for society. Peaceful existence is ensured when all remain quietly and humbly in their place, submitting gladly to those who wield authority in whichever sphere."[140] In this sense, 1 Clement represents a quite different model for the relationship between the church and wider society than we have observed in the Shepherd of Hermas, its literary Roman companion.

There is little to suggest that the author has given much thought to the place of the *ethnē* within this model, as it pertains either to the church or to the Roman Empire. Still, the fact that both church and empire are subsumed under the same hierarchical model with the "Heavenly King" (61.2) at its apex suggests that elements were in place for such thinking to take place—something to bear in mind as we proceed.[141]

The anonymous writing that has come down to us as the Epistle of Barnabas bears this name on account of the belief, appearing as early as Clement of Alexandria, that its author was Barnabas, the companion of Paul and (according to Acts) a prominent member of the churches in Jerusalem and Antioch.[142] Given Barnabas's close association with Jewish Christ-groups in the first generation of the movement and his apparent sympathy for the sensitivities of Jewish Christ-believers, it is surprising (to say the least) that his name would come to

---

140. Horrell, *Social Ethos of the Corinthian Correspondence*, 277. See also Klaus Wengst, *Pax Romana and the Peace of Jesus Christ*, trans. John Bowden (Philadelphia: Fortress, 1987), 106–17.

141. Also bearing in mind Barbara E. Bowe's cautionary word: "It goes without saying, however, that such a positive view of the existing political reality contains within it a dangerous precedent"; "Prayer Rendered for Caesar? *1 Clement* 59.3–61.3," in *The Lord's Prayer and Other Prayer Texts from the Greco-Roman Era*, ed. James H. Charlesworth (Valley Forge, PA: Trinity Press International, 1994), 93.

142. *Miscellanies* 2.6.31.2; 2.7.35.5; 2.20.116.3–4 and passim.

Ethnē and Gentile Christian Identity (Before 135 CE)

be attached to what Ehrman calls "the most virulently anti-Jewish" writing of this period.[143]

The Epistle of Barnabas can be classified as a letter, though one with significant didactic and homiletical elements.[144] The body of the letter falls into two unequal parts: chapters 2–17, which begins with a declaration that God has shown "through all the prophets ... that he has no need of sacrifices" (2.4) and which then continues with an extended scriptural argument for a categorical distinction between "them" (the people of Israel) and "us" (the people of the church); and chapters 18–20, a description of the "Two Ways," the way of darkness and the way of light. Among the many puzzles presented by the work is that of the relationship between these two apparently disparate sections. Related to this is the striking contrast between the author's familiarity with Jewish literary and exegetical traditions (including the two-ways material) and his categorical rejection of any Jewish claim to the covenantal underpinnings of these traditions.[145]

The author, who is well known to the recipients of the letter (Epistle of Barnabas 1.4-8), is clearly a teacher, though he is hesitant to emphasize this status (1.8), even though he also feels that he has received "perfect knowledge" that he would like to impart to them (1.5). His hesitancy perhaps reflects some awareness of potential resistance to the arguments of his letter.[146] As we will see when we look at the occurrences of *ethnē* in the letter, the author clearly identifies himself and his readers as gentile Christians. To be sure, the issue has been debated; the Jewish elements in the letter have led some to argue that the author was indeed Jewish.[147] Most interpreters, however, point to several passages as evidence that both the author and (at least most of) his readers were non-Jews: the concern that "we not be dashed against their law as proselytes" (3.6);[148] and the descriptions of their former state ("after redeeming our hearts from darkness" [14.6];

---

143. Ehrman, *Apostolic Fathers*, 2:3.

144. On the question of genre, see Reidar Hvalvik, *The Struggle for Scripture and Covenant: The Purpose of the Epistle of Barnabas and Jewish-Christian Competition in the Second Century*, WUNT 2.82 (Tübingen: Mohr Siebeck, 1996), 66-81.

145. For a helpful summary of the Jewish material, including postbiblical traditions known only through rabbinic material, see James Carleton Paget, *The Epistle of Barnabas: Outlook and Background*, WUNT 2.64 (Tübingen: Mohr Siebeck, 1994), 7-8.

146. Wilson, *Related Strangers*, 127-28.

147. For details, see Hvalvik, *Struggle for Scripture and Covenant*, 43-44.

148. There is a textual variant here: *epēlytoi* is found in one Greek MS (Sinaiticus); *prosēlytoi* appears in the other main Greek MS (H) and is reflected in the Latin version (*proseliti*). This has little bearing on the meaning of the statement, however; as Philo's usage indicates, the two terms are more or less synonymous in this context.

"before we believed in God" [16.7]).[149] As we will see, his use of *ethnē* provides additional evidence in this regard.

Even so, the author is clearly preoccupied with questions concerning Jews and Judaism and the relationship between Judaism and the church. While some interpreters have seen this as an abstract concern—that is, one arising from internal considerations of identity and scriptural interpretation—it more probably had to do with an actual situation in which Jews, Jewish Christ-believers, and gentile Christians lived in close social proximity.[150] The author seems to be responding to a situation in which gentile Christians were attracted to Jewish beliefs and practices, as found either in Jewish synagogues or in Jewishly oriented Christ-groups, and writes to warn his own circle of the dangers of such attraction.

The question of the letter's context also comes up in discussions of its date, in that the most pertinent evidence concerning date is provided by a passage that speaks of a possible rebuilding of the Jerusalem temple.[151] The passage appears in chapter 16, where the author argues that the true temple of God is to be found not in Jerusalem but in the hearts of believers. In the course of this argument, however, he refers to the Jerusalem temple in a citation of an unknown text: "See, those who have destroyed this temple will themselves build it" (16.3). Then he continues: "This is happening. For because of the war, it was destroyed by their enemies. And now the servants of the enemies will themselves rebuild it" (16.4). While the passage has engendered considerable discussion, with scholarly

---

149. See Hvalvik, *Struggle for Scripture and Covenant*, 43–46; Wilson, *Related Strangers*, 128; Peter J. Tomson, "The Didache, Matthew, and Barnabas as Sources for Early Second Century Jewish and Christian History," in Tomson and Schwartz, *Jews and Christians in the First and Second Centuries*, 361. Nevertheless, there continues to be room for disagreement; see Paget, *Epistle of Barnabas*, 7–9.

150. See the survey in Hvalvik, *Struggle for Scripture and Covenant*, 6–16. For a more general development of the former approach, see Miriam S. Taylor, *Anti-Judaism and Early Christian Identity: A Critique of the Scholarly Consensus*, StPB 46 (Leiden: Brill, 1995).

Taking the latter approach, Tomson draws our attention to the evident links connecting the Epistle of Barnabas, the Didache, and Matthew, links suggesting that the "three texts belonged to a larger Christian milieu of mixed Jewish-gentile ethnicity," one in which "ample use was made of Jewish traditions," even though the texts reflect strikingly different positions on the status of Jews and Jewish traditions within the Christian milieu; "The Didache, Matthew and Barnabas," 355.

151. The reference in the Epistle of Barnabas 4.3–5 to Daniel's "ten kingdoms" and "the fourth beast" might also have some bearing on the issue, though scholarly discussion has been quite inconclusive.

Ethnē and Gentile Christian Identity (Before 135 CE)

opinion coalescing around dates either during the reign of Nerva (96–98 CE) or during the reign of Hadrian, but prior to the outbreak of the Bar Kokhba revolt (i.e., ca. 130 CE), for present purposes it is not necessary to decide between the two.[152] What is more pertinent is that the passage seems to reflect a situation in which the Jewish community was poised to regain some of the social status it had lost during the Flavian period, and thus one in which attraction to Jewish belief and practice might have intensified.

There are seven occurrences of *ethnē* in the letter, six of which are contained in scriptural quotations. In these six occurrences, however, *ethnē* is not simply a passing reference; in each of them, the term is central to the citation, and the citation is embedded in the surrounding argument sufficiently enough that we can readily discern the author's understanding and use of the term. We begin, however, with the one occurrence that is not a citation, which is also the one instance in which the term refers to outsiders.

The verse in question stands at the beginning of the section we have just noted, in which the author speaks of the rebuilding of the Jerusalem temple. After denouncing the Jews ("those wretches") for their false belief that the temple "was actually the house of God," he continues: "For they consecrated him in the Temple almost like the *ethnē* do" (Epistle of Barnabas 16.1–2). In contrast to the occurrences that we have examined to this point, here *ethnē* refers not simply to non-Christian outsiders but to a group that is differentiated from the Jews as well. In other words, here the original sense of the term—that is, as non-Jewish outsiders—is also in view. But even as it evokes the difference, however, it simultaneously negates it. That is, the author perceives Jewish temple worship as almost equivalent to paganism; Jews are virtually indistinct from the *ethnē*. This leads us into the most stunning (and distressing) aspect of the Epistle of Barnabas.

The author's introductory statement about sacrifice, with its language about "the new law of our Lord Jesus Christ" and the nullification of the sacrificial system (noted above; Epistle of Barnabas 2.4–6), might seem to suggest that the author holds to a temporally progressive concept of supersessionary fulfillment.[153] But while there is a temporal element, the process of supersession (if that is even the appropriate category) is much more radical than anything encountered in other early Christian literature. In the Epistle of Barnabas's

---

152. For thorough discussions, see Hvalvik, *Struggle for Scripture and Covenant*, 17–34; Paget, *Epistle of Barnabas*, 9–30. Hvalvik opts for Hadrian, Paget for Nerva. See also Peter Richardson and Martin B. Shukster, "Barnabas, Nerva and the Yavnean Rabbis," *JTS* 34 (1983): 31–55.

153. Wilson recognizes the possibility but rightly rejects it; *Related Strangers*, 129. In addition to "the new law," see also the expression "new people" (5.7; 7.5).

view, the covenant was nullified even before it was enacted. As Moses was receiving it on Mount Sinai, the people of Israel "turned back to idols" in their worship of the golden calf. Perceiving their sin, Moses "cast the two tablets from his hands," thus smashing "their covenant" irrevocably: "They permanently lost it ... that the covenant of his beloved, Jesus, might be established in our hearts."[154] The sole purpose of the subsequent laws of Moses, the writings of the prophets, and of Israel's Scripture as a whole was to speak of this true covenant, something that could be perceived only by those whose hearing and hearts had been circumcised (10.12). It was only because they had been led astray by "an evil angel" that the people of Israel thought that circumcision and other provisions of the law were to be understood in a fleshly way (9.4; cf. 2.10).[155] Indeed, the author cites Jer 9:26 ("See, says the Lord, all the *ethnē* are uncircumcised in their foreskins, but this people is uncircumcised in their hearts"; 9.5) to suggest that a people unable to see that circumcision is a matter of the heart rather than of the flesh is no better than the *ethnē*. For the Epistle of Barnabas, then, the religious and cultic life of Israel as a whole was the result of demonic deception.

The author's argument that the people of Israel permanently lost the covenant because of the golden calf incident is prefaced with his denunciation of "some people" who say "that the covenant is both theirs and ours" (Epistle of Barnabas 4.6).[156] Here we need not linger over the identity of these people. As we have already observed, the author seems to be reacting against Judaizing in some form, probably one in which gentile believers were attracted to mixed-ethnic Christ-groups where they adopted some Jewish observances and thus were considered as sharing in God's covenant with Israel. What is of greater interest at this point is how he conceives of the two groups that he typically refers to as "them" and "us."

154. Quoted material from 4.6–8.
155. As Ferdinand R. Prostmeier puts it: "Because Scripture as a whole promises Christ and Christians, there is no salvation story that precedes God's investment of salvation in Christ. Everything that happened then, including circumcision, the Sabbath, and the Day of Atonement, and the like, exhausts itself pointing to the Christ event"; "The Epistle of Barnabas," in Pratscher, *Apostolic Fathers*, 35.
156. This reading follows the Latin text, which is probably closest to the original. Robert A. Kraft has argued for a reading based primarily on H, with some modifications from S ("by claiming that your covenant is irrevocably yours"), thus understanding the verse as a warning against complacency (cf. 4.14); see *Barnabas and the Didache*, vol. 3 of *The Apostolic Fathers: A New Translation and Commentary* (New York: Thomas Nelson, 1965), 90. Most commentators, however, prefer the reading preserved in Latin; see, e.g., Hvalvik, *Struggle for Scripture and Covenant*, 90.

Ethnē and Gentile Christian Identity (Before 135 CE)

When he speaks of "them," it goes without saying that he has the people of Israel in view. At the end of chapter 4, for example, he instructs his readers "to observe that Israel was abandoned even after such signs and wonders had occurred in it" (Epistle of Barnabas 4.14). But what about "us"? In chapter 13 he returns to the question of which group ("this people or the first one") "receives the inheritance, and whether the covenant is for us or for them" (13.1). The antecedent for "this people" (i.e., the Christians) is found in the preceding verse, which concludes an extended section on the christological meaning of Scripture (chs. 11–12) by citing a text from Isaiah:[157] "The Lord said to Christ my Lord, 'I have grasped his right hand that the *ethnē* will obey him, and I will shatter the power of kings'" (12.11). Clearly, the author here identifies the Christian "people" with the obedient *ethnē* of Isa 45:1.

Such an identification of "us" with the *ethnē* is confirmed and reinforced in the argument contained in the next two chapters, which consists of commentary on a running series of scriptural citations, several of which make reference to the *ethnē*. To be sure, we cannot place much weight on the first of these, a passage having to do with the twins in Rebecca's womb (Epistle of Barnabas 13.2): "the Lord said to her, 'There are two *ethnē* in your womb and two peoples [*laoi*] in your belly, and one people will dominate the other and the greater will serve the lesser'" (Gen 25:21–23). But after another example of a favored younger son, the author turns to the case of Abraham, where non-Jewish *ethnē* are clearly in view: "What then does [God] say to Abraham, when he alone believed and was appointed for righteousness? 'See, Abraham, I have made you a father of the *ethnē* who believe in God while uncircumcised'" (13.7).[158] Further, in the following chapter, as he brings his argument to a conclusion, he cites several passages from Isaiah in which the "holy people," which came into being after Christ "redeemed us from darkness," is identified with the *ethnē* who are to be illuminated through the worldwide mission of the servant of the Lord ("I have given you as a covenant of the people, as a light to the *ethnē*"; "I have set you as a light to the *ethnē* that you may bring salvation to the end of the earth").[159]

The author's answer to the question "whether the covenant is for us or them"

---

157. Albeit as filtered through Christian tradition. The original Isaianic text referred to Cyrus (*Kyrō*) as God's anointed. In Barnabas's rendering, *Kyrō* (Cyrus) has become *Kyriō* (Lord), and it is unlikely that he was responsible for the change. See the discussion in Paget, *Epistle of Barnabas*, 161.

158. The echo of the Pauline formulation (cf. Rom 4:11) is probably due to a free-floating tradition rather than to any direct dependence on Paul; see, e.g., Kraft, *Apostolic Fathers*, 123.

159. 14.7, citing Isa 42:6-7; 14.8, citing Isa 49:6-7.

is not simply "us" as believers in Christ but "us" as distinctly gentile people—"a people not of Jews, but of Gentiles."[160] While in one place he can use the term *ethnē* as a designation for outsiders (Epistle of Barnabas 16.2), the emphasis in his usage falls on *ethnē* as a continuing identity rather than an identity left behind. He and those like him are "*ethnē* who believe in God" (13.7) rather than simply a new people called out from among the *ethnē*.

Nevertheless, the term is of interest to the author only within a very limited sphere. It provides convenient scriptural reinforcement for the sharp distinctions he wants to make between his group and mixed-ethnic Judaizing Christians, between "the new law of our Lord Jesus Christ" (2.6) and the malevolent interpretive influence of evil angels (cf. 9.4), and between "this people [and] the first one" (13.1). No doubt it also reflected his own native identity as a non-Jew. Apart from this, however, the term is of little apparent interest, its usefulness restricted to the internal identity concerns of his own group and its relations to other Christian and Jewish groups.

The author's attitudes to the wider world of the non-Jewish *ethnē* are shaped by the same sort of dualistic outlook that characterizes his internal identity concerns: "The days are evil and the one who is at work holds sway" (Epistle of Barnabas 2.1); "hate the error of the present age, that we may be loved in the age to come" (4.1); the "path of light" is under the supervision of "light-bearing angels of God" (who is "the Lord from eternity past to eternity to come"), while the "path of darkness is governed by "angels of Satan" (who is "the ruler over the present age of lawlessness") (18.1–2). The Roman imperial character of the "present evil age" probably comes into view in the author's citation of texts from Enoch and Daniel, as he informs his readers that "the final stumbling block is at hand" and that God's "Beloved One" will soon "arrive at his inheritance" (4.3–5).[161] In such a dualistic and apocalyptic understanding of the wider world in which he and his readers find themselves, a world categorically divided between those on "the path of light" and those on "the path of darkness," their identity as "*ethnē* who believe in God" is of limited additional usefulness.

In the remaining four writings to be considered here, *ethnē* is not used as a term for outsiders; otherwise, the ways in which the term is used are quite varied. Again, we will deal with the material in the order of increasing interest in *ethnē* as an identity term.

With the majority of commentators, I take the Pastoral Epistles to be pseudonymous, written after Paul's death by a leader within a group of churches that

---

160. Hvalvik, *Struggle for Scripture and Covenant*, 147.
161. On the "strongly apocalyptic anti-Roman sentiment" of 4.3–5, see Paget, *Epistle of Barnabas*, 7, n. 25.

traced their origins to the apostle, who wrote to bring Paul's voice and authority to bear on issues facing these churches in his own day.[162] To be sure, one needs to recognize that there are differences between 2 Timothy and the other two epistles, which have suggested to some that it was written by Paul himself or by someone other than the author of the other two and in a different context.[163] For my part, I see no need to postulate separate authorship, but I nevertheless consider it prudent to treat 2 Timothy on its own terms, rather than simply lumping it together with the others.

While this is not the place for any detailed discussion of the Pastoral Epistles, some comments are in order about the ethnicity of the author. As was observed above, in contrast to the issue of pseudonymity, scholarly discussions of the author's ethnic identity are rare. One way of framing the issue is to ask this question: If we start from the position that the epistles were written by someone other than Paul, in a situation some time after his death, is there any compelling reason to believe that the author was Jewish? As a useful point of reference, we can consider the cases of Ephesians, Colossians, and 1 Peter. As we observed in chapter 4, in each of them, the author simply assumes that "Jews" and "gentiles" are familiar and significant categories and addresses gentile readers from the perspective of a Jewish Christ-believer. In the Pastoral Epistles, however, this is simply not the case.

We begin with 1 Timothy, where the issue of authorial ethnicity can conveniently be discussed in the context of the two instances of *ethnē* (2:7; 3:16) itself. The first of these appears in a section dealing with the practice of prayer in the context of communal worship (2:1–8). The section begins with an exhortation that prayers of various kinds be offered "for all human beings [*pantōn anthrōpōn*]." While the text continues with a more specific reference—"for kings and all who are in high positions"—the universal scope quickly reappears: "This is right and acceptable in the sight of God our Savior who desires all human

---

162. For me, the issue was largely settled when I read P. N. Harrison's study of vocabulary and style while I was still a student; *The Problem of the Pastoral Epistles* (Oxford: Oxford University Press, 1921). Although some of his statistical analysis has been shown to be in need of correction, the overall impact of his study remains unchanged. For attempts to put the analysis on a sounder footing, see K. Grayston and G. Herdan, "The Authorship of the Pastoral Epistles in the Light of Statistical Analysis," *NTS* 6 (1959–60): 1–15; Kenneth J. Neumann, *The Authenticity of the Pauline Epistles in the Light of Stylo-Statistical Analysis* (Atlanta: Scholars Press, 1990).

163. See, e.g., Michael Prior, *Paul the Letter-Writer and the Second Letter to Timothy*, JSNTSup 23 (Sheffield: Sheffield Academic, 1989); Jerome Murphy-O'Connor, "2 Timothy Contrasted with 1 Timothy and Titus," *Revue Biblique* 98 (1991): 403–18.

beings [*pantas anthrōpous*] to be saved and to come to the knowledge of the truth" (vv. 3-4).¹⁶⁴ This leads into a quasi-creedal formulation, again within a universal framework: "For there is one God; there is also one mediator between God and humankind [*anthrōpōn*], the human Christ Jesus, who gave himself a ransom for all [*pantōn*]" (vv. 5-6). The reference to *ethnē* appears in the following verse, where the author declares emphatically that he "was appointed a herald and apostle" of this message — "a teacher of *ethnē* in faith and truth" (v. 7).

The NRSV renders *ethnē* here as "Gentiles," and this translation cannot be ruled out. Any reader of 1 Timothy who was familiar with the other letters bearing Paul's name would be aware that Paul understood himself to be the apostle of the *ethnē* in the sense of non-Jewish nations and individuals.¹⁶⁵ Going further than this, some commentators have argued that a Jew-gentile contrast has been evoked implicitly already in the epistle, in the context of the admonition with which the epistle begins. Here the author warns Timothy about people who were teaching a "different doctrine" (1 Tim 1:3), which a little later is restated in terms of their desire "to be teachers of the law [*nomodidaskaloi*]" (1:7).¹⁶⁶ As the argument unfolds, this polemical admonition concerning teachers of the law is then linked with key aspects of the passage under discussion (i.e., 2:1-7): the theme of universality, including the emphasis on God's desire that all be saved; the appeal to the oneness of God (*heis gar theos*: "God is one") as the basis of this universal desire; the vehement assertion of Paul's apostleship ("I am telling the truth, I am not lying"). Linking the warning against false "teachers of the law" in 1:6-7 with the universality of the message about Christ in 2:4-6, such commentators have argued "that the inclusion of Gentiles alongside Jews in salvation is the primary issue here" and "that the point of stressing God's desire to save all people is to indicate that his desire includes Gentiles as well as Jews."¹⁶⁷

To be sure, some early readers of the epistle might have understood it this

---

164. "This" probably refers to vv. 1-2 as a whole, rather than just to the more limited statement about "kings and all who are in high positions" (v. 2).

165. E.g., *eimi egō ethnōn apostolos* (Rom 11:13).

166. The phrase in 1 Tim 1:3 renders a stand-alone verb: *heterodidaskalein* (to "other-teach"; "to teach otherwise").

167. I. Howard Marshall, with Philip H. Towner, *A Critical and Exegetical Commentary on the Pastoral Epistles*, ICC (Edinburgh: T&T Clark, 1999), 425. Likewise Luke Timothy Johnson: "Paul's insistence on the title 'teacher' [*didaskalos*] here, then, and his placing it in direct connection with 'Gentiles' — as well as his insistence that he is telling the truth — draws our attention to the probable polemic function of his self-designation in this specific situation. Against those would-be teachers of Law who seek to impose it on Gentile Christians, Paul teaches the primacy of God's grace, which empowers humans to have faith"; *The First and Second Letters to Timothy*, AB (New York: Doubleday, 2001), 195.

Ethnē and Gentile Christian Identity (Before 135 CE)

way and could well have appealed to other letters of Paul for support. But it is quite an overstatement to say that the text itself invites such a reading. For one thing, there is no hint in 1 Tim 1:3-11 that the problematic teaching about the law had anything to do with those aspects of the law that differentiated Jews from gentiles and thus would exclude non-Jews from a universal message of salvation. Instead, the problem had to do with "myths and endless genealogies that promote speculations" in place of the "household administration of God that is in faith" (1:4).[168] Further, the author's attempt to set out the legitimate use of the law in 1:8-11 provides no reason to believe that he was polemicizing against an illegitimate attempt to exclude gentiles from "the glorious gospel of the blessed God" (1:11).[169] Indeed, nothing in these verses would lead us to believe that the author had any inside knowledge of what a torah-centered life might have been like at all.

There is little to suggest, then, that distinctions between Jews and gentiles, and issues concerning the inclusion of non-Jews within the sphere of the gospel, would have been to the fore as readers reached the end of chapter 1.[170] With respect to 1 Tim 2:1-7, apart from the reference to Paul's status as "apostle of the *ethnē*" in v. 7, the universal thrust of the passage has to do more with an undifferentiated humanity—"all human beings" (*pantes anthrōpoi*), "humankind" (*anthrōpoi*), "all" (*pantes*)—than with the incorporation of the two parts of a bifurcated humanity. Would the reference to Paul as a "teacher of the *ethnē*," then, be sufficient in itself to bring a Jewish bifurcation of humanity into view?[171] Here we need to remember that ancient readers of a Greek text did not face the

---

168. A literal rendering of *oikonomian theou tēn en pistei*.

169. Older arguments that the Pastorals were written to counter "a kind of Judaizing Gnosticism (with speculation and observance of the law)" may have been overstated and one-dimensional, but the evidence to which such arguments appealed is certainly pertinent here; see Martin Dibelius and Hans Conzelmann, *The Pastoral Epistles: A Commentary*, trans. Philip Buttolph and Adela Yarbro, Hermeneia (Philadelphia: Fortress, 1972); the quoted material appears on p. 3.

170. Indeed, given the polemic in the epistle against "what is falsely called *gnōsis*" (6:20), the universal emphases in the epistle could just as easily be read in contrast to the sorts of anthropological distinctions that appear in groups that have traditionally been labeled "Gnostic"; see, e.g., Raymond F. Collins, *1 & 2 Timothy and Titus: A Commentary*, NTL (Louisville: Westminster John Knox, 2002), 60.

171. Johnson points to Rom 3:29-30, where the similar assertion "God is one [*heis ho theos*]" (cf. 1 Tim 2:5) is used in the context of such a bifurcation ("Or is God the God of Jews only? Is he not the God of Gentiles also?"); *First and Second Letters to Timothy*, 197. But the assertion of God's oneness stands on its own; its use in 1 Timothy is quite different from that in Romans.

kind of either-or decision that is present for modern English readers, who need to decide whether to read *ethnē* as "nations" or "gentiles."[172] The term itself is bivalent—carrying in itself the potential to be taken in two different (though closely related) ways, with various additional factors coming into play in the determination of which sense is most appropriate. While a Jewish reader might have been inclined to read *didaskalos ethnōn* as "a teacher of the non-Jews," in the absence of clear textual signals (such as are found in Ephesians, for example), the default reading for non-Jews would be "a teacher of the nations." In short, while the alternative reading cannot be completely excluded, it is more likely that non-Jewish readers would have taken their clues from the expressions of undifferentiated humanity that permeate the passage as a whole. It is also likely that such a reading was in keeping with the author's intentions as well; that is, from the author's perspective a "teacher of the *ethnē*" (2:7) is one who would lead "all human beings [*pantes anthrōpoi*] to come to a knowledge of the truth" (2:4).

The second instance of *ethnē* in 1 Timothy (3:16) is found in the context of another christological hymn, this time as part of the hymn itself. Coming at a transitional point in the letter, the hymn quite clearly is a piece of preformed tradition, which the author has cited to punctuate his admonition to Timothy about "how one ought to behave in . . . the church of the living God, the pillar and bulwark of the truth" (3:15). Introduced as "the mystery of our *eusebeia* [piety, devotion]," the hymn consists of six participial phrases that each refer to Christ.[173] *Ethnē* appears in the fourth line: "proclaimed among *ethnē*."

A certain element of structuring can be discerned in the hymn as a whole, though not without some uncertainty. The first two lines seem to constitute a contrasting pair ("revealed in flesh"/"vindicated in spirit"), and the last two lines seem to follow a similar pattern ("believed in throughout the world [*kosmos*]"/"received in glory"). In each case, the first line can be seen as having to do with the earthly realm, the second with the heavenly. The pattern seems to be broken with the middle pair, however, where the earthly/heavenly sequence is inverted: "seen by angels"/"proclaimed among *ethnē*." Perhaps, as Hurtado has suggested, the presence of earthly and heavenly planes in each pair is more significant than the sequence.[174] Alternatively, one might posit a chronological

---

172. On this point, see Johnson, *First and Second Letters to Timothy*, 197.

173. Though not explicitly; as with other christological hymns (e.g., Phil 2:6; Col 1:15), it begins with a relative pronoun. On the christological hymns, see Larry W. Hurtado, *Lord Jesus Christ: Devotion to Jesus in Earliest Christianity* (Grand Rapids: Eerdmans, 2003), 146-49, 514-15 (on 1 Tim 3:16).

174. He describes it as "a symmetrical alternation between actions on the two planes," by which he means that the sequence in the middle pair is opposite to that in the pairs

sequence, which seems to be discernible in the first five elements at least: earthly life ("revealed in flesh"); resurrection ("vindicated in spirit"); postresurrection exaltation ("seen by angels"); proclamation ("proclaimed among *ethnē*"); response ("believed in throughout the *kosmos*").[175] As an alternative sequence, some commentators have suggested that *angeloi* in the third line should be rendered "messengers"—that is, the apostolic witnesses to the resurrection who then proclaimed it among the *ethnē*.[176] Either way, however, it is not readily apparent how we are to understand "taken up in glory" as something sequential to the worldwide acceptance of that truth for which the church is "the pillar and bulwark."

Nevertheless, we do not need to resolve these questions before we can say anything about the proclamation "among the *ethnē*." Here the matter is more straightforward than was the case with the previous passage. The fourth and fifth phrases in the hymn are tightly related: the proclamation "among the *ethnē*" results in belief "throughout the *kosmos*"; *ethnē* and *kosmos* stand in parallel. Unless one can imagine an early Christ-hymn that would disregard entirely the initial proclamation to Jews, *ethnē* here cannot carry the distinctively Jewish sense of "gentiles."[177] The worldwide spread of belief in Christ has resulted from the proclamation of this message to the nations of the world. While a phrase such as "proclaimed among the *ethnē*" might have originally emerged in the discourse of early Christ-believers as a reference to the gentile mission, its use in 1 Tim 3:16 needs to be seen as evidence that the distinctively Jewish sense of the term could recede into the background as its more basic sense moved to the fore.

This leads to a further observation about the epistle as a whole. As we have seen, literature produced by Jewish Christ-believers is marked by a concern to provide a rationale for the inclusion of Christ-believing gentiles, by linking it in some way with the people of Israel and with the belief that Christ represents the fulfillment of Israel's hopes. In 1 Timothy, such a concern is severely attenuated

---

that flank it; Hurtado, *Lord Jesus Christ*, 514, n. 54. For an earlier two-planes reading of the hymn, see Dibelius and Conzelmann, *Pastoral Epistles*, 61–62.

175. Hurtado also discerns a chronological sequence, though without highlighting it.

176. See, e.g., Johnson, *First and Second Letters to Timothy*, 233.

177. Even Marshall, who sees the inclusion of the gentiles as an important theme in 1 Timothy, recognizes this: "Through the apostle's ministry, the Gentiles have been reached . . . , but the scope is doubtless wider. Ἔθνη (2.7: 2 Tim 4.17), which does not necessarily exclude Jews, regards the gospel ministry in its universal scope"; *Pastoral Epistles*, 527. Some other commentators slide back and forth between "nations" and "Gentiles" without addressing the difference between the two renderings; e.g., Dibelius and Conzelmann, who see "the missionary term 'nations,' 'pagans'" as synonymous with "man"; *Pastoral Epistles*, 62; also Collins, *1 & 2 Timothy and Titus*, 110–11.

at best. Christ's significance has to do with generic humankind tout court: Christ as the one who "came into the world to save sinners" (1:15); Christ as the "one mediator between God and humankind" (2:5); Christ as "believed in throughout the world" (3:16). Israel and its history are simply cut out of the picture. Even where there is a reference to the law (1:7-11) or to the Scripture (5:18), there is nothing to suggest that these existed in an inextricable relationship with a specific people.[178] This observation tends to confirm the perception that the epistle was written by a gentile Christian and provides one window into the sense of Christian identity within which he writes.

Ethnē appears once in 2 Timothy (4:17), in the account of Paul's first defense in Rome (cf. 1:17), with which the body of the epistle comes to a conclusion (4:16-18).[179] Despite the fact that "no one came to [Paul's] support," he was strengthened by the Lord, "so that through me the message might be fully proclaimed and all the *ethnē* might hear it." The account represents one of the strikingly personal and detailed passages that are especially prominent in 2 Timothy and that have led some to postulate that they were excerpted from earlier letters written by Paul himself, and others to believe that 2 Timothy as a whole was authentic.[180] However, the retrospective tone of the warning about what would come "in the last days" (3:1) is a strong indication that the letter was written after Paul's death, and the similarities between various passages in 2 Timothy and the other two Pastorals suggest that the same author was responsible for all three. So even if it were the case that the passage under discussion here depends on earlier material, we are justified in taking it, in its present form and context, as the work of the same author.

On the most straightforward reading of it, the "full proclamation of the message" referred to in v. 17 was part of what Paul said in his own defense (the basic sense of *apologia*; 4:16), a proclamation that was made possible by the fact that "the Lord stood by [him] and gave [him] strength."[181] In this reading, "all the

---

178. The only biblical personages who receive mention are Adam and Eve (4:13-15), the primordial "man" (*anēr*; 4:8, 12) and "woman" (*gynē*; 4:9, 10, 11, 12).

179. Some MSS add *ethnōn* after *didaskalos* in 1:11 ("for this gospel I was appointed a herald and an apostle and a teacher of the *ethnē*"; so ℵ2 C D F G K L P Ψ). The shorter reading is to be preferred, both on manuscript grounds (omit: ℵ* A D* vgmss) and the probability of influence from 1 Tim 2:7.

180. For the former view, see, e.g., Harrison, *Problem of the Pastoral Epistles*, 87-135, esp. 121-22. And for the latter, see, e.g., Jerome Murphy-O'Connor, *Paul: A Critical Life* (Oxford: Clarendon, 1996), 356-59. A compelling aspect of his argument is that an authentic 2 Timothy helps to explain both why the later pseudonymous epistles (1 Timothy and Titus) were readily accepted and why there were two letters addressed to Timothy.

181. The *hina* (so that) clause is an expression of purpose or, less likely, of result.

Ethnē and Gentile Christian Identity (Before 135 CE)

ethnē" denotes the audience at his hearing. There is something odd, however, about the use of the phrase (*panta ta ethnē*) to denote the collection of individuals who happened to be present at the hearing. It should be noted that if the phrase refers to individuals, *ethnē* must have the sense of non-Jewish individuals; only in such cases can *ethnē* be used of individuals. Unless we are to assume that there were Jews present as well, why use such a grandiose term (*panta ta ethnē*) to denote a small group of people ("all the non-Jews who were there")?[182] The statement about "the message [*to kērygma*]" being "fully proclaimed [*plērophorēthē*]" to the *ethnē*, however, with its echoes of Rom 11:25 ("until the fullness [*to plērōma*] of the *ethnē* come in"), might suggest a reading in which the successful outcome of the hearing ("I was rescued from the lion's mouth") opened up the possibility of further proclamation among "all the *ethnē*."[183] But such a reading would strain the syntax of the sentence: the proclamation in question was made possible not by the divine rescue but by the divine presence and empowerment during the defense itself.

The verse, then, presents some puzzling problems. Perhaps the phrase *panta ta ethnē* appeared in a source used by the author in which it was appropriate for the context but then was rendered problematic in its new setting. Or perhaps the term was chosen by the author himself, because of its Pauline overtones (cf. Rom 1:5; 15:11; 16:26; Gal 3:8) or the symbolic place of Rome at the center of a worldwide empire.[184] For our purposes, there is no need to settle on a specific solution. It is sufficient to note that the phrase depicts the *ethnē* as targets of mission and that non-Jews are probably in view, though this is not made explicit.

Turning briefly to a consideration of this reference to the *ethnē* in its larger context, we can note that, in the epistle, there is a little more evidence of a Jewish framework than we observed in 1 Timothy. The gospel proclaimed by Paul is said to consist of "Jesus Christ, raised from the dead, a descendant [*ek spermatos*] of David."[185] The scriptural account of Korah's rebellion is cited in 2 Tim 2:19 (a citation of Num 16:5, together with a pastiche drawn from various other passages).[186] Reference is made to "Jannes and Jambres" as opponents of Moses (2 Tim 3:8), using names for Pharaoh's magicians that are known from Jewish tradition (CD V, 17–19) but that do not appear in the scriptural account (Exod 7:11).

---

182. And if it were a mixed group—i.e., a group that included some Jews—why exclude them from the hearing of the message?

183. So Collins, *1 & 2 Timothy and Titus*, 286.

184. Cf. Marshall, *Pastoral Epistles*, 824.

185. 2 Tim 2:8; "gospel" (*euangelion*) also appears in 1:8, 10.

186. See the discussions in Johnson, *First and Second Letters to Timothy*, 386–87; and Marshall, *Pastoral Epistles*, 757–59.

At the same time, however, except for the description of Christ as being "from the seed of David," there is no evident interest in the relationship between the community of those "who want to live a godly life in Christ Jesus" (2 Tim 3:12) and the people of Israel. The story of salvation moves directly from "the grace [that] was given to us in Christ Jesus before the ages began" to its revelation "in the appearing of our Savior Christ Jesus" (2 Tim 1:9–10). Timothy may have known from childhood "the sacred writings that are able to instruct you in salvation through faith in Christ Jesus" (2 Tim 3:15), but the letter contains no indication that these Scriptures also told the story of Israel and the promises of salvation made to them. Both 1 and 2 Timothy reflect a form of gentile Christianity for which the Jewish origins of the faith could simply be disregarded or left behind.

While the Apology of Aristides betrays no awareness that *ethnē* could be used as an identity term for non-Jewish Christians, the term does appear as part of an extended exercise in competitive ethnography. As will be readily apparent, the ethnographical argument is much more rudimentary than most of those that have come into view in previous chapters. Nevertheless, it represents perhaps the earliest explicit attempt on the part of a gentile Christian writer to enter this arena of identity negotiation.

Up until the latter part of the nineteenth century, the Apology was known only indirectly through statements by later writers, the earliest of whom was Eusebius. Before the end of the century, however, two full versions of the work came into public view through separate manuscript discoveries, one in Syriac and the other in Greek. Since the latter was embedded in a longer narrative, however, we cannot simply assume that it is closer to the original.[187] There are differences between the two, several of which have a bearing on our own discus-

---

187. The Syriac manuscript was discovered by Agnes and Margaret Smith in St. Catherine's Monastery in Sinai and published by J. Rendel Harris. The Greek version was discovered by Harris's Cambridge colleague J. Armitage Robinson, who, having read a prepublication version of Harris's translation, recognized it as a somewhat longer version of something embedded in the *Life of Barlaam and Joasaph*, an early Christian narrative with which he was familiar. The two versions were published together in a single volume: J. Rendel Harris and J. Armitage Robinson, *The Apology of Aristides on Behalf of the Christians, from a Syriac Ms. Preserved on Mount Sinai, with an Appendix Containing the Main Portion of the Original Greek Text* (Piscataway, NJ: Gorgias, 2004). For the story of the Smith sisters, including an account of the discovery, see Janet Soskice, *The Sisters of Sinai: How Two Lady Adventurers Discovered the Hidden Gospels* (New York: Alfred A. Knopf, 2009). In addition to the full versions, fragmentary portions of the work are extant in Armenian and Greek; for a full discussion of the manuscript tradition, see Bernard Pouderon and Marie-Joseph Pierre, eds., *Aristide: Apologie*, SC 470 (Paris: Cerf, 2003), 107–41; a survey of patristic references to Aristides is provided on pp. 25–31.

Ethnē and Gentile Christian Identity (Before 135 CE)

sion. The Syriac version is longer than the Greek by about a half, as it contains both longer versions of common material and segments not contained in the Greek. In addition, one segment of particular interest—the description of the Jews in chapter 14—differs considerably between the two. Robinson believed that the Greek version preserved the original work, except for "the very few places in which modification was obviously needed" in order to incorporate it into the longer narrative.[188] While his arguments were initially influential, closer examination has led to a shift of opinion, so that the common view now is that the Syriac more closely reflects the original for the most part.[189]

Eusebius makes two statements about the Apology of Aristides, each of which connects it with the reign of Hadrian. The first simply describes it as "a defense [*apologian*] of the faith addressed to Hadrian" (*Ecclesiastical History* 4.3.3). The second appears in his *Chronicle*, a chronological work that contains a section in which events are listed in correlation with the years in which they were presumed to have taken place. Here Eusebius says that the Apology was presented to Hadrian in Athens in the eighth year of his reign (i.e., 124 or 125 CE). At first glance, this information appears to receive general confirmation from the prescript in the Syriac manuscript: "Apology made by Aristides the philosopher before Hadrianus the King, concerning the worship of almighty God."[190] However, this is immediately followed by what appears to be a second prescript, this time addressed to Antoninus Pius: "Caesar Titus Hadrianus Antoninus Augustus Pius, from Marcianus Aristides, a philosopher from Athens." Although Harris took this second prescript to be the original, so that the work should be dated in the time of Antoninus Pius (138–61), current scholarly opinion tends to favor the time of Hadrian.[191]

The Apology begins with a short chapter in which Aristides presents the "king" (*mlk'* [Syr.]; *basileu* [Gk.]) with his understanding of the nature of God—an all-powerful, immortal, incomprehensible, unmoved first mover.[192] Then he

188. Harris and Robinson, *Apology of Aristides*, 80.
189. Nils Arne Pedersen, "Aristides," in *In Defence of Christianity: Early Christian Apologists*, ed. Jakob Engberg, Anders-Christian Jacobsen, and Jörg Ulrich, Early Christianity in the Context of Antiquity 15 (Frankfurt am Main: Peter Lang, 2006), 37–38. For a full discussion, see Pouderon and Pierre, *Aristide*, 143–71.
190. The Armenian is similar, at least in content: "To the autocratic Caesar Adrianos from Aristides, Athenian Philosopher" (Harris and Robinson, *Apology of Aristides*, 30). Given its context in the continuing narrative of the *Life of Barlaam and Joasaph*, the Greek version has no prescript.
191. Pouderon and Pierre, *Aristide*, 32–46. But for a recent argument in support of Harris's original position, see Pedersen, "Aristides," 43–47.
192. The following discussion is based on the Syriac version, using Harris's translation,

moves quickly to the human race and the question of "which of them hold any part of that truth which we have spoken concerning Him, and which of them are in error" (2.1). He asserts that "there are four races [*gns*'; *genē*] of men in this world: Barbarians and Greeks, Jews and Christians,"[193] something he believes that the king will accept as clearly evident (2.2).[194] With this fourfold division of humankind in place, he proceeds to assess them one by one on the basis of their deities and conception of the divine, with some attention to religious observance and moral life.

As he treats these four races or types of humankind, he also uses the category of "nations" (all but once in the plural). Where the Greek overlaps with the Syriac, the term is *ethnē*. The Syriac (with vocalization) is *'amma'*. While we might have expected a form of *gôy*, it is apparent that in Syriac usage *'amma'* has replaced the Hebrew and Aramaic term *gôy*, especially in its sense of pagan or gentile nations.[195] In what follows, then, I will use *ethnē* in citations of the English translation of the Syriac, instead of an English equivalent for *'amma'*.[196]

The term first appears as Aristides picks up the case of the barbarians: "Let us begin with the barbarians, and by degrees we will proceed to the rest of the *ethnē*" (Apology of Aristides 3.1). Given the way he has set up his discourse, *ethnē* is to be understood as referring to the four races or types (*genē*) that constitute humankind; that is, each of the types constitutes a nation. The characteristic feature of the barbarians is that they failed to comprehend God and thus "began to serve created things instead of the Creator of them" (3.1). This leads into an extended catalog of the things worshiped (humanly created idols and images,

---

with references to the Greek version where appropriate. References are based on the versification of Pouderon and Pierre.

193. The Syriac *gns'* is a Greek loanword; see Michael Sokoloff, *A Syriac Lexicon: A Translation from the Latin: Correction, Expansion, and Update of C. Brockelmann's Lexicon Syriacum* (Winona Lake, IN: Eisenbrauns; Piscataway, NJ: Gorgias, 2009), 249.

194. The Greek version has just three categories: aside from the Jews and the Christians, the rest of humankind is lumped into the group of those who "worship the gods acknowledged among you" (2.2). Both categorizations, however (the threefold and the fourfold), are somewhat arbitrary. The Greek version subdivides the first category into three: the Chaldeans, the Greeks, and the Egyptians. The Syriac treats the Egyptians as a subcategory of the Greeks (chs. 12–13). For our purposes, it is not necessary to decide which of these categorizations is original.

195. See the entry in Sokoloff, *Syriac Lexicon*, 1112. Sokoloff cites as an example the Harklean version of Matt 18:17, where *'amma'* renders *ethnikos*. The term appears for *gôyîm* in the Peshitta; see, e.g., Takamitsu Muraoka, *Classical Syriac: A Basic Grammar with a Chrestomathy*, PLO 19 (Wiesbaden: Harrassowitz, 1997), 12 (in the Chrestomathy section).

196. Harris uses "the peoples," Pouderon and Pierre "les peuples."

elements, water, fire, sun, great men of old, etc.), with a typical denunciation of the folly of it all (chs. 3–7).

In chapter 8 he turns to the case of the Greeks, whose greater wisdom simply means that they "have erred even more than the barbarians" (Apology of Aristides 8.1). He describes the Greek pantheon in considerable detail (Kronos, Zeus, Hephaestus, Hermes, Asclepius, and so on down the list), highlighting the moral and sexual misbehavior of each and making the point that the character of the gods has provided human beings with license to behave the same way (chs. 8–11).

In chapter 12 he moves on to the Egyptians, who presumably are to be classified with the race or type of the Greeks. The Egyptians, "because they are more evil and ignorant than all the *ethnē* upon the earth" (Apology of Aristides 12.1), have added to the idolatrous sins of the barbarians and Greeks not only some new gods of their own (e.g., Isis and Osiris) but also the worship of animals. On two other occasions in his account of the Egyptians, he describes them as worse than the rest: "the Egyptians are more ignorant than the rest of the *ethnē*" (12.4); "The Egyptians have erred with a great error, above all the *ethnē* that are upon the face of the earth" (13.1). With these references to "all the *ethnē*" on the face of the earth, Aristides seems to have set his fourfold categorization to one side for a moment and to have in view a human population divided more generically into a larger number of constitutive *ethnē*.

In contrast to the barbarians, Greeks, and Egyptians, the Jews receive a surprisingly positive assessment (ch. 14).[197] In their recognition that "God is one, Creator of all and almighty," who alone is to be worshiped, the Jews "appear to be much nearer to the truth than all the *ethnē*" (Apology of Aristides 14.3). Also commendable is that they "imitate God" in their compassion for the poor, their concern for the captive, and their burying of the dead. Where they fall short, however, is in their observation of "sabbaths and new moons and the passover

---

197. Here the Greek version differs considerably. Despite the many wonders and signs they had experienced, the Jews were stubborn and sinful; they "often served the idols of the *ethnē* and put to death the prophets and just men who were sent to them," including (finally) the Son of God himself. Although they "worship the one God almighty," in that they reject the Son of that one God, they are "very much like the *ethnē*" (14.2–3). Pouderon and Pierre have attempted to argue that both sets of material—the more laudatory material in the Syriac, and the christological polemic of the Greek—were present in the original Greek version (Pouderon and Pierre, *Aristide*, 57–58). It seems difficult to imagine, however, that the two could have gone their separate ways so neatly in the subsequent textual tradition. It is much more likely that the Syriac version preserves the original and that this was replaced with a more typical Christian critique of the Jews when the Apology came to be incorporated into *Barlaam and Joasaph*.

and the great fast, and the fast, and circumcision and cleanness of meats" (14.4). While they think that they are serving God in all this, in reality, "their service is to angels." In this way, they "have gone astray from accurate knowledge."

Finally, then, he comes to the Christians, who through "seeking have found the truth" and thus "are nearer to the truth and to exact knowledge than the rest of the *ethnē*" (Apology of Aristides 15.1). The extended description of the Christians (chs. 15–16) is striking for the absence of Christian distinctives.[198] What Aristides presents instead is what might be seen as an expanded description of the kind of ethical monotheism that he praised in his chapter on the Jews, with a few added references to "their Christ" (15.7, 8; 16.2). As Wilson has observed, chapters 15–16 "amount to little more than Jewish apologetic arguments lightly adapted for Christian use: a commitment to monotheism and to the virtuous life."[199] Aristides concludes this section by characterizing the Christians as "a new *ethnos*" in that "there is something divine mingled with it" (16.3). Further, "the world stands by reason of the intercession of Christians, but the rest of the *ethnē* are deceived and deceivers" (16.6).

In Aristides's ethnographical map of the world, then, the nations of the world can be grouped into four distinct types, which he can also call *ethnē*. The Christians constitute the newest and best of these *ethnē*, in that they have discovered the truth about God and have mirrored the divine nature in their own ethical way of life. While they resemble the Jews to a certain extent, the resemblance is analogical rather than genealogical. That is, Aristides is unaware—or chooses to appear unaware—that the first Christians were Jews and that the Christian movement began within the *ethnos* of the Jews. In this connection, it is not without significance that he describes Jesus's mother as a "Hebrew virgin" and Jesus himself as "born of the tribe of the Hebrews" (Apology of Aristides 2.4). He makes no reference whatsoever to Israel's Scriptures, and he certainly shows no interest in rooting the Christian faith in the scriptural promises.[200] While the Christians may represent a new *ethnos*, in no way do they see themselves as a new Israel. They might stand alongside the Jews in a fourfold classification of the nations of the world, but they are a distinct and separate people. As a non-Jewish people, they might be seen from one angle as a gentile people, a people drawn from the *ethnē*; Aristides, however, betrays no awareness of this alternative ethnographical map of the world.

---

198. Though a more creedal form of the faith comes to expression in ch. 2.

199. Wilson, *Related Strangers*, 31.

200. The closest he gets is his statement that the Jews have derived their commendable qualities from "things that they have received from their fathers of old" (14.3). By contrast, in the case of the Christians, he makes more explicit reference to their "writings" (15.1; 16.4; cf. 2.4).

Ethnē and Gentile Christian Identity (Before 135 CE)

Nevertheless, in contrast to the material we have looked at to this point, the Apology of Aristides represents a significant attempt to engage the wider Greek world on terms that outsiders would recognize.[201] Presenting the Christians as an *ethnos*—a new *ethnos* perhaps, but one that can be classed alongside the other *ethnē*—he redraws the ethnic map of the world so as to locate the Christian *ethnos* in the most advantageous position.[202]

In contrast to other pertinent literature from this period, Luke-Acts is marked by the frequency with which it uses *ethnē* as an identifier for non-Jews, especially as an identity term for Christians, and by the thematic significance of the mission to the *ethnē* within the work as a whole. From the Song of Simeon in the Jerusalem temple ("a light for revelation to the *ethnē*" [Luke 2:32]) to Paul's closing declaration in Rome ("this salvation of God has been sent to the *ethnē*" [Acts 28:28]), the geographical arc of the narrative is matched by the progressive expansion of the ethnic sphere of the "salvation of God." Further, this geographical arc is securely moored in the time frame and territory of the Roman Empire. The story of Jesus's birth and the beginnings of Jesus's public ministry are each introduced chronologically with references to the currently ruling emperor ("a decree went out from Caesar Augustus" [Luke 2:1]; "in the fifteenth year of the reign of Tiberius Caesar" [Luke 3:1]); the story ends with a meeting between Paul and the Jews of Rome, at which he informs them that he was there because he was "compelled to appeal to Caesar" (Acts 28:17).[203]

The secondary literature on Luke-Acts is immense, and we will need to forgo anything like a full discussion in order to keep our treatment within limits commensurate with our treatment of other literature in this section.[204] Some introductory issues can be dealt with briefly. Luke and Acts are clearly the work of the same author (whom for convenience we will call Luke), writing sometime toward the end of the first century CE. Further, Luke and Acts should be seen as

---

201. Despite the address to the emperor, Rome does not come into view in the Apology itself.

202. As Aaron P. Johnson observes: "Aristides bases his whole argument on an ethnic legitimation of Christianity. That is, his defence of Christianity rests upon a distinctively *ethnic* conceptualization of the Christians"; *Ethnicity and Argument in Eusebius' Praeparatio Evangelica* (Oxford: Oxford University Press, 2006), 6.

203. As Luke reminds his readers, who have already encountered seven references to the appeal to Caesar.

204. I have dealt elsewhere with the issues to be considered in resolving questions about identity construction in Luke-Acts, with particular attention to the relative place and status of Jewish and gentile believers in the early Christ-movement; see Terence L. Donaldson, *Jews and Anti-Judaism in the New Testament: Decision Points and Divergent Interpretations* (London: SPCK; Waco, TX: Baylor University Press, 2010), 55–80.

parts of a single, two-volume work (Luke-Acts). Luke's interest in the *ethnē* and their place in the Christian movement is just one of a number of themes that run through the two writings and bind them together in a single work.[205] This interest in the *ethnē* is also one of the considerations that has led most interpreters (though not all) to believe that the author was a gentile, perhaps originally a Godfearer of the type that frequently comes into view in the work. The evidence is not conclusive, however, and so we will return to the question a little later.[206] With respect to genre, Luke-Acts can be fruitfully read as an example of apologetic historiography, even though there are differences in genre between the two parts of the work.[207]

The plural form *ethnē*, used to denote non-Jewish nations or individuals, appears some forty times in Luke-Acts. More than thirty of these are in Acts, and these will be of primary interest to us here. The majority of these occurrences are linked explicitly with Christ-belief. In some cases, the *ethnē* appear simply as the sphere of mission in general.[208] After Paul's conversion, it is revealed to Ananias that Paul "is an instrument whom I have chosen to bring my name before *ethnē* and kings and the people of Israel" (Acts 9:15). Later in Pisidian Antioch, Paul declares to a Jewish audience: "Since you reject [the word of God] and judge

---

205. Geography is another theme: the centrality of Jerusalem in Luke (the narrative begins [1:8-9] and ends [24:53] in the temple); and the expansion from Jerusalem to Rome in Acts (though not without recurring reconnections with Jerusalem). The role of witnesses is another (Luke 24:47-49; Acts 1:8; etc.), especially in view of the qualifications for a witness expressed in Acts 1:21-22. Still, the unity of the two writings is not beyond question; see Mikeal C. Parsons and Richard I. Pervo, *Rethinking the Unity of Luke and Acts* (Minneapolis: Fortress, 1993).

206. While a broad segment of scholarly opinion has taken the author's identity as a gentile to be almost self-evident (e.g., Werner Georg Kümmel, *Introduction to the New Testament*, trans. Howard Clark Kee [Nashville: Abingdon, 1975], 149; Barrett, *Acts of the Apostles*, 2:xxx), more recently some have suggested that he was Jewish, pointing especially to his familiarity with Israel's Scriptures and his sympathies for traditional, torah-observant Judaism; see Gregory E. Sterling, *Historiography and Self-Definition: Josephos, Luke-Acts, and Apologetic Historiography*, NovTSup 64 (Leiden: Brill, 1992), 327-28, and the scholars cited in n. 86; V. George Shillington, *An Introduction to the Study of Luke-Acts* (London: T&T Clark, 2007), 10. See also the more general discussion in Craig S. Keener, *Acts: An Exegetical Commentary* (Grand Rapids: Baker Academic, 2012-15), 1:404-5.

207. See Sterling, *Historiography and Self-Definition*.

208. This is signaled already by a statement of the risen Jesus at the end of Luke: "repentance and forgiveness of sins is to be proclaimed in his name to all the *ethnē*, beginning from Jerusalem" (Luke 24:47). The Jerusalem starting point seems to imply that the *ethnos* of the Jews is included here.

yourselves to be unworthy of eternal life, we are now turning to the *ethnē*," punctuating the declaration with a statement drawn from Isa 42:6: "I have set you to be a light for the *ethnē*" (13:46–47).[209] Usually the mission to the *ethnē* is spoken about in optimistic terms ("they will listen"; 28:28), and so it is not surprising that it almost invariably brings positive results. After the conversion of Cornelius, "the apostles and the believers who were in Judea heard that the *ethnē* had also accepted the word of God" (11:1). Somewhat later in the chapter, Peter declares: "you know that in the early days God made a choice among you, that I should be the one through whom the *ethnē* would hear the message of the good news and become believers (v. 7).[210] In Luke's view, then, the mission to the *ethnē* is a decided success. Further, those *ethnē* who believe continue to be identified as *ethnē*. Speaking of "the *ethnē* who are turning to God," James describes them as "the *ethnē* over whom [God's] name is called" (v. 17). Elsewhere in the chapter, they are described as "brothers from the *ethnē*" or "those of the *ethnē* who turn to God" (vv. 23, 19). While in some of the other occurrences, the *ethnē* are presented in negative terms, there is no sense that negative behavior is to be seen as such a defining characteristic of the *ethnē* that non-Jews necessarily cease to be *ethnē* when they became believers.[211] In other words, the idea that *ethnē* is an identity that believers left behind is not present in Acts. God may have decided to take "a people for his name" "from the *ethnē*," as James declares in Acts 15:14, but these believers "from the *ethnē*" remain *ethnē*, "*ethnē* over whom [God's] name has been called" (v. 17).

To be sure, within the narrative itself, nothing explicitly indicates what gentile characters thought of the term. Nowhere in the narrative do gentiles use *ethnē* of themselves.[212] In the two episodes in which Jewish characters use the term in direct address to non-Jews, although the non-Jews in each case respond positively to the address as a whole, the term itself receives no attention.[213] The

209. Other statements about a mission to the *ethnē* are found in Acts 18:6; 22:21; 26:17–18, 23; 28:28.

210. Also Acts 11:18; 14:27; 15:3, 14–18, 23; 21:25.

211. E.g., "For in this city, in fact, both Herod and Pontius Pilate, with the *ethnē* and the peoples of Israel, gathered together against your holy servant Jesus, whom you anointed" (Acts 4:27); also 14:2, 5; 21:11.

212. Non-Jewish believers get speaking parts only rarely in Acts—the Ethiopian official (8:31, 34, 36); Cornelius (10:4, 30–33); the man from Macedonia whom Paul saw in a vision (16:9); Lydia (16:15); the Philippian jailor (16:30, 36); the Ephesians who had received John's baptism (19:2–3)—all of them brief and perfunctory.

213. Paul's declaration to a mixed crowd of Jews and non-Jews in Pisidian Antioch (13:47–48) and the letter from the Jerusalem apostles and elders "to the brothers from the *ethnē* in Antioch and Syria and Cilicia" (15:23, with the response in 15:31).

most one can say is that Luke assumed that there was no resistance to the term. But if the author of Luke-Acts was gentile himself, the positive place of the *ethnē* within its overall themes and narrative progression can be taken as evidence of a readiness on the part of gentile Christ-believers to accept the ascribed identity and to make positive use of it.

While these narratively developed themes raise many interpretive questions, there is general agreement on the broad outline of the author's interests and concerns. First, he clearly wants to convince his readers that the *ekklēsia* stands in legitimate continuation with the scriptural people of Israel and their history.[214] Second, as already noted, the author wants to set the story of "the events that have been fulfilled among us" (Luke 1:1) in the broader context of the Roman world and to present the Christians as a legitimate people deserving a place of recognition and respect within it. In addition, these two concerns are related to a third, having to do with the delay of the parousia (Luke 19:11; Acts 1:6) and the construction of a period in the divine purposes, occupying the space between the resurrection and the final restoration, for the *ekklēsia* and its mission.

These generally recognized concerns provide the context within which we need to locate an issue of more particular interest—that of the relationship between Jewish and gentile believers in the *ekklēsia*. A striking feature of Acts is Luke's concern to maintain the distinction between Jews and the *ethnē*, not only generally but within the community of Christ-believers as well. In Luke's view, the *ekklēsia* is a community that contains both torah-observant Jews (even those who are "zealots for the Torah" [21:20]) and God-fearing *ethnē*, distinct yet equally significant. On one side, the leaders of the *ekklēsia* reject the position that *ethnē* be required (in effect) to become proselytes to Judaism as a condition of membership (ch. 15). On the other, they reject just as firmly any suggestion that Jewish Christ-believers should be pressured to compromise their torah-observance in order to accommodate non-Jewish believers (21:18–26).

To be sure, there is considerable room for discussion about how this dual-identity *ekklēsia* is to be understood. For one thing, Luke seems to present two distinct theological rationales for the inclusion of the *ethnē*. The more widely recognized of these is one in which the gentile mission is predicated on the failure of Jews to respond. This sequence of rejection (by Jews) and extended mission (to the *ethnē*) comes into view especially in the three scenes in which Paul declares that he is turning from the Jews to the *ethnē* (Acts 13:46; 18:6; 28:25–28). But this theme of rejection should not be allowed to overshadow another aspect of the narrative. Luke also goes out of his way to emphasize the great numbers of Jews

---

214. "It is universally agreed that Luke wishes to present Christianity as an extension of Judaism"; Wilson, *Related Strangers*, 64.

Ethnē and Gentile Christian Identity (Before 135 CE)

who became Christ-believers, from the three thousand on the day of Pentecost (2:41) to the "many thousands" reported by James in his meeting with Paul (21:20), with many other mass conversions in between.[215] Here another rationale can be discerned, one in which gentiles come in not to replace unbelieving Jews but to share in the saving blessings that have been granted to the already-existing community of Jewish Christ-believers.[216]

These two rationales are probably not to be seen as incompatible. Perhaps the key to Luke's view is to be found in statements he attributes to Peter at the end of his sermon in Acts 3, a sermon in which he identifies Jesus as the promised prophet like Moses of Deut 18:15-19. On the one hand, he identifies his hearers as descendants of the covenant that God gave to Israel in the promise to Abraham: "And in your seed all the families [*patriae*] of the earth shall be blessed" (3:25). On the other, those who do not listen to the prophet like Moses "will be utterly rooted out of the people" (3:23). The picture that emerges here is one that includes both a division within Israel and the extension of the blessing to "all the families of the earth." The preaching to Israel takes temporal priority: "When God raised up his servant, he sent him first to you" (3:26). When Jews have had a chance to respond, the message is extended to the *ethnē*, who then have the opportunity to share in the blessing that is already enjoyed by the believing Jews.

In chapter 4, I argued that in the early chapters of Acts, Luke was drawing on source material stemming from earlier groups of Jewish Christ-believers. Further, in that chapter, I also constructed a typology of the ways in which Jewish Christ-believers conceived of the salvation of the *ethnē*. One of the types, which was based on Peter's sermon in Acts 3:11-26 along with other related material—"Christ as inaugurating a new era of fulfillment for (a remnant within) Israel, which gentiles were invited to share"—was very similar to the position I have just attributed to Luke himself. While there might be a perception of circular reasoning here, the existence of the type is not dependent on Acts alone. The more pertinent observation, I believe, is that Luke appears to endorse a rationale for the salvation of the *ethnē* that originated with Jewish Christ-believers and thus as-

---

215. Acts 4:4; 5:14; 6:1, 7; 9:42; 12:24; 13:43; 14:1; 17:12; 19:17-20. Jacob Jervell was one of the first to recognize this aspect of Acts and its significance; see his *Luke and the People of God* (Minneapolis: Augsburg, 1972).

216. Oskar Skarsaune labels these two rationales the "substitution model" and the "association model," respectively; *The Proof from Prophecy: A Study in Justin Martyr's Proof-Text Tradition; Text-Type, Provenance, Theological Profile*, NovTSup 56 (Leiden: Brill, 1987), 326. See also Susan J. Wendel, *Scriptural Interpretation and Community Self-Definition in Luke-Acts and the Writings of Justin Martyr*, NovTSup 139 (Leiden: Brill, 2011), 214-24.

signs a much more positive role to torah-observant Jewish Christ-believers than can be found in any other gentile Christian writing under consideration here.

Still, this is not the whole picture. For the most part, this positive role comes into view primarily with respect to the Christ-groups in Jerusalem and Judea. In the latter half of the work—that is, the account of Paul's missionary travels in the gentile world (Acts 13–28)—Luke places much more emphasis on the hostility of the unbelieving Jews than on the positive response of a Jewish remnant. Indeed, even when he does note a positive response on the part of some Jews, he often attributes subsequent hostility simply to "the Jews" without qualification.[217] Further, this portrayal of "the Jews" as implacably hostile stands in sharp contrast to the depiction of Roman officials, who tend to appear as fair-minded protectors of the Christians in situations of conflict.[218] While this is not to say that Luke-Acts should be seen as a full-throated endorsement of Roman rule and an *apologia* for Christian acquiescence to the imperial state,[219] the contrasting portrayal of Roman officials and "the Jews" in the narrative is striking nonetheless.[220] All of this gives added force to the final scene in the narrative, in which Paul denounces his Jewish hearers in the words of Isaiah (Isa 6:9–10) and declares, "Let it be known to you then that this salvation of God has been sent to the *ethnē*; they will listen" (Acts 28:25–28). It is hard to avoid the conclusion that, for Luke, "the time of mass conversions lies . . . in the past," and the bipartite character of the *ekklēsia*—a Jewish remnant supplemented by a company of believing *ethnē*—is largely confined to the transitional first generation.[221] It is for this reason that, despite his Jewish sympathies and thoroughgoing familiarity with Jewish Scripture, the author of Luke-Acts is probably to be seen as a gentile.

With its dual apologetic concerns—the (largely gentile) *ekklēsia* as the legit-

---

217. See Acts 13:45, 50; 17:5; 18:5–6, 12, 14; 20:3; but cf. 14:2, where he adds a qualifier ("the unbelieving Jews").

218. See Acts 13:7–12; 16:35–40; 18:12–16; 19:35–41; 21:27–40; 22:22–29; 23:16–35; 24:22–23; 25:1–27; 26:24–32; 27:42–44; 28:16.

219. C. Kavin Rowe has demonstrated convincingly that, far from cozying up to imperial power, Luke with skill and subtlety confronts the claims of empire with the subversive proclamation of an alternative Lord; see *World Upside Down: Reading Acts in the Graeco-Roman Age* (Oxford: Oxford University Press, 2009). For an earlier example of a similar argument, see Richard J. Cassidy, *Society and Politics in the Acts of the Apostles* (Maryknoll, NY: Orbis, 1987). Cf. Drew W. Billings, *Acts of the Apostles and the Rhetoric of Roman Imperialism* (Cambridge: Cambridge University Press, 2017).

220. On this aspect of Luke-Acts, see Paul W. Walaskay, *"And So We Came to Rome": The Political Perspective of St. Luke*, SNTSMS 49 (Cambridge: Cambridge University Press, 1983); Wengst, *Pax Romana and the Peace of Jesus Christ*, 89–105.

221. The quoted material is from Wilson, *Related Strangers*, 66; see also Jervell, *Luke and the People of God*, 68–69.

Ethnē and Gentile Christian Identity (Before 135 CE)

imate continuation of the story of Israel and as a legitimate people deserving a place of recognition and respect within the Roman Empire—Luke-Acts anticipates gentile Christian material that will come more fully into view in the next chapter. Before turning to this, however, it will be useful to make a few summarizing observations about the material examined in this section.

The ten pieces of literature examined in this section were all written in the period between the two Jewish wars (or perhaps a little later in one or two cases); all of them, we can say with a reasonable level of confidence, were written by gentile authors for a primarily gentile readership; and all of them use the term *ethnē* in one or more senses. In most cases, the use of *ethnē* suggests some degree of dependence on the original use of the term by Jewish Christ-believers as an ascribed identity for non-Jewish believers. And with perhaps two exceptions, these writings display little interest in the term as a positive identity marker.

The most frequently encountered use of the term is as a designation for outsiders, the others who do not share a faith in Christ. *Ethnē* is used in this way in six of the writings we have examined. The usage is especially frequent in the Shepherd of Hermas (a dozen times). Elsewhere, it is used on three occasions as part of an admonition to believers not to behave in a way that would cause God's name to be blasphemed by outsiders (Polycarp, *To the Philippians* 10.2; 2 Clement 13.1–2; Ignatius, *To the Trallians* 8.2), an admonition based on LXX Isa 52:5.[222] The other two writings are 1 Clement and the Epistle of Barnabas.

Ethnē is used as an identity term for gentile Christ-believers in a couple of writings. As we have just seen, Luke uses it in this sense. The most explicit instance, however, is found in the Epistle of Barnabas. In addressing the question "whether the covenant is for us or them" (where "them" refers clearly to the Jews), he sets out a catena of scriptural citations having to do with the salvation of the *ethnē* (13.1 and following), thus clearly identifying "us" Christ-believers as *ethnē*.[223] More generally, *ethnē* are also depicted as the targets of mission in Luke-Acts and 2 Timothy.

Ethnē is also used in a universal sense, to refer to the whole of humankind as comprising distinct ethnic people groups. The Shepherd of Hermas speaks of the "twelve *ethnē*" "that inhabit the entire earth" and of "all the *ethnē* that dwell under the sky" (Similitudes 9.17.2, 4).[224] In a different way, Aristides speaks of "all the *ethnē* upon the earth" (Apology of Aristides 12.1), which he also classifies

---

222. Explicitly in Polycarp and 2 Clement; implicitly in Ignatius.

223. Cf. Ignatius, *To the Smyrnaeans* 1.2: "so that through his resurrection he might eternally lift up the standard for his holy and faithful ones, whether among Jews or *ethnē*, in the one body of his church." It is clear, however, that Ignatius sees these identities as superseded by a Christian identity.

224. He also uses "twelve tribes" as an equivalent of "twelve nations." While this seems to echo Jewish usage, any Jewish sense of the term has been eclipsed here.

383

according to four types (*genē*) or *ethnē* (2.2). In 1 Timothy, the statements about Paul as a "teacher of the *ethnē*" (2:6) and about Christ as having been "proclaimed among the *ethnē*" (3:16) seem to use the term in a universal sense as well.

Turning from matters of usage, let us look at two broader questions, the first of which concerns the way in which Christian identity is construed in these writings with respect to the Scriptures, religion, and people of Israel. One striking thing to emerge from our examination of these writings is that a number of them display very little awareness of the Jewish origins of the Christian movement and very little interest in questions of the relationship between the two. Polycarp speaks of "the prophets who preached, in advance, the coming of our Lord" (*To the Philippians* 6.3) but does not quote any of them, despite his frequent quotations of and allusions to apostolic writings. While the Shepherd of Hermas contains a number of Jewish-sounding themes and material, the closest it gets to the question of the relationship between the believers of the present and Israel in the past is the concern about the salvation of the righteous who lived in the previous era. In Aristides's depiction of the four basic types (or *ethnē*) into which humankind can be grouped, while he presents Jews as being much closer to the Christians in their conceptions of God than are the Greeks or barbarians, he is neither interested in nor troubled by the historical relationship between the two. The form of belief reflected in 1 Timothy, and to a slightly lesser extent in 2 Timothy, is one in which Christ is the savior of an undifferentiated humanity and in which Paul's differentiated world of Jews and gentiles has receded into the background.

First Clement is the sole representative of another way of construing the relationship between the Christian movement and scriptural Israel. Clement simply assumes, in a naive and straightforward way, that the church bears the identity of scriptural Israel. There is no hint of any kind of temporal progression in which the identity that once belonged to the people of Israel has now passed to the new people of Christ. Rather, what we encounter is an unreflective appropriation of the identity markers of Israel: "we" are the special portion that God has chosen from out of all the *ethnē* of the world (Deut 32:8–9), a people that includes Christ-believers as well as the saints of Scripture without any apparent differentiation (1 Clement 29–30). In this sense, 1 Clement can be seen as holding to a gentile version of the type of identity construction found in Jewish Christ-group literature such as 1 Peter.[225] First Clement is also marked by the complete absence of any *adversus Judaeos* polemic or hostility toward contemporary Jews.

Another way of construing the relationship between the church and Israel

---

225. Which I defined in this way: "Christ as inaugurating a new era and a new Jewish-centered people, in which the traditional distinction between Jews and gentiles has been transcended or overshadowed (though not eliminated)"; see type 3 in ch. 4 ("Ascribed

Ethnē and Gentile Christian Identity (Before 135 CE)

comes into view in the Epistle of Barnabas and in Ignatius. In both cases, Christianity and Judaism are categorically distinct, a distinction that extends back into the pre-Christian past. In both cases, torah-observant Judaism represents a false path; any mingling of faith in Christ with Jewish observance is categorically excluded. In both cases, the patriarchs and prophets, along with a few other righteous people, were in effect Christians before Christ, as they recognized that the real purpose of Scripture was to speak in a symbolic way about the coming of Christ.[226] The relationship between Christians and Jews in the present, then, is just a continuation of a duality that has characterized Israel from the beginning.[227]

Finally, Luke-Acts represents another construal, one in which a church consisting of a torah-observant core of Jewish Christ-believers, together with a growing number of gentile believers (whom God has called as "a people for his name" [Acts 15:14]), is seen as the legitimate continuation of scriptural Israel. This conception corresponds closely with one of the types that was present among early Jewish Christ-believers, though we have also seen reasons to believe that Luke saw this as a transitional stage on the way to a predominantly gentile church.

The second question has to do with attitudes toward the outside world and the place of (gentile) Christ-believers within it. A number of the writings examined in this section are marked by a sharp duality between the church and the outside world, set within an eschatological framework of judgment, vindication, and reversal. Such a view is present to a certain extent in 2 Clement, especially in the sharp contrast between "this age and the age to come" (6.3) and the expectation that in the day of judgment unbelievers will "be shocked when they see that the rulership of this world has been given to Jesus" (17.5).[228] We find more explicit hints of an expected eschatological triumph over the powers that be in the Shepherd of Hermas, the Epistle of Barnabas, and Ignatius. Hermas's Similitudes, which have to do with the possibility of repentance up to the time of the final judgment, are prefaced with a comparison between the believer's life in

---

Identities"). In the case of 1 Clement, however, the Jewish elements have fallen away, and the identity of the Jewish people has simply been assumed by a gentile church.

226. "For the most divine prophets lived according to Jesus Christ" (Ignatius, *To the Magnesians* 8.2). "Because the prophets received his gracious gift, they prophesied looking ahead to him" (Epistle of Barnabas 5.6).

227. With its contrast between the Jews ("those who appear to have God" [2.3]) and the Christians ("our people" [2.3]; "the church that was created before the sun and moon" [14.1]), 2 Clement might be included here as well.

228. Cf. Polycarp's expectation that "the saints will judge the world" (*To the Philippians* 11.2); "the world" stands in parallel with "the *gentes*" in the previous sentence.

the present world and the situation of a resident alien in a foreign city, who lives under the whims of the city's "ruler" (*kyrios*; 1.1–6).²²⁹ The Epistle of Barnabas warns its readers that "the final stumbling block is at hand," citing passages from Dan 7, which could only have been read in an anti-Roman way.²³⁰ And Ignatius, writing during his journey to Rome, claims that the victory over "the ancient realm [*palaia basileia*]" has already been accomplished in the incarnation.²³¹

Alongside this stance of separation from the wider world and of hope for the final overthrow of the rulers of the earth, some of the literature under examination here displays a more nuanced readiness to engage with the outside world and its leaders. This is present to a certain extent in Polycarp's call to pray for "kings and magistrates and rulers."²³² More pointedly, Aristides, with his reconstruction of the ethnic map of the (Greek) world, and Luke, with his account of the emergence of the Christian movement within Judaism and its spread outward into the Roman world, represent attempts to engage with the wider Greek and Roman world and to negotiate a favorable place for the Christians within it. The author of 1 Clement seems to move beyond engagement and negotiation and in the direction of obedient subservience, as he prays that God would allow Christians "to be obedient to your all powerful and all virtuous name, and to those who rule and lead us here on earth," whose "authority to rule" has been given directly by God (60.4–61.1).

In the literature to which we now turn, both questions—the way Christian identity is construed with respect to the Scriptures, religion, and people of Israel; and the place of Christians within the wider Greek and Roman world—are taken up in a more deliberate and thoroughgoing way. As we will see, *ethnē* as a positive identity term plays a much more central role in the ensuing discourse.

---

229. At the final judgment, "the *outsiders* [*ethnē*] will be burned for not knowing the one who created them" (4.4).

230. Epistle of Barnabas 4.3–5. See Paget, *Epistle of Barnabas*, 7, n. 25.

231. "Hence all magic was vanquished and every bondage of evil came to nought. Ignorance was destroyed and the ancient realm was brought to ruin, when God became manifest in a human way" (*To the Ephesians* 19.3).

232. Polycarp, *To the Philippians* 12.3; also 1 Tim 2:1–2.

CHAPTER 7

Ethnē *and Gentile Christian Identity (After 135 CE)*

Toward the end of his *Dialogue with Trypho*, Justin recounts a debate concerning the identity of the *ethnē* who are referred to in one of Isaiah's servant passages: "I have given you to be the light of the *ethnē*, that you may be their salvation even to the farthest part of the earth" (Isa 49:6; *Dialogue with Trypho* 121.4). In response to a claim by Trypho and his companions that Isaiah was speaking of Jewish proselytes, Justin declares: "since God foretold that he would send a new testament, and an eternal law and commandment, we should not apply the above-quoted passage to the Old Law and its proselytes [*prosēlytous*], but to Christ and his proselytes, that is, us Gentiles [*hēmas ta ethnē*] whom he has enlightened" (122.5).[1] This self-designation—"us *ethnē*"—is striking, especially in view of the widespread reticence to use *ethnē* as an identity term in the literature surveyed in the previous chapter. But it is by no means an isolated case. Not only does Justin speak of "us [or we] *ethnē*" on two other occasions in the *Dialogue with Trypho*,[2] he frequently and consistently uses *ethnē*, in the specific sense of

---

1. Citations from the *Dialogue with Trypho* are based (with some adaptation) on the translation of Thomas B. Falls, trans., Thomas P. Halton, rev., Michael Slusser, ed., *St. Justin Martyr: Dialogue with Trypho* (Washington, DC: Catholic University of America Press, 2003); those from the *Apologies* are based on Denis Minns and Paul Parvis, eds. and trans., *Justin, Philosopher and Martyr: Apologies*, OECT (Oxford: Oxford University Press, 2009).

2. Here as well the term appears in the context of scriptural exegesis. In *Dialogue with Trypho* 41.3 he reads Mal 1:10-12 as referring to "the sacrifices which we *ethnē* offer

"gentiles" or "gentile nations," as a term of identification for himself and other members of the body of Christians to which he belongs.³

Further, the use of *ethnē* as an identity term is not a sideline concern for Justin, something restricted to a narrow bilateral debate with Jewish critics such as Trypho and his more combative companions. Similar arguments *adversus Judaeos* ("against the Jews") play an important part in his *First Apology*, addressed to none other than the current emperor, Antoninus Pius.⁴ And the *Dialogue with Trypho* itself is addressed to a certain Marcus Pompeius (*Dialogue with Trypho* 141.5), presumably a Roman gentile.⁵ As we will see in more detail presently, it was important for Justin in his apologetic engagement with the wider Greco-Roman world that he could present himself and those like him as a new transethnic people, distinct from the Jews and drawn "from all the *ethnē*" (e.g., *First Apology* 32.4). Taken as a whole, the resultant presentation can be seen as the first thoroughgoing instance of a Christian pattern of competitive ethnography that drew on patterns already present in the wider culture, that developed in significant ways in subsequent gentile Christian literature, and that, as we have seen in chapter 1, came to full flower in the work of Eusebius a century and a half later.

Our goal in this chapter, then, is to trace this process of development in more detail. We will begin by looking more closely at Justin's use of *ethnē* and related terminology as he attempted to negotiate a place for Christians within the currently prevailing ethnographical maps of the Greco-Roman world. Then, with his apologetic enterprise as a basis, we will turn our attention to other pertinent gentile Christian material.⁶

---

to him in every place, namely, the bread of the Eucharist and the chalice of the Eucharist"; in *Dialogue with Trypho* 130.2 he interprets Deut 32:43 as indicating "that we *ethnē* rejoice with his people, I mean, Abraham, Isaac, Jacob, the prophets, and quite simply all those from that people who are pleasing to God." Portions of the following section are drawn from my article "'We Gentiles': Ethnicity and Identity in Justin Martyr," *Early Christianity* 4 (2013): 213–41.

3. Of the 157 occurrences in his work (132 in the *Dialogue with Trypho*, 24 in *First Apology* and 1 in *Second Apology*), the great majority are used in this way.

4. Along with his adopted sons Marcus Aurelius (here addressed by his nickname Verissimus) and Lucius.

5. In 8.3, we find the vocative *philtate* with no proper name, presumably an address to the same person. The Latin has "Markus" at this point, though it is not clear whether it reflects the original Greek or is a later attempt at clarification.

6. On the problems associated with apologetic as a category, see Sara Parvis, "Justin Martyr and the Apologetic Tradition," in *Justin Martyr and His Worlds*, ed. Sara Parvis and Paul Foster (Minneapolis: Fortress, 2007), 115–27.

Ethnē and Gentile Christian Identity (After 135 CE)

ETHNĒ AS AN IDENTITY TERM IN THE WRITINGS OF JUSTIN MARTYR

In contrast to much of the gentile Christian literature examined in the previous chapter, where, to the extent that it was used at all, *ethnē* functioned primarily as a term for outsiders (and thus perhaps as an identity left behind, though this remained implicit at best), for Justin it was clearly a very useful instrument of self-identification. As has already been suggested, it was useful in two broad ways. Recalling our previous examination of the role of boundaries in identity construction, we can say that these two ways align with the two significant boundaries experienced by the gentile church: Jews and Judaism, on one side, and the wider world of Greeks, barbarians, and Romans, on the other. The processes of identity negotiation across these two boundaries were certainly not independent; perceptive observers on the Greco-Roman side raised troubling questions about the nature of the relationship between gentile Christians and the Jewish origins of the movement, which meant that the argument *adversus Judaeos* was directed at a Greco-Roman audience as much as a Jewish one.[7] We begin, however, with the Jewish side of the process.

Justin's use of *ethnē* as an identity term for Christians is part of a more complex pattern of ethnographical self-presentation.[8] In addition to *ethnē*, he also uses the singular *ethnos* along with both *genos* and *laos* as designations for the Christian collective. His usage is quite complex, interwoven as it is with his incorporation of a variety of self-definitional models—that is, different conceptions of how the church is related to the Israel of Scripture, on the one hand, and of the relative place of Jews and gentiles within the church, on the other. A section from chapter 119 of the *Dialogue with Trypho* provides an instructive case in point.[9]

---

7. Of course, the internal audience—Christians needing reassurance in face of external critiques—was equally important.

8. The groundbreaking work of Denise Kimber Buell has been quite influential in drawing scholarly attention to the importance of ethnic language and categories for Justin Martyr; see *Why This New Race? Ethnic Reasoning in Early Christianity* (New York: Columbia University Press, 2005). Published at about the same time, Daniel Boyarin's work is significant as well, though he ends up arguing that Justin abandoned ethnic categories for "an entirely novel form of identity"; *Border Lines: The Partition of Judaeo-Christianity* (Philadelphia: University of Pennsylvania Press, 2004), 17.

9. On this passage and Justin's construction of Christian identity, see Judith M. Lieu, *Christian Identity in the Jewish and Graeco-Roman World* (Oxford: Oxford University Press, 2004), 265–66; David Rokéah, *Justin Martyr and the Jews*, JCP 5 (Leiden: Brill, 2002), 82–85; Philip S. Alexander, "'The Parting of the Ways' from the Perspective of Rabbinic Judaism," in *Jews and Christians: The Parting of the Ways, A.D. 70 to 135*, ed. James D. G. Dunn (Grand Rapids: Eerdmans, 1999), 84–86.

After citing Deut 32:16–23 as evidence that Moses foresaw the emergence of the Christians (119.2), he continues:

> And after that Just One was put to death, we blossomed forth as another people [*laos*], and sprang up like new and thriving wheat, as the prophets exclaimed: "And many *ethnē* shall flee unto the Lord in that day and they shall be for him a people [*laon*]; and they shall dwell in the midst of the whole earth" [Zech 2:11]. But we are not only a people [*laos*],[10] but a holy people [*laos*], as we have already shown: "And they shall call it a holy people [*laon*], redeemed by the Lord" [Isa 62:12]. Wherefore, [not only] are we are not a contemptible people [*dēmos*], nor a tribe [*phylon*] of barbarians, nor *ethnē* such as the Carians or the Phrygians,[11] but God even chose us and appeared to those who did not seek him. "Behold," he said, "I am God to a nation [*ethnei*] which has not called upon my name" [Isa 65:1]. For, this is really the nation [*ethnos*] promised of old to Abraham by God, when he told him that he would make him a father of many *ethnē*. (*Dialogue with Trypho* 119.3–4)

After going on to assert that Christians would "inherit the Holy Land together with Abraham," on the grounds that "we have abandoned our former way of life" and "by our similar faith we have become children [*tekna*] of Abraham" (119.5), he concludes with this declaration to Trypho: "Thus God promised Abraham a religious and righteous nation [*ethnos*] of like faith, and a delight to the Father; but it is not you, in whom there is no faith" (119.6).[12]

The passage is densely packed with ethnic terms, used in several different ways. On the one hand, Christians constitute a new and distinct "people" (*laos*), one that has come into being after the death of Jesus; they are a "holy people" and thus stand in contrast to the Jews as "another people." They are also a "nation" (*ethnos*), chosen by God even though they did not seek him. Presumably they are also the "foolish nation" (Deut 32:21; cited just previously, in *Dialogue with Trypho* 119.2) that God would use as a means to provoke the people of Israel. On the other hand, however, this new people and nation, distinct from the Jews, is also and at the same time "the nation [*ethnos*] promised of old to Abraham by God." Its members are Abraham's children (*tekna*); for this reason, they, and not the Jews, will inherit the Holy Land. Nevertheless—and here we turn to the

---

10. Falls and Halton render it "we Christians," but "Christians" is not in the Greek text.

11. Falls and Halton translate it "nor just any nation as the Carians or the Phrygians," but the term is plural.

12. The word translated "religious" here is *theosebēs* ("God-fearing"). On its significance, see Judith M. Lieu, "The Race of the God-Fearers," *JTS* 46 (1995): 483–501.

Ethnē and Gentile Christian Identity (After 135 CE)

plural forms—this new/old nation is drawn from the *ethnē*, the (non-Jewish) nations. The "other people" (*laos*; sg.) is the same group as the "many *ethnē*" (pl.) who "shall flee unto the Lord in that day" and who thereby become "for him a people," a people dwelling "in the midst of the whole earth." The nation of Christians is the same group that was in view when God told Abraham that he would be "a father of many *ethnē*," not a multiplicity of nations such as the Arabs, Egyptians, or Idumeans (or, even less, a contemptible population [*dēmos*] or a tribe [*phylos*] of barbarians), but a gathering of *ethnē*—that is, non-Jews who "have abandoned [their] former way of life" and have, by their "similar faith," become "children of Abraham."

In a highly condensed fashion, this passage demonstrates characteristic features of Justin's use of ethnic and racial terminology with respect to the Christian group. His use of these terms oscillates between two poles. At one end, the church is a new race, people, or nation, set over against the Jewish nation by its newness. At the other, this new race, people, or nation is at the same time the nation promised to Abraham—that is, Israel itself. And, most importantly for our purposes, all along the spectrum, this new entity consists, almost entirely and categorically, of (non-Jewish) *ethnē*.

To be sure, from time to time, Justin can use *ethnē* in reference to polytheistic outsiders. In *Dialogue with Trypho* 35, for example, in the context of a denunciation of false Christians ("those who profess Jesus in name only"), he draws an analogy with "those among the *ethnē* [who] engrave the name of God upon their statues, and then indulge in every kind of wicked and atheistic rite" (35.5, 6). Again, because "all the *ethnē* . . . commit idolatry, seduce youths, and perform other wicked deeds," they are under a curse (95.1).[13] Further, to differentiate Christians from such unbelieving *ethnē*, he sometimes speaks of them as being from (*ek, apo*) the *ethnē*: for example, "those from the *ethnē* whom Christ circumcised from all error" (47.1); or "people from all the *ethnē* will await him who is to come again" (*First Apology* 32.4).[14] This could easily have slidden over into the idea that, while Christians were drawn from the gentiles, by coming to believe in Christ they were gentiles no longer; but Justin does not make this move. As will become abundantly clear in what follows, for Justin such Christians continue to be identified as *ethnē*. Further, it is a measure of the term's usefulness that he employs it despite his awareness that his readers would find it odd. In *First Apology* he helps his readers out with an explanatory aside: "For all the other races of humans [*genē anthrōpeia*] are called *ethnē* by the prophetic Spirit, but the Jewish and Samaritan are called the tribe of Israel and the house of Jacob" (53.4).

---

13. Also *Dialogue with Trypho* 10.3; 17.2.
14. Also *Dialogue with Trypho* 53.4; 64.1; 91.3.

GENTILE CHRISTIAN IDENTITY

In this section, we are concerned with the ways in which Justin's ethnic terminology figures into his more extensive arguments against the Jews. Looking at his work as a whole, we can identify a number of broad themes. The themes are well known, constituting an early version of what Soulen calls "Christianity's traditional canonical narrative," a supersessionistic interpretive framework, developed by Justin and others in the second century, that undergirded what came to be the standard way of "reading the Christian Bible as a theological and narrative unity."[15]

(1) *The christological meaning of Scripture.* Basic to this interpretive framework as it appears in Justin's work is the belief that the real intent and true meaning of Scripture is Christ—the biographical details of his life, his accomplishment of salvation, his divine identity (in Justin's case, as the Logos), and so on. (2) *The ineffectiveness of Judaism and the sinfulness of the Jews.* The fundamental failure of the Jews was their inability to recognize the christological and spiritual meaning of Scripture, which led to the mistaken belief that the Mosaic law, with its commandments and institutions, was to be understood in a literal and fleshly way. Partly as a result of their blindness to the true intent of Scripture, the Jews were from the beginning susceptible to sin and idolatry. In fact, it was because of their inveterate sinfulness that God had imposed the law on them in the first place. The culmination of their history of rebellion, blindness, and sin was their rejection of Christ. (3) *The rejection of the Jewish nation in favor of the gentile church.* For Justin, the recent history of the Jews—their defeat in the two wars with Rome, the destruction of Jerusalem and the temple, the banishment of the Jews from Jerusalem, and its reestablishment as a pagan city—was to be understood as divine punishment of the Jews for their rejection of Christ and the pattern of sinfulness that preceded it. One dimension of this punishment was that many commandments of the law, dependent as they were on the existence of the temple and life in the land, could no longer be observed, which in itself demonstrated that God had rendered the Mosaic covenant, in its literal sense, obsolete. At the same time, God had rejected the Jews in favor of the Christians—a new people, drawn primarily from the gentiles.[16] (4) *All of this was foretold by the*

---

15. R. Kendall Soulen, *The God of Israel and Christian Theology* (Minneapolis: Fortress, 1996), 13-16, 33-40. Simon identifies a similar set of themes as characteristic of the *adversus Judaeos* tradition as a whole; see Marcel Simon, *Verus Israel: A Study of the Relations between Christians and Jews in the Roman Empire, 135-425* (New York: Oxford University Press, 1986), 156.

16. Justin recognizes the continuing existence of Jewish Christ-believers and is prepared to see them as legitimate members of Christ's new people, under certain conditions. See further below.

Ethnē and Gentile Christian Identity (After 135 CE)

prophets in the Scriptures. While this theme is related to the first one, it is worth listing it separately. The christological meaning of Scripture had to do not simply with Christ himself but with all of the elements in this canonical narrative. The sinfulness of the Jews, their rejection of Christ, God's judgment of the Jews by means of the Romans, the rejection of the Jews and the turn to the gentiles, the spread of Christian belief among all the *ethnē*—all this was foreseen by the prophets and can be found in the Scriptures themselves. As Justin declares to Trypho, everything that he has been saying is "contained in your scriptures, or rather not yours, but ours. For we believe and obey them, whereas you, though you read them, you do not grasp their spirit" (*Dialogue with Trypho* 29.2).

Of course, the elements of this canonical narrative were not constructed out of whole cloth. We have seen aspects of them in gentile Christian literature examined already. In addition, some of them have antecedents in literature produced by Jewish Christ-believers, albeit as part of an *intra muros* debate and thus as based on a different canonical narrative. Justin was certainly dependent on such material to some extent.[17] Further, although Trypho seems at times to be an overly compliant and cooperative dialogue partner, it is generally agreed that Justin is conversant with the kind of Judaism that a figure such as Trypho would represent and is aware of the kind of criticism that such Jews would have of Christian claims.[18] Still, whatever sources or traditions he might have drawn on, he has left his own distinctive stamp on the material as a whole, and his writings mark the beginning of a new stage in the process of gentile Christian self-definition.

Justin's development of these *adversus Judaeos* themes are sufficiently well known that we do not need to explore them further here in general terms. Instead, we will focus our attention on the more particular matter of the place of *ethnē* as an identity term within them. In what follows, we will organize our ob-

---

17. Indeed, Skarsaune has argued that it is possible to identify two bodies of traditional source material, both dating from the period after the Bar Kokhba revolt, one of them produced by Jewish Christ-believers, the other by gentile Christians. The first of these is marked by what he calls an "association model," in which Jewish Christ-believers represent the restored people of Israel, a body to which gentile Christians are added. The other is based on a "substitution model," in which a largely gentile Christian church replaces the rejected Jewish people. See Oskar Skarsaune, *The Proof from Prophecy: A Study in Justin Martyr's Proof-Text Tradition: Text-Type, Provenance, Theological Profile*, NovTSup 56 (Leiden: Brill, 1987). For the two models, see p. 326.

18. On this point, see Stephen G. Wilson, *Related Strangers: Jews and Christians, 70-170 C.E.* (Minneapolis: Fortress, 1995), 260-61. One can only speculate about what further insight into such interaction might have been gained from the (lamentably lost) *Controversy between Jason and Papiscus*.

servations under three slightly different headings. Given the exegetical character of the *adversus Judaeos* tradition, many of the passages of interest will center on scriptural texts containing references to the *ethnē*.[19]

Scripture, Christ, and the Ethnē

Here we are primarily interested in Justin's appeal to Scriptures that, in his view, include the *ethnē* within the sphere of Christ's activity, and the ways in which these appeals are formulated. Most of what he has to say in this regard centers on three clusters of texts that he reads in christological terms. Two of these clusters—royal psalms (Pss 2, 71 [MT 72]) and the servant passages of Isaiah—are perhaps to be expected. The third, Jacob's blessing of Judah (Gen 49:8-12), is more surprising. We will begin with it.

Genesis 49 contains Jacob's final deathbed words to his twelve sons, in which he says something to each of them under the general theme of "what will happen to you at the last of the days" (LXX Gen 49:1). Justin adduces the patriarch's address to Judah on four occasions, in each case identifying Christ as the one indicated by Jacob in these words: "A ruler [*archōn*] shall not be wanting from Judah, and a leader [*hēgoumenos*] from his thighs, until the things stored up for him come, and he is the expectation of *ethnē*" (LXX Gen 49:10). In the four instances, he highlights different aspects of the address as a whole and develops a range of themes.

The two instances in the *First Apology* come at key transitional points in the argument. The first (32.1) comes at the start of an extended argument carried out on the basis of fulfilled prophecy (chs. 30-53). In chapter 31 he provides a list of things that were prophesied about Christ (31.7), including the fact that in the prophetic writings, "we found certain people sent by him to every race of people [*pan genos anthrōpōn*] to proclaim these things, and that it was people from the *ethnē* [*tous ex ethnōn*] rather who believed in him."[20] The argument that follows ranges over a number of scriptural texts, but he begins with Gen 49, Moses

---

19. Rajak suggests that the *Dialogue with Trypho* can be seen as "less a discussion than a Christian *pesher* on Isaiah and the other prophets"; Tessa Rajak, "Talking at Trypho: Christian Apologetic as Anti-Judaism in Justin's *Dialogue with Trypho the Jew*," in *Apologetics in the Roman Empire: Pagans, Jews, and Christians*, ed. Mark Edwards, Martin Goodman, and Simon Price, in association with Christopher Rowland (Oxford: Oxford University Press, 1999), 80.

20. On the creedal shape of this list, see, e.g., Skarsaune, *Proof from Prophecy*, 139-40; Leslie William Barnard, ed. and trans., *St. Justin Martyr: The First and Second Apologies*, ACW 56 (Mahwah, NJ: Paulist, 1997), 148, n. 215.

Ethnē and Gentile Christian Identity (After 135 CE)

being "the first of the prophets" (32.1). After citing the passage (extending to a portion of Gen 49:11), he begins by claiming that the period during which "the Jews had their own ruler and king" lasted "until the appearing of Jesus Christ" (32.2), which was followed shortly afterward by direct Roman rule of the Jewish land.[21] Then he picks up the phrase about the *ethnē*. This, he says, "signified that people from all the *ethnē* will await him who is to come again," adding that his readers can see the evidence of this with their own eyes (i.e., in the multitude of gentile Christians; 32.4). In 32.5–11 he interprets the portion added from Gen 49:11 ("tethering his colt at the vine, and washing his robe in the blood of the grape") as a prophecy of Jesus's entry into Jerusalem (on the colt of a donkey) and subsequent crucifixion. At the end of the chapter, he sets up his transition to the prophecies of Isaiah with a combined quotation, "prophesying the same things in different words": "A star will rise from Jacob [Num 24:17], and a flower will spring up from the root of Jesse [Isa 11:1], and *ethnē* will hope in his arm [Isa 51:5]" (32.12).[22]

With chapter 54 Justin begins a section (*First Apology* 54–58) in which he develops the claim that various "myths invented by the poets" were actually the work of "evil demons" who had a garbled understanding of the prophecies about Christ and on this basis created myths in imitation of the prophecies in order to deceive the "human race" (*tou anthrōpeiou genous*; 54.1–4). Again he begins with Moses and a citation of Gen 49:10 (54.5). While the examples that follow do not refer to the *ethnē* explicitly, it is significant that he introduces them as things that circulated "both among Greeks and among all *ethnē*" (54.3).[23]

The other two instances occur in the *Dialogue with Trypho*. In 52.2 Justin cites the whole of Gen 49:8–12, in the context of a larger section (chs. 48–54) in which he argues that the two comings of Christ were prophesied in Scripture. He introduces the citation in support of the claims that after the first coming "your people would have neither prophet nor king, and that the *ethnē* who believe in the suffering Christ would look forward to his second coming" (52.1). As in *First Apology* 32 he makes the temporal argument that Christ appeared in conjunction with the end of the period in which the Jewish people were under a continuous succession of leaders (cf. "a leader out of Judah shall not fail, nor a ruler from his thigh"), though to make the argument work he includes prophets and high

---

21. "And you [i.e., the Roman emperors], after his appearing occurred, came to rule over the Jews and achieved mastery of all their land" (*First Apology* 32.3).

22. On the composite quotation, see Skarsaune's analysis (*Proof from Prophecy*, 143–44).

23. He links the story of Dionysus, "the discoverer of the vine," to Moses's references to the "vine" and the "grape" and that of Bellerophon and his horse Pegasus to the "foal" (54.6–7)—garbled imitations indeed.

priests among the leaders (52.3–4), conveniently overlooking their membership in tribes other than Judah. Then he turns to the *ethnē* (52.4–53.4), repeating the argument as it appeared in *First Apology* 32 but with some differences. Here he makes it a little clearer that his argument about the two comings of Christ is based on a distinction between things that have already occurred (the end of the period of continuous leadership and the coming of a new situation) and the fact that the *ethnē* are still expecting something more. He also makes an extended attempt (not present in *First Apology* 32) to interpret the foal of Gen 49:11 (linked with Jesus's entry into Jerusalem, as in *First Apology* 32) as a prophecy "of the *ethnē* who would believe in him" (52.1–4).

The final instance is found in *Dialogue with Trypho* 120.4. In the previous chapter, Justin has made the claim that "the nation promised of old to Abraham by God" is to be found in "us," gentile believers in Christ, and not in "you," Trypho and other Jews (119.4, 6). In support of the claim, Justin first cites the promises to the patriarchs that "in your offspring shall all the *ethnē* be blessed" and argues that the line of "offspring" is restricted to the line of descendants that includes Judah, David, and ultimately Christ (120.1–2). Then he brings the argument to what he sees as a decisive conclusion by citing Gen 49:10, with its declaration that one will come from the line of Judah who "shall be the expectation of the *ethnē*" (120.3–4).

The second set of passages that Justin puts forward as speaking of the *ethnē* as belonging to Christ's sphere of activity consists of royal psalms. Two psalms are used in this way—Ps 2 and Ps 71 (MT 72).[24] In *First Apology* 40, in the context of an extended section of christological exegesis (chs. 30–53), Justin cites the whole of Pss 1 and 2, which he apparently considers to be a single psalm.[25] He introduces the citation by listing the things that "the prophetic Spirit" was prophesying through David (40.5–7). Included in the list is the prophecy that Christ "would be believed in by those from every race of human beings [*ek pantos genous anthrōpōn*]." While Justin does not make the connection explicit, there can be little doubt that he is thinking of Ps 2:7–8, with God's promise to the royal Son: "Ask of me and I will give you *ethnē* as your inheritance and the ends of the earth as your possession" (cited in 40.14–15).

The other citation of Ps 2:7–8 appears in *Dialogue with Trypho* 122, a passage that came into view at the beginning of this chapter when we observed Justin's use of the phrase "we *ethnē*" (122.5). While he uses the phrase in the context of

---

24. He also cites Ps 109 (110) on several occasions, though he passes over v. 6 ("he will exercise judgment among the *ethnē*") without comment.

25. As was common in MSS and interpretive traditions; see Minns and Parvis, *Justin, Philosopher and Martyr*, 189, n. 1.

Ethnē and Gentile Christian Identity (After 135 CE)

an argument that the references to the *ethnē* in Isaiah's servant passages are to be understood as referring to Christians rather than to proselytes, he concludes his argument with a citation of Ps 2:7–8 (122.6).[26]

The other royal psalm to be considered here is LXX Ps 71 (72), which Justin cites on two occasions in the *Dialogue with Trypho*. The first citation appears in the context of a more extended argument for the christological meaning of Scripture. In *Dialogue with Trypho* 34 he cites the psalm in its entirety, in the process of arguing that a psalm "which you [pl.] erroneously think refers to your King Solomon . . . in reality refers to our Christ." While the focus of his argument is christological, he also cites a verse of the psalm that contains a statement about the *ethnē* (v. 17): "And in him shall all the tribes [*phylai*] of the earth be blessed, all the *ethnē* shall call him blessed" (34.6). After listing the ways in which the psalm could not be applied to Solomon, including the fact that "his power [did not] extend to the ends of the earth," he adds a further, unexpected item, having to do with Solomon's idolatry. Here the contrast is drawn, not with Christ, but with "the *ethnē* who know God . . . through the crucified Jesus," who would even face death rather than worship idols (34.8). What seems to be at work here is an almost instinctive reaction to read positive *ethnē* references as referring to Christians.

The other citation of LXX Ps 71 (72) appears in *Dialogue with Trypho* 121, in the context of a larger section (119–22) that has already drawn our attention and to which we will return. Here he cites just v. 17, in order to make the point that "when [God] through David speaks of Christ, it does not say 'in his seed shall the *ethnē* be blessed,' but 'in him'" (121.1). After quoting the verse, he continues: "But, if all the *ethnē* are blessed in Christ, and we who are from all the *ethnē* believe in him, then he is the Christ, and we are they who are blessed through him." The argument is an odd one—Christ is the one in whom all nations are blessed; we from all nations believe in Jesus; thus Jesus is the Christ—but it demonstrates again Justin's readiness to interpret scriptural statements about the *ethnē* as references to Christians.[27]

The third set of christological passages that Justin understands as referring to gentile Christians is drawn from the servant passages of Deutero-Isaiah. All of the citations, drawn from Isa 42:1–7 and Isa 49:6–8 in particular, are found in the *Dialogue with Trypho*, the majority of them appearing in chapters 121–23. We will begin here and then look briefly at the remainder.

26. We will return presently to Isaiah's servant passages.

27. With respect to the appearance of *ethnē* in another (nonroyal) psalm, Justin cites LXX Ps 46:7 (47:7) ("For God is the king of all the earth, sing wisely. For God has reigned over the *ethnē*; God sits on his holy throne"; *Dialogue with Trypho* 37.1) in the context of an argument that "the Holy Spirit . . . called Christ God" (36.2). While he does not spell out his logic here, the assumption seems to be that since the passage is talking about the *ethnē* in positive terms, the king who reigns over them must be Christ.

GENTILE CHRISTIAN IDENTITY

The first citation appears in *Dialogue with Trypho* 121.4, where it sums up the argument that we have just considered, having to do with LXX Ps 71:17 and its statement about all the *ethnē* being "blessed in him" (121.1). After describing the accomplishments of Christ and the "special grace" that "we" have received, he cites Isa 49:6, in which the servant is identified as the one who is "to be the light of the *ethnē*." Having cited the passage, Justin goes on to say that, while Trypho and his fellow Jews interpret it as having to do with proselytes, "in reality it refers to us, who have been enlightened by Jesus" (122.1). Then, after citing Isa 42:6–7 ("I will give you . . . for a light of the *ethnē*"; 122.3), he goes on to make the assertion that we observed at the outset of the chapter, namely, that the passage should not be applied "to the Old Law and its proselytes, but to Christ and his proselytes, that is, us *ethnē* whom he has enlightened." He seals the assertion with a citation of Isa 49:8 (and, as we have seen, of Ps 2:7–8; 122.5–6) and then sums up the whole argument in these terms: "Now, since all these passages refer to Christ and the *ethnē*, you should concede that those others do also" (123.1)

A little later, having made further statements that Trypho perceives as a claim "that you are Israel, and that God says all this about you," Justin declares that Trypho is absolutely right (*Dialogue with Trypho* 123.7).[28] To develop the point, he cites Isa 42:1–4 in its entirety. His argument is that, by addressing the servant as Jacob (the one who "shall bring forth judgment to the *ethnē*," and the one "in [whom] shall the *ethnē* trust"), God was, through Isaiah, "speaking of Christ in parable, call[ing] him Jacob and Israel" (123.7–8). Somewhat later (135.1–3) he repeats the argument, citing Isa 42:1–4 again in support of his claim that "as Christ is called Israel and Jacob, so we, hewn out of the side of Christ, are the true Israelite race [*genos*]."

Finally, Justin cites Isa 42 on two other isolated occasions earlier in the *Dialogue with Trypho*. In chapter 65, Trypho objects to Justin's elevated claims about Christ by citing Isa 42:8, "in which God states that he shares his glory with no one else" (65.1). In response, Justin cites more of the passage (Isa 42:5–13), arguing "that God affirms that he will give his glory to him alone whom he has appointed to be the light of the *ethnē*" (65.4–7).

The other passage raises an issue that we will have to return to later. In *Dialogue with Trypho* 26.2 Justin cites Isa 42:6–7 as part of his response to Trypho's objection to what he seems to be saying—"that none of us [i.e., Jews] will inherit anything on the holy mountain of God" (25.6). While Justin seems to have pro-

---

28. More precisely, he says that this conclusion should have been obvious from everything he has said to this point and that he would prefer to think that Trypho raised the question not out of ignorance but to give Justin an opportunity to repeat his arguments for others who had arrived more recently. Compliant to a fault, Trypho nods in agreement.

Ethnē and Gentile Christian Identity (After 135 CE)

vided Trypho with plenty of reasons to believe that this was exactly what he was saying, his answer is surprising: "I didn't say that but I do say that those who have persecuted Christ in the past and still do, and do not repent, shall not inherit anything on the holy mountain, unless they repent." While this seems to imply that there are Jews who have not persecuted Christ and who therefore will inherit future blessings, the rest of his answer focuses on the *ethnē*: "Whereas, the *ethnē* who believe in Christ and are sorry for their sins shall receive the inheritance, along with the patriarchs, the prophets, and every just descendant of Jacob" (26.1). He then justifies the statement with the citation of Isa 42:6–7 ("I have given you for a covenant of the people, for a light of the *ethnē*"). While Justin frequently implies that the Christian church is categorically gentile, we will see that he makes more allowances than some other Christian writers for the legitimacy of torah-observant Jewish believers. But whether he really envisages a share in the inheritance for Jews who are not Christ-believers is much more doubtful.

The Jews and the Ethnē

As has already become apparent, "Jews" (or its equivalent) and *ethnē* function for Justin as fundamentally contrasting terms. We have already observed how he explains the terms for readers who might not be familiar with the usage: "For all the other races of humans [*genē anthrōpeia*] are called *ethnē* by the prophetic Spirit, but the Jewish and Samaritan are called the tribe of Israel and the house of Jacob" (*First Apology* 53.4). Although he attributes the usage to the Spirit rather than to the Jews, it would not be wrong to say that he uses the terms in much the same way as the Jews did—as a fundamental identity binary—but with an inversion of the values attached to the two terms. To be sure, this is not the whole picture. The *ethnē* on the positive side of the binary are not simply non-Jews in general, as in the traditional Jewish usage, but those *ethnē* who believe in Christ in particular. Further, as we will see, he is prepared to classify some Jews along with believing *ethnē* on the positive side of the binary: righteous patriarchs and prophets from the past; the apostles and the first believers; even some Jewish Christians in the present. Thus it might be more correct to say that he redraws the Jewish map so that the fundamental boundary is drawn between those who believe in Christ and the rest, Jews and gentiles alike. Even so, when he is thinking of the boundary between Christians and Jewish outsiders, it is often expressed simply in terms of *ta ethnē* and *hoi Ioudaioi*.[29] The contrast (explicit or implied) is so basic to his use of *ethnē* that it will be sufficient here to note a few examples.

29. Rokéah may go a little too far when he says that "for Justin 'Gentiles' is a synonym for 'Christians,'" but the statement is not far off the mark; *Justin Martyr and the Jews*, 84.

Justin constructs the contrast in terms of Jewish blindness and sinfulness on one side, gentile Christian faith and spiritual understanding on the other. Given the exegetical nature of his work, it is not surprising that the contrast is often developed on the basis of Scripture. Malachi 1:10–12 is a passage to which he turns on several occasions; here is one instance:

> God has therefore announced in advance that all the sacrifices offered in his name, which Jesus Christ commanded to be offered, that is, in the Eucharist of the Bread and of the Chalice, which are offered by us Christians in every part of the world, are pleasing to him. But he refuses to accept your sacrifices and those offered through your priests, saying, "And I will not receive your sacrifices at your hands. For from the rising of the sun even to the going down, my name is glorified among the *ethnē*; but you profane it." (*Dialogue with Trypho* 117.1)

On the one hand, we have the "Christians . . . among the *ethnē*" and, on the other, a group ("you") that is clearly identified as "Israelites" and "Jews" in the discourse that follows (117.2, 4). A similar use of Mal 1:10–12 appears in *Dialogue with Trypho* 41.2–3, where the contrast is between "we *ethnē*" who glorify God's name and "you" who profane it.[30]

Another pertinent case in point appears in *First Apology* 49.1–5, this time citing a passage from Isaiah: "It is said through the same Isaiah that the peoples of the *ethnē* who did not expect him will worship him, but that the Jews who always expect him will not recognize him once he comes." After citing Isa 65:1–3 ("I was found by those who were not seeking me"), he continues:

> For the Jews, who have the prophecies and who were always expecting the Christ to come, did not recognize him when he came, and not only that, but they also treated him with contempt. But those who were from the *ethnē* never heard anything about the Christ until the time when his apostles went out from Jerusalem and indicated the things concerning him and handed over the

---

See also Werline: "Justin makes Abraham the father of the Gentiles only" (Rodney A. Werline, "The Transformation of Pauline Arguments in Justin Martyr's *Dialogue with Trypho*," *HTR* 92 [1999]: 93); and Adam Gregerman (citing Jeffrey Siker): "For Justin, 'to be a Christian is to be a Gentile'" (*Building on the Ruins of the Temple: Apologetics and Polemics in Early Christianity and Rabbinic Judaism*, TSAJ 165 [Tübingen: Mohr Siebeck, 2016], 46).

30. See also *Dialogue with Trypho* 28.5.

Ethnē and Gentile Christian Identity (After 135 CE)

prophecies. Then, being filled with joy and faith, they renounced the idols and dedicated themselves through Christ to the unbegotten God.³¹

As this last comment indicates, the distinction between Jews and *ethnē* is not simply a matter of a static contrast. Rather, the coming of Christ has effected a thoroughgoing change of affairs that alters the status and situation of both groups. We have seen some of this already in our examination of the use Justin makes of Jacob's speech to Judah, with its promise of "one awaited by the *ethnē*" (Gen 49:8-12) in *First Apology* 32.1-4. With respect to the Jews, the "appearing of Jesus Christ," by which Justin means his birth, was followed shortly afterward by the establishment of direct Roman rule "over the Jews and their land." His subsequent crucifixion was followed by the loss of the land itself: "the land of the Jews was given in captivity to you [i.e., the Roman rulers]." As Barnard notes, "Justin sees a connection between the subjugation of Judaea and the birth of Christ, and later between the fall of the Jewish state and the death of Christ."³² But these events, with such dire results for the Jews, at the same time effected a much brighter change for "all the *ethnē*," who, as Moses had foretold, began to "await him who is to come again."

The nature of these changes is very much in view in the first main section of Justin's argument in the *Dialogue with Trypho* (11-30), in which he sets out many of the themes that he will develop in the rest of the work. He begins with the declaration that the "law promulgated at Horeb," which "was intended for you [Jews] only," "is already obsolete," having been replaced by "an everlasting and final law," which is "for all" (11.2). He immediately provides justification for this declaration by citing Isa 51:4-5: "a law shall go forth from me, and my judgment shall be a light to the *ethnē* . . . my salvation shall go forth, and *ethnē* shall have hope in my arm" (11.3). Linking this with the "new covenant" promised in Jer 31:31-32, he continues to present this new state of affairs as having to do with the *ethnē* in particular: "If, therefore, God predicted that he would make a new covenant, and this for a light to the *ethnē*, and we see . . . that people have turned to God, leaving behind them idolatry and other sinful practices," then it should be apparent to all that Christ is "the expectation of those who, from all the *ethnē*, have awaited the blessings of God" (11.4).³³ From this he draws the further conclusion that "we are the true spiritual Israel, and the descendants [*genos*] of Judah, Jacob, Isaac and Abraham," adding that "all this shall be proved as we proceed" (11.5).³⁴

---

31. For a similar reading of Isa 65:1-3, see *Dialogue with Trypho* 24.3, as well as 119.4.
32. Barnard, *St. Justin Martyr*, 148, n. 219.
33. Falls and Halton render *ethnē* "every nation," but the term is plural.
34. Peter Richardson has observed that Justin is the first Christian writer to identify

401

As he proceeds, he continues to present the *ethnē* as the beneficiaries of this new covenant. In support of what he has just argued, he immediately cites another passage from Isaiah (Isa 55:3-5), which speaks of an "everlasting covenant" and the expectation that "*ethnē* who do not know you shall call upon you" (*Dialogue with Trypho* 12.1). He cites the passage again for good measure in 14.4.³⁵ In chapter 13, where he points to the suffering servant of Isa 53 in order to argue that salvation can be found only through "the blood and the death of Christ," he begins his lengthy citation of the passage a few verses earlier at Isa 52:10: "The Lord shall bare his holy arm in the sight of all the *ethnē*, and all the *ethnē* and the ends of the earth shall see the salvation that is from God" (13.2). Later (24.1-3), just before turning his attention to another topic, he supports his claim that "another covenant, another law has gone forth from Zion, Jesus Christ," by citing texts first from Jeremiah ("come, all the *ethnē*, let us assemble at Jerusalem"; Jer 3:17) and then Isaiah: "I was made manifest to them that seek me not; I was found of them that asked not for me. I said, 'Behold me,' to *ethnē* that did not call upon my name" (Isa 65:1). Not surprisingly, he underlines the contrast between the *ethnē* of the new covenant and the Jewish people of the old by continuing the citation: "I have extended my hands all the day to an unbelieving and contradicting people, who walk in a way that is not good, but after their own sins. It is a people that provokes me to my face" (Isa 65:2-3).

In addition to the new covenant or law, Justin has plenty to say about the old one as well. This whole discourse was precipitated by Trypho's challenge concerning circumcision and the law: "You ... scorn this covenant [i.e., of circumcision], spurn the commands that come afterwards, and then you try to convince us that you know God, when you fail to do those things that every God-fearing person would do" (*Dialogue with Trypho* 10.3). Justin's response to this challenge moves along two lines.

First, he argues that the law, which "was intended for you [Jews] only" (*Dialogue with Trypho* 11.2), was given only because of the sinfulness of the Jewish people. "We, too," he says, "would observe your circumcision of the flesh, your Sabbath days, and, in a word, all your festivals, if we were not aware of the reason why they were imposed upon you, namely, because of your sins and your

---

the church, clearly and equivocally, as Israel; *Israel in the Apostolic Church*, SNTSMS 10 (Cambridge: Cambridge University Press, 1969), 1, 10-14. In this connection, we can note that Justin emphasizes the references to the *ethnē* in the patriarchal narratives: Abraham as "the father of many *ethnē*" (*Dialogue with Trypho* 11.5; Gen 17:4-5); "in your [Isaac's] offspring shall all the *ethnē* be blessed" (*Dialogue with Trypho* 120.1; Gen 26:4).

35. On the differences in wording between the two citations of Isa 55:3-5, see Skarsaune, *Proof from Prophecy*, 63-64.

hardness of heart" (18.2). A little later, he makes a similar statement about the sacrificial system: "Therefore God, adapting his laws to that weak people, ordered you to offer sacrifices to his name, in order to save you from idolatry, but you did not obey even then, for you did not hesitate to sacrifice your children to the demons" (19.6). But as this latter statement indicates, Justin charges that, despite the restraining influence of the law, the Jews continued to sin, a lineage of transgression that continues into the present: "You have murdered the Just One, and his prophets before him; now you spurn those who hope in him, and in him who sent him" (16.4).

This leads to his second line of response, having to do with the two disastrous wars with Rome and their consequences. Not only were the present circumstances in which the Jews found themselves a just punishment for their sin, but the special marks of the covenant had actually been given in order that the punishment might be carried out more easily. Circumcision

> was given to you as a distinguishing mark, to set you off from the other nations [*apo tōn allōn ethnōn*] and from us. The purpose of this was that you and only you might suffer the afflictions that are now justly yours; that only your land be desolate, and your cities ruined by fire; that the fruits of your land be eaten by strangers before your very eyes; that not one of you be permitted to enter Jerusalem. Your circumcision of the flesh is the only mark by which you can certainly be distinguished from other men.... Therefore, the above-mentioned tribulations were justly imposed upon you. (*Dialogue with Trypho* 16.2-3)

And again: "circumcision is not essential for all, but only for you, to mark you off for the suffering you now so deservedly endure ... [and] in order that, as Hosea ... says, 'your people should not be a people, and your nation not a nation'" (19.2, 5).[36] Later in the dialogue, Justin has similar things to say about the Jerusalem temple.[37]

While Justin continues to develop these themes through the remainder of the *Dialogue with Trypho*, this is sufficient to bring into focus his perception of the Jews and the *ethnē*, together with the covenants associated with each. Before mov-

---

36. On Justin's reinterpretation of Jewish circumcision, see Paula Fredriksen, *Augustine and the Jews: A Christian Defense of Jews and Judaism* (New York: Doubleday, 2008), 250-51.

37. In 40.1-2 Justin says, in effect, that God concentrated the sacrificial system in Jerusalem, forbidding sacrifices to be offered anywhere else, so that the destruction of Jerusalem would bring this (temporary) system to an end.

ing on, however, we need to pick up one thread. A little earlier we noted Trypho's objection to what he took to be the logical outcome of Justin's argument—that law-observant Jews would not "inherit anything on the holy mountain of God" (*Dialogue with Trypho* 25.6). Justin's ambiguous response—"I didn't say that, but I do say that" Jews who persecute Christ and his followers will not—might seem to imply that there were other Jews who, without believing in Christ, would nevertheless have a share in the future redemption.[38] Given what we have seen about Justin's argument in chapters 11–30, however, this appears to be unlikely. Indeed, toward the end of the section, he tells Trypho that conversion is the only positive option: "There is only a short time left for conversion. If Christ should come again before your conversion, you will weep and repent in vain, for then he will not heed you" (28.2). This seems to suggest, then, that for Justin, only those Jews who did "acknowledge Christ," which he repeatedly urges Trypho and his companions to do, would join "the *ethnē* who believe in Christ" in the inheritance (cf. 26.1).[39] As he says to Trypho later: "There is no other way" (44.4).

Nevertheless, despite his emphasis on the significance of Christ for the *ethnē*, Justin is aware of Jewish believers and, within certain limits, is more prepared than some of his co-religionists to recognize them as fellow Christians. In *Dialogue with Trypho* 39.2, for example, he observes "that every day some of you are forsaking your erroneous ways to become disciples in the name of Christ." A little later Trypho asks him about the status of someone who "profess[es] Jesus to be the Christ ... yet desires also to observe the commandments of the Mosaic law." Justin replies that, as long as such a person did not also attempt to convince believers "from the *ethnē*" that they need to observe the Jewish law in order to be saved, then he believes that gentile Christians "should receive them and associate with them in every way as kinsmen and brethren" (47.1–2). While Trypho's question was somewhat hypothetical, Justin's response makes it clear that he is well aware of the existence of Jewish believers in Christ. He also makes it clear that there were other gentile Christians who saw Christ-belief and law-observance as mutually exclusive.

Further, Justin seems prepared to see Jewish believers (from the time of the apostles to the present day) as constituting a recognizable entity within the Christian group. In other words, there is a certain limit to his *ethnē*-centeredness. In the passage cited above, for example, in which he observes the number of Jews who day by day become believers (*Dialogue with Trypho* 39.1–2), he identifies them as a contemporary example of the kind of remnant that existed in the days of Elijah.[40] Again, in one of his expositions of Jacob's deathbed words

---

38. On the ambiguity, see the helpful discussion in Wilson, *Related Strangers*, 272–74.
39. In the present passage (28.3) and elsewhere (8.2; 32.2; 44.4; 137.1–2; 142.2–3).
40. Citing Elijah's lament ("I am left alone") and God's reply ("I still have seven thou-

to Judah (Gen 49:8-12), Justin interprets the reference to a "foal" and a "foal's ass" as a prophecy "that both you coming from the synagogue and those who would come from the *ethnē* would believe in him" (53.1-4). In another passage (130.1-2), he interprets Deut 32:43 ("Rejoice, you *ethnē*, with his people") as an indication "that we *ethnē* rejoice with his people, I mean, Abraham, Isaac, Jacob, the prophets, and quite simply all those from that people who are pleasing to God." Then he adds: "But we know that these words do not apply to all members of your race [*genos*]."

As this passage indicates, for Justin the group of Jews "who are pleasing to God" consists not simply of Christ-believers in the present but also of the patriarchs, prophets, and others in the period before Christ. In his view, the present situation is a continuation of a bifurcation within the people of Israel that goes back to the beginning. He spells this out in some detail in chapter 120, where once again he considers Gen 49:8-12. He begins by noting that, with respect to the promises made to Abraham and his descendants, the line of descent narrows progressively—first through Isaac (excluding Ishmael) and then through Jacob (excluding Esau). Then he extends this principle to Jacob's sons: "For the offspring is divided after Jacob, and comes down through Judah and Perez and Jesse and David"—and presumably on down the line of descent to Christ, as in the Matthean genealogy. He continues: "Now, this was a sign that some of your race [*genos*] would certainly be children of Abraham, and at the same time would share in the lot of Christ; but that others, also children of Abraham, would be like the sand on the sea shore, which, though vast and extensive, is barren and fruitless, not bearing any fruit at all." After providing this rather jaundiced interpretation of the patriarchal promise,[41] he adds that "a great part of your people" will belong to this barren portion of Abraham's offspring (*Dialogue with Trypho* 120.1-2). Then after pausing to emphasize once again the promise to the *ethnē* (120.3), he finds another image of the bifurcation in "the death of Isaiah, whom you sawed in half with a wooden saw." This, he says, "was a symbol of Christ, who is going to cut your race [*genos*] in two, and to admit the worthy half into his eternal kingdom with the holy patriarchs and prophets. But the rest, he has said, he will condemn to the undying flames" (120.5).[42]

Given Justin's belief that the real intended meaning of Israel's Scriptures was

---

sand men, whose knees have not been bowed before Baal") (1 Kgs 19:10, 18). He uses the passage as a warning to Trypho: it is only the existence of this remnant that holds back God's "judgment of you."

41. "I will make your offspring as numerously numerous as the stars of the sky and as the sand that is by the seashore" (LXX Gen 22:17).

42. See also *Dialogue with Trypho* 55.3.

to point to Christ and that the prophets denounced the people of Israel precisely for their failure to perceive this, one can readily conclude that the basis of the bifurcation that began in the time of Abraham and continued down to Justin's own day was the christological meaning of Scripture. More precisely, the "holy patriarchs and prophets" were, in a sense, proto-Christians—Christ-believers ahead of their time. While he does not state this as clearly as Ignatius,[43] this seems to be the sense of his statement to Trypho concerning his reading of Scripture:

> For the words which I use are not my own, nor are they embellished by human rhetoric, but are the words as David sang them, as Isaiah announced them as good news, as Zechariah proclaimed them, and as Moses wrote them. Aren't you acquainted with them, Trypho: You should be, for they are contained in your Scriptures, or rather not yours, but ours. For we believe and obey them, whereas you, though you read them, do not grasp their spirit. (*Dialogue with Trypho* 29.2)

In other words, to the extent that Justin grants Jews a distinct place in the community of Christians, it is a place in which the traditional Jewish identity markers, rooted in covenant and torah, carried no positive significance whatsoever, neither in the past nor in the present. Jews who were "pleasing to God" were those—and only those—who recognized the true christological meaning of Scripture, not only in the situation of present fulfillment but also in that of the anticipatory past.

The Christianization of the Ethnē

To bring to a conclusion our consideration of Justin's identity negotiations at the boundary with Jews and Judaism, a few additional observations are in order about what he has to say about the *ethnē* and the emergence of the new Christian reality. Much of the pertinent material has come up already, and so we can afford to be relatively brief.

One theme that comes up repeatedly has to do with the mission of the apostles to the *ethnē*. In *First Apology* 39, for example, after citing the prophecy in Isa 2:2–3 ("the word of the Lord [will go forth] from Jerusalem, and it will judge between *ethnē*"), he declares that this has now been fulfilled: "For men twelve in number went out from Jerusalem into the world, and they were unskilled in

---

43. See *To the Magnesians* 8.2; *To the Philadelphians* 9.2. However, he is prepared to include Abraham and others, along with Socrates and other Greek philosophers, as people "who lived with Logos" and thus "are Christians" (*First Apology* 46.3).

rhetoric, but through the power of God they signified to the whole human race [*genos*] how they were sent by Christ to teach the word of God to all." Justin makes a similar declaration a little later. In *First Apology* 42, having just cited a version of Ps 96 (97) that included the phrase "Let them rejoice among the *ethnē*,"[44] and having claimed that no one before Christ "gave joy to the *ethnē*," Justin continues: "and on account of those things which were proclaimed from him by the apostles among all the *ethnē*, there is joy afforded to those who look forward to the immortality promised by him."[45] Turning to the *Dialogue with Trypho*, he cites Mic 4:1-7 (which includes the expectation that "many *ethnē* will come in pilgrimage to Zion to learn God's ways) in order "to prove that the *ethnē* would repent of the evil in which they, being deceived, were leading their lives, once they heard and learned the doctrine preached by the apostles from Jerusalem" (*Dialogue with Trypho* 109.1-3).[46]

As is already apparent in these passages, Justin also makes the point that the mission of the apostles led to positive results. In response to the mission, the *ethnē* abandoned their old way of life, turned to believe in Christ, and thus became part of a new pious and peaceable people. In *First Apology* 49, for example, as Justin is contrasting the response from the Jews and the *ethnē*, he declares that "those who were from the *ethnē* never heard anything about the Christ until the time when his apostles went out from Jerusalem. . . . Then, being filled with joy and faith, they renounced the idols and dedicated themselves through Christ to the unbegotten God" (49.5). Again, in *Dialogue with Trypho* 83.1-4 Justin continues his christological reading of the Scriptures with an argument that Ps 109 (110) refers to Christ. Although he does not cite v. 6 ("He will judge among the *ethnē*"), he probably has it in mind as he says:

> although our Jesus has not yet returned in glory, he has sent forth into Jerusalem the scepter of power, namely, the call to repentance to all the *ethnē* over which the demons used to rule, as David testifies: "The gods of the *ethnē* are demons." And the power of his word compelled many to abandon the demons whom they used to obey, and through him to believe in almighty God, because "the gods of the *ethnē* are demons." (83.4)

---

44. Justin introduces the passage cited in 41.1-4 as a psalm of David, but it is closer in some respects to 1 Chr 16:23-31; see Minns and Parvis, *Justin, Philosopher and Martyr*, 189, n. 2.

45. *First Apology* 42.4. Here I am using Barnard's translation, which more clearly highlights the point I want to make.

46. For other expressions of the theme, see *First Apology* 31.7; 45.5; 49.5; 50.12; *Dialogue with Trypho* 83.4.

As we will see in more detail in the next section, Justin believes that the polytheistic worship of the *ethnē* is the work of malevolent demons who lurk behind their gods. Psalm 95:5 (96:5)—"the gods of the *ethnē* are demons"—is an important text in this connection.[47] Here the point to note is the way he uses it with respect to the *ethnē* who come to believe in Christ: We used to worship demons along with the rest of the *ethnē*, but now we have abandoned them and turned to Christ. This is not the only place where Justin takes a scriptural text with a negative thrust and uses it to speak about the conversion of the *ethnē*. Analogous instances are found in *Dialogue with Trypho* 69.4 (citing Isa 6:10) and 91.1–4 (citing Deut 33:13–17).[48]

The transition from the demons to Christ was more than simply a shift of allegiances or identity groups. In making this transition, new believers became part of a new race or nation, one that was characterized by a different way of life (*politeia*).[49] This theme is frequently developed on its own terms, but occasionally it comes to expression with respect to the *ethnē*.[50] In *Dialogue with Trypho* 52.4, for example, in one of his commentaries on Jacob's blessing of Judah ("he shall be the expectation of the *ethnē*"; Gen 49:10), Justin declares that "we, from all the *ethnē*, have become pious and just [*theosebeis kai dikaioi*] through our faith in Christ." A more extended example is found in *Dialogue with Trypho* 109–10, a passage that has already come into view. Justin begins with the claim that, according to Scripture, "the *ethnē* would repent of the evil in which they, being deceived, were leading their lives," a claim that he substantiates with a quotation of Mic 4:1–7 ("many *ethnē*" will come to Zion, where God "will instruct

---

47. Cited also in *First Apology* 41.1; *Dialogue with Trypho* 73.3; 79.4.

48. In Christian interpretation Isa 6:9–10 is usually cited as a denunciation of Israel for its inability to see, hear, and understand (Mark 4:12; and parr.; Acts 28:26–27; also *Dialogue with Trypho* 12.2). Here, however, Justin uses it with respect to "the *ethnē*," who would eventually "abandon their idols and place their hope in Christ." Nevertheless, he can exercise some selectivity; Matthew W. Bates has observed that, despite his frequent use of Isaianic *ethnē* passages, he passes over all those passages that speak of their subjugation, "substituting the theme of the destruction of disobedient Israel in its place"; see "Justin Martyr's Logocentric Hermeneutical Transformation of Isaiah's Vision of the Nations," *JTS* 60 (2009): 538–55, here 549.

What captures Justin's attention in Deut 33:13–17 is an odd statement in Moses's blessing of Joseph: "with them [his horns] shall he push *ethnē*, even to the ends of the earth" (v. 17). Evidently the combination of *ethnē* and "the ends of the earth" was enough to convince him that the verse must be speaking about gentile believers.

49. Justin refers to the Christian way of life as a *politeia* in *First Apology* 4.2 ("our name [Christians] and our *politeia*").

50. See, e.g., the extended "before and after" in *First Apology* 14.2–3. The whole of chs. 14–17 are pertinent here.

Ethnē and Gentile Christian Identity (After 135 CE)

us in his way, and we will walk in his path"). Then he points with pride to the results of this instruction:

> And we who delighted in war, in the slaughter of one another, and in every other kind of iniquity, have in every part of the world converted our weapons of war into implements of peace—our swords into ploughshares, our spears into farmers' implements—and we cultivate piety [*eusebeian*], justice [*dikaiosynēn*], brotherly charity [*philanthrōpian*], faith [*pistin*], and hope [*elpida*], which we derive from the Father through the crucified Savior. (*Dialogue with Trypho* 110.3)

Finally, Justin emphasizes the expansion of the Christian faith among the *ethnē*, most often in terms of extent but also in terms of numbers. Both come to expression in *First Apology* 53.3. Here Justin is arguing that Christian belief is based on scriptural prophecies that are being fulfilled in his own day:

> We see the desolation of the land of the Jews, and those from every *ethnos* of human beings persuaded through the teaching from his apostles, and scorning their old ways in which they had conducted themselves erroneously, . . . knowing those from the *ethnē* to be more numerous and more genuine Christians than those from the Jews and the Samaritans.

With respect to extent, as we have already seen, he frequently speaks of Christian believers from "all the *ethnē*" (e.g., *First Apology* 32.4; 40.7; *Dialogue with Trypho* 11.4). A more extended example appears in *Dialogue with Trypho* 117. Here he is making the case that Mal 1:10–12 ("from the rising of the sun even to the going down, my name is glorified among the *ethnē*") refers to Christians rather than Jews. After a paraphrase of Mal 1:11—"it says that their prayers and sacrifices were pure and acceptable in every place"—he declares to Trypho that the prophet could not have had Jewish worship in mind, for "there are *ethnē* among which none of your race [*genos*] has ever lived" (117.4). Then he continues:

> But there is not a single race [*genos*] of men, whether barbarians, or Greeks, or persons called by any other name, nomads, or vagabonds, or herdsmen dwelling in tents, among whom prayers and thanksgivings are not offered to the Father and Creator of the universe in the name of the crucified Jesus. (117.5)

Justin makes the grandiose claim, then, that the Christian *politeia*, this new people of peace and piety, can now be found among all the *ethnē* of the world, from the sun's rising to its setting, with no human *genos* excepted.

These, then, are the main aspects of the place of the *ethnē* in Justin's enterprise of identity construction at the boundary with Jews and Judaism. In turning to the other boundary, however—that with the wider Greco-Roman world—we are not turning to an entirely new topic. As we have seen and will see in more detail as we proceed, self-definition vis-à-vis the Jews was also significant for Christian identity construction in the wider Greco-Roman world. For one thing, the *adversus Judaeos* material was designed in part to address challenges and critiques lobbed across the boundary by perceptive and intelligent polytheists. As Wilken has rightly observed, the *adversus Judaeos* tradition was not "an idle construct patched together after hours while Christian apologists rested from their debates with the Greeks."[51] Rather, in order to make headway in the Greco-Roman world, apologists such as Justin had to address the vexed issue of the relationship between the Christians and the Jews. And for another, some of the material surveyed above was pertinent in its own right for Justin's engagement with the Greco-Roman world and its competitive ethnographies. Justin's construction of Christian identity vis-à-vis Israel and the Jews is just a portion of his redrawn version of the larger map of the human world, the world that encompasses Jews, barbarians, Greeks, Romans, the *ethnē* in general—and the new Christian *ethnos* drawn from all the *ethnē*.

The most convenient point of entry into a discussion of Justin's version of competitive ethnography is his oft-repeated dictum "The gods of the *ethnē* are demons." This is not to be seen as simply an opportunistic use of a scriptural text (i.e., Ps 95:5 [96:5]) to talk about Christian conversion; rather, it represents a key element in a larger construction of ethno-anthropology. Justin begins with divine creation: God created the world "for the sake of the human race [*genos*]" (*Second Apology* 3[4].2),[52] providing human beings with intelligence and free will, so that "they have been born capable of exercising reason [*logikoi*] and intelligence" (*First Apology* 28.3).[53] Thus, "the whole race [*genos*] of human beings" shares in the *logos* (46.2), something that provides Justin with the basis and starting point of his petition to the emperor: "Reason [*ho logos*] prescribes that those who are truly pious and philosophers should honor and hold in affection the truth alone" (2.1).

In addition to "the implanted seed of the *logos*" (*Second Apology* 13.5), however, God provided "providential care over human beings and of things beneath

---

51. R. L. Wilken, "Judaism in Roman and Christian Society," *Journal of Religion* 47 (1967): 313–30, here 323.

52. Following the chapter numbers of Minns and Parvis, who (for compelling reasons) transfer ch. 3 to a position after ch. 7; see Minns and Parvis, *Justin, Philosopher and Martyr*, 54–56. The number in square brackets represents the traditional numbering.

53. Again using Barnard's rendering, which captures the point well.

the firmament" in the form of "angels whom he had established over them" (4[5].2). But these angels quickly lost sight of their appointed task; they "succumbed to intercourse with women, and begot children—who are called demons [*daimones*]" (4[5].3). The origins of Justin's demonology are readily apparent in this account, with its allusion to the story of the "sons of God" and the "daughters of human beings" in Gen 6:4 and its elaboration in Jewish Enochic traditions.[54] As the account continues (4[5].4–6), Justin describes how these demons "went on to enslave the human race to themselves," demanding "sacrifices and incense and libations" and leading people to commit "murders, wars, adulteries, licentiousness, and every kind of evil." Enter the "poets and storytellers," who compounded the problem. Failing to recognize that it was fallen angels and demons who were doing these things "to men and women and cities and nations [*ethnē*]," they ascribed them instead to gods. The names they gave these gods were simply the names given by the angels to their demonic offspring.

Thus the indwelling *logos* proved to be no match for the power of the demons. Because people "did not rationally [i.e., "with *logos*"] evaluate what the demons were doing," in their ignorance and fear they mistook the demons for gods (*First Apology* 5.2). The demons, in turn, used "the myths invented by the poets," which were subsequently spread "both among the Greeks and among all the *ethnē*," as instruments "for the deception and misdirection of the human race [*genos*]" (54.1, 3), with the result that people in "every *ethnos*" were led to "commit unspeakable acts" (27.1). Further, it is at their instigation, Justin asserts, that Christians are subject to punishment by the ruling authorities (5.1).

Justin acknowledges that Scripture assigns Israel a special place among the nations, though he adds a characteristically negative twist to the story of Israel's election. In *Dialogue with Trypho* 130–31 he cites Deut 32:7-9, "the words which show that God divided up all the *ethnē*" (131.1), as part of his account of how "in the beginning God dispersed all human beings according to races [*genos*] and languages, and from all these races he chose for himself yours." To this point,

---

54. On these Jewish traditions and their subsequent influence in Christian writings, see Annette Yoshiko Reed, *Fallen Angels and the History of Judaism and Christianity: The Reception of Enochic Literature* (Cambridge: Cambridge University Press, 2005); Adolf von Harnack, *The Mission and Expansion of Christianity in the First Three Centuries*, trans. James Moffatt (London: Williams & Norgate, 1908), 125–46. For Justin in particular, see pp. 161–74 of Reed's work; see also Jeremy M. Schott, *Christianity, Empire, and the Making of Religion in Late Antiquity* (Philadelphia: University of Pennsylvania Press, 2008), 40–41; Barnard, *St. Justin Martyr*, 108, n. 30; Jörg Ulrich, "Justin Martyr," in *In Defence of Christianity: Early Christian Apologists*, ed. Jakob Engberg, Anders-Christian Jacobsen, and Jörg Ulrich (Frankfurt am Main: Peter Lang, 2006), 58–59.

Trypho may well have nodded in agreement; but Justin adds an unpalatable descriptor: "a useless, disobedient, and faithless race" (130.3). In Justin's view, Israel's election provided no immunity to the general human lot; Israel too had succumbed to the worship of demons. His most frequent charge is that Israel sacrificed its children to demons, a charge that apparently depends on Ps 105:37 (106:37), though it is not cited directly (19.6; 27.2; 73.6; 133.1). In addition, he accuses them more generally of worshiping demons, citing Deut 32:17 (119.2) and Isa 65:11 (135.4).[55]

Nevertheless, despite the deceptive wiles of the demons, there were some who, because of the "implanted seed of logos," were able to catch partial glimpses of the truth (*Second Apology* 13.5). Many of these were "hated and put to death" (7[8].1), including Socrates, who was killed precisely because he had "attempted with true reason [*logos*] and judicious inquiry to bring these things into the open and to draw people away from the demons" (*First Apology* 5.3).

This is probably the point at which to mention Justin's belief—a major plank in his apologetic platform—that Christ and the *logos* were one and the same. What Socrates (and others like him) were able to perceive "by reason [*logos*]" was precisely what was revealed "by the Logos himself, who acquired physical form and became a human being and was called Jesus Christ" (*First Apology* 5.4). Justin's roll call of those in the past "who lived with Logos" comprised some from "among the Greeks—Socrates and Heraclitus and those similar to them," and some from "among the barbarians—Abraham and Ananias and Azarias and Misael and Elijah and many others" (46.3). Indeed, Justin is even prepared to recognize all of these as Christians: "those who lived or do live with Logos are Christians" (46.4).[56] Thus, in Justin's program of identity construction, he blurs the distinction between Greeks and barbarians, on the one hand, and between Jews and the *ethnē*, on the other, as he declares that among both the Greeks and the barbarians (Israel and the Jews included in the latter) there were those who "lived with Logos." Identifying the latter as Christians ahead of time, he thus aligns his own group drawn from all the nations ("we *ethnē*") with this ancient line of those who were able to resist the power of the demons and to live in accordance with the Logos/Christ.

Although Christ as the Logos was discernible in the past, now that Christ has come in the flesh, a new state of affairs has come into being, and the demons have begun to lose their grip over the human race. To be sure, Justin sees the final defeat and destruction of the demons as something to take place in the

---

55. On this aspect of Justin's argument, see Fredriksen, *Augustine and the Jews*, 246–47.

56. Elsewhere he mentions Plato (*Second Apology* 13.2), the Stoics (*Second Apology* 7[8].1), the Sibyl (*First Apology* 20.1), and others like them.

future (*First Apology* 28.1; *Second Apology* 6[7].1). Present realities—the persecution of Christians and the activity of heretics, both of which he attributes to demonic influence (*First Apology* 5.1; 26.5)—hold him back from any exaggerated triumphalism. Even so, this reticence is more apparent in the *Apologies*, where he places the emphasis on God's decision to delay the final punishment "on account of the human race" (*First Apology* 28.2) and on the preserving presence of the Christians themselves (*Second Apology* 6[7].1–2). In the *Dialogue with Trypho*, however, Justin is prepared to place greater emphasis on Christ's present power over the demons. Through his crucifixion and resurrection, Christ has been given "such a great power" that "even the demons shudder" at his name (30.3). And again: "the hidden power of God was in the crucified Christ, before whom even the demons and, in short, all the powers and authorities of the earth tremble" (49.8). He provides only one concrete example, but it is telling nonetheless. The journey of the magi to offer worship to Christ was a fulfillment of the prophecy "that the power of the wicked demon that dwelt in Damascus should be crushed by Christ at his birth."[57] While he could have easily located the magi somewhere farther east, safely beyond the boundaries of the Roman Empire, he chose Damascus instead.

The primary manifestation of Christ's power, however, is to be seen in the mission to the *ethnē*. In the context of this mission, the rule of the demons can be seen as a thing of the past: "he has sent forth into Jerusalem the scepter of power, namely, the call to repentance to all the *ethnē* over which the demons used to rule" (*Dialogue with Trypho* 83.4). Later he declares to Trypho that present realities demonstrate that the prophecies are being fulfilled—prophecies that "the demons were to be destroyed, and to shudder at his name; and that all the authorities and kingdoms were likewise to tremble before him; and that out of every nationality [*genos*] those who believe in him would be shown to be pious and peaceful" (131.5). As the final clause indicates, one result of Christ's power over the demonic "gods of the *ethnē*" was the emergence of a new "pious and peaceful [*eusebeis kai eirēnikous*]" people, something that we observed in more detail in the previous section.

Finally, Justin's claims about Christ's power with respect to "all the authorities and kingdoms" and the emergence of a new pious and peaceful people from all the *ethnē* lead to some observations about the place of the Roman Empire with respect to the new state of affairs brought into being by Christ.

First, as we have already observed, Justin seems to discern some form of providential purpose at work in the events of Roman rule in Judea, as he considers

---

57. *Dialogue with Trypho* 78.9; he interprets the magi's journey as an "[open revolt] against the power that had possessed them," linking it to Isa 8:4.

them in the light of Gen 49:10-11 (*First Apology* 32.1-5). At the very least, he sees significant coincidences. The birth of Jesus occurred around the time that Herodian rule of Judea came to an end and direct Roman rule began. Justin sees this as a fulfillment of the prophecy that "a ruler shall not fail from Judah ... until the one for whom it lies in store should come" (32.1). After Jesus's crucifixion, the mission to the *ethnē* began to bear fruit, and the Judean war with Rome resulted in the end of the Jewish state and the full incorporation of Judea into Roman territory ("the land of the Jews was given in captivity to you"). Justin sees this as a fulfillment of the prophecy that "the one for whom it lies in store" would be "the one awaited by the *ethnē*" (32.4). Precisely what he thinks about the role of Rome in these events is not made clear. He has nothing to say about Rome's role with respect to the *ethnē*, nor does he provide any indication that the *pax Romana* might be seen as beneficial for the apostolic mission. Still, it seems that something more than mere coincidence is in view. Somehow there seems to be a causal connection between the birth and subsequent crucifixion of Christ, the onset of direct Roman rule over Judea, the end of the temple and the Jewish state, and the emergence of those "from all the *ethnē*" who are "await[ing] him who is to come again."[58]

Second, Justin is concerned to present the new race or nation drawn "from all the *ethnē*" as a community of loyal and model citizens.[59] Not only are they a "pious and peaceful" people, as we have seen; in addition, he declares to the emperor that "we more than all people are your allies and fellow soldiers for peace" (*First Apology* 12.1). Since Christians are answerable ultimately to the God who will punish wickedness, he argues, the emperor is working against his own best interests in punishing them. Further, in accordance with the teaching of Christ, Christians willingly pay their taxes and levies (17.1). Taking it a step further, he declares: "while we worship only God we serve you joyfully in other respects, acknowledging you as kings and rulers within the human sphere" (17.3).

Justin, then, does not present his redrawn map of the human race as a direct challenge to the Roman one (at least, not in the *Apologies*).[60] While he praises the admirable qualities of Christians and even describes their way of life as a

---

58. On Justin's apologetic use of the destruction of the temple, see Gregerman, *Building on the Ruins of the Temple*, 26-34.

59. On this point, see Ulrich, "Justin Martyr," 57-58.

60. As was noted above, in the *Dialogue with Trypho* he claims that the power of the demon that controlled the people of Damascus had been "crushed by Christ" at his birth and that, in journeying to worship Christ, the magi were "revolting openly" against the demon (78.9). He gives his readers no reason to believe that a similar statement could not be made about the demon in control of Rome itself.

politeia (*First Apology* 4.2), he does not seem to suggest that this might represent an alternative to the *politeia* of the Roman Empire.[61] As far as the expressed purposes of his *Apologies* are concerned, his account of the identity and *politeia* of the Christians functions in support of an appeal that they be judged fairly and "in accordance with careful and exacting reason" (*First Apology* 2.3). Nevertheless, as this reference to reason (*logos*) indicates, he couches his appeal in terms that convey at least an implicit challenge. He implores his readers—from Antoninus Pius on down—to choose between two alternatives. They can allow themselves to be governed by reason and thus align themselves with the *logos* that has been "implanted in the whole human race" (*Second Apology* 7[8].1); or they can give in "to senseless passion" and the influence "of wicked demons" (*First Apology* 5.1; cf. 14.1), the demons whose aim is "the deception and misdirection of the human race [*genos*]" (*First Apology* 54.1). And he at least hints at these alternatives in the opening address of *First Apology*, which is addressed not only "to the emperor Titus Aelius Hadrian Antoninus Pius Augustus Caesar" but also to the emperor's two sons—Verissimus (i.e., Marcus Aurelius), whom he describes as a philosopher, and Lucius, "a lover of learning [*paideia*]." In other words, *First Apology* is addressed to those who might be expected to be controlled by reason (*logos*) rather than by the demons. In addition, Justin makes his "address and petition" precisely as a representative "of people of every race [*genos*] of human beings who are being unjustly hated and abused." Justin, then, addresses the emperor on behalf of that portion of the human race that is hated and abused by those who choose demons over reason, calling on them to choose reason (*logos*)—even the Logos—instead.

Our examination of Justin's two-pronged apologetic enterprise—vis-à-vis Jews and Judaism, on one side, and Greco-Roman opinion-makers, on the other—has made it readily apparent that the identification of Christians both as *ethnē* and as a distinctive people drawn from "all the *ethnē*" plays an important part in his efforts at identity negotiation across both boundaries. In both cases, the usefulness of the term is also readily apparent. On one side, Justin's Greek version of the Scriptures contained hundreds of instances of *ethnē*, and he shows himself capable of seeing any and all of them as references to, or prophecies of, the Christians.[62] He is willing to adopt *ethnē* as a self-descriptor precisely because it allows him to claim a scriptural pedigree for the gentile church to

---

61. Elsewhere he uses the term with respect to Athens in the time of Socrates (*Second Apology* 10.6), the Jewish way of life (*Dialogue with Trypho* 47.4), that of the Pharisees in particular (*Dialogue with Trypho* 105.6), and the former way of life of gentile Christians (*Dialogue with Trypho* 119.5).

62. Almost six hundred instances, not including the Apocrypha.

which he belongs. Central to his strategy for claiming the Scriptures of Israel for the church is an interpretive program in which the multitude of scriptural references to the *ethnē* are understood to be anticipations of the gentile church. His exegetical enterprise is thus not only *adversus Judaeos* but also *pro gentibus*; not only "against the Jews" but also "for the gentiles." The readiness of Justin to identify himself and others like him as *ethnē* is driven by the desire to demonstrate, as he says to Trypho, that the Scriptures are "not yours but ours" (*Dialogue with Trypho* 29.2).

On the other side, competitive ethnology was, as we have seen, a common feature of the Greco-Roman world. In the jostle for recognition and relative power in an imperial context, people groups found it necessary to define their identities in such a way as to position themselves advantageously on the map of the nations. In Greco-Roman identity discourse, the language of ethnicity—nation, race, people—was an essential element. In such a context, gentile Christians were at an obvious disadvantage. A new group, with none of the usual features of an ethnic people group except for their common deity and (unconventional) pattern of worship, standing in a complicated and problematic relationship with the Judean nation, sprinkled among the nations rather than existing as a nation in any recognizable sense of the term, Christians might seem to have had little chance of positioning themselves anywhere on the map at all, let alone in an advantageous location.

From this perspective, one can see how the two prongs of Justin's apologetic enterprise fit together. By identifying Christians as the actualization of the divine promise to Abraham that he would be the father of a multitude of *ethnē*, merging this with the promise that he would be the progenitor of a great *ethnos*, and pressing great swaths of Israel's Scriptures into the service of this new ethnic identity, Justin was able both to find a point of access into the discourse of competitive ethnology and to make a plausible claim that Christians were really an ancient people with a long and honored pedigree. In addition, as we have seen, the gods who were worshiped by the various nations of the world he identified as demons, malevolent spiritual powers who had enslaved the human race and were the source of evil and human suffering but whose power had now been broken by Christ. While this was a riskier move, it nevertheless allowed him to place the concept of an *ethnos* drawn from all the *ethnē* of the world within a larger cosmic construction of the origin, pathology, and destiny of the nations. With this construction, he was able to position the Christian *ethnos*, drawn from all the *ethnē*, as a visible manifestation of the divine solution to the problems faced by the nations as a whole—"murders, wars, adulteries, licentiousness, and every kind of evil" (*Second Apology* 4[5].4), all of which were instigated by the demons who exercised control over the nations.

Ethnē and Gentile Christian Identity (After 135 CE)

What we encounter in Justin's work—for the first time, as far as our sources can tell us—is both a wholehearted and consistent adoption of *ethnē* as a term of gentile Christian self-identification and the use of this term (along with related ethnic terms) as a central element in an energetic and thoroughgoing enterprise of competitive ethnography.[63] To be sure, he was by no means the first to use the term as an instrument of group self-identification. As we have seen in chapter 6, there are several instances in the Epistle of Barnabas where *ethnē* appears in scriptural quotations that the author takes as references to gentile Christians. The term is also used with a similar reference in Acts, at least if the author of Luke-Acts was himself gentile. Further, if Skarsaune is correct in identifying a gentile Christian source behind some portions of the *Dialogue with Trypho*, this can be added as well.[64] With respect to other aspects of Justin's enterprise, we have already seen how some components can be found in analogous or more primitive

---

63. In different ways, Yoder, Buell, and Boyarin place Justin in a context where Jewish and Christian identities were fluid and overlapped in significant ways, and they see him as playing a decisive role in the separation of the two: John Howard Yoder, *The Jewish-Christian Schism Revisited*, ed. Michael G. Cartwright and Peter Ochs (Grand Rapids: Eerdmans, 2003), 53–61; Buell, *Why This New Race?*, 94–115; Boyarin, *Border Lines*, 37–73. While I cannot interact in any detail here with these works (from each of which I have learned much), it seems to me that Yoder and Buell do not give sufficient latitude to the already-existing distinction between Jews and *ethnē*, and to the resultant emergence of largely gentile congregations and church groupings. Boyarin gives greater recognition to the existence of gentile Christianity and to the emerging question of identity: "These Christians, whom I will call by virtue of their own *self*-presentation, Gentile Christians (The Church from the Gentiles, *ek tōn ethnōn*), were confronted with a dilemma: Since we are no longer 'Greeks' and not 'Jews,' to what kind of group do we belong?" He continues: "These Christians had to ask themselves: What is this *Christianismos* in which we find ourselves? Is it a new *gens*, a new *ethnos*, a third one, neither Jew nor Greek, or is it an entirely new something in the world, some new kind of identity completely?" He concludes that Justin and the form of Christianity to which he belonged chose the latter: "Christianity was a new thing, a community defined by adherence to a certain canon of doctrine and practice" (p. 17). This "new thing" came to be known as a "religion." While there are insights here that I can appreciate, it seems to me that this is to disregard the importance for Justin of an identity grounded in the idea of a race or nation whose members were drawn from "all the *ethnē*" of the world. *Ethnē*-existence, for Justin, was not a dilemma to be solved but an opportunity for identity negotiation in the world of the *ethnē*.

64. Specifically, *Dialogue with Trypho* 32–38 and portions of a more extended section beginning at ch. 66. He also suggests that this source, which he calls the "recapitulation source," might be identified with the *Controversy between Jason and Papiscus*, no longer extant but mentioned by Origen and other later writers; see Skarsaune, *Proof from Prophecy*, 234–42; cf. Will Rutherford, "*Altercatio Jasonis et Papisci* as a Testimony Source

forms in earlier gentile Christian literature—*adversus Judaeos* arguments in the Epistle of Barnabas, for example, or competitive ethnography in the Apology of Aristides, or Ignatius's cryptic reference to christologically significant celestial signs that had "escaped the notice of the ruler of this age" (*To the Ephesians* 19.1–3).[65] And to take a further step back, some of this can be seen as gentile transformations of material produced by Jewish Christ-believers in the context of sectarian engagement with the larger Jewish world.

Nevertheless, the point remains: both in its importance as an identity term and in the central role it plays in his two-pronged apologetic enterprise, Justin's use of *ethnē* represents the beginning of a new stage in early Christian identity negotiation. Or, if we want to give maximum latitude to the possible evidence from reconstructed sources (such as Skarsaune's "recapitulation source") or lost documents (such as the *Controversy between Jason and Papiscus*), Justin's work represents a clear and invaluable window into this new stage of development.[66] Even so, it needs to be seen not simply as a repository of previous work but as a distinctive construction and a substantial achievement in its own right.

This is not to overlook the deficiencies of Justin's work at the literary level, especially in the *Dialogue with Trypho*—repetitive treatment of material, often with little apparent organizing structure; lengthy scriptural citations, introduced in support of a particular argument but whose point often gets lost in the sheer length of the citation itself; condescending and dismissive treatment of Trypho, coupled with unfounded self-satisfaction in arguments that would have been convincing only to the already convinced.[67]

Further, as we will see in a bit more detail as we proceed, the shape of Justin's construction is determined to a significant extent by the complex social, cultural, political, and religious milieu in which he existed. While it is not inappropriate to speak of his work of identity construction as taking place along two boundar-

---

for Justin's 'Second God' Argument," in Parvis and Foster, *Justin Martyr and His Worlds*, 137–45.

65. See the summary at the end of ch. 6.

66. According to Origen, who describes it as a dialogue between a Christian and a Jew on the topic of Christ and the Scriptures, the *Controversy between Jason and Papiscus* was mentioned by Celsus (*Against Celsus* 4.52). Thus it would have been extant in Justin's time, perhaps prior to the writing of his own *Dialogue with Trypho*.

67. This is not the whole picture, to be sure. Trypho is more than a pliable and unresisting straw man; to a certain extent, he is, as Wilson observes, "a significant conversational partner as he probes and queries the Christian position with point and skill"; *Related Strangers*, 260. See also Timothy J. Horner, *Listening to Trypho: Justin Martyr's Dialogue Reconsidered* (Leuven: Peeters, 2001).

Ethnē and Gentile Christian Identity (After 135 CE)

ies, in Justin's case in particular, as Rebecca Lyman has observed, this boundary territory was also a complex hybrid space:

> every element in Justin's self-identification in the *First Apology* is a product of the rapidly changing circumstances under the Roman Empire: his descent from Greek parentage in a Roman colony established in a city built by Vespasian in Samaria after the destruction of the Jerusalem temple. His subsequent search for truth through varied philosophies from this origin also sums up the social and cultural life of many educated men of the second century: colonization, educational mobility, religious interchange.[68]

To the extent, then, that Justin's project of group identity construction can be described as an achievement, it was the achievement of one whose personal identity was marked by complexity, change, and a striving after creative self-actualization. His project, in turn, can be seen as the kind of "social articulation of difference" that Bhabha describes as "a complex, on-going negotiation that seeks to authorize cultural hybridities that emerge in moments of historical transformation."[69]

If Justin's work can be described as an achievement, however, it was one that ran a number of risks and eventually brought with it considerable negative consequences. This was especially the case on the *adversus Judaeos* side of the identity negotiations. As we have seen, Justin's construction of gentile Christian identity comprised a number of distinct elements: (1) Christians are to be identified with the *ethnē* who appear in Israel's Scriptures. (2) At the same time, those from the *ethnē* who believe in Christ constitute a new nation, race, or people. (3) This new race is also the nation promised to Abraham and thus rightly bears the identity Israel. (4) Nevertheless, this race is not really new at all, in that it stands as the continuation of a people marked by a form of religion that predated the law, was found among the righteous patriarchs (including Abraham), and was carried on by the prophets and other heroes of Scripture. (5) The law of Moses played no role as an identity marker for members of this race; its only positive value was as a symbolic pointer to Christ, something that had been recognized by the true members of this race from the beginning.[70]

---

68. Rebecca Lyman, "Justin and Hellenism: Some Postcolonial Perspectives," in Parvis and Foster, *Justin Martyr and His Worlds*, 160–68, here 163.

69. Homi K. Bhabha, *The Location of Culture* (London: Routledge, 2004), 2.

70. On Justin's various views of Christians as a nation, race, or people, see Buell, *Why This New Race?*, 98–99.

Elements 1 and 2 posed no substantial dangers in and of themselves. With respect to 1, one of the few positive features of the *adversus Judaeos* tradition was the extent to which it encouraged gentile Christians to identify with the *ethnē* in Israel's Scripture, rather than with Israelites or Jews in any direct and arrogating way. Nor was there any inherent danger in seeing the new group of Christian believers drawn from all the *ethnē* as constituting a new nation, race, or people. Problems emerge, however, with element 3 and its collapsing of the difference between the "great nation" of Abraham's descendants and the "multitude of nations" who were to be blessed through Abraham and his descendants.[71] With this move, gentile believers were encouraged to find their place in the story not by identifying with the *ethnē* who were to be blessed but by arrogating to themselves the identity of the Israelite and Jewish descendants of Abraham who were to be the means of blessing. Put differently, a problematic aspect of Justin's identity construction is that it posits a gentile church that both is constituted of *ethnē* and claims to be the *ethnos* promised to Abraham.

Admittedly, versions of these elements were present—or, at least, could be perceived—in material written by Jewish Christ-believers, which meant that they could readily be perceived as part of the identity that they were ascribing to gentile believers. Nevertheless, in contrast to Paul, say, or to Matthew, addressing mixed communities in a context where the Jewish origin and nature of the movement was taken for granted, Justin was a gentile, speaking for a gentile church in a situation where gentile Christianity was dominant and Jewish Christ-believers were an increasingly separate and probably minority group for the most part.[72] Further, elements 4 and 5, which were argued by constraint-driven logic that we will explore presently, served to compound the problem by encouraging an anti-Jewish reading of Scripture that emptied the covenantal-historical dimensions of the text of any meaning. While such a reading has often been classified as supersessionistic, the term is not entirely adequate.[73] Supersession—where a superior entity comes to occupy a position once held by another, the displaced entity becoming outmoded or obsolete in the process—necessarily implies that

---

71. Justin "sees no distinction between the descendants of Abraham who become a blessing for the Gentiles and the Gentiles themselves"; Rokéah, *Justin Martyr and the Jews*, 84.

72. On Justin and Paul, see Werline, "Transformation of Pauline Arguments."

73. So, e.g., Oskar Skarsaune, "Does the Letter to the Hebrews Articulate a Supersessionist Theology? A Response to Richard Hays," in *The Epistle to the Hebrews and Christian Theology*, ed. Richard Bauckham and et al. (Grand Rapids: Eerdmans, 2009), 177; Bruce Chilton, "Justin and Israelite Prophecy," in Parvis and Foster, *Justin Martyr and His Worlds*, 83–84.

the superseded entity possessed some original value or legitimacy. The relationship that comes into view here in Justin's work, however, is one in which the displacement serves to deny any value or legitimacy to the displaced entity at all. The image that seems to be called for in this case is not one in which one entity is displaced by another but one in which an entity consisting of two disparate elements is broken into two entities as a result of some subsequent event or factor. In this aspect of Justin's view of things, Israel can be said to have contained within it two opposing groups from the beginning—those who "lived with Logos" and perceived that the law pointed to Christ, and those who (mis)understood the law in a literal and fleshly way. The coming of Christ served to effect a definitive separation of these two disparate and opposing groups.

A discussion of the factors that served to determine this particular view of Israel and the church takes us into the Greco-Roman side of Justin's identity negotiations and his attempt to construct Christian identity on terms that would resonate with Greco-Roman discourse. What is of immediate interest here is his adoption of two assumptions that were widely held in the Greco-Roman world and that proved to be of decisive importance with respect to his treatment of Israel. One was the idea of divine immutability. For Justin, it would be "ridiculous and preposterous" to think that God would "not wish each succeeding generation of humanity always to perform the same acts of righteousness" (*Dialogue with Trypho* 23.1)—that is, to think that God would give one set of good commandments and laws through Moses and then, in an abrupt change, issue another set through Christ. The specific provisions of the Mosaic law, then, must have been given for a particular—and negative—reason: Israel's characteristic propensity for sin and idolatry. The other was the Greco-Roman valuation of antiquity, especially (as we have seen) in the context of ethnic origins and competitive ethnology. Although Justin can speak of a "new covenant" or a "new race" on occasion (but only in the *Dialogue with Trypho*), the idea of newness concedes antiquity to the Jews.[74] Hence the more dominant insistence is to present Christians as the continuation of an ancient people, one that even antedated the time of Moses—Christians not simply as a new Israel but as true Israel, the continuation of a line that goes back to Ur-Israel.

The factors that pushed Justin's thinking in these directions were not unique to his situation, of course, but served to constrain the development of gentile

---

74. "In contrast to his practice in the *Dialogue*, in his *Apology* Justin avoids the language of newness"; Judith M. Lieu, *Marcion and the Making of a Heretic: God and Scripture in the Second Century* (Cambridge: Cambridge University Press, 2015), 407. In the *Dialogue with Trypho*, "new covenant" language appears in 11.3; 43.1; 122.5; 123.1; he speaks of a "new race" or "people" in 119.3; 138.2.

GENTILE CHRISTIAN IDENTITY

Christian identity construction throughout the period up to Eusebius. We will examine these factors in more detail in the next section, as we look at Celsus's critique of the kind of arguments made by Justin (and others). But Justin was acutely aware of an additional constraint coming from another direction—from Marcion and his version of gentile Christian identity, which dispensed with many of the problems Justin had to wrestle with simply by doing away with any attempt to align Christians with Israel and its Scriptures entirely. In the next section, we will look at Marcion as well.

Before turning to this directly, we should highlight one other aspect of the Greco-Roman side of Justin's identity negotiations—specifically, statements that suggest, at least in a rudimentary way, a kind of providential relationship between Rome and the Christian movement. As we have seen, Justin sees something more than coincidence at work in the fact that the subjugation and defeat of the Jews took place around the time of Christ's birth, death, and resurrection. To this he adds some affirmations about the willingness of Christians to be good citizens of the empire and about the preservative effect of the Christian presence in the world.[75] In the final section, where we move beyond Justin to sketch out subsequent developments in gentile Christian identity construction, we will see how this providential relationship becomes a more dominant theme.

Constraints: Celsus and Marcion

Justin and Marcion were contemporaries and probably (for a time) co-residents of Rome, and thus Justin was well aware of his ideas and the dangers they posed to his own proto-orthodox view of things.[76] By contrast, Celsus's extended critique of the Christian movement, *True Doctrine*, probably appeared ten or fifteen years after Justin's death,[77] and thus it does not represent something to which

---

75. See especially *First Apology* 12.1, where he tells the emperor that "more than all other people we are your helpers and allies in the cause of peace."

76. He provides brief descriptions of Marcion's views in *First Apology* 26.5; 58.1–3.

77. Celsus's work is usually dated toward the end of the rule of Marcus Aurelius (161–80 CE), while Justin's martyrdom probably occurred in the first half of his rule. For a recent discussion of Celsus's dates, including an attempt to date *True Doctrine* to the period immediately following the Bar Kokhba revolt, see Marco Rizzi, "Some Reflections on Origen, Celsus and Their Views on the Jews," in *Jews and Christians in Antiquity: A Regional Perspective*, ed. Pierluigi Lanfranchi and Joseph Verheyden (Leuven: Peeters, 2018), 37–59. For the traditions about Justin's martyrdom and its probable date, see Minns and Parvis, *Justin, Philosopher and Martyr*, 32–33.

Ethnē and Gentile Christian Identity (After 135 CE)

Justin was responding directly.[78] Nevertheless, it seems likely that, as Frede has argued, Celsus relied on "an already substantial tradition of Jewish and pagan criticism of Christianity."[79] This, together with the fact that many of Justin's own apologetic arguments seem to address the kind of criticisms that appear in the *True Doctrine*, suggests that we can reasonably use Celsus's work as a window into Justin's own environment. In any case, here we are interested in Marcion and Celsus not so much for what they might tell us about Justin in particular but for their significance for the ongoing process of gentile Christian identity construction that first comes into view in his work. To be sure, the task is complicated by the fact that neither Marcion's *Antitheses* nor Celsus's *True Doctrine* has survived, being accessible only through later Christian refutations. Nevertheless, what has survived is sufficient to provide us with valuable insight into the particular constraints within which this process of identity construction took place.

We begin with Celsus, whose extensive and well-informed critique of Christianity comes into view in Origen's detailed point-by-point refutation (*Against Celsus*).[80] His work represents both a counteridentity that is thereby being ascribed to the Christian movement by a perceptive pagan outsider and an indication of the extent to which the relationship between Christianity and Judaism was perceived to be a problem for Christians attempting to negotiate a place for themselves in the wider Greco-Roman world.[81] Here we will not attempt anything like a full descriptive analysis.[82] What is important for our purposes is

---

78. Indeed, the reverse may well have been the case. The title of Celsus's work—*True Doctrine* (*Logos Alēthēs*)—has led some interpreters to make the plausible suggestion that he was responding to Justin; see, e.g., Robert L. Wilken, *The Christians as the Romans Saw Them* (New Haven: Yale University Press, 1984), 101; Schott, *Christianity, Empire, and the Making of Religion*, 45.

79. Michael Frede, "Origin's Treatise *Against Celsus*," in Edwards et al., *Apologetics in the Roman Empire*, 132. And in the forward direction, Celsus stands at the start of an ongoing tradition of pagan critique that includes Porphyry's *Against the Christians* and Julian's *Against the Galileans*.

80. Written at the request of Ambrose (*Against Celsus* preface 1), during the reign of Philip the Arab (244–49 CE) (according to Eusebius [*Ecclesiastical History* 6.36.2]). Origen regularly incorporates extensive and apparently verbatim quotations in his work; in what follows I have depended on Chadwick's identification of these in his standard translation: Henry Chadwick, ed. and trans., *Origen: Contra Celsum* (Cambridge: Cambridge University Press, 1953).

81. On the latter point, see Wilken, *Christians as the Romans Saw Them*, 112–17.

82. Wilken's account is very helpful: *Christians as the Romans Saw Them*, 94–125; see also Frede, "Origin's Treatise *Against Celsus*," 133–35; Chadwick, *Origen*, xvi–xxii.

to observe the extent to which Celsus's critique is formulated with reference to nations and ethnic identity.[83]

While Celsus made use of a wide variety of pagan and Jewish criticisms of Christianity, he used them within his own coherent framework, something that can be described as a form of religious ethnography.[84] He argues that, among all the nations worthy of the name, there was a shared view of the world—"an ancient doctrine [*archaios anōthen logos*] which has existed from the beginning, which has always been maintained by the wisest *ethnē* and cities and wise men" (*Against Celsus* 1.14). While he gives pride of place to the Greeks (for "the Greeks are better able to judge the value of what the barbarians have discovered, and to establish the doctrines and put them into practice by virtue"), he readily includes most barbarian nations within this transethnic collective as well (for "the barbarians [are] capable of discovering doctrines"; 1.2).[85]

Central to this true and ancient doctrine is the recognition of an ultimate deity—"the God over all things [*ton epi pasi theon*]" (*Against Celsus* 1.24), the God by whose will "all things are indeed administered" and from whom "all providence [*pronoia*] [is] derived" (7.68). Even though different ethnic groups might use different names for this supreme deity, this monotheistic belief is held in common and is readily apparent to all.[86] In governing the world, the supreme God is aided by a variety of lesser gods or subordinate beings ("angels or other daemons or heroes"), all of whom have received authority from God over the various nations or other aspects of earthly life and carry out their tasks according to "a law given by the greatest God."[87] Thus each of them is also worthy of human recognition and veneration for their part in the overall divine order of

---

83. A rough indication of this is provided by the frequency with which *ethnos* appears in the work (73 occurrences in the singular, 139 in the plural, for a total of 212), a substantial minority of them occurring in material attributed to Celsus (which also constitutes a much smaller proportion of the whole work).

84. Wilken, *Christians as the Romans Saw Them*, 96.

85. Among those excluded are the Scythians, the Nomads of Libya, the Senes "who believe in no gods," and "other nations [*ethnē*] that are most impious and have no regard for law" (7.62).

86. "It makes no difference whether one calls the supreme God [*ton epi pasi theon*] by the name used among the Greeks, or by that, for example, used among the Indians, or by that among the Egyptians" (1.24).

87. "Are not all things indeed administered [*dioiketai*] according to God's will, and is not all providence [*pronoia*] derived from him? And whatever there may be in the universe, whether the work of God, or of angels, or of other daemons or heroes, do not all these things keep a law given by the greatest God? And has there not been appointed over each particular thing a being who has been thought worthy to be allotted power?" (7.68).

things. Just as one honors a human emperor by showing due respect to his "satrap and subordinate governor or officer or procurator," so by worshiping God's own subordinate governors, one is thereby worshiping the supreme God.[88]

To be sure, Celsus's ethnography provides considerable latitude for differences among nations in their customs and patterns of worship. In the context of a lengthy description of differences among a number of named nations, he declares: "Thus there is nothing wrong if each of them observes its own laws of worship. Actually we will find that the differences from nation to nation [*kata ethnē*] are very considerable" (*Against Celsus* 5.34).[89] In accounting for the differences, he makes some allowance for the unpredictability of human nature ("it came into the head of different people to think differently"), but he places more emphasis on the discretion allowed to the various heavenly overseers: "it is probable that from the beginning the different parts of the earth were allotted to different overseers, and are governed in this way by having been divided between certain authorities" (5.25). In the end, however, what seems to carry most weight for him is the antiquity of the traditions. It would be "impious to abandon the customs which have existed in each locality from the beginning"; their very antiquity offers proof that "they are done in the way that pleases the overseers" and thus "are right" (5.25).

Within Celsus's religious ethnography, the Jews occupy an ambiguous place. On the one hand, he gives grudging recognition to the antiquity of their traditions and, on this basis, is prepared to count them among the nations. The passage that was cited in the previous paragraph begins with this comment about the Jews:

> Now the Jews became an individual nation [*ethnos idion*], and made laws according to the custom of their country; and they maintain these laws among themselves at the present day, and observe a worship which may be very peculiar but is at least traditional [*patrion*]. In this respect they behave like the rest of mankind [*tois allois anthrōpois*]. (*Against Celsus* 5.25)

However, as Origen complains on several occasions, Celsus refuses to include the Jews among the number of those nations with venerable traditions and honorable histories. Although there were "many of the nations [*ethnē*]"—the "wisest" of them—that held to the same "doctrine," Celsus would not count the Jews as

---

88. *Against Celsus* 8.35; see the whole of 8.33–35; also 7.68; 8.2. On the place and role of the gods of the *ethnē* in the Greco-Roman world, see especially Paula Fredriksen, "How Jewish Is God? Divine Ethnicity in Paul's Theology," *JBL* 137 (2018): 193–212.

89. He adds: "and nevertheless each one of them think its own by far the best."

"a very wise nation [*ethnos*]" like "the Egyptians, Assyrians, Indians, Persians, Odrysians, Samothracians, and Eleusinians."[90] None of the Jews "ever did anything of importance"; "they were of no significance or prominence whatsoever" (4.32).[91]

The issue for Celsus was the refusal of the Jews to acknowledge the gods of the other nations and their corresponding arrogance in insisting that their national god was the supreme deity. This was the work of Moses, a sorcerer and deceiver, who "heard of this doctrine which was current among the wise *ethnē* and distinguished men" and, through trickery, was able to convince a motley group of Egyptian goatherds and shepherds "that there was only one God," with the result that "without any rational cause these goatherds and shepherds abandoned the worship of many gods" (1.21, 23). The Jewish nation, then, began as a rebellion on the part of a seditious group of people who "were Egyptian by race [*tō genei*], and left Egypt after revolting against the Egyptian community and despising the customs of Egypt" (*Against Celsus* 3.5).[92]

This leads to Celsus's attack on Christians, who, in his view, exhibit most of the faults of the Jews with none of their redeeming features. Their shared faults go back to the beginnings of each group. Just as the Jewish people began as a seditious separation from the Egyptians, so the Christians originated out of a similar "revolt" (*to stasiazein*) against the Jews (*Against Celsus* 3.5); just as the earliest Jews were "deluded" by Moses (1.23), so the earliest Christians were "deluded by Jesus" (2.1).[93] Celsus recognizes the irony: "what they [the Jews] did to the Egyptians they suffered in turn through those who followed Jesus and believed him to be the Christ" (3.5), whom he describes elsewhere as "the author of their sedition [*tēs staseōs*]" (8.14).

In their revolt against the Jews, the Christians nevertheless retained the absurd Jewish notion that worship of their own god meant that they could not "render the due honors" to other gods, the subordinate divine beings who had

---

90. *Against Celsus* 1.14; a similar passage, with another roll call of "inspired nations [*ethnē*]" from which the Jews were excluded, appears in 6.80.

91. On Celsus's depiction of the Jews among the nations of the world, see N. R. M. de Lange, *Origen and the Jews: Studies in Jewish-Christian Relations in Third-Century Palestine* (Cambridge: Cambridge University Press, 1976), 64–65.

92. The term *stasiazein*, translated "revolting," has to do with the activity of a seditious faction. On the political significance of *stasis* in the Greek and Roman periods, see Rizzi, "Some Reflections on Origen, Celsus and Their Views on the Jews," 48. Recall the concern about *stasis* in 1 Clement, as discussed in ch. 6.

93. In adding that they "have left the law of their fathers," Celsus demonstrates his awareness that the earliest followers of Jesus were Jews.

Ethnē and Gentile Christian Identity (After 135 CE)

been entrusted with the supervision of various aspects of human life. Like the Jews, they "refuse to worship" God's own appointed spiritual agents "in the proper way" and thus have cut themselves off from normal society (*Against Celsus* 8.55).

As we have seen, while Celsus is generally disparaging in his comments about Jewish worship, he nevertheless concedes that it "is at least traditional [*patrion*]"; in this way, he says, the Jews resemble the other nations (*Against Celsus* 5.25). The Christians, however, can make no legitimate claim to ancient tradition. It was only "a very few years ago" that the founder of the Christian group "taught this doctrine" (1.26).[94] Speaking in a more contemptuous tone, Celsus says:

> I will ask them where they have come from, or who is the author of their traditional laws [*patriōn nomōn*]. Nobody, they will say. In fact, they themselves originated from Judaism, and they cannot name any other source for their teacher and chorus-leader. Nevertheless they rebelled against the Jews. (5.33)

For Celsus, proper worship is indissolubly bound up with an identifiable people group—a city or nation with its own place, shared history, and ancestral traditions.[95] In rebelling against the Jews, then, the Christians have forfeited any claim to be a legitimate people.

To be sure, Celsus is aware to a certain extent that Christians laid claim to Israel's Scriptures and attempted to root their beliefs about Christ and their own existence in the writings of the Jewish prophets. Speaking in the voice of a Jewish interlocutor, however, he accuses them of trying to have it both ways: "Why do you take your origin from our religion [*hierōn*], and then, as if you are progressing in knowledge, despise these things, although you cannot name any other origin for your doctrine than our law?" For, as the interlocutor goes on to point out, the Christians attempt to legitimize their doctrine by appealing to the prophets.[96] Later, speaking in his own voice, Celsus ridicules the Christians for the picture of a befuddled and capricious god that emerges, a god who gives one set of laws through Moses and then replaces them with something different through Jesus: "Who is wrong? Moses or Jesus? Or when the Father sent Jesus had he forgotten what commands he gave to Moses? Or did he condemn his

---

94. Again: "he was most dishonourably arrested and punished to his utter disgrace, and though quite recently he wandered about most shamefully in the sight of all men" (6.10).

95. Described perceptively by Wilken, *Christians as the Romans Saw Them*, 124–25.

96. "For if there was anyone who proclaimed to you that the son of God would come down to men, it was our prophet, the prophet of our God" (2.4).

own laws and change his mind, and send his messenger for quite the opposite purpose?" (*Against Celsus* 7.18).

For Celsus, then, while most of the nations of the world are bound together by their adherence to a "true doctrine," the Christians, with their exclusive monotheism, antisocial posture, and recent origins, simply do not qualify. Rather than being a legitimate people group, he says at the outset, they are a secret society and, as such, they are dangerous and their associations are illegal (*Against Celsus* 1.1). Further, toward the end of the work, he seems to recognize that the Christians, like the Jews before them, harbored dreams that eventually the Romans, together with the people of the world, would abandon their own gods, "call upon your Most High," and thus recognize the Christians as "masters of the whole world" (8.69). While he dismisses it as a ludicrous pipe dream, his comments nevertheless betray a certain nervousness about a transethnic group that separated itself from the normal structures of society.[97] And so, while he began his *True Doctrine* with a condemnation, he ends with an appeal. In his conclusion, he calls on Christians to render appropriate worship to the divinely established gods, to support the emperor, to accept public office in their homeland (*patris*), and, in short, to participate in the common life of the human race.[98]

Looking back at Justin's apologetic project through the lens provided by Celsus's *True Doctrine* helps us gain perspective on two aspects of Justin's argument that were highlighted at the end of the previous section. One had to do with his unambiguous claim that the church was Israel. It was not enough for Justin that the church represented the fulfillment of the scriptural promises concerning all the (non-Jewish) nations; he felt compelled to go further and to claim for the church the identity of Israel itself. Christians, then, were not only the multitude of *ethnē* who were to be blessed through Abraham's descendants; they also constituted the great *ethnos* that, according to the divine promise, Abraham's descendants would become.

In the previous section, it was suggested that in his construction of this (rather self-contradictory) identity for the Christian group, Justin was influenced by a concern for antiquity. In earlier chapters, we have already seen how a claim

---

97. In the case of the Jews, he says, things did not work out that way at all. A little later, he declared that it was simply impossible "to unite under one law the inhabitants of Asia, Europe, and Libya, both Greeks and barbarians even at the furthest limits" (8.72). On this aspect of Celsus's critique, see Henry Chadwick, "Christian and Roman Universalism in the Fourth Century," in *Christian Faith and Greek Philosophy in Late Antiquity: Essays in Tribute to George Christopher Stead*, ed. L. R. Wickham and C. P. Bammel, VCSup 19 (Leiden: Brill, 1993), 26–42, esp. 33–36.

98. *Against Celsus* 8.55, 73, 75.

to antiquity was important in the competitive ethnology of the Greco-Roman world in general; Celsus's critique gives us a clearer insight into how it became especially important for Christian identity in particular. As has already been observed, for Celsus and the world he inhabited, the proper domain for religious worship was an ethnic people group (a nation or a city), a group associated with a specific locale and bound together by communal laws, ancestral traditions, and shared history.[99] As a group with relatively recent origins—a group that, in addition, had severed its ties with Judaism—the Christians represented none of these things. In such an environment, one can readily understand Justin's desire to lay claim to Israel's tradition—in the form of not only its Scriptures, with their promises of future salvation, but also its identity as an ancient nation.

The second highlighted aspect had to do with the Christians' rejection of Jewish ancestral traditions and patterns of worship. Not only did this seem to subvert any Christian claim to antiquity, it also implied unpalatable things about the nature of God. What kind of a God would enact one set of laws through Moses and another through Jesus? One of the appealing things about the idea of a supreme God was that such a being with an immutable character transcended the changeable and capricious behavior exhibited by many of the ethnic, civic, or other gods of the ancient world. The God of Moses and Jesus, however, might seem to belong to the latter category. From this perspective, one can get a better understanding of Justin's moves to shift the problem from God to the Jews. The law was given because of the particular and persistent sinfulness of the Jews; now that the Jews have been punished for their sinfulness and Christ has established a new people (which was also the reestablishment of an ancient line of those who had "lived with Logos"), the purpose of the law had run its course.

Turning from Celsus to Marcion, here we encounter someone whose thinking and influence posed similar challenges for the proto-orthodox project of identity construction, though coming from quite a different angle. Since this "wolf of Pontus," as Eusebius later called him,[100] was a Christian thinker who was likewise

---

99. Louis H. Feldman recognizes the close connection here between antiquity and ethnicity: "The attack on Christianity in pagan literature was on two fronts: first, it was the first religion devoid of a nationalistic connection; and second, it was new and had no real roots in the past"; "Origen's *Contra Celsum* and Josephus' *Contra Apionem*: The Issue of Jewish Origins," *VC* 44 (1990): 107. Schott notes the centrality of ethnic people groups in Celsus's conception of the human world: "Celsus sees Greeks, Egyptians, Phoenicians, Thracians, and other *ethne* as the natural building blocks of the empire. Celsus understands these distinctions to be the consequence of both the natural development of human civilization and divine fiat"; *Christianity, Empire, and the Making of Religion*, 49.

100. *Ecclesiastical History* 5.13.4.

wrestling with issues of Christian identity in a gentile environment and whose differences with the proto-orthodox were recognized by perceptive outsiders such as Celsus (*Against Celsus* 5.61), Justin and those who followed him needed to engage the external critique of Celsus in ways that did not cede ground to the internal challenge of Marcion and his followers.[101]

While Marcion's work has likewise not survived, in his case, unlike that of Celsus, we have several substantial accounts of its arguments and major themes.[102] While this puts us potentially in a better position, at the same time it complicates the situation, in that the varying accounts alert us to the extent to which the differing portraits have been shaped in accordance with the concerns and perspectives of the portrayers.[103] Nevertheless, with the exercise of due critical caution, a reasonably reliable portrait emerges.

What comes immediately into view in any discussion of Marcion is his radical duality of Gods. The Father God revealed by Jesus is a different—and higher— deity than the creator God revealed in the Scriptures and worshiped by Israel.[104] The creator God is a God of law and justice, ruling the world with severity and temperamental caprice, and distressingly entangled with the created order. In contrast, the Father God of Jesus, "who is above the God who made the world" (Irenaeus, *Against Heresies* 1.27.2), exists above all this and is thoroughly good— "the good God of Marcion," as Irenaeus refers to him (2.1.2). What is important for our purposes, however, though it is not always recognized, is the way this duality also has to do with a duality of peoples—the Jews and the gentiles.[105]

---

101. See Lieu, *Marcion and the Making of a Heretic*, esp. 436-39.

102. Justin provides the earliest (albeit brief) accounts (*First Apology* 26.5; 58.1-3); the most extensive and detailed discussion is that of Tertullian (*Against Marcion*), though others appear in Irenaeus, Clement of Alexandria, Origen, Hippolytus, and Epiphanius.

103. E.g., "At every point Tertullian's own convictions and his construction of Marcion play off against each other like a light and the shadows it throws, the sound and its echo"; Lieu, *Marcion and the Making of a Heretic*, 84. In her comprehensive treatment, Lieu proceeds in two stages: first she describes the various "Marcions" that are reflected in the writings of his opponents; then she carries out her own reconstruction by means of a critical analysis of these ancient accounts (she describes her procedure on pp. 10-11). Of course, modern reconstructions (including her own) result in further "Marcions"; among the most influential of these has been that of Adolf von Harnack, *Marcion: The Gospel of the Alien God*, trans. John E. Steely and Lyle D. Bierma (Durham, NC: Labyrinth, 1990; German original, 1921).

104. This duality of deities appears consistently in the sources, beginning with Justin: "Marcion, from Pontus, who even now is still teaching those he can persuade to consider some other, greater than the Creator God" (*First Apology* 26.5).

105. Though note this straightforward comment by Kenneth W. Clark: "The Matthean

Of course, this is inherent in his identification of the God of Israel, the God of (Israel's) Scriptures, as the inferior creator God. But this contrast between Israel and non-Israel does not remain latent; it appears to have been an important aspect of his construction. Further, it is just as apparent that Marcion describes this other people—those with whom Jesus and his Father God are particularly concerned—as the *ethnē*.

Despite Marcion's deprecation of Israel's God, it is clear that he does not call into question this God's existence, his special relationship with the Jews, the validity of his revelation in the Scriptures, and so on. Indeed, he even accepts the reality of a Jewish messiah, who will come at some time in the future to fulfill the scriptural promises and to restore Israel.[106] Addressing himself to Marcion, Tertullian declares: "your Christ promises the Jews their former estate, after the restitution of their country, and, when life has run its course, refreshment ... in Abraham's bosom" (*Against Marcion* 3.24.1). Tertullian understands Marcion to have thought in terms of two Christs: a "Judaic Christ [who] was intended by the Creator for the regathering out of dispersion of the people [*populi*] and no others," and "your Christ [who] has been advanced by the supremely good God for the deliverance of the whole human race [*omni humano generi*]" (3.21.1). Again: "Marcion lays it down that there is one Christ who in the time of Tiberius was revealed by a god formerly unknown, for the salvation of all the nations [*omnium gentium*]; and another Christ who is destined by God the Creator to come at some time still future for the reestablishment of the Jewish kingdom" (4.6.3).

Marcion's concept of two Christs means that when he speaks of Christ who has come "for the salvation of all the nations [*omnium gentium*]," a Christ who is set over against another Christ for the Jews, we need to understand *gentes* in its specific sense of "non-Jewish nations," that is, "gentiles." This comes to expression in a different way in Irenaeus's account of how Marcion understood Christ's descent into hell; in this curious account, Christ's role as Savior of the non-Jews is clearly in view:

> Cain and those like him, the Sodomites and the Egyptians and those like them, and all the pagans [*omnes gentes*] who walked in every mess of wickedness were all saved by the Lord when he descended into the netherworld and they met him, and he took them into his kingdom. But Abel, Enoch, Noah, and the rest of the righteous and the patriarchs who came from Abraham,

---

thesis is not ... like the later message of Marcion that Jews and gentiles have different gods and separate identities"; "The Gentile Bias in Matthew," *JBL* 66 (1947): 166.

106. On this aspect of Marcion's thought, see especially Wilson, *Related Strangers*, 214–17.

together with all the prophets and those who pleased God, did not share in salvation. (*Against Heresies* 1.27.3)

This specific sense of *gentes* is also in view in the Latin translation of Origen's *Commentary on the Epistle to the Romans*, where, with Marcion evidently in mind, Origen speaks of "those who want there to be one God of the Jews and another God of the Gentiles [*gentes*]."[107] To come at the point from another angle, Marcion seems to have been well aware of the proto-orthodox argument that positive statements about the *ethnē* in Isaiah and the other prophets were prophecies of the apostolic mission to the *ethnē* and the resultant gentile church. In response, as Tertullian reports, he argued that these people "from among the gentiles [*nationibus*]" "are passing over to the Creator" (rather than to the supreme God) and thus are proselytes to Judaism (*Against Marcion* 3.21.2–3), rather than those for whose salvation Jesus was sent by the supreme God.

One consequence of this is that, if one brackets out Marcion's duality of Gods for a moment, his interpretation of Scripture is aligned with Jewish interpretation in significant ways. One may well imagine Trypho or Celsus's Jew nodding in agreement with Marcion's defense of Jewish messianic expectation and his rejection of the strained arguments by which interpreters such as Justin attempted to demonstrate that such prophetic expectations were fulfilled in Christ. Some modern interpreters have noted that, aside from the matter of the two Gods, Marcion represents a kind of two-covenant approach to Christian and Jewish identity.[108] Tertullian seizes on this as an opportunity, denouncing Marcion for having been "compelled to form an alliance with Jewish error" (*Against Marcion* 3.6.1) and having "borrowed his guidance in this discussion" from the Jews themselves (3.7.1).

Of course, one cannot bracket out Marcion's duality of Gods for long; to the extent that there are parallels between his position and a two-covenant approach to things, the covenants are given by two different and unequal Gods, which represents a denigration of Judaism that Trypho would have found equally offensive. Still, looking at Marcion from this angle, we can recognize the extent to which both he and the proto-orthodox interpreters were wrestling with the same issues—how to understand the emergence of gentile Christianity out of its Jewish beginnings and to construct an account of gentile Christian identity

---

107. Thomas P. Scheck, trans., *Origen: Commentary on the Epistle to the Romans*, FC 103 (Washington, DC: Catholic University of America Press, 2001), 230.

108. See, e.g., John W. Marshall, "Misunderstanding the New Paul: Marcion's Transformation of the *Sonderzeit* Paul," *JECS* 20 (2012): 1–29.

Ethnē and Gentile Christian Identity (After 135 CE)

in ways that would make sense in a Greco-Roman environment.[109] Justin and his proto-orthodox successors tended to prioritize the Greco-Roman ideal of antiquity, claiming Israel's Scriptures and (idealized) identity for themselves and subordinating the Jewish people, together with the Mosaic covenant by which they were identified, to a primordial (Christian) Israel. On the other side, if Lieu is right, Marcion seems to have prioritized an idealized Platonic concept of God, identifying Jesus as this God's emissary and thus avoiding altogether the problems associated with the need to align the gentile Christians with the God of Scripture and his dealings with the Jews. The popularity of Marcion's position seems to provide one measure of the extent to which the proto-orthodox interpretation of Israel's Scripture was perceived by many gentile Christians to be problematic.

Looking at Marcion from the perspective of Justin and other proto-orthodox interpreters, however, we can understand how the popularity of Marcionism served both to intensify the kind of constraints that were represented by Celsus and other perceptive pagan critics of the movement and to compel other aspects of their apologetic response to follow particular channels. As we have seen, Celsus's critique of the Christian movement consisted of several distinct elements: some of them directed at the Jews as well (the claim that a local ethnic god was the sole and supreme God; the origins of both groups in acts of sedition); and some of them specific to the Christians (God's capriciousness in sending Moses and Jesus on contradictory missions; the lack of correspondence between prophetic promise and christocentric fulfillment; Christians as a new people with no claim to antiquity and legitimacy). Marcion, by abandoning the last of these (i.e., by presenting Jesus as the emissary of a hitherto unknown god, with the result that Christians were a new and unprecedented people), was able simply to sidestep the others.

On the proto-orthodox side of things, identification of Jesus as the promised Messiah and of his work as the fulfillment of Scripture had been too deeply embedded in the movement from the beginning to be called into question or abandoned. At the same time, however, their opposition to Marcion reinforced their desire to prioritize antiquity and to present themselves as the current embodiment of an ancient people with a long history. It also meant that, in dealing with the other elements of pagan critique, they needed to respond in ways that

---

109. Lieu suggests that we see Marcion and other Christians of his era as addressing "the fundamental challenge of the second century, namely of introducing the Christian message, rooted in the Scriptures and received tradition, to a new audience whose world view was shaped by the philosophical, and particularly by the popularised Platonic, tradition"; *Marcion and the Making of a Heretic*, 439.

did not concede any ground to Marcionism. If Marcion wanted to dismiss the Old Testament as the Scripture of the Jews, this was all the more reason to hang on to it as distinctly Christian Scripture. The result was a reinforcement of the anti-Jewish character of their response: the special sinfulness of the Jews as the reason for God's giving of the law;[110] the Christians as true Israel, the continuation of a people predating the law and thus distinct from the Jews; the christological meaning of Scripture.

All of this is well known, though we will observe further aspects of it as we sketch out the further development of gentile Christian identity in the last part of this chapter. One might wonder in passing, however, whether an opportunity was lost here on the part of gentile Christians, an opportunity to read their Old Testament as it presents itself—that is, as the Scriptures of Israel, but Scriptures that also offer a place for the *ethnē* in the story they have to tell. The decision on the part of the proto-orthodox Christians to prioritize antiquity resulted in a reading of Scripture in which gentile Christians claimed the center for themselves, identifying themselves not only with the *ethnē* (important secondary characters in the story) but also with the main (human) character—the people of Israel, the seed of Abraham, the "great *ethnos*" promised to Abraham by God. How might history have been different if gentile Christians had been content to identify with the multitude of *ethnē* to be blessed through Abraham's promised *ethnos*, rather than going on to claim the identity of the Jewish *ethnos* as well?

Ethnē and Christian Identity Construction after Justin

We began our study by looking at the remarkable oration that Eusebius delivered in defense of the Christian emperor Constantine at the dedication of the emperor's newly completed Church of the Holy Sepulchre in Jerusalem. Setting this oration alongside Luke's account of Paul's speech before the Roman governor Festus and the Jewish king Agrippa II, in which he defended his mission to the gentiles and appealed his case to the emperor, we identified some questions about gentile Christian identity—specifically, what gentile Christ-believers did with the ascribed identity *ethnē* and how to understand the process of develop-

---

110. On this point, Dunn observes that Tertullian, in his response to Marcion, "insisted that the one God acted more harshly in the Old Testament than in the New because God had been dealing with a more difficult people, the Jews"; further, citing Efroymsen: "Thus the God of the Hebrew Bible was 'salvaged' for Christians precisely by means of the anti-Judaic myth"; Geoffrey D. Dunn, *Tertullian*, ECF (London: Routledge, 2004), 33.

Ethnē and Gentile Christian Identity (After 135 CE)

ment that resulted in the kind of theological ethnology exhibited in Eusebius's work as a whole.

Our investigation has covered a lot of territory, both conceptual and evidentiary. With the work of Justin Martyr, however, the answers to our questions have started to become clear. Indeed, looking again at Eusebius, we can observe that, to a significant extent, his construction of gentile Christian identity—both in its general contours and in many of the fine details—was present already in Justin's work. At the same time, comparing Justin to his predecessors, we can readily see the extent to which his work represents the beginning of a new stage. Except for Luke-Acts, gentile Christian writings in this earlier period display little interest in *ethnē* as an identity term. Where it does appear, it is used primarily to refer to outsiders, nonbelievers. For Justin, however, and the gentile Christian groups with which he identifies, *ethnē* (together with related ethnographic terms and concepts) has obviously become a very useful and important term of self-definition and identity negotiation. While Justin's contributions in this regard should not be undervalued, it is probably the case that he was building on work that had already been started by others. Still, with respect to the writings that have survived, his work serves to mark the beginning of a new stage.

What remains to be done is to look (more briefly) at this stage and to sketch out the developments that we can discern in the period after Justin. On the Jewish side of the identity negotiations, these developments have primarily to do with matters of detail. On the Greco-Roman side, we can discern more substantial developments, especially with respect to Roman imperial realities. To keep this study within reasonable limits, we will focus our attention on the first half of this period (roughly to the end of the Severan dynasty), during which time most of the developments of interest to us become apparent. Further, we will not attempt detailed examinations of individual authors and literature, such as we have carried out in chapter 6 and earlier in this chapter. Rather, we will organize our observations according to the same thematic categories that we used in our analysis of Justin's work, which had to do first with the Jewish boundary and then with the Greco-Roman. Of the literature, the most important for our purposes will be that produced by proto-orthodox writers, especially work of an apologetic/theological nature. In addition, we will look at some ecclesiastical literature (church order and liturgical material), popular literature in genres represented in the New Testament, and literature stemming from other varieties of gentile Christianity (Marcion and literature traditionally described as Gnostic).

Before turning to gentile Christian identity construction vis-à-vis Israel and the Jews, we should make a few observations about terminological usage more generally. We are primarily interested in the terms denoting non-Jews—*ethnē* in Greek, *gentes* and *nationes* in Latin—though we will also take some note of terms used to speak of Christians as constituting a single race, nation, or people.[111] In the material to follow, it will become abundantly clear that *ethnē* and related terms continue to be just as important for gentile Christian self-definition as they were for Justin. To be sure, these terms are also used on occasion with reference to polytheistic outsiders,[112] though just as often we find *ethnikoi* (Gk.), *ethnici* (Lat. loanword), or *gentiles* (Lat.).[113] And, from time to time, the terms denote what gentile Christians used to be.[114] But very frequently—and especially in apologetic discourse about gentile Christian identity—these terms function as standard forms of self-reference.

To illustrate the point in a preliminary way, we can note that Justin was not the only one to speak of "us *ethnē*." At the outset of Tertullian's treatise *Against the Jews*, for example, he cites the statements in Genesis "that in his [Abraham's] offspring all the nations [*omnes nationes*] of the earth would be blessed and that from Rebekah's womb two peoples and two clans [*duo populi et duae gentes*] were about to come forth," and then he continues: "They are, of course, the Jews—that is, Israel—and the Gentiles—that is, us [*et gentium, id est noster*]" (*Against the Jews* 1.3). Several other equivalent assertions appear later in the work.[115] Also referring to Abraham, Irenaeus describes him as "the father of those who from among the Gentiles [*ex gentibus*] believe in Jesus Christ, because his faith and ours are one and the same" (*Against Heresies* 4.21.1). Origen, referring to Paul's analogy in his homily on Joshua, says that "we [are] the branches of the wild olive taken up from the nations [*ex gentibus*]" (*Homilies on Joshua* 7.5).

---

111. *Gentes* and *nationes* tend to be interchangeable (as they were later in the Vulgate). For example, in *Against the Jews* 10.7–8 Tertullian cites a passage (Deut 33:17) containing a reference to *nationes* but then uses *gentes* in his own discussion. A little later in the work (12.1–2), we find the inverse: he makes a statement about *nationes* but then cites two passages (Ps 2:7–8; Isa 42:6–7) containing *gentes*. The phenomenon is frequently encountered; e.g., *Against the Jews* 14.12; *Against Marcion* 3.18.3–4; 3.20.2–4.

112. Very frequently in Clement (e.g., *Christ the Educator* 3.11.53.3; *Miscellanies* 3.1.3.4), though he is not very interested in positioning Christians with respect to Jews or scriptural categories. The usage is common in the *Martyrdom of Polycarp* as well (9.2; 12.2; 19.1); also Tertullian (*The Apparel of Women* 2.1.2; *Idolatry* 2.4; 10.1; *To the Heathen* 1.17.3; *Prayer* 15.1; *Repentance* 2.1); Origen (*Against Celsus* 8.20, 23). In the Nag Hammadi literature, it appears in Gospel of Philip 52.16–24 (NHC II 3); Interpretation of Knowledge 21.30–34 (NHC XI 1).

113. *Ethnikoi*: Clement, *Miscellanies* 4.9.72.4. *Ethnici*: Irenaeus, *Against Heresies* 4.30.1; Tertullian, *Against Marcion* 3.24.4; *Idolatry* 14.4; 15.1; *The Shows* 3.1. *Gentiles*: Tertullian, *The Apparel of Women* 2.11.3; *Prayer* 15.1; *Patience* 7.11.

114. Clement, *Christ the Educator* 3.12.85.2; *Exhortation to the Greeks* 9 (83.3); *Miscellanies* 2.15.68.1.

115. *Against the Jews* 3.9; 7.1; 13.24; also *Against Marcion* 5.17.12–14.

Ethnē and Gentile Christian Identity (After 135 CE)

Turning from terminology to matters of substance, we begin with identity construction at the boundary between gentile Christians and the Jews.[116] As has already been mentioned in passing, the pattern of gentile Christian apologetic *adversus Judaeos* was largely in place by the time of Justin Martyr; most of what we observed at the outset about Eusebius's apologetic can be found already in Justin. One indication of this is provided by Cyprian's *Testimonies against the Jews*. The list of headings for books 1 and 2 contains no surprises for someone familiar with Justin's work; likewise, the Scriptures that are cited under Cyprian's heads, with their emphasis on Genesis, the Psalms, and Isaiah, overlap in large measure with those appealed to by Justin.[117] Another indication can be found in standard treatments of the *adversus Judaeos* tradition,[118] whose authors are content to deal with the topic thematically, with no felt need to differentiate the material with respect to authors or periods.[119] For present purposes, then, there is no pressing need for extensive documentation and discussion. The point to be made is that what we have observed in Justin's *adversus Judaeos* discourse about the importance of *ethnē* as a term of self-definition continues to be the case for his immediate successors. For each of the three broad themes that we used in our analysis of Justin's work, we will make the point by looking at a representative sample of material.[120]

---

116. On Christian apologetic discourse as "border discourse," that is, "discourse poised at the frontiers between rival identities," see Aaron P. Johnson, *Ethnicity and Argument in Eusebius' Praeparatio Evangelica* (Oxford: Oxford University Press, 2006), 2.

117. Also cited are one or two isolated passages such as Mal 1:10-12.

118. Especially James Parkes, *The Conflict of the Church and the Synagogue: A Study in the Origins of Antisemitism* (London: Soncino, 1934), 95-115; Simon, *Verus Israel*, 135-78 (first published in 1948: *Verus Israel: Étude sur les relations entre Chrétiens et Juifs dans l'Empire Romain, 135-425* [Paris: E. de Boccard, 1948]); Rosemary R. Ruether, *Faith and Fratricide: The Theological Roots of Anti-Semitism* (Minneapolis: Seabury, 1974), 117-82; John G. Gager, *The Origins of Anti-Semitism* (Oxford: Oxford University Press, 1983), 117-73; cf. Fredriksen, *Augustine and the Jews*, xiv-xv, 84-87. This is not to deny the importance of finer-grained studies of individual authors (e.g., de Lange, *Origen and the Jews*), works (e.g., Geoffrey D. Dunn, *Tertullian's Aduersus Iudaeos: A Rhetorical Analysis*, Patristic Monograph Series 19 [Washington, DC: Catholic University of America Press, 2008]), and themes (e.g., Jeffrey S. Siker, *Disinheriting the Jews: Abraham in Early Christian Controversy* [Louisville: Westminster John Knox, 1991]).

119. As Ruether observes: "The *adversus Judaeos* tradition was a literary tradition, the themes of which remain quite constant from the second to the sixth centuries"; *Faith and Fratricide*, 123.

120. Much of the material that we will draw on here is concentrated in a few specific works or sections of works, especially Tertullian (*Against the Jews, Against Marcion*); Ori-

The first theme has to do with the Scriptures, Christ, and the *ethnē*. In one aspect of their christological exegesis of Scripture, gentile Christians argued that, according to Scripture, gentiles would be the primary beneficiaries of Christ's life and mission. As we have seen, this is an important aspect of Justin's apologetic, and it continues to be important in subsequent tradition, where we encounter most of the texts that are prominent in Justin's discourse, together with an expansion of the set of texts that are used to make the argument.

The importance of the term is readily apparent in Cyprian's *Testimonies against the Jews*. The term *gentes* appears some fifty times in the (relatively short) work;[121] the longest section in (the more pertinent) book 1 is 1.21, where testimonies are collected under the head "That the Gentiles [*gentes*] should rather believe in Christ." Analogous general statements about the prophets—that they made "pronouncements about the future such as ... that the *ethnē* would believe in the Savior"—appear frequently in other pertinent literature.[122]

Most of the scriptural passages that Justin uses in support of this theme are included in Cyprian's list of testimonies and are frequently cited elsewhere. Jacob's deathbed blessing of Judah (Gen 49:8–12)—"A ruler shall not be wanting from Judah, and a leader from his thighs, until the things stored up for him come, and he is the expectation of *ethnē*" (v. 10)—continues to be important. Cyprian cites it (*Testimonies against the Jews* 1.21); Irenaeus alludes to an extended typological reading;[123] Origen links it to Isa 11:10 in one passage (*Against Celsus* 1.53) and, in another, declares that it "is clearly seen to have been fulfilled in the multitude of those who, from different nations [*gentibus*], have believed through

---

gen (*Against Celsus*); Irenaeus (*Against Heresies*, especially book 4); Cyprian (*Testimonies against the Jews*). However, the documentation of our observations could be expanded almost indefinitely. As Ruether has observed, it is misleading "simply to list treatises, sermons, dialogues and major sections of writings devoted to this theme," for "[a]ny sermons, commentaries, or teachings based on scriptural exegesis of the Old Testament, and even of the New Testament texts where Jews are mentioned, will reflect this tradition of anti-Judaic midrash"; *Faith and Fratricide*, 121.

121. The first two (of the three) books of the work are more pertinent; *gentes* appears thirty-four times in book 1 and sixteen times in book 2; *nationes* (twice) and *populi* (six times) also appear.

122. The cited passage appears in Origen, *Against Celsus* 1.37. For Tertullian, the fact that "we—that is, the Gentiles [*gentes*]—would believe" in Christ was something prophesied by the prophets (*Against the Jews* 7.1). See also, e.g., Irenaeus, *Against Heresies* 4.34.3; Origen, *Against Celsus* 1.54.

123. In which he declares that the various elements in the passage—vine, ass's colt, clothing, eyes, teeth, wine—all refer to Christ, "who is the hope of the nations [*gentium*]" (*Against Heresies* 4.10.2).

Ethnē and Gentile Christian Identity (After 135 CE)

Christ in God" (*First Principles* 4.1.3). Similar observations can be made about other passages cited by Justin in this regard (Pss 2:7-8; 72:17 [71:17]; Isa 42:1-7; 49:6-12).[124] Further, Justin's interpretation of the odd statement in Moses's blessing of Joseph—"with them [his horns] shall he push the *ethnē* even to the ends of the earth" (Deut 33:17)—as a reference to gentile believers (*Dialogue with Trypho* 91.1-4) also finds an echo in later material. Like Justin, Tertullian sees in the horns an allusion to the cross and, by extension, to Christ, who is "even now winnowing all the nations [*gentes*] through faith, lifting them up from earth into heaven" (*Against Marcion* 3.18.3-4).

Another aspect of Justin's exegesis that is found more extensively in later interpreters is his readiness to find references to gentiles in passages where *ethnē* (or related terms) does not appear at all. A prime example is his reading of the story of Laban, Jacob, and the sheep (Gen 30:29-43). Justin reads the story as a typological anticipation of Christ: "Jacob served Laban for the spotted and speckled sheep, and Christ served, even to the servitude of the cross, for men of different colors and features from every nationality [*genos*], redeeming them by his blood and the mystery of the cross" (*Dialogue with Trypho* 134.5). The typological reading is used later, but with more precise terminology, by Irenaeus: "the wages of Christ are human beings, who from various and diverse nations [*gentibus*] come together into one cohort of faith" (*Against Heresies* 4.21.3). And Origen uses it as well: "the story in the Bible about Laban and Jacob refers to those *ethnē* who believe in Him," "the different *ethnē* [who] become branded and are ruled by the Word of God" (*Against Celsus* 4.43). In further instances, Irenaeus declares that "the church taken from among the Gentiles [*ethnōn*; *gentibus*]" is typologically prefigured by the stories of Hosea and his wife, Moses and his Ethiopian wife, and Rahab (*Against Heresies* 4.20.12). Elsewhere he sees

---

124. Cyprian cites Ps 2:7-8 in *Testimonies against the Jews* 2.8. Irenaeus describes Christians as those "who from various and diverse nations [*gentibus*] come together into one cohort of faith, as the Father promised Him," going on to cite Ps 2:8 (*Against Heresies* 4.21.3). See also, e.g., Tertullian, *Against Marcion* 3.20.2-3; 4.25.9; 5.17.6.

While Cyprian does not cite Ps 72:17 (71:17), it is used by Tertullian, who cites the verse ("In him shall all the nations [*gentes*] be blessed") and then, like Justin, declares, "In Solomon no gentile nation [*natio*] is blessed, but in Christ every one of them" (*Against Marcion* 5.9.11).

Citations of Isa 42:1-7 appear in Cyprian, *Testimonies against the Jews* 2.7; Tertullian, *Against Marcion* 3.20.4-5; *Against Praxeas* 11.5. And citations of Isa 49:6-12 in Cyprian, *Testimonies against the Jews* 1.21 (via Acts 13:47); Tertullian, *Against Praxeas* 11.5. Other *ethnē* texts from Isaiah that are open to messianic interpretation come into view as well: e.g., Isa 9:1-2 (Cyprian, *Testimonies against the Jews* 1.21; Origen, *Against Celsus* 6.66); Isa 11:10 (Cyprian, *Testimonies against the Jews* 1.21).

GENTILE CHRISTIAN IDENTITY

the exodus from Egypt in its entirety as a type and image of "the exodus of the church which should take place from among the Gentiles [*gentibus*]" (4.30.4).

The second broad theme that we used in our analysis of Justin's *adversus Judaeos* argumentation had to do with the Jews and the *ethnē*, especially the idea that God has rejected the Jews because of their sinfulness and unbelief and has turned instead to the gentiles. In one version of this theme, the gentile church has replaced Israel in God's purposes. Since this conceded antiquity to the Jews, however, this version tended to give way to another—the idea that the gentile church is in reality a continuation of a true people of God that was represented first by the pre-Mosaic patriarchs and then by the prophets and other righteous heroes, who recognized that the sole positive purpose of the law was to point forward in a spiritual way to the coming of Christ. As with the first theme, this one has already attained its full-blown form in Justin's work, with later writers reproducing its main elements and supplementing it with additional exegetical embroidery. While this aspect of the *adversus Judaeos* tradition is well known, here we are particularly interested in noting the centrality of *ethnē* and related terms in the rejection-replacement theme.

Cyprian signals the importance of the theme at the outset of his *Testimonies against the Jews*. In his preface, he declares that his purpose in book 1 was

> to show that the Jews, according to what had before been foretold, had departed from God, and had lost God's favor, which had been given them in past time, and had been promised them for the future; while the Christians had succeeded to their place, deserving well of the Lord by faith, and coming out of all nations [*gentibus*] and from the whole world.

While several of the headings to follow give explicit expression to the theme of rejection and replacement, the theme runs through book 1 as a whole.[125]

More generally, the theme runs through the pertinent literature as a whole.[126]

---

125. "19. That two peoples [*populi*] were foretold, the elder and the younger; that is, the ancient people of the Jews, and the new one which should be of us.

20. That the Church, which had previously been barren, should have more sons from among the Gentiles [*gentibus*] than the synagogue had had before.

21. That the Gentiles [*gentes*] should rather believe in Christ.

22. That the Jews should lose the bread and the cup of Christ, and all His grace; while we should receive them, and that the new name of Christians should be blessed in the earth.

23. That rather the Gentiles [*gentes*] than the Jews should attain to the kingdom of heaven."

126. In addition to the passages cited below, see, e.g. (all with a reference to nations),

Ethnē and Gentile Christian Identity (After 135 CE)

Tertullian and Origen express it in terms of a transfer of God's favor. Origen, for example, after citing Isa 6:9–10, declares:

> Yet indeed, it is obvious that although they saw Jesus, they did not know who he was, and although they heard him they did not comprehend the divinity within him from his sayings, so that God's care of the Jews was transferred to those from the *ethnē* who believe in him. (*Against Celsus* 2.8; also 4.22; 5.50)

Tertullian says that the prophets repeatedly warned Israel "that the day should come when in the last courses of time God would from every race [*gens*], people [*populus*] and place gather Himself worshipers far more faithful, to whom He would transfer his favor" (*Apology* 21.6). Irenaeus, alluding to such exegesis and using the image of inheritance, declares:

> For if they had known that we would ever exist and could use the testimonies of the Scriptures, they would never have hesitated to burn the Scriptures that make it clear that all the other nations [*reliquas omnes gentes*] all have a share in life, and that show that those who boast that they are the house of Jacob and the people of Israel are disinherited from the grace of God. (*Against Heresies* 3.21.1)

As these examples indicate, Christian apologists were determined to anchor this theme in Israel's Scriptures themselves. Jacob's blessing of Judah, which figured prominently in the previous section, is used to full advantage here as well. The coming of the one who would be "the expectation of the *ethnē*" coincided with the end of the Jewish line of leaders, together with that of the temple and all the other "Jewish institutions in which they prided themselves."[127]

Also popular were texts in which Israel was more explicitly contrasted unfavorably with the gentiles. Among these, pride of place goes perhaps to Mal 1:10–12, which we have encountered already in Justin's work. As cited by Irenaeus, the passage reads:

Epistle to Diognetus 11.2–3; Irenaeus, *Against Heresies* 3.17.3; 4.34.4; 4.36.2; Clement of Alexandria, *Miscellanies* 2.9.43.3; Tertullian, *Against Marcion* 4.31.6; *Modesty* 7; Origen, *Against Celsus* 2.5, 78; 7.26; 8.42; *Homilies on Joshua* 2.40; Teaching of the Apostles (*Didascalia Apostolorum*) 21.5.16.7; 23.6.5–7; 5 Esdras 2:33–34.

127. Origen, *First Principles* 4.1.3; also, e.g., Cyprian, *Testimonies against the Jews* 1.21; Irenaeus, *Against Heresies* 4.10.2.

> I have no pleasure in you, saith the Lord Omnipotent, and I will not accept sacrifice at your hands. For from the rising of the sun, unto the going down [of the same], my name is glorified among the Gentiles [*gentibus*], and in every place incense is offered to my name, and a pure sacrifice; for great is my name among the Gentiles [*gentibus*], saith the Lord Omnipotent.

According to Irenaeus, with these words the prophet was "indicating in the plainest manner ... that the former people shall indeed cease to make offerings to God, but that in every place sacrifice shall be offered to Him, and that a pure one; and His name is glorified among the Gentiles [*gentibus*]."[128] In addition to Mal 1:10–12, Cyprian cites a number of other *testimonia* in support of his proposition "that the Gentiles [*gentes*] should rather believe in Christ" (*Testimonies against the Jews* 1.21), including Deut 28:44: "Ye Gentiles [*gentes*] shall be for the head; but this unbelieving people [*populus*] shall be for the tail" (also Jer 6:18; Ps 17:43–44 [18:43–44]).

Here we might also mention the use made of contrasting pairs as types of Israel and the gentile church. Such a typological argument appears already in Justin, who sees in Leah and Rachel a convenient foreshadowing of the two ("As the eyes of Leah were weak, so too are the eyes of your souls exceedingly weak"; *Dialogue with Trypho* 134.5). Cyprian cites this example with explicit reference to the *gentes* (*Testimonies against the Jews* 1.20), along with a number of others: Jacob and Esau (1.19); the two sons of Joseph (1.21); and the two wives of Elkanah (Peninah and Hannah; 1.20).[129] Assisting with this interpretation is the fact that both Isaac's blessing of Jacob and Jacob's blessing of Joseph's younger son include references to the gentiles (as cited in 1.21).

In addition to these passages in which the church is understood to consist of gentiles or to have been drawn from all the gentiles, it is also presented as constituting a nation (*ethnos, gens, natio*) or people (*laos, populus*) in and of itself. We will look at some stand-alone versions of this idea a little later; here we are interested in those versions in which this Christian nation is set over against that of the Jews or is seen as replacing Israel in God's purposes.[130]

We begin again with Cyprian, who devotes one heading to the theme: "That two peoples [*duo populi*] were foretold, the elder and the younger; that is, the

---

128. Irenaeus, *Against Heresies* 4.17.5; also, e.g., Cyprian, *Testimonies against the Jews* 1.16; Tertullian, *Against the Jews* 5.4, 7; 13.26; *Against Marcion* 3.23.6; 4.1.8.

129. On Jacob and Esau, see also Irenaeus, *Against Heresies* 4.21.2–3; Tertullian, *Against the Jews* 1.2; *The Soul* 26.1–2.

130. We will pick up the idea of Christians as a "third race [*genos, genus*]" (e.g., Tertullian, *To the Heathen* 1.8.1) a little later as well.

Ethnē and Gentile Christian Identity (After 135 CE)

old people of the Jews, and the new one which should consist of us" (*Testimonies against the Jews* 1.19). The terms in which he states the theme echo Gen 25:2–3, which he goes on to cite: "And the Lord said unto Rebekah, Two nations [*duo gentes*] are in thy womb, and two peoples [*duo populi*] shall be separated from thy belly; and the one people [*populus populum*] shall overcome the other people; and the elder shall serve the younger." He supplements this with Hos 1:10; 2:2–3: "I will call them my people [*populum*] that are not my people [*populum*], and her beloved that was not beloved. For it shall be, in that place in which it shall be called not my people [*populus*], they shall be called the sons of the living God" (1.19).

Both texts are cited elsewhere in the service of the same point. Tertullian, for example, cites the story of Rebekah at the outset of his treatise *Against the Jews*, where he interprets the text as having to do with two groups, each of which "was called a people [*populus*] and a nation [*gens*]," the former that of the Jews or Israel, the latter that of the gentiles [*gentes*] or Christians (1.2–6).[131] Irenaeus, for his part, in an allusion to Hos 2:2–3, says with reference to Christians that "those who were not a people might be a people [*non populus populus*]," linking this transformation to John the Baptist's declaration that God is able to create descendants of Abraham from "these stones" (*Against Heresies* 3.9.1).[132] Tertullian and Origen made use of a similar-sounding verse in Deuteronomy, in which God says of Israel, "So I will make them jealous with what is no nation [*ethnos*], provoke them with a nation [*ethnos*] lacking understanding" (Deut 32:21), to speak of the gathering of the gentiles, thus designating gentile Christians as a nation.[133]

In addition to these recurring *testimonia*, we also find isolated references to the church as a nation or people. Irenaeus refers to the community of gentile believers as "a sanctified people [*populus*]" (*Against Heresies* 3.5.3). Origen speaks of the events that happened after Jesus's death—the calamity experienced by "the city [i.e., Jerusalem] and all the nation [i.e., the Jews], and the sudden birth of the nation [*ethnos*] of Christians" (*Against Celsus* 8.43). Clement, using the language of 1 Pet 2:9, describes Christians ("we") as "the chosen race [*genos*], the royal priesthood, the holy nation [*ethnos*], the peculiar people [*laos*], who once were not a people [*laos*], but are now the people [*laos*] of God" (*Exhortation to the Greeks* 4 [59.2–3]).

---

131. Also, e.g., Irenaeus, *Against Heresies* 4.21.2–3. Here he also draws on Jacob's appropriation of Esau's blessing.

132. Irenaeus is fond of this statement by John the Baptist (see *Against Heresies* 4.7.2; 4.8.1; 4.25.1; 5.34.1), linking this reference to "stones" to the fact that, as idolaters, gentile believers used to worship stones.

133. Tertullian, *Against Marcion* 4.31.6; Origen, *Against Celsus* 2.78.

As should be apparent, in much of this material, the church and Israel, or gentile Christians and Jews, are set over against each other as alternative nations or peoples.[134] In some material, the relationship between the two is described in terms of old and new, as in a number of Cyprian's headings (especially 1.10–20).[135] Elsewhere the same idea is expressed as a transfer from one to the other—a transfer of God's care, favor, grace, invitation to blessedness, promised inheritance, and so on.[136] From this idea of transition or supersession, it is but a short step to say that the identity Israel was transferred from one to the other as well. For various reasons, however, writers under review here seem to have been a little more reticent than was Justin to make this claim straightforwardly and without further ado. To be sure, the identification is not absent. Irenaeus, for example, drawing on his argument that God is able "to raise up from the stones descendants for Abraham," sees Ezek 28:25-26—"These things saith the Lord, I will gather Israel from all nations [*ex omnibus gentibus*] whither they have been driven, and I shall be sanctified in them in the sight of the sons of the nations"—as referring to the church drawn from all the nations ("those that shall be saved from all the nations [*ex omnibus gentibus*]").[137] But where the identification is made, it is done so with hesitation and qualification.[138]

To the extent that there was reticence, it can be explained in part by the fact that some of the texts used in argumentation *adversus Judaeos* addressed Israel in negative terms (e.g., Isa 1:3-4; Jer 9:26). But a more important factor prob-

---

134. In addition to passages mentioned already, see, e.g., Melito, *On the Passover* 92 (672-77): "But you cast the opposite vote against your Lord. For him whom the Gentiles [*ethnē*] worshipped and uncircumcised men admired and foreigners [*allophyloi*] glorified, over whom even Pilate washed his hands, you killed him at the great feast"; 5 Esdras 2:33-34: "I, Ezra, received a command from the Lord on Mount Horeb to go to Israel. When I came to them they rejected me and refused the Lord's commandment. Therefore I say to you, O nations [*gentes*] that hear and understand. . . ."

135. Also to be included here is Melito's description of Israel as a "preliminary sketch" or a scale "model" for the church as the finished product (*On the Passover* 35 [218]; 36 [224-34]), though he does not highlight *ethnē* as a descriptor for the church as much as other literature of the period (but see 76 [537-44]; 92 [672-77]).

136. Origen, *Against Celsus* 2.8; 4.22; 5.50; Tertullian, *Apology* 21.6; Irenaeus, *Against Heresies* 3.21.1.

137. *Against Heresies* 5.34.1; see also 3.9.1; 4.7.1-2; 4.8.1; 4.25.1; in addition, Origen, *Homilies on Joshua* 22.6.

138. One indication of this is that *adversus Judaeos* writers themselves were quite prepared to use *Israel* in negative ways: e.g., Melito, *On the Passover* 76 (538); Irenaeus, *Against Heresies* 3.21.1; Tertullian, *Against the Jews* 1.3; Origen, *Against Celsus* 1.37; 5 Esdras 2:33-34.

Ethnē and Gentile Christian Identity (After 135 CE)

ably is to be seen in another aspect of gentile Christian identity construction, found already in Justin. As we have observed in our discussion of Celsus, the argument that gentile Christians represented a new Israel that replaced the old was vulnerable on two counts: that it conceded antiquity to the old ethnic Israel; and that it suggested a capricious and changeable God.[139] In the literature under examination here, we find a continuation of the line of response that we have seen already in Justin's work: namely, that Christians represent a continuation of the positive side of a duality found in the story of Israel from the beginning; and that the elements that characterized the Jews as a distinct nation—that is, the law of Moses and the practices associated with it—are to be seen simply as an indication of the deficiencies and special sinfulness of the Jews.

Tertullian provides us with a succinct account of both themes in his tractate *Against the Jews*. He begins with the particularity of the Mosaic law. Why, he asks, is God, "the governor of the whole world, the creator of humankind, the instigator of universal nations [*universarum gentium*], believed to have given the law through Moses to one people [*uni populo*] and is not said to have given it to all nations [*omnibus gentibus*]?" (2.1). His answer in part is that the law of Moses was a more detailed form of a "general and original law" given first to Adam and Eve and subsequently to "all nations [*omnibus gentibus*]." Thus, "before the law of Moses was written on stone tablets there was an unwritten law, which was understood naturally and was kept by the ancestors" (2.7). But the law of Moses, given to the particular nation of the Jews, had a particular character because of the special sinfulness of the Jewish people. As with Justin before him, he argues that the purpose of the law was primarily punitive. Taking one of the most ethnic-specific aspects of the law, he argues that circumcision was given as a negative sign, "by which Israel, in more recent times, was to be distinguished [from other people], when it was justly prohibited from entering the holy city" (3.4), and this because, as the prophets ceaselessly declared, they were a "sinful nation, people saturated in sin, wicked sons, [who] have abandoned the Lord and have provoked to indignation the Holy One of Israel" (3.5, citing Isa 1:4).

There were those, however, who responded in a more faithful way to the original "natural law." The patriarchs—Noah, Abraham, Melchizedek—all kept this law and thus were accounted righteous (*Against the Jews* 2.7). And now that the story of the Jews has run its course, the primordial law, as the prophet Isaiah had anticipated, has gone out from Zion in a new form and has been embraced by a new people—that is, says Tertullian, by "us, who have been called from the

---

139. Cf. Tertullian, *Apology* 19.1: "Supreme antiquity, then, claims for these books [i.e., of Moses] the highest authority. And among you it is almost a superstition to make credit depend on time elapsed."

nations [*ex gentibus*]" (3.9). While he does not connect the dots explicitly, there can be little doubt that he sees his own group of gentile Christians, who have "been instructed in the new law" (3.10), as standing in line with those who had been accounted righteous by the primordial law from the beginning.

This twofold account of Israel, the law, and the nations appears elsewhere as well. On one side, the idea that the law of Moses was given because of Israel's particular sinfulness appears, for example, in Irenaeus. The natural law, written in their hearts, was sufficient to preserve righteousness in the case of the patriarchs. But because of the baleful effect of their time in Egypt, "this righteousness and love to God had passed into oblivion and became extinct," as was evidenced especially by their turn to idolatry in the incident of the golden calf, and God deemed it necessary to impose "laws of bondage" "on account of their hardness [of heart], and because of their unwillingness to be obedient."[140]

On the other side, we also frequently encounter the idea that the gentile Christians stand in a line of the righteous that began with the patriarchs, continued with the heroes and prophets during the period of the Mosaic covenant, and was established in a new way through the apostles.[141] To draw on Irenaeus again, he describes the righteous people prior to the time of Christ as those "who from the beginning, according to their capacity, in their generation have both feared and loved God, and practiced justice and piety toward their neighbors, and have earnestly desired to see Christ, and to hear his voice" (*Against Heresies* 4.22.2).[142] The existence of this line of those who from ancient times "earnestly desired to see Christ" serves to demonstrate the antiquity of the Christian people. Hippolytus, for example, claims that "the race [*genos*] of the God-fearers is obviously proved to be older than all the Chaldeans, Egyptians, and Greeks."[143]

As a nation or people, then, the church on one side is drawn from all the non-Jewish *ethnē*, which has replaced the Jews in God's purposes; and on the other, it stands as the culmination of a race of righteous people that predated the people of the Jews. This line included some Jews—Moses, the prophets, other righteous Jews who lived during the interim period of the Mosaic covenant, the apostles, and other early Jewish believers. However, their membership in this race has to do more with their Christian identity—as Christians before Christ or, in the case

---

140. See *Against Heresies* 4.14.1–4.16.5. The quoted material is from 4.16.3, 4.16.5, and 4.15.2.

141. Clement of Alexandria extends it to include some from the gentiles as well; *Miscellanies* 2.9.43.3.

142. Melito says of Abel, Isaac, Joseph, Moses, David, and the prophets that they all "suffer[ed] for the sake of Christ"; *On the Passover* 59 (415–21).

143. *Refutation of all Heresies* 10.30.8; the theme is developed in 10.30.1–10.31.5 as a whole; also, e.g., Tertullian, *Apology* 19.1–7.

of the apostles and their Jewish converts, simply as Christians — than with any identity derived from the Mosaic covenant and their adherence to it. Indeed, for most of the proto-orthodox tradition, continuing observance of the Mosaic law was virtually incompatible with Christian identity.[144]

While it is probably an oversimplification to say that proto-orthodox Christians laid claim to the name *Israel* in any comprehensive or straightforward way, they certainly identified themselves with all that was positive in Israel's story and laid claim to all that they felt was of value. They were not content simply to identify with the nations that appeared as secondary characters in Israel's scriptural story (though they definitely made use of this material in accordance with their purposes); in addition to this, they laid claim to the center of the story (even as they reconstrued it in their own way). To the extent that they saw the church as having replaced the Jewish people in God's purposes, they were identifying themselves as a new Israel. To the extent that they saw the history of Israel from the time of Abraham in binary terms, and themselves as standing in continuity with those who perceived the true spiritual and christological meaning of the law, they were identifying themselves as "the true spiritual Israel" (Justin, *Dialogue with Trypho* 11.5).

To be sure, this was not the only option; while the proto-orthodox voices are the loudest in the material that has survived, other voices can be discerned. Marcion represents an extreme voice on one side. The extensive growth of Marcionite churches indicates that many gentile Christians found his categorical distinction between Jewish Israel and the gentile church to be more appealing than proto-orthodoxy with its strained scriptural exegesis. To the other side, the ongoing proto-orthodox struggle with Judaizers indicates that other gentile Christians

---

144. Of course, it was recognized that the apostles and the earliest Christians were Jewish (e.g., Teaching of the Apostles 19.5.5.1). But the level of tolerance toward torah-observant Jewish Christ-believers that is found in Justin Martyr is the exception; in becoming Christians, Jews were ipso facto abandoning Jewish customs and observances. This is probably the framework in which we should understand the occasional comments about the church incorporating both Jews and gentiles (see especially Irenaeus, *Against Heresies* 3.5.3; 3.12.13, 15; 3.15.1; 3.17.1-2; 4.21.1-2; 4.25.2; 4.31.2, 5.34.3; also Tertullian, *Prescription against Heretics* 20.2; *The Resurrection of the Flesh* 22.2; Origen, *Against Celsus* 1.31; *Commentary on Romans* 160; Epistle of the Apostles 30; Acts of Peter 16). For the most part, such comments pertain to an apostolic era that now lies in the past. Nevertheless, one occasionally encounters statements anticipating a future salvation of Jews at the parousia (Tertullian, *Against Marcion* 5.9.9; Origen, *Commentary on Romans* 8.9.4-7; 8.12.1-8; but cf. 8.12.6: "Who the 'all Israel' are who will be saved, and what that fullness of the Gentiles [*gentes*] will be, only God knows and his only-begotten").

might have been prepared to construe the relationship between the church and Israel in terms that were less starkly supersessionistic.

This issue of the way in which proto-orthodox gentile Christians conceived of their relationship with Israel leads into the third broad theme that we used in our analysis of Justin's identity negotiation, having to do with the Christianization of the *ethnē*. Justin's concerns in this area—the mission of the apostles to "all the *ethnē*," the success of this mission in the extensive geographical spread of the faith, and the emergence of a new peaceable people of virtue and piety—continue to find expression in subsequent gentile Christian material.

The first aspect of the theme has to do with the universal mission of the apostles who were sent by Christ to preach to the nations.[145] Tertullian provides us with a typical example of the theme, which appears in the context of his *Prescription against Heretics*. After a reference to Christ's "disciples, of whom he had chosen the twelve chief ones to be at his side, and whom he destined to be the teachers of the nations [*nationibus*]," and an allusion to the fate of Judas, he continues: "Accordingly, . . . he commanded the eleven others, on his departure to the Father, to 'go and teach the nations [*nationes*], who were to be baptized into the Father, and into the Son, and into the Holy Ghost.'" These apostles immediately set out to carry out this task: "after first bearing witness to the faith in Jesus Christ throughout Judaea, and founding churches (there), they next went forth into the world [*in orbem*] and preached the same doctrine of the same faith to the nations [*nationes*]. They then in like manner founded churches in every city" (20.2–4). The theme is widespread, appearing not only in apologetic and antiheretical material but also in church orders and popular Christian literature.[146] In the former, it appears in both straightforward declarations and scriptural interpretation.[147] Occurrences in popular literature include the oddly romantic notion of the apostles dividing up the various nations of the world among themselves.[148] The universal scope of the mission is expressed in a

---

145. The sources often identify the apostles as the Twelve (Tertullian, *Prescription against Heretics* 20.2; Teaching of the Apostles 15.3.6.2; 23.6.8.1; Martyrdom of Isaiah 3.16–20) or the disciples (Origen, *Against Celsus* 2.42; 3.40)—those sent to preach or teach (Irenaeus, *Against Heresies* 3.5.3; Tertullian, *Prescription against Heretics* 20.2–3; Martyrdom of Isaiah 3.16–20) or make disciples (Teaching of the Apostles 15.3.6.2).

146. For the former, see, e.g., Irenaeus, *Against Heresies* 3.1.1; 3.5.3; 3.12.6; Tertullian, *Flight in Persecution* 6.1–3; Origen, *Against Celsus* 2.42; 3.40. And for the latter, e.g., Teaching of the Apostles 15.3.6.2; 23.6.8.1; Acts of John 112; Acts of Thomas 1; cf. Infancy Gospel of Thomas 1.

147. Irenaeus sees references to the gentile mission in the parables of the wedding feast (*Against Heresies* 4.36.5–8) and the mustard seed (frag. 31).

148. Teaching of the Apostles 23.6.8.1: "But when we had divided all the world among

Ethnē and Gentile Christian Identity (After 135 CE)

variety of ways: all the nations; (all) the world; the ends of the earth; those who come from east and west; and so on.[149]

Further, the universal scope of the mission is matched by its universal success. The literature under review here places considerable emphasis on the spread of the Christian faith among "all the nations," in terms both of geographical extent and of numerical growth. Melito of Sardis declares that the Christian presence is found "not in one place nor in a little plot" but in "all the ends of the inhabited earth [*oikoumenē*]" (*On the Passover* 45 [294-99]). Analogous comparative constructions appear elsewhere: Irenaeus says that the new covenant "has also been diffused, not throughout one nation [*gens*] [only], but over the whole world [*mundus*]" (*Against Heresies* 4.9.2); Clement declares that, in contrast to the teaching of the philosophers, which was restricted "to the Greeks alone," the teaching of Christ "was diffused over the whole world [*oikoumenē*], over every nation [*ethnos*], and village, and town" (*Miscellanies* 6.18.167.2-3). More general statements about the church's universal extent are also common: the name of Christ "now glorified in the Church among all nations [*in omnibus gentibus*]" (Irenaeus, *Against Heresies* 4.19.1); the church "disseminated throughout the world, even to the ends of the earth (Irenaeus, *Against Heresies* 1.10.1); "the universal nations [*universas nationes*] thenceforth emerging from the vortex of human error to the Lord God the Creator and His Christ" (Tertullian, *Against the Jews* 12.1); "the spread of his doctrine over the whole world [*oikoumenē*]" (Origen, *Against Celsus* 1.27).[150]

Of particular interest are passages in which the spread of the Christian movement is expressed in ways that correlate with the geographical, ethnic, and imperial structures of the world. In this passage from Origen's *Against Celsus*, for example, the providential spread of Christianity is described with reference to

---

ourselves into twelve parts, and had gone out to the nations so that we could preach the word in all the world."

149. All the nations: Tertullian, *Flight in Persecution* 6.3; Origen, *Against Celsus* 3.40; Martyrdom of Isaiah 3.16-20; also, the "universal nations" (*universas nationes*; Tertullian, *Against the Jews* 12.1). (All) the world: Tertullian, *Prescription against Heretics* 20.4; Origen, *Against Celsus* 2.42; Teaching of the Apostles 106; Acts of Thomas 1 (the regions of the world). The ends of the earth: Irenaeus, *Against Heresies* 3.1.1; frag. 31. Those who come from east and west: Irenaeus, *Against Heresies* 4.36.8.

150. Tertullian again, after speaking of Christians as a *gens*: "We are but of yesterday, and we have filled everything you have—cities, islands, forts, towns, exchanges, yes! and camps, tribes, decuries, palace, senate, forum. All we have left to you is the temples!" (*Apology* 37.4).

the *oikoumenē*, the hierarchical ruling structure of the Roman Empire, and the division of the inhabited world into Greeks and barbarians:[151]

> From the beginning everyone opposed the spread of his doctrine over the whole world [*oikoumenē*], the emperors in each period, the chief generals under them, and all governors [*hēgemones*], so to speak, who had been entrusted with any power at all, and furthermore, the rulers [*archontes*] in each city, the soldiers and the people. Yet . . . as it was stronger than all these adversaries it overcame all Greece and the most part of the barbarian countries, and converted innumerable souls to follow its worship of God. (1.27)

In a similar passage later in the work, Origen speaks of the numbers of "those from the *ethnē*" who believed in Christ despite the efforts of "emperors and rulers of *ethnē* [*basileis kai ethnōn hēgoumenoi*]" (7.26). Given the fact that *ethnē* was used in this period to denote Roman provinces, it is probable that Origen's statement about the "rulers of the *ethnē*" at least includes provinces, though it need not be read as restricted to them.[152] From another angle, Irenaeus describes the extent of the church with a geographical list—Germany, Spain, Gaul, the East, Egypt, Libya, the central regions of the world—a representative collection of Roman provinces and other places in the empire (*Against Heresies* 1.10.2).

Finally, as with Justin before them, Christian authors during this period claim that the significance of the Christian movement is to be measured not only by its extent but also by the piety, virtue, and peaceable way of life exhibited by its members. An important scriptural text in this regard is Isa 2:2–4, with its anticipation of a (new) law being promulgated from Zion and the *ethnē* coming to learn the ways of the Lord. Irenaeus, for example, quotes the passage in order to say of Christians that they have converted their weapons of war "into instruments used for peaceful purposes, and that they are now unaccustomed to fighting, but when smitten, offer also the other cheek" (*Against Heresies* 4.34.4). Tertullian says that "as soon as they have believed," they begin to convert "their formerly fierce and savage minds into honest thoughts productive of a good result" (*Against Marcion* 4.1.4); further, since "the Christ who was promised was not one powerful in war, but a bringer of peace" (*Against Marcion* 3.21.4), "the observance of the new law" among Christians "has shone forth in peaceful obe-

---

151. For other references to the *oikoumenē*, see the previous paragraph. For additional references to the spread of the church through Greek and barbarian peoples, see, e.g., Epistle to Diognetus 5.1–5; Irenaeus, *Against Heresies* 3.4.2; Origen, *Against Celsus* 1.26.

152. We observed this use of *ethnē* as a designation for Roman provinces in ch. 5; for another early Christian instance of this, see Athenagoras, *Embassy for the Christians* 34.3.

Ethnē *and Gentile Christian Identity (After 135 CE)*

dience" (*Against the Jews* 3.6–11).[153] And Origen declares to Celsus: "No longer do we take the sword against any nation [*ethnos*], nor do we learn war any more, since we have become sons of peace" (*Against Celsus* 5.33).

In addition to *testimonia* such as these, Christian writers can speak of the exemplary character of their group more generally, without making explicit reference to Scripture. Athenagoras, for example, who in his appeal to the emperors Marcus Aurelius and Commodus takes his standpoint within "all the cities and all the *ethnē*" of the empire, concludes by claiming that he has "proved that we are pious [*theosebeis*], and gentle, and temperate in spirit" (*Embassy for the Christians* 37.1).[154] Clement of Alexandria, speaking of the new "children of Abraham" (cf. Matt 3:9) that have been raised up out of the *ethnē*, describes them as exhibiting a new character of piety (*theosebeia*) and virtue (*aretē*) (*Exhortation to the Greeks* 1 [4.2]). The author of the Epistle to Diognetus, who describes himself as "a teacher of the *ethnē*" (11.1), writes to inform his readers about the "way of life" (*epitēdyma*; 1.1) or "citizenship" (*politeia*; 5.4) of the new Christian "race" (*genos*; 1.1), describing the virtues of this race in a series of paradoxes (5.1–17): for example, "they love everyone and are persecuted by all"; "they do good and are punished as evil."

This reference in the Epistle to Diognetus to the new *politeia* of the Christian *genos* touches on an aspect of gentile Christian identity construction that serves as a convenient point at which to turn from their boundary with Jews and Judaism to that with the wider Greco-Roman world.[155] To be sure, the two are not easily separated. The argument *adversus Judaeos* is carried out with one eye on the exigencies of their apologetic *ad nationes*; some aspects of the apologetic enterprise vis-à-vis the Greco-Roman world overlap with aspects of the *adversus Judaeos* material. Still, the two can be differentiated. One difference, as we will see, is that more development beyond the work of Justin Martyr can be discerned at the second boundary, especially having to do with Christian positioning with respect to the Roman Empire. Another is that a number of authors and texts that engage in identity apologetics with respect to the Greco-Roman world pay little attention to *adversus Judaeos* arguments.[156]

---

153. Elsewhere Tertullian uses Ps 2:8—where Christ is given "the *gentes* for his heritage, and the ends of the earth for his possession"—to say that through Christ the love commandment, formerly given only to the Jews, was now extended "to the whole race [*genus*] of mankind" (*Against Marcion* 4.16.11–13).

154. Though without using *ethnē* with reference to Christians more explicitly (*Embassy for the Christians* 14.2).

155. The idea of a Christian *politeia* is common; e.g., Tatian, *Address to the Greeks* 28.1; 40.1; Clement, *Miscellanies* 5.14.98.4.

156. In varying degrees, this is true of Tatian, Theophilus of Antioch, the Epistle to

We begin with a general observation, one that should not be surprising by this point in our discussion, though it has not always been sufficiently recognized: As gentile Christians thought about their identity and engaged in self-presentation to the wider Greco-Roman world, they did so by creatively utilizing the categories of nations, ethnicity, and competitive ethnology. As Johnson has observed, "Christianity was conceived not merely as one among many separate religious positions, but, rather, was mapped into the imaginary and constructed national and ethnic landscape."[157]

This has come into view already in the characterization of the Christians as constituting a new "race" (*genos*) with its own "citizenship" (*politeia*; Epistle to Diognetus 1.1; 5.4). Elsewhere Tatian uses the idea that there should be "one common way of life [*politeia*]" for all in order to tout Christian superiority in comparison with various ethnic groups (Greeks, Persians, Romans)—thus placing the Christian group in the same category of ethnicity.[158] In his appeal to the emperors (Marcus Aurelius and Commodus), Athenagoras uses different terms toward the same end. Observing that "the nations [*ethnē*] and peoples [*dēmoi*]" of the empire are allowed to follow their own distinctive "customs and laws" (*Embassy for the Christians* 1.1), he goes on to argue that Christians should be granted the same freedom. The assumption—that Christians belong to the same category—becomes explicit a little later on: "If, then, we are guilty of impiety because we do not practise a piety corresponding with theirs, then all cities and all nations [*panta ethnē*] are guilty of impiety, for they do not all acknowledge the same gods" (14.3).

More generally, the literature under consideration here displays broad familiarity with the kind of ethnographical discourse that was widespread in the Greco-Roman world.[159] Most of this can be left until later, when we look more closely at specific aspects of Christian apologetic (ethnic gods and the demons; the antiquity of the Christian *politeia*; the victory of Christ over the demons; and so on). Here, though, we can note a number of more general aspects: lists or surveys of diverse ethnic groups, both well-known and exotic;[160] the mapping of

---

Diognetus, Clement of Alexandria, Athenagoras, and Minucius Felix, among others.

157. Johnson, *Ethnicity and Argument*, 9.

158. *Address to the Greeks* 28.1; see also Clement, *Miscellanies* 5.14.98.1–4.

159. E.g., Origen's account of what constitutes a nation: "Each nation [*gens*], for example, the Egyptians or the Syrians or the Moabites, is designated as this or that nation in view of the fact that it is distinguishable by its own particular borders, language, disposition, customs, and institutions. Syrians are never called Egyptians, nor are Moabites named Idumeans, nor Arabs, Scythians" (*Commentary on Romans* 8.6.6).

160. Minucius Felix pairs the following *gentes* with their gods: Eleusinians, Phrygians, Epidaurians, Chaldeans, Syrians, Taurians, Gauls, Romans (*Octavius* 6.1); see also Tatian,

Ethnē and Gentile Christian Identity (After 135 CE)

ethnic distinctives in terms of custom, language, or worship;[161] cultural invention and borrowing;[162] the emergence of new nations through migration or historical development;[163] an interest in chronology and antiquity more generally.[164]

But the category *nation* had its limits. As the Epistle to Diognetus recognizes, in many ways, they did not resemble a nation; the *politeia* of the Christians was a paradoxical one: "They live in their respective countries [*patrides*], but only as resident aliens [*paroikoi*]; they participate in all things as citizens [*politai*], and they endure all things as foreigners [*xenoi*]. Every foreign territory [*xenē*] is a homeland [*patris*] for them, every homeland foreign territory" (5.5). Origen addresses the same issue when he observes, "Christians are not a single nation but are one people from all nations. And for this reason . . . [they] can be called a nation of all nations [*gentium gens*]."[165]

Thus the Christians also strove to locate themselves with respect to larger people groups, especially the fundamental binary of Greeks and barbarians. The binary is pervasive in Christian literature and does not need any further documentation. Here, though, we need to note the ways in which the Greek-barbarian binary is complicated by the Jewish origins of the Christian movement. In some cases, Christians for this reason identify themselves with the barbarian nations. Tatian, for example, identifies Christians as following a "barbarian code of law" (*barbarikē nomothesia*)—that is, the law of Moses, properly understood—and thus attempts to align Christians with those other barbarian nations from which

---

Address to the Greeks 1.1–3; Athenagoras, *Embassy for the Christians* 1.1–2; Hippolytus, *Refutation of All Heresies* 10.26(30).4–8; 10.30(34).1.

161. E.g., Clement's account of the frugal customs of various *ethnē* (*Christ the Educator* 3.3.24.2); see also Tatian, *Address to the Greeks* 28.1. On the differentiation of nations by their gods, see, e.g., Athenagoras, *Embassy for the Christians* 1.1–2; 14.1–2; Minucius Felix, *Octavius* 6.1–3; 20.1–3; Clement, *Exhortation to the Greeks* 3 (42.1)–4 (54.5); on the role of language, see Tatian, *Address to the Greeks* 1.2; Clement, *Miscellanies* 1.21.142.1.

162. E.g., Tatian's long list of nations whose inventions the Greeks have borrowed and his screed against them for "calling imitations inventions"; *Address to the Greeks* 1.1–2; also Clement, *Exhortation to the Greeks* 6 (70.1).

163. According to Tertullian, "transmigrations were made by the swarms of redundant nations [*gentes*]. The exuberance of the Scythians fertilizes the Persians; the Phoenicians gush out into Africa; the Phrygians give birth to the Romans; the seed of the Chaldeans is led out into Egypt; subsequently, when transferred thence, it becomes the Jewish race [*gens*]" (*The Pallium* 2.6); see also Hippolytus, *Refutation of All Heresies* 10.30.4–7.

164. Substantial portions of Tatian, *Address to the Greeks*; Theophilus, *To Autolycus*; Hippolytus, *Refutation of All Heresies*.

165. *Commentary on Romans* 8.6.6, a continuation of the passage cited in a footnote just above (n. 159).

the Greeks have not disdained to borrow (*Address to the Greeks* 12.5; 1.1–3). Origen also is willing to accept Celsus's classification of Judaism (and Christianity as its derivative) among the barbarians.[166]

Elsewhere the barbarian element recedes from view, and Christians attempt to position themselves as a third entity alongside the Jews and a different transethnic grouping. Most commonly this position in the triad is occupied by the Greeks:[167] in a passage from the *Kerygma Petri* cited by Clement;[168] in Clement's own formulations;[169] in the Epistle to Diognetus.[170] Elsewhere Clement speaks of the *ethnē*, the Jewish people, and the church (*Miscellanies* 3.10.70.2). Also, as we have seen, the Syriac version of the Apology of Aristides contains four "races"—barbarians, Greeks, Jews, and Christians (2.2). The Greek version speaks of "three races," the first of which is constituted by "the worshipers of the gods acknowledged among you, and Jews, and Christians." Since the work is addressed to the emperor Hadrian, the first "race" is the Roman Empire itself. Tertullian for his part knows of a triad comprising "the Romans, the Jews and the Christians" (*To the Heathen* 1.8.9–13), though in his case the idea that the Christians constitute a third race (*genus*) or nation (*gens*) is an insult contemptuously flung at them by outsiders (*To the Heathen* 1.20.4; *Antidote for the Scorpion's Sting* 10.9). Here we do not need to delay ourselves in an attempt to trace

---

166. "Next he [Celsus] says that the doctrine (obviously meaning Judaism with which Christianity is connected) was originally barbarian" (*Against Celsus* 1.2). Origen goes on to applaud Celsus's readiness to acknowledge the possibility that barbarians can make worthwhile discoveries, though he also takes issue with Celsus's additional comment that "the Greeks are better able to judge the value of what the barbarians have discovered" and to put them to good use.

167. Perhaps in this material, the Jews as a barbarian people are occupying the barbarian slot in the triad.

168. "The one and only God was known by the Greeks in a Gentile way [*ethnikōs*], by the Jews Judaically [*Ioudaikōs*], and in a new and spiritual way by us" (*Miscellanies* 6.5.41.7). Cf. Harnack: "The religious philosophy of history set forth by Clement of Alexandria rests entirely upon the view that these two nations, Greeks and Jews, were alike trained by God, but that they are now . . . to be raised into the higher unity of a third nation"; *Mission and Expansion*, 248–49.

169. The Greeks with their philosophy, the Jews with their prophets, both transcended by "the one race [*genos*] of the saved people" (*Miscellanies* 6.5.42.2). Clement also knows of a Christian interpretation of a passage in Plato in which Plato's reference to three classes of people is understood as having to do with three *politeiai*—those of the Jews, Greeks, and Christians (*Miscellanies* 5.14.98.1–4).

170. Christians as a new "race" (*genos*) "neither giving credence to those thought to be gods by the Greeks nor keeping the superstition of the Jews" (Epistle to Diognetus 1.1).

the development of the idea or to sort out the relationship between its various manifestations.[171] The thing to observe is simply that gentile Christians sought to locate themselves on the map of the nations with respect to variously recognized transethnic groupings.[172]

At the same time, however, the terms on which this map was constructed were significantly reformulated. We begin with conceptions about nations, gods, and demons, which, as we have seen (in the case of Justin earlier and Eusebius later), had a central role to play in gentile Christian identity negotiations. Irenaeus gives voice to the common view when he declares that "the gods of the nations [*gentium*] not only were no gods at all, but even the idols of demons" (*Against Heresies* 4.24.2). His declaration echoes Ps 95:5 (96:5), a text that serves as the scriptural linchpin for the idea that worship offered to the various gods of the nations was in effect offered to the demons who were ultimately behind their religious practices and traditions.[173] By virtue of their control over the nations, the demons, like "plagues invading cities and nations [*ethnē*]" (Clement, *Exhortation to the Greeks* 3 [42.1]), were responsible for all that was wrong in the world—strife, armed conflict and human slaughter, depravities of all kinds,[174] and even the foul accusations against Christians for the kind of outrageous sexual behavior that in reality originated in "your own nations [*gentibus*]."[175]

The story of how this lamentable state of human affairs came to be is one with which we are familiar. It is a story that begins with the emergence of demons as a result of a rebellion on the part of some of God's angels; in Tertullian's words: "the story how certain angels corrupted themselves and how from them was produced a brood of demons yet more corrupt, condemned by God with the authors of their race and that prince whom we have named [i.e., Satan]."[176] Athenagoras, who says that the demons work in various ways, with "individuals and nations

---

171. For discussions of the idea in its larger context, see Harnack, *Mission and Expansion*, 240–77; Lieu, *Christian Identity*, 239–68; and, more generally, Buell, *Why This New Race?*

172. While gnosticizing groups tended to divide humankind into a triad on other grounds (spiritual, psychic, material), occasional references to ethnic groupings (Greeks, barbarians, Hebrews) do appear; see Tripartite Tractate 109.24–111.5 (NHC I 5).

173. Cited explicitly, e.g., by Clement, *Exhortation to the Greeks* 4 (62.4); Tertullian, *Idolatry* 20.4; Origen, *Against Celsus* 3.2; 7.69; 8.3.

174. Clement, *Exhortation to the Greeks* 3 (42.1–5); Tatian, *Address to the Greeks* 8; Irenaeus, *Against Heresies* 5.28.

175. As Octavius says to Caecilius (Minucius Felix, *Octavius* 31.2). Origen accuses them more generally of "stirr[ing] up the emperors, and the senate, and the local governors everywhere, and even the populace" in opposition to the Christians; *Against Celsus* 4.32.

176. Tertullian, *Apology* 22.3; see also, e.g., Tatian, *Address to the Greeks* 7.2–3.

[*ethnē*]," refers allusively to the story in Gen 6:4 about the "sons of God" and the birth of the *nephilim*.[177]

From here the story can continue along two lines, though the end result is the same. One is the account in Deut 32:8–9 of angelic beings whom God set over the nations: "when the most High divided the nations [*ethnē*], as he scattered the sons of Adam, he set the boundaries of the nations [*ethnē*] according to the number of the angels of God."[178] After their rebellion, they then sought to consolidate their demonic hold over the nations by encouraging idolatry, their "basic principle" being to encourage the worship of created things and beings.[179] The other line of development has to do with the human origins of polytheistic worship. Some gods originated as founders or heroes of the past; Tertullian refers to situations in which "aforetime the gods themselves of the nations [*nationes*] were men" (*Idolatry* 15.2). Origen asks rhetorically: "did not all Gentile error [*totius gentilitatis error*] receive a beginning from the fact that men want those things which they love much to be gods and they ascribe a divine name to each of the human vices and desires?" (*Homilies on Judges* 57). From there it was a short step to a demonic takeover of humanly constructed religion.

This story has its polytheistic counterpart, as can be seen in the position argued by Celsus (see *Against Celsus* 5.25–29). In his view, the gods of each nation serve both as national overseers (*epoptai*) and as agents of the ultimate deity. Origen acknowledges the similarity but takes issue with Celsus's corollary that

---

177. Athenagoras, *Embassy for the Christians* 24.1–25.4; quotation from 25.3.

178. Origen, *Against Celsus* 4.8; see also, e.g., Clement, *Miscellanies* 7.2.6; Irenaeus, *Against Heresies* 3.12.9; Origen, *Against Celsus* 5.29. According to Irenaeus, Gnostic ideas about the cosmic angelic powers display some similarity, in that "the angels who rule the lowest heaven . . . made all the things which are in the world and portioned out for themselves the earth and the nations [*gentes*] that are upon it" (1.24.4); the highest of these was the god of the Jews. A somewhat similar picture of angelic supervision appears in Tripartite Tractate 99.34–100.18 (NHC I 5). The idea expressed in Deut 4:19—that "God has allotted to all the nations [*panta ta ethnē*] beneath the sky" the heavenly bodies for worship—receives less attention (cf. Origen, *Against Celsus* 5.10), though Clement does understand it as a divinely provided opportunity for the nations "to rise up to God" (*Miscellanies* 6.14.110.3–111.1). Clement also believes that God gave philosophy to the Greeks through one of the subordinate angels set over "the nations [*ethnē*]" (*Miscellanies* 7.2.6.4). Cf. Origen's idea that the "provinces" each have good angels as well as evil ones (*Homilies on Luke* 49 [12.4]).

179. Tatian, *Address to the Greeks* 9.1. Cf. Clement: "to build up the stupidity of the nations [Lat. *gentium*; Gk. *ethnous*] with blocks of wood and stone"; *Exhortation to the Greeks* 1 (3.1); see also 1 (7.4–6).

Ethnē and Gentile Christian Identity (After 135 CE)

therefore "the practices done by each nation are right when they are done in the way that pleases the overseers" (5.26).[180]

The passage about God's appointment of angelic beings as national overseers (Deut 32:8–9) has something to say about Israel as well: while God may have "set the boundaries of the nations [*ethnē*] according to the number of the angels of God," he reserved Israel for himself: "the Lord's portion was Jacob his people, Israel the lot of his inheritance."[181] This brings us to the topic of the nations, Israel, and the church, and thus to an overlap between gentile Christian identity negotiation with respect to the Greco-Roman world and the *adversus Judaeos* tradition that we have already explored. For this reason, we can be brief, noting two aspects of the area of overlap in particular.

First, as we might have expected, Christian interpreters read Deut 32:8–9 as part of a longer narrative of sin, rejection, and replacement, one that is on full view in the *adversus Judaeos* material. Despite Israel's privileged position as the only nation under God's direct supervision, they nevertheless succumbed to the baleful influence of the demons, fell into idolatry (including the worship of the golden calf), and were punished by God, who eventually rejected them and replaced them with a new people drawn from all the nations. In Origen's response to Celsus, for example, as soon as he has cited Deut 32:8–9, he goes on to say that this was a thing of the past, now replaced by a different divine ordering of human affairs. "Formerly," he says, "the Lord's portion was Jacob his people, Israel the lot of his inheritance"; but now the operative Scripture is what "the Father said to the Savior" (in Ps 2:8): "Ask of me and I will give thee the nations [*ethnē*] for thine inheritance, and the bounds of the earth for thy possession" (*Against Celsus* 4.8). A little later he recounts the narrative that, in his view, has led from one to the other. While Israel differed from the other nations in that "they alone" were under the direct charge of God, they nevertheless sinned repeatedly, to the point that God "purposely takes no notice of them when they are carried off by the rulers of the other nations [*tois loipois ethnesin*]." Abandoning them to their punishment and, as it were, "avenging himself," God turns instead to the other nations to establish a different people: "detaching those whom he could from the other nations [*tōn loipōn ethnōn*], . . . appoint[ing] laws for them and show[ing] them a life which they should follow" (5.31).

As he continues, however, he makes an additional statement that alludes to the other aspect of gentile Christian self-positioning with respect to Israel. God's purpose in seeking a new people from "the other nations" was "to lead them on to the end to which he led those of the earlier nation [*tou proterou ethnous*]

---

180. "Nation" is supplied from the context; see 5.25.
181. To complete Origen's citation of the passage (*Against Celsus* 4.8).

who did not sin." This idea that there were those of the "earlier nation"—that is, Israel—"who did not sin" and who had already arrived at God's intended "end" touches on something that we have already seen in the *adversus Judaeos* tradition—namely, the distinction between the Hebrews and the Jews. According to this line of differentiation, the Hebrews were the pre-Mosaic patriarchs, together with the prophets and other heroes of the earlier dispensation, who were able to live in accordance with God's will and to discern God's ultimate purposes. The Jews, by contrast, were those who had fallen away from this level of communion with God, who had been lured into polytheistic habits in Egypt, who thus became subject to the remedial provisions of the Mosaic law, and who (most of them, at least) resisted God's call and continued in sin. As we have seen, this distinction allowed gentile Christians to identify themselves as the inheritors of an honored pedigree and as the continuation of a devout and virtuous people who not only predated any of the proffered alternatives but who also was the source of any insight or wisdom that was to be found among the Egyptians, Greeks, or any other ancient people.

While we do not need to establish this aspect of gentile Christian self-definition again, it is nevertheless important to note how prominent this argument for antiquity is in their identity negotiations with the Greco-Roman world. One measure of this is the fact that it figures prominently in apologetic literature that (except for the antiquity of Moses and the message of the prophets) pays little attention to Jewish matters and *adversus Judaeos* material and is oriented primarily to a Greco-Roman readership.[182] Here a few examples will have to suffice, again with particular attention to *ethnē*, *gentes*, and related terms.

In his *Address to the Greeks*, Tatian denounces the shortcomings of the Greeks, describes his conversion, which came about while reading "some barbarian writings," and then uses the remainder of his work to argue that these works, written by Moses, were "older by comparison with the doctrines of the Greeks, more divine by comparison with their errors" (29.1). Further, not only was Moses prior to the others, he was also the source of anything that was valuable in their work: the Greeks "learned his doctrines at second hand," and the sophists "tried to counterfeit all they knew from Moses' teaching" (40.1). Thus the Christian "way of life" (*politeias*) is not only older than all the others (40.1), it alone is able to serve as the desired "common *politeia*" for all cities and nations (28.1).

In his attempt to convince Autolycus of the truth of the Christian faith, Theophilus of Antioch depends almost entirely on a similar argument—that Moses, along with "most of the prophets after him," "proves to be more ancient than all

---

182. Worthy of particular mention here are the writings of Tatian, Theophilus of Antioch, Clement of Alexandria, and Hippolytus of Rome.

writers" who are usually cited as authoritative sources (*To Autolycus* 3.29) and that any truth found in their writings was derived from these "Christian" predecessors. In his accounts of the Sybil, of Plato, and of the other "wise men or poets or historiographers," he mentions that they dealt with "kings, nations and wars," "the Greeks and the other nations," and "the various cities in the world and the habitations and the nations," thus placing the work of Moses and the prophets in the same world of ethnic discourse.[183]

In the case of Clement of Alexandria, much of his energy was devoted to the related themes that the Greeks and the Jews represented parallel preparatory stages to the coming of Christ, but that the philosophy of the Jews was earlier and original.[184] Addressing Plato, for example, he claims that, while the Greeks learned many practical things from more ancient races (Egyptians, Babylonians, Thracians, Assyrians), "for the laws that are consistent with truth, and your sentiments respecting God, you are indebted to the Hebrews" (*Exhortation to the Greeks* 6 [70.1]). The truth about God—"that it is not possible to touch the highest good" through idols or images of the divine, but only "through the mind"—was a "philosophy" that was introduced to the world "thanks to Moses" and then reached a climax long ago among the barbarians as something precious and shone brightly through the nations (*ethnē*) until it finally came to Greece (*Miscellanies* 1.15.71.1, 3). Thus "every nation [*ethnos*]," Greek or barbarian, has some access to the knowledge of God (*Miscellanies* 5.14.133).

As a final example, we turn to the *Refutation of All Heresies*, commonly attributed to Hippolytus. After a lengthy (nine-book) survey of "all the dogmas of Greeks and barbarians" (9.31.1), he sums up his argument for the "true doctrine [*logos*] of the divine" (10.34.1). Addressing himself to a lengthy list of Greek and barbarian nations, he presents himself and his fellow Christians as members of "the race [*genos*] of the God-fearers" (10.30.8) that predates them all, including those particular "nations [*ethnē*] schooled in philosophy," the Chaldeans, Egyptians, and Greeks (10.31.5).[185] He concludes by calling on all the learned

---

183. *To Autolycus* 2.33, 36; 3.16; *ethnē* in each case.

184. "To the Jews belonged the law, and to the Greeks philosophy, until the Advent; and after that came the universal calling to be a peculiar people [*laos*] of righteousness, through the teaching which flows from faith, brought together by one Lord, the only God of both Greeks and barbarians, or rather of the whole race [*genos*] of men" (*Miscellanies* 6.17.159.9).

185. He addresses "Greeks and barbarians, Chaldeans and Assyrians, Egyptians and Libyans, Indians and Ethiopians, Kelts and Latins who lead in war—all you dwelling in Europe, Asia and Libya" (10.34.1).

and barbarian *ethnē* of the world to "master this logic" and to learn from him about "the nature of the divine and the nature of his well-ordered craftsmanship" (10.31.6).

Finally, to complete our examination of gentile Christian identity negotiations with respect to the Greco-Roman world, we need to look at Christ, the church, and the Roman Empire. Aspects of this topic overlap with what we have already seen in our discussion about the Christianization of the *ethnē*. Here, though, we need in addition to look at the theme of Christ as one who has overcome the power of the demons and the ways in which the church drawn from all the *ethnē* attempted to position itself with respect to the transethnic Roman Empire. It is in this latter aspect that we will see significant advances beyond the work of Justin Martyr.

Continuing a line of apologetic that we have encountered in Justin's work, subsequent proto-orthodox writers present Christ as having effected an overthrow of the demonic powers that have held the nations under their sway. Both Tertullian and Minucius Felix, for example, make reference to Christian exorcisms, presenting them as public demonstrations of Christ's power over the demons.[186] In his response to Celsus's argument that the gods who oversee each area of the world should, for that reason, be respected, Origen declares that Jesus has "proved himself to be purer and more powerful than all rulers," and that God has given to him the "nations [*ethnē*] for [his] inheritance and the uttermost parts of the earth for [his] possession."[187] Further, in his *Homilies on Luke*, we find a passage in which Christ's overthrow of the demons is linked explicitly with Deut 32:9-8, the text that speaks about God's division of "the nations [*ethnē*] according to the number of the angels of God." After citing the text and identifying these angels as national rulers, Origen continues: "Christ our Lord conquers all rulers. He crosses their borders and brings captive peoples over to himself for salvation" (145-46 [35.6-7]).

As this latter passage suggests, there is a tight link between the defeat of the demons and the expansion of the church among the nations. In his *Homilies on Joshua*, for example, Origen interprets the conquest narrative as a representation of Christ's victorious battle against the "diabolical nations [*gentes*] of powerful adversaries," which seem to be both the fallen angels themselves and the nations over which they held sway, and of the church's own mission: "However many

---

186. Comparing polytheistic *spectacula* to the more noble ones of the Christians, Tertullian asks: "What nobler than to tread under foot the gods of the nations [*nationum*]—to exorcise evil spirits—to perform cures—to seek divine revealings—to live to God?" (*The Shows* 29.3); also *Apology* 37.9-10; see also the whole of Minucius Felix, *Octavius* 27.

187. *Against Celsus* 5.32, citing Ps 2:8.

Ethnē and Gentile Christian Identity (After 135 CE)

of these races we set under our feet, however many we conquer in battle, we shall seize their territories, their provinces, and their realms, as Jesus our Lord apportions them to us" (1.6).

Before looking further at this quasi-military way of describing the geographical spread of the church, it is worth pausing for a moment. To identify your group as a new nation drawn from all the nations—a group brought into being by the defeat of the demonic powers who have held all nations in a tyrannical grip—is to describe the group in terms that mirror the Roman Empire. Even if there had been no attempt to set the transethnic church over against the empire in any explicit way, this form of self-representation would necessarily suggest an implicit counterclaim to that of the Roman Empire. In reality, however, the proto-orthodox gentile Christians did not stop here but engaged in much more explicit discourse that both portrayed the church in empire-like terms and set it in contrast to the Roman Empire in particular.[188]

This discourse becomes apparent, for example, in another passage in Origen's response to Celsus: "Because God wanted the word of Jesus to succeed among men, daemons have been powerless, even though they have exerted every effort, to put a stop to the further existence of Christians" (*Against Celsus* 4.32). As he continues, he takes the battle imagery one step further by identifying the human agents of these demons: "For they have stirred up the rulers, and the senatorial council, and the local governors everywhere, and even the populace, who do not perceive the irrational and wicked activity of the daemons, to oppose the Gospel and those who believe in it."[189] In other words, the spread of Christian faith among all the nations is depicted as a struggle against the ruling powers of the Roman Empire, a struggle that has been increasingly successful, for "the word of God is mightier than them all."

In a remarkable passage (*Against the Jews* 7.1–9), Tertullian provides us with an even more explicit portrayal of the geopolitical expansion of the church as a Roman-like conquest of the nations. He begins by citing several scriptural passages (Isa 45:1; LXX Ps 18:5) as referring to Christ, the one "whom the prophets prophesied would come and in whom they announced we—that is, the nations [*gentes*]—would believe." Then he continues:

---

188. To be sure, since Christians also identified themselves as a nation, they could on occasion present themselves as analogous to one of the nations or provinces within the empire. Tertullian, for example, complains that while "every individual province, every city, has its own god," "we alone are forbidden a religion of our own" (*Apology* 24.7).

189. "Senatorial council" translates *synklētos*: a council called together; used frequently of the Roman senate; see *LSJ* ad loc.

In fact, in whom else have the nations [*gentes*] of the world believed if not in the Christ who has come already? For in whom have the other nations [*gentes*] believed—the Parthians, Medes, Elamites and those who inhabit Mesopotamia, Armenia, Cappadocia, those dwelling in Pontus and Asia, Phrygia and Pamphylia, those remaining in Egypt and those inhabiting parts of Africa beyond Cyrene, Romans and foreign residents, then also Jews in Jerusalem and the remaining nations [*gentes*], as now the various Gaetulians and the many territories of the Moors, all [within] the boundaries of both Spains, the diverse tribes of the Gauls, and the region of the Britons that is inaccessible to the Romans but subject to Christ, and the Sarmatians, Dacians, Germans, Scythians, and the many concealed nations and provinces and islands unknown to us that we are less able to count?

Many of the "nations and provinces and islands" that have been subjugated to Christ fall within the boundaries of the Roman Empire, but Tertullian's extensive list also includes lands beyond the Roman borders, even territory "inaccessible to the Romans."

Echoing the language of Isa 45:2, Tertullian continues to describe the progression of Christ through the world in military terms: "In all of these places the name of Christ, who is come already, reigns, in as much as the gates of every city have been opened before him and none has been closed to him, before whom iron bolts have been smashed and bronze folding-doors have been opened." While he acknowledges a certain spiritual aspect to the language—"the hearts of individuals besieged by the devil in various ways may be saved by faith in Christ"—he nevertheless insists that it is a reality on the plane of ethno-imperial geography as well.[190] The domain over which Christ holds sway—the territory occupied by "the people [*populus*] of the name of Christ"—is larger than the empires of Solomon, Darius, Pharaoh, Nebuchadnezzar, Alexander, and even of the Romans, "who fortify their empire [*imperium*] with garrisons of their own legions, and who are not able to extend the force of their rule across those nations [*gentes*]." By contrast, "the name of Christ is extended everywhere, believed everywhere, honored by all the above-mentioned nations [*gentes*]. It reigns everywhere. It is cultivated in worship everywhere." To present Christ as reigning (*regnat*) over a multitude of nations (*gentes*) that both includes and exceeds those within the Roman Empire (*imperium*) is not only to present "the people

---

190. A little later in the work, he argues that the gifts of the magi represent the "plunder of Samaria" (cf. Isa 8:4) and thus the firstfruits of the victory spoils of all the nations (*Against the Jews* 9.4); see also *Against Marcion* 3.12.1; 3.13.7–8. On the figurative or spiritual meaning of military language, see also *Against Marcion* 3.14.5–7.

Ethnē and Gentile Christian Identity (After 135 CE)

of the name of Christ" as a kind of empire in general but also to set it in a direct competitive relationship with the Roman Empire in particular.

This passage is indeed remarkable, but it is not unique. Other writers of the period engage in similar apologetic discourse, interacting with the themes of Roman imperial ideology, presenting the church as an empire-like people drawn from all the nations, and positioning it variously as an oppositional counterempire or as a beneficial force for good within the Roman Empire itself. In all this, the identification of the Christians as gentiles—as *ethnē* or *gentes* who have been liberated by Christ, who give him their allegiance, and who are formed by him into a new people or nation—is a central and foundational element.

To begin with, as is the case in this passage from Tertullian, Christian writers display easy familiarity with Roman imperial ideology. This is especially the case in Minucius Felix's *Octavius*, in which the polytheist Caecilius is given free rein to expound the Roman point of view, though it is the Christian Octavius who makes reference to the stories of Romulus's asylum and the abduction of the Sabine women (*Octavius* 25). Rome's conquest of the nations, which is why the empire consisted of nations, and the universality of Roman rule are all mentioned as a matter of course by Minucius Felix and other writers.[191] Rome's establishment of peace and freedom of travel, the benevolence of Roman rule, Roman respect for "the divinities they have conquered," its adoption of "the rites of all nations [*gentium*]," and Rome's pride in bringing *humanitas* to the barbarian nations—all are mentioned in the context of various arguments or appeals, as is Rome's claim that its success is due to the favor of the gods.[192]

But it is not simply a matter of familiarity with Roman imperial ideology; Christians appropriated imperial themes for their own use, presenting the church

---

191. E.g., "you ... rulers of the nations [*gentium*]" (Tertullian, *Apology* 21.28); "their triumphs over ... nations [*gentibus*]" (Tertullian, *Apology* 25.15); "your nations [*ethnesin*]" (Melito, as cited by Eusebius, *Ecclesiastical History* 4.26.7); "all the cities and all the nations [*ethnē*]" of the empire (Athenagoras, *Embassy for the Christians* 14.3).

192. Quoted material from Minucius Felix, *Octavius* 6.2–3; see also in 6.3: "Thus, by adopting the rites of all nations [*gentium*] in this way, they have won their empires as well"; and Tertullian, *Apology* 25–26; *To the Heathen* 2.17.1–19. Also, e.g., Irenaeus speaking of the Romans: "through their instrumentality the world is at peace, and we walk on the highways without fear, and sail where we will" (*Against Heresies* 4.30.3); Athenagoras addressing the emperors: "with admiration of your mildness and gentleness, and your peaceful and benevolent disposition towards every man, individuals live in the possession of equal rights; and the cities, according to their rank, share in equal honour; and the whole empire, under your intelligent sway, enjoys profound peace" (*Embassy for the Christians* 1.2). Tertullian's reference to Roman *humanitas* is much less flattering (*Apology* 21.30).

from all the nations as a kind of empire. One might even say as an empire within the Roman Empire, except that this empire-like Christian church has conquered territory outside the Roman imperial boundaries as well. Such a strategic appropriation of imperial discourse is on full display in the passage from Tertullian's treatise cited above, *Against the Jews* 7.2–9. There he treats Christ as belonging to the same category as those rulers who have aspired "to reign over all nations [*omnes gentes*]" and thus the nations among whom "the people of the name of Christ" are to be found: the empires of Nebuchadnezzar, Darius, Alexander, and the Romans themselves. The same category, perhaps, but an empire superior to all the others: "For who could have reigned over all but Christ, God's Son, who was ever announced as destined to reign over all nations [*omnibus gentibus*] to eternity?"

Hippolytus takes this one step further, presenting the Roman Empire as a satanic counterpart of the new nation called by God through the mission of the apostles to "all the nations":

> as the Lord also called all the nations [*panta ta ethnē*] and tongues by means of the apostles and fashioned believing Christians into a people [*ethnos*], the people of the Lord, and the people which consists of those who bear a new name—so was all this imitated to the letter by the empire [*hē basileia*] of that day, ruling according to the working of Satan: for it also collected to itself the highest-born of all the nations [*pantōn tōn ethnōn*], and, dubbing them Romans, got ready for the battle.[193]

In effect, here the Christian *basileia* is the original, of which the Roman Empire is a Satan-inspired imitation.

Of course, this is not a new observation; scholars have generally recognized parallels between Christian portrayals of Christ, regional authority structures, and corporate self-perception, on the one hand, and Roman imperial counterparts, on the other.[194] What needs to be noted here is the important role played by the vocabulary of nations in what Cameron calls this Christian "rhetoric of empire."[195]

---

193. *Commentary on Daniel* 4.9.2; English translation from Harnack, *Mission and Expansion*, 262 (slightly adapted).

194. See, e.g., Leif E. Vaage, "Why Christianity Succeeded (in) the Roman Empire," in *Religious Rivalries in the Early Roman Empire and the Rise of Christianity*, ed. Leif E. Vaage (Waterloo, ON: Wilfrid Laurier University Press, 2006), 253–78.

195. "But it is still useful and important to ask how Christians, the quintessential outsiders as they appeared to men like Nero, Pliny, Tacitus, and Suetonius, talked and wrote

Ethnē and Gentile Christian Identity (After 135 CE)

There is one other point to note before looking more closely at this rhetoric of empire, though it has been touched on already. The idea that the church constituted a kind of empire within the Roman Empire was one that could be spun in different ways. In the passage from Tertullian cited above, the emphasis falls on the contrasting or oppositional relationship between the two—the church as counterempire. In other passages, however, the emphasis is more complementary or beneficial—the church as a beneficial component of the empire and the empire itself as a potential partner. The two are not mutually exclusive, of course; one could recognize opposition as the present reality while still holding out partnership as a hoped-for ideal. And so we can find a single author making statements that place the emphasis at different points. Nevertheless, the range of emphases between opposition and partnership is readily apparent. Our observations in what follows will be organized around three nodes: providence, God, and the gods; the emperor; and the subjects of the empire.

On the negative side of the theme of providence, we find direct challenges to the Roman idea that their success in conquering the nations and gathering them into an empire was both due to their own reverence for the gods and a sign of divine favor on the empire itself. Hippolytus's assertion that the Roman Empire was in actuality a satanic counterfeit of the kingdom of Christ (*Commentary on Daniel* 4.9.2) represents at least an implicit challenge to the Roman theme. A more explicit and particularly striking example appears in Minucius Felix's *Octavius*. Beginning with Romulus and Remus, he turns Roman history on its head, arguing that Rome's success was due not to its piety but to its criminal ferocity and cruel disregard for the gods of the nations: "And so the number of Roman triumphs means an equal number of desecrations; the victorious trophies won over other nations [*gentibus*] mean an equal number of robberies of their gods. It follows that Rome is so great not because she has been devoutly religious but because she has been sacrilegious and gone unpunished" (*Octavius* 25.6–7).

---

themselves into a position where they spoke and wrote the rhetoric of empire. For it is perfectly certain that had they not been able to do this, Constantine or no Constantine, Christianity would never have become a world religion"; Averil Cameron, *Christianity and the Rhetoric of Empire: The Development of Christian Discourse* (Berkeley: University of California Press, 1991), 14.

While explicit references to *ethnē* are not present, it is worth noting also Origen's depiction of the church as a counter fatherland (*patris*), existing in all the cities of the empire (*Against Celsus* 8.75), and the encounter between Paul and Nero in the Acts of Paul 11.2–3, in which Paul's mission is described as enlisting soldiers for a counterempire ("And he [Nero] said to him, 'Man of the great king, now my prisoner, what induced you to come secretly into the Roman empire and to enlist soldiers in my territory?'").

Tertullian provides a similar (and perhaps linguistically related) argument in his *Apology*. After a lengthy development of the theme that "the Romans were not religious before they were great; and, it follows, they are not great because they were religious," he concludes: "Then the sacrileges of the Romans are exactly as many as their trophies; their triumphs over gods as many as over nations [*gentibus*]; their spoils in war as many as the statues still left of captured gods."[196]

Another aspect of this theme of providence in a negative key is the assertion that although Rome has attempted to hinder the spread of the Christian faith among the nations, the God of the Christians has overruled and has rendered these attempts ineffectual. We find this aspect at several points in Origen's *Against Celsus*. In 5.50, for example, after identifying "we Christians" as "those from the nations [*apo tōn ethnōn*] who believed in him," he makes this claim:

> although the Romans have wanted to do much against the Christians to prevent their further existence, they have not been able to achieve this. For the hand of God was fighting for them and wanted to scatter the word of God from one corner in the land of Judaea to the whole race [*genos*] of humankind.

Somewhat later, in a passage where Christians are likewise identified as "those from the nations [*apo tōn ethnōn*]," he makes a similar claim: "and the more emperors [*basileis*] and rulers of nations [*ethnōn*] and peoples in many places have humiliated them, the more they have increased in number so that 'they have become exceedingly strong.'"[197]

Also in a negative key is the more general assertion that the rise and fall of empires, including that of the Romans, is the providential result of the will and supervision of God. Tertullian provides us with a pertinent example. After listing the various nations (*nationes*) that "have possessed empire," a list that concludes with the Romans ("until at last almost universal dominion has accrued to the Romans"), he encourages his readers to "inquire who has ordained these changes in the times." It is God, he says, "who dispenses kingdoms, and has now put the supremacy of them into the hands of the Romans." Then he adds, with a note of warning: "What he has determined concerning it, they know who are the nearest to him" (*To the Heathen* 2.17.18–19).

A much more positive view of the role of divine providence in the rise of Rome, however, is also apparent in this period. As we have already seen, Justin seems to have discerned some divine providence at work in the fact that the birth of Christ coincided with the reign of Augustus (*First Apology* 32.1–5), though

---

196. See the whole of ch. 25; quoted material from *Apology* 25.13, 15.
197. *Against Celsus* 7.26, echoing Exod 1:7.

he is more concerned with the onset of direct Roman rule over Judea. We have also seen Hippolytus's negative interpretation of this coincidence: the empire as a satanic imitation of the emergent kingdom of Christ. Others, however, put the coincidence in a much more positive light.

Eusebius preserves several passages from an address by Melito to the emperor (Marcus Aurelius), including this one: "Our philosophy first flourished among barbarians, but it blossomed out among your nations [*ethnesin*] during the great reign of your ancestor Augustus" (*Ecclesiastical History* 4.26.7). Melito's primary concern has to do with the benefits that, in his view, accrued to the Roman Empire ("your nations") by means of this "philosophy" (a point to which we will return). But he also believes that the church benefited as well: "it was for good that our thinking flourished together with the empire which began so well—the fact that nothing ignoble befell it from the rule of Augustus, but on the contrary everything splendid and glorious in accordance with the prayer of all." While he does not mention God's providential activity explicitly, the idea is close to the surface.

A more explicit example appears in Origen's *Against Celsus*.[198] In response to Celsus's statement that a true Son of God would have made himself as visibly manifest as does "the sun which illuminates everything else," Origen asserts that there is such a visible manifestation in the correlation of the *pax Romana* and the gentile mission. If the world had consisted of a large number of warring kingdoms, it would have been "more difficult for Jesus' apostles to do what he commanded them when he said, 'Go and teach all nations [*panta ta ethnē*].'" But, says Origen, "it is quite clear that Jesus was born during the reign of Augustus, the one who reduced to uniformity, so to speak, the many kingdoms on earth so that he had a single empire." All of this was anticipated by the Scriptures: "For 'righteousness arose in his days and abundance of peace' began with his birth." Thus all of this is due to the activity of God: "God was preparing the nations [*ethnē*] for his teaching, that they might be under one Roman emperor."[199]

As with the idea of divine providence, a similar bivalent attitude is apparent with respect to the emperors and Christ. On the one hand, the emperors can be seen as opponents and enemies. This is decisively the case in the passage from Hippolytus that we have already looked at, in which Augustus (along with his successors, presumably) is seen as the emperor of a satanic empire drawn from "all the nations [*pantōn tōn ethnōn*]" and engaged in battle with the people of Christ, drawn from "all the nations [*panta ta ethnē*] and tongues" (*Commen-

---

198. On the connection between this passage and the one from Melito just discussed, see Schott, *Christianity, Empire, and the Making of Religion*, 154.

199. *Against Celsus* 2.30; the scriptural citation is from Ps 71:7.

tary on Daniel 4.9.2). Origen, for his part, identifies the "emperors and rulers of nations [*ethnōn*]" as working to hinder the spread of the teaching about Jesus among "those from the nations [*apo tōn ethnōn*]" (*Against Celsus* 7.26).[200]

But on the other hand, the emperors frequently appear as more positive figures. In keeping with the idea of divine providence, emperors can be seen as having been appointed by God. Tertullian, for example, says that "we respect the judgment of God in the emperors, who has set them over the nations [*gentibus*]" (*Apology* 32.2). A little earlier in the same work, after declaring that Pilate was "in his secret heart already a Christian," he goes on to say that "the Caesars also would have believed on Christ, if Caesars had not been necessary for the world, or if the Caesars, too, could have been Christians" (21.24). Athens may have not had anything to do with Jerusalem, but perhaps he was prepared to think differently of Rome.

Further, apologies addressed to the emperors praise them for their piety, *humanitas,* and adherence to a proper form of philosophy. Returning to the passage from Melito discussed above (Eusebius, *Ecclesiastical History* 4.26.7–11), Melito acclaims Marcus Aurelius as the successor of Augustus and the "great and splendid empire" ("your nations") that began with him. Of his other predecessors, all were pious (*eusebeis*) except for Nero and Domitian, and some rebuked those who resorted to violence against the Christians. As for Marcus Aurelius, "since you hold the same opinion as they did concerning these men, and are in your humanity and your philosophy far greater, we are even more convinced that you will do all we ask you."

Athenagoras strikes a similar tone in his appeal to Marcus Aurelius and Commodus, an appeal in which he describes the empire a number of times as consisting of "nations [*ethnē*]" (*Embassy for the Christians* 14.2; 23.2; 25.3; 34.3). In his opening address to the emperors, he speaks of "your mildness and gentleness, and your peaceful and benevolent disposition toward every man," which have produced an empire that, "under your intelligent sway, enjoys profound peace" (1.2). Nevertheless, he laments, this "peaceful and benevolent disposition" has not extended to the Christians: "you allow us to be harassed, plundered, and persecuted, the multitude making war upon us for our name alone" (1.3). At the end of the appeal, however, having argued the case that Christians too "are pious, and gentle, and temperate in spirit," he resumes his praise of the emperors: "you, who are entirely in everything, by nature and by education, upright,

---

200. Although the passage contains no reference to the nations, the Acts of Paul contains an episode similar to the story of Eutychus (Acts 20:9–12), in which the young man (Patroclus) is a cupbearer for Nero, with the result that the story becomes one of a confrontation between Christ and the emperor (11.1–4).

and moderate, and benevolent, and worthy of your rule" (37.1). Then he assures them that he and his fellow Christians "pray for your government," a prayer not only that their line ("son from father") continue but also "that your empire may receive increase and addition, all men becoming subject to your sway" (37.2). It is by any account a remarkable prayer—Christians, who are struggling to find a place for themselves in an empire that often opposes them, nevertheless praying that the empire would expand and become fully universal.

Finally, we come to the subjects of the empire and the place of Christians among them. Again we find a contrast, though here a difference not so much of substance as of emphasis. The negative side of the contrast is particularly to the fore in Tertullian's work. In one passage, he picks up a common aspect of Roman self-justification—having to do with bringing *humanitas* to the barbarians. In the first part of the passage, he describes the universal mission of the apostles ("preaching throughout the world [*per orbem*]"), a mission that was met with persecution and bloodshed on the part of the Romans (*Apology* 21.23–28). Then, addressing the Romans as the "rulers of the nations [*gentium*]," he describes their so-called humanizing mission as one that brings only demonic terror—a mission that attempted to "mould men, stockish and still savage, to civilization [*humanitatem*] by terrorizing them with such a crowd of gods to worship as Numa did."[201] Set in contrast to this, Christ's mission was one that gave people "eyes to recognize the truth" (21.29–30).

In another passage (*To the Heathen* 1.17.1–6), Tertullian contrasts the character of the Christians, those who worship Christ and refuse to worship the Caesars, with that of the other subjects of the empire who are prepared both to "propitiate their images [and to] swear by their genius." On the one hand, he presents the Christians as subservient and peaceable people, not guilty of any conspiracy, insurrection, or acts of violence against the emperor or his officials. On the other hand, they stand in contrast to many of the nations (*nationes*) in the empire, who were originally conquered enemies and continue to harbor enmity, and also to many of the common Roman people, who are rebellious "in tongue" if not "in arms."

Elsewhere Tertullian comes at the topic of Rome's enemies and the place of Christians in the empire from another angle (*Apology* 37.4–8). Noting that Rome considers the Christians as "enemies of the human race [*generis humani*]," he conducts a kind of thought experiment in which they would indeed "play the part of open enemies." Here he compares the Christians with hostile nations (*gentes*) such as the Moors or the Parthians, arguing that, because Christians

---

201. Numa Pompilius, the second king of Rome in Roman tradition, was believed to have initiated the basic elements of Roman worship.

were spread throughout the territory and structures of the whole Roman Empire rather than being concentrated in a single bounded region, they would constitute a more dangerous enemy: "we have filled everything you have—cities, islands, forts, towns, exchanges, yes! and camps, tribes, decuries, palace, senate, forum. All we have left to you is the temples!" He concedes that Christian teaching would prohibit them from actually taking up arms ("in our doctrine we are given ampler liberty to be killed than to kill"), but he says that they could achieve much the same result simply by a passive-aggressive withdrawal from the empire:

> Why! without taking up arms, without rebellion, simply by standing aside, by mere ill-natured separation, we could have fought you! For if so vast a mass of people as we had broken away from you and removed to some recess of the world apart . . . you would have shuddered at your solitude, at the silence in the world, the stupor as it were of a dead globe. You would have had to look about for people to rule. You would have had more enemies left than citizens.

Implicit in this passage is the other, more positive side of the theme—that Christians were loyal citizens rather than enemies and thus a source of benefit to the empire as a whole. As he continues, Tertullian turns to this positive side, arguing that "as things are, you have fewer enemies because of the multitude of the Christians" and claiming that, because of their power over the demons through Christ, Christians also keep another kind of enemy in check.[202]

This positive side of the theme is emphasized elsewhere as well. Athenagoras calls on the emperors to recognize the benefits of having subjects who are "pious, and gentle, and temperate in spirit" (*Embassy for the Christians* 37.1). In a passage that has already drawn our attention for its discussion of the temporal overlap between Augustus and Christ, Melito asserts that the empire has benefited from this coincidence as much as the Christians. Addressing the emperor, he claims that as "our philosophy . . . blossomed out among your nations [*ethnē*] during the great reign of your ancestor Augustus, [it] became especially for your empire an auspicious benefit. For from that time the power of Rome grew to become great and splendid" (*Ecclesiastical History* 4.26.7). And Irenaeus, after speaking of the miraculous deeds of healing that Christians have performed for the benefit of others, sums it up in this way:

> What more can we say? It is impossible to count up all the favors that the church performs daily throughout the whole world for the help of the nations

---

202. *Apology* 37.8–9; a little earlier he asserts that, through their prayers, the Christians ensure the security and stability of the empire (32.1–3).

Ethnē and Gentile Christian Identity (After 135 CE)

[*tōn ethnōn, gentium*].... In this she neither misleads them nor accepts bribes from them. For just as she has received gratuitously from God, so she renders service gratuitously. (*Against Heresies* 2.32.4)

He sees a church drawn from all the nations and spread throughout the Roman world, bringing benefits to the nations within the Roman Empire. Such is the positive portrait of the church that Irenaeus and other fellow Christians painted of themselves and presented to the larger Roman world.

In various ways, then, Christian writers in this period appropriated the vocabulary and rhetoric of empire, constructing and projecting an identity for themselves as an empire-like, transethnic people drawn from all the (non-Jewish) nations—especially those nations that were part of the Roman Empire, though, when it suited their purpose, also including nations even beyond the Roman borders. Sometimes the emphasis was placed negatively, on the side of contrast—Christians as a counterempire engaged in conflict with the empire it mirrored. At other times the emphasis was more positive—Christians as a supportive element within the empire, willing to be constructive partners (within certain limits) of the imperial agents. As we have seen, the two emphases were not necessarily mutually exclusive.

Rhetoric and reality are often not coterminous, and especially not in this case. Nevertheless, the significance of this project of identity construction is not to be diminished by its rhetorical character. To quote Cameron again, "a large part of Christianity's effectiveness in the Roman Empire lay in its capacity to create its own intellectual and imaginative universe."[203] At the same time, however, the contours and structures of this universe were adaptations of those that shaped and undergirded the Roman Empire itself. Even in its negative form as a counterempire, the "intellectual and imaginative universe" of the Christians was one that absorbed aspects of imperial ideology into itself.[204] The positive form—Christians as an ideal empire within an empire—was one that could readily be merged with the larger empire if circumstances changed.

But this is not the whole story. Christian engagement with the rhetoric of empire was just part of a larger tradition of competitive ethnography, one in which most ethnic groups (and larger groupings of nations) were involved—and

---

203. Cameron, *Christianity and the Rhetoric of Empire*, 6.

204. Cf. Schott: "Thus, the apologists did not offer a discourse that erased the effects of empire. Mimicry reiterates, even if partially, confusedly, and disruptively, the conditions of its own possibility. Apologetics was a discourse of resistance *within*, not liberation from, the asymmetries of power and prestige"; *Christianity, Empire, and the Making of Religion*, 51.

had been involved, even before the Mediterranean had become a Roman pond. The Jews, with their distinctive worship and customs, had developed their own distinctive strategies for this competition. Gentile Christians in turn adopted and adapted some of these strategies, even as they turned them back against the Jews, the Jewish origins of the Christian church having become a problem for Christians in the larger competitive field.

One of the aims of this work has been to demonstrate that this story can be told, to a considerable extent, by tracing the use of the term *ethnē* and related ethnic language, particularly the identification of non-Jewish Christians as constituted by *ethnē* or as drawn from all the *ethnē*. This language came into the story as an identity ascribed by Jewish Christ-believers to those non-Jews who became part of the movement in its early stage. Once gentile Christ-groups began to exist as separate entities, independent of Jewish believers, the evidence suggests that the term initially lost its rationale for the most part; where it did appear, it was used to denote outsiders and thus, in some cases, an identity that had been left behind. By the middle of the second century, however, especially among the proto-orthodox churches, the term took on increased usefulness as they attempted to negotiate a place for themselves within the larger Greco-Roman world.[205]

This usefulness was probably first apparent with respect to the church's need to define itself over against the Jews (*adversus Judaeos*) by anchoring its corporate identity in the *ethnē* who appeared in Israel's Scriptures. This move having been made, the term then began to prove its usefulness with respect to the church's related need to define itself within the larger Roman world. As Schott has observed, Christians did not need to create a new identity term for themselves; Rome provided them with one that was already deeply rooted in their past: "*ta ethnē*, or *gentes*, in Latin, was the same terminology used by Romans of previous centuries to classify the peoples they ruled."[206]

We should not imagine, however, that Christians picked up this term with any conscious prior intention of fashioning themselves as an empire-like entity that would go head-to-head with the Roman Empire in a battle for supremacy. Rather, the fact that there was a certain isomorphic relation between *ethnē* in the church and *ethnē* in the empire—in both cases a community of *ethnē* being drawn into a larger transethnic kingdom characterized in part by worship and

---

205. The term seems to have had little currency among gnosticizing groups, who had different ways of classifying the people of the world. Among Marcionites, however, it was a useful term, as we have seen.

206. Schott, *Christianity, Empire, and the Making of Religion*, 133.

projects of human transformation—led naturally and increasingly to the kind of imperial discourse that we have observed.

This aspect of the Christian "imaginative universe"—the idea of the church as an empire-like body within the Roman Empire—was present only in an incipient way in Justin's work. Otherwise, gentile Christian strategies for engaging in the competitive ethnographical fray were largely in place by the time of Justin. These were continued and amplified by his successors, who also carried out significant developments in the presentation of the church in empire-like terms, as we have seen.

When Eusebius stood in the Church of the Holy Sepulchre to praise the emperor, to exult in the possibilities of a Christian empire and to provide Constantine's less enthusiastic subjects with a theo-ethnographical rationale for the emperor's patronage of the church, he was in all probability standing not far from where the first debates over the admission of gentiles into the new Jewish renewal group had taken place. A short walk, perhaps, but in all other respects the two events were separated by a considerable distance—in time, to be sure, but also in ethnic makeup, social location, and group identity.

In this work, we have attempted to traverse this distance, to trace the stages of development, and to demonstrate that much of the theological ethnography that comes into view in Eusebius's *On the Holy Sepulchre* was in place at least a century before. Indeed, a considerable proportion of Eusebius's own work predated the new Constantinian state of affairs and so can be seen as a culmination of the project of identity construction that first comes into clear view in the work of Justin. With Constantine's defeat of Licinius in 324 and his consequent accession to the position of sole emperor, however, these apologetic constructions of Christian history and (gentile) Christian identity were soon modulated into a new imperial key.

Afterword

A lot of water has flowed under the Milvian Bridge since Eusebius stood inside the new Church of the Holy Sepulchre in Jerusalem and delivered his address in praise of the emperor who built it. While Constantine's embrace of Christianity was motivated no doubt by a real religious commitment at some level, it also reflected the realpolitik of a shrewd imperial ruler.[1] The forces set in motion by his patronage of the church have had profound consequences: in the short term, for Christian self-identification and the emergence of the church in its orthodox form, for the social location of the church and its members, for the integration of ecclesial structures into the political structures of the empire in its western and eastern forms, and so on; and in the long term—as these forces flowed through the subsequent centuries—for the development of Christian cultures in northern and eastern Europe, for the competition for colonial territory and the spread of Christianity to the "New World," for the emergence of new empires and of nation-states, and so on into our own day. In addition, these chains of development have had profound consequences for the Jewish people among whom the Christian movement first came into being, as they faced an ongoing struggle to maintain their own identity and existence within the emergent, often hostile, Christian world.

Of course, these developments fall well outside the limits of this study, and any attempt to pursue the themes of the study beyond these limits falls well

---

1. See Timothy D. Barnes, *Constantine and Eusebius* (Cambridge, MA: Harvard University Press, 1981), 48.

outside the competence of its author. At the same time, however, it is readily apparent that the themes of the study—the role of *ethnē* (nations) as a term by which gentile Christians negotiated a place for themselves with respect to Jews and Judaism, on the one hand, and the Roman Empire, on the other—represent a not insignificant component of the forces set in motion by Constantine's adoption of the church. Christian claims that, as a nation drawn from all the *ethnē*, they both replaced the Jews in God's purposes and constituted a counterempire within the Roman Empire continued to have social and political consequences within the Christian world long after the Roman Empire had faded into the past. Thus some reflections are in order on the manner in which the church got to the point where it could become an imperial partner of the Roman emperor.

Before saying anything else, it is appropriate first to recognize the magnitude of the achievement. To return to an observation by Rodney Stark that we noted in chapter 1, it is an improbable and remarkable story—the story of "how . . . a tiny and obscure messianic movement from the edge of the Roman Empire dislodge[d] classical paganism and [became] the dominant faith of Western civilization."[2] We have traced one element of the story—how *ethnē* as a sometimes derogatory Jewish term for outsiders became a central element in the apologetic narrative that undergirded the gentile Christian sense of who they were and thus played a part in the Christianization of the empire—and from this vantage point, we have been able to glimpse the remarkable nature of the story itself. While the story might have unfolded in another way with a different emperor, the outcome was much more determined by the compelling way in which Christians learned to speak and write the "rhetoric of empire" than it was by the whims of a single emperor.[3] So while we from our vantage point may be able to see some of the darker consequences of the story, we should not allow this to prevent our appreciation of the achievement itself.

My reflections are oriented around the two boundaries at which the gentile Christians constructed their sense of identity; they thus correspond to two strands indicated in the subtitle (the parting of the ways, Roman imperial ideology). I begin with gentile Christian identity construction at the boundary with Jews and Judaism. In my view, one of the positive things about the early Christian apologists is their recognition of themselves as gentiles, *ethnē*. The Scriptures—both Israel's Scriptures and the writings of the New Testament—provide a natural point of entry for gentile readers. Israel's Scriptures tell the

2. Rodney Stark, *The Rise of Christianity: A Sociologist Reconsiders History* (Princeton: Princeton University Press, 1996), 3.

3. Averil Cameron, *Christianity and the Rhetoric of Empire: The Development of Christian Discourse* (Berkeley: University of California Press, 1991), 14.

Afterword

story of God's covenantal relationship with Israel, a story in which the nations are present as secondary characters—sometimes as hostile outsiders, sometimes as potential worshipers of Israel's God, and ultimately as secondary beneficiaries of God's redemption of Israel. The writings of the New Testament reflect a Jewish-centered movement into which gentiles have been invited to participate. In identifying themselves as *ethnē* (or a group drawn from "all the *ethnē*"), then, the proto-orthodox Christians were taking advantage of these natural points of entry to align themselves with the place of non-Jews in the story of Israel and its continuation in the figure of Jesus.

In addition to this, they identified themselves as a particular nation (*ethnos*), people (*laos*), or race (*genos*). This was not problematic in itself. Religious worship was considered to be an aspect of ethnic people groups, which meant that group identification in these terms was very helpful as Christians engaged in the kind of identity negotiation that was necessary if they were to achieve recognition and respect. Further, these terms were also common as identifiers in the New Testament writings.

As we have seen, however, gentile Christians took the additional step of identifying themselves with the nation or people of Israel in particular. It must be conceded that, in doing so, they could claim New Testament grounds for the identity. The author of 1 Peter, as we have observed, takes scriptural identity terms that were characteristically used to describe Israel and applies them to the mixed community of Christ-believers that includes his gentile readers (1 Pet 2:9);[4] Paul invites the gentile believers in Corinth to join Jewish believers in considering the exodus generation as "our fathers" (1 Cor 10:1); he also declares that gentile believers are part of Abraham's "seed" (Gal 3:29; Rom 4:13–16), a term that in Israel's Scripture is restricted to circumcised descendants of Abraham (Gen 17:7–14). However, a status offered by Jews to gentiles in the context of a recognizably Jewish movement, led primarily by Jewish Christ-believers, is one thing. A status unilaterally claimed by gentile Christians—who identify themselves with a church that is categorically non-Jewish and who engage in ungenerous and derogatory apologetic against the Jews—is quite another. Seen from our own perspective, where we are aware of the tragic history of Christian anti-Judaism and its role in generating anti-Semitic attitudes, policies, and programs of violence, the persistence with which gentile Christians pressed their claim to the identity of Israel may well appear to have been both ill-advised and fraught with danger.

This is especially the case when one takes into consideration an additional identity move that was made by gentile Christians. As we have seen, they made a

---

4. "A chosen race [*genos*], a royal priesthood, a holy nation [*ethnos*], a people for [God's] possession" (cf. LXX Exod 19:6; LXX Isa 43:20–21).

distinction between Hebrews (i.e., the righteous pre-Mosaic patriarchs, together with the heroes, saints, and prophets of the subsequent period) and the Jews (i.e., most of the people identified with the law of Moses and the patterns of worship centered on the temple). On the one hand, this move emptied the Mosaic covenant of any positive significance in itself, as they understood it instead as having been given as a means of restraining and punishing the excessive sinfulness of the Jews. On the other, this allowed the gentile Christians to redefine the Hebrews as Christians before Christ—people who were able to live in righteous relationship with God without any need for law and temple, and people who recognized that the true positive significance of the law, the temple, and the Scriptures was as a typological revelation of Christ.

With this move, the Christian claim to the identity of Israel shifted from one of supersession—in which the gentile church took over the identity and role of Israel after these had been forfeited by the Jews (new Israel)—to one of arrogation or appropriation, in which the gentile church redefined the dramatis personae in Israel's story in such a way that the positive human characters in the story were identified as prototypical Christians (true Israel), while the negative characters constituted the people of the Jews. By defining themselves as Israel in this way, the church laid claim to the center of the scriptural story of Israel.

As is readily apparent, this move carried with it the potential for exacerbating the negative consequences of Christian attitudes and teaching with respect to the Jews, especially in situations where the authority of the church was undergirded by its relationship to political power. But there were negative consequences for other peoples as well. In his important and groundbreaking study of theology and race in the period of New World exploration, territorial conquest, and colonial establishment, Willie Jennings has shown how such readings of the Old Testament from the standpoint of the center allowed Christian colonizers not only to identify themselves as Israel but also to identify native peoples as the gentiles—the pagan nations, the dangerous other—with often disastrous results.[5] His book also issues a call to contemporary Christians that they reorient themselves with respect to the story of Israel and the story of Jesus, and that they learn to read them again as gentiles and to enter into them by identifying with the gentile characters in the story.

My purpose in the preceding pages has been to engage in a historical investigation, and so I am not suggesting that they be read as the preamble to an analogous call to action. Nevertheless, in the course of carrying out this

---

5. Willie James Jennings, *The Christian Imagination: Theology and the Origins of Race* (New Haven: Yale University Press, 2010).

Afterword

historical study, I have come increasingly to the opinion that gentile Christians should learn to read the Scriptures—the Scriptures of Israel and the New Testament—as gentiles, and that such a reading would make a positive contribution to Christian self-understanding generally and to the ongoing dialogues between Christians and Jews in particular. To the extent that early gentile Christian self-identification included an identification with the *ethnē* in Israel's Scripture, it can provide us, if not with a model of such a reading, at least with an instructive case study.

The reference to the church's involvement in the colonial era brings us to the other identity-construction boundary, that with the Greco-Roman empire. Here we also encounter a claim to the center—a claim that was realized with Constantine's embrace of Christianity but was prepared for by two overlapping Christian enterprises of competitive identity construction. One of these had to do with the map that gave shape to the arena within which ethnographical competition took place in the Greek world, a map whose primary boundary was between Greeks and barbarians. Here the Christians worked with a version of the map that already included the Jews and thus contained another primary boundary, one lying between polytheists and monotheistic Jews, a map that they redrew in such a way to position themselves at the center by virtue of their alignment with the Hebrews as primordial monotheists.

The other enterprise of Christian identity construction had to do with Roman imperial ideology, with its image of an ideal transethnic empire, one in which the Greek project of humanization was being more fully realized by drawing all the nations into a new imperial entity and making it possible for them to participate in the culture and benefits of the empire.[6] In this case, Christians conceived of themselves in analogous terms, an alternative empire in which Christ was drawing all the nations into a new transethnic community, one in which baleful demonic influences were overcome and the possibilities of a new pious and peaceable people were being realized. Some forms of this identity stressed difference and opposition—the church as a counterempire involved in battle with Rome. Other forms saw Rome as having a more providential role to play in the emergence of the transethnic church—the church and Rome as at least potential partners in a larger divine enterprise.

Counterempire or partners in empire—with Constantine's embrace of Chris-

---

6. Rome's self-positioning with respect to the Greek tradition might be viewed as another example of supersessionism, though one in which the virtues and accomplishments of the old entity were valued more highly (though not without reservation) by the shapers of the new.

tianity, the differences tended to disappear, as the church suddenly found itself in a position close to the center of imperial power. Thus began a period of almost a millennium and a half in which Christian existence, for better or worse, was closely aligned with the power and identity structures of empires and nations. The effects of this alignment, of course, continue to be felt in our own contemporary world.

In his study of the "construction of nationhood," Adrian Hastings has drawn attention to two contrasting effects of the kind of Christian alignment with imperial power that is reflected in a writer such as Eusebius. He identifies two models, the first of which is the modern notion of the nation-state:

> The nation and nationalism are both, I wish to claim, characteristically Christian things which, in so far as they have appeared elsewhere, have done so within a process of westernisation and of imitation of the Christian world, even if it was imitated as western rather than as Christian.[7]

While the claim has to do more with the historical development of the European nation-state, it does have contemporary resonances. In this connection, while finishing this book my attention was caught by a statement made by Ukrainian President Petro Poroshenko, who was celebrating the creation of a new Ukrainian Orthodox Church separate from Moscow and the Russian Orthodox Church. Speaking on a Ukrainian television network, he declared that "the creation of an independent Ukrainian Orthodox church is a necessary attribute of nation-building."[8]

In contrast to this idea of the church as an essential element of a nation-state, the other model emerges from the idea of Christianity as a transethnic and universalizing phenomenon and thus a component in the building of empires and other multinational political constellations. Hastings again:

> We have seen the national model recur again and again, yet if one looks at some of the central areas of Christian history, one also sees a quite different one—acceptance of a world empire, the continuation of Rome. Here, Chris-

---

7. Adrian Hastings, *The Construction of Nationhood: Ethnicity, Religion, and Nationalism* (Cambridge: Cambridge University Press, 1997), 186; Eusebius comes into view on p. 199. See also Halvor Moxnes, *Jesus and the Rise of Nationalism: A New Quest for the Nineteenth-Century Historical Jesus* (London: I. B. Taurus, 2012).

8. Sommer Brokaw and Allen Cone, "Ukraine Splits from Russian Orthodox Church," *United Press International*, December 15, 2018, https://www.upi.com/Top_News/World-News/2018/12/15/Ukraine-splits-from-Russian-Orthodox-church/2631544889703/#ixzz5dkX7E9VU.

tians were able to feel no less at home. A world empire corresponded geographically and politically to the sort of religious society they saw themselves to be.[9]

With its jurisdiction over most of the Orthodox Churches in the former Soviet Union, the Russian Orthodox Church can be seen as representative of this other model—the church as a means of binding a number of national groups into a larger political entity.

I have nothing substantial to say about the place of the church in the conflict between the Ukraine and Russia, except to make the more general observation that the countervailing effects of these two models have the potential of providing Christians with opportunities for tempering the extremes that can be found in blood-and-soil nationalisms, on the one hand, and totalizing empires, on the other. My purpose here is to reflect on the pre-Constantinian situation—specifically, on the manner in which the church got to the point where it could become an imperial partner of the Roman emperor, and on the advisability of that partnership.

In his own reflection on these matters, John Howard Yoder has invited us to consider "how things could have been otherwise" and has suggested that we look at the experience of the Jews as representing an alternative model.[10] Without following his own analysis any further here, I would like at least to pick up his suggestion. Through its history up to the time of Constantine, the Jewish people had accumulated plenty of experience living with empires and under imperial rule. The Assyrians, the Babylonians, the Persians, the Greeks, the Romans—they had experienced them all, and through it all, they had learned to maintain their separate identity even as they adapted to changing circumstances. What is of particular interest to me here is not so much the Judean state as the Jewish diaspora existence. During the period when the church was developing its presence throughout the Mediterranean world as a new people drawn from all the nations, the Jewish people were already present in their own communities among all the nations. While they too were engaged in competitive ethnography and the attempt to articulate their tradition in terms that educated outsiders could appreciate, they did not envision themselves as occupying the center (at least in this age) but were content with a diaspora existence. While they were prepared to seek the welfare of the city (cf. Jer 29:7), they did not aspire (as it were) to obtain the keys to city hall.

9. Hastings, *Construction of Nationhood*, 198–99.
10. John Howard Yoder, *The Jewish-Christian Schism Revisited*, ed. Michael G. Cartwright and Peter Ochs (Grand Rapids: Eerdmans, 2003), 44.

AFTERWORD

It is not my intention here either to idealize the Jewish diaspora or to denigrate the early Christians. Still, one way in which the outcome might have been different is to imagine the early Christians as constructing an Israel-like stance with respect to the empire, rather than the kind of empire-like identity that turned out to be so easily absorbed into the empire itself. An Israel-like stance toward the empire and a gentile self-awareness in its approach to Israel's Scriptures—there are things yet to be learned by pondering "how things could have been otherwise."

Bibliography

Primary Texts and Translations

Except where otherwise noted, citations of classical Greek and Latin texts and translations depend on the pertinent volumes of the Loeb Classical Library (LCL). Citations of other Greek texts are drawn from the *Thesaurus Linguae Graecae* (*TLG*), where these are available. With respect to ecclesiastical literature, where more recent editions are not available, citations of Greek and Latin texts are drawn from J.-P. Migne's Patrologia Graeca and Patrologia Latina; where more recent translations are not available, citations in English depend on *Ante-Nicene Fathers* (*ANF*) or *Nicene and Post-Nicene Fathers* (*NPNF*). All other texts and translations are listed in the bibliography.

Albeck, Chanoh, ed. *Shishah Sidre Mishnah*. Jerusalem: Bialik Institute, 1952–58.
Arbesmann, Rudolph, Emily Joseph Daly, and Edwin A. Quain, trans. and eds. *Tertullian, Apologetical Works, and Minucius Felix, Octavius*. FC 10. New York: Fathers of the Church, 1950.
Barnard, Leslie William, ed. and trans. *St. Justin Martyr: The First and Second Apologies*. ACW 56. Mahwah, NJ: Paulist, 1997.
Behr, Charles A. *P. Aelius Aristides: The Complete Works*. 2 vols. Leiden: Brill, 1981–86.
Behr, John, ed. and trans. *Origen: On First Principles*. OECT. Oxford: Oxford University Press, 2018.
Blümel, Wolfgang, ed. *Die Inschriften von Knidos I*. Inschriften griechischer Städte aus Kleinasien 41. Bonn: R. Habelt, 1992.

Bruce, Barbara J., trans., Cynthia White, ed. *Origen: Homilies on Joshua*. FC 105. Washington, DC: Catholic University of America Press, 2002.

Brunt, P. A., and J. M. Moore, eds. and trans. *Res Gestae Divi Augusti: The Achievements of the Divine Augustus*. London: Oxford University Press, 1967.

Burke, Tony, trans. and ed. *De Infantia Iesu Evangelium Thomae Graecae*. Turnhout: Brepols, 2010.

Chadwick, Henry, ed. and trans. *Origen: Contra Celsum*. Cambridge: Cambridge University Press, 1953.

Charlesworth, James H., ed. *The Old Testament Pseudepigrapha*. 2 vols. Garden City, NY: Doubleday, 1983–85.

Clarke, G. W., trans. *The Octavius of Marcus Minucius Felix*. ACW 39. New York: Newman, 1974.

Crehan, Joseph Hugh, trans. *Athenagoras: Embassy for the Christians; The Resurrection of the Dead*. ACW 23. Westminster, MD: Newman, 1956.

Dessau, Hermann. *Inscriptiones Latinae Selectae*. Berlin: Weidmann, 1892–1916.

Drake, H. A. *In Praise of Constantine: A Historical Study and New Translation of Eusebius' Tricennial Orations*. Berkeley: University of California Press, 1976.

Dunn, Geoffrey D. *Tertullian*. ECF. London: Routledge, 2004.

Elliott, J. K., ed. *The Apocryphal New Testament: A Collection of Apocryphal Christian Literature in an English Translation*. Oxford: Clarendon, 1993.

Evans, Ernest, ed. and trans. *Adversus Marcionem*. OECT. Oxford: Clarendon, 1972.

Falls, Thomas B., trans., Thomas P. Halton, rev., Michael Slusser, ed. *St. Justin Martyr: Dialogue with Trypho*. Washington, DC: Catholic University of America Press, 2003.

Ferguson, John, trans. *Clement of Alexandria: Stromateis; Books One to Three*. FC 85. Washington, DC: Catholic University of America Press, 1991.

Ferrar, W. J. *The Proof of the Gospel: Being the* Demonstratio Evangelica *of Eusebius of Caesarea*. London: SPCK; New York: Macmillan, 1920.

Finkelstein, L. *Sifra on Leviticus*. New York: Jewish Theological Seminary of America, 1983–91.

García Martínez, Florentino, and Eibert J. C. Tigchelaar, eds. *The Dead Sea Scrolls: Study Edition*. Leiden: Brill, 1997.

Gifford, Edwin Hamilton. *Eusebii Pamphili Evangelicae Praeparationis*. Oxford: Typographeo Academico, 1903.

Grant, Robert M., trans. *Theophilus of Antioch: Ad Autolycum*. OECT. Oxford: Clarendon, 1970.

Hall, Stuart George, ed. and trans. *Melito of Sardis:* On Pascha *and Fragments*. Oxford: Clarendon, 1979.

Harris, J. Rendel, and J. Armitage Robinson. *The Apology of Aristides on Behalf of the Christians, from a Syriac Ms. Preserved on Mount Sinai, with an Appen-*

dix Containing the Main Portion of the Original Greek Text. Piscataway, NJ: Gorgias, 2004.

Henderson, Jeffrey, ed. *Loeb Classical Library Online*. Cambridge, MA: Harvard University Press, 2014.

Jones, F. Stanley. *An Ancient Jewish Christian Source on the History of Christianity: Pseudo-Clementine Recognitions 1.27–71*. Texts and Translations. Atlanta: Scholars Press, 1995.

Lauro, Elizabeth Ann Dively, trans. *Homilies on Judges*. FC 119. Washington, DC: Catholic University of America Press, 2010.

Lauterbach, J. Z., trans. and ed. *Mekilta de Rabbi Ishmael*. Philadelphia: Jewish Publication Society of America, 1933–35.

Lieberman, Saul, ed. *The Tosefta*. New York: Jewish Theological Seminary of America, 1955–88.

Lienhard, Joseph T., trans. *Homilies on Luke: Origen, Fragments on Luke*. FC 94. Washington, DC: Catholic University of America Press, 1996.

Litwa, M. David. *Refutation of All Heresies*. WGRW 40. Atlanta: SBL Press, 2016.

McCabe, Donald F., ed. *Ephesos Inscriptions: Texts and List*. The Princeton Project on the Inscriptions of Anatolia. Princeton: Institute for Advanced Study, 1991.

McGiffert, Arthur Cushman, trans. *The Church History of Eusebius*. In vol. 1 of *Nicene and Post-Nicene Fathers*, Series 2. Grand Rapids: Eerdmans, 1989.

Migne, J.-P., ed. *Patrologia Cursus Completus: Series Graeca*. Paris, 1857–86.

———, ed. *Patrologia Cursus Completus: Series Latina*. Paris, 1844–64.

Minns, Denis, and Paul Parvis, eds. and trans. *Justin, Philosopher and Martyr: Apologies*. OECT. Oxford: Oxford University Press, 2009.

Neusner, Jacob. *The Mishnah: A New Translation*. New Haven: Yale University Press, 1988.

———, trans. *Sifra: An American Translation*. Atlanta: Scholars Press, 1988.

———, trans. *The Tosefta*. Peabody, MA: Hendrickson, 2002.

Pantelia, Maria C., ed. *Thesaurus Linguae Graecae: A Digital Library of Greek Literature*. Irving, CA: University of California, 2001.

Petzl, Georg, and Elmar Schwertheim. *Hadrian und die dionysischen Künstler: Drei in Alexandria Troas neugefundene Briefe des Kaisers an die Künstler-Vereinigung*. Asia Minor Studien 58. Bonn: Habelt, 2006.

Pietersma, Albert, and Benjamin G. Wright, eds. *A New English Translation of the Septuagint and the Other Greek Translations Traditionally Included under That Title*. New York: Oxford University Press, 2007.

Pouderon, Bernard, and Marie-Joseph Pierre, eds. *Aristide: Apologie*. SC 470. Paris: Cerf, 2003.

Robinson, James M., ed. *The Nag Hammadi Library in English*. 3rd ed. Translated and introduced by Members of the Coptic Gnostic Library Project of the Institute for Antiquity and Christianity. San Francisco: Harper & Row, 1988.

Robinson, James M., Paul Hoffmann, and John S. Kloppenborg, eds. *The Critical Edition of Q*. Hermeneia. Minneapolis: Fortress, 2000.

Rossi, Filippo de, ed. *Iscrizioni Dello Estremo Oriente Greco: Un Repertorio*. Inschriften griechischer Städte aus Kleinasien 65. Bonn: Habelt, 2004.

Scheck, Thomas P., trans. *Origen: Commentary on the Epistle to the Romans, Books 1–5*. FC 103. Washington, DC: Catholic University of America Press, 2001.

———, trans. *Origen: Commentary on the Epistle to the Romans, Books 6–10*. FC 104. Washington, DC: Catholic University of America Press, 2002.

Stewart-Sykes, Alistair, ed. *The Didascalia Apostolorum: An English Version*. Studia Traditionis Theologiae 1. Turnhout: Brepols, 2009.

Tomkins, Frederick, and William George Lemon. *The Commentaries of Gaius on the Roman Law with an English Translation and Annotations*. London: Butterworth, 1869.

Unger, Dominic J., trans. and ed., with further revisions by John J. Dillon and Irenaeus M. C. Steenberg. *St. Irenaeus of Lyons: Against the Heresies*. ACW 55. New York: Newman, 1992.

Warmington, E. H. *Archaic Inscriptions*. Vol. 4 of *Remains of Old Latin*. LCL 359. London: W. Heinemann, 1940.

Wood, Simon P., trans. *Clement of Alexandria: Christ the Educator*. FC 23. New York: Fathers of the Church, 1954.

Secondary Sources

Abraham, Susan B. "Critical Perspectives on Postcolonial Theory." Pages 24–33 in *The Colonized Apostle: Paul in Postcolonial Eyes*. Edited by Christopher Stanley. Minneapolis: Fortress, 2011.

Alexander, Philip S. "'The Parting of the Ways' from the Perspective of Rabbinic Judaism." Pages 1–25 in *Jews and Christians: The Parting of the Ways, A.D. 70 to 135*. Edited by James D. G. Dunn. Grand Rapids: Eerdmans, 1999.

Anderson, Benedict. *Imagined Communities: Reflections on the Origin and Spread of Nationalism*. Rev. ed. London: Verso, 2006.

Ando, Clifford. *Imperial Ideology and Provincial Loyalty in the Roman Empire*. Berkeley: University of California Press, 2000.

Ascough, Richard S., Philip A. Harland, and John S. Kloppenborg, eds. *Associations in the Greco-Roman World: A Sourcebook*. Waco, TX: Baylor University Press, 2012.

Aune, David E. *The New Testament in Its Literary Environment*. Philadelphia: Westminster, 1987.
———. *Revelation 1–5*. WBC. Nashville: Thomas Nelson, 1997.
———. *Revelation 6–16*. WBC. Nashville: Thomas Nelson, 1998.
Avidov, Avi. *Not Reckoned among Nations: The Origins of the So-Called "Jewish Question" in Roman Antiquity*. TSAJ 128. Tübingen: Mohr Siebeck, 2009.
Badian, Ernst. "Alexander the Great and the Unity of Mankind." *Historia: Zeitschrift für alte Geschichte* 7 (1958): 425–44.
Bainbridge, William Sims. "The Sociology of Conversion." Pages 178–91 in *Handbook of Religious Conversion*. Edited by H. Newton Malony and Samuel Southard. Birmingham, AL: Religious Education Press, 1992.
Baird, William. *History of New Testament Research*. 3 vols. Minneapolis: Fortress, 1992–2003.
Balsdon, J. P. V. D. *Romans and Aliens*. London: Duckworth, 1979.
Bamberger, Bernard J. *Proselytism in the Talmudic Period*. New York: Ktav, 1968.
Barclay, John M. G. "Constructing Judean Identity after 70 CE: A Study of Josephus's *Against Apion*." Pages 99–112 in *Identity and Interaction in the Ancient Mediterranean: Jews, Christians and Others*. Edited by Zeba A. Crook and Philip A. Harland. Sheffield: Sheffield Phoenix, 2007.
———. *Jews in the Mediterranean Diaspora: From Alexander to Trajan (323 BCE–117 CE)*. Edinburgh: T&T Clark, 1996.
Barnes, Timothy D. *Constantine and Eusebius*. Cambridge, MA: Harvard University Press, 1981.
Barrett, C. K. *A Critical and Exegetical Commentary on the Acts of the Apostles*. 2 vols. ICC. Edinburgh: T&T Clark, 1994–98.
Barth, Fredrik, ed. *Ethnic Groups and Boundaries: The Social Organization of Culture Difference*. Boston: Little, Brown, 1969.
———. *Process and Form in Social Life: Selected Essays of Fredrik Barth*. London: Routledge & Kegan Paul, 1981.
Bates, Matthew W. "Justin Martyr's Logocentric Hermeneutical Transformation of Isaiah's Vision of the Nations." *JTS* 60 (2009): 538–55.
Bauckham, Richard. *The Climax of Prophecy: Studies on the Book of Revelation*. Edinburgh: T&T Clark, 1993.
———. "The Continuing Quest for the Provenance of the Old Testament Pseudepigrapha." Pages 9–29 in *The Pseudepigrapha and Christian Origins: Essays from the Studiorum Novi Testamenti Societas*. Edited by Gerbern S. Oegema and James H. Charlesworth. London: T&T Clark, 2008.
———. *Jesus and the God of Israel: God Crucified and Other Studies on the New Testament's Christology of Divine Identity*. Grand Rapids: Eerdmans, 2008.
———. "The Parting of the Ways: What Happened and Why." *Studia Theologica* 47 (1993): 135–51.

BIBLIOGRAPHY

Bauer, Walter. *Orthodoxy and Heresy in Earliest Christianity*. Philadelphia: Fortress, 1971.

Baur, Ferdinand Christian. *Paul: The Apostle of Jesus Christ*. Translated by Allan Menzies. London: Williams & Norgate, 1876.

———. *Paulus, Der Apostel Jesu Christi*. Stuttgart: Becher & Müller, 1845.

Becker, Adam H., and Annette Yoshiko Reed, eds. *The Ways That Never Parted: Jews and Christians in Late Antiquity and the Early Middle Ages*. Minneapolis: Fortress, 2007.

Becker, Jürgen. *Paul: Apostle to the Gentiles*. Louisville: Westminster John Knox, 1993.

Beker, J. Christiaan. *Paul the Apostle: The Triumph of God in Life and Thought*. Philadelphia: Fortress, 1980.

Berger, Peter L., and Thomas Luckmann. *The Social Construction of Reality: A Treatise in the Sociology of Knowledge*. Garden City, NY: Doubleday, 1966.

Berthelot, Katell. "Grecs, Barbares et Juifs dans l'oeuvre de Philon." Pages 47–61 in *Philon d'Alexandrie: Un penseur à l'intersection des cultures gréco-romaine, orientale, juive et chrétienne*. Edited by Baudouin Decharneux and Sabrina Inowlocki. Turnhout: Brepols, 2011.

Betz, Hans Dieter. *Galatians: A Commentary on Paul's Letter to the Churches in Galatia*. Hermeneia. Philadelphia: Fortress, 1979.

Bhabha, Homi K. *The Location of Culture*. London: Routledge, 2004.

Bickerman, Elias. "*Origines Gentium*." CP 47 (1952): 65–81.

Billings, Drew W. *Acts of the Apostles and the Rhetoric of Roman Imperialism*. Cambridge: Cambridge University Press, 2017.

Bird, Michael F. *Jesus and the Origins of the Gentile Mission*. LNTS 331. London: T&T Clark, 2006.

Birnbaum, Ellen. *The Place of Judaism in Philo's Thought: Israel, Jews, and Proselytes*. Atlanta: Scholars Press, 1996.

Bosch, David J. *Transforming Mission: Paradigm Shifts in Theology of Mission*. American Society of Missiology Series 16. Maryknoll, NY: Orbis, 2011.

Bowe, Barbara Ellen. *A Church in Crisis: Ecclesiology and Paraenesis in Clement of Rome*. HDR 23. Minneapolis: Fortress, 1988.

———. "Prayer Rendered for Caesar? *1 Clement* 59.3–61.3." Pages 85–102 in *The Lord's Prayer and Other Prayer Texts from the Greco-Roman Era*. Edited by James H. Charlesworth. Valley Forge, PA: Trinity Press International, 1994.

Boyarin, Daniel. *Border Lines: The Partition of Judaeo-Christianity*. Philadelphia: University of Pennsylvania Press, 2004.

Bremmer, Jan N. *The Rise of Christianity through the Eyes of Gibbon, Harnack and Rodney Stark*. Groningen: Barkhuis, 2010.

Brett, Mark G. *Ethnicity and the Bible*. Biblical Interpretation Series. Leiden: Brill, 1996.

Brown, Raymond E. *The Birth of the Messiah: A Commentary on the Infancy Narratives in the Gospels of Matthew and Luke.* ABRL. New York: Doubleday, 1993.

———. "Not Jewish Christianity and Gentile Christianity, but Types of Jewish/Gentile Christianity." *CBQ* 45 (1983): 74–79.

Brunt, P. A. *Roman Imperial Themes.* Oxford: Oxford University Press, 1990.

Buell, Denise Kimber. *Why This New Race? Ethnic Reasoning in Early Christianity.* New York: Columbia University Press, 2005.

Bultmann, Rudolf. "Paul." Pages 111–46 in *Existence and Faith.* Translated and introduced by Schubert M. Ogden. New York: Meridian, 1960.

Burton, Ernest de Witt. *A Critical and Exegetical Commentary on the Epistle to the Galatians.* ICC. Edinburgh: T&T Clark, 1921.

Caird, G. B. *The Apostolic Age.* London: Duckworth, 1955.

Cameron, Averil. *Christianity and the Rhetoric of Empire: The Development of Christian Discourse.* Berkeley: University of California Press, 1991.

Cameron, Ron, and Merrill P. Miller, eds. *Redescribing Christian Origins.* SBL Symposium Series. Atlanta: Society of Biblical Literature, 2004.

Cassidy, Richard J. *Society and Politics in the Acts of the Apostles.* Maryknoll, NY: Orbis, 1987.

Chadwick, Henry. "Christian and Roman Universalism in the Fourth Century." Pages 26–42 in *Christian Faith and Greek Philosophy in Late Antiquity: Essays in Tribute to George Christopher Stead.* Edited by L. R. Wickham and C. P. Bammel. VCSup 19. Leiden: Brill, 1993.

Chilton, Bruce. "Justin and Israelite Prophecy." Pages 77–87 in *Justin Martyr and His Worlds.* Edited by Sara Parvis and Paul Foster. Minneapolis: Fortress, 2007.

Clark, Kenneth W. "The Gentile Bias in Matthew." *JBL* 66 (1947): 165–72.

Cohen, Shaye J. D. *The Beginnings of Jewishness: Boundaries, Varieties, Uncertainties.* Berkeley: University of California Press, 1999.

———. "The Ways That Parted: Jews, Christians, and Jewish-Christians, Ca. 100–150 CE." Pages 307–39 in *Jews and Christians in the First and Second Centuries: The Interbellum 70–132 CE.* Edited by Joshua Schwartz and Peter J. Tomson. CRINT 15. Leiden: Brill, 2018.

Collins, Adela Yarbro. *Mark: A Commentary.* Hermeneia. Minneapolis: Fortress, 2007.

Collins, John J., ed. *Apocalypse: The Morphology of a Genre.* Semeia 14. Missoula, MT: Scholars Press, 1979.

———. *The Apocalyptic Imagination: An Introduction to Jewish Apocalyptic Literature.* 2nd ed. Grand Rapids: Eerdmans, 1998.

———. *Between Athens and Jerusalem: Jewish Identity in the Hellenistic Diaspora.* 2nd ed. Grand Rapids: Eerdmans, 2000.

———. *The Scepter and the Star: Messianism in Light of the Dead Sea Scrolls*. Grand Rapids: Eerdmans, 2010.

Collins, Raymond F. *1 & 2 Timothy and Titus: A Commentary*. NTL. Louisville: Westminster John Knox, 2002.

Concannon, Cavan W. *"When You Were Gentiles": Specters of Ethnicity in Roman Corinth and Paul's Corinthian Correspondence*. New Haven: Yale University Press, 2014.

Conzelmann, Hans. *1 Corinthians: A Commentary on the First Epistle to the Corinthians*. Translated by James W. Leitch. Hermeneia. Philadelphia: Fortress, 1975.

Crüsemann, Frank. "Human Solidarity and Ethnic Identity: Israel's Self-Identification in the Genealogical System of Genesis." Pages 57–76 in *Ethnicity and the Bible*. Edited by Mark G. Brett. Leiden: Brill, 1996.

Dahl, Nils A. "The Messiahship of Jesus in Paul." Pages 37–47 in *The Crucified Messiah, and Other Essays*. Minneapolis: Augsburg, 1974.

———. "Nations in the New Testament." Pages 54–68 in *New Testament Christianity for Africa and the World: Essays in Honour of Harry Sawyerr*. Edited by Mark E. Glasswell and Edward W. Fasholé-Luke. London: SPCK, 1974.

Dahlheim, Werner. *Gewalt und Herrschaft: Das provinziale Herrschaftssystem der römischen Republik*. Berlin: de Gruyter, 1977.

Davila, James R. *The Provenance of the Pseudepigrapha: Jewish, Christian, or Other?* JSJSup 105. Leiden: Brill, 2005.

Dench, Emma. *From Barbarians to New Men: Greek, Roman, and Modern Perceptions of Peoples of the Central Apennines*. Oxford Classical Monographs. Oxford: Oxford University Press, 1995.

———. *Romulus' Asylum: Roman Identities from the Age of Alexander to the Age of Hadrian*. Oxford: Oxford University Press, 2005.

Derks, Ton, and Nico Roymans, ed. *Ethnic Constructs in Antiquity: The Role of Power and Tradition*. Amsterdam Archaeological Studies. Amsterdam: Amsterdam University Press, 2009.

Dibelius, Martin, and Hans Conzelmann. *The Pastoral Epistles: A Commentary*. Translated by Philip Buttolph and Adela Yarbro. Hermeneia. Philadelphia: Fortress, 1972.

Dilke, O. A. W. *Greek and Roman Maps*. Ithaca, NY: Cornell University Press, 1985.

Dobbeler, Axel von. "Die Restitution Israels und die Bekehrung der Heiden: Das Verhältnis von Mt 10,5b–6 und Mt 28,18–20 unter dem Aspekt der Komplementarität: Erwägungen zum Standort des Matthausevangeliums." ZNW 91 (2000): 18–44.

Dodd, C. H. *According to the Scriptures: The Sub-structure of New Testament Theology*. London: James Nisbet, 1952.

Donaldson, Terence L. "'The Field God Has Assigned': Geography and Mission in

Paul." Pages 109–37 in *Religious Rivalries in the Early Roman Empire and the Rise of Christianity*. Edited by Leif Vaage. ESCJ 18. Waterloo, ON: Wilfrid Laurier University Press, 2006.

———. "'Gentile Christianity' as a Category in the Study of Christian Origins." *HTR* 106 (2013): 433–58.

———. *Jews and Anti-Judaism in the New Testament: Decision Points and Divergent Interpretations*. London: SPCK; Waco, TX: Baylor University Press, 2010.

———. *Judaism and the Gentiles: Jewish Patterns of Universalism (to 135 CE)*. Waco, TX: Baylor University Press, 2007.

———. "Paul, Abraham's Gentile 'Offspring' and the Torah." Pages 135–50 in *Torah Ethics and Early Christian Identity*. Edited by David M. Miller and Susan Wendel. Grand Rapids: Eerdmans, 2016.

———. *Paul and the Gentiles: Remapping the Apostle's Convictional World*. Minneapolis: Fortress, 1997.

———, ed. *Religious Rivalries and the Struggle for Success in Caesarea Maritima*. ESCJ 8. Waterloo, ON: Wilfrid Laurier University Press, 2000.

———. "'Riches for the Gentiles' (Rom 11:12): Israel's Rejection and Paul's Gentile Mission." *JBL* 112 (1993): 81–98.

———. "Supersessionism and Early Christian Self-Definition." *JJMJS* 3 (2016): 1–32.

———. "'We Gentiles': Ethnicity and Identity in Justin Martyr." *EC* 4 (2013): 213–41.

Donfried, Karl Paul. *The Setting of Second Clement in Early Christianity*. SupNovT 38. Leiden: Brill, 1974.

Draper, Jonathan A. "Do the Didache and Matthew Reflect an 'Irrevocable Parting of the Ways' with Judaism?" Pages 217–41 in *Matthew and the Didache: Two Documents from the Same Jewish-Christian Milieu?* Edited by Huub van de Sandt. Assen: Royal Van Gorcum; Minneapolis: Fortress, 2005.

———. "Missing Pieces or Wild Goose Chase? A Retrospect and Prospect." Pages 529–43 in *The Didache: A Missing Piece of the Puzzle in Early Christianity*. Edited by Jonathan A. Draper and Clayton N. Jefford. ECL 14. Atlanta: Society of Biblical Literature Press, 2015.

———. "'You Shall Not Give What Is Holy to the Dogs' (*Didache* 9.5): The Attitude of the *Didache* to the Gentiles." Pages 242–58 in *Attitudes to Gentiles in Ancient Judaism and Early Christianity*. Edited by David C. Sim and James S. McLaren. LNTS 499. London: Bloomsbury T&T Clark, 2013.

Draper, Jonathan A., and Clayton N. Jefford, eds. *The Didache: A Missing Piece of the Puzzle in Early Christianity*. ECL 14. Atlanta: SBL Press, 2015.

Dunn, Geoffrey D. *Tertullian's* Aduersus Iudaeos: *A Rhetorical Analysis*. Patristic Monograph Series 19. Washington, DC: Catholic University of America Press, 2008.

Dunn, James D. G. *Beginning from Jerusalem.* Vol. 2 of *Christianity in the Making.* Grand Rapids: Eerdmans, 2009.

———. *Christology in the Making: A New Testament Inquiry into the Origins of the Doctrine of the Incarnation.* 2nd ed. London: SCM, 1989.

———. *Jesus Remembered.* Vol. 1 of *Christianity in the Making.* Grand Rapids: Eerdmans, 2003.

———, ed. *Jews and Christians: The Parting of the Ways, A.D. 70 to 135.* Grand Rapids: Eerdmans, 1992.

———. *The Partings of the Ways between Christianity and Judaism and Their Significance for the Character of Christianity.* Philadelphia: Trinity Press International, 1991.

———. *Romans 1–8.* WBC. Dallas: Word, 1988.

———. *Romans 9–16.* WBC. Dallas: Word, 1988.

———. *The Theology of Paul the Apostle.* Grand Rapids: Eerdmans, 1998.

Edwards, Catharine. "Incorporating the Alien: The Art of Conquest." Pages 44–70 in *Rome the Cosmopolis.* Edited by Catharine Edwards and Greg Woolf. Cambridge: Cambridge University Press, 2003.

Edwards, Catharine, and Greg Woolf. "Cosmopolis: Rome as World City." Pages 1–20 in *Rome the Cosmopolis.* Edited by Catharine Edwards and Greg Woolf. Cambridge: Cambridge University Press, 2003.

———, eds. *Rome the Cosmopolis.* Cambridge: Cambridge University Press, 2003.

Ehrman, Bart D., ed. and trans. *The Apostolic Fathers.* 2 vols. LCL. Cambridge, MA: Harvard University Press, 2003.

Elgvin, Torleif. "Jewish Christian Editing of the Old Testament Pseudepigrapha." Pages 278–304 in *Jewish Believers in Jesus.* Edited by Oskar Skarsaune and Reidar Hvalvik. Peabody, MA: Hendrickson, 2007.

Elliott, Mark Adam. *The Survivors of Israel: A Reconsideration of the Theology of Pre-Christian Judaism.* Grand Rapids: Eerdmans, 2000.

Elmer, Ian J. "Fishing the Other Side: The Gentile Mission in Mark's Gospel." Pages 154–72 in *Attitudes to Gentiles in Ancient Judaism and Early Christianity.* Edited by David C. Sim and James S. McLaren. LNTS 499. London: Bloomsbury T&T Clark, 2013.

Enslin, Morton Scott. "Parting of the Ways." *JQR* 51 (1961): 177–97.

Esler, Philip F. *Conflict and Identity in Romans: The Social Setting of Paul's Letter.* Minneapolis: Fortress, 2003.

Evans, Craig A. "The Jewish Christian Gospel Tradition." Pages 241–77 in *Jewish Believers in Jesus.* Edited by Oskar Skarsaune and Reidar Hvalvik. Peabody, MA: Hendrickson, 2007.

Feldman, Louis H. *Jew and Gentile in the Ancient World: Attitudes and Interactions from Alexander to Justinian.* Princeton: Princeton University Press, 1993.

———. "Origen's *Contra Celsum* and Josephus' *Contra Apionem*: The Issue of Jewish Origins." *VC* 44 (1990): 105–35.

Ferguson, Niall. *Empire: The Rise and Demise of the British World Order and the Lessons for Global Power*. New York: Basic, 2003.

Filtvedt, Ole Jakob. *The Identity of God's People and the Paradox of Hebrews*. WUNT 2.320. Tübingen: Mohr Siebeck, 2015.

Finlan, Stephen. "Identity in the *Didache* Community." Pages 17–32 in *The Didache: A Missing Piece of the Puzzle in Early Christianity*. Edited by Jonathan A. Draper and Clayton N. Jefford. ECL 14. Atlanta: Society of Biblical Literature, 2015.

Foakes-Jackson, F. J., ed. *The Parting of the Roads: Studies in the Development of Judaism and Early Christianity*. London: Edward Arnold, 1912.

Frede, Michael. "Origen's Treatise *Against Celsus*." Pages 131–55 in *Apologetics in the Roman Empire: Pagans, Jews, and Christians*. Edited by Mark Edwards, Martin Goodman, and Simon Price, in association with Christopher Rowland. Oxford: Oxford University Press, 1999.

Fredriksen, Paula. *Augustine and the Jews: A Christian Defense of Jews and Judaism*. New York: Doubleday, 2008.

———. "How Jewish Is God? Divine Ethnicity in Paul's Theology." *JBL* 137 (2018): 193–212.

———. "Paul and Augustine: Conversion Narratives, Orthodox Traditions and the Retrospective Self." *JTS* 37 (1986): 3–34.

———. *Paul: The Pagans' Apostle*. New Haven: Yale University Press, 2017.

Frend, W. H. C. *The Rise of Christianity*. London: Darton, Longman and Todd, 1984.

Freyne, Seán. *The Jesus Movement and Its Expansion: Meaning and Mission*. Grand Rapids: Eerdmans, 2014.

Fuller, Reginald H. *The Formation of the Resurrection Narratives*. New York: Macmillan, 1971.

———. *The Foundations of New Testament Christology*. New York: Scribner, 1965.

Gager, John G. *The Origins of Anti-Semitism*. Oxford: Oxford University Press, 1983.

Garber, Zev, ed. *The Jewish Jesus: Revelation, Reflection, Reclamation*. West Lafayette, IN: Purdue University Press, 2011.

Gardner, Gregg, and Kevin L. Osterloh. "The Significance of Antiquity in Antiquity: An Introduction." Pages 1–23 in *Antiquity in Antiquity: Jewish and Christian Pasts in the Greco-Roman World*. Edited by Gregg Gardner and Kevin L. Osterloh. TSAJ 123. Tübingen: Mohr Siebeck, 2008.

Gaston, Lloyd. "The Messiah of Israel as Teacher of the Gentiles: The Setting of Matthew's Christology." *Int* 29 (1975): 24–40.

Gaventa, Beverly Roberts. *From Darkness to Light: Aspects of Conversion in the New Testament*. Philadelphia: Fortress, 1986.

Geiger, Joseph. "The Jew and the Other: Doubtful and Multiple Identities in the Roman Empire." Pages 136–46 in *Jewish Identities in Antiquity: Studies in Memory of Menahem Stern*. Edited by Lee I. Levine and Daniel R. Schwartz. Tübingen: Mohr Siebeck, 2009.

Gibbon, Edward. *The History of the Decline and Fall of the Roman Empire*. Edited by J. B. Bury. London: Methuen, 1909–26.

Gilbert, Gary. "Gentiles, Jewish Attitudes Towards." Pages 670–73 in *The Eerdmans Dictionary of Early Judaism*. Edited by John J. Collins and Daniel C. Harlow. Grand Rapids: Eerdmans, 2010.

Goffman, Erving. *Stigma: Notes on the Management of Spoiled Identity*. Englewood Cliffs, NJ: Prentice-Hall, 1963.

Goldenberg, Robert. *The Nations That Know Thee Not: Ancient Jewish Attitudes towards Other Religions*. Sheffield: Sheffield Academic, 1997.

Goldhill, Simon, ed. *Being Greek under Rome: Cultural Identity, the Second Sophistic and the Development of Empire*. Cambridge: Cambridge University Press, 2001.

Goodman, Martin. *Mission and Conversion: Proselytizing in the Religious History of the Roman Empire*. Oxford: Clarendon, 1994.

———. *Rome and Jerusalem: The Clash of Ancient Civilizations*. New York: Vintage, 2008.

Grabbe, Lester L. *Judaism from Cyrus to Hadrian*. Minneapolis: Fortress, 1992.

Grant, Robert M., and Holt H. Graham. *First and Second Clement*. Vol. 2 of *The Apostolic Fathers: A New Translation and Commentary*. New York: Thomas Nelson, 1965.

Grayston, K., and G. Herdan. "The Authorship of the Pastoral Epistles in the Light of Statistical Analysis." *NTS* 6 (1959–60): 1–15.

Gregerman, Adam. *Building on the Ruins of the Temple: Apologetics and Polemics in Early Christianity and Rabbinic Judaism*. TSAJ 165. Tübingen: Mohr Siebeck, 2016.

Gruen, Erich S. *Cultural Identity in the Ancient Mediterranean (Issues & Debates)*. Los Angeles: Getty Research Institute, 2011.

———. *Culture and National Identity in Republican Rome*. London: Duckworth, 1993.

———. "Jews and Greeks as Philosophers: A Challenge to Otherness." Pages 402–22 in *The "Other" in Second Temple Judaism: Essays in Honor of John J. Collins*. Edited by Daniel C. Harlow et al. Grand Rapids: Eerdmans, 2011.

———. "Kinship Relations and Jewish Identity." Pages 101–16 in *Jewish Identities in Antiquity: Studies in Memory of Menahem Stern*. Edited by Lee I. Levine and Daniel R. Schwartz. Tübingen: Mohr Siebeck, 2009.

———. *Rethinking the Other in Antiquity*. Princeton: Princeton University Press, 2011.

Grundeken, Mark. *Community Building in the Shepherd of Hermas: A Critical Study of Some Key Aspects*. VCSup 131. Leiden: Brill, 2015.

Hagner, Donald Alfred. *The Jewish Reclamation of Jesus: An Analysis and Critique of Modern Jewish Study of Jesus.* Grand Rapids: Baker Academic, 1984.

———. *The Use of the Old and New Testaments in Clement of Rome.* NovTSup 34. Leiden: Brill, 1973.

Hahn, Ferdinand. *Mission in the New Testament.* Translated by Frank Clarke. London: SCM, 1965.

Hall, Edith. *Inventing the Barbarian: Greek Self-Definition through Tragedy.* Oxford: Clarendon, 1989.

Hall, Jonathan M. *Ethnic Identity in Greek Antiquity.* Cambridge: Cambridge University Press, 1997.

———. *Hellenicity: Between Ethnicity and Culture.* Chicago: University of Chicago Press, 2002.

Halliday, Michael A. K. *Language as Social Semiotic: The Social Interpretation of Language and Meaning.* London: Edward Arnold, 1978.

Hannestad, Niels. *Roman Art and Imperial Policy.* Aarhus: Aarhus University Press, 1986.

Hardwick, Lorna. "Concepts of Peace." Pages 335–68 in *Experiencing Rome: Culture, Identity and Power in the Roman Empire.* Edited by Janet Huskinson. London: Routledge, 2000.

Hare, Douglas R. A., and Daniel J. Harrington. "'Make Disciples of All the Gentiles' (Mt 28:19)." *CBQ* 37 (1975): 359–69.

Harland, Philip A. *Associations, Synagogues, and Congregations: Claiming a Place in Ancient Mediterranean Society.* Minneapolis: Fortress, 2003.

———. *Dynamics of Identity in the World of the Early Christians: Associations, Judeans, and Cultural Minorities.* New York: T&T Clark, 2009.

Harnack, Adolf von. *The Acts of the Apostles.* Translated by J. R. Wilkinson. London: Williams & Norgate, 1909.

———. *Einführung in die alte Kirchengeschichte: Das Schreiben der Römischen Kirche an die Korinthische aus der Zeit Domitians.* Leipzig: Hinrichs, 1929.

———. *Marcion: The Gospel of the Alien God.* Translated by John E. Steely and Lyle D. Bierma. Durham, NC: Labyrinth, 1990.

———. *The Mission and Expansion of Christianity in the First Three Centuries.* Translated by James Moffatt. London: Williams & Norgate, 1908.

Harris, William V. *War and Imperialism in Republican Rome, 327–70 B.C.* Oxford: Clarendon, 1979.

Harrison, P. N. *Polycarp's Two Epistles to the Philippians.* Cambridge: Cambridge University Press, 1936.

———. *The Problem of the Pastoral Epistles.* Oxford: Oxford University Press, 1921.

Hartin, Patrick J. *James and the Q Sayings of Jesus.* JSNTSup 47. Sheffield: JSOT Press, 1990.

Hartog, Paul, ed. *Polycarp's Epistle to the Philippians and the Martyrdom of Polycarp: Introduction, Text, and Commentary.* OAF. Oxford: Oxford University Press, 2013.

Hastings, Adrian. *The Construction of Nationhood: Ethnicity, Religion, and Nationalism.* Cambridge: Cambridge University Press, 1997.

Hayes, Christine. *Gentile Impurities and Jewish Identities: Intermarriage and Conversion from the Bible to the Talmud.* Oxford: Oxford University Press, 2002.

Hays, Richard B. "'Here We Have No Lasting City': New Covenantalism in Hebrews." Pages 151–73 in *The Epistle to the Hebrews and Christian Theology.* Edited by Richard Bauckham et al. Grand Rapids: Eerdmans, 2009.

Hellerman, Joseph H. *Jesus and the People of God: Reconfiguring Ethnic Identity.* Sheffield: Sheffield Phoenix, 2007.

Hellholm, David. "The Shepherd of Hermas." Pages 215–42 in *The Apostolic Fathers: An Introduction.* Edited by Wilhelm Pratscher. Waco, TX: Baylor University Press, 2010.

Hengel, Martin. *Between Jesus and Paul: Studies in the Earliest History of Christianity.* Translated by John Bowden. Philadelphia: Fortress, 1983.

Hill, Craig C. *Hellenists and Hebrews: Reappraising Division within the Earliest Church.* Minneapolis: Fortress, 1992.

Hill, Jonathan. *Christianity: How a Despised Sect from a Minority Religion Came to Dominate the Roman Empire.* Minneapolis: Fortress, 2011.

Himmelfarb, Martha. "The Parting of the Ways Reconsidered: Diversity in Judaism and Jewish-Christian Relations in the Roman Empire; A Jewish Perspective." Pages 47–61 in *Interwoven Destinies: Jews and Christians through the Ages.* Edited by Eugene J. Fisher. Mahwah, NJ: Paulist, 1993.

Hingley, Richard. *Globalizing Roman Culture: Unity, Diversity and Empire.* London: Routledge, 2005.

Hirschberg, Peter. "Jewish Believers in Asia Minor according to the Book of Revelation and the Gospel of John." Pages 217–38 in *Jewish Believers in Jesus.* Edited by Oskar Skarsaune and Reidar Hvalvik. Peabody, MA: Hendrickson, 2007.

Hodge, Caroline Johnson. *If Sons, Then Heirs: A Study of Kinship and Ethnicity in the Letters of Paul.* Oxford: Oxford University Press, 2007.

Holmberg, Bengt, and Mikael Winninge, eds. *Identity Formation in the New Testament.* Tübingen: Mohr Siebeck, 2008.

Holmes, Michael W. *The Apostolic Fathers.* Grand Rapids: Baker, 2006.

Horner, Timothy J. *Listening to Trypho: Justin Martyr's Dialogue Reconsidered.* CBET 28. Leuven: Peeters, 2001.

Horrell, David G. "'Race', 'Nation', 'People': Ethnic Identity-Construction in 1 Peter 2:9." *NTS* 58 (2011): 123–43.

———. *The Social Ethos of the Corinthian Correspondence: Interests and Ideology from 1 Corinthians to 1 Clement.* Edinburgh: T&T Clark, 1996.

Howard, George. *The Gospel of Matthew according to a Primitive Hebrew Text*. Macon, GA: Mercer University Press, 1987.
Hubbard, Benjamin J. *The Matthean Redaction of a Primitive Apostolic Commissioning: An Exegesis of Matthew 28:16-20*. SBLDS 19. Missoula, MT: Society of Biblical Literature, 1974.
Hultgren, Arland J. *The Rise of Normative Christianity*. Minneapolis: Fortress, 1994.
Hurtado, Larry W. *Lord Jesus Christ: Devotion to Jesus in Earliest Christianity*. Grand Rapids: Eerdmans, 2003.
Huskinson, Janet. "Élite Culture and the Identity of Empire." Pages 95-123 in *Experiencing Rome: Culture, Identity and Power in the Roman Empire*. Edited by Janet Huskinson. London: Routledge, 2000.
———, ed. *Experiencing Rome: Culture, Identity and Power in the Roman Empire*. London: Routledge, 2000.
———. "Looking for Culture, Identity and Power." Pages 3-27 in *Experiencing Rome: Culture, Identity and Power in the Roman Empire*. Edited by Janet Huskinson. London: Routledge, 2000.
Hvalvik, Reidar. "Jewish Believers and Jewish Influence in the Roman Church until the Early Second Century." Pages 179-216 in *Jewish Believers in Jesus: The Early Centuries*. Edited by Oskar Skarsaune and Reidar Hvalvik. Peabody, MA: Hendrickson, 2007.
———. *The Struggle for Scripture and Covenant: The Purpose of the Epistle of Barnabas and Jewish-Christian Competition in the Second Century*. WUNT 2.82. Tübingen: Mohr Siebeck, 1996.
Inge, William Ralph. "Essay I: Introductory." Pages 1-14 in *The Parting of the Roads: Studies in the Development of Judaism and Early Christianity*. Edited by F. J. Foakes-Jackson. London: Edward Arnold, 1912.
Isaac, Benjamin H. *The Invention of Racism in Classical Antiquity*. Princeton: Princeton University Press, 2004.
Isacson, Mikael. *To Each Their Own Letter: Structure, Themes, and Rhetorical Strategies in the Letters of Ignatius of Antioch*. ConBNT 42. Stockholm: Almqvist & Wiksell, 2004.
Jackson-McCabe, Matt, ed. *Jewish Christianity Reconsidered: Rethinking Ancient Groups and Texts*. Minneapolis: Fortress, 2007.
Jacobs, Andrew S. "The Lion and the Lamb: Reconsidering Jewish-Christian Relations in Antiquity." Pages 95-118 in *The Ways That Never Parted: Jews and Christians in Late Antiquity and the Early Middle Ages*. Edited by Adam H. Becker and Annette Yoshiko Reed. Minneapolis: Fortress, 2007.
Jenkins, Richard. *Social Identity*. 4th ed. New York: Routledge, 2014.
Jennings, Willie James. *The Christian Imagination: Theology and the Origins of Race*. New Haven: Yale University Press, 2010.
Jeremias, Joachim. *Jesus' Promise to the Nations*. SBT 24. London: SCM, 1958.

Jervell, Jacob. *Luke and the People of God*. Minneapolis: Augsburg, 1972.
Johnson, Aaron P. *Ethnicity and Argument in Eusebius' Praeparatio Evangelica*. Oxford: Oxford University Press, 2006.
Johnson, Luke Timothy. *The First and Second Letters to Timothy*. AB. New York: Doubleday, 2001.
Jonge, Marinus de. *The Testaments of the Twelve Patriarchs: A Critical Edition of the Greek Text*. Leiden: Brill, 1978.
Jossa, Giorgio. *Jews or Christians? The Followers of Jesus in Search of Their Own Identity*. WUNT 1.202. Tübingen: Mohr Siebeck, 2006.
Kaden, David A. "Flavius Josephus and the *Gentes Devictae* in Roman Imperial Discourse: Hybridity, Mimicry, and Irony in the Agrippa II Speech (*Judean War* 2.345–402)." *JSJ* 42 (2011): 481–507.
Kahl, Brigitte. *Galatians Re-imagined: Reading with the Eyes of the Vanquished*. Minneapolis: Fortress, 2010.
Kaminsky, Joel S. "Israel's Election and the Other in Biblical, Second Temple and Rabbinic Thought." Pages 17–30 in *The "Other" in Second Temple Judaism: Essays in Honor of John J. Collins*. Edited by Daniel C. Harlow et al. Grand Rapids: Eerdmans, 2011.
———. *Yet I Loved Jacob: Reclaiming the Biblical Concept of Election*. Nashville: Abingdon, 2007.
Kampen, John. *Matthew within Sectarian Judaism*. AYBRL. New Haven: Yale University Press, 2019.
Katz, Steven T. "Issues in the Separation of Judaism and Christianity After 70 CE: A Reconsideration." *JBL* 103 (1984): 43–76.
Käsemann, Ernst. *Commentary on Romans*. Translated and edited by Geoffrey W. Bromiley. Grand Rapids: Eerdmans, 1980.
Keener, Craig S. *Acts: An Exegetical Commentary*. 4 vols. Grand Rapids: Baker Academic, 2012–15.
Kelley, Shawn. *Racializing Jesus: Race, Ideology, and the Formation of Modern Biblical Scholarship*. London: Routledge, 2002.
Khomych, Taras. "Another Gospel: Exploring Early Christian Diversity with Paul and the Didache." Pages 455–76 in *The Didache: A Missing Piece of the Puzzle in Early Christianity*. Edited by Jonathan A. Draper and Clayton N. Jefford. ECL 14. Atlanta: Society of Biblical Literature, 2015.
Klausner, Joseph. *From Jesus to Paul*. New York: Macmillan, 1943.
———. *Jesus of Nazareth: His Life, Times and Teaching*. London: George Allen & Unwin, 1929.
Klijn, A. F. J. *Jewish-Christian Gospel Tradition*. VCSup 17. Leiden: Brill, 1992.
Kloppenborg Verbin, John S. *Excavating Q: The History and Setting of the Sayings Gospel*. Minneapolis: Fortress, 2000.

Knox, John. *Chapters in a Life of Paul*. 2nd ed. Macon, GA: Mercer University Press, 1987.
Konradt, Matthias. *Israel, Church, and the Gentiles in the Gospel of Matthew*. Translated by Kathleen Ess. Baylor-Mohr Siebeck Studies in Early Christianity. Waco, TX: Baylor University Press, 2014.
Kraft, Robert A. *Barnabas and the Didache*. Vol. 3 of *The Apostolic Fathers: A New Translation and Commentary*. New York: Thomas Nelson, 1965.
Kümmel, Werner Georg. *Introduction to the New Testament*. Translated by Howard Clark Kee. Nashville: Abingdon, 1975.
Lampe, Peter. *From Paul to Valentinus: Christians at Rome in the First Two Centuries*. Edited by Marshall D. Johnson. Translated by Michael Steinhauser. London: T&T Clark, 2003.
Lange, N. R. M. de. *Origen and the Jews: Studies in Jewish-Christian Relations in Third-Century Palestine*. Cambridge: Cambridge University Press, 1976.
Le Bas, Philippe, and W. H. Wadding. *Voyage archéologique en Grèce et en Asie Mineure*. Paris: Firmin-Didot, 1888.
Lechner, Thomas. *Ignatius adversus Valentinianos? Chronologische und theologiegeschichtliche Studien zu den Briefen des Ignatius von Antiochien*. VCSup 47. Leiden: Brill, 1999.
Levine, Amy-Jill. *The Social and Ethnic Dimensions of Matthean Salvation History*. Studies in the Bible and Early Christianity 14. Lewiston, NY: Edwin Mellen, 1988.
Levine, Lee I. "Jewish Identities in Antiquity: An Introductory Essay." Pages 12–40 in *Jewish Identities in Antiquity: Studies in Memory of Menahem Stern*. Edited by Lee I. Levine and Daniel R. Schwartz. Tübingen: Mohr Siebeck, 2009.
Lietzmann, Hans. *A History of the Early Church*. Translated by Bertram Lee Woolf. London: Lutterworth, 1961.
Lieu, Judith M. *Christian Identity in the Jewish and Graeco-Roman World*. Oxford: Oxford University Press, 2004.
———. *Image and Reality: The Jews in the World of the Christians in the Second Century*. Edinburgh: T&T Clark, 1996.
———. *Marcion and the Making of a Heretic: God and Scripture in the Second Century*. Cambridge: Cambridge University Press, 2015.
———. "'The Parting of the Ways': Theological Construct or Historical Reality?" *JSNT* 56 (1994): 101–19.
———. "The Race of the God-Fearers." *JTS* 46 (1995): 483–501.
Lightfoot, J. B. *The Apostolic Fathers: Clement, Ignatius, and Polycarp: Revised Texts with Introductions, Notes, Dissertations and Translations*. 5 vols. Peabody, MA: Hendrickson, 1989.

Lindemann, Andreas. *Die Clemensbriefe*. HNT 17. Die Apostolischen Väter 1. Tübingen: Mohr Siebeck, 1992.

Lofland, John, and Rodney Stark. "Becoming a World-Saver: A Theory of Conversion to a Deviant Perspective." *American Sociological Review* 30 (1965): 862–75.

Löhr, Hermut. "The Epistles of Ignatius of Antioch." Pages 91–115 in *The Apostolic Fathers: An Introduction*. Edited by Wilhelm Pratscher. Waco, TX: Baylor University Press, 2010.

Longenecker, Richard N. *Galatians*. WBC 41. Waco, TX: Word, 1990.

Lopez, Davina C. *Apostle to the Conquered: Reimagining Paul's Mission*. Minneapolis: Fortress, 2008.

Luz, Ulrich. *Matthew 21–28: A Commentary*. Translated by Wilhelm C. Linss. Hermeneia. Minneapolis: Fortress, 2005.

Lyman, Rebecca. "Justin and Hellenism: Some Postcolonial Perspectives." Pages 160–68 in *Justin Martyr and His Worlds*. Edited by Sara Parvis and Paul Foster. Minneapolis: Fortress, 2007.

Mack, Burton L. *The Christian Myth: Origins, Logic, and Legacy*. New York: Continuum, 2001.

——— . *A Myth of Innocence: Mark and Christian Origins*. Philadelphia: Fortress, 1988.

MacMullen, Ramsay. *Christianizing the Roman Empire (A.D. 100–400)*. New Haven: Yale University Press, 1984.

Maier, Harry O. *The Social Setting of the Ministry as Reflected in the Writings of Hermas, Clement, and Ignatius*. Waterloo, ON: Wilfrid Laurier University Press, 1991.

Malkin, Irad, ed. *Ancient Perceptions of Greek Ethnicity*. Center for Hellenic Studies Colloquia 5. Cambridge, MA: Harvard University Press, 2001.

Malony, H. Newton, and Samuel Southard, eds. *Handbook of Religious Conversion*. Birmingham, AL: Religious Education Press, 1992.

Marcus, Joel. "The Circumcision and the Uncircumcision in Rome." *NTS* 35 (1989): 67–81.

Marshall, I. Howard, with Philip H. Towner. *A Critical and Exegetical Commentary on the Pastoral Epistles*. ICC. Edinburgh: T&T Clark, 1999.

Marshall, John W. "Misunderstanding the New Paul: Marcion's Transformation of the *Sonderzeit* Paul." *JECS* 20 (2012): 1–29.

Martyn, J. Louis. *Galatians: A New Translation with Introduction and Commentary*. AB. New York: Doubleday, 1997.

Mason, Steve. *A History of the Jewish War, A.D. 66–74*. Cambridge: Cambridge University Press, 2016.

——— . *Josephus and the New Testament*. Peabody, MA.: Hendrickson, 2003.

——— . "'Should Any Wish to Enquire Further' (*Ant*. 1.25): The Aim and Audience of Josephus' *Judean Antiquities/Life*." Pages 64–103 in *Understanding Josephus:*

Seven Perspectives. Edited by Steve Mason. JSPSup 32. Sheffield: Sheffield Academic, 1998.
Mattingly, David J. *Imperialism, Power, and Identity: Experiencing the Roman Empire.* Princeton: Princeton University Press, 2011.
McKnight, Scot. *A Light among the Gentiles: Jewish Missionary Activity in the Second Temple Period.* Minneapolis: Fortress, 1991.
McNicol, Allan J. *The Conversion of the Nations in Revelation.* LNTS 438. London: T&T Clark, 2011.
Meier, John P. "Nations or Gentiles in Matthew 28:19?" *CBQ* 39 (1977): 94–102.
Meissner, Stefan. *Die Heimholung des Ketzers: Studien zur jüdischen Auseinandersetzung mit Paulus.* WUNT 2.87. Tübingen: Mohr Siebeck, 1996.
Meyer, Ben F. *The Early Christians: Their World Mission and Self-Discovery.* Wilmington, DE: Michael Glazier, 1986.
Miles, Richard, ed. *Constructing Identities in Late Antiquity.* London: Routledge, 1999.
Montefiore, Claude G. *Judaism and St. Paul: Two Essays.* London: Max Goschen, 1914.
———. *The Synoptic Gospels.* London: Macmillan, 1927.
Moore, George Foot. *Judaism in the First Centuries of the Christian Era.* 3 vols. Cambridge, MA: Harvard University Press, 1927–30.
Moxnes, Halvor. *Jesus and the Rise of Nationalism: A New Quest for the Nineteenth-Century Historical Jesus.* London: I. B. Taurus, 2012.
Muraoka, Takamitsu. *Classical Syriac: A Basic Grammar with a Chrestomathy.* PLO 19. Wiesbaden: Harrassowitz, 1997.
Murphy-O'Connor, Jerome. *Paul: A Critical Life.* Oxford: Clarendon, 1996.
———. "2 Timothy Contrasted with 1 Timothy and Titus." *RB* 98 (1991): 403–18.
Murray, Michele. *Playing a Jewish Game: Gentile Christian Judaizing in the First and Second Centuries CE.* ESCJ 13. Waterloo, ON: Wilfrid Laurier University Press, 2004.
Nasrallah, Laura, and Elisabeth Schüssler Fiorenza, eds. *Prejudice and Christian Beginnings: Investigating Race, Gender, and Ethnicity in Early Christian Studies.* Minneapolis: Fortress, 2009.
Neumann, Kenneth J. *The Authenticity of the Pauline Epistles in the Light of Stylo-Statistical Analysis.* Atlanta: Scholars Press, 1990.
Nicolet, Claude. *Space, Geography, and Politics in the Early Roman Empire.* Ann Arbor: University of Michigan Press, 1991.
Niederwimmer, Kurt. *The Didache: A Commentary.* Translation by Linda M. Maloney. Hermeneia. Minneapolis: Fortress, 1998.
Nock, Arthur Darby. *Conversion: The Old and the New in Religion from Alexander the Great to Augustine of Hippo.* London: Oxford University Press, 1933.
North, John. "The Development of Religious Pluralism." Pages 174–93 in *The Jews among Pagans and Christians in the Roman Empire.* Edited by Judith Lieu, John North, and Tessa Rajak. London: Routledge, 1992.

Novenson, Matthew V. *Christ among the Messiahs: Christ Language in Paul and Messiah Language in Ancient Judaism*. New York: Oxford University Press, 2012.

Oakes, Peter S. *Reading Romans in Pompeii: Paul's Letter at Ground Level*. Minneapolis: Fortress, 2009.

Ophir, Adi, and Ishay Rosen-Zvi. *Goy: Israel's Others and the Birth of the Gentile*. Oxford: Oxford University Press, 2018.

Osiek, Carolyn. *Rich and Poor in the* Shepherd of Hermas: *An Exegetical-Social Investigation*. CBQMS 15. Washington, DC: Catholic Biblical Association of America, 1983.

———. *Shepherd of Hermas: A Commentary*. Hermeneia. Minneapolis: Fortress, 1999.

Overman, J. Andrew. *Matthew's Gospel and Formative Judaism: The Social World of the Matthean Community*. Minneapolis: Fortress, 1990.

Paget, James Carleton. *The Epistle of Barnabas: Outlook and Background*. WUNT 2.64. Tübingen: Mohr Siebeck, 1994.

———. "Jewish Revolts and Jewish-Christian Relations." Pages 276–306 in *Jews and Christians in the First and Second Centuries: The Interbellum 70–132 CE*. Edited by Joshua Schwartz and Peter J. Tomson. CRINT 15. Leiden: Brill, 2018.

———. *Jews, Christians and Jewish Christians in Antiquity*. WUNT 1.251. Tübingen: Mohr Siebeck, 2010.

Parkes, James. *The Conflict of the Church and the Synagogue: A Study in the Origins of Antisemitism*. London: Soncino, 1934.

———. *The Jew and His Neighbour: A Study of the Causes of Anti-Semitism*. London: SCM, 1930.

Parsons, Mikeal C., and Richard I. Pervo. *Rethinking the Unity of Luke and Acts*. Minneapolis: Fortress, 1993.

Parvis, Sara. "Justin Martyr and the Apologetic Tradition." Pages 115–27 in *Justin Martyr and His Worlds*. Edited by Sara Parvis and Paul Foster. Minneapolis: Fortress, 2007.

Pedersen, Nils Arne. "Aristides." Pages 35–49 in *In Defence of Christianity: Early Christian Apologists*. Edited by Jakob Engberg, Anders-Christian Jacobsen, and Jörg Ulrich. Early Christianity in the Context of Antiquity 15. Frankfurt am Main: Peter Lang, 2006.

Pernot, Laurent. "Aelius Aristides and Rome." Pages 175–201 in *Aelius Aristides between Greece, Rome, and the Gods*. Edited by William V. Harris and Brooke Holmes. Columbia Studies in the Classical Tradition 33. Leiden: Brill, 2008.

Pfleiderer, Otto. *Primitive Christianity*. Translated by W. Montgomery. Edited by W. D. Morrison. London: Williams & Norgate, 1906.

Porton, Gary G. *Goyim: Gentiles and Israelites in Mishnah-Tosefta*. BJS 155. Atlanta: Scholars Press, 1988.

———. *The Stranger within Your Gates: Converts and Conversion in Rabbinic Literature*. Chicago: University of Chicago Press, 1994.
Pratscher, Wilhelm, ed. *The Apostolic Fathers: An Introduction*. Waco, TX: Baylor University Press, 2010.
———. "The Second Epistle of Clement." Pages 71–90 in *The Apostolic Fathers: An Introduction*. Edited by Wilhelm Pratscher. Waco, TX: Baylor University Press, 2010.
———. *Der zweite Clemensbrief*. Kommentar zu den Apostolischen Vätern 3. Göttingen: Vandenhoeck & Ruprecht, 2007.
Preston, Rebecca. "Roman Questions, Greek Answers: Plutarch and the Construction of Identity." Pages 86–119 in *Being Greek under Rome: Cultural Identity, the Second Sophistic and the Development of Empire*. Edited by Simon Goldhill. Cambridge: Cambridge University Press, 2001.
Prior, Michael. *Paul the Letter-Writer and the Second Letter to Timothy*. JSNTSup 23. Sheffield: Sheffield Academic, 1989.
Prostmeier, Ferdinand R. "The Epistle of Barnabas." Pages 27–45 in *The Apostolic Fathers: An Introduction*. Edited by Wilhelm Pratscher. Waco, TX: Baylor University Press, 2010.
Pummer, Reinhard. *The Samaritans: A Profile*. Grand Rapids: Eerdmans, 2016.
Räisänen, Heikki. "Paul's Conversion and the Development of His View of the Law." *NTS* 33 (1987): 404–19.
Rajak, Tessa. "Talking at Trypho: Christian Apologetic as Anti-Judaism in Justin's *Dialogue with Trypho the Jew*." Pages 59–80 in *Apologetics in the Roman Empire: Pagans, Jews, and Christians*. Edited by Mark Edwards, Martin Goodman, and Simon Price, in association with Christopher Rowland. Oxford: Oxford University Press, 1999.
Rambo, Lewis R. "The Psychology of Conversion." Pages 159–77 in *Handbook of Religious Conversion*. Edited by H. Newton Malony and Samuel Southard. Birmingham, AL: Religious Education Press, 1992.
———. *Understanding Religious Conversion*. New Haven: Yale University Press, 1993.
Rauschenbusch, Walter. *A Theology for the Social Gospel*. New York: Macmillan, 1917.
Reed, Annette Yoshiko. *Fallen Angels and the History of Judaism and Christianity: The Reception of Enochic Literature*. Cambridge: Cambridge University Press, 2005.
———. "'Jewish Christianity' as Counter-History? The Apostolic Past in Eusebius' *Ecclesiastical History* and the Pseudo-Clementine *Homilies*." Pages 171–216 in *Antiquity in Antiquity: Jewish and Christian Pasts in the Greco-Roman World*. Edited by Gregg Gardner and Kevin L. Osterloh. TSAJ 123. Tübingen: Mohr Siebeck, 2008.
Richardson, John. *The Language of Empire: Rome and the Idea of Empire from the*

Third Century BC to the Second Century AD. Cambridge: Cambridge University Press, 2008.

Richardson, Peter. *Israel in the Apostolic Church*. SNTSMS 10. Cambridge: Cambridge University Press, 1969.

Richardson, Peter, and Martin B. Shukster. "Barnabas, Nerva and the Yavnean Rabbis." *JTS* 34 (1983): 31–55.

Richter, Daniel S. *Cosmopolis: Imagining Community in Late Classical Athens and the Early Roman Empire*. Oxford: Oxford University Press, 2011.

Rives, James B. "Animal Sacrifice and Political Identity in Rome and Judea." Pages 105–25 in *Jews and Christians in the First and Second Centuries: How to Write Their History*. Edited by Peter J. Tomson and Joshua Schwartz. CRINT 13. Leiden: Brill, 2014.

———. "Religion in the Roman Empire." Pages 245–75 in *Experiencing Rome: Culture, Identity and Power in the Roman Empire*. Edited by Janet Huskinson. London: Routledge, 2000.

Rizzi, Marco. "Some Reflections on Origen, Celsus and Their Views on the Jews." Pages 37–59 in *Jews and Christians in Antiquity: A Regional Perspective*. Edited by Pierluigi Lanfranchi and Joseph Verheyden. Leuven: Peeters, 2018.

Robinson, James M. "LOGOI SOPHON: On the Gattung of Q." Pages 71–113 in *Trajectories through Early Christianity*. Edited by James M. Robinson and Helmut Koester. Philadelphia: Fortress, 1971.

Robinson, John A. T. "The Most Primitive Christology of All?" *JTS* 7 (1956): 177–89.

Robinson, Thomas A. *Ignatius of Antioch and the Parting of the Ways: Early Jewish-Christian Relations*. Peabody, MA: Hendrickson, 2009.

Rokéah, David. *Justin Martyr and the Jews*. JCP 5. Leiden: Brill, 2002.

Rosen-Zvi, Ishay, and Adi Ophir. "*Goy*: Toward a Genealogy." *Diné Israel* 28 (2011): 69–122.

———. "Paul and the Invention of the Gentiles." *JQR* 105 (2015): 1–41.

Rowe, C. Kavin. *World Upside Down: Reading Acts in the Graeco-Roman Age*. Oxford: Oxford University Press, 2009.

Rowland, Christopher. *Christian Origins: An Account of the Setting and Character of the Most Important Messianic Sect of Judaism*. 2nd ed. London: SPCK, 2002.

Ruether, Rosemary R. *Faith and Fratricide: The Theological Roots of Anti-Semitism*. Minneapolis: Seabury, 1974.

Runesson, Anders. *Divine Wrath and Salvation in Matthew: The Narrative World of the First Gospel*. Minneapolis: Fortress, 2016.

Runia, David T. "Philo and the Gentiles." Pages 28–45 in *Attitudes to Gentiles in Ancient Judaism and Early Christianity*. Edited by David C. Sim and James S. McLaren. LNTS 499. London: Bloomsbury T&T Clark, 2013.

Rutherford, Will. "*Altercatio Jasonis et Papisci* as a Testimony Source for Justin's 'Sec-

ond God' Argument." Pages 137-45 in *Justin Martyr and His Worlds*. Edited by Sara Parvis and Paul Foster. Minneapolis: Fortress, 2007.
Saldarini, Anthony J. *Matthew's Christian-Jewish Community*. Chicago: University of Chicago Press, 1994.
Sanders, E. P. *Jesus and Judaism*. Philadelphia: Fortress, 1985.
———. *Paul and Palestinian Judaism*. Philadelphia: Fortress, 1977.
Sandt, Huub van de. "Was the Didache Community a Group within Judaism? An Assessment on the Basis of Its Eucharistic Prayers." Pages 85-107 in *A Holy People: Jewish and Christian Perspectives on Religious Communal Identity*. Edited by Marcel Poorthuis and Joshua Schwartz. JCP 12. Leiden: Brill, 2006.
Schäfer, Peter. *Judeophobia: Attitudes toward the Jews in the Ancient World*. Cambridge, MA: Harvard University Press, 1997.
Schiffman, Lawrence H. *Who Was a Jew?* Hoboken, NJ: Ktav, 1985.
Schnabel, Eckhard J. *Early Christian Mission*. 2 vols. Downers Grove, IL: InterVarsity, 2004.
Schoedel, William R. *Ignatius of Antioch: A Commentary on the Letters of Ignatius of Antioch*. Hermeneia. Philadelphia: Fortress, 1985.
Schott, Jeremy M. *Christianity, Empire, and the Making of Religion in Late Antiquity*. Philadelphia: University of Pennsylvania Press, 2008.
Schüssler Fiorenza, Elisabeth. *In Memory of Her: A Feminist Theological Reconstruction of Early Christian Beginnings*. New York: Crossroad, 1983.
Schweitzer, Albert. *The Mystery of the Kingdom of God: The Secret of Jesus' Messiahship and Passion*. Translated by Walter Lowrie. New York: Dodd, Mead, 1914.
———. *The Mysticism of Paul the Apostle*. Translated by W. Montgomery. London: A. & C. Black, 1931.
———. *Paul and His Interpreters*. Translated by W. Montgomery. London: A. & C. Black, 1950.
Scott, James C. *Domination and the Arts of Resistance: Hidden Transcripts*. New Haven: Yale University Press, 1990.
Scott, James M. *Paul and the Nations*. WUNT 1.84. Tübingen: Mohr Siebeck, 1995.
Sechrest, Love L. *A Former Jew: Paul and the Dialectics of Race*. London: T&T Clark, 2009.
Segal, Alan F. *Paul the Convert: The Apostolate and Apostasy of Saul the Pharisee*. New Haven: Yale University Press, 1990.
———. *Rebecca's Children: Judaism and Christianity in the Roman World*. Cambridge, MA: Harvard University Press, 1986.
Sevenster, J. N. *The Roots of Pagan Anti-Semitism in the Ancient World*. NovTSup 41. Leiden: Brill, 1975.
Shillington, V. George. *An Introduction to the Study of Luke-Acts*. London: T&T Clark, 2007.

Siker, Jeffrey S. *Disinheriting the Jews: Abraham in Early Christian Controversy.* Louisville: Westminster John Knox, 1991.
Sim, David C. *The Gospel of Matthew and Christian Judaism: The History and Social Setting of the Matthean Community.* Edinburgh: T&T Clark, 1998.
Simon, Marcel. *Verus Israel: Étude sur les relations entre Chrétiens et Juifs dans l'Empire Romain, 135–425.* Paris: E. de Boccard, 1948.
———. *Verus Israel: A Study of the Relations between Christians and Jews in the Roman Empire, 135–425.* Translated by H. McKeating. New York: Oxford University Press, 1986.
Skarsaune, Oskar. "The Development of Scriptural Interpretation in the Second and Third Centuries—Except Clement and Origen." Pages 373–442 in *Hebrew Bible/Old Testament: The History of Its Interpretation.* Vol. 1, *From the Beginnings to the Middle Ages (Until 1300).* Edited by Magne Sæbø. Göttingen: Vandenhoeck & Ruprecht, 1996.
———. "Does the Letter to the Hebrews Articulate a Supersessionist Theology? A Response to Richard Hays." Pages 174–82 in *The Epistle to the Hebrews and Christian Theology.* Edited by Richard Bauckham et al. Grand Rapids: Eerdmans, 2009.
———. *The Proof from Prophecy: A Study in Justin Martyr's Proof-Text Tradition; Text-Type, Provenance, Theological Profile.* NovTSup 56. Leiden: Brill, 1987.
Skarsaune, Oskar, and Reidar Hvalvik, eds. *Jewish Believers in Jesus: The Early Centuries.* Peabody, MA: Hendrickson, 2007.
Smith, Anthony D. *The Ethnic Origin of Nations.* Oxford: Blackwell, 1986.
Smith, Daniel A. *The Post-mortem Vindication of Jesus in the Sayings Gospel Q.* LNTS 338. London: T&T Clark, 2006.
Smith, R. R. R. "*Simulacra Gentium*: The *Ethnē* from the Sebasteion at Aphrodisias." *JRS* 78 (1988): 50–77.
Snow, David A., and Cynthia L. Phillips. "The Lofland-Stark Conversion Model: A Critical Reassessment." *Social Problems* 27 (1980): 430–47.
Snow, David A., and Richard Machalek. "The Convert as a Social Type." Pages 259–89 in *Sociological Theory.* Edited by Randall Collins. San Francisco: Jossey-Bass, 1983.
———. "The Sociology of Conversion." *Annual Review of Sociology* 10 (1984): 167–90.
Snyder, Graydon F. *The Shepherd of Hermas.* Vol. 6 of *The Apostolic Fathers: A New Translation and Commentary.* Camden, NJ: Thomas Nelson, 1967.
Soards, Marion L. *The Speeches in Acts: Their Content, Context, and Concerns.* Louisville: Westminster John Knox, 1994.
Sokoloff, Michael. *A Syriac Lexicon: A Translation from the Latin: Correction, Expansion, and Update of C. Brockelmann's Lexicon Syriacum.* Winona Lake, IN: Eisenbrauns; Piscataway, NJ: Gorgias, 2009.

Sollors, Werner. "Foreword: Theories of American Ethnicity." Pages x–xliv in *Theories of Ethnicity: A Classical Reader*. Edited by Werner Sollors. London: Macmillan, 1996.
Soskice, Janet. *The Sisters of Sinai: How Two Lady Adventurers Discovered the Hidden Gospels*. New York: Alfred A. Knopf, 2009.
Soulen, R. Kendall. *The God of Israel and Christian Theology*. Minneapolis: Fortress, 1996.
Spawforth, Antony. "Shades of Greekness: A Lydian Case Study." Pages 375–400 in *Ancient Perceptions of Greek Ethnicity*. Edited by Irad Malkin. Center for Hellenic Studies Colloquia 5. Cambridge, MA: Harvard University Press, 2001.
Spilsbury, Paul. *The Image of the Jew in Flavius Josephus' Paraphrase of the Bible*. TSAJ 69. Tübingen: Mohr Siebeck, 1998.
Spitta, Friedrich. *Jesus und die Heidenmission*. Giessen: Alfred Töpelmann, 1909.
Stanton, Graham. "Jewish Christian Elements in the Pseudo-Clementine Writings." Pages 305–24 in *Jewish Believers in Jesus*. Edited by Oskar Skarsaune and Reidar Hvalvik. Peabody, MA: Hendrickson, 2007.
Stark, Rodney. *The Rise of Christianity: A Sociologist Reconsiders History*. Princeton: Princeton University Press, 1996.
Sterling, Gregory E. *Historiography and Self-Definition: Josephos, Luke-Acts, and Apologetic Historiography*. NovTSup 64. Leiden: Brill, 1992.
Stern, Menahem. *Greek and Latin Authors on Jews and Judaism*. 3 vols. Jerusalem: Israel Academy of Sciences and Humanities, 1974–84.
Stewart-Sykes, Alistair. *From Prophecy to Preaching: A Search for the Origins of the Christian Homily*. VCSup 59. Leiden: Brill, 2001.
Swain, Simon. *Hellenism and Empire: Language, Classicism, and Power in the Greek World, AD 50–250*. Oxford: Oxford University Press, 1996.
Tajfel, Henri, ed. *Social Identity and Intergroup Relations*. European Studies in Social Psychology. Cambridge: Cambridge University Press; Paris: Editions de la maison des sciences de l'homme, 1982.
———. *Human Groups and Social Categories: Studies in Social Psychology*. Cambridge: Cambridge University Press, 1981.
Tarn, William W. "Alexander the Great and the Unity of Mankind." *Proceedings of the British Academy* 19 (1933): 123–66.
Taylor, Brian. "Conversion and Cognition: An Area for Empirical Study in the Micro-Sociology of Religious Knowledge." *Social Compass* 23 (1976): 5–22.
———. "Recollection and Membership: Converts' Talk and the Ratiocination of Commonality." *Sociology* 12 (1978): 316–24.
Taylor, Miriam S. *Anti-Judaism and Early Christian Identity: A Critique of the Scholarly Consensus*. StPB 46. Leiden: Brill, 1995.
Tomson, Peter J. "The Didache, Matthew, and Barnabas as Sources for Early Second

Century Jewish and Christian History." Pages 348–82 in *Jews and Christians in the First and Second Centuries: How to Write Their History*. Edited by Peter J. Tomson and Joshua Schwartz. CRINT 13. Leiden: Brill, 2014.

———. "The Halakhic Evidence of *Didache* 8 and Matthew 6 and the *Didache* Community's Relationship to Judaism." Pages 131–41 in *Matthew and the Didache: Two Documents from the Same Jewish-Christian Milieu?* Edited by Huub van de Sandt. Assen: Royal Van Gorcum; Minneapolis: Fortress, 2005.

Trebilco, Paul R. *Outsider Designations and Boundary Construction in the New Testament: Early Christian Communities and the Formation of Group Identity*. Cambridge: Cambridge University Press, 2017.

Trevett, Christine. *A Study of Ignatius of Antioch in Syria and Asia*. Studies in the Bible and Early Christianity 29. Lewiston, NY: Edwin Mellen, 1992.

Tromp, Johannes. *The Assumption of Moses: A Critical Edition with Commentary*. SVTP 10. Leiden: Brill, 1993.

Tucker, J. Brian. *You Belong to Christ: Paul and the Formation of Social Identity in 1 Corinthians 1–4*. Eugene, OR: Pickwick, 2010.

Turner, John C., and Michael A. Hogg. *Rediscovering the Social Group: A Self-Categorization Theory*. Oxford: Blackwell, 1987.

Ulrich, Jörg. "Justin Martyr." Pages 51–66 in *In Defense of Christianity: Early Christian Apologists*. Edited by Jakob Engberg, Anders-Christian Jacobsen, and Jörg Ulrich. Frankfurt am Main: Peter Lang, 2006.

Vaage, Leif E. "Why Christianity Succeeded (in) the Roman Empire." Pages 253–78 in *Religious Rivalries in the Early Roman Empire and the Rise of Christianity*. Edited by Leif E. Vaage. Waterloo, ON: Wilfrid Laurier University Press, 2006.

VanderKam, James C. *The Book of Jubilees: English and Ethiopic*. CSCO 510–11. Leuven: Peeters, 1989.

Vogt, Katja Maria. *Law, Reason and the Cosmic City: Political Philosophy in the Early Stoa*. Oxford: Oxford University Press, 2008.

Voltaire. *Histoire de l'établissement du Christianisme*. Pages 43–116 in *Oeuvres complètes*, vol. 31. Paris: Garnier frères, 1877–85.

Walaskay, Paul W. *"And So We Came to Rome": The Political Perspective of St. Luke*. SNTSMS 49. Cambridge: Cambridge University Press, 1983.

Walker, Rolf. *Die Heilsgeschichte im ersten Evangelium*. FRLANT 91. Göttingen: Vandenhoeck & Ruprecht, 1967.

Wallace-Hadrill, Andrew. *Rome's Cultural Revolution*. Cambridge: Cambridge University Press, 2008.

Webster, Jane, and Nicholas J. Cooper. *Roman Imperialism: Post-colonial Perspectives*. Leicester: University of Leicester, 1996.

Wells, Peter S. *The Barbarians Speak: How the Conquered Peoples Shaped Roman Europe*. Princeton: Princeton University Press, 1999.

Wendel, Susan J. *Scriptural Interpretation and Community Self-Definition in Luke-Acts and the Writings of Justin Martyr.* NovTSup 139. Leiden: Brill, 2011.
Wengst, Klaus. *Pax Romana and the Peace of Jesus Christ.* Translated by John Bowden. Philadelphia: Fortress, 1987.
Werline, Rodney A. "The Transformation of Pauline Arguments in Justin Martyr's *Dialogue with Trypho.*" *HTR* 92 (1999): 79-93.
White, Benjamin L. "The Eschatological Conversion of 'All the Nations' in Matthew 28.19-20: (Mis)Reading Matthew through Paul." *JSNT* 36 (2014): 353-82.
Wilken, Robert L. *The Christians as the Romans Saw Them.* New Haven: Yale University Press, 1984.
Wilson, Stephen G. *Leaving the Fold: Apostates and Defectors in Antiquity.* Minneapolis: Fortress, 2004.
———. *Related Strangers: Jews and Christians, 70-170 C.E.* Minneapolis: Fortress, 1995.
Wire, Antoinette Clark. *The Corinthian Women Prophets: A Reconstruction through Paul's Rhetoric.* Minneapolis: Fortress, 1990.
Woolf, Greg. "Becoming Roman, Staying Greek: Culture, Identity and the Civilizing Process in the Roman East." *Proceedings of the Cambridge Philological Society* 40 (1994): 116-43.
———. *Rome: An Empire's Story.* Oxford: Oxford University Press, 2012.
———. *Tales of the Barbarians: Ethnography and Empire in the Roman West.* Malden, MA: Wiley-Blackwell, 2011.
Yoder, John Howard. *The Jewish-Christian Schism Revisited.* Edited by Michael G. Cartwright and Peter Ochs. Grand Rapids: Eerdmans, 2003.
Zahn, Theodor. *Ignatius von Antiochien.* Gotha: F. A. Perthes, 1873.
Zangenberg, Jürgen K. "Reconstructing the Social and Religious Milieu of the Didache: Observations and Possible Results." Pages 43-69 in *Matthew, James, and Didache: Three Related Documents in Their Jewish and Christian Settings.* Edited by Huub van de Sandt and Jürgen K. Zangenberg. SBL Symposium Series 45. Atlanta: Society of Biblical Literature, 2008.
Zanker, Paul. *The Power of Images in the Age of Augustus.* Translated by Alan Shapiro. Ann Arbor: University of Michigan Press, 1988.

Author Index

Abraham, Susan B., 67
Alexander, Philip S., 52, 389
Anderson, Benedict, 64
Ando, Clifford, 80, 83, 84, 88, 91, 92, 99
Ascough, Richard S., 77, 255
Aune, David E., 164, 223, 224, 225, 226
Avidov, Avi, 88

Badian, Ernst, 73
Bainbridge, William Sims, 319
Baird, William, 156
Balsdon, J. P. V. D., 88, 93, 94, 98, 101
Bamberger, Bernard J., 115, 116
Barclay, John M. G., 81, 117, 118, 122
Barnard, Leslie William, 394, 401, 411
Barnes, Timothy D., 14, 475
Barrett, C. K., 153, 156, 167, 170, 185, 211, 326, 378
Barth, Fredrik, 56–59, 320
Bates, Matthew W., 408
Bauckham, Richard, 47, 51, 171, 199, 222, 223, 225, 241, 420
Bauer, Walter, 49

Baur, F. C., 43, 156, 157, 166
Becker, Adam H., 14, 41, 47, 48, 49, 198
Becker, Jürgen, 160
Beker, J. Christiaan, 160
Berger, Peter L., 58, 76
Berthelot, Katell, 147
Betz, Hans Dieter, 192
Bhabha, Homi K., 67–69, 419
Bickerman, Elias, 71, 72, 94, 95
Billings, Drew W., 382
Bird, Michael F., 181
Birnbaum, Ellen, 145
Bosch, David J., 182
Bowe, Barbara Ellen, 354
Boyarin, Daniel, 48, 49–50, 52–53, 417
Bremmer, Jan N., 16
Brett, Mark G., 60, 109
Brown, Raymond E., 170, 187, 205
Brunt, P. A., 84, 85, 90
Buell, Denise Kimber, 55, 60, 65, 389, 417, 419, 455
Bultmann, Rudolf, 160
Burton, Ernest de Witt, 160

AUTHOR INDEX

Caird, G. B., 179
Cameron, Averil, 464–65, 471, 476
Cameron, Ron, 163
Carleton Paget, James, 14, 312, 359
Cassidy, Richard J., 382
Chadwick, Henry, 423, 428
Chilton, Bruce, 420
Clark, Kenneth W., 195, 215, 430
Cohen, Shaye J. D., 106, 116
Collins, John J., 108, 117, 169, 228, 340
Collins, Raymond F., 367, 369, 387
Concannon, Cavan W., 119, 310, 323, 324
Conzelmann, Hans, 176, 367, 369
Cooper, Nicholas J., 80
Crüsemann, Frank, 109

Dahl, Nils A., 222
Dahlheim, Werner, 79, 80
Davila, James R., 199
Dench, Emma, 60, 72, 74, 79, 83, 84, 86, 87, 88, 92, 94, 100, 281
Dibelius, Martin, 367, 369
Dilke, O. A. W., 83
Dobbeler, Axel von, 217
Dodd, C. H., 169, 181
Donaldson, Terence L., 15, 18, 41, 42, 112, 114, 117, 122, 126, 131, 180, 184, 189, 205, 213, 227, 234, 240, 326, 377, 388
Donfreid, Karl Paul, 334
Draper, Jonathan A., 196, 219, 220, 221, 222
Dunn, Geoffrey D., 50, 434, 437
Dunn, J. D. G., 47, 48, 52, 156, 159, 160, 162, 171, 172, 174–75, 178, 184, 185, 186, 191, 214, 239, 389

Edwards, Catharine, 83, 84, 87, 95, 247
Edwards, Mark, 394, 423
Ehrman, Bart D., 334, 348, 353, 354, 359
Elgvin, Torleif, 199, 227, 228, 229–30
Elliott, Mark Adam, 183

Elmer, Ian J., 197
Enslin, Morton Scott, 47
Esler, Philip F., 60, 67
Evans, Craig A., 198, 209

Feldman, Louis H., 104, 317, 429
Ferguson, Niall, 77
Filtvedt, Ole Jakob, 241
Finlan, Stephen, 222, 233
Foakes Jackson, F. J., 38, 46
Foster, Paul, 388, 418, 419, 420
Frede, Michael, 423
Fredriksen, Paula, 66, 185, 320, 327, 403, 412, 425, 437
Frend, W. H. C., 16
Freyne, Seán, 165, 178, 182
Fuller, Reginald H., 170, 191

Gager, John G., 104, 317, 437
Garber, Zev, 46
Gardner, Gregg, 14, 83, 109, 111
Gaston, Lloyd, 195, 215
Gaventa, Beverly Roberts, 66, 320
Geiger, Joseph, 101
Gibbon, Edward, 16
Gilbert, Gary, 107
Goffman, Erving, 62
Goldenberg, Robert, 106, 119
Goldhill, Simon, 60, 98, 100
Goodman, Martin, 113, 180, 394
Grabbe, Lester L., 113
Graham, Holt H., 353
Grant, Robert M., 353
Grayston, K., 365
Gregerman, Adam, 400, 414
Gruen, Erich S., 59, 60, 72, 111, 112
Grundeken, Mark, 341, 345

Hagner, Donald A., 46, 353, 354
Hahn, Ferdinand, 165, 174, 181, 182, 183
Hall, Edith, 60, 72

512

Hall, Jonathan, 55, 57, 58, 60, 70, 72, 74
Halliday, Michael A. K., 149
Hannestad, Niels, 84
Hardwick, Lorna, 90, 98, 101
Hare, Douglas R. A., 215
Harland, Philip A., 60, 77, 118, 255
Harnack, Adolf von, 16, 44, 50, 156, 169, 180, 182, 354, 411, 430, 454, 455, 464
Harrington, Daniel, 215
Harris, J. Rendel, 372, 373, 374
Harris, William V., 7, 79
Harrison, P. N., 331, 332, 365, 370
Hartin, Patrick J., 163
Hartog, Paul, 331, 332
Hastings, Adrian, 64, 480–81
Hayes, Christine, 107, 116, 143
Hays, Richard B., 241, 420
Hellerman, Joseph H., 60
Hellholm, David, 340, 341
Hengel, Martin, 165, 166, 167, 174, 178, 179, 187
Herdan, G., 365
Hill, Craig C., 166
Hill, Jonathan, 16
Himmelfarb, Martha, 47, 51
Hingley, Richard, 59, 78, 79, 80, 84, 87, 88, 91, 92, 93
Hirschberg, Peter, 224, 225
Hodge, Caroline Johnson, 60
Hogg, Michael A., 79, 205
Holmberg, Bengt, 60
Holmes, Michael W., 332, 336
Horner, Timothy J., 418
Horrell, David G., 242, 354, 358
Howard, George, 198
Hubbard, Benjamin J., 191
Hultgren, Arland J. 163
Hurtado, Larry, 157, 163, 164, 171, 172, 368–69
Huskinson, Janet, 78, 80, 84, 90, 94, 95, 96, 98, 101

Hvalvik, Reidar, 14, 198, 199, 224, 346, 354, 357, 359, 360, 361, 362, 364

Inge, W. R., 45–46, 78
Isaac, Benjamin H., 60, 104, 317
Isacson, Mikael, 347

Jackson-McCabe, Matt, 14
Jacobs, Andrew S., 49
Jefford, Clayton N., 219, 220, 222
Jenkins, Richard, 56, 57, 58, 59, 61, 62, 63, 129, 321, 322
Jennings, Willie, 478
Jeremias, Joachim, 181
Jervell, Jacob, 381, 382
Johnson, Aaron P., 16, 377, 437, 452
Johnson, Luke Timothy, 366, 367, 368, 369, 371
Jonge, Marinus de, 227
Jossa, Giorgio, 51

Kaden, David A., 285
Kahl, Brigitte, 84, 302, 323
Kaminsky, Joel S., 106
Käsemann, Ernst, 214
Katz, Steven T., 48
Keener, Craig S., 154, 211, 378
Kelley, Shawn, 60
Khomych, Taras, 219
Klausner, Joseph, 46, 47
Klijn, A. F. J., 198
Kloppenborg, John S., 77, 162, 163, 195, 208, 255
Knox, John, 160
Konradt, Matthias, 195, 215, 216, 217
Kraft, Robert A., 362, 363
Kümmel, Werner Georg, 378

Lampe, Peter, 340, 341, 354
Lange, N. R. M. de, 426, 437
Le Bas, Philippe, 254

513

AUTHOR INDEX

Lechner, Thomas, 332
Levine, Amy-Jill, 216, 217, 232
Levine, Lee I., 102, 106, 112
Lietzmann, Hans, 16
Lieu, Judith M., 47–49, 50, 113, 348, 389, 390, 421, 430, 433, 455
Lightfoot, J. B., 332, 333, 334, 336, 347, 348, 354
Lindemann, Andreas, 353, 354, 355
Lofland, John, 319
Löhr, Hermut, 347
Longenecker, Richard N., 159
Lopez, Davina C., 309, 323
Luckmann, Thomas, 58
Luz, Ulrich, 232
Lyman, Rebecca, 419

Machalek, Richard, 66, 319
Mack, Burton L., 163
MacMullen, Ramsay, 16
Maier, Harry O., 340, 341
Malkin, Irad, 55, 60, 73
Malony, H. Newton, 66, 319
Marcus, Joel, 200
Marshall, Howard, 366–67, 369, 371
Marshall, John W., 432
Martyn, J. Louis, 158, 174, 236, 327
Mason, Steve, 118, 122, 130, 285
Mattingly, David J., 77, 78, 79, 80, 81, 98, 101
McKnight, Scot, 180
McNicol, Allan J., 222, 223, 226
Meier, John P., 215, 216
Meissner, Stefan, 47
Meyer, Ben F., 164, 165, 174, 178, 179, 182, 187
Miles, Richard, 80, 81
Miller, David M., 126
Miller, Merrill P., 163
Minns, Denis, 387, 396, 407, 410, 422
Montefiore, Claude, 46, 47

Moore, George Foot, 46
Moxnes, Halvor, 64, 480
Muraoka, Takamitsu, 374
Murphy-O'Connor, Jerome, 157, 159, 365, 370
Murray, Michele, 226

Nasrallah, Laura, 60
Neumann, Kenneth J., 365
Nicolet, Claude, 83, 84, 86, 87, 90, 281, 288–89
Niederwimmer, Kurt, 218, 219, 220
Nock, Arthur Darby, 16
North, John, 113
Novenson, Matthew V., 164

Oakes, Peter S., 323
Ophir, Adi, 108, 135, 136, 144
Osiek, Carolyn, 254, 340, 341, 344, 345
Osterloh, Kevin L., 14, 83, 109, 111
Overman, J. Andrew, 216, 217

Parkes, James, 38–39, 41, 46, 47–48, 51, 437
Parsons, Mikeal C., 378
Parvis, Paul, 387, 396, 407, 410, 422
Parvis, Sara, 388, 418, 419, 420
Pedersen, Nils Arne, 373
Pernot, Laurent, 7, 31, 32
Pervo, Richard I., 378
Pfleiderer, Otto, 45
Phillips, Cynthia L., 319
Pierre, Marie-Joseph, 372, 373, 374, 375
Porton, Gary G., 115, 116, 143
Pouderon, Bernard, 372, 373, 374, 375
Pratscher, Wilhelm, 333, 334, 337, 362
Preston, Rebecca, 100
Prior, Michael, 365
Prostmeier, Ferdinand R., 362
Pummer, Reinhard, 153

Räisänen, Heikki, 160
Rajak, Tessa, 113, 394
Rambo, Lewis, 66, 319
Rauschenbusch, Walter, 44
Reed, Annette Yoshiko, 14, 41, 47, 48, 49, 198, 411
Richardson, John, 77, 83, 87, 257
Richardson, Peter, 236, 361, 401
Richter, Daniel, 7, 33, 59, 72, 73, 74, 75, 76, 94, 95, 98, 100–101, 109, 111
Rives, James B., 101, 327
Rizzi, Marco, 422, 426
Robinson, J. Armitage, 372, 373
Robinson, James M., 162, 163, 195, 208
Robinson, John A. T., 170
Robinson, Thomas A., 47, 347, 352
Rokéah, David, 389, 399, 420
Rosen-Zvi, Ishay, 108, 135, 136, 144
Rowe, C. Kavin, 382
Rowland, Christopher, 174, 394
Ruether, Rosemary R., 437–38
Runesson, Anders, 195, 217, 232
Runia, David T., 121, 145, 149–50
Rutherford, Will, 417

Saldarini, Anthony J., 216, 217
Sanders, E. P., 181, 182, 237
Sandt, Huub van de, 219, 222
Schäfer, Peter, 104, 317
Scheck, Thomas P., 432
Schiffman, Lawrence H., 52
Schnabel, Eckhard J., 182, 184
Schoedel, William R., 347, 348, 349–50, 351, 352
Schott, Jeremy M., 71, 74–75, 80, 81, 88, 95, 112, 411, 423, 429, 467, 471, 472
Schüssler Fiorenza, Elisabeth, 60, 323
Schweitzer, Albert, 44–45, 181
Scott, James C., 67–68, 89, 293, 297
Scott, James M., 254
Sechrest, Love L., 60

Segal, Alan F., 48, 52, 66, 320
Sevenster, J. N., 104
Shillington, V. George, 378
Shukster, Martin B., 361
Siker, Jeffrey S., 400, 437
Sim, David C., 121, 196, 197, 216, 217, 232
Simon, Marcel, 50, 392, 437
Skarsaune, Oskar, 14, 198, 199, 224, 227, 346, 356, 381, 393, 394, 402, 417, 418, 420
Smith, Anthony D., 60, 106
Smith, Daniel A., 163
Smith, R. R. R., 83–84, 247, 258, 281
Snow, David A., 66, 319
Snyder, Graydon F., 345, 346
Soards, Marion L., 164–65
Sokoloff, Michael, 374
Sollors, Werner, 58–59
Soskice, Janet, 372
Soulen, R. Kendall, 42, 392
Southard, Samuel, 66, 319
Spilsbury, Paul, 145
Spitta, Friedrich, 181
Stanton, Graham, 199, 209
Stark, Rodney, 15, 16, 33, 319, 476
Sterling, Gregory E., 110, 156, 378
Stern, Menahem, 102, 106, 109, 317
Stewart-Sykes, Alistair, 333
Swain, Simon, 74, 98

Tajfel, Henri, 58, 62–64, 65, 67
Tarn, William W., 73
Taylor, Brian, 66, 320
Taylor, Miriam S., 50, 360
Tomson, Peter J., 219, 311, 313, 327, 360
Towner, Philip H., 366
Trevett, Christine, 348, 349, 352
Tromp, Johannes, 139
Tucker, J. Brian, 67
Turner, John C., 67, 205

Ulrich, Jörg, 373, 411, 414

Vaage, Leif E., 189, 464
VanderKam, James C., 140
Vogt, Katja Maria, 75
Voltaire, 16

Wadding, W. H., 254
Walaskay, Paul W., 382
Walker, Rolf, 195, 215
Wallace-Hadrill, Andrew, 78, 80, 81, 97, 101–2, 105, 119
Webster, Jane, 80
Wells, Peter S., 60
Wendel, Susan J., 126, 381
Wengst, Klaus, 358, 382
Werline, Rodney A., 400, 420

White, Benjamin L., 217
Wilken, Robert L., 410, 423, 424, 427
Wilson, Stephen G., 48, 65, 241, 350, 359, 360, 361, 376, 380, 382, 393, 404, 418, 431
Winninge, Mikael, 60
Wire, Antoinette Clark, 323
Woolf, Greg, 59, 60, 70, 77, 80, 83, 87, 88, 91, 92, 95, 98, 101, 112, 247

Yarbro Collins, Adela, 191
Yoder, John Howard, 417, 481

Zahn, Theodor, 347, 348
Zangenberg, Jürgen K., 219
Zanker, Paul, 83, 84, 85, 87, 89, 90, 92, 93, 94, 97

Subject Index

Abraham, 106, 109, 113, 228, 228n214, 229n217, 363, 405, 445; Apocalypse of, 127; as a Chaldean by birth, 114–15; children/descendants of, 390–91, 420, 477; Jewish ancestors of, 111n22; journey of, to Ur of the Chaldees, 112; role of, as father, 115–16; seed of (*sperma*), 235–36, 240–41n232, 434

Acts of Augustus (Augustus), 85, 86, 86n143, 89–90, 246, 257, 279, 292, 302n116, 451; on the establishment of peace, 295; on the temple of Janus, 298

Acts of the Apostles, 11, 151, 152n2, 157, 195, 325

Adam, contrast with Christ, 235

Address to the Greeks (Tatian), 458

adversus Judaeos, 38, 40, 42, 357, 384, 388, 410, 416, 418, 437, 440, 444, 457–58; depiction of Judaism in, 49–50n38; Justin Martyr's development of, 393–94; as a literary tradition, 437n119

Aelius Aristides, 1, 7–11, 12, 26–29, 27nn49–52, 89, 92, 97, 98, 123n63, 259–60n45, 290, 298, 377n202; description of the metaphorical clothing of the nations, 303–4, 303n117; oration of, in the court of Antoninus Pius, 32; on the pantheon of Greek gods, 10; view of barbarians, 374–75.

Aeneid (Virgil), 86–87, 94–95, 287, 292

Against Apion (Josephus), 110

Against Celsus (Origen), 449, 456, 456n178, 467

Against the Jews (Tertullian), 436, 445

Agrippa II, 11, 13, 89n158, 123n64, 285–86, 434

Alexander the Great, 8, 73–74, 100, 285, 462, 464

Altar of Peace, 85–86, 90

Antioch, 186–87, 311, 326, 358; church of, 154, 155; mixed-ethnic community in, 160

Antiochus, 300

Antiquities (Josephus), 71, 110, 142

anti-Semitism, 38, 40, 40–41n11, 47, 477

517

SUBJECT INDEX

Antitheses (Marcion), 423
Apocalypse of Abraham, 108
Apollonius of Tyana, 74n99
"Apologia for Jewish Believers" (Pseudo-Clementine), 228–29
Apology of Aristides, 330, 372–77
apostleship, 183–84, 192, 192n115
Appian, 258–59, 268–69, 284, 290, 302–3
Aristobulus, 111n25
Arminius, 249n16
Aseneth, 113, 114; otherness of, 113–14n33
astrology: Chaldean, 112; polytheistic, 112
Athenagoras, 259, 452, 468–69
Augustus (Caesar Augustus), 4, 24, 82, 83, 87, 260, 272, 279, 301, 377; inscriptions of, 85–86; triumphs of, 283, 304. *See also Acts of Augustus*

Babylon, 134, 141, 241n233
Balaam, 123, 124, 148
Balak, 123, 148
barbarians, 4, 10, 14, 22, 29, 30, 71–72, 72n95, 96, 100, 101, 147, 148n150, 374, 384, 410, 412; Aristides's view of, 374–75; characteristics of, 69–70; distinction of, from Greeks, 74, 253; division of the world into Greeks and barbarians, 93, 116, 146, 308, 450, 453–54, 479; Josephus's view of, 147–48; and Judaism, 454, 454n166; Rome's position concerning, 245, 277, 279, 296–97, 301n114, 309, 469; and the truth about God, 459, 459n184
Bar Kokhba revolt, 40, 40n9, 313–14; *ethnē* and identity between destruction of Jerusalem and Bar Kokhba revolt, 329–86 *passim*; outbreak of, 361

Barnabas, 154, 155, 156, 186
Bernice, 11
Berosus of Babylon, 263
Biblical Antiquities (Pseudo-Philo), 125, 126, 139
bifurcation: bifurcation models, 44–45; within Judaism, 45
"biographical reconstruction," 66
Birkat Haminim, 39, 39n5, 40n9
Book of Eldad and Modat, 346
boundary/boundaries: between Greeks and barbarians, 74, 119, 253, 479; between Jews and gentiles, 17, 49, 51, 53, 106–7, 218–19, 239, 399, 406, 410, 435; between Jews and Judaism, 400, 410, 451, 476–77; between Jews and non-Jews, 108, 117, 120–21, 124, 129–30, 322; language of, 17–18
Byzantine Caesarea, 15n19

Caesennius Gallus, 258
Calpurnius Siculus, 287n96
Cassius Dio, 259, 260, 260n46, 284, 302, 302n116
Celsus, 422–29, 422n77, 445; attack of, on Christians, 426, 429n99; on proper worship, 427; and religious ethnography of the Jews, 425–26
Cestius, 258
Chaldeans, 446
Christ-belief/believers, 38, 159, 162, 165, 168, 171, 177, 181, 182, 191, 225, 230, 243, 311–14, 378, 381; among Christians, 404; among non-Jews, 153, 206; early form of, 169, 170–71, 173, 179–80, 230, 369; evangelizing activity of, 186; gentile, 194, 197n129, 206–7, 226, 312, 314, 323, 335–36, 369, 385; Jerusalem Christ-believers, 188; Jewish, 176–79, 179–80n82, 194, 197,

Subject Index

198, 199, 208, 209–11, 211n170, 226–27, 229, 230–31, 239, 240n232, 321, 328–29, 344n95, 346, 381–82, 392n16, 393, 420, 447n144, 472, 477; non-Jewish, 204, 379; Paul's view of, 174; primary types of, 315–17; relationship of, with Israel, 316–17; spread of, 245
Christian identity, gentile, 6–7, 37–54 *passim*, 98, 152, 237–38n229; and the antipodal model, 42–43, 44; ascribed identities, 194–243 *passim*, 207n156, 207–8n157; construction of, 13–36 *passim*; and concept of replacement, 41–43; ethnicity and social identity, 54–69; significance of, 51; social identity as dynamic, 63; and social mobility, 65–66; typology of, 206–12. *See also* parting-of-the-ways model
Christianity, 14, 14n16, 17, 23, 32, 34, 35, 37, 39n4, 53n45, 179n81, 417n63, 420; Catholic Christianity, 46; as continuation of a bifurcation already present in Judaism, 43–44; diversity as a feature of, 15; early Christianity, 43, 45; Hellenistic Jewish Christianity, 166–67; Ignatius's view of, 351–52; Jewish origins of, 384; Orthodox Christianity, 48; proto-orthodox forms of, 42–43, 312, 447; and race, 64–65n72; relationship with Judaism, 423–24; spread of, 449–50. *See also* Jewish Christianity
Christianization: of the *ethnē*, 406–22, 448, 460; of the Roman Empire during the imperial period, 15, 33, 78, 81–82, 476
Christians, 23, 29–30, 40–41n11, 42, 69, 351, 363, 374, 382, 385, 388, 400, 422, 433, 454–55, 466–67, 472–73; as the actualization of the divine promise to Abraham, 416; adherence of, to "true doctrine," 428; Celsus's attack on, 426; early, 39, 39n6; gentile, 360, 417, 434, 447–48, 477–79; Jewish (Judeo-Christians), 39–40, 40n9; as "masters of the whole world," 428; as a nation, 461; as a new and distinct "people," 390–91; non-Jewish, 54–55, 61, 472; and observance of the new law, 449–50; origins of, 163n39, 384; place of, in Roman Empire, 469–70; rejection of Jewish ancestral traditions by, 429; revolt against the Jews, 426–27; and the rhetoric of empire, 464–65n195
Christology, 168–69, 177, 188, 348; Christological meaning of Scripture, 392; exaltation Christology, 172, 172n66
Chrysippus, 75
Cicero, 82, 91, 262, 278–79, 281–82, 291, 294n106, 295, 295n107, 304; on Roman clemency (benevolent character of Roman rule), 294–97; on Roman imperial ideology, 299
Cilicia, 326
circumcision, 148–49n152, 159, 159–60n28, 187, 200n140, 207–8n157, 403
citizenship, 114, 451, 452; Athenian, 88; Roman, 88, 296, 299, 299n112, 300–301; Zeno's conception of, 75–76
classics/classical studies, 79, 79n116
Claudius, 85, 95, 97, 247, 260, 266, 281
Clement of Alexandria, 45, 358–59, 384, 449, 451; philosophy of, 454n168
Commodus, 451, 452, 468
Conflict of the Church and the Synagogue, The (Parkes), 38
Constantine, 1, 2, 2n1, 31, 434; embrace of Christianity by, 479–80

SUBJECT INDEX

Controversy between Jason and Papiscus, 418
conversion, 66
Corinth, 203, 235, 236, 314, 334, 353, 355, 358
Corinthians, 323–24n36
Cornelius (of Caesarea), 34, 153n6, 153–54n7
cosmopolitanism, 75n104; Stoic, 75, 76; transethnic, 70, 116
Crassus, 279
criteria/indicia distinction, 57n50
"cultural triangulation," 101
Cyprian, 437–39, 439n124, 444
Cyrus (*Kyrō*), 363n157

David, 397, 406
Dead Sea Scrolls, 47
Demetrius the Chronographer, 110
demons, 2–4, 6, 20–21, 452, 455, 457, 470; defeat of, 460–61; demonic forces at work in the polytheistic structure of nations, 5; power of, 3, 19, 23, 411–13, 415–16, 460; resistance to, 412, 460; "wicked demons," 415
Demonstration of the Gospel (Eusebius), 23–24, 23–24n36, 35
Dialogue with Trypho (Justin Martyr), 49, 387–88, 387–88n2, 389–90, 407–9, 413, 418
Didache, 196, 196n123, 202, 218–21, 218n187, 231, 233, 339, 360n150
Dio Chrysostom, 252, 261–62, 262n50
Diodorus Siculus, 69, 71, 265, 265n57, 268, 270n61, 271, 276, 292; on Roman citizenship, 300–301
Dionysius of Corinth, 354
Dionysius of Halicarnassus, 90n160, 98, 99–100, 266n59, 267–68, 280, 289, 296; on Roman citizenship, 300–301;
on Rome's ambition, 280, 289; on Rome's rise to prominence, 296
disciples, the, 4, 44, 154, 164–65, 168, 181, 183, 231, 233, 448; of Galilee, 167; gentile, 217–18, 232; Jesus's command to, 19, 202, 208, 209n161, 214–16, 232n220; mission of, 6, 190, 314
docetism, 348, 348n11
Domitian, 283, 354, 468
Dulgubnii, the, 273

Egypt/Egyptians, 74–75, 74–75n102, 101, 138, 229, 334, 446; polytheism of, 458
ekklēsia, 152, 173, 179n81, 204, 233–36, 238, 380, 382–83; of Antioch, 185, 186; earthly, 337; Jewish, 161n131, 184, 185–86n95; Paul on, as new human community, 236–37; spiritual, 337
Eleazar, 120, 126
Enlightenment, 43
Epistle of Barnabas, 330, 358–64, 360n150, 385, 386, 417; author of, 359–60; occurrences of *ethnē* in, 361, 363
Epistle of Jeremiah, 141
Epistle to Diognetus, 451, 454
Erfinder motif, 71–72, 74, 110, 116
eschatology, 45, 168, 172, 177, 188, 206, 226; Jewish, 165; national, 120–21; Zion, 227–28
ethnē, 17–19, 23, 33, 69, 73, 132–33, 137, 138, 141, 141n130, 142, 194, 237–38n229, 238, 239, 241, 242, 247n13, 277–78, 472–73; appearance of, in 2 Timothy, 370–71; "believers from the *ethnē*," 204–5; Christ-believing *ethnē*, 243; Christianization of, 406–22, 448, 460; of foreign nations, 154–55; governors of, 259n43; as an identity term, 54–55, 308–9; in inscriptions, 257n37, 258n42,

520

275n74; and the Jewish nation, 193; Justin Martyr on the Jews and, 399–406; for nations other than the Greeks, 254n26; as the other, 62; Paul's use of the term, 204–5; people of, 211–12; perspective of, in Ephesians, 197n128; plural forms of, 222–23, 378–79; as referencing those outside the Christ community, 203–4, 383; Roman interpretation of, 255–56; scriptural citations of, 199–201; structural role of, 272–73; twofold aspect of, 223–25; use of, in the universal sense, 383–84; various uses of, 60–61. *See also ethnē* and gentile Christian identity

ethnē, and gentile Christian identity, 310–11, 367–68, 383, 387–88; *ethnē* and identity construction after Justin, 434–73 *passim*; *ethnē* and identity construction between destruction of Jerusalem and Bar Kokhba revolt, 329–86 *passim*; *ethnē* and identity up to 70 CE, 322–29; questions concerning, 311–22

ethnicity, and identity, 35, 54–69 *passim*; Barth's view of, 56–59; shared characteristics of ethnic identity, 55–56; and the study of nations/groups in antiquity, 59–60. *See also* Jewish identity construction, in the Greco-Roman world

ethnography/ethnographers, 69–70; theological ethnography, 17, 20, 30

ethnology: aggregative, 112, 113; competitive, 109, 124, 128, 277, 307, 309, 416, 421, 429, 452; theological, 34, 435

ethnos, 222, 222n198, 242, 245, 246, 246n5, 247n13, 257, 308–9, 424n83; the "great *ethnos*" promised to Abraham, 434; of the Jews, 274n71; Josephus's use of, 258; use of, to denote jurisdictional territories, 258–59

Eusebius, 1, 7n6, 12, 23n34, 32, 429, 435, 467, 473; Church of the Holy Sepulchre oration of, 13; as a debater, 30; distinction of, between Hebrews and Jews, 21; on ethnic maps of the world, 22–23; on a nation's *politeia*, 3; on political disputes, 3; and praise of Greeks, 22–23; theological ethnography of, 17, 20, 30; on transethnic character of the Christian movement, 16; three modes of religion of, 23–25; use of Roman imperial ideology by, 30–31; on the victory of Christ's death, 4

evangelization, 153, 160

Exposition, the, 121, 121n58

external categorization/internal self-definition dialectic, 61–62

Festus, 11, 13

First Apology (Justin Martyr), 318n20, 388, 391, 394–96, 400, 401, 406–7, 409, 412–15, 419

First Clement, 353-58

Flaccus, 119–20

Florus, 279, 282, 289n99

Gaius (emperor), 297
Gaius (*Institutes*), 91, 253
Gaius Gracchus, 248n14
Gaius Memmius, 279
Galatia, 326–27
Galilee, 154, 163, 167, 258
Gallogrecians, 264–65, 276
Gaul/Gauls, 264–65, 265n57, 266n59, 270–71, 274n72
Genesis, genealogical system of, 109n12
genos ("race," "human race"), 8, 18,

521

SUBJECT INDEX

27, 74, 101, 200n138, 242, 245, 246n5, 405, 407, 409, 415; as designation for the Christian collective, 389; of the "God-fearers," 446, 459; *pan genos anthrōpōn*, 2, 146, 147, 252, 394; of the righteous, 345

gens/gentes, 139, 139–40n127, 246, 246n7, 247nn12–13, 248–50, 249n17, 250–51, 257, 277–78, 385n228; Alpine *gentes*, 275n74; as denoting a group of individuals, 260–61n47; *exterae gentes*, 255–56; as interchangeable with *nationes*, 436n111; structural role of, 272–73; as term for outsiders, 333

gentiles, 12, 18–19, 161n31, 184, 202, 237, 350, 352, 369–70; Paul's mission among, 51. *See also* boundary/boundaries: between Jews and gentiles; Christ-belief/believers: gentile; Christian identity, gentile; disciples: gentile

Geography (Strabo), 87, 263–64, 272

German Idealism, 43

Germany/Germans, 265–67, 270–71, 273, 273n68, 274n72, 283

Gnosticism, 312, 348n112, 367n169

God, 106, 123–25, 130–31, 134, 164, 337–38n70, 367, 398; covenant of, 107; as Creator, 375–76; forgiveness of, 237; as the God of Jesus, 430; as the God over all things, 424; providence of, 229n216; purpose of, in seeking a new people from "the other nations," 457–58; transfer of favor of, from Israel to the gentile church, 440–45; will of, 424n87

Gospel of Thomas, 161n32

gôyîm, 18n25, 115, 142n131, 143; plural of, 131–32, 131n79, 137, 143–44; representational overtone of, 140–41

Greeks, 4, 9n11, 10, 14, 29, 30, 31–32, 71–72, 130, 147, 148n150, 266n59, 294, 374, 374n194, 384, 446; belief of civilization's origins in Egypt, 74–75n102; distinction of, from barbarians, 74, 253; division of the world into Greeks and barbarians, 93, 116, 146, 308, 450, 453–54, 479; Greek pantheon of gods, 375; Josephus's view of, 147–48; Rome's position concerning, 245, 277; under the Ptolemies, 105

heavenly bodies, worship of, 20, 20–21n31

Hebrew Gospel of Matthew, 198, 198n133

Hebrews, 240–41n232; distinction of, from Jews, 42–43; nation of, 23–25; relevance of, 196n125

Hellenism/Hellenists, 88, 116, 186; spread of, 72–73

Hellenization, 101, 104

Herod, 24

Herodotus, 55, 55–56n46, 69, 74, 273n67

Hesiod, 10, 107n8

Hippolytus, 459–60, 467

history/historiography, 116; ethnic historiography, 71–72; historical writing, 69–70

Holocaust, 47

Holy Spirit, the, 174–75, 177, 183, 187, 448; outpouring of, "on the nations," 228

Horace, 252–53

Hosea, 439

humanitas, 91–92, 93–94, 97, 98, 100, 294, 308; alignment of, with *paideia*, 98

Hymn for a New Age (Horace), 87

hymns, christological, 368–69

522

Subject Index

identity binary, 131–32, 135–36, 333, 399
idolatry, 112, 112n30, 115, 391–92, 401, 403, 421, 426, 456–57; folly of, 127; lawless, 204, 241; of Solomon, 397
ideology. *See* Roman imperial ideology
Idumea, 134
Ignatius, 330, 331, 352n123, 383n223, 386; on Christianity, 351–52; letters of, 346–51; use of *ethnē* by, 349
imperialism, 82; anti-imperialism, 80n118; cultural, 104; modern, 79
India, 274n70
Institutes (Gaius), 253
internal/external perception distinction, 64
Irenaeus, 438, 439n124, 443; on Gnosticism, 456n178
Israel, 211–12, 316–17; commonwealth of, 239, 240; institutions of, 189; nation of, 123; rejection of the Jewish nation, 392; special status of, 232

Jacob, 24, 404–5; and Laban, 439
Jeremiah, 134
Jerusalem, 184, 358; banishment of Jews from, 392; centrality of, 378n205; destruction of temple and, 18n26, 25–26, 42, 128n73, 194, 313, 322, 392, 403n37, 419. *See also* Jerusalem community; Jerusalem Council
Jerusalem community, 51, 154, 158–59, 166, 167n53, 187, 194, 208, 215n180
Jerusalem Council, 185–86n95, 190–91, 203
Jesus Christ, 2, 30, 207, 209, 232, 238, 337–38n70, 348, 350, 372, 384n225, 385, 419, 449–50; birth of, 422; contrast with Adam, 235; death of, 157; as firstborn of all creation, 238n230; *gentes* heritage of, 451n153; as the *logos*, 412–13; as Messiah, 316, 346, 433; mission of, 181–82; mistreatment of, 228; and the new covenant, 25, 240–41n232; new law of, 361; power of, 413–14, 414n60; resurrection of, 164–65, 165n45; revelation of, 3–4; significance of, for the *ethnē*, 404; as the Son of God, 375n197; teaching/message of, 6, 17; soteriological significance of death of, 176; sovereignty of, 191; victory of, 4
Jewish Antiquities (Josephus), 119n54, 123–24n26, 145n139, 148n150
Jewish Christianity, 14–15, 14–15nn17–18
Jewish Christ-movement, 151, 162–63, 162n33, 167, 176, 184, 187–88, 206; Jewish-Christ communities, 161; Jewish Christ-communities and the gentiles, 152–93 *passim*
Jewish diaspora, 180, 182–83n89
Jewish identity construction, in the Greco-Roman world, 103–28 *passim*. *See also* identity binary
Jews, 21, 29–30, 73, 108, 124, 237, 240–41n232, 242, 349–50, 352, 374, 374n194, 375–76, 376n200, 428n97, 454–55; Alexandrian, 119–20; distinction of, from Hebrews, 42–43; Greco-Roman attitude toward, 40; as a new race, 454n170; punishment of, 25–26, 25n41; revolts of, 312–14; within Celsus's religious ethnography, 425–26. *See also* boundary/boundaries: between Jews and gentiles; boundary/boundaries: between Jews and Judaism; Christians: Jewish (Judeo-Christians); Jewish Christianity; Judaism; Jewish identity construction, in the Greco-Roman world; Law of Moses

523

SUBJECT INDEX

John (author of Revelation), 226n210
John, Gospel of, 240–41n232
John the Baptist, 161–62, 443
Jonathan, 113
Josephus, 24, 85, 118, 118n50, 119n54, 122, 135, 258n41, 286; account of the Jewish war with Rome, 292–93, 306–7; on the misfortunes of the Jews, 124; readings of the blessings by, 123–24; view of Greeks and barbarians, 147–48
Jubilees, 108, 124, 125, 127n71, 130–31, 139, 140–41n129, 147; character of, 139–40n127
Judah, 24, 134; Jacob's blessing of, 441; revolt, of against Rome, 151
Judaism, 37, 39, 39n4, 40, 42, 50, 53n45, 350, 351, 454, 454n166; bifurcation within, 45–47; Christian movement within, 163n39, 384, 386; first-century, 44n20; Hellenistic, 44; ineffectiveness of, 392; pre-rabbinic, 108n10; rabbinic, 48; and rabbinic literature, 143n135; relationship of, with Christianity, 423–24. *See also* boundary/boundaries: between Jews and Judaism; Second Temple Judaism
Judaizing, 348, 348n112, 350, 362, 364, 367n169
Judas, 138
Julius Caesar, 244, 244n2, 270, 274n72, 282
justification by faith, 235
Justin Martyr, 49, 53, 62, 227n212, 318n20, 421, 428, 430, 435, 437, 447n144, 451, 460; development of the *adversus Judaeos* by, 393–94. *See also* Justin Martyr, *ethnē* as an identity term in the writings of
Justin Martyr, *ethnē* as an identity term in the writings of, 389–94, 417n63; and the Greek version of the Scriptures, 415–16; on the Jews and the *ethnē*, 399–406; on the redrawn map of the human race, 414–15; Scripture, Christ, and the *ethnē*, 394–99, 397n27, 398n28

kalōs, 214, 214n175
Kerygma Petri, 454
Kulturbringer motif, 71–72, 110, 112, 116

laos (people), 65, 132–34, 146, 245, 246n5, 355, 357, 390–91, 442–43, 459n184; as a designator for the Christian collective, 389
Law of Moses, 23, 25, 26, 40n8, 42, 117, 120, 187, 326, 421, 445, 453–54, 458; at the level of symbol and shadow, 21–22
legalism, 45
Letter of Aristeas, 120
literature, Jewish, 134–35
Livy, 95, 252, 272, 276, 279, 281n85, 287, 299–300
logos, 415; Christ as, 412–13; indwelling of, 411; seed of, 410–11, 412
Lucius, 415
Luke-Acts, 377–85, 417

Maccabees, nationalism of, 44, 44n20
Marcion, 429–34; and concept of the two Christs, 430–33; as the "wolf of Pontus," 429
Marcionism, 433
Marcus Agrippa, 83, 96, 302
Marcus Aurelius, 247n13, 388n4, 415, 451, 452, 467, 468
Martial, 283
Matthew, Gospel of: gentile bias of, 215; and the Torah, 232n220

524

Subject Index

Melchizedek, 445
Melito of Sardis, 444n134, 446n142, 449, 467, 468, 470
migration, 112–13; transmigrations, 453n163
Minucius Felix, 463, 463n192
Moab, 134
Moessian, 279
monotheism, 424; ethical, 116–17, 217n185
Mosaic covenant, 231, 237, 315, 392, 433, 446–47, 478
Moses, 111, 111n23, 147, 209, 229, 381, 406, 427, 433, 446; blessing of Joseph by, 408n48; and Rahab, 439–40. *See also* Law of Moses; Mosaic covenant; Testament of Moses

natio/nationes, 246, 246n7, 248–49, 250–51, 275n74, 277–78, 448; as interchangeable with *gentes*, 436n111; structural role of, 272–73
nations, in Roman imperial discourse, 244–45, 286, 307; general considerations of vocabulary and usage concerning, 245–77 *passim*
Neoplatonism, 76, 116
Nicolas of Damascus, 302
Nicolaus of Antioch, 184
Noah, 242, 431, 445
non-Jews, 108, 117, 124, 130, 141, 186, 239, 323, 325, 325–26n40; Christ-belief among, 153, 206; non-Jewish Christians, 54–55, 61, 472; non-Jewish nations, 125, 135, 136; sexual intercourse with, 139; terms denoting, 435–36

On Architecture (Vitruvius), 87
144,000, in Revelation, 224, 224n205, 225–26

On Rewards and Punishments (Philo), 121
On the Holy Sepulchre (Eusebius), 1–7, 15, 17, 28, 473; as an apologetic work, 29; contrast between Jews and gentiles in, 19
orbis terrarum ("the whole earth," "the inhabited world"), 82, 85, 86n143, 87–88, 92, 244, 252, 262, 277; and Caesar, 279, 282; civilizing agent within, 96
Origen, 418n66, 423n80, 425, 438–39, 441, 443, 449–51, 461, 468; on Jesus as more powerful than all rulers, 460; on what constitutes a nation, 452n159
"other," the, 62, 253

paganism, 166n49, 361; classical, 15, 33, 476
panta ta ethnē (all the nations), 6, 16, 24, 122, 133, 134, 190, 193, 201–2, 216–17, 216–17n183, 224n207, 227, 231–32, 268, 371, 452, 456, 464; as a collection of individuals, 371; inclusive reading of, 216, 232–33; and the people of Christ, 467; plural form of, 222; as a reference to humankind in its totality, 338; as the sphere of apostolic proclamation, 346; universal denotation of, 252
parousia, 176, 193, 194, 207, 208, 217, 232, 316–17; delay of, 173–75, 380
particularism, Jewish, 64
parting-of-the-ways model, 35, 37–39, 41–42, 47–54, 48–49n35, 64, 312, 476
Pastoral Epistles, 197, 329, 364–65, 367n169, 368–70
Paul, 1, 17, 19, 20, 32, 46–47, 156, 157–58, 186, 211n170, 366, 370, 379n213; apostolic commission of, 189–90, 192, 192n115; as the apostle of the *ethnē*,

366; on the collection of the saints, 212; Damascus experience of (conversion of), 12–13, 155, 157, 157n18, 158, 160, 378; early years of, as believer in Christ, 154–55; on the *ekklēsia* as a new human community, 236–37; on the Holy Spirit, 175; letters of, 152n2, 155–57, 159–60, 171–72, 213, 234–35, 237, 324–25; mission of, among the gentiles, 51, 154–55; persecuting activity of, 159, 160n30; speech of, recorded in Acts 25:23–26:32, 11–13; and term "the Israel of God," 236, 236n227

Persian Empire, 291

Peter, 18, 153–54, 164, 172n66, 189, 190, 197n129, 229; as the "apostle for the circumcised," 158–59

Pharisaism/rabbinism, 39

Philip the Arab, 423n80

Philip V of Macedon, 74, 299, 300

Philo, 44, 114, 115, 118, 119n54, 121, 135, 145n139, 147n148, 297; and account of benevolent Roman rule, 301, 301n115; attitude of, toward gentiles, 149; on location of Jews as barbarian, 147n148; and realities of Jewish existence, 122

philosophy, 130n78, 459–60; Greek, 117

piety, Christian doctrine of, 4–5

Plato, 111, 147n148, 454n169, 459

Pliny the Elder, 85, 272, 275n74, 277n75, 279, 282n87; on divine providence for Rome, 305–6, 306n119

Pliny the Younger, 94, 282

Plutarch, 73, 98, 99, 100, 284, 305

politeia, 3, 20, 99, 118, 298n10, 353, 358, 454n169; Christian, 409, 451, 452–53; common, 27, 458; of Israel, 239; Mosaic, 25; Roman, 415

political discourse, 68n84

Polybius, 82, 98, 99, 271, 290n103; on fall of Carthage, 261

Polycarp, 330, 330n52, 331–33, 335, 346, 385n228

Polyhistor, Alexander, 110

Pompey, 282, 284, 286, 300

populi, 245, 257n35, 260, 272, 280, 431, 438n121; *duo populi*, 440n125, 442–43; *omnes populi*, 91n135, 252, 253; *populi Romani*, 255, 277

populus, 248, 248–49n15

Porticus Vipsania, 83, 85

postcolonialism, 67, 68, 80n118, 81n121

Preparation for the Gospel (Eusebius), 29, 35

Prescription against Heretics (Tertullian), 448–49

prophets, on the rejection of the Jews foretold by God, 392–93

proselytism, 113, 126, 179, 185, 187n99, 198, 210n168, 221; criticism of, 232; hard-line, 131n79

provincia, 257–58, 257n39

Psalms of Solomon, 128n73, 138

Pseudo-Clementine, 198, 209, 228–29

Pseudo-Philo, 125

Q document, 162, 163, 163n36, 195–96, 195n120, 202, 208, 322

Quintilian, 250, 262

Quintus, 294

Recognitions (Pseudo-Clementine), 209, 209nn162–63

Refutation of All Heresies (Hippolytus), 459–60

Regarding Rome (Aelius Aristides), 7–11, 26, 30–31, 89, 297, 302–3; as a representation of imperial ideology, 29, 30–31

Subject Index

replacement model, 41–43, 50, 211n167, 213–14, 214n177, 457; and rejection, 328, 440, 457; replacement theology, 336, 337
Rhetoric for Herennius, 278
rhetoric versus reality debate, 49–50n38
R. Judah, 115
Roman Antiquities (Dionysius of Halicarnassus), 280
Roman Empire/Rome, 26, 28–29, 35–36, 67, 128, 184n93, 249n16, 260, 334, 358; benefits of rule of, 90–91, 97, 298–99n111, 301–4; Christianization of, 15, 33, 78, 476; clemency of, in victory (benevolent character of rule of), 291–305; coinage of, 84; conception of the Roman *imperium*, 278, 279; connection of Roman rule to Roman law, 91–92; as conqueror, 284–85; examples of imperial inscriptions, 85–86, 270, 302n116; extent of, 26–27, 291; founding of, 265n56; government of, 9; and Greece, 97–98; identity, ethnicity, and power in, 69–102 *passim*; and ideology that empire was foreordained by the gods (divine providence), 92–93, 305–6; and language of empire, 82–83; and markers of imperial reality, 82–83, 86–87, 88–89; mixed-ethnic community in, 160; narrative of progress in, 77–78; nations as a fundamental constituent of, 278; and the *pax Romana*, 87–88; sovereignty of, 280, 287, 288, 290, 297, 299, 305; transcending of ethnic boundaries in, 76–77; and transformation of Romans into Greeks, 99–100; universality of rule of, 89–90, 287–88, 289, 290n103, 307–8; visual representations of, 83–85, 83–84n130, 88–89. *See also* citizenship: Roman; nations, in Roman imperial discourse; Roman imperial ideology
Roman imperial ideology, 32, 123, 245, 269, 272–73, 277–309 *passim*, 476, 479; Cicero's view of, 299; dual message of, 96; and the gods, 92–93, 304–6; main themes of, 307–8, 463; place of nations in, 277; use of, by Eusebius, 30–31
Romanization, 78–79, 80–81, 92, 104, 105
Romulus, 97
Rullus, 287

salience, concept of, 205, 205n150
salvation, 188, 191, 334, 362n156; gentile, 212–13; opportunity for, 210–11
Samaritans, 153
Sebasteion in Aphrodisias, 83–84, 90, 247, 281
Second Clement, 333–38, 338n59
Second Jewish Revolt, 40n9
Second Sophistic, 98, 98n194
Second Temple Judaism, 47, 107, 135, 137, 165n45, 178, 188
Seleucids, 105
Severan dynasty, 34, 82
Shepherd of Hermas, 330, 338–46, 341n84, 342n90, 345–46n100, 385; use of *ethnē* in, 343n94, 345
Simon, 138, 145n139
Socrates, 72n95, 76, 412
Solomon, 397, 462
sons of light/sons of darkness binary, 108–9n11
soteriology, 168, 175, 177, 188; and significance of Christ's death, 176
Spain, 266, 283n88
Stoicism, 75–76; pantheistic *logos* of, 116

527

SUBJECT INDEX

Strabo, 87, 253–54n25, 263–65, 264–65nn53–55, 268n60, 272
Suebi, the, 244, 244n2, 249–50, 267
Suetonius, 279–80, 295
supersessionism, 42, 211, 239, 329, 336, 361, 392, 448, 478, 479n6; ethnic, 207n156, 316n16; forms of, 42n15; proto-, 324, 328; theology, 211n167
Syria, 101, 326, 334, 348

Tacitus, 130n76, 244n2, 264, 267, 273n66, 282
Tatian, 452, 458
Tertullian, 430n103, 434n110, 443, 445–46, 460n186, 464, 468; on Christians as a *gens*, 449n150; on the geographical expansion of the church, 461–63; on the place of Christians in the Roman Empire, 469–70; on transmigrations, 453n163
Testament of Moses, 108, 124–25, 127n72, 139, 161
Testaments of the Twelve Patriarchs, 200, 227, 229–30
Testimonies against the Jews (Cyprian), 437–39, 439n124
theocracy, 118
theology, 40, 42, 76, 205, 332; geopolitical, 92; natural, 127–28; penitential, 340; replacement, 336; supersessionist, 211
Theophilus of Antioch, 458–59
Tiberius Caesar, 282n87, 283, 377
Titus, 302, 306
Torah, 106–7, 221, 232n220; translation of, into Greek, 120
To the Philippians (Polycarp), 330, 330n52, 331–33, 335
Trajan, 39n7, 255n32, 282n87, 300, 347

transethnic concepts, 73, 275, 320, 388; and Christianity, 480; transethnic character of the Christian movement, 16; transethnic character of Jewish identity, 104; transethnic church, 17, 461, 479; transethnic communities, 76; transethnic cosmopolitanism, 70, 116; transethnic grouping, 454–55; transethnic ideals/aspirations, 31, 54, 55; transethnic identity, 74; transethnic kingdom/empire, 472, 479; transethnic mission, 26; transethnic social construction, 75
transcripts: hidden transcript, 67; public transcript, 67
True Doctrine (Celsus), 422–23
Turdetanians, 301n114

Ukraine/Russia conflict, 481
universalism, 35, 43, 44n20, 131; non-ethnic universalism, 64; universality of Israel's God, 107
universal mission, 189, 191, 192n109

Velleius, 282, 283–84
Verissimus (Marcus Aurelius), 415
Vespasian, 293
Virgil, 86–87, 94–95, 260n46, 280, 287, 307
Virtue/Fortune, and the creation of Rome, 305–6
Vitruvius, 276–77, 287

Zechariah, 406
Zeno, 75, 75n104
Zeus, 10
Zion, 136, 184, 402, 407, 408, 445, 450; eschatology, 227–28

Index of Ancient Sources

HEBREW BIBLE

Genesis
4:22	110
6:4	410, 456
12:1–3	139
12:2	131, 132
12:3	180, 192, 199
17	236
17:2	229
17:4	236
17:4–5	402
17:5	115, 192, 199
17:7–14	477
17:9–14	180
17:12	132
18:18	199
22:17	229, 405
22:18	192
25:2–3	443
25:21–23	363
26:4	402
30:29–43	439
49:1	394
49:8–12	394, 395, 401, 405, 438
49:10	24, 131, 394, 395, 408, 438
49:10–11	414
49:11	395, 396

Exodus
1:7	466
1:9	132
7:11	371
12:2	135
12:43	132, 143
14:1–5	225
14:4	225
15:14	132
19:5	132, 225
19:5–6	225
19:6	131, 132, 233, 242, 477
21:8	132
22:20	115
22:27	119
22:29(28)	356
23:27	132
33:16	132

Leviticus
17:8–14	185
18:26	185
20:2	132
20:24	132
20:26	132
25:47–55	140

Numbers
11:26–30	346
16:5	371
18:27	356
22–24	123
23:9	148
24:8	148
24:17	395

Deuteronomy
1:28	132
2:10	132
2:21	132

529

INDEX OF ANCIENT SOURCES

2:25	132	**1 Samuel**		2:8–9	191
4:6	132	8:5	132	9:20	19
4:19	20, 456	8:20	132	10:16	132
4:27	148			17:43–44 (18:43–44)	442
4:34	356	**2 Samuel**		18:5	461
6:5	115	7	169	18:44	132
6:14	132	7:23	132	18:49	199
10:15	132	22:50	132	22	169
18:15–19	381			22:8	132
23:1	154	**1 Kings**		33:10	131
27–30	121	8:41	107	44:2	132
27:26	25	19:10	405	45:5	131
28:25	242	19:18	405	46:7 (47:7)	397
28:44	442			47:3	132
29:24	131	**1 Chronicles**		59:6	131
30	218	14:17	131	69	169
30:1–5	121	16:23–31	407	71 (72)	394, 396–97
30:4	242	16:24	131	71:7	467
32:7–9	148, 411			71:17	397, 398
32:8	20, 125, 132	**2 Chronicles**		72:7	6
32:8–9	355, 356, 384, 456, 457	32:23	131	72:8	6
				72:17 (71:17)	439
32:16–23	390	**Ezra**		95:5 (96:5)	408, 410, 455
32:17	412	4:10	132		
32:21	390, 443			96 (97)	407
32:43	199, 388, 405	**Nehemiah**		96:3–8	19
33:13–17	408	1:9	242	96:10	19
33:17	436, 439	5:8	132	98:1–3	19
				105:37 (106:37)	412
Joshua		**Psalms**		109 (110)	191, 396
3:17	132	1	396	110	191
4:1	132	2	169, 191, 394, 396	110:1	171
5:6	132	2:1	132, 200	110:5–6	191
5:8	132	2:7	172	115:2	132
10:13	132	2:7–8	357, 396–97, 398, 436, 439	116:1 (117:1)	199
				135:15	132
Ruth		2:8	132, 439, 451, 457, 460	144:7	132
2:10	132			146:2	242

530

Index of Ancient Sources

Isaiah

1:3–4	444
1:4	445
2:2	131
2:2–3	406
2:2–4	165, 450
2:3	19
2:4	6
5:26	349
6:9–10	382, 408, 441
6:10	408
8:4	413, 462
9:1–2	200, 439
9:1–7	169
10:33–34	140
11:1	395
11:1–9	169
11:10	438, 439
14:2	131
14:6	131
14:26	131
17:13	132
33:3	131
34:1	132
34:2	131
40:17	131
42:1	132, 200
42:1–3	192
42:1–4	398
42:1–7	397, 439
42:4	200
42:5–13	398
42:6	192, 379
42:6–7	363, 398–99, 436
42:8	398
43:20–21	242, 477
45:1	363, 461
45:2	462
49:1	132, 192
49:6	192, 242, 325, 387, 398
49:6–7	363
49:6–8	397
49:6–12	439
49:8	398
49:22	131, 349
51:4	131, 132
51:4–5	401
51:5	131, 395
52:5	199, 332, 333, 335–36, 349, 383
52:10	402
53	176, 357
54:1	336, 337
55:3–5	402
56:3	132, 134
56:3–5	154
56:6	132
56:6–8	133
56:7	133, 193, 201
58:2	132
58:9	336
62:10	349
62:12	390
65:1	390, 402
65:1–3	400, 401
65:2–3	402
65:11	412
66:18	338
66:19	184
66:20	131
66:24	336

Jeremiah

3:17	131, 402
6:18	442
9:26	362, 444
28:11	131, 134, 193
28:14	131, 134, 193
29:7	481
31:31–32	401
34:2	134
34:3	134
34:6	134
34:8	134
34:12	134
34:16	134
35:11	133, 134, 193
35:11–14	134
35:14	133, 134, 193
46:1	132
51:58	132
66:24	336

Lamentations

1:10	141, 142, 144

Ezekiel

2:3	131, 132
5:8	132
20:14	132
25:8	132
28:25–26	444
36:15	131
37:22	131
39:21	131
44:7	132
44:9	132

Daniel

3:2	133, 193, 338
3:4	132
3:7	132, 133, 193, 338
3:31	132
4:1	132
4:37	133
4:37c	193

INDEX OF ANCIENT SOURCES

5:19	132	**Malachi**		2:29	136, 137
6:26	133, 193	1:10–12	387, 400, 409,	4:6	136, 137
7	386		437, 441–42		
7:13–14	191	1:11	200, 220, 409	**Epistle of Jeremiah**	
7:14	132, 191	1:14	200, 220	1:4	141
				1:4–5	136
Hosea		**DEUTEROCANONICAL**		1:50	136
1:10	443	**BOOKS**		1:50–51	136, 137
2:2–3	443				
9:1	132	**Tobit**		**Prayer of Azariah**	
10:10	131	1:10	136, 137	1:14	136
		1:17	136		
Joel		3:4	136, 137	**Bel and the Dragon**	
3:2	131	13:3	135, 137	28	114
		13:5	136, 137		
Amos		13:11–17	165	**1 Maccabees**	
9:11–12	188, 200, 211	14:5–7	165	1:11	135, 136
		14:6	136	1:13	136
Micah		14:6–7	135, 137	1:14	141
1:2	131			1:14–15	136, 137
4:1	131	**Judith**		1:43	135
4:1–7	407, 408–9	3:8	133, 136, 193	2:12	141
4:3	131	4:12	135, 137	2:18	136
5:1–5	169	9:14	136, 224	2:19	136, 137
				2:40	141
Habakkuk		**Wisdom of Solomon**		2:44	141
2:13	131, 132	10:5	145	3:10	138
		10:15–11:11	112	3:25	138
Zephaniah		12:12	145	3:52	137, 138
3:9	131	14:11	136, 137, 145	4:1	138
		15:15	136, 137, 145	4:6	138
Haggai				4:7	141
2:7	131	**Sirach**		4:11	135, 136, 137
		10:15	136, 137	4:12–14	137–38
Zechariah		17:17	137	4:45	141, 142
2:11	390	36:1	136	4:54	141
8:20	131	36:2	136	4:58	136
8:22	131			4:60	141
14:2	131	**Baruch**		5:9–10	138
		2:13	136, 137	5:19	136

5:22	138	14:14	138	48:40	126, 127
5:43	136	14:34	224	48:43	126
6:53	141			51:4	126
7:23	135, 137	**3 Maccabees**		54:13–19	127
8:22–32	85, 247, 281	1:11	136, 224	54:14	127
9:29	136, 224	2:27	136, 224	54:17	127
10:20	224	2:33	136, 224	54:18	127
11:21	224	4:1	138	67:2	136
11:25	224	4:1–2	136	67:5–6	136
12:1–23	113	5:13	136, 137	68:5–7	136
12:3	224	6:9	141	72–74	128
12:6	224	6:13	136, 137	72:1–6	135, 137
13:6	224	7:3–4	136	72:2	136
14:4	224	7:4	136	72:4	136
14:6	224			72:5	136
14:28	224	**4 Maccabees**		82:6	126
14:29	224	1:11	136		
14:30	224			**4 Baruch**	
14:32	224	**PSEUDEPIGRAPHA**		6:19	141
14:35	224			7:37	141
14:36	138, 141	**Apocalypse of Abraham**			
16:3	224	1–8	112	**1 Enoch**	
		7:10	127	10:21	136, 137
2 Maccabees		8:1–6	127	83–90	108
4:10	104	21:7–22:4	124	90:6–39	165
4:13	104	27:1	137, 139	90:13–39	223
5:19	224	29:3–13	228	90:37	165
5:19–20	136	29:4	228		
5:20	224	29:8	228	**2 Enoch**	
6:4	137, 138, 141–42	29:9	228	70:7	136
6:14	136, 224	29:11	228		
6:31	224	29:12	228	**4 Ezra**	
7:37	224	29:17–19	228	3:36	125
8:9	138	31:6	127	4:23	135
8:16	137, 138			7:20–24	126–27
10:8	224	**2 Baruch**		7:24	125
11:27	224	29–34	128	7:37–38	136, 137
12:13	138	39:1–40:4	128	7:72	127
13:11	136, 137	41:4	126, 128	7:72–74	125, 127
14:5	136	42:5	126	7:82	125

8:55-61	125, 127	190-91	146	Testament of Asher	
9:9-12	125, 127	208	146	7:3	200, 227
11:1-12:39	128	235	111		
13:1-58	128	257	146	Testament of Benjamin	
		259	146	3:8	200
Joseph and Aseneth				9:2-3	227
1:5	113-14	**Martyrdom of Isaiah**		9:8	227
8:9	113-14	3.16-20	448, 449	11:2-5	227
Jubilees		**Psalms of Solomon**		**Testament of Joseph**	
1:8-10	136	1:8	136	19:10-11	227
1:13	136, 137	2	128		
1:15	136, 137	2:2	138, 141	**Testament of Judah**	
1:19	136, 137	2:19	138	22:2	200
2:19	124, 137	2:22	136, 137, 138	24:4-6	122
3:31	137	7:3	136, 137	24:6	145
11:14-13:9	112, 127	7:6	138	25:5	122
12:12-14	127	8	128		
12:22-23	139	17	128	**Testament of Levi**	
12:23	136, 137	17:3	136, 137	2:10-11	227
15:26	125	17:28	142	14:1-2	136
15:31	125	17:34-35	136, 137	14:1-4	137, 145
16:17-18	136, 137			14:4	136, 137
18:16	136, 137	**Sibylline Oracles**		15:1	145
22:11	136	3	145	15:1-2	136, 137
22:16	137, 139-41	3:97-161	110	16.3-5	228
30:1-17	139	3:191-95	122	18:2-9	122
30:11	139-40	3:218-19	110		
30:11-14	137	3:218-30	112	**Testament of Moses**	
30:13-14	139	3:556-72	122	1:11-13	124-25, 127, 136, 137
		3:667-795	165		
Letter of Aristeas		3:710-23	122	8:3	139
6	146	3:732-33	122	10:7-8	135
9	146	3:762-75	122		
16	120	4	145	**Testament of Naphtali**	
120-27	120	5	145	8:1-4	122
139	120, 146, 149	5:247-80	122	8:3-4	135
143-66	120	5:420-31	122	8:3-6	137, 145
184	120	5:484-503	122		
184-85	120				

Index of Ancient Sources

Testament of Simeon		
7:2	227	
Testament of Zebulun		
9:8	122, 145	
9.8–9	228	

Dead Sea Scrolls

1Q27 frag.1	
I, 8–9	136
1QM	
XIV, 4–5	136, 137
1QM	
XIX, 10	136
1QM	
XV, 1–2	135, 137
1QM	
XVI, 1	135, 136
1QpHab	
III, 4–6	136
1QpHab	
V, 3–5	136
1QpHab	
VIII, 5	136
1QpHab	
XII, 12–14	136, 137
1QpHab	
XIII, 1–2	136, 137

1QS	
III, 17–IV, 26	218
4Q159 frag. 2–4	
1–3	140
4Q161 frag. 8–10	
1–4	140
4Q228 frag. 1	
II, 1–2	140
4Q269 frag. 8	
II, 1–2	136
4Q271 frag. 5	
I, 9	140
4Q372 frag. 1	
4–11	135
4Q378 frag. 3	
I, 9	135
4Q394 frag. 3–7	
I, 6–11	136
4Q504 frag. 1–2	
III, 2–7	135, 136, 137
4Q504 frag. 1–2	
IV, 2–12	136
4Q504 frag. 1–2	
V, 9–12	135, 137
4Q504 frag. 6	
6–9	136

11QTempleª	
XLVIII, 6–14	137
XLVIII, 11–13	140, 142
LI, 19–21	137, 140
11QTemple	
LXIV, 9–11	135, 136
CD	
V, 17–19	371
XI, 8–9	140
XI, 14–15	140
XII, 6–7	136

Nag Hammadi Literature

Gospel of Philip	
52.16–24 (NHC II 3)	436
Interpretation of Knowledge	
21.30–34 (NHC XI 1)	436
Tripartite Tractate	
99.34–100.18 (NHC I 5)	456
109.24–111.5 (NHC I 5)	455

Ancient Jewish Writers

Josephus

Against Apion

1.1	71, 110, 146
1.59	146
1.172	145
2.48	117

535

INDEX OF ANCIENT SOURCES

2.122	146	10.275	145	20.38	114
2.163	111	10.276	145	20.44	126
2.165	118	11.3	145, 146	20.256	146
2.168	111	11.19	146	20.262	149
2.209	146	11.138	145		
2.220	145	11.140–41	149	*Jewish War*	
2.237	119	11.140–52	146	2.85–86	146
2.281	111	11.145	149	2.192–98	122
		11.151–52	149	2.340–41	117
Jewish Antiquities		11.184	145	2.342–407	89
1.10	118	11.185	145	2.345–401	122, 285
1.15–26	111	11.207	146	2.361	123
1.19	147	11.211	146	2.362	146, 280, 286
1.25	118, 130	11.299	148	2.364	146
1.107	148	11.303	145	2.382	146
1.154–57	112	11.326	145	2.390	92, 123
1.192	148	11.331–36	117	2.397	146, 286
2.151	71	12.7	145	2.412	146
2.215–16	146	12.241	146	2.417	146
3.23	146	13.78	117	2.463	186
4.12	148	13.200	145, 146	2.510	258
4.112–30	123, 307	13.242–44	117	3.34	258
4.114–16	146	13.257–58	114	3.41	146
4.116	148	13.419	145	3.402	146
4.125	124	14.110	117, 146	4.181	117
4.128	124	15.136	148	4.261–62	146, 149
4.190	148	15.417	146	4.265	114
4.207	119	16.2	146	4.275	117
4.262	146	16.14	117	4.323	92
6.32	145	16.31–57	122	4.323–25	123
6.61	146	16.36	146, 302	4.397	146
6.342	146	16.39	302	5.15–18	117
8.116	146	16.177	148	5.233	145
8.116–17	117	18.1	258	5.367	122, 306–7
8.120	145, 146	18.122	117	5.376–419	307
8.284	148	18.345	146, 149	5.378	123
10.183	146	19.290–91	85, 247, 281	5.408–12	123
10.195–210	123, 307	19.328	145	5.562–64	117
10.210	123	19.329	146	5.563	146
10.271	145	19.330	146	5.563–64	149

6.102	146, 149	8–13	121	189	146
6.199	148	12–13	301		
6.250–51	123	143–47	121	*On the Migration*	
6.328–50	122	144	146	*of Abraham*	
6.340–42	293	144–47	301	53–61	145
6.341–42	302	183	146	60	146
6.442	146	200	146	89–93	119
7.45	150, 186, 311	211	146	93	119
7.351	146	306	117	98	119
7.423	145	*On the Life of Abraham*		*On the Posterity of Cain*	
		56	146	89	146
Philo		66–71	112	89–93	145
Against Flaccus		98	117	*On the Sacrifices of Cain*	
43	120, 148	226	146	*and Abel*	
				7	146
On Dreams		*On the Life of Joseph*			
2.230	146	19	146	*On the Special Laws*	
		56	146	1.51	114
On Planting		134	146	1.52	114
59	146, 148	135	146	1.52–53	114
		242	146	1.56	146
On Rewards and		*On the Life of Moses*		1.97	117
Punishments		1.2	146	1.124	146
14	146	1.87	146	1.153	119
123	146	1.139	146	1.168	117
126–27	121	1.149	117	1.190	117
127–61	121	1.195	146	1.211	146
162	121	1.278	146, 148	1.303	146
163	121	2.12	147	1.308–9	114
164	121	2.17–21	147	2.44	130
165	121	2.25–28	146	2.162	117
168	121	2.27	147	2.162–63	147
On the Change of Names		2.41–42	150	2.162–68	117
148–150	146	2.41–44	122	2.163	146
		2.49–51	118	2.165	146
On the Decalogue		2.165	146	2.188–92	117
37	146	2.205	119, 146	3.8	146
153	146	2.225	146	3.29	146
On the Embassy to Gaius		2.271	146	4.19	146
8–10	290, 297			4.178	114

4.180	117	11.1	125, 126, 136, 137	16:28	173
		11.2	126	18:17	142, 204, 314, 318
On the Virtues		20.4	136	20:25	214
65	111, 130	27.7	136, 137	21:43	216
102	114	30.4	136	22:34–40	217, 232
108	118			22:44	171
147	146	**NEW TESTAMENT**		23:15	232
160	146			23:23	217, 232, 233
178	114	**Matthew**		24:7	216
179	114	3:9	451	24:9	199, 201
184–85	146	4:15	199–200	24:14	191, 199, 201, 215
186	146	5:19	217, 233	24:34	173
210–19	112, 114–15	5:23–24	233	25:31–45	182
222	146	5:43–47	220	25:32	199, 201, 215
		5:46	208	27:25	215
Questions and Answers on Exodus		5:47	202, 208, 214	28:18	191
		6:5–18	219	28:18–20	201, 215–16
2.5	119	6:7	202, 214	28:19	133, 193, 199,
2.22	145	6:16–18	219		201, 202, 215–17,
		6:32	202, 214, 314		231–32, 314
Questions and Answers on Genesis		7:12	217, 232	28:19–20	19, 190
		8:5–13	182, 215, 231	28:20	217, 221
3.60	145	8:10	215		
		8:11	182, 231	**Mark**	
That Every Good Person Is Free		8:11–12	215	1:11	191
		8:12–13	182	1:16–20	181
57	112	9:13	217, 232	3:13–19	181
72–73	130	10:5	199	4:12	408
72–74	146	10:5–6	182, 208, 214–15,	7:24–30	182, 196
160	111		231	7:27	193
		10:6	232	9:1	173
That God Is Unchangeable		10:18	191	10:33	196
		10:23	208, 217, 232	10:42	196, 202, 314
144	146	12:7	217, 232	11:17	196, 199, 201
148	146	12:18	200, 215	12:36	171, 191
		12:18–20	192	13:10	191, 193, 196,
Who Is the Heir?		12:21	199, 200, 215		202, 314
272	146	12:41–42	215	13:26	191
278	146, 148	13:52	214	13:30	173
		15:21–28	215, 231	14:9	193
PSEUDO-PHILO		15:24	214, 215, 231	14:62	191
Biblical Antiquities					
9.5	139				

Index of Ancient Sources

15:39	196	9:22	196	3:25	164, 170, 184, 192, 381
16:14–16	191	10:16	196, 240		
16:15	191, 193	11:52	196, 240	3:26	184, 381
16:19–20	191	12:20–21	196, 240	4:4	381
		12:42–43	196	4:11	172
Luke		20:19–23	191	4:25	199, 200
1:1	163, 380	21:22–23	173	4:25–26	191
1:1–4	156			4:27	199, 379
1:8–9	378	**Acts**		4:32–35	152
1:54–55	170	1:6	170, 173, 380	4:36–37	154
1:72–73	170	1:7–8	174	5:12–16	153
2:1	377	1:8	153, 154, 191, 192, 193, 326, 378	5:14	381
2:25	170			5:31	171, 172, 176
2:32	199, 201, 377	1:14	154	5:32	174
2:38	170	1:21–22	192, 378	5:36	167
3:1	377	2:7	167	5:42	153
7:1–10	182	2:10	184	6:1	381
9:27	173	2:16–21	175	6:1–8:8	166
9:52–55	153	2:16–22	174	6:5	154, 167, 312
10:1–16	181	2:32	164	6:7	153, 167, 381
10:30–37	153, 182	2:33	174	6:14	179
12:30	202, 208	2:33–35	171, 172	7:2–53	164
13:28	182	2:34–35	191	7:5	179
13:28–29	182	2:36	164	7:37	164
13:29	182	2:38	174, 176	7:39	164
17:11–19	153	2:41	381	7:51–53	164
17:18	142	2:43–47	152	7:52	357
19:11	173, 380	3:11–26	381	8:1	153, 167
20:42–43	171	3:12	170	8:4–25	153
21:32	173	3:12–26	164, 170, 172	8:5	153
24:21	168	3:15	170	8:5–25	153
24:33	192	3:18	169	8:26–39	153, 184
24:45–47	192	3:19	173, 176	8:31	379
24:46–48	192	3:19–21	170, 172	8:34	379
24:47	190, 193, 378	3:20	170, 316	8:36	379
24:47–49	378	3:20–21	176	9:3	157
24:53	378	3:21	179, 184, 316	9:10–22	154
		3:22	164	9:15	192, 199, 378
John		3:22–24	164, 328	9:23	155
4:19–21	153	3:23	381	9:26	154, 155
7:35	196, 240			9:26–30	154, 166

539

INDEX OF ANCIENT SOURCES

9:28	154	13:45	382	16:35–40	382
9:29	155	13:46	193, 380	16:36	379
9:31	153, 154	13:46–47	379	17:5	382
9:42	381	13:47	192, 439	17:12	381
10	325	13:47–48	379	18:5–6	326, 382
10–11	192	13:48	325	18:5–7	20
10:1–11:18	153	13:50	382	18:6	379, 380
10:4	379	14:1	381	18:12	382
10:28	142, 188, 318	14:2	379, 382	18:12–16	382
10:30–33	379	14:4	192	18:14	382
10:34–35	188	14:5	379	18:22	154
10:42	172	14:14	192	18:22–23	154
10:43	176	14:27	379	19:2–3	379
10:45	325	15	154, 211, 380	19:17–20	381
11:1	154, 203, 314, 379	15:1	211, 327	19:35–41	382
11:1–3	166	15:1–2	166, 187	20:3	382
11:7	379	15:2	155	20:9–12	468
11:17	379	15:3	153, 379	21–23	154
11:18	154, 379	15:5	167	21:11	379
11:19	179, 185, 379	15:7	190, 202, 314	21:18–26	380
11:19–26	154, 155	15:7–11	155	21:20	380, 381
11:20	179	15:10	327	21:20–21	51, 167
11:23	379	15:12	155	21:21	178
11:23–26	154	15:14	155, 199, 203, 211, 379, 385	21:25	185, 379
11:29–30	155			21:27–40	382
12:17	154	15:14–18	379	22:6	157
12:24	153, 381	15:15–17	188	22:14–15	192
13–28	382	15:16–17	211	22:21	192, 379
13:1–14:28	154	15:17	199, 200, 379	22:22–29	382
13:2	155	15:19	155, 211, 310	23:16–35	382
13:7–12	382	15:23	160, 203, 314, 326, 379	24:22–23	382
13:9	155			25:1–27	382
13:13	155	15:23–29	326	25:6–12	11
13:16	325	15:28	327	25:15	11
13:31	167	15:29	185, 326	25:19	11
13:33	191	15:31	326, 327, 379	25:23	11
13:42	155	15:36–41	154, 156	25:23–26:32	11–13
13:43	325, 381	16:9	379	25:27	12
13:44–48	20	16:15	379	26	15, 17, 19, 32
13:44–52	325	16:30	379	26:2	12

Index of Ancient Sources

26:4	12	3:9	234	10:12	234
26:5	12	3:20	237	11:7	213
26:6	12	3:21–26	237	11:7–12	190
26:9	12	3:22	234	11:7–24	214
26:12	157	3:22–24	234	11:11	190, 200
26:13	12	3:25	158, 237	11:11–15	213
26:17–18	379	3:28	235	11:11a	213
26:17–28	192	3:29	190, 199, 200, 234	11:11b	213
26:18	12, 19			11:12	190, 199, 213
26:20	20	3:29–30	367	11:12–15	234
26:22	19	4:11	236, 363	11:13	xiii, 152, 189, 190, 192, 199, 200, 203, 204, 314, 325, 328, 366
26:23	12, 17–18, 20, 24, 379	4:13	180		
		4:13–16	236, 477		
26:24	12, 13	4:16–17	180		
26:24–32	382	4:17	192, 199, 236	11:13–14	200
26:31–32	13	5:5	174	11:13–32	324
27:42–44	382	5:12	235, 239	11:15	213
28:13–14	154	5:12–21	235	11:17	214, 328
28:15	154	5:15	235	11:19	214
28:16	382	5:18	235	11:20a	214
28:17	377	5:19	235	11:20b–21	214
28:17–28	326	5:20	237	11:23–24	213
28:23–28	20	6:6	235, 239	11:25	188, 190, 200, 213
28:25–28	380, 382	7:5	237		
28:26–27	408	7:7	237	11:25–26	234
28:28	377, 379	7:8	237	11:26	213
		7:10	237	13:3	15
Romans		7:11	237	14:9	172
1:3–4	158, 171	7:22	235	15:8–9	190, 200, 213
1:5	189, 190, 192, 199, 314, 371	8:1–27	174	15:9	199, 201
		8:15	158	15:9–12	190
1:5–6	203, 314, 325	8:23	175	15:10	190, 199, 200, 201
1:13	189, 200, 203, 314, 325	8:34	171		
		9:5	164	15:11	199, 371
1:16	193	9:24	190, 199, 200, 203	15:12	199
2:9–10	193			15:16–18	189
2:13	237	9:30	190, 199	15:18	199, 201
2:14	199, 201	9:30–31	200	15:19	158, 190
2:16	235	10:8–9	158	15:19–29	190
2:24	199, 349	10:9	171	15:25	212

541

INDEX OF ANCIENT SOURCES

15:25–29	158
15:26	158, 161, 212
15:26–27	161, 190, 200
15:27	201, 212, 234
15:29	212
15:31	159
16:25–27	188
16:26	324, 371

1 Corinthians

1:12	158
1:23	199, 200
2:4	174
2:14	235
3:4	158
3:5	158
3:6	158
3:16	174
3:22	158
4:6	158
5:1	203, 314
7:29–31	173
9:1	152, 158
9:1–2	183
9:5	158
9:6	158
10:1	477
10:6–11	236
10:11	175
10:32	235
11:1	236
11:23–25	157
12:2	199, 200, 204, 310, 314
12:3	158, 171
12:13	174, 234
15	235
15:3	157, 176
15:3–7	157–58, 164, 169
15:3–8	176
15:7	183
15:8–11	152, 183, 192
15:9	159
15:10	152
15:12–28	164
15:21	235
15:22	235
15:23	175
15:24–28	171
15:28	164
15:45	235
15:51	173
16:1–4	158
16:12	158
16:22	158, 171

2 Corinthians

1:20–22	175
4:5	171
4:16	235
5:5	175
5:14–15	235
8	158, 212
8:14–15	212
9	158, 212
10:13–16	190
11:5	158
11:21–23	158
11:22	195
11:26	199, 200, 201
12:11	158
12:11–12	183

Galatians

1:1	183, 192
1:6	327
1:11–14	211
1:13	159
1:13–14	152, 159
1:13–2:10	158
1:13–2:14	155
1:15	192
1:15–16	324
1:16	160, 189, 190, 202, 314
1:17	152, 155, 157, 158, 192
1:17–19	158
1:18	155, 157, 158
1:18–24	155
1:19	158
1:21	187
1:22	158
1:22–23	159
2	211
2:1	155, 158, 186
2:1–10	152, 159, 189, 193, 324
2:2	155, 186, 190, 324
2:3	318
2:3–5	152
2:4	152, 159
2:5	324
2:6	152
2:7	155, 158, 160, 190, 192
2:7–8	158, 173, 190
2:8	192, 200, 328
2:9	155, 158, 186, 190, 200, 201, 328
2:10	158, 212
2:11	187
2:11–12	203, 314
2:11–14	156, 158, 159, 187, 324
2:12	17–18, 152, 158, 159, 200, 318, 328

Index of Ancient Sources

2:13	158	2:15	238	**1 Thessalonians**	
2:14	142, 156, 180, 200, 328	2:16	238	1:1	158
		2:19	239	1:6	174
2:15	199, 200, 204, 205, 328	2:21	239	1:9–10	158
		3:1	197, 203, 238, 314	1:10	173
2:16	235	3:1–6	238	2:14–16	159, 160, 200
2:21	237	3:1–9	188, 189	2:15	158, 202
3:1	327	3:3–6	240	2:16	189, 201, 314
3:1–5	174	3:6	201, 203, 314	4:5	201, 310
3:3	328	3:8	202	4:8	174
3:8	180, 190, 192, 199, 371	3:9	240	4:15	173
		4:17	204, 239, 314		
3:11	237			**1 Timothy**	
3:13–14	213	**Philippians**		1:3	366
3:14	175	2:2–3	187	1:3–11	367
3:15	204	2:6	368	1:4	367
3:28	35, 234, 235, 236, 238	2:10	235	1:6–7	366
		2:11	171	1:7	366
3:29	180, 235, 477	3:5	195	1:7–11	370
4:6	174	3:6	152, 159	1:8–11	367
4:9	327, 328			1:11	367
4:21	327	**Colossians**		1:15	370
5:2	327	1:6	238	2:1–2	366, 386
6:12	160	1:15	238, 368	2:1–7	366, 367
6:16	236	1:15–20	238	2:1–8	365
		1:16	238	2:2	366
Ephesians		1:20	238	2:3–4	366
1:3–14	238	1:21	239	2:4	368
1:9	240	1:23	238	2:4–6	366
1:9–13	188	1:25–26	237	2:5	367, 370
1:10	238	1:25–27	197, 238	2:5–6	366
1:21–23	238	1:25–28	189	2:7	189, 197, 365, 366, 367, 368, 369, 370
1:22–23	239	1:26–27	240		
2:11	200, 238, 239	1:27	238	3:15	368
2:11–12	197, 238	2:11–12	239	3:16	197, 365, 368, 369, 370, 384
2:11–22	238, 239	3:9–10	239		
2:12	239, 240	3:11	238, 239	4:8	370
2:13	239			4:9	370
2:14–15	238			4:10	370

543

4:11	370	9:25–26	241	7:3–4	233
4:12	370	9:27	241	7:9	201, 202, 222, 224, 233
5:18	370	10:1	240		
6:20	367	13:23	196	7:9–12	224
				7:9–17	224

2 Timothy

1 Peter

				7:14	224
1:8	371	1:1	241, 242	9:4	224
1:9–10	372	1:1–2	242	10:11	201, 202, 222, 233, 251
1:10	371	1:10–12	242		
1:11	370	1:14	241, 242	11:1	226
1:17	370	1:18	197, 241, 242	11:1–2	201, 222–23, 226
2:8	371	1:21	241	11:2	222, 226, 314
3:1	370	2:9	242, 443, 477	11:8	223, 226
3:8	371	2:11–12	242	11:9	201, 202, 222, 233, 251
3:12	372	2:12	197, 201, 203, 241, 314		
3:15	372			11:18	222, 223
4:16	370	3:6	242	12:5	199, 222, 223
4:16–18	370	4:3	197, 201, 204, 241, 242, 314	13:7	201, 202, 222, 233
4:17	197, 369, 370				
		4:16	242	14:4	224
Philemon		4:18–20	242	14:6	201, 202, 222, 225, 233
24	158	5:1	241		
		5:13	241	14:8	199, 222, 223
				15:3	222
Hebrews		**2 Peter**		15:4	199, 222, 223
1	357	3:16	212	16:19	222, 223
1:13	171			17:15	199, 201, 202, 222, 233, 251
2:1–2	241	**3 John**			
2:9	196, 241	7	196, 330	17:18	223
2:10–18	241			18:3	199, 222, 223
2:16	241	**Revelation**		18:10	223
3:1–6	241	1:6	225, 233	18:16	223
4:8	241	2:9	226, 349	18:18	223
4:8–10	241	2:26	222, 223	18:19	223
5:1–10	241	3:9	226, 349	18:21	223
6:5	175	5:9	201, 202, 222, 233	18:23	199, 222, 223
7:5–6	241			19:15	222, 223
8:13	240	5:9–10	225, 233	19:15–21	223
9:6–12	241	7:1–8	224	20:3	222, 223
9:15	240				

Index of Ancient Sources

20:8	222, 223	m. Ketubbot		Midrash Exodus	
21:2	223	2:9	135	1:36	115
21:24	201, 222, 223, 233	m. Nedarim		Midrash Genesis	
21:24–26	223	3:11	136	39.16	115
21:26	201, 222, 223, 233	4:3	135, 143	Sipre Deuteronomy	
22:2	222, 223	m. Pe'ah		32.3	115
22:22	201, 233	2:7	143	t. Berakhot	
		4:6	143	5:31	143, 144
Rabbinic Literature		m. Shabbat		6:18	143
		1:8	143	t. Demai	
b. Sukkah		23:4	143, 144	1:12–13	135, 143
49b	115	m. Shevi'it		4:25–27	143
		5:7	144	6:12	143
b. Yevamot				6:13	143, 144
47b	115	m. Ta'anit		t. Eruvin	
		3:7	135, 143	3:8	143
m. Bava Metzi'a		m. Terumot		5:19	143
5:6	143	8:12	135, 143	t. Gittin	
m. Bava Qamma		m. Yevamot		3:13	144
4:3	144	16:5	143	3:13–14	143
m. Bikkurim		Mekilta Nezikin		t. Ketubbot	
1:4	115	18	115	3:2	143
m. Demai		Mekilta Tractate Pisha		t. Megillah	
3:4	143	2:35–40	143	2:16	143
5:9	144	2:39–40	135	t. Pe'ah	
6:1	144	9:34–37	143	2:9	144
6:10	143	15:19	144	2:9–11	143
m. Eruvin		15:19–20	143	3:1	135, 136
3:5	135, 143				

INDEX OF ANCIENT SOURCES

t. Pesahim

2:5	143
2:12	143, 144

t. Sanhedrin

13:2	115

t. Sheqalim

3:11	143, 144

t. Yevamot

14:7	143, 144

y. Bikkurim

1:4 64a	115

EARLY CHRISTIAN WRITINGS

Athenagoras

Embassy for the Christians

1.1	452
1.1–2	453
1.2	463, 468
1.3	468
14.1–2	453
14.2	451, 468
14.3	452, 463
23.2	468
24.1–25.4	456
25.3	456, 468
34	260
34.3	450, 468
37.1	451, 469, 470
37.2	469

Barnabas

1.4–8	359
1.5	359
1.8	359
2–17	359
2.1	364
2.4	359
2.4–6	361
2.6	364
2.10	362
3.6	359
4.1	364
4.3–5	360, 364, 386
4.6	362
4.6–8	362
4.14	362, 363
5.6	385
5.7	361
7.5	361
9.4	362, 364
9.5	362
10.12	362
11–12	363
12.11	363
13.1	363, 364, 383
13.2	363
13.7	363, 364
14.6	359
14.7	363
14.8	363
16.1–2	361
16.2	364
16.3	360
16.4	360
16.7	360
18–20	359
18.1–2	364

Clement of Alexandria

Christ the Educator

3.3.24.2	453
3.11.53.3	436
3.12.85.2	436

Exhortation to the Greeks

1 (3.1)	456
1 (4.2)	451
1 (7.4–6)	456
3 (42.1)	455
3 (42.1–5)	455
3 (42.1)–4 (54.5)	453
4 (62.4)	455
4 (59.2–3)	443
6 (70.1)	453, 459
9 (83.3)	436

Miscellanies

1.15.71.1	459
1.15.71.3	459
1.21.142.1	453
2.6.31.2	358
2.7.35.5	358
2.9.43.3	441, 446
2.15.68.1	436
2.20.116.3–4	358
3.1.3–4	436
4.9.72.4	436
5.14.98.1–4	452, 454
5.14.98.4	451
5.14.133	459
6.5.41.7	454
6.5.42.2	454
6.14.110.3–111.1	456
6.17.159.9	459
6.18.167.2–3	449
7.2.6	456
7.2.6.4	456

Index of Ancient Sources

1 Clement	
1.1	353
3	353
3.3	353
5.1	354
5.6–7	355
6.4	354
29–30	384
29.1	355
29.2	355
30.1	356
31.2	356
32.2–4	356
36.4	357
41	357
42	353
44.6	353
45.2–5	357
53–55	354
53.4	355
54	354
54.2	353
55.1	354, 355
55.2	355
55.5–6	355
59.3–61.3	353, 356, 358
59.4	357
60.4	358
60.4–61.1	386
61.1	358
61.2	358
63.3	354

2 Clement	
1–18	334
1.4	336
1.6	334, 335, 336
1.8	337
2.1–2	336, 337
2.3	336, 385
3.1	334, 335
3.2	335
5.5–6	334
6.3	335, 385
7.6	336
11.1–4	336
13.1	335
13.1–2	383
13.1–3	332, 338
13.2	335, 349
13.3	335
14.1	336, 337, 385
14.2	337
15.3	336
17.1–3	337
17.4–5	337
17.5	385
17.5–6	338
17.7	338
19–20	334
19.1	333–34

Cyprian

Testimonies against the Jews

preface	440
1.10–20	444
1.16	442
1.19	442, 443
1.20	442
1.21	438, 439, 441, 442
2.7	439
2.8	439

Didache	
1–4	233
1–6	218, 221
1.1	219
1.3	202, 220, 314
2–6	221
2.1	219
2.2	220
3.4	220
4.13	218
6.2	221, 233
6.2b	221
7–10	218
7–15	218
7.1	233
8.1	219
8.2	219
9.2	218
9.5	196
10.6	218
11–15	218
12.4	218
13.3	218
14	220
14.1	218
14.1–3	218
14.3	200, 218, 220
16	218
16.8	218

Epiphanius

Panarion against Heresies

30.13	208

5 Esdras

2:33–34	441, 444

547

INDEX OF ANCIENT SOURCES

Eusebius

Demonstration of the Gospel

1.1.4	20
1.1.8	20, 24, 25
1.1.15–16	18
1.2.4	21
1.2.5	21
1.2.8	20
1.2.8–16	20
1.2.9	23
1.2.10	23
1.2.12	24
1.2.16	22
1.4.1	19
1.5.2	23
1.6.30	20
1.6.31	22, 24
1.6.38	25
1.6.38–39	25
1.6.54	20
1.6.60	20
1.6.62	23
1.6.63	23
1.6.75	23
1.7.6	19
1.9.2	20
1.10.6	20
2.1.1	19, 24
2.1.1–2.2.19	23
2.2.20	24
2.2.21	24, 25
2.3.1–29	25
2.3.30	24
2.3.32	24
2.3.48	24
2.3.78	24
3.2.40	23
4.7.1	20
4.9.1–12	21
5.1.28	20
6.13.26	20
8.3.13	17

Ecclesiastical History

1.1.2	25
1.2.21	21
1.2.22	21
1.3.6	19
1.4.2	16, 23
1.4.5	16
1.6.1	19
1.6.1–4	24
1.6.4	19
2.1.8	19
2.1.13	19
3.4.1	19
3.5.7	25
3.7.5	19
3.36.1–11	347
4.3.3	373
4.6.3	19
4.23.9–13	354
4.26.7	463, 467, 470
4.26.7–11	468
5.1.4	24
5.13.4	429
6.36.2	423
10.4.20	23

In Praise of Constantine (On the Holy Sepulchre narration chs. 11–18)

11.2	6, 27
11.5	2, 23
11.7	2
13.1–6	2
13.4–5	27
13.4–6	3
13.5	2, 20
13.7–8	3
13.8	2
13.9	3, 27
13.9–10	27
13.9–14	3
13.14	3, 27
13.15	3
15.7	4
15.8	2
15.11	4
16.2	3
16.3	3, 4
16.4	4, 6, 27
16.5	6, 18
16.5–6	5
16.5–7	31
16.6	6, 23, 26, 29
16.7	2, 5–6, 27
16.8	4, 5, 6
16.10	5, 16
17.1	26
17.6	5
17.8	16, 18
17.9	4, 18
17.12	16, 27
17.13	5, 26
18.3	2

Preparation for the Gospel

1.1.6	23
1.2.1–4	29, 30
1.2.5–8	30
1.3.14	19
1.4.9	23
1.4.11	14, 23
1.4.13	23
1.5.1	23
1.5.2	23
1.6.30	23

Index of Ancient Sources

1.6.54	23
1.6.62	23
1.9.15	20
2.5.2	23
7.1.3	22
7.3.1	21
7.6.2	21
7.6.4	21
7.7.1	23
7.8.36	23
7.8.37	21
7.8.38	21
7.8.39	22
7.8.40	24
7.16.8	21
9.18.1	111, 112
9.19.4	110
9.21.1–19	110
9.23.1	112
9.23.2–3	111
9.26.1	111
9.27.3	111
9.27.4	111
9.27.10	111
9.29.1–3	110
9.29.15	110
9.29.16	110
10.1.1	22
10.1.1–3	22
10.3.26	22
10.14.19	22
12.12.4	112
12.32.7	23
13.12.1	112
13.12.8	111

Hebrew Gospel of Matthew

10.5–6	208–9

Hippolytus

Commentary on Daniel

4.9.2	464, 465, 467–68

Refutation of All Heresies

9.31.1	459
10.26(30).4–8	453
10.30.1–10.31.5	446
10.30.4–7	453
10.30.8	446, 459
10.30(34).1	453
10.31.5	459
10.31.6	460
10.34.1	459

Ignatius

To the Ephesians

1.2	347
3.1	347
19.1–3	353, 418
19.3	386
21.2	347

To the Magnesians

5.2	352
8.1	350, 351
8.2	351, 385, 406
9.1	351, 352
10.3	350, 351
14	347

To the Philadelphians

5.2	351, 352
6.1	350, 352
8.2	349
9.1–2	351
9.2	406
10.1	347

To the Romans

9.1–3	347

To the Smyrnaeans

1.1–2	348
1.2	349, 352, 383
11.1–3	347
11.2	347

To the Trallians

6–10	349
8.2	349, 383
10	348
13	347

Infancy Gospel of Thomas

1	448

Irenaeus

Against Heresies

1.10.1	449
1.10.2	450
1.24.4	456
1.27.2	430
1.27.3	432
2.1.2	430
2.32.4	470–71
3.1.1	448, 449
3.4.2	450
3.5.3	443, 447, 448
3.9.1	443, 444
3.12.6	448
3.12.9	456
3.12.13	447
3.12.15	447
3.15.1	447
3.17.1–2	447
3.17.3	441
3.21.1	441, 444
4.7.1–2	444
4.7.2	443
4.8.1	443, 444

INDEX OF ANCIENT SOURCES

4.9.2	449	11.3	401, 421	41.2–3	400
4.10.2	438, 441	11.4	401, 409	41.3	387
4.14.1–4.16.5	446	11.5	401, 402, 447	43.1	421
4.15.2	446	12.1	402	44.4	404
4.16.3	446	12.2	408	47.1	391
4.16.5	446	13.2	402	47.1–2	404
4.17.5	442	14.4	402	47.4	415
4.19.1	449	16.2–3	403	48–54	395
4.20.12	439	16.4	403	49.8	413
4.21.1	436	17.2	332, 349, 391	52.1	395
4.21.1–2	447	18.2	403	52.1–4	396
4.21.2–3	443	19.2	403	52.3–4	396
4.21.3	439	19.5	403	52.4	408
4.22.2	446	19.6	403, 412	52.4–53.4	396
4.24.2	455	23.1	421	52.5	395
4.25.1	443, 444	24.1–3	402	53.1–4	405
4.25.2	447	24.3	401	53.4	391
4.30.1	436	25.6	398, 404	55.3	405
4.30.3	463	26.1	399, 404	64.1	391
4.30.4	440	26.2	398–99	65.1	398
4.31.2	447	27.2	412	65.4–7	398
4.34.3	438	28.2	404	69.4	408
4.34.4	441, 450	28.3	404	73.3	408
4.36.2	441	28.5	400	73.6	412
4.36.5–8	448	29.2	393, 406, 416	78.9	413, 414
4.36.8	449	30.3	413	79.4	408
5.28	455	32–38	417	83.1–4	407
5.31.1	444	32.2	404	83.4	407, 413
5.34.1	443	34	397	91.1–4	408, 439
5.34.3	447	34.6	397	91.3	391
frag. 31	449	34.8	397	95.1	391
		34.17	397	105.6	415

Justin Martyr

		35	391	109–10	408
		35.5	391	109.1–3	407
Dialogue with Trypho		35.6	391	110.3	409
8.2	404	36.2	397	117.1	400
8.3	388	37.1	397	117.2	400
10.3	391, 402	39.1–2	404	117.4	400, 409
11–30	401, 404	39.2	404	117.5	409
11.2	401, 402	40.1–2	403	119–22	397

550

Index of Ancient Sources

119.2	390, 412	2.3	415	46.3	406, 412
119.3	421	4.2	408, 415	46.4	412
119.3–4	390	5.1	411, 413, 415	49.1–5	391, 400
119.4	396, 401	5.2	411	49.5	407
119.5	390, 415	5.3	412	50.12	407
119.6	390, 396	5.4	412	53	318
120.1	402	12.1	414, 422	53.3	408, 409
120.1–2	396, 405	14–17	408	53.4	391, 399
120.3	405	14.1	415	54–58	395
120.3–4	396	14.2–3	408	54.1	411, 415
120.4	396	17.1	414	54.1–4	395
120.5	405	17.3	414	54.3	395, 411
121	397	20.1	412	54.5	395
121–23	397	26.5	413, 422, 430	54.6–7	395
121.1	397, 398	27.1	411	58.1–3	422, 430
121.4	387, 398	28.1	413		
122.1	398	28.2	413	**Second Apology**	
122.3	398	28.3	410	3[4].2	410
122.5	387, 396–97, 421	30–53	394, 396	4[5].3	411
122.5–6	398	31.7	394, 407	4[5].4	416
123.1	398, 421	32	395–96	4[5].4–6	411
123.7	398	32.1	394–95, 414	5[5].2	411
123.7–8	398	32.1–4	401	6[7].1	413
130–31	411	32.1–5	414, 466	6[7].1–2	413
130.1–2	405	32.2	395	7[8].1	412, 415
130.2	388	32.3	395	10.6	415
130.3	412	32.4	388, 391, 395, 409, 414	13.2	412
131.1	411			13.5	410–11, 412
131.5	413	32.5–11	395		
133.1	412	39	406	**Martyrdom of Polycarp**	
134.5	439, 442	40	396	9.2	331, 436
135.1–3	398	40.5–7	396	12.2	331, 436
135.4	412	40.7	409	13.1	331
137.1–2	404	40.14–15	396	17.2	331
138.2	421	41.1	408	18.1	331
141.5	388	41.1–4	407	19.1	331, 436
142.2–3	404	42	407		
		42.4	407	**Melito**	
First Apology		45.5	407	*On the Passover*	
2.1	410	46.2	410	35 (218)	444

36 (224–34)	444	2.78	441, 443	8.72	428
45 (245–99)	449	3.2	455	8.73	428
59 (415–21)	446	3.5	426	8.75	428, 465
76 (537–44)	444	3.40	448, 449		
76 (538)	444	4.8	456, 457	*Commentary on Romans*	
92 (672–77)	444	4.22	441, 444	8.6.6	452, 453
		4.32	426, 455, 461	8.9.4–7	447
Minucius Felix		4.43	439	8.12.1–8	447
		4.52	418	8.12.6	447
Octavius		5.10	456	160	447
6.1	452	5.25	425, 427, 457		
6.1–3	453	5.25–29	456	*First Principles*	
6.2–3	463	5.26	457	4.1.3	439, 441
6.3	463	5.29	456	*Homilies on Joshua*	
20.1–3	453	5.31	457	1.6	460–61
25	463	5.32	460	2.40	441
25.6–7	465	5.33	427, 451	7.5	436
27	460	5.34	425	22.6	444
31.2	455	5.50	441, 444, 466		
		5.61	430	*Homilies on Judges*	
Origen		6.10	427	57	456
		6.66	439	*Homilies on Luke*	
Against Celsus		6.80	426	49 (12.4)	456
preface 1	423	7.18	428	145–46 (35.6–7)	460
1.1	428	7.26	441, 450, 466,		
1.2	424, 454		468	**Polycarp**	
1.14	424, 426	7.62	424		
1.21	426	7.68	424, 425	*To the Philippians*	
1.23	426	7.69	455	1–12	332
1.24	424	8.2	425	3.1	332
1.26	427, 450	8.3	455	4.1	332
1.27	449–50	8.14	426	6.3	333, 384
1.31	447	8.20	436	7.1	332
1.37	438, 444	8.23	436	8	332
1.53	438	8.33–35	425	9	332
1.54	438	8.35	425	9.2	331
2.4	427	8.42	441	10.1–3	335
2.5	441	8.43	443	10.2	332, 383
2.8	441, 444	8.55	427, 428	10.2–3	335, 349
2.30	467	8.69	428	11.2	332, 333, 385
2.42	448, 449			12.1	333

Index of Ancient Sources

12.3	386	11.1.4	343	2.2.4–6	340
13–14	331	12.4.7	339	2.2.5	342
13.1	331			2.2.6	339
13.2	331	*Similitudes*		2.3.1	338
		1.1.4	342	2.3.4	346
Pseudo-Clementine		1.1.6	385–86	2.4.1	338
		1.10	342	2.4.3	341, 354
Homilies		4.1.4	343	3.3.3	339
8.6.1–8.7.5	199	4.4	342, 386	3.7.7	338
		8.1.1	343	4.2.1	339
Recognitions		8.3.2	343	4.2.4–5	339
1.27–71	199, 209, 228–29	8.9.1	343	5.1	339
		8.9.3	343	5.3	339
1.32.1–1.34.1	229	9.1.1	339	5.6	339
1.36.1–2	229	9.1.4	344	5.7	339
1.42.1	203, 229, 314	9.3.3	344		
1.43.1	229	9.4.2–3	344	**Tatian**	
1.43.1–2	229	9.4.5	344		
1.43.2	209	9.14.3	339	*Address to the Greeks*	
1.43.3	209	9.15.4	345	1.1–2	453
1.50.5–6	209	9.16.7	345	1.1–3	453, 454
1.70.1	209	9.17.1	345	1.2	453
1.71.3–4	209, 229	9.17.2	345, 383	7.2–3	455
4.5.5–9	199	9.17.4	345, 383	8	455
		9.17.5	345	9.1	456
Q		9.23.5	339	12.5	454
6:34	163	9.24.4	339	28.1	451, 452, 453, 458
7:34	163	9.25.1–2	345		
9:58	163	9.28.8	342	29.1	458
12:30	163, 208			40.1	451, 458
12:40	163	*Visions*			
13:28	163, 208	1.1.1–9	338	*Teaching of the Apostles (Didascalia Apostolorum)*	
13:29	163, 208	1.2.2	338		
17:24–30	163	1.3.1–3	338		
		1.3.2	341	15.3.6.2	448
Shepherd of Hermas		1.3.3	341	19.5.5.1	447
		1.3.4	342	21.5.16.7	441
Mandates		1.4.2	342, 343	23.6.5–7	441
4.1.8	339	2.2.2–3	338	23.6.8.1	448
4.1.9	342	2.2.4	339	106	449
10.1.4	343				

INDEX OF ANCIENT SOURCES

Tertullian

Against Marcion
3.6.1	432
3.7.1	432
3.12.1	462
3.13.7–8	462
3.14.5–7	462
3.18.3–4	436, 439
3.20.2–3	439
3.20.2–4	436
3.20.4–5	439
3.21.1	431
3.21.2–3	432
3.21.4	450
3.23.6	442
3.24.1	431
3.24.4	436
4.1.4	450
4.1.8	442
4.6.3	431
4.16.11–13	451
4.25.9	439
4.31.6	441, 443
5.9.9	447
5.9.11	439
5.17.6	439
5.17.12–14	436

Against Praxeas
11.5	439

Against the Jews
1.2	442
1.2–6	443
1.3	436, 444
2.1	445
2.7	445
3.4	445
3.5	445
3.6–11	451
3.9	436, 446
3.10	446
5.4	442
5.7	442
7.1	436, 438
7.1–9	461–62
7.2–9	464
9.4	462
10.7–8	436
12.1	449
12.1–2	436
13.24	436
13.26	442
14.12	436

Antidote for the Scorpion's Sting
10.9	454

Apology
19.1	445
19.1–7	446
21.6	441, 444
21.23–28	469
21.24	468
21.28	463
21.29–30	469
21.30	463
22.3	455
24.7	461
25–26	463
25.13	466
25.15	463, 466
32.1–3	470
32.2	468
37.4	449
37.4–8	469
37.8–9	470
37.9–10	460

The Apparel of Women
2.1.2	436
2.1.3	436

Flight in Persecution
6.1–3	448
6.3	449

Idolatry
2.4	436
10.1	436
14.4	436
15.1	436
15.2	456
20.4	455

Modesty
7	441

The Pallium
2.6	453

Patience
7.11	436

Prayer
15.1	436

Prescription against Heretics
20.2	447, 448
20.2–3	448
20.2–4	448
20.4	449

Repentance
2.1	436

The Resurrection of the Flesh
22.2	447

The Shows
3.1	436
29.3	460

Index of Ancient Sources

The Soul
26.1–2   442

To the Heathen
1.8.1   442
1.8.9–13   454
1.17.1–6   469
1.17.3   436
1.20.4   454
2.17.1–19   463
2.17.18–19   466

Theophilus of Antioch

To Autolycus
2.33   459
2.36   459
3.16   459
3.29   458–59

GRECO-ROMAN LITERATURE

Aelius Aristides

Regarding Rome
2–5   8
6–13   8
10   8, 26
13   8
15–23   8
20   9, 27
23   8, 298
24   8
24–57   8
28   123, 278, 290, 291
29   8, 9, 90, 280
31   9, 280
34   90, 97
36   9
51   8, 9, 31, 91, 118, 298
57–106   8
58   8
59   32, 118
60   10
61   10, 303
61–65   97
63   10, 27
65   9, 303
67   8, 9, 260, 262, 280
88   9, 27, 262
90   9, 27, 298
90–91   118
91   9, 298
92   9, 91, 303
92–94   27
92–104   302–4
93   303
94   303
95   9, 303
96   303
97   9, 10, 27, 304
100   9, 10, 27
102   97
103   10, 27
103–4   10
104   9, 10, 27, 92, 304
105   10
106   10
107   11
107–9   8

Appian

Civil Wars
1.5   280, 290
2.13   259
2.17   259
2.18   259
2.27   259
2.48   259
2.106   259
2.107   259
4.137   253

Roman History
preface.1   280
preface.6   257, 280
preface.7   280, 290, 302
preface.8–9   291
preface.12   259
preface.15   259
6.38   259
7.61   259
8.1.132   261
10.3   273
10.6   258, 268–69, 275
12.118   284

Aristophanes

Frogs
888   214

Women of the Assembly
1092   214

Aristotle

Politics
1324b   254

Augustus

Acts of Augustus (Res Gestae)
3   246, 279, 292
3.1   97
8.2   86
12   85
13   86, 90, 298
15–23   90
24   90

555

INDEX OF ANCIENT SOURCES

25	257
25–33	86
26	86, 90, 246, 257, 279, 295
27	246, 257, 279, 295
28	90
30	246, 279, 283
31	86
32	246, 295
33	246, 295
appendix 4	90

Calpurnius Siculus

Eclogue

1.74–76	287, 298

Cassius Dio

Roman History

37.16.5	274
37.17.1	114
37.17.2	274
37.20.2	302
39.5.1	284
48.28.4	260
51.18.1	260
52.19.1–3	260
52.22.1	280
52.27.1	260
53.4.3	260
53.5.4	260
53.8.1	280
53.9.6	260
53.12.1	260
53.12.8	260
53.13.1	260
53.15.1–4	260
56.4.4	260
56.34.1–2	284

Cicero

Against Catalina

4.2	295
4.11	295
4.22	256

Against Piso

16	256
16.38	255

Concerning the Consular Provinces

33	249, 289

In Defense of Balbus

5.13	278
6.16	256, 282
13.31	299
16.39	286
28.64	286

In Defense of Cluentius

134	255

In Defense of Sestius

1.67	282
51	251, 295, 298
67	251, 287
132	246

Letters to Quintus

1.9–10	294
1.27–28	294

On Behalf of Fonteius

35	251, 255

On Behalf of King Deiotarus

15	82, 282

On Behalf of Marcellus

8–9	282, 292

On Behalf of Milo

19	256, 295
77	299
90	295

On Duties

2.26–27	292, 294–95
3.69	91, 260

On the Agrarian Law

1.18	287, 295
2.33	262, 87
2.39	251, 287
2.98	261, 278

On the Laws

2.8	248
2.33	251

On the Making of an Orator

1.14	278, 287
2.18	266, 275
2.76	281, 286

On the Manilian Law

44	256
56	286

Philippic

2.15	286
4.13	248, 280
4.15	256, 281, 286
5.12	255
6.12	281, 286
6.19	304
7.3	249
7.19	286
8.10	286

The Republic

1.26	288
3.33	260

Index of Ancient Sources

The Speech concerning the Response of the Soothsayers

19	304

Tusculan Disputations

1.2	294

Dio Chrysostom

Kingship 3 [Or. 3]

45	262

Man's First Conception of God [Or. 12]

39.5	252

On Tyranny [Or. 6]

56	262

Opinion [Or. 68]

4	275

Refusal of the Office of Archon [Or. 49]

1	262

Retirement [Or. 20]

17	262

Diodorus Siculus

Historical Library

1.9.3	71
1.14–15	71
1.53–57	71

Library of History

1.3.2	271
1.8.4	252
2.38.1	265, 274, 276
2.45.3	270
3.14.6	271
3.23.1	271
3.35.1	270, 271
4.1.5	274
4.1.5–6	271
5.25.1	265
5.32.1	268
21.9	253
32.4.4–5	289, 292, 296, 301
40.4	247, 289

Dionysius of Halicarnassus

Roman Antiquities

1.3.3	90
1.3.5	280, 289
1.9.4	296, 301
1.25.2	266
1.25.5	266
1.29.1–2	267–68, 274, 275
1.89.1	100
6.63	253
7.70.1	296

Epictetus

Discourses

2.19.19–21	114

Florus

Epitome of Roman History

1.introduction.1	289
1.introduction.1–2	286
1.introduction.2	248
2.13	285
2.26	279, 282, 286
2.34	288, 298–99

Gaius

Institutes

1.1	91, 253, 260

Herodotus

Histories

1.1	69
8.144	56, 244, 273

Horace

Epistles

2.1.156–57	93

Odes

1.3.25–28	253
1.12.49–50	248

Isocrates

Panegyric

24–25	71
50	73–74

Julius Caesar

Civil War

3.47.5	282

Gallic War

1.1	270
4.1	244
4.1–3	244
6.11	270, 275
6.11–28	274
6.16	274
8.24	283

Juvenal

Satires

3.62	96

Livy

History of Rome

1.preface.1	272
1.preface.7–8	272

INDEX OF ANCIENT SOURCES

1.preface.8	279
5.48.8	279, 287
9.17.3	285
26.49.7–9	295
26.49.8	255
28.12.2–4	273
28.12.3	265, 274
30.16.9	256
30.30.1	252
30.32.2	288
30.34.2	265
30.35.7	265
33.4–6	299–300
33.32.4–6	275
33.32.5–7	299
36.17.13–16	286
36.17.16	248
37.38.3	265
37.54.15–28	300
38.17.2	266
38.17.8–12	265
38.17.9	274
38.17.9–12	276
38.17.12	274
42.52.10	266
42.52.11	266
45.18.1	300

Lucian

Demonax

38.4	214

Martial

Epigrams

8.65	283
12.6	251, 257

Ovid

Fasti

1.599–600	284
2.683–84	260, 287

Petronius

Poems

24	130

Satyricon

102	130

Plato

The Republic

5.21	214

Pliny the Elder

Natural History

preface.16	272, 281
2.189	277
3.5	272, 281
3.20.136	275, 279
3.20.136–37	85
3.39	305
4.40	251, 266
6.187–88	270
7.1	262
7.6	248, 253, 262
16.5	283

Pliny the Younger

Letters

8.24.1	94

Panegyric

17.2	283
29.1	300
32.1	300
32.2	300
51.3	281
56.4	255, 282
59.3	255

Plutarch

Caesar

15.3	284

The Fortune of the Romans

2	305–6
8	306
11	305, 306

Marcellus

1	306
3	306

Pompey

67.6	284

Roman Questions

22	306

Polybius

Histories

1.1.5	82, 99
1.2.1–8	271, 289, 291
1.3.8–10	290
6.2.5	99
9.1.3–5	271
36.9.9	266
38.9.6–8	266
38.22	261

Quintilian

An Orator's Education

1.5.55	255, 273
11.3.87	262, 273

Index of Ancient Sources

Rhetoric for Herennius (unknown author)

4.13	255, 278, 287, 288, 299

Sallust

Histories

4.17	286

The War with Catiline

6.1–2	265

The War with Jugurtha

31.20	279, 284, 287

Strabo

Geography

1.1.1	278
1.1.6	272
1.1.16	87, 263
1.2.27	264
1.2.34	267, 273
2.1.31	266
2.3.1	266
2.5.28	253, 268
3.2.15	301
3.3.8	301
4.1.5	301
4.3.2	85, 247, 281
4.4.2	266
9.2.2	290, 297, 301
9.5.8	264
9.5.12	265
9.5.21	263
12.1.2	264
12.4.6	264
14.2.28	253
14.5.27	254, 264
17.3.25	87

Suetonius

Augustus

2.21.1	279
2.21.2	288
48.1	295

Claudius

5.25.3	260, 266

Divus Julius

84.5	275

Nero

6.46.1	247, 283

Tacitus

Agricola

12	249

Annals

2.22	282
2.44	249
3.59	248, 286
11.24	95, 97
13.54	296
14.44	275, 280

Germany

1	271
2	266, 269, 274
4	264, 265–66, 273, 276
27	249, 266, 275
29	251, 264
33	256
34	249, 273
38	249–50, 267, 275
38–41	244
46	267

Histories

5.5.1–2	130

Velleius Paterculus

Compendium of Roman History

1.12.7	286
1.13.2	284
2.5.1	266, 278
2.36.1	287
2.37.3–4	305
2.37.4	266
2.38	258
2.38.1	250
2.39.2	247, 266, 283
2.40.2	282
2.92.2–3	249
2.97.3–4	266, 273
2.106.1	249, 282
2.106.2	266, 273
2.106.3	282
2.107.3	282
2.110.2	249
2.110.3	260
2.131.1–2	305

Virgil

Aeneid

1.12–22	288
1.15–18	304
1.32–33	266
1.33	260
1.235–36	86
1.261	260
1.261–64	304
1.277–82	304
1.277–87	286
1.278	86
1.286–87	304
2.282	260
6.788	260
6.788–89	260

INDEX OF ANCIENT SOURCES

6.851–53	90, 280, 283, 292, 293	**Vitruvius**		2.1.1	276
7.720–23	304	*On Architecture*		2.1.4	275
8.327	260	1.preface.1	256, 279, 285, 287	2.1.6	276
8.626–728	86			6.1.5–11	276
8.720–23	283	1.preface.1–2	272	6.1.9	249
12.838	248	1.preface.2	87	6.1.10–12	87
				9.2.1	263

www.ingramcontent.com/pod-product-compliance
Lightning Source LLC
Chambersburg PA
CBHW031538300426
44111CB00006BA/102